D0473928

Teaching English Learners

Strategies and Methods

Lynne T. Díaz-Rico

California State University, San Bernardino

PEARSON

Boston ✦ New York ✦ San Francisco
Mexico City ✦ Montreal ✦ Toronto ✦ London ✦ Madrid ✦ Munich ✦ Paris
Hong Kong ✦ Singapore ✦ Tokyo ✦ Cape Town ✦ Sydney

Series Editor: Aurora Martínez Ramos
Editorial Assistant: Erin Beatty
Senior Marketing Manager: Elizabeth Fogarty
Editorial-Production Service: Omegatype Typography, Inc.
Manufacturing Buyer: Andrew Turso
Composition and Prepress Buyer: Linda Cox
Cover Administrator: Linda Knowles
Electronic Composition: Omegatype Typography, Inc.

For related titles and support materials, visit our online catalog at www.ablongman.com.

Between the time website information is gathered and then published, some sites may have closed. Also, the transcription of URLs can result in typographical errors. The publisher would appreciate notification where these errors occur so that they may be corrected in subsequent editions.

Many of the designations used by manufacturers and sellers to distinguish their products are claimed as trademarks. Where those designations appear in this book, and Allyn and Bacon was aware of a trademark claim, the designations have been printed in initial or all caps.

Library of Congress Cataloging-in-Publication Data

Díaz-Rico, Lynne T.
    Teaching English learners : strategies and methods / Lynne T. Díaz-Rico.
      p. cm.
    Includes bibliographical references and index.
    ISBN 0-205-35543-9
    1. English language—Study and teaching—Foreign speakers.   I. Title.

PE1128.A2D453 2004
428'.0071—dc21

                                  2003052430

Printed in the United States of America

10 9 8 7 6 5 4 3 2 1   08 07 06 05 04 03

Photo Credits: p. 2: Will Hart; p. 3: T. Lindfors/Lindfors Photography; p. 9: Will Hart; p. 35: T. Lindfors/Lindfors Photography; p. 79: Will Hart; p. 113: Will Hart; p. 140: T. Lindfors/ Lindfors Photography; p. 159: Will Hart; p. 195: Will Hart; p. 213: T. Lindfors/Lindfors Photography; p. 218: Will Hart; p. 261: Paul Conklin/Photo Edit; p. 281: Gary Conner/Photo Edit; p. 294: Will Hart; p. 302: Will Hart; p. 332: Will Hart; p. 356: Will Hart; p. 380: Will Hart; p. 391: Will Hart; p. 411: Will Hart

To Phillip, Voltaire, Daniel, and Eva:
Thank you for your love and care.

To Sondra, Simon, Ian, and Liana:
Love to my extended family.

To my students, who work so hard as learners and as teachers:
Thank you for your devotion to the success of English learners.

To my colleagues:
Thank you for making TESOL a worthy profession.

To all my teachers, past, present, and future:
Thank you for your help and guidance.

Brief Contents

Contents

5 Learner Strategies and Learner-Focused Teaching   101

7 The Learning Process and the Imaginary   200

8 Grammar through Integrated Language Skills and Wonderful English   239

9 Culturally Based Language Teaching   266

15 Learning English through Service to the Community   402

Appendix A   Influencing Language Policies to Benefit English Learners   417

List of Figures and Tables

Figures

Tables

Preface

This book offers an overview of basic principles, practices, and methods that provide a broad foundation in educating English learners. It covers the issues and techniques of second-language acquisition, as well as attending to such topics as the influence of culture on schooling, the cultural practices of schooling, and the sociopolitical context of education. This book is designed to increase teachers' effectiveness in expanding English learners' access to the core curriculum, instructing all students with a rich and demanding curriculum, and making crosscultural connections by means of teaching practices and curricular content.

ESL (English as a second language) and EFL (English as a foreign language) teachers with multicultural sensitivity and knowledge of intercultural communication can be expected actively to build a base of personal knowledge about the ways in which language, culture, and schooling are connected. This book is designed to offer a solid foundation in core techniques, in a manner that balances a growth in theoretical understanding with exposure to effective practice. Most important, it is designed to work at many levels simultaneously, so that participants can organize and verbalize what they know, make professional presentations, and pursue a teaching career graced with knowledge, empathy, and dedication. The best teaching model is one that is open-ended, furthers understanding, and encourages learners to take responsibility for what they have learned by actively reaching out to apply it.

Teacher education is open-ended and neverending. One goal of this book is for teachers to gain more confidence in their own teaching ability and become more competent teachers. This book does not use a *behaviorist* model of teacher training (in which one is told exactly how to behave as a teacher), but rather a *cognitive/humanist/constructivist* model of teacher education, in which one receives fundamental principles and then fashions one's own version of what constitutes good teaching.

Simultaneously, a dedication to social equity and justice broadens the focus of education to include attention to issues of social context, cultural values, and individual rights and responsibilities within a democratic framework. This adherence to democratic ideals is a given, despite the wide variety of cultures and societies that now use English for their own purposes. Although English grew from a limited language of five to seven million speakers to a global language through a combination of imperialism, global militarism, and ambitious economic agendas, it is still the language of the Declaration of Independence and the Bill of Rights. One must never lose sight while teaching English of the possibilities of human freedom, equality of opportunity, and justice, ideals exquisitely expressed in the English language.

The terms "strategies and methods" in the title of this book have been chosen to reflect current practice in the field of teaching English learners, with the full knowledge that the terms have a multitude of meanings and connotations. Such an undertaking— delineating strategies for a broad field— is easily criticized. Some educators may feel that to recommend teaching strategies is futile. Paulo Freire (1987), in his letter to North American educators, warned against uncritically importing and exporting strategies and methods with no regard for sociocultural contexts. For Freire, it is vital that teachers possess both knowledge of their content area *and* the political clarity to be able to apply this knowledge with confidence that the learner will be both challenged and treated with respect. It is my hope that educators will learn how to adapt teaching strategies and methods to the learning contexts of English learners.

In this book, I use the word *strategy* to mean "an idea that a learner can use to increase learning." This book features strategies that the prospective teacher may acquire and deploy *as a learner of teacher education*—these may also be called methods or teaching techniques. Some learner strategies, in turn, are appropriate for the learner of the second language. These are "learner strategies applied to the SLA context."

I use the term *megastrategy* to denote "a large idea that guides practice and hosts a set of matching strategies consonant with its theme." There are fifteen megastrategies, one corresponding to each of the fifteen chapters of the book. Sixty-eight matching strategies align with these megastrategies. Each strategy is accompanied by a set of tactics. A *tactic* is a recommended practice aligned with a given strategy.

The term "megastrategy" is used instead of "principle" because a "principle" connotes "postulate in a grand, unifying theory." To educate English learners, one needs to draw upon many disciplines, including philosophy, psychology, linguistics, anthropology, and sociology. A single unifying theory therefore, is neither appropriate nor available, but this does not mean that the education of English learners is not based upon theoretical foundations.

Often, teacher education that is systemic and organized—in other words, theoretical—is mistrusted by the classroom teacher. Practitioners often call themselves "eclectic," meaning that they borrow classroom techniques from a variety of sources and synthesize them into craft, that is, daily practice built upon "what works" for that individual. Those who use this approach may distrust the process of identifying and discussing teaching practices as being "too theoretical." An assumption, then, is that theory and practice are somehow opposite, and that theory is "not useful." In contrast, what is "useful" is craft that allows the teacher and student some smooth function within the given setting.

This functional view, however, seems to reduce the concept of theory to the idea that the test of a successful theory of teaching would be its power to alter conditions for individual learners. This is a fundamentally Western liberal notion, that worth is measured by the actions of individuals, and that the sum total of success or failure of individuals can somehow be equated with the success of an entire enterprise. Anyon (1994) argued for a broader view, stating that "such a theory would make useful recommendations to those who work for a more humanitarian, more equitable society, and consequently, this theory will have a progressive effect on society itself" (p. 117). Thus the standards for a successful theory are higher; it must be aimed at improving social conditions, rather than merely improving the lot of individuals in the hope that somehow this process will amass positive change as an aggregate.

Moreover, this book is built upon a fundamental rejection of any dichotomy of theory and practice. I visualize the tool kit of theory and the practice as components in a cycle of stance (see Figure P.1). Gramsci (Adamson, 1980) has conceptualized

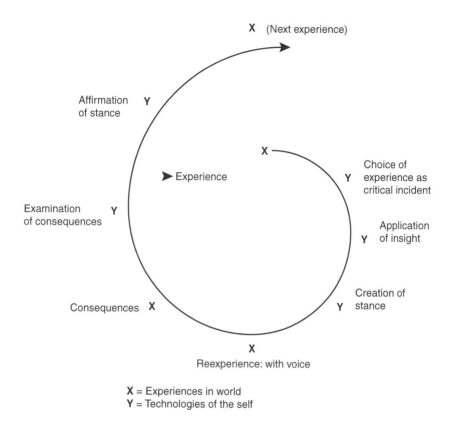

X   (Next experience)

Affirmation   Y
of stance

X

Choice of
Y   experience as
critical incident

► Experience

Examination   Y
of consequences

Application
Y   of insight

Creation of
Consequences   X   Y   stance

X
Reexperience: with voice

X = Experiences in world
Y = Technologies of the self

FIGURE P.1   ♦   Components in a cycle of stance.

theory and practice as a linked set, in which theory and practice are linked by the identification of how individuals come to constitute—and therefore also can reconstitute—
their worlds. In this instance I conceive of *theory* as a tool kit of megastrategies,
strategies, and tactics. *Practice* is the deployment of the self with a repertoire of these
megastrategies, strategies, and tactics within a specific context. (Critical theorists might
call this *praxis* rather than practice.) *Insight* into a specific occurrence, together with
the *creation of stance and voice*, followed by the *ongoing affirmation of the stance* in
view of real consequences, becomes the chief technology (set of techniques) of deploying the self (Foucault, 1988) within an individual's profession.

The concept of "stance" is an individual instantiation of what Gramsci called
the "war of position" (Simon, 1982). In advanced capitalist societies in which civil
society is highly developed, a "war of position" is required. The power exercised by
the status quo is often unquestioned; but in order to create social change, members
of society who wish to transform relationships within the civil society must deliberately take positions to interrupt this status quo. For this reason I consider "stance"
an individual analog of the war of position, in which individuals engage in transformative practices using a cycle of stance.

What kinds of transformative practices are required? Experienced teachers assert themselves on a daily basis to sustain support for effective teaching. Educators who teach English learners in the United States sometimes face multiple obstacles to school success: poverty, stress, discrimination, and increasing academic demands are often blamed as educators struggle to explain the frustration faced by English learners. Educators who teach English as a foreign language abroad face a different set of frustrations: the risks of marginalization or intercultural miscommunication. Appendix A includes a discussion of how U.S.-based educators can exert power to maintain their profession on the cutting edge of educational progress. Similar techniques may be adapted for teaching abroad, taking into consideration the particular context.

In the process of using the cycle of stance, an individual chooses a particular challenge to face. This challenge may include trying a new teaching tactic, or asserting influence within an institution. Experiencing that tactic creates a critical incident. By applying reflective insight, the practitioner evaluates the incident and creates a stance. The stance is a position taken by a practitioner with a voice. The "voice" speaks up for change; if the practice failed for a specific reason, the voice advocates for change in the social context to allow the next trial of the tactic to be a success. The cycle continues as the consequences of this reexperience with voice are examined. If the stance is affirmed, the tactic, with its attendant social change, was successful. If so, the cycle spirals to a new level of implementation. If not, the failure becomes a new critical incident. Thus the individual creates experiences in the world using the technologies of the self.

The cycle of stance provides a clear process for using and evaluating tactics. It does not, however, place blame on the tactic or the practitioner if success is not attained. Neither does it encourage the practitioner to quit trying. Rather, it acknowledges that the practitioner needs to examine the incident, choose points of leverage in the stance to apply the self within the social context, and then reexperience and evaluate the consequences. Only in this way can the practitioner learn to examine the social context and act meaningfully within that context.

Use of a carefully structured tool kit of megastrategies, strategies, and tactics, with a clear process for use, permits the educator to act clearly and consistently as a professional. In addition, the educator can attain a lucid and concise picture of a complex and demanding profession. This view moves beyond the concept of teaching as a collection of "methods," which some have defined as "decontextualized techniques." In reality, the complex texture of native and target cultures, native languages, social and political situations, socioeconomic status, and individual differences in learners that one faces when teaching English learners means that one must continually innovate and experiment with teaching and learning strategies.

Beneath the complexity of teaching English learners lies yet another layer of complication: second-language acquisition (SLA) theory. Despite over fifty years of research into language acquisition, the process of learning a second language (defined as learning any language other than one's native language) remains poorly understood, with conflicting results and poorly generalizable findings across learner and language task. For this reason, and due to constraints of time and space, this book does not delve deeply into SLA theory. I refer readers to specific sources for deeper study in specific areas, such as Gass and Selinker's *Second Language Acquisition: An Introductory Course* (2nd ed., 2001).

Also, due to constraints of time and space, this book does not include provisions for reasoned acquisition of strategies. Hence this book is short on processes for convincing the practitioner of the worth and efficacy of the strategies, such as the inclusion of such devices as "point/counterpoint" to offer both sides of the debate on contentious issues, discussion questions, or specific training activities. Those who seek such teaching tools may wish to refer to Díaz-Rico and Weed's (2002) *Crosscultural, Language, and Academic Development Handbook* as a useful supplement. This book may also be short on specific, anecdotal documentation of the use and success of specific strategies in the context of the classroom. Such examples in the book are drawn from classrooms ranging from kindergarten through adult levels, with some attempt to draw upon both ESL and EFL teaching.

This book emphasizes a commitment to social justice and a moral commitment to democracy. I offer my thanks and tribute to colleagues in the profession of teaching English learners whose like-minded dedication has sustained and inspired me throughout my professional life. If the reader disagrees with this position and does not support these social goals, I invite dialogue, autonomy, and resistance, using a cycle of reflection, stance, and voice.

Acknowledgments

This book was made possible through the help of many people. I credit my editor, Aurora Martínez Ramos, with the persuasive power that moved me to undertake the project. I thank my colleague Dr. Kathryn Z. Weed for her help. I acknowledge the support of my students, who gave me feedback on early drafts. Thanks to Dr. Patricia Arlin, dean of the College of Education at CSUSB, and my colleagues for their patience.

I would also like to thank the reviewers of this book for their insight and feedback: Sue Atkinson, University of Houston; Irma N. Guadarrama, University of Houston; Nancy Hadaway, University of Texas, Arlington; Linda Lippitt, College of Santa Fe; and Elba Maldonado-Colón, San José State University.

Strategies for Teaching English Learners: A Summary

❖ **MEGASTRATEGY 1**   Professionalize the teaching of English learners
   ◆ **STRATEGY 1.1**   Become familiar with the profession of teaching English learners.
   ◆ **STRATEGY 1.2**   Know who your learners are and why they need English.
   ◆ **STRATEGY 1.3**   Join with other professionals to facilitate teaching.

❖ **MEGASTRATEGY 2**   Advance the interests of the learner
   ◆ **STRATEGY 2.1**   Set professional goals with the learner's best interests in mind, as the learner defines them.
   ◆ **STRATEGY 2.2**   Critique the social conditions of the learner.
   ◆ **STRATEGY 2.3**   Use power and policy issues to support English learners.

❖ **MEGASTRATEGY 3**   Teach the whole person—beliefs, body, brain, emotions, and culture—within a positive social environment
   ◆ **STRATEGY 3.1**   Take into consideration your philosophy and beliefs, as well as the philosophies and beliefs of the learner.
   ◆ **STRATEGY 3.2**   Use behavioral training for accurate pronunciation and rote memory of information such as object and motor vocabulary.
   ◆ **STRATEGY 3.3**   Align learning with the brain and its natural way of knowledge acquisition.
   ◆ **STRATEGY 3.4**   Reduce tension and support a positive emotional state in the learner.
   ◆ **STRATEGY 3.5**   Be aware of the effect of the sociocultural context on cognitive and language development.
   ◆ **STRATEGY 3.6**   Place learning in the context of contemporary social change.

❖ **MEGASTRATEGY 4**   Maximize learning by basing performance on measurable outcomes
   ◆ **STRATEGY 4.1**   Align instruction with local, state, and national standards.
   ◆ **STRATEGY 4.2**   Understand the purposes and functions of assessment.
   ◆ **STRATEGY 4.3**   Expect the highest performance possible in the time available.
   ◆ **STRATEGY 4.4**   Plan cooperatively and flexibly for maximum student involvement and achievement.
   ◆ **STRATEGY 4.5**   Set criteria for effective performance and assess attainment of those criteria.
   ◆ **STRATEGY 4.6**   Adjust instruction to attain performance criteria.

Who Are English Learners and Their Teachers?

❖ **MEGASTRATEGY 1**: Professionalize the teaching of English learners

Language is a powerful means to communicate the deepest and highest desires, dreams, and ideals of humanity. Language helps us to fulfill our potential, to share our inner selves with others, or to act upon the world powerfully. We use language to participate in private and public life with our families, community, or nation. As teachers, we use language to help others reach higher states of knowledge, emotion, or spirit. These are among the strongest drives of humankind, and language has proved to be a superior tool for those ends. But how frustrating that no common language exists among peoples of the world! The world today stands on the brink of an opportunity never before available: the use of a world language, English, that can sustain intercultural contact between individuals who would otherwise have no mutual means of communication.

Teaching English learners is one of the fastest-growing professions in today's world. But who are "English learners"? In countries such as the United States, Canada, the United Kingdom, and Australia, native speakers of English study their own language as they progress through school. They do so first in elementary classrooms, where the focus is on learning to read and write English as one of several subjects, and later in secondary schools, where they attend classes taught by English teachers. Such instruction is not considered "teaching English learners"; even though English is being taught on a daily basis, the fact that the learners are native speakers of English means they are not "English learners." The term "English learners" means those who are learning English who are not native speakers.

However, in many English-speaking countries, traditional academic English classes increasingly serve students who, although they are being schooled entirely in English, speak other languages at home. These have been termed "Generation 1.5 students" (Harklau, Losey, & Siegal, 1999)—caught between generations, having acquired some proficiency in two or more languages but not truly native speakers of English. Even though they take classes with native speakers, they may not actually have attained academic competence in English. To teach these students, English teachers in classes designed for native speakers may also benefit from a focus on "English learners."

Thus the answer to the question, "Who is an English learner?" may not simply be, "One who is taught by an ESL/EFL teacher." English learners are also taught by

1

English learners comprise a growing proportion of school children in the United States.

teachers whose primary responsibility is to teach a primary language in a so-called bilingual classroom, as well as by English and other elementary school teachers who treat their students as native English speakers even if they are not. This situation creates a complex set of professional loyalties on the part of teachers.

◆ STRATEGY 1.1: Become familiar with the profession of teaching English learners

The term "teaching English to speakers of other languages" (TESOL) includes teaching English learners in general, although classroom teachers may think of themselves as "elementary teachers," "bilingual teachers" or "English teachers." Teaching English learners is a broad and flexible profession: TESOL educators can be found in kindergartens in Seattle, college classrooms in Korea, adult education classes in Texas, "cram" schools in Thailand, precollege preparation courses in Michigan, middle school social studies classes in California, five-year vocational colleges in Taiwan, private schools in the United Arab Emirates, or summer intensive programs in Uzbekistan. They operate at a myriad of levels in a host of countries around the world, working with learners at levels ranging from preschool to postgraduate. TESOL educators are represented professionally by the organization TESOL, Inc. (www.tesol.org).

However, many teachers of English learners do not identify themselves as TESOL educators. They may choose other professional affiliations, such as the National Association for Bilingual Education (NABE, www.nabe.org); National Council of Teachers of English (NCTE, www.ncte.org); International Reading Association (IRA, www.ira.org); International Association of Teachers of English as a Foreign Language (IATEFL, www.iatefl.org); or state, regional or local affiliates of these organizations. Although these organizations increasingly focus on the education of English learners in their publications and conference sessions, TESOL, Inc. is the only U.S.-based professional organization whose central mission is the teaching of English to speakers of other languages.

To prepare for teaching English learners, one can pursue various stages of career preparation, from B.A. programs with a special emphasis on language teaching, through twelve-hour certificate or endorsement programs, to M.A. programs, to doctoral study in academic departments of education, linguistics, applied linguistics, or English. The website of TESOL, Inc. (www.tesol.org) has a link (www.tesol.org/careers/seekers-faq1.html#2) that may help to clarify these terms and the important differences that distinguish these preparation programs and levels of career training. Despite the widely varying career ladders available to educators, the demand for professional English-language teachers has grown steadily around the world. In all parts of the world, at all times of the day, someone is teaching or studying English.

The field of teaching English learners is equally open to those whose native language is English and those who are nonnative speakers. Although some employers may specify "native-speaker-like proficiency" in their job ads, positions are available worldwide with employers who recognize that those who have learned English as an additional language and have achieved some measure of bilingual competence are uniquely qualified to understand the needs of English learners (see Brutt-Griffler & Samimy, 1999). TESOL's Nonnative English Speakers in TESOL (NNEST) Caucus (nnest@tesol.org) can provide more information about this topic.

The Internet can help to provide a broad picture of the possibilities available to those who specialize in teaching English learners. Bilingual and ESL educators in the United States may enjoy the Bilingual ESL Network (http://ben.nabe.net/ben.htm) or the professional information available from the National Clearinghouse for Bilingual Education (http://ncbe.gwu.edu), including the online library (hundreds of full-text articles and other documents for educators); useful links to national, regional, and state

Non-native English speakers outnumber native English speakers around the world.

educational resources and databases; a conference calendar; lesson plans; and other practical classroom information. Dave's ESL Cafe (online at www.eslcafe.com) is a popular site for English learning, featuring chat rooms; a "bookstore"; job listings; and sections on slang, idioms, and other language-teaching tips. The *Internet TESOL Journal* (www.aitech.ac.jp/~iteslj) connects to 3,500 additional links of interest to ESL/EFL students and teachers. *Eflweb* (www.u-net.com/eflweb) is an online magazine for those learning English as a foreign language in general, and Englishtown (www.englishtown.com) is an EFL site for Portuguese educators. Boot up, click, and enjoy the international flavor of the profession of teaching English learners.

❖ **Tactics for teachers to find out more about teaching English learners:**

- ◆ Investigate the career possibilities of teaching English learners using the Internet.
- ◆ "Job shadow" an educator to observe the challenges and opportunities.

Once the door to English is opened, learners who acquire basic tools of language acquisition may proceed at their own pace. In some countries, English skills can be a key to social and economic success. However, in the United States, as in other target cultures, entrenched social class privileges, politics, and economic realities present obstacles that must be overcome. Assisting English learners to adapt to, or adopt the ways of, a particular target culture as they learn English is an increasingly important facet of teaching. In the process, educators of many backgrounds, not solely native speakers of English, may learn much about themselves and their own unwitting internalization of monocultural values and assumptions. Such cultural broadening as an outcome of teaching offers the possibility of valuable personal growth, which is often the result of reflecting on one's gaffes in intercultural communication. One learns from mistakes, and when teaching English learners, many more errors are possible than in a monocultural setting. But they will be fascinating errors!

Aside from the intellectual and pedagogical challenges of teaching in a language acquisition classroom, those who teach in multicultural classrooms reap what they sow. Those who offer cultural understanding receive it; those who offer language exchange expand their foreign-language skills; those who offer empathy grow as human beings. No other area of teaching extends as rich an opportunity for intercultural communication, literacy development, creative instructional delivery, or reflective social praxis. And few other teaching areas involve such hard work!

Language learning is a complex, dynamic process that forms the foundation for academic skills. Beginning with basic communication skills, English learners face an uphill battle to acquire the sophisticated verbal skills needed for college entry or career success. An array of educational policies and practices either helps or hinders this process. Part of the challenge of educating learners of a second language is discovering what works and doing more of it, and then supporting other educators who are making similar discoveries and achieving similar successes.

In the past, students without English skills may have sat silent, excluded from instruction, because the classroom teacher was unable to teach them. Thankfully, those days are over. Teachers today are challenged to prepare all students to succeed in life, including those learners who enter schools speaking a language other than English. Schools and school systems must ensure that all students have access to an excellent education. Part of the repertoire of the contemporary teacher is a set of English-teaching strategies to reach those students whose English proficiency is emergent.

Educational Terminology

As in other professions, teaching English learners requires mastering a unique jargon. Table 1.1 offers a look at the terminology in this field.

As in other fields, when teaching English learners, one occasionally meets controversy over terminology. This book uses the term *English learner* ("English *language* learner" is redundant) rather than the term *language minority student*, although Skutnabb-Kangas insists that the term "minority" is correct, and its use in reference to populations whose language is a minority actually preserves legal protections for students' language rights under international agreements (see Wink, 2000). The acronyms ELL (English language learner), FEP (fluent English proficient), FES (fluent English-speaking), LEP (limited English proficient), LES (limited English-speaking), NEP (non-English proficient), and NES (non–English-speaking) are not used because they have often been misused as acronym-jargon.

The term *bilingual* has a wide variety of meanings and connotations. It can be used to designate the linguistic skills of individuals competent in two or more languages. The term *bilingual education* is also used to characterize types of educational programs (see Díaz-Rico & Weed, 2002) and is sometimes used erroneously by beginning teachers to refer to the composition of the students in their class. "I have a bilingual class" may mean, "My students do not speak English."

Like other aspects of education, the profession of teaching English learners seems to thrive on acronyms of all sorts. Rose (2001) offered a list of fifty-five entries to the alphabet soup that is used in California alone. Other states and countries probably have an equal amount of professional jargon. Learning this "lingo" may help educators to understand what learners of English have to suffer when they face long lists of new vocabulary words! Many other terms will arise in the quest to supply a glossary of words and ideas useful in teaching English learners. These will be defined as they arise.

Teachers of English learners draw upon such disciplines as linguistics, English literature and language study, foreign-language teaching pedagogy, sociology, anthropology, psychology, philosophy, and computer-assisted learning, as well as specific fields of study (medicine, engineering, aviation) that have their own distinctive glossaries in English (creating the field known as English for Special Purposes or ESP). Terminology from these associated disciplines will be introduced through this book as needed.

Critical Perspectives

This book adopts a critical perspective in regard to the education of English learners. The term *critical* has been used by sociologists and social philosophers who study language and society and who have urged a wider perspective on the social tensions that

TABLE 1.1 ◆ Educational Terminology for Teachers of English Learners

Term	Meaning
English learners, EL students	Anyone learning to speak English whose native language is not English
Teachers of English to Speakers of Other Languages (TESOL)	The discipline of instructing English learners
Teachers of English to Speakers of Other Languages, Inc. (TESOL, Inc.)	International professional association that represents TESOL educators
English Speakers of Other Languages (ESOL)	Elementary, secondary, higher, and adult education English language learners or programs
English as a second language (ESL)	Learners whose primary language is not English, yet who live in places where English has some sort of special status or public availability
Teaching English as a second language (TESL)	Teacher education programs whose candidates will teach ESL
English as a foreign language (EFL)	Learners of English who live in places where English is, by and large, an academic subject, functioning narrowly in that culture as a tool for communicating with outsiders
Teaching English as a foreign language (TEFL)	Teacher education programs whose candidates will teach EFL
English as a new language (ENL)	Term coined by the Educational Testing Service to represent ESOL, but with limited currency
English-language development (ELD)	Term used in the United States to refer to ESL services
English-language teaching or English-language training (ELT)	Term used internationally to refer to EFL services
Language acquisition (includes language learning)	Learning language in a natural context or formally through rules of grammar and usage
First language (L1)	The language learned at home from the primary caregivers (mother tongue, primary language, or native language)
First-language acquisition (FLA)	Acquiring mother tongue, primary language, or native language
Second language (L2)	Any language (whether third or twentieth) that is learned after the first language
Second-language acquisition (SLA)	Learning any language (whether third or twentieth) in school or in some other way after the first language
Target language (TL)	The language that is being learned in SLA
Minority-language student	Student whose native language is not the main language spoken in that country (a misleading term, however, because a language other than English is the *majority* language in many classrooms of English learners)
ELL	English-language learner (English learner)
Fluent-English-proficient (FEP), or Fluent-English speaker (FES)	English learner who is ready for redesignation (mainstreaming)
Limited-English-proficient (LEP), or Limited-English speaker (LES)	English learner who is not yet ready for redesignation
Non–English-proficient (NEP), or Non–English speaker (NES)	English learner who is in the first stages of learning English

underlie language usage. A critical perspective is one that looks at broad social issues of dual-language proficiency and language policy from a point of view that promotes social transformation. It asks teachers to develop a deeper understanding of the effects of culture and language on the success—or disenfranchisement—of minority students by school culture, curriculum, and instructional methods in order to promote social change toward increased social equity and social justice.

As Wink (2000) has stated, "Critical does not mean to criticize. Rather, it means seeing beyond. It means looking within and without and seeing more deeply into the complexities of teaching and learning" (p. 29). It is my hope that those who use this book will become inspired to look within, around, and beyond social and educational issues; to ask probing questions concerning the role of educators in the struggle to attain fairness, justice, equity, and equal opportunity in the world; and also to work toward social equity and justice as part of their role a language educators.

Equity issues connected to the teaching of English do not disappear when English is taught as a foreign language. The same social, political, and economic forces that have mandated English learning in countries around the world have created layers of access and disenfranchisement that facilitate enrollment in English courses for social elites while barring the door to the poor. English as an international language (EIL) is an area of sociological and linguistic study that traces the impact of English on societies around the world. Those who equate English with traditions of social justice and democracy may be in for a rude awakening, for English is deployed within a wide variety of nations without democratic goals and ideals as well as in countries which share liberal Western cultural values.

Challenges for Teachers of English Learners

The first challenge is to teach English effectively, to motivate English learners to achieve the highest possible level of proficiency possible under the circumstances, and to gain a sensitive and complex understanding of the target culture. In this process, teachers of English who represent the highest ideals of the American target culture will work to create a classroom environment characterized by equal opportunity and democratic process. One can only wish that English learning represents a positive experience for the majority of English learners.

The second challenge for the teacher of English learners is to respect the native language and the rights of its speakers. Those who teach speakers of other languages are language acquisition experts. English teachers who make sincere attempts to learn the languages of their students and build English on students' prior language expertise will model expert learning. Teachers of English learners are intercultural educators, whose understanding of crosscultural similarities and differences will further the abilities of the learners to acquire appreciation for the target culture.

Languages at Risk

Unfortunately, the rich linguistic heritage of the peoples on earth today is at risk. Of course the dominant languages of the world are not threatened—the 1,113 million Chinese speakers, for example, outnumber the native 352 million English speakers by a ratio of three to one. By the year 2050, 556 million speakers of Urdu and Hindi, 486 million speakers of Spanish, and 482 million speakers of Arabic will more than hold their own numerically against 508 million speakers of English (Wallraff, 2000).

Minor languages, however, are in jeopardy. According to Woodbury (1997), there are roughly 5,000 to 6,000 languages spoken in today's world. A century from now, the number will almost certainly fall to the low thousands or even the hundreds. Even now, fewer than 300 of these languages have more than one million speakers; half of the world's languages have fewer than 10,000 users (Skutnabb-Kangas, 2001). Nearly half of the world's languages are already moribund, that is, they are no longer being learned by children. Many linguistic communities find themselves under intense pressure to adopt the language of powerful neighbors or invaders, often jeopardizing their own languages, and even their ethnic identity, in the process. The linguistic diversity most at risk includes the tribes of Papua New Guinea, who alone speak as many as 900 languages; the native peoples of the Americas, who in ever-smaller numbers still retain 900 or so of their indigenous languages; national and tribal minorities of Africa, Asia, and Oceania, speaking several thousand more languages; and marginalized European peoples such as the Irish, the Frisians, the Provençaux, and the Basques. (See the website www.yourdictionary.com for an Endangered Language Repository.)

The single greatest threat to languages with tiny numbers of speakers is often the language of the colonizer, of the most profitable trading partner, or of a more numerous and aggressive nearby population. In California, for example, the number of speakers of the 100 Native American languages spoken 150 years ago at the time of the arrival of English-speaking settlers has dwindled decade by decade. At present, there are about 1,000 speakers of these languages, representing 27 languages or language families (Hinton & Montijo, 1994). English is the native language of the children of these native groups, with the exception of the Spanish-speaking Indian people (Kumeyaay, Ipai, Tipai, and Quechan) residing on the border of Mexico and the United States. In San Bernardino, California, where I reside, the native Indian language Serrano has two remaining native speakers. Part of the work of the M.A. in Education, TESOL Option program at my university is to teach young people to respect Serrano as part of the heritage of the local area.

What happens when a language dies? Woodbury (2001, p. 1) described this damage in eloquent terms: "Language loss entails the loss of much of the cultural, spiritual, and intellectual life of a people as experienced through language, ranging from prayers, myths, ceremonies, poetry, oratory, and technical vocabulary, to everyday greetings, leave-takings, conversational styles, humor, ways of speaking to children, and unique terms for habits, behavior, and emotions." When a language is lost, there is no guarantee that all this can be refashioned in the new language; when it does take place, such refashioning involves abrupt loss of tradition. More often, replacement cultural forms from other languages take over, transmitted often by schools or by television; this process may be accelerated by force, by intolerance practiced by the powerful against the weak, or by what Skutnabb-Kangas (1993) called *linguistic genocide*, "systematic extermination of a minority language."

Aside from the toll on specific human cultures, social groups, and individuals' personal identities, the impending loss of linguistic diversity will limit scientific knowledge about the human mind. Language diversity tells us about the types of languages

Native American students need maintenance bilingual programs as well as cultural content in English to preserve the Native American languages.

people can and cannot learn, how these differ, what such limitations may reveal about human cognition, and what this can tell us about the ways in which infants and young children acquire the range of diverse language structures now known to us.

Educators can address the problem of language endangerment in two positive ways. One is to volunteer to work with communities around the world who wish to preserve their languages, offering technical and other assistance in programs of language teaching, language maintenance, and even language revival. The other approach is to assist English learners to grow toward full bilinguality while documenting the primary language using videotape, audiotape, and written records of both formal and informal language use. Only in the context of full support for the bilingual, bicultural learner does the teaching of English respect the learner's linguistic and cultural heritage. Boseker (1999/2000) suggested ways in which educators can strengthen the capacity of indigenous communities to preserve their linguistic heritage. Chapter 2 and Appendix A explore in more depth the role of educators in language planning and policy issues, and Chapter 7 examines ways in which educators can involve the broader heritage language community in English learning.

❖ **Tactics for teachers to support heritage languages:**

- ◆ Further the teaching of English while respecting native language rights.
- ◆ Volunteer to learn an endangered language.
- ◆ Help speakers of endangered languages to speak, read, or write in that language.

Who Are English Learners and What Are Their Needs?

Before looking at English teaching around the world, some fundamental questions need to be posed. Asking these questions helps frame the context for English instruction (Kaplan, 2001).

> Why will English be taught, and what variety?
>
> Who are the learners?
>
> Who are the teachers, and how are they trained?
>
> When will instruction begin, how long will it last, and who will pay the expenses?
>
> Who prepares the syllabus and teaching materials?
>
> Who determines what methods are appropriate, how the success of students is assessed, and whether or not the teaching program is effective?
>
> What role do the learners, or parents of learners, play in decision making?

From these questions it is clear that language teaching is intricately interwoven with language planning and policy decisions (see Chapter 2). The following overview of the education of English learners in the United States and in selected countries around the world is presented with the above questions in mind.

◆ **STRATEGY 1.2:** Know who your learners are and why they need English

U.S. Demographics

Higher birthrates among nonwhites than among whites, together with steady immigration rates, have impacted U.S. demographics and created a need for ESL services. California still leads the United States in demographic changes, as "minorities" became the majority in California in the year 2000. The U.S. Census Bureau estimates that whites are 49.9 percent of the state's 33.1 million residents. Latinos follow at 31.6 percent, Asians, 11.4 percent, African Americans, 6.7 percent, and American Indians less than 1 percent (Nelson & O'Reilly, 2000).

The number of students in the United States from non–English-speaking backgrounds, including those who are exposed to English only at school, is large and growing. In 2001 this number stood at roughly 3.4 million. English learners and their families are increasingly living in places like the Midwest and the South that have not previously needed to hire English-language development teachers. The largest populations of English learners are Hispanic/Latino and Asian/Pacific Islander.

In 2000, 32.8 million Latinos resided in the United States, accounting for 12 percent of the total U.S. population. Of these, 66.1 percent were of Mexican origin (meaning either from Mexico or of Mexican American origin), 14.5 percent were Central and South American, 9 percent were Puerto Rican, 4 percent Cuban, and 6.4 percent of other Hispanic origin (the terms "Hispanic" and Latino" are used interchangeably in the 2000 census reports). Latinos of Mexican origin live mostly in the West (56.8 percent) and South (32.6 percent); Cubans predominate in the South (80.1 percent); Puerto Ricans in the Northeast (63.9 percent); and Central and South Americans in the

Northeast (32.3 percent), the South (34.6 percent) and the West (28.2 percent) (U.S. Census Bureau, 2001b). Hispanics make up more than 30 percent of the population of New York City (Wallraff, 2000). Nearly half of all Hispanics live in the center of a city within a metropolitan area (46.4 percent). In 1999, 22.8 percent of all Hispanics were living in poverty (compared to 7.7 percent of non-Hispanic whites). In addition, Hispanic children under eighteen were more likely than non-Hispanic white children to be living in poverty (30.3 percent versus 9.4 percent) (U.S. Census Bureau, 2001b).

In March 1999 the Asian and Pacific Islander population in the United States numbered 10.1 million, constituting 4 percent of the population. ("Asian" refers to those belonging to any of the original peoples of the Far East, Southeast Asia, or the Indian subcontinent including Cambodia, China, India, Japan, Korea, Malaysia, Pakistan, the Philippine Islands, Thailand, and Vietnam. "Pacific Islander" refers to those belonging to any of the original peoples of Hawaii, Guam, Samoa, or other Pacific islands.) Approximately 2.4 percent of these Asians are Chinese speakers, and of these more than 80 percent prefer to speak Chinese at home (Wallraff, 2000). Nationally, 96 percent of the Asian and Pacific Islander population currently live in metropolitan areas, with 45 percent living in central cities—double the proportion for non-Hispanic whites (22 percent) (U.S. Census Bureau, 2001a).

Nationwide, in 1990 about one in seven people spoke a language other than English at home. By 2001, that number had risen to 18 percent of the population (U.S. Census Bureau, 2001c). States vary in this percentage, with California leading at 40 percent, followed by New Mexico at 36 percent and Texas at 32 percent. Swerdlow's (2001) detailed population maps show when and where immigration occurred within the continental United States. In 1998 California, with a school enrollment of approximately 1.4 million English learners, led the states in the need for ESL services at the K–12 level (California State Department of Education, 2001).

ESL Services for English Learners

By and large, then, in the United States, those who educate English learners are more likely to find employment in California, New Mexico, New York, or Texas, and in schools in city centers, serving Hispanics or Asians and Pacific Islanders. Aside from this employment likelihood, demographics indicate that services for English learners are needed in every state and large city.

From these demographics, it should be clear that ESL education in the United States is deeply bound up with the problems of inner-city education. There are many English learners among the 50 percent yearly dropout population of the Boston public school system, or the 70 percent dropout population in the New York public schools. Macedo & Freire (1998, p. ix) claimed that the United States is experiencing the "Third-Worldization" of North America, with high levels of poverty, violence, homelessness, and human misery in the inner cities of the United States that approach proportions seen in the shantytowns of the disadvantaged nations of the world. According to the latest statistics found in *The State of America's Children Yearbook 2000* (Children's Defense Fund, 2000), one in five, or 13.5 million, children are living in poverty in the United States, 5.8 million of them in extreme poverty in households with an income of less than $6,500 a year for a family of three. To educate these students, resources are badly needed, resources that are often not available to inner-city schools. The richest school districts spend 56 percent more per student than do the poorest; schools with large numbers of poor children tend to have fewer books and supplies and teachers with less training and experience. Thus the urgent need for excellence in education for English learners is further complicated by the fact that many of the very students enrolled in these programs in the United States are poor and attend poorly equipped schools.

Career Preparation for ESL Teaching

In states that support bilingual education, teachers with bilingual fluency who can deliver primary-language education K–6 in the languages of demand often receive hiring preference over educators who do not have bilingual certification. In the course of their primary-language instruction in literacy and in content areas, these teachers are then expected also to deliver English language development (ELD) instruction. In states where structured immersion (content delivery in English, usually without support for primary-language literacy) is the norm for K–12 English learners, teachers may be asked to use specially designed academic instruction in English (SDAIE) strategies (see Chapter 3) in addition to ELD. Elementary and secondary school teachers in most states must have a degree in education. Most elementary or secondary education teaching positions in school districts heavily impacted by English learners also require a ESL/TESL/ESOL/TESOL certification or an add-on endorsement in ESL.

For teacher education positions as well as community college and precollege preparation of international students (intensive English programs, or IEPs), an M.A. degree is the basic requirement. The website for TESOL, Inc. offers an online directory of teacher education programs in North America.

For teachers who plan to teach outside the United States and later return to the United States for a master's degree, certification in ESL/TESL/ESOL/TESOL (not TEFL) may count toward the completion of the M.A. degree or state certification upon return to the United States.

Teaching adult immigrants to function successfully in an ESL environment can be richly rewarding, for seldom does one find a more grateful or devoted group of students. Aside from the level of survival skills (gaining employment, finding housing, and providing vocational English), higher levels of professional ESP can include worksite training for engineering and computer professionals and other career-enhancing efforts. When such training is offered by high-level consultants to Fortune 500 companies, the pay for teachers/trainers can be lucrative.

Certification for teaching in adult English programs in the United States is less standardized than are requirements in K–12 schools. Some states have statewide certification, but in others the professional requirements vary from one service provider to the next. Each employer can make the local requirements and training options available to prospective employees.

The availability of teaching employment in the United States, then, depends on the population, the role of ELD teaching in relation to bilingual education, and the local need for qualified ESOL experts. One fact, however, remains a constant: The current shortage of teachers in U.S. classrooms will worsen in the decade 2000–2010, with urban school districts facing the most extreme shortfalls. The United States is expected to need at least two million teachers by 2011. Districts are setting aside funds for teacher bonuses, training, and recruitment; raising starting salaries for teachers; and recruiting abroad for teachers in such specialty areas as bilingual education. The employability outlook has never been better for teachers who specialize in teaching English learners.

❖ Tactics for teachers that increase employability:

◆ Be aware of the connection between local language populations and career opportunities in teaching.
◆ Engage in career preparation that certifies instruction at more than a single level.
◆ Find out what specific kind of ESOL instruction is offered at various levels of education.

International Demographics of English

Shakespeare's English at the end of the sixteenth century was the native speech of between five and seven million Britons. Today, English is used by at least 750 million people, although barely half of those speak it as a mother tongue. Three quarters of the world's written communications, more than half of the world's technical and scientific periodicals, 80 percent of the information stored in the world's computers, and nearly half of all business deals in Europe are conducted in English (McCrum, Cran, & MacNeil, 1986). In fact, despite the admission of ten additional states to the European Union and the establishment of eleven languages with equal rights, English is nudging out French as the language of diplomacy in Europe (Phillipson, 2003). Estimates of the number of people who have studied English as a foreign language vary widely—it could be as low as 100 million or as high as a billion.

No one is sure, moreover, what level of mastery of English determines whether a user of the language is proficient. Richard Parker, in his book *Mixed Signals: Prospects for Global Television News* (1995) reported that a study in the early 1990s tested 4,500 Europeans for "perceived" versus "actual" English skills and found that in countries such as France, Spain, and Italy, fewer than 3 percent had an excellent command of English. Only in Scandinavia, the Netherlands, and Belgium did the number rise above 10 percent. These sobering statistics indicate that English may not, after all, be the perfect international communication tool. In fact, several factors may be putting at serious risk the idea that English will continue to dominate worldwide discourse (Wallraff, 2000): the backlash against American values and culture in the Middle East and other places; the rise of regional trading zones in Asia, Latin America, and the Middle East; and the demographic surge of young non–English speakers in Asia, Africa, and the Middle East.

Many have touted the Internet as a medium that will circulate English around the world. However, as the technology becomes more widely available, people will naturally prefer to use the Web in their home language. Of the 56 million who use languages other than English on the Internet, nearly 25 percent are Spanish speakers, and 13.1 percent speak an Asian language at home (Wallraff, 2000). In fact, the Internet has proved useful in pulling together speakers from obscure languages such as Basque in order to slow the speed of linguistic eradication. No matter how much material is available on the Web, one cannot simply assume that people will use the medium as a tool to practice English. After all, most people want television delivered in their native language. As the Internet is more widely available for recreation and entertainment, it may become more and more similar to television: People may consume and use it in their native language in preference to English. After all, 5,700 million people in the world are *not* native speakers of English.

Hot on the heels of research in developing enhanced Internet capacity are programs that translate from one language to another, such as Alta Vista's free translator, Babel Fish (although the quality is not entirely accurate). Machine translation may not reduce the need for an international language, but there is no guarantee that someday this may not reduce the need for English proficiency worldwide.

Given these conditions, one cannot simply assume that the demand for English will develop apace with world population growth. The presence of a variety of trends argues as much *for* the increasing role of global English as *against*. Despite the culture shock they may face by going overseas to teach—and the shock of cultural "reentry" they often face when returning—many educators cherish the time spent working abroad and gain much self-esteem by teaching in countries in which the profession of English teaching is held in highest regard. Whatever the long-range opportunities, for the present, teaching English learners is among the world's fastest-growing occupations.

Contexts for English Teaching Worldwide

Despite concerns that call into question the value and utility of English to the world's cultures and peoples, there is no doubt that many countries are eager for ESOL services. Following is a brief sampling of the conditions in which English is taught in various countries and areas of the world. In Japan it is widely believed that people who can speak English well have an advantage in obtaining and advancing their careers, and such individuals are seen as having a sophisticated manner and a broad and flexible sense of the world as international businesspeople (Ikenaga, 1979). However, few Japanese people need English skills in their everyday life. Teachers who are native speakers of English are employed by the Japanese Exchange Teacher (JET) program at the high school level, but there is also work in the private *eikaiwa* (conversation) schools (Morrison, 1997).

In South Korea, English plays a crucial role in academic performance as a requirement for admission to competitive universities, as well as in entering prestigious occupations and, later, obtaining advancement at work. Since 1994 communicative language teaching, emphasizing listening and speaking, has been featured in secondary schools, and English has been required in elementary schools since 1997. An impetus to learning English for many Koreans is the desire to live in the United States, which is home to over two million expatriate Koreans, 600,000 of whom live in the Los Angeles area (van der Woude, 1998).

In Taiwan most students study English beginning in junior high school or earlier. About 80 percent of the economy of Taiwan relies on importing and exporting with English being the most commonly used language in the global economic system as well as in trade between other Asian countries. Many students study English in order to visit, study, or live in the United States. English is largely a tool for passing senior high school or university entrance examinations. However, five-year vocational colleges feature curricula rich in ESP opportunities in such areas as computer training, business management, or import-export trade. Other openings for English teaching are in the private after-school or after-work "cram" schools, in which creative alternatives to rote classroom instruction are possible.

In the People's Republic of China, English is widely taught, although the preferred target language is British English. The demand for teachers who are native speakers of English is high, although the pay is low by Western standards. Those who have an M.A. in TESOL may find themselves teaching English teachers or preparing advanced students for the required nationwide English examinations. Conversational classes are also popular (Ness, 1998).

In 2001 France announced a package of government reforms aimed at lowering the age at which French children start studying a foreign language to six in 2004 and five in 2005. Since 1998 students have had the opportunity to begin learning a foreign language at age ten, although it is mandatory by age eleven. These changes will require the employment of 1,850 language assistants in the schools per year. Not all French citizens are happy with these policies, however. Many teachers fear that the new policy will result in the dominance of English (Pugliese, 2001).

In Tunisia most students learn English as a fourth language, after Tunisian Arabic, classical Arabic, and French. Despite the dominance of French as a Western language, English is gradually gaining ground in some sectors of society (Battenberg, 1997).

In Israel all university students need a high level of reading comprehension in English, for the vast majority of courses feature reading assignments in English. However, as written and oral assignments and class lectures take place in Hebrew, students tend to prioritize learning the meaning of technical vocabulary words in English (Kirschner, 1993).

In eastern Europe, the breakup of the Soviet Union and the declining influence of Russian culture and language has brought new life into English studies in former Soviet-bloc countries such as Hungary, the Czech Republic, and Poland. In former republics of the Soviet Union, however, the surge of nationalist sentiments and the scramble for economic survival has served to emphasize communication in the native language and in the language of nearby trading partners over a large-scale push for English proficiency (Darian, 2001). In Russia students generally begin to learn English at the age of ten but may start as early as age five or six. However, outside Moscow or St. Petersburg, there are few opportunities to use English outside the classroom. Teaching positions for foreigners are limited at the primary and secondary levels, but institutions of higher education and foreign-language institutes employ native speakers, and exchange programs are available (Menconi, 1996).

In Mexico, English is in high demand in the wake of the North American Free Trade Agreement (NAFTA) and the opening of the Mexican economy. Anglo-American culture is extremely popular, represented by subtitled Hollywood movies, dubbed American television shows, American baseball and football news, and various forms of pop and rock music in English on radio and television. Positions for English teachers are found mainly in private schools, private English institutes, or in businesses (Wall, 2001).

In Colombia the extreme economic and security situation, as well as the number of multinational companies doing business in Colombia, have created a surge of interest in engineering and technical English. All universities offer two semesters of English, usually focused on reading comprehension, with courses taught largely by nonnative English-speakers (Deer, 2001). Ecuador, in contrast, has much to offer EFL teachers with M.A. degrees, who may receive a reasonable teaching load at a provincial university, free health insurance, and paid vacations (Owens, 1998). In Uruguay, English is taught as a required subject at the secondary level and, since 1993, in the primary schools. Even small towns have English institutes, in which students work to complete international certificates. Teacher training is also available through distance learning (Pérez de Lima, 1996).

In Cuba, English is a compulsory subject in secondary school for pre-university majors. English is the most widely-spoken foreign language in Cuba, where English-language magazines are available in hotels, and at least one television program that teaches English is broadcast nationwide (Irizar, 2001).

Teaching English around the World

TESOL professionals seeking to work globally may find that the era is over in which native English-speakers could be hired to teach English solely on the basis of their native speech. The M.A. in TESOL is a better "ticket" abroad than a teaching credential or a certificate from a TESL or TEFL training course, especially in westernized countries. Racial discrimination also plays a part in hiring in many countries. One native speaker of English of Korean background who was raised in Chicago encountered difficulties when applying to teach English in an Asian country. The reason? He did not "look" like a native English speaker! In many countries there are no laws prohibiting discrimination and few laws to protect foreigners' employment rights.

There is increasing evidence that being a native English-speaker will be less and less of a hiring advantage in the coming years. In fact, as the twenty-first century advances, English will be shaped less and less by the cultures of English-speaking countries and will show more and more influence of "fusion," in which the language is subject to hybridization (this is already the case for "fusion cuisine," as English-speakers routinely order *lattes,* tacos, *sushi,* and pita bread).

It is a desirable goal overseas, if not actually an attainable one, for TESOL educators to be aware of the local flavor of the language. For example, the website India World (www.indiawebservices.net) offers a search for travel and tourism that reveals a guide to "himachal pradesh of India covering chamba and its attractions, temples, resorts, hotels, destinations, business, Chaugan, minjar, salooni, bharmour, sarol, pangi, maninahesh, ravi, caddies, gaddi, vishnuman, chaurassi, himachalonline, megri, hadsar, pangwala, champawati, chhariyatra, and dhanchho." Good luck, and I advise taking a glossary. And this is a country in which English has an official function! English in India is definitely not the English of Kansas.

It may well be, in fact, that the English spoken in Nigeria, Trinidad, Scotland, and Montana may already be mutually unintelligible, with the gap worsening moment by moment. Whole lists of lexical entries differ from one English country to another: In South Africa, a *robot* is a traffic light; in England, a *lift* is an elevator, a *lorry* is a truck, and a *boot* is the trunk of a car; in Massachusetts, a *frappe* is a milkshake; and in South Asia, a *hotel* is a restaurant. It may be that the concept of English as an international language is already passé, as the English of India is far enough from the

English of Nigeria to be no longer considered the same language. English may soon find itself in the quandary of Chinese: the written language is shared, but Cantonese and Mandarin are considered separate languages.

English teaching is an attractive international career, one that, although imperfect, offers interesting professional and personal growth opportunities. As Wall (2001) states, "Teaching English in a foreign country has its own rewards: viewing your native language from another perspective, living and working in a foreign country not as a tourist but as an insider, and the exhilaration of really communicating in a foreign language." According to Johnston (1997), TESOL is the quintessential postmodern profession, featuring an international perspective, translinguistic work at the borders of culture, and the necessity to deploy a flexible, self-constructed identity. What more could one ask?

One is best advised to prepare carefully for a job overseas; TESOL, Inc. offers articles in the Placement E-Bulletin (PEB) that may often provide additional articles and tips for working outside the United States (sample tip: Candidates should take plenty of official transcripts and copies if planning to teach abroad—they may need to change jobs while overseas). Whether you are looking for a teaching position or are just curious about ESL/EFL employment trends, PEB is a useful resource. To subscribe to PEB, you must be a TESOL member.

❖ **Tactics for teachers to teach successfully abroad:**

- Be prepared for local adaptation and adjust your teaching to local needs.
- Despite the fact that you may have native-like or native-speaker proficiency in English, you may not understand the English of the natives!
- Gain experience teaching English overseas while the demand for instructors who are native-English speakers is high.
- Negotiate job details carefully before accepting an overseas position.

English as an International Language (EIL)

No one will question the fact that English has achieved some sort of global status. Three linked events created the opportunity for English to spread worldwide and fulfill social and economic functions in the lives of people from many nations: (1) the global military, political, and economic imperialism of Great Britain and the United States; (2) the defeat of Japan and Germany in World War II, with the subsequent reconstruction of their cultures and economies more aligned with English-speaking cultures; and (3) the global deployment of the Internet, resulting from a communication matrix connecting the technical and scientific universities in the United States (Wark, 2001). As such, English has become an international language, used by many the world over as a common linguistic currency.

Many regard the spread of English around the world as the beneficial result of a natural process, in which English is benignly chosen as a trade lingo of choice because as a language it is somehow neutral in its social, political, and economic entailment. In reality, nothing could be further from the truth. Researchers who have looked closely at the role of English as an international language have challenged the spread of English in its global and local contexts. What are the implications of using English globally? Pennycook (1994) frames the issue with the following questions: To what uses is English put? What different meanings does it come to carry? Is the spread of English indeed *natural, neutral,* and *beneficial*?

Is English Natural?   To see the domination of English as *natural* is to believe that EIL is the result of inevitable global forces; that some language would eventually come to dominate others; and that, as it happened, English filled this slot. This conviction in effect excuses international English from the sins of its perpetrators. To choose one example, the use of English on the part of the people of Puerto Rico, one of the foremost colonies of the United States (Pérez, 1976), is the result of a series of coercive government policies that have mandated English instruction at one level or another in Puerto Rican schools from 1905 to the present (Cebollero, 1975). To choose another example, English use in Japan would be much lower if China instead of the United States had occupied Japan after World War II. Yet another example is the way in which U.S. foreign policy created connections with populations abroad that pulled certain groups to the United States. For example, the conquest of the Philippines at the beginning of the twentieth century eventually resulted in large Philippine immigration to the United States. Later, during the Vietnam War and its aftermath, Cambodians who cooperated with the U.S. military immigrated to the United States (Gillett, 1989). Imperialism and wars are not new, however; the British forced their way into mainland China in the nineteenth century using opium addiction as a tool, and to this day English-language newspapers in Beijing use British spelling as the norm. Basically, English has spread around the world in most unnatural ways (unless war, addiction, and coercion can be considered the natural state of humankind). One can only hope that the twenty-first century brings English to speakers of other languages using kinder means.

Is English Neutral?   Is English a *neutral,* transparent medium of communication, detached from its original cultural contexts and not ideologically encumbered? First, one may hope that English will remain "ideologically encumbered" with the highest ideals: equality of opportunity, social justice, and human rights. However, it is naive to believe that people around the world are choosing to study English in a neutral way. To do so would be tantamount to denying that English proficiency worldwide is associated with middle- or upper-class status, access to higher education, and cultural encumbrances including the embrace of modernity.

Teaching English is therefore not only a matter of efficiency, involving innocent quests for effective methods and communicative access. EIL is heavily implicated in many social systems abroad that reproduce inequities in wealth, power, and privilege. Because English is the means to achieve education, employment, and social position, its use creates and maintains social divisions dominated by elites. Like access to technology, English is a player in a system that is widening the gap between global "haves" and "have-nots," with the ownership of knowledge becoming ever more one-sided. In many countries, not speaking or reading English is an assurance that one will remain in an unskilled job. Even in America's premier colony, Puerto Rico, those who have learned English successfully may answer telephones in the executive suites of international pharmaceutical companies, while those who speak only Spanish may find themselves hauling boxes on the loading dock of the same company, paid minimum wage or less (Díaz, 1988).

Is English Beneficial?   One final question that Pennycook posed is this: Is the spread of English *beneficial*? Can one adopt the blandly optimistic view that international communication in English is a positive force for international understanding? To believe that English is solely beneficial and that there is no downside to its hegemony is to deny its threat to other languages, to assume that English plays no role in the "linguistic genocide" (Skutnabb-Kangas, 1993, 2000) of other languages. Such a belief also assumes that this spread occurs on a cooperative and equitable footing, denying the role that English plays in many countries as a gatekeeper to social and economic progress. Like the spread of capitalism, international development aid, American media-disseminated popular culture, and international academic relations, the drive to attain English proficiency has its good and bad points. Just as consumers can become dependent on store-bought goods that were not considered necessary in traditional cultures, students can become dependent not only on knowing English for academic purposes but also on English-language media to spur desires that are, in the final analysis, irrelevant for their own best needs and purposes. This is the danger inherent in a world language when the world is not an equal playing field.

The changing nature of English—its evolution en route to becoming "the world's language," and the pros and cons of this process—are a part of the curriculum in educating teachers of English to speakers of other languages (Brown, 2001). Teachers are becoming increasingly aware that like many other aspects of teaching, teaching English involves power and politics.

❖ Tactic for teachers to understand English as an international language:

◆ Don't be naive about the social and economic forces that coexist with the demand for English worldwide.

Professional Organizations for Teachers of English Learners

◆ **STRATEGY 1.3:** Join with other professionals to facilitate teaching

TESOL, Inc. as an Organization

TESOL, Inc. promotes excellence in education for English learners and a high-quality professional environment for their teachers. TESOL's mission is to develop the expertise of its members and others involved in teaching English to speakers of other languages to help them foster effective communication in diverse settings while respecting individuals' language rights. To this end, TESOL articulates and advances standards for professional preparation and employment, continuing education, and student programs; links groups worldwide to enhance communication among language specialists; produces high-quality programs, services, and products; and promotes sound, research-based education policy and practices that increase awareness of the strengths and needs of English learners and further appreciation of diverse linguistic and cultural backgrounds.

TESOL is organized around twenty interest sections, offering the opportunity for members to focus on particular areas of expertise such as Teacher Education, ESOL in Adult Education, Intercultural Communications, and Computer-Assisted Language Learning, to name but a few. Associated regional organizations comprise over 100 affiliates, with such titles as Thailand TESOL (ThaiTESOL), IATEFL Hungary, Moroccan Association of Teachers of English (MATE), and California/Nevada TESOL (CATESOL). Most affiliates hold yearly conferences or institutes for professional development so that teachers, administrators, and researchers with a distinct focus on areas such as elementary, secondary, adult, and university education can meet and share expertise.

Finding a Job Teaching English Learners

To become better qualified to teach ESL or EFL, it may be wise to subscribe to TESOL's Employment Clearinghouse, in which one can browse the Career Center articles, request a printed Career Counsel, or use the *JobFinder*. This is a Web-based job bank in which one can research jobs from around the world, post a resume, apply for jobs online, or even set up search agents that send e-mail when a job is posted that fits the seeker's criteria. TESOL's in-person Employment Clearinghouse, held in concert with the annual convention, serves as a networking event in the field of TESOL where job seekers can meet face to face with prospective employers.

❖ Tactics for teachers to meet, "network," and enhance employment options:

- Investigate the local and regional TESOL affiliates.
- Explore the TESOL interest sections available with membership.
- Use sample job search Internet programs.

The best educators are those whose passion for teaching and learning nurtures within their students the capacity for critical literacy and joyful lifelong learning, along with a sense of respect and pride regarding human diversity and the desire to promote intercultural understanding. This accomplishment is made possible through professional collaboration among colleagues who together undertake the task of achieving full literacy and social justice, accompanied by equal access to, and opportunity for, quality education for all students. Critical educators become advocates for a more inclusive society, in which language, literacy, and culture play a central, integrated role in the understanding, communication, and respect needed to improve and transform education in local and global communities.

Those who teach English learners work within a full range of social, cultural, and linguistic contexts. They engage in reflective practice, promote reciprocal teaching/learning relationships, develop pedagogical knowledge that is socioculturally based, and honor in themselves and others the diversity in culture, language, socioeconomic status, and talents that makes us all uniquely human.

Critical Roles for Teachers

Teachers influence the daily lives of students in their classrooms. They can create a climate of warmth, acceptance, and high achievement for English learners, supporting the home language while fostering the growth of English. Conversely, they can allow policies of the school to benefit the English-dominant students at the expense of English learners. As relative newcomers to English, English learners may need their instructor's support to negotiate their way in a new culture. Teachers of English learners cannot ignore the effects of power and policy issues. A critical stance is necessary in order to understand these issues.

❖ **MEGASTRATEGY 2:** Advance the interests of the learner

Educators as Critical Pedagogists

Teachers of English learners have a special role in the classroom: as language emissaries and mediators; as agents of introduction to the target culture; and as sources of professional knowledge for their colleagues. Teachers who are aware of students' needs at various stages of their adjustment to the academic demands of schools and the stresses of life will help students to be more successful learners and intellectual partners.

◆ **STRATEGY 2.1:** Set professional goals with the learner's best interests in mind, as the learner defines them

What Is Critical Pedagogy?

The term *critical pedagogy* originated in the work of Paulo Freire. In the 1950s and early 1960s, Freire ran an adult native-language literacy project in northeast Brazil. Rather than using a standard text, Freire and his teachers taught using "generative" words based on the learners' social conditions and environment, such as *slum, land, salary, government, wealth*, and so on. Freire chose these words because they had special affective importance to the learners and reflected their social, cultural, and political contexts (Spener, 1992).

Using this method, Freire aimed to develop literacy built upon the themes and actions identified in everyday life. By learning to read and write, students would also learn to criticize and act upon their conditions (Brown, 1987). They could seize ownership of the written code to change their lives and social circumstances and gain the confidence to begin to free themselves from oppression and exploitation. Freire believed that one of the main tasks of adult education was to increase people's belief in themselves (Freire, 1973).

Freire popularized the term "conscientization," which means to learn to perceive, resist, and transform the social, political, and economic contradictions within the learner's everyday world as well as within society in general (Freire, 1970, p. 28). When Freire's work became more widely known in Brazil, he was eventually jailed and exiled. After Brazil's military regime was overthrown, Freire served as the education minister of the province containing São Paulo, Brazil's largest city.

Glass (2001) has offered a eulogy to Freire that is both eloquent and comprehensive:

> Nearly four years after his death, a world still mourns Paulo Freire. Freire's theory about the relationship between liberation and education has inspired and informed countless efforts to make life more human for those oppressed by economic and ideological structures that denied them their dignity, rights, and self-determination. The ideas in *Pedagogy of the Oppressed* (1970) have been applied in every continent, in projects ranging from grassroots basic literacy programs to national educational policies. Many people engaged in progressive struggles for justice—teachers, students, community organizers, workers, movement activists, and citizens from every walk of life—who studied his work discovered practices worth translating into their own contexts. Freire's legacy is unprecedented for an educator: None other has influence practice in such a wide array of contexts and cultures, or helped to enable so many of the world's disempowered turn education toward their own dreams. (p. 15)

Educators around the world who understand his pedagogy of hope (Freire, 1987, 1994, 1998) have adopted Freire's learner-centered literacy approach in native- and second-language literacy projects in both rural and urban settings (Spener, 1992). In the United States, many community-based organizations have used the approach to developing basic literacy in English, in native languages other than English, and in English as a second language. In the process these methods, originally designed for native-language literacy, are adapted to the education of English learners (see Auerbach, 1995; Graman, 1988). As Hones (1999) put it, "Critical pedagogy is a way of teaching and learning that poses problems about the world, with the goal of helping all participants become more fully human and transform the reality around them" (p. 27).

Critical Pedagogy as a Method

Critical pedagogy begins with *problem posing*. Teachers help learners to draw upon their experiences, culture, and personal strengths to try to resolve problems in their everyday lives. Teachers learn about problems in the community by walking through students' neighborhoods with students or alone, talking to people on the street, and observing living conditions, habits, and material objects. Conversations with students reveal as much as they are willing to relate about their home country, how their lives compare in their previous and new countries, and what values they want to retain.

To verify what topics are vital for the students, teachers select and present familiar situations to students. Photographs, drawings, collages, stories, written dialogues, movies, or songs are used as stimulus situations called *codes*. Each situation contains personal or social conflicts that are emotionally charged. The teacher asks a series of open-ended questions about these materials so that students can elaborate upon what they see, in this way defining the real-life problem being represented, discussing its causes, and proposing actions that can be taken to solve it (Wallerstein, 1983).

Inductive questions move students from the concrete to a more analytical level: "What do you see?" (students describe and name the problem); "How does this apply to you?" (students define and personalize the problem); "How does the problem apply to your own situations?" (students describe connections); "Why does this problem exist?" (students fit their individual experiences into a larger historical, social, or cultural context); "What are some solutions?" (students discuss alternatives). This last step leads students into plans for action. During the use of the code, teachers avoid asking for information that would jeopardize students' legal or work status.

In developing the content of the curriculum, teachers and students work as partners, with equal status as learners. Freire described their dialogue as an "I–thou relationship between two subjects" in which both parties confront each other as knowledgeable equals in a situation of genuine two-way communication (Freire, 1973, p. 52). Teachers possess knowledge of reading and writing; students possess equally valuable knowledge, the concrete reality of their lives. Freire contrasts the problem-posing approach with problem-solving instructional approaches, in which educators identify students' life problems for them and then design lessons to give students the knowledge they need to solve those problems (Auerbach & Burgess, 1985).

Contrasting Critical Pedagogy with Banking Models of Instruction

The technique described above clearly contrasts with ESL lessons that stem from what Freire calls the "banking model" of education, in which the teacher treats students as though their minds were empty accounts in which to deposit information. The banking model is predicated on two deeply entrenched misconceptions. The first is the belief that learners are empty, devoid of useful culture and knowledge. To the contrary, learners are not empty—they lead complex lives full of thoughts, dreams, emotions, families, loyalties, problems, friendships and enmities that can enrich their language life in L2 as in L1.

The second misconception of the banking model is that "standard" knowledge is useful for everyone. In fact, this material is drawn from a "central bank of knowledge" selected and authorized by those with the power to set standards (Shor, 1992). From a critical point of view, existing curricula often exclude the achievements, idioms, and themes important to groups outside the elite. Even if they purport to address the daily challenges met by immigrants, ESL books often contain dialogues featuring survival role-plays that are unrealistic, patronizing, or do not accurately describe social realities (cf. Mosteller & Haight, 1994, for an example of "survival ESL" materials). When students generate their own dialogues, they have more chance to address those issues that they find meaningful.

Sample Topics Used for Problem Posing

The U.S. system of justice furnishes rich discussion. Hones (1999) used ESL instruction based on social studies to study the incarceration of Philadelphia death-row inmate Mumia Abu-Jamal. During reading assignments, class discussions, debates, and field trips to local courts, police stations, and protest sites, students posed problems relating to the criminal justice system in the United States, especially for prisoners whose race, socioeconomic status, and/or politics differ significantly from the mainstream. Hones specifically related race relations to Foucault's analysis of discipline and punishment (Foucault, 1979). Because Hones's students were drawn from a variety of nations, their contrasting views and experiences with social justice enabled a rich dialogue among students.

Problem posing has been used as well in teacher education. Schleppegrell (1997, p. 9) engaged prospective teachers in a critical view of language teaching. Candidates in a teacher education course viewed a videotape of an education class and worked in groups to answer questions about the role of the teacher and students, type of language generated, and tasks performed. Then the class as a whole discussed the question, "Is this good language teaching?" Next, the candidates wrote individually to answer the question, "What questions does this video and our discussion raise for you about your own lessons?" Candidates read relevant source materials to research the effect on learner participation of the methods they had observed. Finally, the teacher candidates revisited the videotaped lesson and planned how they might teach differently in that context.

Using these methods to generate student language using codes drawn from both their daily lives and current social issues, teachers bring English into the classroom that is useful and powerful in ways that students need it to be powerful. Auerbach and Wallerstein's workplace handbook, *ESL for Action* (1987), offers a possible set of codes and questions for discussion. But how can critical pedagogy be modified for use in K–12 classrooms? Chapter 14, which discusses project-based learning, lays out a rapidly growing alternative to lockstep, sequenced, banking-model lesson planning. Both approaches hold fruitful potential for teaching English learners.

❖ **Tactics for teachers who see the possibilities of English learners as problem solvers:**

- Listen and observe as learners tell you who they are and what are their passions.
- Build codes based on students' lives to stimulate discussion.
- Invest in long-term issues in order to grow language that is meaningful to students.

A Critical Sociological Look at Language and Power

◆ **STRATEGY 2.2:** Critique the social conditions of the learner

Teaching methods are not carried out in a vacuum. Sociologists and social philosophers who study language and society have urged a wider perspective on the social tensions that underlie educational language usage. Critical-language theorists offer tools of analysis that unveil language–power relations. Teachers who take a critical stance understand that the everyday realities of schooling—including the oral language of the classroom, the texts, and the written and unwritten practices and policies at the school site, district, and government levels—work in powerful ways to benefit or disadvantage English learners. Critical analysis can uncover ways to oppose discriminatory institutional and social inequities.

A critical perspective, one that looks at broad social issues of dual-language proficiency and language policy, has developed from the work of five theorists in particular: Tollefson, Foucault, Bourdieu, Cummins, and Fairclough. These five theorists represent critical sociological points of view and offer insights about language policies in education.

Tollefson: Power and Inequality in Language Education

Tollefson (1995) has compared language policy issues across a variety of countries, researching the inequity created by social policies and practices that undermine the academic achievement of nonnative language speakers. He has laid the foundation for a worldwide vision of language equity issues.

Tollefson contrasted *descriptive* and *evaluative* ways to understand language behavior (Tollefson, 1991). The descriptive approach examines such linguistic phenomena as low-status versus high-status language, code switching by bilingual speakers in various social contexts, and the way language is used to establish and maintain social position. An evaluative approach, on the other hand, looks at efforts to standardize or purify language, to preserve or revive endangered languages, to establish national languages, or to legislate language usage. Both approaches help to understand issues relating to language and power.

One might view language diversity as a *problem, right,* or *resource* (Ruiz, 1984). The view that bilingualism is a *problem* is at best socially and economically shortsighted. A country with bilingual citizens benefits economically and socially in commerce with other countries. Those who view language diversity as a *right* understand language rights in two ways: "(1) the right of freedom from discrimination on the basis of language; and (2) the right to use your language(s) in the activities of communal life" (Macías, 1979, p. 41). As a *resource*, dual-language proficiency, the attainment of advanced skills in more than one language, will be the source of employment advancement for job seekers in the coming global economy. Tollefson and his colleagues have documented that the struggle to achieve language equity has profound worldwide ramifications.

Foucault: The Power of Discursive Practices

Foucault, a twentieth-century social historian, documented the means by which language practices sustain the spread of power relations in the modern world. Foucault emphasized that the struggle for power is "a struggle for the control of discourses" (Corson, 1999, p. 15). In several important treatises (1973, 1979, 1980, 1984, 1988) Foucault outlined the ways in which authorities have used language to repress and disempower social groups in favor of those in power, and how certain social groups have appropriated language practices for their own ends.

Foucault's contribution to the study of language policy, although indirect, is profound. He has shown that language is not neutral; language is inseparable from the workings of power. Power, however, is neutral; it can be either a creative force for those who use discourse masterfully or a destructive force that excludes those without effective language practices. As Ewald (1992) put it, "We have a responsibility with regard to the way we exercise power: we must not lose the idea that we could exercise it differently" (p. 334).

Bourdieu: Language as Social Capital

According to the French sociologist Bourdieu, language functions as *social capital*, a major form of cultural capital, that is, as a part of the social "goods" that people accumulate and use to assert power and social class advantage. Language is an asset, just as physical resources are. In a capitalist society, those who are native speakers of a high-status language receive their language skills as a part of their social capital, but those born into a language with lower social status have a lack of language capital to overcome. Those without capital largely remain in that condition.

Bourdieu (1977, 1991) recognized the key role of education in the determination of social success, emphasizing that schools reproduce the existing distribution of capital, permitting the "haves" to succeed at the expense of the "have nots." In the classroom, those children who already appear to be successful can attract a teacher's attention, admiration, and reinforcement at the expense of those who appear to lack social capital. The teacher's attention is an important facet of a teacher's social capital. Bourdieu placed schooling, with its behaviors and practices, squarely in the context of the surrounding economic reality.

Cummins: Language Policies as Emancipatory

Cummins (1989, 1996) contrasted educational practices that serve as *collaborative* relations of power with those that are *coercive*. Cummins cautioned that children who enter schools in which diversity is *not* affirmed soon perceive that their "difference" is not honored. Often English learners are not encouraged to think critically, to reflect, and to solve problems. This attitude on the part of teachers communicates a sense of reduced worth, resulting in poor motivation to achieve.

Pressuring students to conform to schooling practices that are unfair or discriminatory results in a loss of their identity as human beings. Cummins called this "identity eradication." To counteract this devaluation of students, teachers who are dedicated to social change must help students to develop the confidence and motivation to succeed academically: they must also be aware of the ways in which spoken and unspoken language can circulate positive attitudes, building strong personal and social identities. Cummins's work highlights the need for schools to support the academic success of English learners.

Fairclough: Critical Language Analysis

Fairclough (1989, 1992) offered critical language analysis (CLA) as a structured means to analyze how power messages are conveyed. Fairclough conceived of discourse as a nested set of boxes: In the inside box is the text itself, the language of the message. In the middle box is the institutional influence on the message. The outer box denotes the social and cultural meanings embedded in the message (see Figure 2.1). Any text, whether spoken or written, has features at these three levels.

In the innermost box, a set of tools is available to describe the features of the text. One might ask, What is the origin of the text? What is the style of writing, level

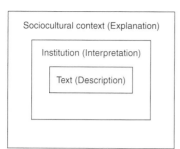

FIGURE 2.1 ◆ Critical language analysis at three levels.
Source: Fairclough, 1989.

of vocabulary, complexity of syntax, and tone of the message? What is said? What is unsaid, but implied? Does the text assume prior knowledge on the part of the reader? Who is responsible for the actions, opinions, or stance taken in the text?

At the middle layer of analysis, one can interpret the institutional influence on the text, asking such questions as, What institution originated the message? What social group (school, club, etc.) supplied the paper, the computer or word processor, or the microphone? Who stands to benefit from the message? What invisible rules or constraints shape or delimit the message?

The outermost layer of analysis is sociocultural. One might ask, How did society's attitudes and treatment of age, gender, and culture influence the text? Is the text biased? How might the text have been different had its origin been a person of different culture, gender, or age? What hidden messages can be understood about this message knowing its social origin?

Fairclough's CLA can be used to examine any item of discourse. For example, one might use CLA to scrutinize an editorial written by an English learner in a high school newspaper. The editorial criticizes local police officers who target minority youth whom they suspect are members of street gangs by stopping individuals on the street and detaining them for informal questioning. The editorial denounces this practice and calls for an immediate end to it. At the level of *text*, the editorial appears to be two columns wide, five paragraphs long, and prominently placed on the editorial page. The text is well edited, and the sentences are simple and uncomplicated. The choice of words— "Unjustified police action," "illegal," "unwarranted"—is unequivocal. The editorial is unattributed.

At the level of *institution*, the editorial is a part of the "school homecoming edition" of the paper, thus assuring that many townspeople and alumni will read the accusations against the police. One must use prior knowledge about newspapers to identify the paper's editor as the author. The editorial reflects on the school, because the newspaper is the official student "voice" of the school.

At the *sociocultural* level, the text assumes that the newspaper staff feels free to criticize the actions of the local police. Publication of the editorial is predicated on the support of the teacher who acts as the faculty sponsor of the student staff. The author of the editorial obviously sides with the minority youth who are being targeted by the police action.

One can see from this example that no published text is devoid of social and political consequences. CLA is a structured means of creating awareness of hidden levels of language. This awareness can then be used to tap previously unacknowledged information about the relationship between power and language and confront assumptions and practices that lie beneath schooling practices. As an analytical tool, it is simple yet easy enough to teach to English learners as they become aware of what is said—and unsaid—in discourse.

Before continuing, two important terms come to mind when critical views are presented: *pedagogy* and *empowerment.* McLaren (1989) suggested that pedagogy is "the process through which students learn to critically appropriate knowledge existing outside their immediate experience in order to broaden their understanding of themselves, the world, and the possibilities for transforming the taken-for-granted assumptions about the way we live" (p. 186). Banks (1991) set empowerment in the context of personal and social change: "A curriculum designed to empower students must be transformative in nature and help students to develop the knowledge, skills, and values needed to become social critics who can make reflective decisions and implement their decisions in effective personal, social, political, and economic action" (p. 131). Wink (2000) cautioned that the verb *empower* should not be used with a direct object, because it is patronizing to believe that one can empower someone else.

To summarize the contributions of the critical social theorists, societies around the world hide power relations within language issues. Language is a chief vehicle for deploying power, whether constructively or destructively. Language is a kind of social asset, and schools are agencies in which language is often used to benefit the privileged and disenfranchise the powerless. Schooling practices can empower or disempower, depending on the language and cultural policies of the school. The tools of the social language critic work to clarify and reveal covert language-power relations.

❖ **Tactics for teachers to critique the power issues that involve the learner:**

- Use critical analyses to expose how power and policy issues affect teaching.
- Understand that language skills constitute an important form of social capital.
- Acknowledge that a critical stance is needed to examine the policies of the school and provoke an improvement in social context for English learners.
- Analyze the English presented to the learner to deconstruct hidden empowering or disempowering messages.

Profession, Policy, and Power in the Education of English Learners

Language policies such as class size, allocation of classrooms, availability of primary-language instruction, availability of support services for English learners, and funds for curricular materials are determined by policies at the school, district, local, state, and federal level. Even the day-to-day influence of teachers amounts to a de facto language policy. Educators can promote the interests of English learners by taking an active role in language policy issues.

Examining the power issues that underlie the social uses of language helps to provide a broader perspective on language policy issues in education. Educators with a critical perspective may choose to influence policy matters at various levels to foster educational opportunities for English learners.

◆ STRATEGY 2.3: Use power and policy issues to support English learners

Language policies are written descriptions or unwritten actions that are taken to support certain languages. In many countries, language decisions are made top down, stemming from the highest levels of policy making; in the United States, on the other hand, language decisions are made at many levels of government. Therefore, it is important to examine language policy decisions at many levels.

Policies can be formal and official; or they can be informal, such as efforts made to manipulate attitudes toward languages and dialects (Corson, 1990). Language policies are not only enacted in government offices and legislative bodies but are also debated in public forums such as newspapers, school board meetings, and radio talk shows. Official policies, such as California's Proposition 227 "outlawing" bilingual education, have intended consequences (that instruction in school take place only in English) as well as unintended consequences, such as the reluctance of Latin American corporations to establish trade centers in California because high school graduates lack bilingual (Spanish-English) skills. Attitudes toward second-language teaching and usage in schools overlap with other kinds of attitudes, such as support for immigration and racial prejudice against speakers of other languages; these attitudes in turn affect language policies. Both formal and informal policies have an impact on teachers, who often work under conditions that are highly political. Appendix A presents ways in which educators can influence policies to benefit English learners.

In the United States, where the majority of the more than 280 million people use English for daily interchange, the language skills and rights of minorities are a fragile resource. These same issues resonate in other countries. Teachers need to use the leadership of large professional organizations wisely to effect constructive change in the education of English learners. Teachers must be willing to step outside the confines of the classroom to help students be successful and learn how to influence policy on a larger scale. The belief that teachers have no role in language politics is a denial of professional responsibility and an abdication of authority. As Kubota (1998) noted,

> Teachers who engage in critical pedagogy thus challenge and question the knowledge that is taken for granted, and explore the creation of new knowledge. In this view, the teacher's role shifts from that of apolitical technician merely transmitting information to a "transforming intellectual" (Giroux, 1991), critically aware of power and discourse, who addresses social and political issues. Thus, teaching is never neutral or apolitical; it legitimizes or challenges a particular discourse that controls social practices. (p. 303)

"To raise critical consciousness means first of all to notice the linguistic and cultural imbalance and contradictions in everyday social and cultural practices that are taken for granted, and to critically reflect on the values attached to those practices:" (Kubota, 1998, p. 303). A teacher who believes in English learners' potential for success is in a strong position to fight for the recognition of their rights and the allocation of resources that make educational success possible.

Views of Teaching and Learning

Philosophy, Psychology, Anthropology, Sociology, and Postmodern Pedagogy

Education is the key not only to survival, but to prosperity. This has been the message to young people throughout the history of human beings. When knowledge was whole—not divided into disciplines and specializations—wisdom was integrated into holistic views about nature and human nature, craft and sorcery, men's and women's knowledge, earth and the universe. Later, the study of ideas, human nature, culture, and language separated into disciplines such as philosophy, psychology, anthropology, and linguistics.

In the late twentieth century these disciplines came together again in the complex endeavor of teaching English to speakers of other languages. Few undertakings combine so many disparate areas of knowledge. It is rare in this age of specialization to encounter a teaching discipline that demands the range of cross-disciplinary expertise required of those who educate English learners.

Second-language acquisition (SLA), as a domain of learning, is difficult, for it requires attaining linguistic and cultural proficiency, precise control of meaning, careful attunement to intonation, and mastery of behavioral subtlety. Unlike other areas of learning, however, prior knowledge of one's own language and culture assists this learning only to a degree, and may actually be counterproductive: What is right at home may be exactly wrong abroad.

To make matters worse, whereas second-language mistakes are often forgiven in a rank novice ("charming accent," "how good of you to try our language"), an advanced speaker of a foreign language faces increasingly negative sanctions for error. Often, "almost there" is more threatening to native speakers than the failings of a beginner, and the better one becomes as a learner, the less one's errors are tolerated. Added to this difficulty is the seductive ease of lapsing into one's native language. Thus, there are multiple cognitive and emotional obstacles to second-language proficiency.

The particular nature of English as a target language compounds this difficulty. The huge vocabulary is a burden. Cultural invention of all kinds promotes continuous linguistic and cultural innovation, making learning English like swimming after a moving ship. Spelling is a learner's headache (compare *come* and *home*). Idiomatic verb-particle combinations provide challenges (compare "put up with" versus "put down" versus "put on"). Finally, different varieties of English worldwide may already be mutually incomprehensible—to pick just two examples, the English spoken in Jamaica versus that spoken in Taiwan.

Educators need every possible tool to create successful learning in the face of these challenges. Pedagogy for English learners draws on philosophy, psychology, anthropology, and sociology. Today, TESOL is a worldwide pedagogy. In this, it must be experimental. Language teachers must be unafraid to be risk takers and innovators in their teaching and must actively apply teaching and learning strategies using a broad, interdisciplinary approach.

Teaching the Whole Person

❖ **MEGASTRATEGY 3:** Teach the whole person—beliefs, body, brain, emotions, and culture—within a positive social environment

Learning a second language involves the whole person. When a word or phrase comes out exactly right, accurate and appropriate for the situation, the whole person benefits. Educators who devote their attention to the whole learner reap the reward of rich, person-to-person interaction. Such education draws upon philosophy, psychology, sociology, and anthropology.

Philosophical Foundations of Education

◆ **STRATEGY 3.1:** Take into consideration your philosophy and beliefs as well as the philosophies and beliefs of the learner

Teaching strategies in many parts of the world are based upon philosophy. In societies around the world, dominant systems of thought and governing ideologies are closely aligned with the policies and curricula in schools. Instruction is designed not to conflict with prevailing values and norms. English instruction in these countries is no exception.

In the United States, however, the First Amendment to the Constitution states, "Congress shall make no law respecting an establishment of religion. . . ." Citizens have the right to freedom of thought, more basic even than freedom of worship or speech. This law has prevented public schools in the United States from promoting specific religious, political, or social philosophies. English teachers who go abroad may find themselves constrained there by the absence of these freedoms.

Progressivism

In the twentieth century, education in the United States was influenced by John Dewey's *progressivism*, which sought to embody in educational practices the American ideals of individual rights, freedom, and creativity. According to Dewey (1916/1963), the learner must participate in forming purposes that direct learning, so that education can develop thinking citizens in a democracy. This philosophy has justified pedagogy based on active learning and liberal social beliefs. Educators from abroad may find this emphasis on activity in U.S. schools to be disconcerting.

Traditionalism

However strong an influence Dewey has had upon education, traditional schooling persists. Traditional schooling features an emphasis on the authority of the teacher and school administration; learning is based upon the discipline of bodies and acquisition of a predetermined body of authorized knowledge, and the maintenance of a stable society is valued over the attainment of individuality. In fact, English is taught around the world in highly traditional contexts.

In various contexts, English instruction is framed by philosophical beliefs. In many parts of the world, religious beliefs based upon the Koran prescribe classroom behavior and curricula. Elsewhere, Confucian or Buddhist values underlie educational principles. Educators in countries with a Western European cultural heritage believe in individual liberty and devotion to the worth of the individual stemming from the Renaissance and Enlightenment eras, beliefs that are often labeled "humanistic."

Belief Systems and Teaching

An educator's personal philosophy inevitably shapes and underlies classroom instruction. Challenges to one's personal philosophy may be superficial or profound, depending on the degree of difference between the cultures of the teacher and students. Intercultural educators are wise to pursue a deeper understanding of philosophical differences in discussions with peers, rather than students, and outside class time. In response, practitioners may adopt educational strategies that are psychological, rather than philosophical, in origin.

Teachers may face ethical dilemmas if they feel at odds with a given student's cultural background. Note the differences between Chad's values and that of the student's family in Box 3.1 (the incident is based on a real occurrence). What should be the recommended course of action in this situation?

> ❖ Tactics for teachers whose instruction is impacted by contrasting teacher-student philosophical belief systems:
>
> - Learn more about the philosophical beliefs of students by finding a neutral context for discussion that does not jeopardize teaching and learning activities.
> - Develop intercultural communication skills to frame discussions of comparative philosophical systems and the effect these may have on TESOL instruction.
> - Be aware that in some cultures, authorities negatively sanction discussion of personal beliefs.

Educational Psychology: Behavioral Methods

Psychology provides a second main foundation for instructional practices. The United States, perhaps because of its tradition of experimentation in natural and social sciences, has embraced a pragmatic orientation to education, formed around the question, "How do individuals learn?" The teaching of English has benefited as a

Chad is a journalism teacher in a large urban high school and the adviser to the school newspaper. Khalia is a young woman who enrolled in an introductory journalism class as a junior. Although English was not her first language, she showed unusual ability and creativity in writing the stories to which she was assigned. Chad routinely advises students on their vocational choices, writes letters of recommendation for them when they apply to college, and en-

courages those who want to further their education. Khalia has told Chad of her difficulty in winning support from her parents to attend college. Her father has already warned her that if her older sister does not receive a proposal of marriage within the year, he will approach a matchmaker to find Khalia a husband. Khalia does not want to enter an arranged marriage and has asked Chad for help in applying to college. Should Chad help Khalia?

discipline from psychological research on teaching and learning. The most successful paradigm in the early days of educational psychology was behaviorism.

* **STRATEGY 3.2:** Use behavioral training for accurate pronunciation and rote memory of information such as object and motor vocabulary

Grammar Translation

The earliest type of language teaching was predicated on authorities having strict control over the learners' behavior. Grammar-translation pedagogy can be seen as a traditional form of behaviorism. As teachers explain the meaning of vocabulary words and the structure of sentences, students learn only what is required, in a system in which the rewards are explicitly connected to precisely defined actions.

The strengths of this methodology are twofold. First, when rewards are explicit, students have a clear choice of how much effort is needed. When grades are a measure of the degree to which the individual is willing to work to attain socially sanctioned rewards, school success clearly predicts social success. Second, the curriculum can be carefully structured and controlled, with students' access to L2 limited to that which the teacher or other authorities determine to be valuable. Grammar-translation pedagogy is thus compatible with traditional education.

There are drawbacks to traditional behaviorism. First, students have little choice in what they might find motivating. Rewards are limited to those aligned with success in the native culture, even if a separate set of rewards may be available in the target culture. Second, grammar translation as a methodology goes against the intrinsic nature of cognition: stimulation of curiosity, playfulness, and exploration. Third, there is often little independent language acquisition. Limited access to the target language and culture means little social interaction with actual speakers of the target language.

The Rise of Experimental Behaviorism

B. F. Skinner's success in formulating principles of behavior management established behaviorism as the dominant paradigm of psychology in the United States from the

1920s to the 1970s. Results from laboratory experiments performed on lower mammals were used to understand human behavior. Skinner's basic principles of reinforcement using reward and punishment were used to explain language-learning behavior.

Principles of behavioral management are based on the Law of Effect: Actions followed by an immediate positive effect (reward) tend to be repeated, and actions followed by an immediate negative effect (punishment) tend to be discontinued. Teachers reward desired actions, using immediate, tangible, and desirable rewards that are verbal (praise), material (candy, etc.), or token (the award of a point or privilege). Similarly, they deal with undesirable actions by imposing immediate and tangible punishments—either verbal (scolding), material (loss of a desirable object), or token (the loss of a point or privilege).

Behaviorism emphasizes the importance of external rewards and incentives. These only work if students value the rewards. If students do not value school-based tokens such as grades, there is little incentive for them to behave as the teacher mandates. Providing grades, stars, and so on to reward learning—or imposing demerits for misbehavior—is an attempt to motivate students by extrinsic means. Unfortunately, overreliance on external rewards tends to decrease internal motivation. Nevertheless, there are situations when incentives and external supports are necessary (Brophy, 1988).

Practices in descriptive and structural linguistics during this era resulted in a kind of behaviorist language-teaching methodology. Linguists whose doctoral research was based upon careful phonological and syntactic description of exotic languages believed that such description should be the basis for teaching foreign languages. They believed that second-language teaching should be based upon training the learners to perform accurate sound and sentence structure behavior. Their findings led to the development of the Audiolingual Method.

The Audiolingual Method

Based on behavioral principles, audiolingual instruction was designed to create correct pronunciation in a second language through oral practice. Students developed correct language habits by repetitious training, often using technology such as tape recordings in language laboratories. Teachers provided pattern drills based on carefully ordered grammatical structures in the target language. The role of the teacher was to direct and control students' behavior, provide a model, and reinforce correct responses (Doggett, 1986). Errors were corrected immediately to discourage "bad" habit formation. Reading and writing were often delayed until the student had an adequate oral base. However, audiolingual instruction alone did not seem to be very successful for second-language instruction beyond a basic level.

Total Physical Response

Total physical response (TPR) was invented by Asher (1982) based on the association between language and body movement. Even though Asher aligned his teaching with Krashen and Terell's Natural Approach, much of TPR teaching actually follows behavioral methods of teaching, such as shaping of response and fading of reward. In

Total Physical Response involves active learning.

TPR, students respond to oral commands that are simultaneously modeled; for example, the teacher says "Stand" while standing up and "Sit" while sitting down, and students follow along. The instructor repeats the commands followed by the appropriate action until students perform them without hesitation. The instructor then begins to delay modeling to allow students the opportunity to respond and thus demonstrate understanding.

Eventually, the number of commands is increased, and novel commands are given that combine previously learned commands in a new way. For example, if the students learn "run," and "touch the chair," they may be given "run to the chair." Students continue to respond in a nonverbal manner until they feel comfortable issuing their own commands. Reading and writing are also introduced through commands. The instructor may write "stand" on the board and gesture to the students to perform the action. TPR is associated with early stages of second-language learning, although efforts have been made to use advanced techniques at higher levels (see the section on TPR storytelling in Chapter 7).

Direct Teaching and Mastery Learning

In direct teaching, the instructor maximizes learning time by careful classroom management, makes clear and organized presentations, and moves at a steady pace to cover key topics. This type of behavioral learning emphasizes explicit instructional objectives for students and promotes the learning of facts, sequenced steps, or rules. A clear and consistent match of instructional objectives with assessment helps students know the goals of study and guides the teacher's content delivery. Two contemporary reading programs, Open Court and Direct Instruction, use the direct teaching approach.

Another type of behaviorist instruction is mastery learning. A course of study is divided into small units with specific objectives. Students progress at their own rate and demonstrate mastery of each unit before proceeding to the next, thus developing basic skills before moving on to more complex skills. As in other systems of behavioral management, mastery learning provides immediate feedback and reinforcement of performance. Students are gradually taught how to self-monitor, regulate, and reward their own actions; to monitor their progress, for example, through journals or study schedules; and reward themselves as they acquire skills.

Advantages of Behavioral Methods

Methods that focus on training the body (oral language behavior as well as kinesthetics) continue to be used in TESOL education. The strength of the audiolingual method is its focus on correct pronunciation. The strength of TPR is the reinforcement to memory provided by physical action. The strength of direct teaching and mastery learning is the ability to build discrete skills.

Disadvantages of Behavioral Methods

A weakness of grammar-translation pedagogy is that it limits exposure to target culture and self-motivated language acquisition. The weakest feature of audiolingual instruction is that learners pressured to perform accurately under classroom or laboratory conditions often find it difficult to communicate spontaneously with native speakers. The drawback of TPR is the tendency to focus on sensory-motor actions. The weakest part of direct teaching is students' lack of ownership of the goals of learning, even though mastery learning may permit students to control their own instructional pacing. Balancing the strengths and weaknesses of behavior-based pedagogy, one might conclude that these teaching techniques have a distinct, yet limited, role in instruction.

❖ Tactics for teachers in the use of behavioral management:

- Direct teaching is useful to maintain class discipline and to teach such topics as precise mastery of grammar, vocabulary, or pronunciation.
- Behavioral management in the classroom is useful when rewards are in demand and the students depend on the teacher for these rewards.
- Balancing external rewards with intrinsic motivation meets the needs of a variety of students.
- Careful alignment of instructional objectives, direct teaching, and assessment is useful for mastering a highly structured curriculum.
- Mastery learning supplements direct instruction by inducing students to achieve incremental, precisely defined objectives.

Educational Psychology: Cognitive Methods

The 1960s saw the birth of cognitive psychology, brought forth through a combination of Piaget's developmental work with children, Chomsky's focus on innate language processing, and the application of information-processing models to human thinking. Cognitive psychologists studied human thinking directly, rather than basing principles of behavior upon animal studies. This research gave rise to studies in generative grammar, information-processing theories of the mind, brain-compatible learning, and neurolinguistics. Language functioning, as a higher-order mental process, began to be better described by cognitive than by behavioral theorists, aided by a vision of language as human communication.

♦ **STRATEGY 3.3:** Align learning with the brain
and its natural way of knowledge acquisition

Generative Grammar

Chomsky's devastating critique in 1959 of Skinner's book *Verbal Behavior* (Chomsky, 1959) helped to break the hold that behaviorism had gained over psychology. Chomsky asserted that if language were learned solely by reinforcement, native speakers would find it impossible to understand sentences that they had never before heard. He claimed that language is not learned solely through a process of behavioral reinforcement, but that the mind contains an active language processor, the language acquisition device (LAD), which generates rules through the unconscious acquisition of grammar.

The fact that preschool children, for example, master several complex aspects of their native language's syntax and semantics suggests that certain aspects of language need not be taught to children. Linguists postulate the existence of linguistic universals—a human "instinct" or biological blueprint for language development—to explain why the first language is mastered so rapidly.

Researchers studying generative grammar examine the language of native speakers, looking for rules used to master syntax. The syntax used by those acquiring a second language often shows characteristic errors, which also demonstrates their use of rules, even if the rules are not correct. Selinker (1972, 1991) used the term *interlanguage* to describe the language created by second-language learners. Interlanguage researchers look for ways in which the rules of both the first and target language influence language learning, as well as asking what rules, and what kinds of rules, are universal to the human mind.

Krashen's Monitor Model

An idea similar to that of Chomsky's LAD was incorporated by Krashen's (1981, 1982) theory of SLA. Krashen's theory included five hypotheses. The *acquisition-learning hypothesis* distinguished acquisition (an unconscious process that occurs when language is used for real communication) from learning (which involves "knowing about" language and its rules). Krashen considered acquisition more important than learning in achieving fluency, and deemphasized direct instruction of syntax rules. In fact, according to Krashen and Terrell (1983), "Error correction in particular does not seem to help" (p. 27) in learning correct sentence syntax.

Krashen's *natural order hypothesis* asserted that language rules are acquired in a predictable order, and certain grammatical rules of the language tend to be acquired before others. Children acquire correct usage of grammatical structures in their first language (L1) gradually, as do children acquiring a second language (L2).

The *monitor hypothesis* postulated that the mind employs an editor, the monitor, which scans utterances for accuracy in order to make corrections. Acquisition initiates an utterance and is responsible for fluency. When an individual initiates an utterance, that individual's monitor edits, that is, confirms or repairs, the utterance either prior to or after attempted communication. This is only useful when there is ample time to be concerned with grammatical correctness, as opposed to situations involving rapid verbal exchange (Krashen, 1981, 1982).

The *input hypothesis* claimed that language is acquired in an "amazingly simple way—when we understand messages" (Krashen, 1985, p. vii). What kind of messages? Simply immersing a learner in a second language is not sufficient. Imagine, for example, listening to Turkish on the radio. Unless you had some knowledge of that language beforehand, there would be no way to understand topics, or even words. Second-language learners are challenged by language that is slightly more complex than they can themselves easily understand. Peer conversation that mixes more and less skilled speakers is the chief means of accelerating a student's SLA.

Teachers may vary their speech to make it more comprehensible to students, using shorter sentences, simple sentence structures, and restricted vocabulary and range of topics. However, just simplifying speech may not be the central facet that makes language comprehensible; it may be necessary instead to focus on the message and its relevance for the language learner within the environment. Many educators have found that when working with English learners, one needs to use a variety of modalities, including visual and kinesthetic, to ensure that speech is comprehensible.

Krashen's *affective filter hypothesis* described the mental and emotional blocks that can prevent language acquirers from fully comprehending input. People acquire a second language only if their affective filters are low enough to allow them to receive adequate input.

Krashen's monitor model has been extensively criticized (some find its constructs vague and difficult to prove, such as Af Trampe, 1994, and Ellis, 1994), but it has nonetheless provided the theoretical base for the Natural Approach, which has had a great impact on second-language instruction in the United States. Krashen's distinction between acquisition and learning is important; teachers can easily see that students produce some aspects of language unself-consciously in a nonstressful, "natural" language-rich environment but need rules and help for other aspects. Moreover, teachers now understand that intensive practice in itself does not produce perfect formation of grammatical structures.

Stages of Development

There appear to be some generally accepted stages of development through which second-language learners progress in spite of human differences. The stages described by the Natural Approach are *preproduction, early production, speech emergence,* and *intermediate fluency.* In natural situations, second-language learners progress through these stages in a predictable order and at their own pace.

In preproduction (also called the *silent period*) the learner absorbs the sounds and rhythms of the new language, learns to identify specific words, relies on contextual clues for understanding key words, and generally communicates nonverbally.

Once a learner feels more confident (the early production stage) words and phrases are attempted, and responses can consist of single words ("yes," "OK," "come"), two- or three-word combinations ("gimme the ball," "don't go"), utterances learned in one piece ("Can-I-go-to-the-bathroom?"), and simple poems and songs. In the third stage (speech emergence) utterances become longer and more complex. In the fourth stage (intermediate fluency) students begin to sustain conversations and can recognize and correct their own errors.

Specific guidelines for students' language behaviors at various levels of proficiency can be found in Richard-Amato (1996, pp. 99–100) and in Bell (1991). These include suggestions for classroom activities that match the acquisition level of the students. Among Bell's recommendations for managing multilevel classes (those that contain students at differing levels of proficiency) are the following: Plan a curriculum in which daily lesson plans feature a variety of activities geared toward differing skill levels. Use assessment frequently and flexibly so that students receive instruction matched to their skill levels. Group students cooperatively and heterogeneously so that skill levels can be combined for effective peer language input or, alternatively, homogeneously so that students at the same skill level can be taught using the same materials and expectations. Vary the size of groups, from pairs to whole-class activities. Provide individual self-access material so that students can work alone. Ask tutors and volunteers to work with students in need of additional mediation.

❖ Tactics for teachers using Krashen and Terrell's Natural Approach:

- Emphasize language acquisition as a by-product of interesting learning activities, rather than direct instruction of grammar or sentence structure.
- Use placement tests to indicate a language acquisition level for each student who enters the class, and match instruction to the student's language ability at that level.
- If the class as a whole has attained a certain level of fluency and one or two students have not, use specific techniques to include the lower-level students during instruction.

Information-Processing Theories of Mental Functioning

For information-processing theorists, the computer serves as a metaphor for human mental activity: The mind processes information by gathering and recognizing it, storing it, retrieving it when needed, and generating responses. The whole system is guided by control processes that determine how and when information will flow through the system. The sensory register (input/recognition), short-term memory (information encoding), and long-term memory (storage) work together during learning.

During information processing, *perception* is the process by which the sensory register receives and briefly holds environmental stimuli, either as images or sound patterns, and selects input for further processing. Meaning is constructed by combining objective reality with existing prior knowledge. However, the mind can pay attention to only one demanding task at a time. Teachers can help students to manage their attention.

Stating the *purpose* of a lesson helps students to focus on how the material will be useful or important to them. Questions such as "What would happen if. . . ." arouse curiosity. Changing the arrangement of the room or moving to a different setting gets attention. Giving lessons that require students to touch, smell, or taste shifts sensory channels. Using movements, gestures, and voice inflection (speaking softly and then more emphatically) or writing with colored pens or chalk stimulates perception.

Table 3.1 offers ways in which teachers can enhance students' perceptions as they process information.

The next phase, short-term memory (STM), receives patterns of images or sounds. Such information lasts only about twenty to thirty seconds at the most; it must be kept activated (by rehearsing or repetition) to be retained, or it decays or fades quickly. STM is sometimes known as *working memory*, because it holds what is being thought about at the moment. Individuals differ in their ability to retain information in STM. Talent for SLA may be associated with differential memory abilities.

To enhance STM, teachers can play short-term memory games such as Fruit Clap-Clap-Click-Click. (Students stand in a circle, and all clap their hands twice and snap their fingers twice; when it is a person's turn, he or she repeats the name of a fruit said by the previous person on the first click and adds a new fruit on the second click. The turn moves around the circle.) To stretch STM for actions, teachers can use a series of three or four commands in TPR situations.

Long-term memory (LTM) is the permanent store of knowledge. Theoretically, storage in LTM is unlimited, but access and retrieval is the problem. To move information into LTM requires time and effort, but once it is securely stored, it can remain there permanently, encoded either as visual images, verbal units, or both. A *schema*

TABLE 3.1 • **Ways to Enhance Students' Perception**

Explanation	Tactics for Teachers
Variation in properties of written or spoken words: intensity, pitch, size, color, or novelty	Use various colored markers on board; teach words that have an unusual sound; use volume change-up (soft, soft, loud, soft).
Manipulating posture, gestures, and movements	Use accompanying gestures to teach action words.
Use of emotion: vivid mental images, metaphors	Teach students to pronounce their names in the second language; use reading material that quickens the pulse.
Use of . . .	
Complexity	Distinguish "the open door," "the opening door," the "opened door."
Ambiguity	Discuss puzzling news headline: "Safety Concerns Warehouse Neighbors."
Incongruity	"The only person at the scene missing was the policeman."
Use of commands (verbal statements with highly probable consequences)	TPR commands

TABLE 3.2 ◆ **Ways to Enhance Storage and Retrieval of Information from LTM**

Prioritizing	separating essential from nonessential details and focusing on meaning
Elaboration	adding meaning to new information by connecting new with existing knowledge to increase retrieval cues
Organization	placing new information in a structure that serves as a guide for retrieval
Context	learning physical or emotional cues connected with information to enhance retrieval cues
Repetition, review	repeated acts of storage and retrieval
Logic, cues, and connected knowledge	adding structure to information to assist recall
Reconstruction	using structure to enhance recall rather than rote memory

is a structure for organizing information or concepts. A *script* stores a common behavioral sequence.

Teachers can help students store data in and retrieve information from LTM. Table 3.2 describes storage and retrieval devices. Whatever devices are used, students get better as they practice, developing their own organizational and elaboration strategies as they mature.

Alternative Theories of Mental Functioning

Some linguists believe that parallel-processing computing models the operation of the brain. Parallel or distributed processing involves a simultaneous adjustment of a net of neural connections in the brain. As information is received, the brain creates a pattern across the net, adjusted over time by repeated exposure (see Clark, 1993). This model is closer to the LAD in operation. It is not, however, as good a model for conscious or strategic learning.

Edelman (1992) saw the development of the brain as a process of evolution, with synapses evolving and competing with one another. In his view, the brain is not programmed from the outside by parents or educators or any other external force. Instead, it is more useful to think of the brain as a messy terrain in which competing capacities vie for dominance. The environment selects from among the built-in options available so that one set of propensities wins out over others (Sylwester, 1995; see also Clark, 1997).

Ratey (2001) used a metaphor of the brain as ecosystem. Four theaters (perception, function, consciousness, and identity) alternately take precedence, depending upon task and predilection. His view, that function and consciousness are partially separate theaters, is an interesting way to look at the use of language, a human skill that often involves simultaneous conscious and unconscious performance. Even in this model, language is a central player, whatever theater is prominent at the moment.

To summarize these alternative views of how the brain functions during learning, learning stimulates the brain to search for the best response to the immediate challenge. The brain contains a basic set of neurons that interconnect to respond to the environment. On top of this innate capacity, culture has added technological components (computers, books) that continually interact with the internal biological brain but in themselves create new stresses and challenges to the brain's innate ability to solve problems (Sylwester & Cho, 1992/1993).

We must be flexible in the discourse we construct about mind, as we evolve the capacity to model a set of ever-more-complex connectionist systems based on qualitatively distinct, situationally responsive modular subsystems that afford humans the capacity to process information and communicate, and simultaneously to do both.

Brain-Compatible Learning

Recent research on how the brain learns has led to exciting ideas about optimizing learning environments. The greatest challenge of brain research for educators lies in comprehending the vastness, complexity, and potential of the human brain. Brain-compatible learning helps to reconceptualize teaching by taking into consideration how the brain learns (D'Arcangelo, 1998; Jensen, 1998; Wolfe & Sorgen, 1990).

The brain is a parallel processor that performs many functions simultaneously. Thoughts, emotions, imagination, and predispositions interact with general socio-cultural knowledge and survival functions in a complex flow of activity. Learning engages the entire physiology and is as natural to humans as breathing. Neuron growth, nourishment, and synaptic interactions are integrally related to the perception and interpretation of experiences. Brain-compatible teaching must fully incorporate stress management, nutrition, exercise, drug education, and other facets of health into the learning process in order to respect and support the brain's complicated functioning.

The brain automatically registers the familiar, while simultaneously searching for and responding to novel stimuli. The brain attempts to discern and understand patterns as they occur and to express unique and creative patterns of its own (Nummela & Rosegren, 1986; Hart, 1983; Caine & Caine, 1997). The search for meaning cannot be stopped, only channeled and focused. This process is impaired when educators impose isolated, unrelated pieces of information that make inefficient use of the brain. Brain-compatible education satisfies the brain's need for complex and meaningful challenges.

Although there is evidence of brain laterality, in a healthy person the left and right brain hemispheres interact, irrespective of whether a person is dealing with words, mathematics, music, or art (Hart, 1975). Good teaching builds understanding and skill over time using both parts (analyzing information in small segments) and the whole (getting the big picture).

Students remember not what they are told, but what they experience. Active processing, through such activities as questioning and genuine reflection, allows learners to internalize learning in a way that is personally meaningful. Teachers should use a great deal of "real life" activity, including classroom demonstrations, projects, field trips, visual imagery, stories, metaphor, drama, interaction of different subjects, and so on. Success depends on making use of all the senses by immersing the learner in a multitude of complex and interactive experiences (Jensen, 1998).

The brain absorbs both information of which it is directly aware and signals that lie beyond the immediate focus of attention. Subtle signals that emanate from a teacher, such as muscular tension and posture, rate of breathing, and eye movements, have a real impact on learning. These unconscious signals convey the importance and value of what is being learned through the enthusiasm and feelings signaled to the learner.

Emotions and cognition cannot be separated. Emotions are crucial to memory because they facilitate the storage and recall of information; optimal cognitive functioning depends on a classroom emotional climate that is supportive and respectful, and creates a state of relaxed alertness in students. Under stress, the brain "down-shifts" (Hart, 1983) as we literally lose access to portions of the brain. Students need projects that include a public demonstration so that they can experience anticipation, concern, excitement, and suspense, but the brain also needs "downtime" (D'Arcangelo, 1998) to relax.

Mental processes are integrated differently in each person's brain. Personal biases and prejudices, self-esteem, and the need for social interaction influence and organize what is learned. Teaching should be multifaceted in order to allow students to express visual, tactile, emotional, or auditory preferences and individual interests. Understanding how the brain learns may require the reshaping of schools toward the complexity found in life. This is the key to optimal brain functioning (Caine & Caine, 1994, 1997).

Multiple Intelligences.   A popular form of brain-compatible teaching is Howard Gardner's theory of multiple intelligences. Gardner (1983) defined intelligence as the ability to solve problems or make things that are culturally valued. According to Gardner, children possess different abilities that naturally direct them to learn in different ways and have at least eight separate kinds of "intelligences": linguistic (verbal), musical, spatial, logical-mathematical, bodily-kinesthetic, interpersonal (understanding of others), intrapersonal (understanding of self), and natural (using cues from nature). Gardner (1993) further stated that teachers who respect multiple intelligences offer a variety of materials and help to ease children into activities that they may find threatening.

Emotional Intelligence.   Emotional intelligence (EI) is a construct proposed by Salovey and Mayer (1990) and popularized by Goleman (1998). According to Goleman, emotional intelligence is "the capacity for recognizing our own feelings and those of others, for motivating ourselves, and for managing emotions well in ourselves and in our relationships" (p. 317). EI consists of five competencies: self-awareness, self-regulation, motivation, social skills, and empathy. Empathy is a foundation for social skills, and includes understanding others, having a service orientation, developing the skills of others, leveraging diversity, and being politically aware (Goleman, 1998, p. 137). Whereas some may argue that identifying the importance of the emotional aspect of life is not new, especially in education, the term EI is a useful shorthand for discussing competencies that need to be encouraged in educating English learners.

Suggestopedia.   Lozanov (1982), in his Suggestopedia method, was a pioneer in brain-based learning. He believed that emphasizing intellectual at the expense of emotional and motivational functions places unnecessary limitations on learning. Directing learning only to the conscious level ignores that which can be learned spontaneously and intuitively. By contrast, Suggestopedia encouraged simultaneous and indivisible participation of conscious and paraconscious processes.

A key condition of the Suggestopedic language program is the inclusion of relaxation, which allows students "undisturbed intellectual and creative activity" (Lozanov, 1982, p. 155). Concentration is directed to the whole communicative aspect of the teacher's message. Pronunciation, vocabulary, and grammar are assimilated and learned intuitively. Music is a vital element in the lesson, especially classical and early Romantic music.

Once material is introduced in a relaxed, supportive atmosphere, students engage in "elaborations"—reading dialogues, songs, games, and conversations. Role playing is another important aspect of the program. Students can take on new identities when they wish, but they are never forced to perform. For more information about schooling based on Suggestopedia, see www.northside.isd.tenet.edu/esparww/s-accel1.htm. Current language instruction may benefit from Suggestopedic techniques such as the relaxation methods, vocabulary presentation, use of creative skits, and involvement of students' personalities.

❖ Tactics for teachers which involve the whole brain in learning (see Lazear, 1993; Armstrong, 1993, 1994):

- Vary methods and media for presentation of new information and problem solving, and invite outcomes that are diverse and varied.
- Provide opportunities for students to develop skills in areas of strength and weakness, especially using both heterogeneous and homogeneous groupings of students based on strengths.
- Invite role models to visit the classroom to offer students contact with someone in their area of strength.
- Frequently demonstrate the interconnections of the multiple intelligences through an interdisciplinary approach.

Neurolinguistic Research Based on Study of Brain Function

How does the brain store words once learned? Do bilinguals store their separate languages in two different parts of the brain? Is the left side of the brain really the language side? Do people who read languages written from left to right (like English) think differently from people who read languages written from right to left (like Hebrew and Arabic)? What about languages written using some other kind of symbols, such as Chinese or Japanese?

Neurolinguists use techniques like event-related potential (ERP), which can show finer and finer details of the brain's constantly changing activity, and functional magnetic resonance imaging (FMRI), which can be used to picture the brain's tissues and functions. However, simple answers about language and the brain are not forthcoming. Evidence shows that listening, understanding, talking, and reading all involve activities in certain parts of the brain, mostly the left hemisphere, regardless of what language serves as input. In contrast, areas in the right side are essential for communicating effectively and for understanding the point of what people are saying (Menn, 2001).

Human brains are not all organized in the same way. Everybody's brain is different in terms of size, structure, and function, independent of the effects of experience and aging (Hotz, 2001). Among cognitive skills, however, language stands apart in several ways. Language is one of the most complex of all human cognitive abilities (Crain, 2001). For one thing, the use of language is universal; all normally developing children learn to speak at least one language, and many learn more than one. By contrast, not everyone becomes proficient at complex mathematical reasoning, few people learn to paint well, and many people cannot carry a tune.

Cognitive Teaching Means a Focus on Learning

In summary, cognitive psychology studies how people transform, elaborate, store, and recover information. According to this view, people are active learners who initiate experiences, seek out information, and reorganize what they already know to achieve new insights, pursue goals, solve personally relevant problems, and attempt to make sense of the world (Bruner, 1986). Information processing can occur at a conscious level of awareness, but this capacity is limited, as people cannot consciously think about and monitor everything. Thus, various automatic mental control processes, schemata, and other mental mechanisms help the brain to deal with both familiar and unfamiliar situations.

Teachers motivate students best by providing course activities and projects that tap students' natural abilities and interests and develop their confidence in their ability to think. Teachers who ask thought-provoking questions and use concrete examples, activities, and demonstrations stimulate students' imaginations and critical thinking skills. This process includes *metacognition* in the form of cognitive self-knowledge (multiple intelligences, learning styles), goal setting, planning, self-monitoring, and self-evaluating.

Cognitive training includes the use of learning strategies, study skills, memory enhancement, text-processing skills, note taking, research skills, test-taking skills, problem solving, making use of transfer, use of graphic organizers, information-processing tips, as well as learning the characteristics of the brain. A cognitivist view of learning means teaching students how to learn. A cognitive lesson needs two kinds of objectives: *content objectives* and *learning strategy objectives*. Teaching content involves knowledge of subject matter. Teaching learning strategies builds cognition.

Comparing the Cognitive View with Behaviorism

Since the era in which behaviorism was dominant, much has been learned about making fuller use of higher-order cognitive functions during learning. Table 3.3 contrasts basic behaviorist assumptions about the nature of learning with later cognitivist views.

Learning Styles and Strategies

A large part of the shift toward a cognitive view of learning has involved research on learning styles and strategies. Chapter 5 explores these areas.

TABLE 3.3 • Comparing Behaviorist and Cognitivist Views of Learning

Component of Learning	Behaviorist	Cognitivist
Belief about the mind	The mind is a blank slate. All minds are basically alike.	The mind is an active organizer. Brains vary, with multiple intelligences and learning styles.
Goal setting	Teacher plans and sets goals.	Students participate in planning and goal setting.
Motivation	Reward is a motivator.	Learning is a motivator.
Teaching styles	Teacher teaches his/her way; one "best" way.	Teacher teaches with variety; no one "best" way.
Content of curriculum	Students are taught "what."	Students are taught "what" and "how."
Assessment: who does it	Teacher assesses.	Students are actively involved in peer- and self-assessment.
Assessment: what is evaluated	Product is important.	Product and process are important.
Role of culture	Culture is irrelevant.	Culture is the basis for social interaction patterns; learning results from social interaction.

Constructivist Learning

Constructivism is an offshoot of the cognitivist tradition, in which complex, challenging learning environments help students to take responsibility for constructing their own knowledge. As students deal with complex situations, the teacher provides support. Thus students and teachers share responsibility for the knowledge construction process, collaborating on the goals of instruction and the planning needed for learning to take place (Fosnot, 1989; Wells & Chang-Wells, 1992).

Key elements of constructivist learning are particularly relevant to learning in multicultural classrooms: the encouragement of student autonomy and initiative, expectation that student responses will drive lesson content and instructional strategies, engendering of learning experiences that will test hypotheses and provoke discussion, focus on students' concept understanding rather than teachers' concept explanation, emphasis on critical thinking and student dialogue (Brooks & Brooks, 1993). A constructivist learning environment is of vital importance in enabling students to balance global issues and understanding—they will, after all, live in a different world than currently exists—against the need to achieve their own orientation to the world's challenges (Brown & Kysilka, 2002).

Constructivist learning makes use of instructional objectives that are tailored to students' differing needs and levels. A wide range of learning materials includes provision for enrichment, remediation, and student self-pacing. Constructivist methods make minimal use of rote memorization and instead focus on problem solving. Students discuss, ask questions, give explanations to one another, and present ideas and solve problems together.

Constructivist learning in the elementary years helps students to maintain their curiosity and zest for learning. English develops as students talk, listen, read, write, and are involved with authentic tasks. Typical constructivist environments are children's museums, rich worlds in which children can be exposed to many different stimuli.

At the middle and high school levels, students use research resources featuring various types of information representation. Conducting research need not be a solitary occupation; project-based learning (PBL), for example, is a constructivist technique in which teams of students pool resources and expertise in the service of large undertakings.

❖ **Tactics for teachers to promote students' construction of knowledge:**

◆ Ensure that instructional objectives involving authentic learning are both compelling and comprehensible.
◆ Realize that complex problems require teachers to become learners as well as students. Constructivism is not for teachers who already know everything!
◆ In schools where students are exposed to a variety of representational formats for knowledge (text, visual, oral, figurative, etc.), students can choose to which modes they are most receptive and in which modes they are most productive.
◆ Facilitate working in teams, not to reduce stress but to distribute the stress across and between individuals. Students need conflict resolution skills as well as receptive and productive language skills.

Humanistic Education: Affective and Emotional Factors

◆ **STRATEGY 3.4:** Reduce tension and support a positive emotional state in the learner

Integrating Cognitive and Affective Learning

Educators have long recognized the advantages of developing both cognitive and affective (emotional) aspects of learning: the head *and* the heart. Students who explore content that interests them, work cooperatively with others, and accept the emotions that accompany learning (joy, curiosity, and excitement as well as frustration and anxiety) will mature as people with unique gifts and talents. Positive emotional factors such as self-esteem, motivation, and proactive attitudes help language acquisition to take place.

Self-Esteem

"Self-esteem" can be defined as having a positive self-concept, or evaluation of oneself. *Self-concept* is "the composite of ideas, feelings, and attitudes people have about themselves" (Hilgard, Atkinson, & Atkinson, 1979, p. 605). High self-esteem may *cause* language success or *result from* language success. Students who feel proud of their successes and abilities, self-knowledge, and self-expression and who have enhanced images of self, family, and culture are better language learners.

Of course the most powerful sense of self-esteem is the result not solely of one's beliefs about oneself but also of successful learning experiences. Practices of schooling that damage self-esteem, such as tracking and competitive grading, undermine authentic cooperation and a sense of accomplishment on the part of English learners.

Classroom texts are available that offer literature and anecdotal readings aimed at the enhancement of identity and self-esteem. *Identity* (Raimes, 1996) includes readings grouped into chapters titled "Name," "Appearance, Age, and Abilities," "Ethnic Affiliation and Class," "Family Ties," and so forth. The readings contain authentic text and may be best used in high school ESL classes of intermediate fluency and above.

A poignant excerpt from the above is from Mike Rose's reminiscences from "Tracking": "Students will float to the mark you set. I and the others in the vocational classes were bobbing in pretty shallow water" (p. 372). Another entry in this genre is *Who Am I* from Perfection Learning (2000), a collection of essays and stories that help students (middle school and above) to examine their identity and values. These anecdotal essays elicit reflective writing from students about their classes and their academic goals. Some stories, particularly those involving the loss of self-esteem through schooling, may provoke students to empathy. In the story "The Cutting of My Long Hair," Zitkala-Sa, a Dakota Sioux sent in 1884 to a missionary school, recounts the final indignity:

> And now my long hair was shingled like a coward's! In my anguish I moaned for my mother, but no one came to comfort me. Not a soul reasoned quietly with me, as my own mother used to do; for now I was only one of many animals driven by a herder. (p. 61)

Materials in the self-esteem genre can be divided into four parts using Siccone's (1995) typology: Type I activities promote an internal sense of individual esteem; Type II enhance students' sense of interdependence, or group esteem; Type III advance a personal sense of responsibility; and Type IV help students to feel a sense of social responsibility. Suggested activities for each type of self-esteem building, along with recommended grade levels for each activity, are presented in Table 3.4 keyed to sources for the activities.

Sapon-Shevin (1999) suggested four books of children's literature with cooperative friendship as a theme. *Friends* (Heine, 1982) is the story of a pig, a duck, and a rooster who learn to play together. In *Amos and Boris* (Steig, 1972) a mouse and a whale forge a deep connection. *Two Good Friends* (Delton, 1974) is about a bear and duck "odd couple." *Some Things You Just Can't Do by Yourself* (Schiff, 1973) can inspire a class-created book of cooperative activities. Sapon-Shevin recommends books for various ages in many self-esteem genres, including books about self-affirmation, family diversity, peers helping each other, social inclusiveness, and social justice. Sapon-Shevin includes a large resource list of books, lists of organizations devoted to social change, songs, and cooperative games.

Related to self-esteem is the concept of *inhibition*. Students are inhibited when they defend themselves against new experiences and feelings. Emphasizing fluency over accuracy in the first stages of language learning may help students feel less

TABLE 3.4 • A Sampling of Self-Esteem–Building Activities by Grade Level

Activity	Description	Type	Grade	Source
The Name Game	Introduce yourself by first name, adding a word that describes how you are feeling today—using a word that begins with the same letter as the first name. (The teacher may provide English learners with an alphabetized list of adjectives so that they can prepare in advance.) Each subsequent person repeats what the others have said in sequence.	I	3–12	Siccone
Name Interviews	Students work in pairs using a teacher-provided questionnaire: "What do you like about your name? Who named you? Were you named for someone? Are there members of your family who have the same name?"	I	1–12 (adapt to grade)	Siccone
Ageless	Think positively about your age and other ages by answering eight questions, such as "What do you like about being your present age?" and "What did you like about being younger?"	I	4–12	Moskowitz
Lifeline	Using a string and index cards, enter six to ten points that represent important events that you are willing to share. Compare your life stories with a partner's.	I	1–12 (adapt to grade)	Canfield & Wells
Friends #1 Chart, Friends #2 Chart	Graphic organizers teach concepts about friendship as a theme, integrating literature, language, art, science, music, and movement at two distinct levels of sophistication.	II	#1, K–2; #2, 1–3	Hopkins & Winters
Autograph Books	Each student makes a book with materials provided by the teacher. Each page has a message from another student.	II	1–12	McCabe & Rhoades
Class Name/ Theme	Class decides on a name and theme. Students must not choose a name that is a put-down ("The Losers") or reflects a competitive orientation ("The Best Third Grade").	II	1–12	Sapon-Shevin
Cooperative Musical Chairs	When the music stops, all must be successfully in a chair for the group to win. With groups of eight students, remove one chair each time.	II	1–4	Sapon-Shevin
Class Meeting	Regularly schedule meetings for event planning, or hold impromptu ones for group problem solving.	II	1–12	McCabe & Rhoades
Me Power	Imagine you are going to give a speech before a large group of people. Write a brief description of your accomplishments for the person who is to introduce you.	III	4–12	Moskowitz

(continued)

TABLE 3.4 • Continued

Activity	Description	Type	Grade	Source
Maybe Yes, Maybe No	Students use a Chinese folktale to learn that events in one's life can be interpreted positively or negatively.	III	4–12	Siccone
Success Story	Describe an incident in which you achieved a victory or reached a goal.	III	1–12	Moskowitz
Crossing the Goal Line	Provide a visual representation of students reaching academic goals.	III	1–12	Siccone
"Why People Speak Many Languages"	A Seneca Indian folktale is used in a lesson that teaches social harmony and conflict resolution.	IV	1-12	Brody, Goldspinner, et al.
Social Responsibility Chart	Graphic organizer teaches concepts about social responsibility as a theme, integrating literature, language, art, science, music, and movement.	IV	4–6	Hopkins & Winters
Lend a Hand	Using a poster displaying prints of everyone's hands, students plan/celebrate giving or receiving help.	IV	1–12	Siccone
A Kid's Guide to Resources for Social Action	Provide a comprehensive list of organizations available for resources on projects of social change.	IV	4–12	Lewis

Sources: Brody, E., Goldspinner, J., Green, K., Leventhal, R., & Porcino, J. (Eds.). (1992). Canfield, J., & Wells, H. (1976). Hopkins, S., & Winters, J. (1990). Lewis, B. (1991). McCabe, M., & Rhoades, J. (1988). Moskowitz, G. (1978). Sapon-Shevin, M. (1999). Siccone, F. (1995).

inhibited. Lozanov's Suggestopedia is a methodology that focuses on a reduction of inhibitions so that students can communicate more freely.

The ability to *take risks,* to "gamble," may facilitate SLA. Learners who are willing to guess at unclear meanings and to risk making errors will progress in language skills more rapidly than their more inhibited colleagues. As Brown (2000) pointed out, however, students who make random guesses and blurt out meaningless phrases have not been as successful. It appears that moderate risk takers stand the best chance of language development.

Motivation

Motivation has been defined as the impulse, emotion, or desire that causes one to act in a certain way. Humans strive to actively acquire knowledge, explore, enhance the ego, achieve an identity within a group, and learn about their world. Various individual, sociocultural, and instructional factors impact motivation. Gardner and Lambert (1972) postulated two types of motivation in learning a second language: *instrumen-*

tal motivation, the need to acquire a language for a specific purpose such as getting a job; and *integrative* motivation, the desire to affiliate with members of the second-language group. Most students experience a mixture of both types of motivation.

Pierce (1995) has reconceptualized motivation in terms of investment, identity, and language choice (see also Brown, 2001). As Brutt-Griffler and Samimy (1999) pointed out, the basic social construction of the identity of native versus nonnative speaker influences motivation. A nonnative speaker must accept the status of a permanent learner (and unfortunately, even at the present time, someone who must learn is socially positioned as unfinished and intellectually marginal, despite the postmodern sheen applied to the concept of marginality).

Motivation can be seen as being a *trait* that is relatively consistent and persistent or as a *state*, a more temporary condition that can be influenced by the use of interesting materials or activities, reward, or punishment (Tharp, 1989). Much depends on a teacher's definition of motivation. The belief that motivation is a *trait* may lead teachers to blame the student, parents, or culture for low student interest or achievement. Conversely, teachers who believe that motivation is a *state* may be motivated to alter their teaching if students appear unmotivated, to make lessons more interesting and involving.

Anxiety

Anxiety about language learning resembles communication anxiety, that is, feelings of self-consciousness, desire to speak perfectly, and fear of making mistakes. SLA anxiety is like other feelings of tension that students may experience in the classroom. In some ways, however, anxiety in a second language is more than simply communication anxiety; using a foreign language can threaten a person's sense of self because speakers know they cannot represent themselves fully in a new language or understand others readily (Horwitz, Horwitz, & Cope, 1991).

Because students learn better in a supportive, nonthreatening environment, several language educators have developed methodologies that make the learning environment as comfortable as possible and reduce tension (e.g., Lozanov's Suggestopedia). Student-to-student communication increases with peer work, small-group work, games, simulations, and an atmosphere of warmth and friendliness.

Classroom techniques can teach students to manage anxiety (Crookall & Oxford, 1991). Agony Column allows students to write a letter to an imaginary Ann Landers, relating a particular difficulty they have in language learning and asking for advice. Students in groups read and discuss the letters, offer advice, and return the letters to their originators for follow-up discussion. This helps students to recognize and deal directly with their anxiety. Mistakes Panel is an activity in which students collect mistakes over a number of classes and, working in groups, assess the errors. They then discuss the errors; rate them on a scale of 1 to 3 for such qualities as amusement, originality, and intelligibility; and tally points to reward the "winning" mistake. Anxious Photos features a series of photos of people in a wide range of communicative contexts, such as a restaurant, a post office, a family visit, and a classroom. Students work in groups to judge the level of anxiety that they would feel in these situations and discuss in pairs why they think anxiety is aroused in each context.

Several types of activities allow all students to participate with little apprehension. Beginning students tend to feel comfortable in activities that require sensorimotor involvement, such as TPR, and playing games that require a combination of language and physical activity, such as Simon Says.

> In Simon Says, contestants make one horizontal line about twenty feet from the leader, who calls out commands to the participants that are a combination of gestures and forward moves. ("Simon says take three steps forward. Simon says touch your nose.") Contestants must listen carefully, though, because commands preceded by "Simon says . . ." should be followed, and those commands that are *not* so preceded should *not* be followed. Those who step forward or gesture in the latter case must go back to the starting line. The first participant to cross the finish line wins the game. Like the commands in TPR, the language in Simon Says is simple, and the activities do not require complex production or a verbal response in English.

Anxiety-reducing tasks at the level of early production might involve hands-on tasks such as working with maps or creating simple puppet shows in which the puppeteer is behind a curtain or below a table. Speech emergence activities may include singing in a group or creating activity books such as "Autumn Leaf Poems." At the level of intermediate fluency, pair interviews help students to get to know a classmate. "Preference ranking" of favorite and less favorite hobby activities, songs, celebrities, or household chores enables students to voice their opinions without using complex language (Koch & Terrell, 1991).

❖ **Tactics for teachers to reduce student anxiety (adapted from Woolfolk, 1998):**

◆ Monitor activities to reduce undue pressure.
◆ Give students in competitive tasks a reasonable chance to succeed.
◆ Avoid making anxious students perform in front of large groups.
◆ Give examples or models of how the task is done when starting a new type of task.
◆ Teach skills explicitly and provide study guides.
◆ Vary assignments over different modes of language learning.
◆ Energize students by giving them a brief chance to be physically active, or by introducing activities that provoke curiosity or surprise.

Attitudes of the Learner

Attitudes toward self, language, peers, the teacher, and the classroom environment play a critical role in learning English (Richard-Amato, 1996). One's *attitude toward the self* involves self-esteem and related emotions, what one believes about one's ability in general as well as the ability to learn language. These cognitions and feelings are often hidden and may be slow to change.

Attitudes toward English, or the primary language, and those who speak it are largely influenced by peers and parents, as well as by prior experience. Negative reactions are often the result of negative stereotypes, discrimination, or racism. Peñalosa (1980) pointed out that if English learners are made to feel inferior because of accent or language status, they may have a defensive reaction or ambivalent feelings about their L1. Some parents may use English only in the home, hoping children will learn English more rapidly. Conversely, students who acquire English while neglecting their primary language may be considered traitors by their peers or families. Either of these situations can cause problems within the family and create a backlash against English or against maintenance of the primary language.

Attitudes toward the teacher and the classroom environment play an important role. Families' positive attitudes toward school can influence their children's success. However, Ogbu and Matute-Bianchi (1986) stated that parents who have had negative experiences at school may subconsciously pass along these attitudes to their children. Students may cling to language behavior that characterizes their group, as opposed to the language group represented by the school, and engage in resistance in the form of misbehavior, vandalism, and poor relationships with teachers (Nieto, 2000). Self-esteem-building techniques (see Moskowitz, 1978) can counteract resistance and foster positive attitudes.

Other Affective Factors

In addition to those affective factors discussed in this section, other affective factors involve the connection of oneself to others. *Empathy* aids language acquisition if the learner is aware of another's feelings, understands the intentions and emotions of a speaker, and attempts to comprehend the message.

> Community language learning (Curran, 1982) provides students with increased opportunities to share with and belong to a learning group and has led to significant language gains. In this method, learners form a circle of about eight to ten members. Facilitators stand behind the circle. When one participant has something to say to another, the facilitator whispers the correct English, and the participant then delivers the message aloud. In this way, English directly serves the desires and needs of the communicators.

Extroversion can be seen as the need to receive ego enhancement or information from other people, which can be a personality factor or a cultural trait. Students' prior schooling may have encouraged them to be more willing to participate in class. Although the extrovert may be perceived as a person who takes more risks with language, an introverted or more reserved person may show more intuitive understanding or empathy with others.

Motivating Students Humanistically

Humanistic approaches promote positive feelings toward learning and respect for the value of every student. Students feel cared for, encouraged, and supported as they learn from their successes and failures, make choices, seek new experiences, work independently, and self-reflect. Students feel able to use their inner resources, competence, and autonomy in the pursuit of knowledge. However, high-quality education is not free of stress. Students need an optimum level of stress in order for school to be effective.

Agne emphasized that humanistic education is not a single technique, but "a deep emotional belief that pervades every teacher's thoughts and behaviors" (1992, p. 123), placing emphasis on the worth of the individual, trusting and accepting the strengths and weaknesses of learners, and empathizing with their thoughts and feelings. Good teachers target a level of performance that is within the learners' skills and abilities. They give positive feedback as often as possible as students pursue personal inquiry and collaboration, and offer the chance for input into course design so that students can explore issues that interest them.

Evidence shows, however, that promoting self-esteem and a warm relationship between teacher and student is not in itself enough to achieve effective education. In fact, "having positive self-esteem is almost impossible for many young people, given the deplorable conditions under which they are forced to live by the iniquities in our society" (Beane, 1991, p. 27). A caring classroom cannot entirely overcome the negative quality of the dehumanizing "get tough" administrative policies of inner-city schools, or the negative messages that students may receive about their home culture.

❖ **Tactics for teachers seeking to motivate students humanistically:**

- Tell students you care for them, and that your high standards for them are the highest form of caring.
- Demonstrate that you value creativity and individual uniqueness.
- Show students you care for them by watching carefully for individual differences: recognize which students will ask for help and which will not, who is afraid, or who wants no help at all.
- Help students distinguish between "eustress" (good stress) and unwarranted pressure.
- Listen to students' opinions about classroom occurrences they deem unfair, teaching practices that bore them, or ideas that would benefit the whole group.

The Teacher as Counselor

English learners may need assistance during their adjustment to language and schooling in a new culture. Teachers may be called upon to do more than facilitate cognitive or language development. They may need to address students' emotional needs by responding to emotional problems or crises, resolving interpersonal conflicts, referring students to school study teams for special education evaluation, or otherwise assessing and guiding students' emotional and social growth (Kottler & Kottler, 1993).

Teachers can help students adjust to school, and to life's "ups and downs," in three ways. First, educators can teach in a way that is "kind and helpful, inviting and stimulating . . . fostering tolerance, cooperation, and self-respect" (Kottler & Kottler, 1993, p. 6). Second, teachers can help students to deal with stresses in daily life, either by one-on-one conversation, by group discussion, or by using a story in class that touches upon a theme relevant to common problems. Lastly, events such as a student's suicide or a community crisis can trigger anxiety on the part of many students, and teachers may offer help in focusing students on their schoolwork or dealing with their emotional unrest.

Bullying—defined as a single or series of intentionally cruel incidents in which the intent is to put the victim in distress—may be a problem for non–English-speaking students as it is for many others. Clifford (2001) claimed that students who are the victims of bullying can become suicidal or suffer lifelong emotional scars. The incidence of bullying is greater than most people believe; one-third of students reported bullying or having been bullied. Victims reported being lonely, had problems making friends, and were more likely to dislike and perform poorly in school (Mestel, 2001; Mestel & Groves, 2001).

Evidence from the workplace suggests that intercultural miscommunication may be a daily feature of life in communities of mixed races. In one example, some American workers in a U.S. technology company talked in a condescending way to Russian coworkers because they unconsciously considered those with Russian accents stupid. In turn, the Russians thought those who smiled at them were mocking them, because Russian culture discourages smiling at work (Vaughn, 2001). Judging from these incidents, schools may benefit from clear antidiscrimination policies, supported with examples of what may be considered prohibited behaviors. Encouraging structured programs of intercultural communication can reduce stress for students in K–12.

Some programs provide training in listening skills and intervention strategies. These skills may assist in other ways besides being able to address students' emotional concerns. Communication training often leads to improvement in interpersonal, collegial relationships; increases respect for teachers from both students and colleagues; and helps teachers themselves cope with job-related stress. As one teacher reports, "Learning to improve my listening skills helped me in a small way to communicate with a parent who blamed me for her son's insubordinate attitude. But it helped me in a big way when I didn't end up blaming myself" (Bider, 2001).

❖ **Tactics for teachers seeking to play a counseling role:**

- Take workshops or academic training in counseling skills if possible.
- Be willing to take time outside class to hear about a student's personal life, if this is appropriate in the context of the school.
- Understand that trust and mutual respect take time to develop, yet all cultures expect a certain level of automatic respect from students toward teachers.
- Be aware that students respond differently to trust from teachers: Those who experience love at home may take this for granted, but those who have been abused may show resistance and distrust.
- Nonjudgmental listening holds back both quick praise and facile advice; students seek their own solutions to their problems.

Cultural Anthropology and Education

- **STRATEGY 3.5:** Be aware of the effect of the sociocultural context on cognitive and language development

In recent years, cultural anthropologists have contributed rich insights into the practices of schools, investigating the relative successes and failures of members of various subcultures of, or immigrants to, the United States who have attended public schools dominated largely by European American educators. This cultural perspective has also been applied to the study of English teaching in a variety of settings, both in English-dominated cultures and in EFL contexts. From this perspective has emerged a vision of TESOL as one of the first truly intercultural teaching professions.

Communicative Competence

Hymes (1972, 1974) introduced the term "communicative competence," meaning the ability that enables language users to "convey and interpret messages and to negotiate meanings interpersonally within specific contexts" (Brown, 1987). Rather than merely knowing grammatical forms, the competent speaker is recognized as one who knows when, where, and how to use language appropriately.

Canale (1983) expanded the components of communicative competence beyond *grammatical competence* to include *sociolinguistic competence*, *strategic competence*, and *discourse competence*. Grammatical competence focuses on accurate knowledge of sentence formation, vocabulary, and so forth. Sociolinguistic competence involves producing and understanding language in different social contexts. Strategic competence involves using language to meet communicative goals, compensate for breakdowns in communication, or enhance the effectiveness of communication. Discourse competence involves the ability to combine utterances (spoken) and sentences (written) into a meaningful spoken conversation or written text.

Teachers can help students to increase their skills in sociolinguistic, strategic, and discourse competence by building experiences into the curriculum that involve solving problems, exploring students' areas of interest, and designing projects. Students carry over knowledge of how to communicate from experiences in their first language. This knowledge can be tapped as they develop specific forms and usage in English.

> In a high school ESL class, Mr. Thurmond demonstrated grammatical, sociolinguistic, strategic, and discourse competence to students by having them role-play a job interview. As students conducted and analyzed the interview situation, they identified such aspects as the need for forms of politeness and the inappropriate use of slang. The final winner was the applicant who, having at first been turned down, used strategic competence—she asked to be put on a waiting list and then got the job when the first-choice candidate accepted "a better offer"!

Communicative Language Teaching.   Communicative competence theory has given rise to communicative language teaching involving social functions of language; for example, talking about oneself, requesting, agreeing, refusing, telling a story, expressing disappointment, and so forth. Students may use conversational gambits (Keller & Warner, 1988), such as those for the expression of opinions ("In my opinion . . . ," "I personally believe . . . ," "You might disagree, but I think . . .") or expressions used to change a subject ("Speaking of . . . ," "That reminds me . . . ," "By the way . . . ," "Oh, before I forget . . ."). Even at the beginning level, one learns how to have one's needs met through communication in L2.

At the intermediate level of instruction, students might listen and repeat conversations or role plays in which someone makes a complaint ("Look, I'm sorry to bother you, but . . .") or an apology ("I can't tell you how sorry I am . . . "). Communicative dialogues help students to identify what functional language is needed in a situation (persuading, stating preferences, etc.), and then provide a variety of ways to express the function ("It might be a good idea to . . . ," "Have you ever thought of . . . ?" "Why don't you . . . ?") (see Jones and von Baeyer's *Functions of American English Student's Book,* 1983). At the intermediate level, students also work to expand their repertoire of common phrases, such as, "How's it going?" "I hope so," "I doubt it," and a hundred other useful expressions (see *Common American Phrases in Everyday Contexts,* Spears, 1992).

At the advanced level of instruction, communicative competence helps the learner to achieve personal goals and desires. For example, Goodale's *The Language of Meetings* (1987, p. 9) gives this example of a communicative interchange:

SPEAKER A: (wants to say) I want to meet on the 24th.

SPEAKER A: (actually says) I was wondering if we could meet again on the 24th.

SPEAKER B: (wants to say) That's not suitable. I want the 31st.

SPEAKER B: (actually says) As a matter of fact, I'm afraid that might be a bit difficult, as I have to contact one or two colleagues who are out of town at the moment. Perhaps we could give ourselves an extra week. Wouldn't the following Thursday, the 31st, be better?

Goodale includes an analysis of the strategic features of this interchange: the use of modals (*could, might*) to make a statement more tentative; using questions rather than statements; adding "I'm afraid" to make it clear that the speaker recognizes the unhelpfulness of the message; using qualifying words ("a bit," "a slight problem") and the continuous form ("I was wondering . . .") to make the position more flexible; and using a comparative ("more convenient") to soften the message. Language is thus taught in a strategic/pragmatic/contextual form, and the learning is immediately useful outside the classroom setting. This demonstrates some of the reasons for the dominance of communicative competence theory as today's paradigm.

Communicative language teaching has also led to greater use of games and communicative activities, which lighten the spirit of learning, reduce the affective filter, add excitement to the lesson, and make review and practice more fun. Box 3.2 offers a variety of resources for communicative games.

Communicative language teaching must do more than entertain students. As Taylor (1987) noted,

> Real communication is a shared activity which requires the active involvement of its participants. . . . We have a responsibility to create an atmosphere in which communication is possible, one in which students can feel free to take communicating initiative and are motivated to do so. Making classes "student-centered" can contribute to creating such an atmosphere.
>
> But creating a supportive, student-centered environment . . . is not enough. True communication to which students are committed will only take place if we also have

BOX 3.2
❖ Resources for Communicative Games

Blair, R. W. (Ed.). (1982). *Innovative approaches to language teaching.* Boston: Heinle & Heinle.

Danesi, M. (1985). *A guide to puzzles and games in second language pedagogy.* Toronto: Ontario Institute for Studies in Education.

Harvey, J. (1982). Communications approach: Games II. In R. W. Blair, (Ed.). (1982). *Innovative approaches to language teaching.* Boston: Heinle & Heinle.

Lewis, G., & Bedson, G. (1999). *Games for children.* Oxford: Oxford University Press.

Lewis, M. (1997). *New ways in teaching adults.* Alexandria, VA: Teachers of English to Speakers of Other Languages.

Maculaitis, J. (1988). *The complete ESL/EFL resource book: Strategies, activities, and units for the classroom.* Lincolnwood, IL: National Textbook Company.

Nation, P. (1994). *New ways in teaching vocabulary.* Alexandria, VA: Teachers of English to Speakers of Other Languages.

Omaggio, A. (1978). *Games and simulations in the foreign language classroom.* Washington, DC: Center for Applied Linguistics.

engaging content that will involve the participants and in which those participants have a stake . . . which focus on issues that are relevant and meaningful to students. (p. 49)

Social Contexts for Language Learning

The Russian psychologist Lev Vygotsky emphasized the role of social interaction in the development of language and thought: language joins with thought to create meaning (Wink, 2000). Interaction occurs in a cultural, historical, and institutional context, which shapes the availability and quality of the tools and signs that mediate higher mental functions.

According to Vygotsky, teaching must take into consideration the student's "zone of proximal development," defined as "the distance between the actual developmental level as determined by independent problem solving and the level of potential development . . . under adult guidance or in collaboration with more capable peers" (1981, p. 86). Social interaction between adults and students operates within this zone.

Children's knowledge develops through their "taking for themselves" the ways of thinking and talking provided by their culture (Kozulin & Presseisen, 1995). This *mediation* of learning—assisting students' performance—requires teachers to adapt to the level of the student, provide help when needed, and to help students to work with one another and the teacher to coconstruct meaning (see Tharp & Gallimore, 1988).

The social uses of language are advanced when students engage in communicative pair or group tasks: practicing Reader's Theater with other students, developing interview questions for a community survey, or planning an exhibition of art or written work to which to invite the public. Students benefit from communication with one another, members of the school community, and members of the community at large.

Vygotsky recognized that all teaching and learning takes place within the context of the memories, experiences, and cultural habits that are found within families. Families form the matrix that underlies the schooling in which students participate. The wise teacher draws upon families' stories and social histories to enrich the classroom. Self-esteem and identity are strengthened as themes and values are expressed through the words of students and their families. Children appreciate their parents and parents' friends more as they see their experiences are worthy of regard.

Activity Theory

Vygotsky's student Leont'ev developed *activity theory,* studying the interaction between the individual, the artifacts (tools) that are situated within the setting, and the other individuals. According to activity theory, the society at large is the sum total of the activity systems that are developed and maintained by its members (Wells, 1998). Activity theory is being extended by current researchers to include the influences of multiple cultural perspectives (Lucero, 1999).

Communities of Practice

Learning is not a separate and independent activity of individuals, but an integral part of participation in a community (Lave & Wenger, 1991). Children return to dynamic and interactive communities after a day of school. Teachers must come to know and respect what the community offers students and encourage knowledge to travel a two-way path as it circulates from school to home and back to school. Thus, learning is both an individual and communal activity (McCaleb, 1994). The "funds of knowledge" approach (see Chapter 13) uses the cultural practices of households and communities as the resources within the students' world that can be connected in a meaningful way to the school curriculum.

Culture and Schooling

Schools, as institutions of learning and socialization, represent the larger culture. Culture, though largely invisible, influences instruction, policy, and learning in schools. A knowledge of the deeper elements of culture—beyond superficial aspects such as food, clothing, holidays, and celebrations—can give teachers a crosscultural perspective that enables them to educate students to the greatest extent possible. Chapter 9 treats this topic in depth.

The Study of Classroom Discourse

Schools, as institutions of learning and socialization, are representatives of a particular society, a *macroculture.* Moreoever, each classroom has a unique *microculture.* Understanding the discourse practices used in the classroom is an important step forward for students who are new to English. Classroom discourse practices will be analyzed in Chapter 10.

Culturally Responsive Teaching

Intercultural educators have a repertoire of teaching and learning strategies available for use in a given context. Should students outside the mainstream change their cultural patterns to match those of the society at large, and should they seek success in mainstream terms? This is an *assimilationist* view. Other teachers believe in *accommodating* instruction to facilitate learning for such students. Culturally responsive teaching strategies help teachers to use the students' own cultures to support their learning. These will be further explored in Chapter 9.

❖ Tactics for culturally responsive teaching (adapted from Ladson-Billings, 1994):

◆ Building upon students' culture supports them as intellectual leaders in the classroom.
◆ Teaching in an integrated, coherent way helps students to feel a part of a learning community.
◆ Student's real-life experiences legitimate their contribution to the "official" curriculum.
◆ A broader conception of literacy includes literature and oratory.

Looking Forward: Postmodernism

◆ **STRATEGY 3.6:** Place learning in the context of contemporary social change

Modernism versus Postmodernism

Schools stand in no privileged position in the contemporary world but must take their place among the institutions that discipline and shape daily life. Schooling has gained in importance as daily life has become ever more knowledge-driven and inundated by information. At the same time, formal schooling may eventually decrease in importance as time goes by and the information age flowers. Formal "seat time" in front of credentialed teachers may lose place to more informal, perhaps more powerful modes of interactive learning. However, at this moment schooling still retains its role as the chief means by which society produces leaders and reproduces followers.

Contemporary schooling is based on assumptions that suit the modern world of the immediate past better than the needs of the future—a future some call "postmodern." Applying ideas adapted from postmodern theory may enable us to learn enough about schools to change them, just in time to preserve them. Apart from public schooling, there is no other shared institution in which all become citizens together. As society pulls people deeper into enclaves separated from common ideals, public schooling is at risk.

Modernism

The modern world encompassed the eighteenth to the twentieth centuries. The Enlightenment led European cultures to a new freedom to pursue scientific questions using rational methods without fear of reprisal from religious authorities. Individuals took on surnames that permitted them to be known outside their village and were thus able to carry this identity forth to trade goods and knowledge, and to build empires capitalized by wealth resulting from new worlds of exploitable raw materials, cheap labor, and mechanization, served by an increasingly large managerial class (see Irvine, 1998).

Based on these trends, mass marketing spread the belief that mass consumption results in a secure, middle-class existence and access to a mass culture for everyone, underpinned by a number of specific certainties: that there exists a unified, centered self; that hierarchies based on social class are natural and inevitable; that the possession of "original" and expensive objects and experiences defines "value," while analysis and access to these objects and experiences constitutes "culture"; and that books contain knowledge, structured as explanations for educated people of history, identity, and core cultural values. "Late capitalism" is a widely used term for consumer economies based on the now global scope of capitalism.

However, one by one these beliefs have been challenged by developments that have taken place in the twenty-first century. As the modern age culminated, humans webbed the earth with knowledge, yet ran a headlong race against the forces of ignorance and injustice. The modern world cannot be stitched back together in a comforting way. Irreversible changes have taken place: an awareness of the limitations of rationality, a shift in what constitutes identity, a loss of belief in progress. It has become difficult to sustain a consistent view of change and growth.

Postmodernism

Postmodernism is a movement in arts and culture that contradicts, subverts, or resists the prevailing assumptions of modernism. The "hippie era" of the 1960s in the United States was the first to exploit mass media to spread the vision of a viable alternative to capitalism. The art and styles of the period successfully countered the centralized culture represented by mass advertising. "Funky," a hippie term connoting "individual, not store-bought, eclectic, odd" was a key move against standardization. A combination of writers, artists, and visionaries pioneered the hybridization of forms and genres, the mix of styles of different cultures or time periods in architecture, visual arts, and literature that has come to be called "postmodern" (as distinguished from poststructuralism; see Klage, 1997).

The term "postmodern" recognizes that globalization of cultures, races, images, and products has eroded national, linguistic, ethnic, and cultural identities, resulting in a global mixing of cultures on a scale unknown to societies before the information era. Using the World Wide Web, people all over the planet are "writing back" to tell their own stories. Some of these positions are postcolonial, with writers expressing the tensions of the previously colonized. At the same time, however, individualism has become elusive. Attempts to provide illusions of individual style (ads for jeans, cars, etc.) through images that define cool, hip, and desirable actually recirculate images, so that every style becomes an echo of something previously seen or heard.

As people live in a world of perpetual images and sound bites, ethnic traditions that had created and supported individual differences blend into a pastiche of recombinant, mutually interchangeable fragments. The individual goes adrift as multiple, conflicting identities, housed in alternative family units, combine with bionic mixes of organic and inorganic, human and electronic, to create a consciousness beyond reality saturated by images that may never have been "real." People have become unable to recognize the genuine, much less honor it.

Implications of Postmodernism for Educators

Teaching English in a postmodern world is a career predicated upon uncertainty. Like colonized people, those who learn English as a second or foreign language may simultaneously both love and hate the colonizer, English. The mother tongue that has nurtured them is no longer sufficient in and of itself and it cannot be protected from the cultural change that has brought the learner to the point of needing a second means of communication. Modernity has caused tensions and contradictions, yet postmodern pedagogies offer possibilities. The four most important implications of postmodernism for teachers of English learners are in areas of teachers' and learners' identities, technologies of knowledge, understandings about power, and changes in the English language.

Identity.   In the modern world, one's *identity* was imprinted by one's primary socialization and encoded in one's native language. In the postmodern shift, identity is investment (see Pierce, 1995). The question is no longer, "What changes take place in my personality as I learn another language?" Instead, identity is seen as an internal resource. What time, energy, and personal characteristics is the learner willing to invest in L2, and how is this done?

Postmodern identity is flexible, multiple, and extended (Weedon, 1987). More and more people are ethnically mixed and culturally porous. Postmodern learners are polycultural, as identity boundaries dissolve and people resonate in brotherhoods and sisterhoods that are self-created.

Identity is a powerful engine for SLA, because cultural resistance is acknowledged in the postmodern shift. Many learners nurture a secret fear that conflicting loyalties between L1/Culture 1 versus English-language target cultures will disrupt family life or cause irreversible change. Teachers can openly discuss fears of cultural detriment and/or change or loss of identity. English is not the enemy of tradition, but rather a vehicle for cultural change. Something is lost and something is gained when cultures change. Dealing with resistance directly makes new identity investments possible, both for the learner and the teacher. Intercultural educators benefit greatly from becoming bicultural, achieving what Bennett (1999) called "dynamic in-betweenness."

By acknowledging inner resistance, the learner is free to adopt a more flexible orientation toward identity. This can foster additive rather than subtractive identity. Teachers of L2 embrace Identity 2 and nourish multicultural hybrid identities that activate and energize SLA and create new connections between motivation and methods.

Technologies of Knowledge.   *Technologies of knowledge* will dramatically change in the postmodern world. The four major components of postmodern techniques of knowledge are *constructivism, intercultural positioning, metarational thinking*, and *cybertutorial technologies* (Díaz-Rico, 1999a). Constructionism endorses interactive creation of meaning. Meaning is not constant within the structure of a language or of a given text, or in the tongue of the teacher. Meaning resides in the hearts, minds, and intent of the learners. In the postmodern world, new teaching tools entail local-focus methodology. Teachers leave behind one-size-fits-all methods and negotiate activities and objectives based upon the needs of the learner, using knowledge of learning styles and multiple intelligences, and encouraging metacognition and self-reflection in order to increase students' self-knowledge and capacity for making conscious meaning.

English teachers will find increasingly powerful ways to incorporate the primary language and the primary culture of the learner. If culture is externalized mind and mind is internalized culture (Cole, 1998), postmodern teaching is about mindful and "culture-ful" learning. This new emphasis radically repositions the teacher and learner in the postmodern classroom. The teacher is the professional learner. Students are apprentices. Intercultural educators who become learners about the language and culture of the students will serve as a model for learners.

Metarational thinking acknowledges that postmodern technologies do not engage solely the rational mind. Good teachers dip into the imaginary to teach, to use that primordial realm of "prepossibility" where dreams originate. This protects the learner from the belief that rationality is the only desirable mode of thinking, permits the yoking of emotion to logic, and sanctions solutions that are neither wholly right nor wholly wrong (see Chapter 7).

Increasing sophistication will characterize the computer-learner connection. These are not preprogrammed tutorials in which basic skills are carefully sequenced in computer-managed "drill and kill." They offer instead learner-managed information access, with project-based learning at the core. The Internet empowers the learner as creator to spin artfully a personal web of knowledge. Students who surf the Web to complete projects for class can process English purposefully and independently, becoming, in effect, their own tutors.

New Conceptions of Power.   Postmodernism will circulate altered understandings about power. In classrooms of the monolingual era, students spoke one language or remained silent. The institution controlled the goals and purposes of students' L2. There was no question that power lay in the hands of the teacher, the authorities, and the L2 deployed by the school (see Darder, 1991). In the postmodern world, however, power circulates, as dual-language acquisition rotates power between peoples and among cultures. Instead of the pretense of institutional nonnegotiability, unavailability, and neutrality, students now have the power to speak, and to use a public voice toward their self-determined ends.

English as a Language Will Become Postmodern.   English will become not "world English," but "the world's English." English as an international language has multiple vernaculars, and speakers have their own dialects and purposes. This notion may unleash chaos, fostering discrimination and misunderstanding; or it may be liberating, expanding the rights of others to access English. The best teachers are not necessarily native speakers, but rather those who have found something to love about English, for themselves and for their students.

Just the fact that English as an international language has multiple purposes, however, does not mean that all of these purposes are noble. Some, indeed, may not be democratic, may not be benevolent, and may not promote human rights. One would hope that the English that is learned favors humanity, equality, and environmental sustainability.

Native speakers of English can learn to practice compassion for others who are learning English and to view varietal English with a sense of equity, respect, and fondness. Teachers trained for ESL/EFL contexts need explicit background in EIL issues. Prospective EFL teachers need to be equipped with insight into power relations and hegemonic practices in countries where English is spoken.

New Roles for English Educators

English-language teachers are poised at the edge of new opportunities, teachers with a truly global mission. Dedication to local learning means taking on flexible identities, affirming primary socialization while adopting a polycultural repertoire. Exploring the mind deeply, evoking its potential for self-regulatory and accelerated learning, and honoring the English of international speakers frees teachers of English learners to embrace postmodernism. Tomorrow calls!

❖ **Tactics for postmodern education:**

- Help learners accept that having a second language means developing a more complex identity, and nurture that complexity.
- Encourage the learner to find meaning using new techniques of intercultural communication, imagination, and computer technologies.
- Examine the social relations of the classroom to see if learners have equal access to power and are treated fairly by the institution.
- Embrace polyvarietal English as equal in status to native speakers' or standard English.

The Future of Teaching English Learners

Strategic English teaching no longer concerns a search for methods and techniques that are so useful that they transcend learner, culture, and context. On the contrary, successful strategies are *built on* these specifics. Learners are most productive when they understand themselves, their capabilities, and predilections—and when they affirm their own culture as they expand their cultural repertoire. Culture, identity, and motivation are inextricably linked. The following chapters position teaching strategies within three layers, following Fairclough's (1989) schema for critical language analysis. Learner strategies are at the core, with strategies influenced by the institution at the next level and those influenced by the sociocultural context at the outermost level (see Figure 3.1).

FIGURE 3.1 ◆ A nested view of strategies for teaching English learners.

Learner Strategies

Chapter 5 details a wealth of strategies that can assist the acquisition and use of a second language. It is important to note that these strategies position the individual acquiring English as a "learner." Most, but not all, learners are students in formal schools. However, some educators may find themselves teaching in a setting devoted to oracy (listening and speaking) skills in which the literacy skills of reading and writing and the larger set of skills necessary for academic success are not emphasized. They can find these strategies easily within the overall schemata devoted to academic competence and focus on them. Chapter 6 treats strategies for both literacy and oracy in depth.

Strategies Influenced by the Institution

A successful teacher needs more than learner strategies. The education of English learners takes place in settings with local institutional norms and values, influenced by larger cultural and political factors. In this book, the contributions and views of critical educators are offered as strategies that take these institutions and contexts into consideration. Chapters 4 and 14 place the learner in the contexts of standards-based education and PBL. Cutting-edge institutions have adopted these learning methods.

Strategies Influenced by the Sociocultural Context

Chapters 8, 11, and 12 place the learner within the context of the English language and its social and cultural contexts for teaching English. Chapters 9 and 10 explore ways in which teachers can act as intercultural educators to serve the communities in which they teach by fostering dual-language acquisition, English teaching that incorporates native culture topics, and service learning.

By seeing strategies for teaching English learners not as narrow techniques that serve the learner but rather as broader techniques that serve the community as well, one can hope that educators who use these strategies will help to bring the language skills of bilingual, bicultural teachers and learners to the forefront of education.

Performance-Based Learning

❖ **MEGASTRATEGY 4:** Maximize learning by basing performance on measurable outcomes

Teaching is both a humanistic endeavor and a science. It is a humanistic endeavor because many psychological and sociocultural factors must be balanced in order to evoke the highest-quality learning from each student. It is a science because the current emphasis on outcome-based learning is based on careful research on teaching and learning over the past one hundred years. Assumptions that underlie this approach are straightforward. In order to achieve learning, one must do the following:

1. Describe what students are expected to accomplish, or perform.
2. Detail what kind of evidence will substantiate this performance.
3. Design learning activities that will accumulate the desired evidence.

Given the complicated social context of schools with English learners, and their pressures to acquire English as rapidly as possible, one can begin to appreciate the complex terrain in which teachers of English learners are employed. "What makes someone want to learn?" and "How can a teacher plan lessons that are driven by the learners' desires to learn?" are even more complex questions than previously thought.

Stakes are high. In a sense, the whole community is invested in the learning that takes place in a classroom, and the whole community suffers if the learning impetus of the young is misdirected, quashed, or squandered. As Einstein said, "The world we created today has problems which cannot be solved by thinking the way we thought when we created them." Teachers must help learners to use psychological tools that are designed for contemporary minds.

What Is Performance-Based Learning?

English is taught for purposes of communication and/or academic achievement. Therefore, a classroom lesson usually contains some content, whether a communication skill or a content concept. Moreover, the current emphasis on students learning *how to learn* entails some learning strategy objective in each lesson. Additionally, because students are English learners, a third type of objective develops language. The objectives for an optimal lesson for English learners fall into three categories:

- content (knowledge, skill, or disposition in a subject area or domain of communicative competence)
- learning to learn (knowledge, skill, or learning strategy that teaches the student how to acquire or process information)
- language (knowledge or skill in some facet of English)

How are these objectives chosen? Schools, school districts, or state agencies publish standards documents that spell out what students should know and be able to do. Curricular programs follow the goals put forth in the documents. A classroom teacher plans instruction using curriculum guides at the specific grade level. Units may be organized based on a theme or, if the course is text-driven, on chapters in the text (instructional planning is presented in greater detail later in this chapter). Units or chapters are further divided into specific lessons. Each lesson contains the essential content area objectives. The classroom teacher is responsible for presenting the material in an understandable way, arranging for students to participate in learning activities, and then measuring the extent of the student's mastery of the material. Thus instruction and assessment are linked.

Objectives may include more than one content area. Both middle school and elementary school instruction increasingly feature thematic units that integrate basic skills and content areas (Short, 1991). In developing a theme, five important questions come to mind: (1) How do activities match standards and curriculum objectives? (2) Are objectives balanced between concrete and abstract? (3) Will students use a range of talents and learning styles in the final assessment? (4) What level of language skills are needed? and (5) How can these language skills be developed? The teacher considers the various tasks that language users must be able to perform in the project (listening, speaking, reading, writing) and makes provision for learning the vocabulary and concepts needed in the discourse of the content areas involved.

The objectives chosen must be matched to a specific level of performance that students will demonstrate. This process is central to the contemporary focus on accountability, because the specific performance expected of the student as a learning outcome can be directly linked to some standard for the performance. Together, these constitute *standards-based learning*.

Standards-Based Learning

At the 1989 Education Summit in Charlottesville, Virginia, President George Bush and the nation's governors proposed a long-term national education strategy (often referred to as "Goals 2000"). The call went out for national professional organizations to articulate clear, high standards for what students should know (content standards) and how well they should know it (performance standards). Then the states were supposed to establish delivery standards declaring what all schools must provide in order for students to achieve these standards. All students were henceforth to be measured at intervals (say, fourth, eighth, and tenth or twelfth grade). These standards and assessment together constitute a voluntary accountability system (Wolf, LeMathieu, & Eresh, 1992).

◆ **STRATEGY 4.1:** Align instruction with local, state, and national standards

TESOL Standards

The organization TESOL, Inc. responded to the call for professional standards by adopting the *ESL Standards for Pre-K–12 Students* in 1997 (see Box 4.1). The document serves as a complement to other standards documents and specifies those language competencies English learners need in order to become fully fluent in English. Using these standards, teachers give students an opportunity to acquire these skills and knowledge. Assessment is a way of ensuring that students are making progress and that instructional activities are used wisely. The use of standards helps ensure that assessment is purposeful and systematic, so that educators can agree on the expectations and content of English-language instruction and be certain that the school successes of English learners are clearly documented.

The standards are organized around three goals, each subdivided into three standards. The goals and standards, divided into grade-level clusters (pre-K–3, 4–8,

---

BOX 4.1
❖ TESOL Standards for Pre-K–12 Students

Goal 1 To use English to communicate in social settings

Standard 1	Students will use English to participate in social interactions.
Standard 2	Students will interact in, through, and with spoken and written English for personal expression and enjoyment.
Standard 3	Students will use learning strategies to extend their communicative competence.

Goal 2 To use English to achieve academically in all content areas

Standard 1	Students will use English to interact in the classroom.
Standard 2	Students will use English to obtain, process, construct, and provide subject matter information in spoken and written form.
Standard 3	Students will use appropriate learning strategies to construct and apply academic knowledge.

Goal 3 To use English in socially and culturally appropriate ways

Standard 1	Students will use the appropriate language variety, register, and genre according to audience, purpose, and setting.
Standard 2	Students will use nonverbal communication appropriate to audience, purpose, and setting.
Standard 3	Students will use appropriate strategies to extend their communicative competence.

Source: TESOL (1997).

9–12) are explained through descriptors, sample progress indicators, and classroom vignettes. The goals represented by the TESOL standards address the language development needed for the purposes of general communication, academic learning, and socioculturally appropriate language use. The descriptors that accompany each goal and standard offer language function equivalents of the standard, and progress indicators expand the concept further.

The standards do not prescribe instructional practices that match the goals. These aspects are covered in five accompanying volumes: *Integrating the ESL Standards into Classroom Practices Grades Pre-K–2* (Smallwood, 2000); *Integrating the ESL Standards into Classroom Practices Grades 3–5* (Samway, 2000); *Integrating the ESL Standards into Classroom Practices Grades 6–8* (Irujo, 2000); *Integrating the ESL Standards into Classroom Practices Grades 9–12* (Agor, 2000); and *Scenarios for ESL Standards-Based Assessment* (TESOL, 2001). Together, these volumes contain curricular units that demonstrate how classroom teachers organize instruction to incorporate the standards.

Program Standards

Standards are also available that assist in the evaluation of programs for English learners. *Program Evaluation: English as a Second Language* (Edwards & Fitzpatrick, 2002) offers guidelines for defining the expectations for student learning, analyzing student performance, identifying priorities for improvement, and collecting and using evidence of instructional and organizational effectiveness. Using the principles provided in this document, schools can formulate plans to improve their education of English learners.

Instruction Aligned with TESOL Standards

In the kindergarten unit "Making Bread Together" (James, 2000), ESL students develop social interaction skills together with academic skills in an inclusion model, in which ESL instruction takes place in the mainstream classroom taught by the kindergarten teacher together with the ESL specialist. The content objectives are based on the science theme of the four main food groups: Students learn to (1) identify different kinds of bread around the world and (2) describe the four food groups. The learning objective is that students work in small groups to complete assignments. The language objectives are that students will (1) respond orally to a story in print, (2) practice oral language, and (3) develop listening skills. The learning activities include story retelling, storybook reading, making a book, making a bread chart and collage, listening and reading a story using the computer, graphing using dry cereal, and taking a field trip to a bakery. Assessment matches the objectives.

"The Most Beautiful Place in the World" is an instructional unit based on the book by the same title (Cameron, 1988) about a young boy in Guatemala who longs to attend school and learn to read (Levine, 2000). Levine found that the Spanish words, foods, and other cultural aspects incorporated in the novel were particularly appropriate for her class, who were all from Spanish-speaking families. The unit also integrated social studies curricular goals as students studied map locations, compass directions, and cultural comparisons. To fulfill language arts goals, they read for comprehension and enjoyment, read for specific information, predicted and inferred from text, answered questions using oral and written sentences, and acquired academic vocabulary. To meet affective goals, they learned to listen to and show respect for peers, help one another learn, and feel secure and successful. To achieve study skills goals, they learned specific techniques to learn vocabulary. In a task-intensive unit that featured the use of reading strategies, map work, and vocabulary self-teaching tools, the assessment focused on continuing cycles of modeling learning behaviors and checking for comprehension.

At the middle school level, Sillivan (2000) used the unit "Mastering the Art of Persuasion: Marketing and the Media" to culminate a yearlong ESL/language arts course. Students worked their way through a standards chart that stipulated the language functions and critical thinking skills used in persuasive media-based writing (creating print, radio, and television advertising). TESOL standards were used in each phase of instruction as students analyzed and created print ads, critiqued radio ads, and wrote and evaluated their own ad copy. Rubrics were used throughout the unit so that students could evaluate their own work as well as that of their peers.

In a high school intermediate/advanced ESL/social studies class using specially designed academic instruction in English (SDAIE, see Chapter 5), standards-based instruction was incorporated into the unit "Exploring World Religions" (Riles & Lenarcic, 2000). Students developed a word web journal to define religion; used reading passages and journals to discuss religion; and conducted library and Internet research to identify important religious figures. Final portfolios were used to archive students' essays and other writings. Throughout the unit, note-taking skills, outlines, time lines, maps, games, and other knowledge technologies were incorporated into group research, oral presentations, paragraph writing, and grammar work. In the unit plan, each activity was closely linked to the descriptors and progress indicators of the TESOL goals and standards.

English-Language Development Standards

The TESOL standards do not define what students should know or be able to do in each level of proficiency. Nor does this document provide educators with directions and strategies to assist English learners. In contrast, California has prepared *English Language Development (ELD) Standards* (California Department of Education, 1999a) to ensure that EL students develop proficiency in both the English language and the concepts and skills contained in the English-Language Arts (ELA) Content Standards (California Department of Education, 1999b) (see Box 4.2 for first-grade ELA Standards). Like the ELA Standards, the California *ELD Standards* are organized into areas of reading, writing, and listening/speaking. The *California English Language Development Test (CELDT)* is aligned with the standards as a placement and achievement test. Using the ELD and ELA standards, teachers can work with students through a developmental framework that stipulates the requirements of each proficiency level. Other standards—standards for effective pedagogy—are available from the Center for Research on Education, Diversity, and Excellence (CREDE) (1999).

Reading

1.0 Word Analysis, Fluency, and Systematic Vocabulary Development

Students understand the basic features of reading. They select letter patterns and know how to translate them into spoken language by using phonics, syllabication, and word parts. They apply this knowledge to achieve fluent oral and silent reading.

Concepts About Print
1.1 Match oral words to printed words.
1.2 Identify the title and author of a reading selection.
1.3 Identify letters, words, and sentences.

Phonemic Awareness
1.4 Distinguish initial, medial, and final sounds in single-syllable words.
1.5 Distinguish long- and short-vowel sounds in orally stated single-syllable words (e.g., *bit/bite*).
1.6 Create and state a series of rhyming words, including consonant blends.
1.7 Add, delete, or change target sounds to change words (e.g., change *cow* to *how*; *pan* to *an*).
1.8 Blend one to four phonemes into recognizable words (e.g., /c/ a/ t/ = cat; /f/ l/ a/ t/ = flat).
1.9 Segment single syllable words into their components (e.g., /c/ a/ t/ = cat; /s/ p/ l/ a/ t/ = splat; /r/ i/ c/ h/ = rich).

Decoding and Word Recognition
1.10 Generate the sounds from all the letters and letter patterns, including consonant blends and long- and short-vowel patterns (i.e., phonograms), and blend those sounds into recognizable words.
1.11 Read common, irregular sight words (e.g., *the, have, said, come, give, of*).
1.12 Use knowledge of vowel digraphs and *r*-controlled letter-sound associations to read words.
1.13 Read compound words and contractions.

1.14 Read inflectional forms (e.g., *-s, -ed, -ing*) and root words (e.g., *look, looked, looking*).
1.15 Read common word families (e.g., *-ite, -ate*).
1.16 Read aloud with fluency in a manner that sounds like natural speech.

Vocabulary and Concept Development
1.17 Classify grade-appropriate categories of words (e.g., concrete collections of animals, foods, toys).

2.0 Reading Comprehension

Students read and understand grade-level–appropriate material. They draw upon a variety of comprehension strategies as needed (e.g., generating and responding to essential questions, making predictions, comparing information from several sources). The selections in *Recommended Readings in Literature, Kindergarten Through Grade Eight* illustrate the quality and complexity of the materials to be read by students. In addition to their regular school reading, by grade four, students read one-half million words annually, including a good representation of grade-level–appropriate narrative and expository text (e.g., classic and contemporary literature, magazines, newspapers, online information). In grade one, students begin to make progress toward this goal.

Structural Features of Informational Materials
2.1 Identify text that uses sequence or other logical order.

Comprehension and Analysis of Grade-Level–Appropriate Text
2.2 Responds to *who, what, when, where,* and *how* questions.
2.3 Follow one-step written instructions.
2.4 Use context to resolve ambiguities about word and sentence meanings.
2.5 Confirm predictions about what will happen next in a text by identifying key words (i.e., signpost words).
2.6 Relate prior knowledge to textual information.
2.7 Retell the central ideas of simple expository or narrative passages.

(continued)

BOX 4.2
❖ Continued

3.0 Literary Response and Analysis

Students read and respond to a wide variety of significant works of children's literature. They distinguish between the structural features of the text and the literary terms or elements (e.g., theme, plot, setting, characters). The selections in *Recommended Readings in Literature, Kindergarten Through Grade Eight* illustrate the quality and complexity of the materials to be read by students.

*Narrative Analysis of Grade-Level–
Appropriate Text*
3.1 Identify and describe the elements of plot, setting, and character(s) in a story, as well as the story's beginning, middle, and ending.
3.2 Describe the roles of authors and illustrators and their contributions to print materials.
3.3 Recollect, talk, and write about books read during the school year.

Writing

1.0 Writing Strategies

Students write clear and coherent sentences and paragraphs that develop a central idea. Their writing shows they consider the audience and purpose. Students progress through the stages of the writing process (e.g., prewriting, drafting, revising, editing successive versions).

Organization and Focus
1.1 Select a focus when writing.
1.2 Use descriptive words when writing.

Penmanship
1.3 Print legibly and space letters, words, and sentence appropriately.

2.0 Writing Applications
(Genres and Their Characteristics)

Students write compositions that describe and explain familar objects, events, and experiences. Student writing demonstrates a command of standard American English and the drafting, research, and organizational strategies outlined in Writing Standard 1.0.

Using the writing strategies of grade one outlined in Writing Standard 1.0, students:

2.1 Write brief narratives (e.g., fictional, autobiographical) describing an experience.
2.2 Write brief expository descriptions of a real object, person, place, or event, using sensory details.

Written and Oral English Language Conventions

The standards for written and oral English language conventions have been placed between those for writing and for listening and speaking because these conventions are essential to both sets of skills.

1.0 Written and Oral English Language Conventions

Students write and speak with a command of standard English conventions appropriate to this grade level.

Sentence Structure
1.1 Write and speak in complete, coherent sentences.

Grammar
1.2 Identify and correctly use singular and plural nouns.
1.3 Identify and correctly use contractions (e.g., *isn't, aren't, can't, won't*) and singular possessive pronouns (e.g., *my/mine, his/her, hers, your/s*) in writing and speaking.

Punctuation
1.4 Distinguish between declarative, exclamatory, and interrogative sentences.
1.5 Use a period, exclamation point, or question mark at the end of sentences.
1.6 Use knowledge of the basic rules of punctuation and capitalization when writing.

Capitalization
1.7 Capitalize the first word of a sentence, names of people, and the pronoun *I*.

(continued)

BOX 4.2
❖ Continued

Spelling

1.8 Spell three- and four-letter short-vowel words and grade-level–appropriate sight words correctly.

Listening and Speaking

1.0 Listening and Speaking Strategies
Students listen critically and respond appropriately to oral communication. They speak in a manner that guides the listener to understand important ideas by using proper phrasing, pitch, and modulation.

Comprehension

1.1 Listen attentively.

1.2 Ask questions for clarification and understanding.

1.3 Give, restate, and follow simple two-step directions.

Organization and Delivery of Oral Communication

1.4 Stay on topic when speaking.

1.5 Use descriptive words when speaking about people, places, things, and events.

*2.0 Speaking Applications
(Genres and Their Characteristics)*
Students deliver brief recitations and oral presentations about familiar experiences or interests that are organized around a coherent thesis statement. Student speaking demonstrates a command of standard American English and the organizational and delivery strategies outlined in Listening and Speaking Standard 1.0.

Using the speaking strategies of grade one outlined in Listening and Speaking Standard 1.0, students:

2.1 Recite poems, rhymes, songs, and stories.

2.2 Retell stories using basic story grammar and relating the sequence of story events by answering *who, what, when, where, why,* and *how* questions.

2.3 Relate an important life event or personal experience in a simple sequence.

2.4 Provide descriptions with careful attention to sensory detail.

Source: © 1999 by the California Department of Education.

Incorporating Standards into Lesson Plans

A standard becomes useful to teachers only when they can identify when the standard has been met or progress is being made toward meeting it (Jametz, 1994). Moreover, when schools communicate performance standards to students, the students know what is considered important for them to be able to do and can more easily judge where they stand within the full range of performance expectations. Students must be prepared to receive targeted feedback on their work in a way that encourages them to compare their work to specific standards. Assessment should provide information on what students already do well and pinpoint what they still need to learn. In this way assessment can provide information about what aspects of instruction need to be redesigned so that both student and teacher performance improves (Jametz, 1994).

What Is the Best Use of Assessment?

Many students feel anxiety when confronting a test and have been conditioned to fear assessment. But assessment means more than scoring high marks on a test, getting good grades, or satisfying the accountability demands of an external authority. Assessment plays a vital role in supporting and enhancing learning. Performance assessment has received attention in contemporary educational practice because of its close association with outcome-based education (OBE) and standards-based education. The goal of these educational reforms is to make schools, teachers, and students accountable for learning. This trend has brought assessment issues to the fore.

Assessment is a process for determining the current level of a learner's performance or knowledge. Assessment for the purpose of placement informs educators about the strengths and needs of the language learner so that students can be appropriately instructed. Classroom instruction that is directly linked to placement tests for English learners permits teachers to begin using effective instructional practices as soon as students enter the classroom. Ongoing assessment informs parents and school authorities of the student's progress and ensures continuous progress. In the current climate of standards-driven instruction, the results of assessment may also be used to assess the effectiveness of the teacher's instruction.

◆ **STRATEGY 4.2:** Understand the purposes and functions of assessment

Various evaluation methods have been used with English learners. Some are required by government programs and legal mandates; others, more informal, are devised by classroom teachers. Educators involved in assessment must be careful to ensure that tests are fair (free from cultural and linguistic bias) and valid (measuring what they purport to measure). If it is to be a valid part of education, assessment should be used not merely for labeling and placing students but also for designing instruction that advances students' understanding and abilities. Testing must therefore be an integral part of learning, helping students to seek meaning and use a second language to fulfill academic and personal goals.

The Changing Nature of Assessment

Three major factors have converged to intensify the focus on new forms of assessment. First, advances in cognitive psychology have led educators to recognize the complex nature of learning. Assessment must be diverse to capture this complexity accurately and fairly (cf. Shuell, 1986). Second, many educators have acknowledged that multiple-choice, standardized achievement tests do not measure the complexity of learning processes despite the fact that educators are increasingly pressured to use such measures to document school improvement (Wiggins, 1989; Guskey, 1994). Third, tests are increasingly being used to measure the success of school reform and to document accountability. Tests used as criteria should be dependable and credible measures of student learning (Linn, 2000).

The passage of the federal "No Child Left Behind" Education Act in 2002 mandates that states periodically test student achievement. Ironically, the increased emphasis on accountability testing results in increased pressure on teachers of English learners to prepare students to succeed on standardized tests. This pressure does not take into consideration the difficulty that English learners experience. The pressure for students to perform well on these tests may detract from time spent on language development activities. Educators have argued that these nationally standardized tests penalize English learners, causing schools with large percentages of EL students to rank comparatively poorly on school achievement indices (Groves, 2000).

Traditional views of testing were based on the behaviorists' belief that knowledge can be analyzed into small skill units which could be taught, measured, and reinforced separately (Shepard, 2000). Objective tests, administered uniformly to all students, were believed to represent scientific measurement of learning.

Classroom assessment based on constructivist, cognitive, and sociocultural theory, in contrast, offered a radically different focus. Rather than seeing the capacity to acquire knowledge as an inborn skill, Vygotsky and his colleagues argued that knowledge is based on a set of cognitive structures that are created through a dynamic, socially based process of meaning making. As a result of this view, thinking and problem-solving skills have come to the fore. Assessment is still used to report on students' ability to others, but it also provides direct feedback to learners so that they can take responsibility for self-correction and improvement.

Standardized testing will probably persist because of the economic and political investment in the type of assessment that compares students with one another. Too often, however, social and economic pressures from testing overshadow the curriculum and the affective goals of schooling. The judgments resulting from this testing may affect students' present adjustment to school and their future academic and social successes, effectively undermining their ability to plan their own learning strategies, activities, and use of time and resources (O'Malley & Pierce, 1996).

Overall, assessment used wisely can become a source of insight, helping to achieve high standards for schooling. Involving students and teachers in collaborative, informative assessment makes the process more authentic and equitable, and "makes it possible to hold students to higher standards because the criteria are clear and reasonable" (Wiggins, 1992, p. 30).

The Role of Assessment in the Integrated Curriculum

The use of an integrated curriculum promotes language and academic development for English learners. Units of study in literature, math, science, and social studies may be combined into an interdisciplinary program in which students can use a variety of communication systems (language, art, music, drama) to pursue open-ended assignments. Students develop proficiency through activities such as silent reading, experiments, questioning, discussion, free writing, focused writing, and other integrated activities. Assessment is a natural part of this curriculum. Student outcomes are documented in a variety of ways—time capsules, surveys, creative works, posters, and so forth. Good records allow teachers to track individual progress and also reflect and store many observations about students' skills and interests. *Scenarios for ESL Standards-Based Assessment* (TESOL, 2001) uses actual classroom settings to illustrate how teachers integrate ongoing assessment with instructional activities.

The unit "Medieval Times" provided a standards-based, integrated thematic unit for a fourth-grade class at St. Ann School in St. Catharines, Ontario. As a culminating activity, students held a medieval fair in the school gymnasium. The teacher, Susan Drake, describes their learning:

> We covered language arts and the arts by asking students to demonstrate their learning. Students designed and constructed a castle, wrote research reports and stories, danced, drew portraits, role-played, and gave oral reports. They also read age-appropriate literature. We explicitly taught and evaluated the skills for each activity. We had an ongoing dialogue about what to evaluate and how. We planned for both ongoing and summative assessment. We checked which standards we had covered after implementing the Peasants and Kings mini-unit. We had actually covered a number beyond our expectations! (TESOL, 2001, pp. 40–41)

What Is Performance-Based Assessment?

Outcome-based performance assessment is designed to provide information about students' proficiency (Marzano, 1994), including the ability to analyze and apply as well as simply recognize or recall information. Performance-based testing procedures can be based on tasks that students are asked to do, including essays, demonstrations, computer simulations, performance events, and open-ended problem solving. Collectively, these measures are referred to as *authentic assessments,* because they are related to a student's ability to think knowledgeably about real-life problems (Linn, Baker, & Dunbar, 1991).

In an example of performance-based assessment, a beginning English learner may be given clues to a treasure hunt to practice the vocabulary associated with schoolroom objects (eraser, chalk, globe). The teacher may observe the student's ability to collect all the relevant items in an informal assessment. The performance assessment is authentic, because the student actually needs to learn the names of common classroom objects and where to find them.

An ideal performance test for reading would be one that contained materials similar to that found in real books, rather than one that reproduced paragraphs written with a controlled vocabulary. The person administering the test would be the concerned adult who is usually present to help (the teacher, or classroom parent volunteer). The test would be observational and interactional, but scores would also be valid and reliable, and available for comparison and reporting purposes. The test would be diagnostic, in order to offer a picture of the student's reading strengths and weaknesses. Ideally, it would be motivating and fun so that students, by taking it, would be encouraged to read more (Bembridge, 1992).

The benefits of performance-based assessments are the match of assessment with instruction and the satisfying feedback provided to the teacher and learner alike about areas of satisfactory attainment and areas of needed improvement. Assessment is an integral part of the instructional process, rather than an "add-on" at the end (Guskey, 1994). At the same time, it provides evidence that a standard of quality has been accomplished. Performance-based assessment is directly related to classroom performance and permits teachers to design and offer the extra mediation that students may need as determined by the assessment.

Performance rubrics are often used to assign grades to performance-based assessment. Students have these available as they begin the task. The results from the task constitute the evaluation product, and in addition, the process itself is assessed. Students, together with the teacher, make judgments about the progress being made in language (Hancock, 1994). Multiple measures may be used for assessment, incorporating nontraditional domains such as the arts and thus providing a wide range of evidence on which to evaluate a student's competence. Some of these methods are discussed below.

Methods of Assessment

Before taking a closer look at performance-based assessment as a method, let us survey a broad range of assessment types and take a closer look at some terms that are used to compare types of assessment. This examination may assist in identifying what separates performance assessment from other approaches.

Assessment Terms

The assessment literature has developed a rich vocabulary of concepts. Allen, Noel, and Rienzi offer the following glossary of terms (see Table 4.1).

Standardized and Less Standardized Assessment

Methods for assessing a performance can be *standardized* (students are scored according to a predetermined outcome) and *less standardized* (scoring is flexibly tailored to the product). A combination of assessment (standardized and less standardized) provides a cross-check of student capabilities. Students may be assessed through standardized means, such as teacher-designed examinations that are intended to be scored quickly. (These, of course, are not as elaborately "standardized" using national norms as are large-scale, commercially published tests.) For example, a teacher uses a structured observation checklist to circulate among students while they are working and monitors specific skills, such as emergent literacy, word identification, and oral reading (Miller, 1995). The advantage of a standardized assessment is its speed of scoring through the use of predetermined questions and answer keys.

Less standardized, open-ended assessment, on the other hand, may be more labor-intensive and subjective, although with effort, acceptable agreement can be achieved among a group of assessors (Maeroff, 1991). Generally speaking, open-ended assessments may feature longer problem-solving exercises, assignments that involve performances or exhibitions, and/or portfolios that contain student work gathered over a longer period of time, such as a semester. Despite the potential drawbacks of open-ended assessment, it can furnish valuable information about students' abilities. Not all open-ended assessments are difficult to grade; teachers can develop *scoring rubrics* before an assignment to help both teacher and student understand in advance the basis for scoring (Jasmine, 1993). Navarrete and Gustke (1996; www.ncbe.gwu.edu/miscpubs/eacwest/performance/index.htm#contents) have written a practical guide that teachers may find useful in helping them develop sound performance assessment.

TABLE 4.1 • Assessment Glossary

Type of Assessment	Definition
Direct measure of learning objective	Students demonstrate that they have achieved an objective.
Indirect measure of learning objective	Students report how well they have achieved an objective.
Traditional measurement	Students exhibit how well they have achieved an objective by taking traditional tests, such as multiple-choice tests.
Performance measure	Students exhibit how well they have achieved an objective by doing it, such as a reciting a poem.
Authentic assessment	The assessment process is similar to or embedded in relevant real-world activities, such as debugging a computer program or providing community service.
Quantitative assessment	Assessment results are summarized in a numerical score.
Qualitative assessment	Assessment results are described verbally and may involve counts of categories (such as those for scoring rubrics or rating scales).
Value-added assessment	Student learning is demonstrated through measuring how much the students have gained through participation in your program. This is usually done by comparing pre- and post-measures of the same group of students or by comparing entering to advanced students.
Embedded assessment	Assessment activities are embedded within courses. Students generally receive grades on this work; some or all of the work also is used to assess specific program learning objectives.
Formative vs. summative assessment	Formative assessment is designed to give feedback to improve what is being assessed. Summative assessment provides an evaluative summary. For example, a student paper receives a C+ (summative), and formative information is written in the margins to help the student improve.

Source: Adapted from Allen, Noel, & Rienzi (2001, p. 5). Used with permission.

Standardized Proficiency Tests

Several large-scale standardized proficiency tests are available for English learners. For example, the ESL curriculum in the United Kingdom uses a standard—the Graded Tests—produced by a national examination board to determine ESL/EFL proficiency and readiness for entry into British universities. The Test of English as a Foreign Language (TOEFL), developed by the Educational Testing Service in Princeton, New Jersey, is a similar test used for nonnative speakers of English who wish to study at universities and colleges in the United States. The benefits of standardized tests include speed in administration and convenience in scoring.

Norm-referenced standardized tests compare student scores against a population of students with which the test has been standardized. Examples of norm-referenced tests are the Language Assessment Scales (LAS), a test designed to measure oral language skills in English and Spanish; and the Woodcock-Muñoz Language Assessment. Results from these assessments are used for multiple purposes, including student placement, school accountability, and program improvement. *Criterion-referenced* standardized tests are used principally to find out how much of a clearly defined domain of language skills or materials students have learned. The focus is on how the students achieve in relation to the material, rather than to one another or to a national sample. In an ELD program with many levels, students may be required to pass criterion-referenced tests to progress from one level to the next. Tests that are norm-referenced (standardized using a large-scale reference group) may be used as a criterion (students must master a level before moving on).

Teacher- and Student-Created Rubrics

Instructionally sound assessment requires more than implementing meaningful tasks and standards. Teachers must develop the capacity to analyze student work, as well as the leadership ability to train students to do this analysis. Together, teachers and students need to practice self-assessment on a daily, ongoing basis so that students can regularly make judgments about their own progress as learners, with the teacher's help.

A rubric is a scoring guide that provides criteria to describe various requirements or levels of student performance. The use of rubrics helps to score student work more accurately, quickly, fairly, and reliably and can lead to shared standards among

Standardized tests are increasingly used to measure educational outcomes.

faculty about what constitutes quality in a response. Rubrics give students a better idea about the qualities their work should exhibit and help them to understand the meaning behind the grades they are given. If the students are given the rubric in advance or if they help to create it, they can self-assess their work before completion and offer feedback to their peers.

Developing a rubric first requires decoding what criteria define "quality performance." Looking at other rubrics from the same discipline is often helpful. Next, samples of work must be assembled that demonstrate a range of quality, according to a three-, four-, or five-point scale. Following this step samples of student work need to be separated into the quality levels represented by the rubric. If the rubric does not permit adequate separation of the work, it may need to be revised. Finally, reliable samples of good, average, and poor work can be shown to students to help them to understand the quality levels.

Marzano (1994) described a performance task with an associated rubric, designed by high school teachers in South Dakota, that dealt with Indian treaties affecting ownership of the Black Hills. The teachers wanted students to show that they were *knowledgeable* (understood the issues), *complex thinkers* (able to make claims that were documented by evidence), *proficient information processors* (could become informed using a variety of sources), and *able communicators* (comfortable using a variety of media). Separate rubrics were therefore used for each of these areas. All rubrics were presented to the students prior to the task. The scoring rubrics each consisted of a fixed scale, with characteristics describing performance for each point on the scale. Below is the four-point rubric for the complex-thinker component of the assessment:

> 4 = Provides a comprehensive argument that represents a detailed survey of the available information relative to the claim; additionally, documents well all important aspects of the argument.
>
> 3 = Provides a well-documented argument that includes all the major evidence supporting this claim.
>
> 2 = Provides support for claim, omits some important points from the argument and/or provides poor documentation for the evidence in the argument.
>
> 1 = Provides little cohesive support for claim and/or presents little documentation for argument. (Marzano, 1994, p. 46)

Some teachers work with students to analyze the standards required for the task and design rubrics together with the students, thus underscoring the importance of the specific criteria. With the evaluative criteria as well as the standards in mind, students are more likely to complete work that they can honor (Perrone, 1994). Particularly important is finding a measure to infer individual performance if the task is based on group performance (Baker, 1994).

Having a role in determining and describing the evaluation criteria also helps students who may be underprepared for regular learning. The emphasis for them is not only how they can attain high standards, but which strategies will be necessary (Dole, 2001). Planning the evaluation criteria with students in advance helps teachers become aware if the rubric should include revised criteria for those at beginning levels of English acquisition.

Teacher-Constructed Tests

Teacher-constructed tests can assess skills in reading comprehension, oral fluency, grammatical accuracy, writing proficiency, and listening. Although they may not be as reliable and valid as tests that have been standardized, the ease of their construction and administration and their relevance to classroom learning have made them a popular basis for awarding grades. Tests may be either highly convergent (one right answer required) or open-ended (many answers possible). Many teachers may have a tendency to devise tests that call for specific items of grammar or vocabulary rather than requiring students to use judgment and skillful language. Teachers can write good communicative tests by using the following criteria (adapted from Canale in Cohen, 1991):

- What is tested is what has been taught; testing should look like learning.
- The focus is on the message, and on authentic problems in language use.
- Tests offer group collaboration as well as individual work.

Portfolio Assessment

The purpose of portfolio assessment is to maintain a long-term record of students' progress, to provide a clear and understandable measure of student productivity, to improve student self-esteem through demonstrating progress and accomplishment, to recognize different learning styles, and to provide an active role for students in self-assessment (Gottlieb, 1995). Portfolios may include writing samples (compositions, letters, reports, drawings, dictation); student self-assessments; audio recordings (retellings, oral think-alouds); photographs and video recordings; semantic webs and concept maps; and/or teacher notes about students (Glaser & Brown, 1993).

No matter what kind of a portfolio system is developed, some common questions arise: What goes into the portfolio? Who decides? Who "keeps" the portfolio, and where? How are the contents of the portfolio used for grading? (Johnson, B., 1996). A *best-works* portfolio might feature the works of which the student is most proud, with reflective writing or audiotaping from the student explaining why the particular works were chosen. A *selection* portfolio contains work samples, for example, what a student considers the most difficult task. A *process* portfolio might contain evidence of developmental work. Each portfolio might contain a table of contents, reflective entries that discuss the work from the student's perspective, and copies of rubrics that explain why certain works received the grades they did. Pierce (1998) and Wolfe-Quintero (1998) offer practical guidelines on planning and implementing portfolio assessment for ESL students.

Portfolios can be used in an ELD program to record students' progress in reading, oral language, and writing. The reading assessment component might begin with an initial reading assessment and include group and individual checklists to document reading-related behaviors. The oral assessment might document the results when students are asked to invent a story, to listen/retell, and to produce spontaneous speech. The writing assessment component features rough drafts as well as final copies. For further information about procedures to implement portfolios, see "A Portfolio Assessment Model for ESL" (Moya & O'Malley, 1994; www.ncbe.gwu.edu/miscpubs/jeilms/vol13/portfo13.htm).

Teacher Observation and Evaluation

Teachers are in the best position to diagnose needs and document student progress. As students interact and communicate using language, an observant teacher can record how a collaborative group works together or how students use oral language. These observations may extend across all areas of the curriculum and in all types of interactional situations. Observations may be formal (e.g., miscue analysis) or informal. They may be based on highly structured content or on divergent and creative activities. Multiple observations show student progress (Crawford, 1993). One observational instrument that is used to assess students' oral proficiency is the Student Oral Language Observation Matrix (SOLOM). The teacher rates students' proficiency in comprehension, fluency, vocabulary, pronunciation, and grammar based on descriptors in a scale from 1 to 5.

Grading

A variety of approaches have been used to assign grades to English learners. Some teachers of English learners assign a traditional A–F grade scale in accordance with grade-level expectations. Performance standards are not lowered for ELD students, although assignments are adjusted to meet the students' language levels. Alternatively, a pass/fail grade scale is used to avoid comparing English learners with English-proficient classmates. A modified A–F grade scale may used for ESL classes, with A–F grades given based on achievement, effort, and behavior and report card grades modified by a qualifier signifying work performed above, at, or below grade level (From the Classroom, 1991).

Student Self-Assessment and Peer Assessment

Many teachers have used self-assessment and peer assessment to help students take responsibility for their own learning, including student portfolios. As part of the reflection on their learning, students can include in the portfolio a letter to the teacher that describes the areas in which they achieved the most growth over a stipulated period, what are now their strongest and weakest areas and why, what is their plan for improving their weakest area, and what grade they would give themselves and why. This task is supplemented by a learning log in which students evaluate their practice and make plans for future effort (McNamara, 1998b). McNamara recommends that teachers offer three types of feedback to this log: *cheerleading feedback*, in which the teacher celebrates, suggests, or offers encouragement; *instructional feedback*, in which the teacher suggests strategies or materials; and *reality-check feedback*, in which the teacher helps students to set more realistic goals or soften their self-criticism.

Brown (1998) offers a rich source for self- and peer assessments in ESL/EFL, including assessment of group work, oral presentation, natural communication, interviews, and so forth. O'Malley and Pierce (1996) provided a useful compendium of assessments for educators, including self- and peer assessments.

Other Types of Tests

Not all testing is performance-based. Several types of tests will be reviewed below, along with some cautions about the use of assessment. Proficiency tests determine a student's level of performance; diagnostic and placement tests provide information to place students in the appropriate level of academic or linguistic courses; achievement tests assess the student's previous learning; and competency tests assess whether or not a student may be promoted or advanced. Teachers and school administrators sometimes have a choice about which tests are used and for what purposes, but often tests are mandated by state authorities. It is usually up to teachers to develop effective grading procedures and communicate assessment results to students, parents, and other educators (Ward & Murray-Ward, 1999). Therefore, it is teachers who must recognize and protest unethical, illegal, and otherwise inappropriate assessment methods and hold the line at unethical uses of assessment information.

Proficiency Tests.   Proficiency tests measure overall ability in English. These tests are sometimes divided into subskills or modes of language (speaking, listening, writing, reading, vocabulary, and grammar). By definition, proficiency tests are not authentic measures of language skill; they are designed to be independent of the curriculum and do not measure the extent to which a student has worked to acquire meaning. Because the tests do not engage the learner's intrinsic interest by providing a story or feature article from which test items are drawn, the learner is unable to assign personal meaning. Educators should be cautious about using proficiency tests to predict academic or vocational success, because language is only one element among many that contribute to success (Alderson, Krahnke, & Stansfield, 1987).

Diagnosis and Placement Tests.   Diagnosis and placement tests are proficiency tests that are used to determine the academic level or the grade level into which students need to be placed. In addition to identifying students who are English learners and determining the level of proficiency, placement tests can be used to monitor the progress of English learners in acquiring English and to assist in transferring students to mainstream classrooms.

Achievement Tests.   Achievement tests measure a student's success in learning specific instructional content. A curriculum-based achievement test is given after instruction has taken place and contains only material that was actually taught. However, many contemporary standardized achievement tests are not aligned with specific curricular content. Teachers who understand the needs of English learners can adjust their instruction to balance lesson planning with the need to prepare students to perform well on standardized achievement tests.

Competency Tests.   Competency tests are achievement tests that are used to identify students who may be promoted or graduate. Many school districts mandate remedial instruction between terms for students who fail to meet minimum competency standards. It is important that such supplementary instruction take into consideration the needs of English learners. Some states have provisions that modify or exempt testing for EL students until they are ready for standardized testing. Other states offer modifications in the testing such as extended time, a separate site, small-group testing, or testing supervised by a familiar person (Evaluation Assistance Center-East, 1990).

Identification, Assessment, and Placement of English Learners in the Schools

Twenty-nine states have specific laws and provide procedural guidelines regarding identification procedures for English learners; others do not have state laws but do provide guidelines for the assessment of EL students. Many states also have procedures for redesignating students and for placing them in mainstream classes. Generally speaking, when students enroll in school, if they are identified as needing ESL services, they are placed in suitable programs, if available. Ideally, students are given placement tests that correspond directly to an instructional plan that can be implemented immediately by a classroom teacher. Once in a program, students are then periodically reevaluated for purposes of reclassification.

Identification Procedures for English Learners

A variety of methods are used to identify EL students needing services. The *home-language survey* is a short form administered by school districts to determine the language spoken at home, but students can be identified by other measures. Among these are registration and enrollment information; staff observation; and interviews or referrals made by teachers, counselors, parents, administrators, or community members (Cheung & Solomon, 1991). Some state and federal mandates require school districts to administer a placement test before assigning a new student to an instructional program if a home language survey indicates that the student's primary language is not English.

Cheng (1987) recommended other ways to gain information about students' language abilities that can be helpful in making placement decisions: Observe students in multiple settings (classroom, home, and playground); obtain history (medical, family, previous education, immigration experience, home languages); interview current or previous classroom teachers for information about learning styles and classroom behavior; seek information from other school personnel (counselor, nurse); and ask the student's parents to characterize a student's language and performance skills in the home and the community. Educators who draw from a variety of information sources can see the students' needs in a broader context and thus design a language program to meet these needs.

Assessment for Placement

Ideally, once students are identified, bilingual staff conduct an assessment to determine placement. Sometimes, however, this assessment consists only of a conversational evaluation in English by an untrained person. School staff need to be trained, aware, and sensitive to the backgrounds and experiences of the student population; in addition, parents and students should be given an orientation about the assessment and placement process and informed about the services of the school system.

Some districts place students using the LAS to measure oral language skills in English and Spanish. Another frequently used proficiency test is the Bilingual Syntax Measure (BSM), which measures oral proficiency in English and/or Spanish grammatical structures and language dominance. The Basic Inventory of Natural Language (BINL) determines oral proficiency in English by means of pictures that are used to elicit natural speech; spoken sentences are analyzed for fluency, average length of utterance, and level of syntactic complexity. The IDEA proficiency test also measures oral language proficiency in English, as students are asked to point to and name objects and complete sentences. These responses are scored for accurate comprehension and production.

A more comprehensive instrument is the English Language Development Monitoring Tool, employed by Hacienda La Puente Unified School District in California. The tool has four components (Listening, Speaking, Reading, and Writing Behaviors) for each of the six levels of placement that correspond to the CELDT. At each level, the placement chart indicates behaviors that show mastery; for example, at the Early Production level, "ability to understand basic survival sentences" is an indicator of performance. As a student demonstrates the corresponding behavior, the teacher attaches a sample of the student's work. The placement instrument travels with the student, permitting a smooth transition from ELD services to mainstream instruction.

Teachers and school personnel need to be cautioned that even after administering placement tests and gathering information, appropriate academic placement may be difficult. Placement tests measure only language proficiency; they are not informative about a student's academic background, which may vary from strong to weak depending on the subject area. Placement by age can also be a problem. Students may need much more time in the system to learn English, but placement in an earlier grade may lead to social adjustment problems. Teacher-devised checklists and observational data from the classroom can be used to confirm or adjust student placement (Lucas & Wagner, 1999).

Redesignation and Exit Procedures

School districts use specific criteria to determine when English learners have attained the language skills necessary to succeed in an English-only classroom. This reclassification (redesignation or exiting) process may use multiple criteria (Rico, 2000), which include, but are not limited to, measures of speaking, comprehension, reading, and writing as well as evidence that students can participate meaningfully in the general program. Some districts organize bilingual education advisory committees to ensure ethnic parent representation and participation in implementing redesignation criteria that are reliable, valid, and useful. Norm-referenced tests—or standardized, criterion-referenced tests using national norms or district, regional, or state nonminority norms—are often employed for purposes of reclassification. The establishment of minimum score levels as criteria for proficiency is often a political issue, because the higher the score that must be attained, the longer the students will remain in a primary-language class.

Limitations of Assessment

Tests play a large role in placing and reclassifying English learners. Often pressure is applied for programs to redesignate students as fluent English-speakers in a short period of time, perhaps before they are ready. Continuing support—such as tutoring, follow-up assessment, and primary-language help—is often not available after reclassification.

Standardized tests, though designed to be fair, are not necessarily well suited as measures of language ability or achievement for English learners. In fact, both the testing situation and the test content may be rife with difficulties and bias for EL students.

Difficulties in the Testing Situation

The context in which a test is administered needs to be examined to understand how students may be affected. Factors within the context of testing such as anxiety, lack of experience with testing materials, time limitations, and lack of rapport with the test administrator may cause difficulties for culturally and linguistically diverse students.

All students experience test anxiety, but this anxiety can be compounded if the test is alien to the students' cultural background and experiences. Allowing students to take practice exams may familiarize them with the test formats and reduce test anxiety. Moreover, students may take longer to answer individual questions because they need more time for mental translation and to formulate a response. Students from other cultures do not necessarily operate under the same conception of time as do European Americans. Some students may need a time extension or should be given untimed tests.

When testers and students do not share the same language or dialect, the success of the testing may be reduced. Students who ostensibly speak the same primary language as the test administrator may not share certain dialectic features, reducing their understanding as a result. Students may not verbalize freely if they are shy or wary in relation to test taking, feel defensive about teachers' negative stereotypes, or resent the testing situation itself. Students from some cultural groups may not feel comfortable making eye contact with a test administrator. Those from cultures that discourage individuals from displaying knowledge may not be quick to answer questions and may be reluctant to guess unless they are certain they are right. They may be embarrassed to volunteer a response or receive positive feedback about their performance (Cloud, Genessee, & Hamayan, 2000).

Tests, however, particularly achievement tests, may have bias that affects the performance of English learners. *Language-specific bias* is created when a test developed for use with one language is simply translated into another language; the translation may fail to furnish equivalent vocabulary items. *Geographic bias* happens when test items feature terms used only in particular geographic regions. *Dialect bias* occurs when certain expressions are used that are relevant only to certain dialect speakers. *Cultural bias* may be present when English learners understand test items derived from mainstream culture differently or not at all (Sattler, 1974). Many students are completely unfamiliar with common European American food items, sports, musical instruments, nursery rhymes, or children's stories. Test content may represent *class bias;* for example, "vacuum cleaner" may be a term familiar only among the middle class.

Cautions about Testing

Tests are an influential part of the U.S. schooling system and are used in every classroom. When choosing standardized tests, teachers can consider the following guidelines to help them determine the benefits and limitations of the test: Does the test correspond to the task that it measures? Is the score a true measure or fair sample of the student's ability? How can the score be supplemented with other information? Is the testing driving the curriculum? Is the test being used unfairly to compare students and schools with one another? (Worthen & Spandel, 1991)

Researchers have the following recommendations for effective practice in the assessment of English learners (August & Pease-Alvarez, 1996; Navarrete & Gustke, 1996):

- Test both content knowledge and language proficiency in the native language and in English.
- Use a variety of techniques to measure content knowledge and skills (e.g., portfolios, observations, anecdotal records, interviews, checklists, exhibits, students' self-appraisals, writing samples, dramatic renditions, and criterion-referenced tests).
- Be sure that the teacher is aware of the purpose of the assessment (e.g., whether the test is intended to measure verbal or writing skills, language proficiency, or content knowledge).
- Take students' backgrounds into account, including their educational experiences and parents' literacy.
- Add context to assessment tasks by incorporating familiar classroom material (brief quotations, charts, graphics, cartoons, works of art) as a stimulus and including questions for small-group discussion and individual writing.
- Mirror learning processes with which students are familiar, such as the writing process and reading conferences.
- Match administration procedures to classroom instructional practices (e.g., cooperative small groups, individual conferences, and assessment in the language of instruction).
- Give extra time to complete or respond to assessment tasks, making accommodations such as simplifying directions in English and/or paraphrasing in the student's native language, as well as permitting students to use dictionaries or word lists.

Academic Expectations

How can English learners achieve the highest possible performance? Without question, there is a connection between teacher expectations for English learners and their subsequent school success, or lack of it. The next section examines teacher expectations for student performance. Overall, the effect of teacher expectations amounts to a de facto ongoing assessment of students' worth and capabilities. Addressing these expectations and how they operate is therefore an integral part of examining the role of performance outcomes in the achievement of English learners.

- **STRATEGY 4.3:** Expect the highest performance possible in the time available

How Teacher Expectations Are Formed and Communicated to Students and How Students Respond

How can teachers communicate positive expectations in order to increase the academic achievement of these students? How do teachers form expectations about student achievement and communicate these during instruction? How do students react?

The "Pygmalion in the classroom" research (Rosenthal & Jacobson, 1968) documented significant intellectual gains on the part of students whose teachers were told to expect such gains. The so-called "Pygmalion" effect was named for the mythical sculptor, Pygmalion, who made a statue and then caused it to be brought to life. In this case, teachers seemed to cause students' intelligence to increase by the effect of their expectations. Despite disagreements over the magnitude of the effects documented in various studies, researchers have conceded that teachers' performance expectations do influence students' actual achievement (Rosenthal, 1987).

A "self-fulfilling prophecy" is defined as "a groundless expectation that comes true simply because it has been expected" (Woolfolk, 1998). Students may perform at levels consistent with the teacher's expectations. Although the expectation may have no basis in fact, the student's behavior comes to match the expectation. This effect can be positive (a teacher overestimates a student's abilities, and the student is stimulated to perform well), or it can be negative (a teacher expects very little from a student, and communicates this expectation so clearly that student performance is affected adversely).

Jussim (1986) offered a general framework for the operation of expectancy effects: Teachers develop expectations, teachers treat students differently depending on their expectations, and students react to this differential treatment in ways that confirm the expectations. According to Jussim, expectation operates through a set of mediating factors.

Teachers Form Expectations.   Teachers first form expectations about students based on *prejudgments* (a student's reputation, inferences from information in cumulative files, experience with older siblings, or anecdotes from other teachers); racial and cultural *stereotypes; scores from placement or standardized tests; observations of a student's classroom performance* compared against memories of previous successful and unsuccessful students; and *naive predictions and fallacies,* for example exaggerating the salience of a few examples of behavior. Together, these factors create an image in a teacher's mind about the likely success or failure of a student.

Teachers' beliefs about students' capabilities may be modified as new information is collected, if teachers alter their expectations in the light of subsequent evidence. When a student's performance is consistent with expectations, these expectations will be confirmed. When student performance does not fit expectations, though, it may take many instances of behavior contrary to a teacher's expectations to change a teacher's beliefs about the ability of a student (Brophy, 1983). People evaluate the same test performance differently, depending upon whether they have been told that the student is from an upper- or lower-class background (Darley & Gross, 1983). High-expectancy students, unlike low-expectancy students, are given the benefit of the doubt in borderline situations (Finn, 1972). Teachers with flexible expectations readily revise their impressions when direct information about student achievement is available (Brophy, 1983).

Differential Treatment of Students.   Expectations and treatment of students are linked. This linkage provides an understanding of the operation of the expectation effect in classroom teaching, both at the psychological level (teachers' actions and reactions) and at the situational level (sociocultural features of schooling).

Perceptions of control alter the instructional environment. Some teachers believe that they need to exert more control over the behavior of students for whom they have low expectations so that these students will learn. Jussim (1986) proposed that this attitude might account for the different feedback provided to "highs" and "lows." It might also lead to less emotional support and praise for the efforts of students for whom expectations are low.

Attributions may explain why students of whom teachers have high expectations receive positive attention. Teachers tend to prefer students who are attentive, cooperative, and conscientious, and time their questions, interruptions, requests, and misbehavior appropriately. They perceive that high-performing students hold similar academic values to their own, and they tend to spend more time with those students to whom they attribute the most potential payoff for their instructional investment. This may explain why teachers spend more time coaching "highs" with more cues and prompts; offer them more feedback, prompts, and response opportunities; are less accepting of poor-quality answers from such students; and design more challenging assignments for them. This closer communication is a factor in students' academic success.

Tracking and ability grouping are ways in which schools make differential curricula available to students in accordance with their beliefs about student ability. In the United States, middle-income students are more often tracked in average and higher groups, while low-income and minority students are found in disproportionate numbers in lower-ability groups (Sleeter & Grant, 1987). Students who are placed in low-ability groups may be systematically denied access to "high-status" knowledge, which includes the academic skills, content, attitudes, and experiences that are inculcated into well-educated members of society.

The social context of the learning environment permeates teachers' expectations. A teacher's behavior must be consonant with the motivational climate of school. If the discipline climate in the school is punitive, a less punitive discipline style on the part of the teacher may be perceived as weak. Conversely, if school discipline is lax, the teaching staff may fail in efforts to create high expectations for homework completion. Students participating in a resistance culture may see teachers' motivational efforts as evidence of weakness or react in a hostile manner to teacher demands (see Díaz-Rico, 1993). A school climate featuring fierce academic competition may exacerbate feelings of helplessness and depression on the part of some students. In these contexts teachers may find it necessary to adapt to the context and behave as expected, opt out and seek a context more suitable to their teaching styles and values, or become advocates for a school climate more supportive of all learners.

Students' Reactions.   Differential treatment received by students alters the potential for achievement. Being called on less and having attempts to speak cut short reduces the chance to think spontaneously and to articulate ideas. When teachers are more concerned with issues of control, their students become intrinsically less interested in school (Deci, Nezlek, & Sheinman, 1981). Such a reduction in their intrinsic interest in school in turn causes them to substitute other interests, leading to an increased need for teachers to control their behavior—and so the cycle perpetuates itself.

If teachers attribute poor performance to students' lack of ability, this assessment is communicated to students, who are likely to lower their level of aspiration.

Teachers can influence students' attributions of the cause of their academic success and failure. When teachers respond to a student's mistakes with pity, praise, or unsolicited help, that student is more likely to attribute the errors to lack of ability. In contrast, a critical, corrective response from the teacher conveys the message that the student is capable of success.

Minority-group students may sometimes be victims of well-meaning pity from teachers who "ease up" on requirements so that students will "experience success" and "feel good about themselves." This attitude, however well meaning, may also communicate the message, "You don't have the ability to do this, so I will overlook your failure." This targeting of minority-group members for pity, praise in the event of failure, or unsolicited help may cause the internalization of low self-esteem (Graham, 1991) and is a subtle form of racial discrimination that detracts from academic motivation. Rather than pitying or excusing students who need additional academic support, teachers can teach them how to learn and hold them accountable.

Attention, participation, and cooperation on the part of students may *cause* positive or negative teacher evaluation or *result* from it. Decreased motivation may follow lowered expectations, and lower motivation may in turn lead to lowered performance, which serves to confirm teacher expectations. Cooperation and participation may be enhanced by an understanding of students' differing ability to understand the participation expectations and perform in ways that are consonant with the culture of the classroom.

Student Control over Classroom Learning

Teachers can reduce the negative effects of teacher-induced achievement via the reinforcement of preconceived expectations by reducing the frequency of teacher-directed lessons and providing an opportunity for more peer interaction and support. This approach allows students' voices to be heard in determining the topics of interest, contributing to these topics, and choosing with whom to work cooperatively. Those students who need more individual attention should be encouraged to attend teacher-led study sessions at predetermined times.

Intercultural Communication of Expectations

Differences in the culture of the teacher and student may cause miscommunication of expectations. Language and word choice are other factors that make intercultural communication challenging. Words that may seem harmless in one context may have a negative connotation within a subculture; teachers have to be careful both to use appropriate terms of address and reference when communicating with students and to be aware of which terms used in the classroom might have an incendiary effect.

Students' response to teacher expectations seems to be highly influenced by cultural background and home discourse patterns. Sato (1982) found that Asian students initiated classroom discourse less often than English learners from other countries. Students who have achieved academic success through individual attainment may resent being grouped with lower-achieving students, particularly if a group grade is given (Bennett, 1990). Some cultures encourage students to set internal standards of worth, and peer pressure devalues dependence on teachers for approval.

Expecting high achievement from English learners and communicating these expectations require specific educational programs that draw attention to the hidden curriculum of the school, quality of dialogue between teachers and students, diverse learning styles, the use of the community as a resource, and a commitment to democratic ideals in the classroom (Gollnick & Chinn, 2002).

"Culturally relevant teaching" is one approach to intercultural communication (Ladson-Billings, 1994). Prospective teachers may need to be observed closely and objectively to offer feedback on practices that encourage classroom equity. Prospective teachers may also need to participate in sessions that raise self-awareness of racism in practice in the classroom (see Díaz-Rico, 1998b, 2000). New forms of instruction are necessary that promote equity, and new forms of communication must be developed that allow teachers to believe in their students' capacity for high achievement, and to communicate that belief to the students.

Planning Instruction

Effective teaching makes a strong connection between goals and outcomes. A teacher who sets precise, well-delineated objectives, plans instruction to teach the targeted skills clearly, and then carefully assesses the results can usually count on most of the students achieving the desired objectives. Does this sound like pedagogical science? Despite the seductive clarity of this approach, it is based on the underlying assumption that good teaching causes learning. The reality of the teaching-learning connection is much more complex. Students who are not involved in the process of setting goals miss out on the opportunity to desire to learn.

◆ **STRATEGY 4.4:** Plan cooperatively and flexibly for maximum student involvement and achievement

The desire to learn, like other kinds of desires, has a specific object. A person who desires, desires *something*—usually something tangible, like a new car, a better house, a video game. People can be socialized to desire intangibles, like victory in a soccer game, more power at work, or high grades at school. But the desire to learn is a tricky intangible, because learning is destabilizing. In Piaget's terms, learning causes disequilibration. Many people dislike learning; they wish to be satisfied by a life in which every question has an answer and every problem has a simple solution. But the central question that drives high-quality teaching is one that in itself is complex, ill defined, and unsettling: "What makes someone want to learn? How can a teacher plan lessons based on the learners' desires to learn?

Constructivist Planning

The teacher may ask that question, but the learner must answer. Cognitive, constructivist teaching asks, "What is interesting here? What about this subject provokes us? What makes us wonder? Why do we care?" Structures such as K-W-L (see Chapter 5) help teachers to bring students' knowledge and interests into the planning cycle. In the long run, the learner is fully engaged only when there is a sense of co-ownership of the learning process so that the learner has a sense of involvement and shared control. This situation is not easy to achieve.

When curriculum and content standards are set by external governing agencies, neither students nor teachers have complete freedom to study what they will. In most school districts, the grade-level curriculum is predetermined, and standards of content mastery are distributed to the teacher before the start of the school year. Co-planning, co-monitoring, and co-evaluation are the hallmark of co-ownership of the instructional process. How can they fit with a standards-driven curriculum?

In its most inclusive sense, a lesson is a plan that affords or allows learning. *Affordance* means that a student can acquire a new concept as a part of a sociocultural process, the activity system that makes this acquisition possible (Van Lier, 2000). The teacher's role is to help the learner to design and perform learning, set learning in motion, identify important problems and make them comprehensible, and set up times and places to showcase discovery and report results. This is the best use of instructional planning.

The Direct Teaching Model

The seven-step lesson plan is a popular one, stemming from the days of direct teaching. In this model, the teacher determines the *objectives* of the lesson; teaching then begins with an *anticipatory set*, in which the teaching materials are displayed and students are told the key topics to be covered. Next, *direct instruction* takes place, in which the teacher presents information and models the activity that constitutes the learning. *Guided instruction* follows, as the teacher continues to model and guide students before they engage in *independent practice*. At this point there may be *supplementary activities* before the *evaluation/summary/closure* (Molina, Hanson, & Siegel, 1997).

Modifying the Direct Teaching Model

Critics of the direct instruction model see a lack of student "ownership" of the design and implementation of this kind of lesson. However, the seven-step model does not have to be teacher-driven. For example, the teacher may involve students in thematic planning before the start of the unit of instruction. The anticipatory set can be used as a means of bringing forth prior knowledge. Direct teaching can be done by students or the teacher, or it can be a very brief stage setting forth instructions for a prolonged practice phase. Students may choose among several different activities to achieve the objective. Finally, students can self-assess or peer-assess in addition to undergoing teacher assessment.

In the long run, however, two major paradigm shifts (learning-centered instruction and standards-based instruction) have made the direct teaching model useful only for small, turn-around lessons that demonstrate a specific skill. Project-based learning—with its extended time frame, complex set of skills to be acquired, and highly visible set of outcomes—is a more robust and authentic model of learning that makes the direct instruction model seem artificial.

> As a part of the César Chávez Community Garden Project, I led a group
> of twenty-two middle school students in constructing a prefabricated

tool shed measuring eight feet by ten feet. Facing a thirty-one–page in-struction manual and a box containing about a hundred parts, I had no time to stop and give every student guided practice. Working in infor-mal teams, we had the shed together in about four hours. Standing in-side on the plywood floor, it felt authentic. But it was certainly more than seven steps!

Matching Performance and Assessment

♦ **STRATEGY 4.5:** Set criteria for effective performance and assess attainment of those criteria

Teachers who have been given the opportunity to think carefully about the connec-tion between assessment and learning understand that learning goals, lesson plans, classroom activities, and evaluations of student learning must be consistent (Jametz, 1994). Most teachers know that they need to plan stimulating, intellectually chal-lenging tasks for students. Performance-based assessments cannot by themselves bring about significant changes in learning unless classroom instruction improves.

Setting Objectives

The cycle of planning begins with a rich question that "stirs up" swirls of interest. To-gether the teacher and learner plan how questions that arise can be addressed. A les-son can be guided by clear objectives that focus instruction; but lessons can also be layered, overlapping, and confusing, with objectives that are hard to grasp, control, and divide into pieces. The teacher helps to refine goals, discover means, set time lines, and define performances that will help students showcase their learning. In this process content, learning, and language objectives go hand in hand as language is used to acquire information and perform written or spoken outcomes.

After teachers and students have determined objectives, they can plan to use many means, such as illustration, dramatization, creating songs, or rewriting stories to demonstrate their performance. The learning tasks then become ways to transform information into knowledge, ways that meet the standards that are set. A variety of ways can be used to employ students' language skills on both formal and informal oc-casions: learning centers; dramatic, visual, or oral presentations; readers' theater; or slide, video, or computer-based audiovisual shows. Re-presentation of knowledge is an important means by which teachers assess student learning and pinpoint areas for reteaching, expansion, and/or modification. In this manner, assessment becomes a part of the learning cycle.

Authentic tasks provide a richer means of assessing English learners than tradi-tional paper-and-pencil tests. In one community college English class that had been in session one block away from the World Trade Center when it crumbled, students gath-ered when class resumed to speak of their shock and horror. The class debated what type of writing project they could initiate that would serve as a collection of their thoughts and reactions and convey their response to the tragedy (Abdoh, 2001). This situation is typical of the power of student-determined goals. Obviously, a teacher-imposed project would not sustain the full measure of their emotions and desire to make meaning, yet the teacher can work with them to evoke and refine their work.

Lessons are performance-based when the objective is stated in measurable terms: What is the student expected to be able to do, or perform, when the objective is mastered? Therefore, the wording of the objective is active, as in the samples below.

- Students will talk about the weather.
- Students will ask for and give opinions and advice.
- Students will describe a sequence of events.

Tasks as Objectives

In *task-based learning* (Nunan, 1989), the goal or objective is linked to the learning activities through *tasks*. A task is "a piece of classroom work which involves learners in comprehending, manipulating, producing, or interacting in the target language while their attention is principally focused on meaning rather than on form" (p. 10). Communication and learning tasks are the central building blocks of a lesson plan. Additional elements, such as a focus on form, may be included as lesson supplements.

Tasks have one central characteristic: They rehearse communicative events that take place in the real world, using language that appears naturally in these events. The social function—perhaps learning to extend an invitation—serves as a goal or performance indicator to be attained.

A classroom lesson involves a clear connection among the objectives, activities, and assessment. After the objectives have been determined, activities are designed that will accomplish these objectives. Tasks are linked to the objectives of the lesson by means of task chains.

Task Chains

A task chain is a linked series of actions that accomplishes a specific objective, performed by the learner under the supervision of the teacher. Tasks are linked thematically to the objective. They may involve a variety of language modes, for example, listening and speaking, reading, writing, and critical thinking.

The tasks may consist of a mix of short activities across various modalities. In the example above, extending an invitation, tasks could be the following: practice in pairs using sentences containing invitation gambits ("How about . . ." "Are you free Friday afternoon . . ."); a listening activity followed by comprehension questions; a writing activity ("Write four sentences that could function as invitations to go roller skating on Saturday morning"); or a role play. Alternatively, the task chain could consist of one complex task built from several steps.

In the curriculum *Atlas* (Level 2, Unit 3, "Old Friends"), the first unit goal is to "Talk about Friends" (see Nunan, 1995, pp. 25–27). Task Chain 1 ("Close Friends") is designed to accomplish this goal. Several of the tasks in Task Chain 1 are summarized as follows (some tasks have been omitted):

Task 1. (Pair work). Circle which of the words below (eleven adjectives are given) that describe your best friend.

(Pair work). Think of three friends and make statements about them using words from the list.

Task 2. Listen to the tape-recorded conversation given in which Tony is talking about his best friends. Using the given chart, circle the names he mentions and write the correct occupation beside each name.

Task 4. (Group discussion). What does Tony do? Is this an unusual occupation for a man? What about in your country? Do men do this type of job? What jobs do men rarely do? Women?

Task 6. Think of three friends and then complete the chart. (The chart has five columns, "Name," "Things You Do Together," "Things You Talk About," "Occupation, " and "Where You Met.")

(Pair work). Use the chart to talk about your friends with a partner.

Assessing the Task Chain

The success of a task chain is evaluated in several ways, through assessment activities at the end of the chain or through a final assessment at the end of the lesson. Using assessment, the teacher is able to measure directly the extent to which students have mastered the objective. Based on this information, the teacher can choose to reteach the task to all or some of the students, or the class may move forward to the next objective.

Figure 4.1 offers a set of criteria for assessing an instructional plan based on task chains. Each objective of the plan is assessed during the task chain or at the end. The tasks themselves are supported by four kinds of materials. *Posters* offer large, whole-class presentation of information; *focus sheets* offer information that can be used as a component of instruction but are not written on by students during the lesson and can be collected for reuse; *work sheets* are completed during the lesson; and *assessment sheets* are used as the test and scored by the teacher or by peers. This can include peer- or self-assessment sheets.

Figures 4.2 through 4.5 show how a TPR-based lesson features some of these components.

Formative Assessment

As students are engaged within the activity system, the teacher can help them to maintain momentum and solve ongoing problems through formative assessment. This process involves progress checks that help students to evaluate their efforts in the light of their goals and to stay on track with benchmark performance measures. The teacher may require formal weekly progress reports, ask for partial products at predetermined times, or set deadlines for circulation of rough drafts. Rich documentation of the progress of an ongoing project helps to create a final product that is not overly dependent on one final spurt of activity that can cause tension and frustration. These requirements help students to avoid procrastination and keep their projects moving forward.

Candidate _____	Assignment: A B C D E
Component of Plan	Point Value/Critique

Introductory Information   _____/10
- Unit/lesson has relevant and appropriate title.
- Level, characteristics of students are specified.
- Materials are listed.
- Provision is made for involving students.

Performance Indicators   _____/10
- Specific
- Feasible in time allotted
- Indicate adequate content
- Matched to TESOL, ELD, district standards

Task Chains   _____/10
- Content is supported using focus sheets or other source materials; matched to performance indicator.
- Activities are relevant; adequate to attain indicator; matched to performance indicator.
- Activity is supported using Worksheets or other practice materials.
- Focus sheets and Worksheets are referenced and source(s) cited.

Assessment   _____/10
- Formative assessment is relevant and adequate to measure attainment of indicator; performance criteria are specified.
- Summative assessment is supported using assessment sheets or other materials.
- Assessment sheets are referenced and source(s) cited.

Format   _____/10
- Consistent format is used throughout.
- Appearance is professional, word-processed.
- Titles of supporting materials match presentation in lesson plan.

TOTAL   _____/50

FIGURE 4.1 ◆ M.A. in Education, TESOL Option program outcome assessment criteria for instructional plan, standards-based.

Summative Assessment, Culminating Performance, and Metalearning

A final performance on a certain day—a play with other students as audience, an exhibit for parents, or a publication with a printer's deadline—helps students to understand the real world of promise and fulfillment. The excitement that these events generate helps to provide community pressure and support for achievement.

Level: Adult—Speech Emergence

Performance Indicators:

Learning Strategy Objective	1. To sequence written directions using context cues
Language Objective	2. To acquire vocabulary for simple sensory-motor actions
Content Objective	3. To make flowers from tissue paper

Warm-Up: Pass out tissue paper flowers and ask who knows how to make one.
                  If someone knows, recruit him/her as assistant in Task Chain 3.

TESOL Standard: Standard 3. Students will use learning strategies to extend their
                  communicative competence.

Task Chain 1. *Sequencing written directions using context cues*

1. Instructor explains task: Sequence written directions using context cues.
2. Pair students. Each pair receives an envelope with directions on how to make a tissue
   paper flower (Focus Sheet 1, cut up). Each pair sequences the strips to re-create the
   proper sequence of instructions.
3. When sequencing task is completed, instructor shows solution on overhead
   (transparency of Focus Sheet 1).
4. Pairs self-assess their versions for accuracy, reordering if necessary. (Pairs keep
   directions spread out before them.)

Task Chain 2. *Acquiring vocabulary for simple sensory-motor actions*

1. Each pair chooses ten new words from the directions.
2. First pair writes their ten new words on board. Second pair writes their ten words;
   if one of their words is already on the board, they put a check beside it, writing only
   words that have not appeared already.
3. When enough pairs have written their words, instructor takes ten words with the
   highest number of checks as vocabulary. These are circled on transparency, and
   pronounced together.
4. Students put strips back in envelopes and return them to instructor.
5. Instructor presents visual representation of six new words (transparency of Focus
   Sheet 2). In pairs, students act out sensory-motor actions.
6. Instructor hands out sets of matching cards; students match in pairs for self-assessment.
   Instructor shows transparency again as self-check.

Task Chain 3. *Making flowers from tissue paper*

1. Instructor demonstrates how to make a flower following directions on transparency
   (see Focus Sheet 1), accentuating (acting out) verbs that are circled as vocabulary items.
2. Students choose tissue paper colors and follow instructions from overhead.
3. Students process-check against models of partially made flowers.

Final Assessment: *Making flowers from tissue paper*

1. Using the Assessment Sheet, students check their awareness of sequence, knowledge
   of vocabulary, and context for sensory-motor actions. Scoring: 18–20, Flower; 15–17,
   Bud; 12–15, Leaf; 8–11, Stem; below 7, Root.

FIGURE 4.2 ◆ **Demonstration instructional plan: Making flowers from tissue paper.**

1. Select six sheets of tissue paper, each 10 inches by 15 inches.
2. Stack neatly. For variety, the four on top should be color A, the other two color B.
3. Stack all six layers together and fold into accordion pleats. The pleat should be 10 inches long. Each pleat should measure about 1.5 inches wide.
4. Fold the pleated strip in half at the 5-inch point.
5. Pinch and wrap tightly in wire. The result should look like a bow tie.
6. Shape ends of petals by making either curved or pointed cuts at both ends of tissue-paper "bow." For curved petals, cut a semicircle at each end of the bow tie. For pointed petals, cut a triangle at the ends.
7. With fingertips, stretch folds outward to shape tissue paper into a bowl.
8. Delicately fluff out the petals, using a gentle touch to separate the layers of tissue.
9. Holding the floral tape in one hand, wind the tape around the wire stem in a spiral, working from the center of the bow to the end of the wire.

FIGURE 4.3 ◆ Focus sheet 1: Sequencing written directions using context cues.

FIGURE 4.4 ◆ Focus sheet 2: Visual images of sensory-motor actions.

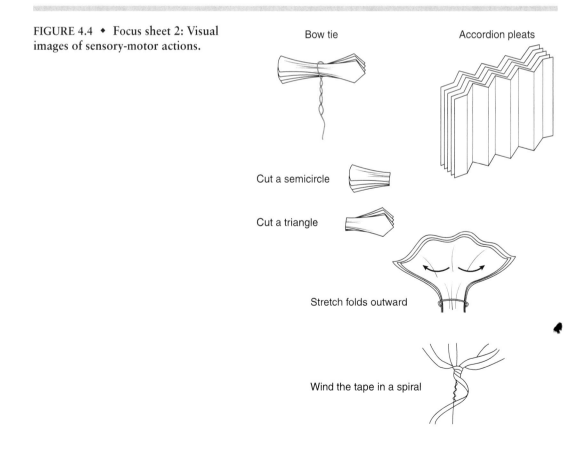

I. *Awareness of Sequence.* Number these steps in the correct order.

_____ Pinch and wrap in wire.

_____ Wind the tape around the wire stem.

_____ Fold the pleated strip in half.

_____ Stretch folds outward.

_____ Fluff out the petals.

_____ Fold in accordion pleats.

_____ Select paper.

_____ Stack neatly.

_____ Cut ends of petals.

II. *Vocabulary for Simple Sensory-Motor Actions.* Draw a circle around the words that describe an *action* that takes place in the directions above.

wire	pinch	outward
wrap	pleated	cut
stem	strip	around
wind	tape	stretch
petal	half	out
pleats	fold	ends
select	accordion	paper
fluff	neatly	stack

III. *Context for Sensory-Motor Actions.* Write "Yes" if the **bold** word is used correctly in the sentence. Write "No" if it is not.

1. _____ We **wrap** gifts in gift wrap paper.
2. _____ **Wind** the turkey in the oven.
3. _____ **Stack** the clean clothes.
4. _____ **Stretch** your legs before running.
5. _____ **Fluff** the dirt under the bed.
6. _____ We can use an **accordion** to play music.

FIGURE 4.5 ◆ **Assessment sheet: Making flowers from tissue paper.**

Despite the satisfaction that these culminating events offer, the substance of assessment remains with the content standards that have been achieved. Peer evaluation, self-evaluation, and teacher evaluation together garner the final wisdom: What did the project achieve? What was learned about the content? What was learned about the process? And, most exciting, what is still not known? What remains to be discovered? This summative assessment is the basis for metalearning, learning about improving learning.

Monitoring and Adjusting Instruction

Formative evaluation can permit much valuable ongoing readjustment of the learning process. The responsibility for this monitoring is shared between teacher and learners, but much of the responsibility for adjustment falls upon the learner.

◆ **STRATEGY 4.6:** Adjust instruction to attain performance criteria

Teachers exercise patience in helping students to monitor and adjust their learning to meet the desired performance standards; vanquish the students' habitudes of sloth or procrastination, if that is a problem; conquer the students' lack of faith in themselves by providing encouragement, structure, and guidelines; overcome students' impatient desire to improve instantly, as they perhaps try and fail several times before succeeding; help students to accept the disappointment of failure if there is some aspect of a complex problem that eludes solution; or make themselves available during the basic struggle to use English as a means of expression.

Not all learning is successful. Sometimes problems that are worth addressing are beyond comprehension, and sometimes problems that are comprehensible are simply not interesting. Most teachers do everything possible to facilitate successful learning. In the last analysis, however, it is not the teacher's job to rescue students from disappointment or failure; these are a part of authentic learning. Sometimes the metalearning—the wisdom about learning—that takes place comes after the learning has taken place, in a process of reflection and hindsight.

The teacher, who is the storehouse of success and failure, can take into consideration the struggles and triumphs of one year's students in order to modify instruction the next time. What is exciting about teaching is the opportunity for metalearning, that is, learning better and better how to learn. This goal is not easily achieved, for one must look clearly at the failure that took place as well as the success. Without failure there is no learning; there is only the "already known." For in the last analysis, errors—when assessment shows these clearly and precisely—are the best teachers, providing the opportunity for failure to be converted to wisdom.

Learner Strategies and Learner-Focused Teaching

Learner Control and Academic Competence

This chapter explores the concepts of learner control: how the learner takes responsibility for second-language acquisition (SLA) and what strategies can be used to foster the ability of the learner to be in charge. This emphasis on learner autonomy places the education of English learners squarely in line with contemporary education that is cognitive and humanistic. To accomplish this, two topics follow: first, a look at learner autonomy as an overall topic and second, a focus on learner strategies.

❖ **MEGASTRATEGY 5:** Increase the learner's control, self-management, and self-motivation

Learner autonomy can be defined as "the learners' feeling that studying is taking place due to their own volition." This autonomy is the basis for self-managed, self-motivated instruction. Such autonomy is more than a preference or strategy by the learner; it must be supported in a systematic way by the teacher and curriculum in order for the learner to benefit.

Given the limited time available for in-class instruction in relation to the vast amount of language there is to learn, educators acknowledge that it is impossible to teach learners everything they need to know while they are in class. Therefore, a major aim of classroom instruction should be to equip learners with learning skills that they can employ on their own. These include the following:

- efficient learning strategies
- identification of their preferred ways of learning
- skills needed to negotiate the curriculum
- encouragement to set their own learning objectives
- support for learners to set realistic goals and time frames
- skills in self-evaluation (Nunan, 1989, p. 3)

Unfortunately, too often educators assume that students at the beginning level of proficiency in English cannot learn advanced skills. In response to this misconception, the intellectual level of the curriculum is adjusted downwards to teach isolated skills that do not foster the cognitive processes necessary for self-directed learning (Hernández, 1993). Strategic teaching addresses the need for educators to promote high-level instruction that will allow English learners to extend their academic potential.

This chapter details a variety of strategies that individuals can use to achieve academic competence (see Adamson, 1993). Not all learners are students in a formal school; some may be learning English informally. This book is devoted to strategies used by teachers in schools—hence the emphasis on academic competence—but strategies are also used by second-language learners outside the school setting (see Figure 5.1 and its equivalent in outline form, Table 5.1). The emphasis on self-directed and self-motivated learning acknowledges that successful SLA takes place outside as well as inside the classroom.

In Figure 5.1 (from Yeh, 2001), academic competence is divided into learner strategies (indirect and direct) and academic/survival skills (indirect and direct). Within the category of learner strategies, some are general; that is, they are not specifically for SLA but can be applied to other content. This chapter focuses not on general strategies but on learner strategies applied to the SLA context.

Cohen (1996) divides learner strategies applied to the SLA context into two parts: second-language use strategies (employed, for the most part, when the learner must extemporaneously speak) and second-language learning strategies (those that assist learners to improve their knowledge in a target language). The distinction contrasts *output* (second-language use strategies) and *input* (second-language learning strategies). Language use strategies primarily employ language that learners already

Academic competence	Learner strategies (indirect and direct)	Learner strategies applied to SLA context	General strategies applied to non-SLA context		
			Indirect: Learning styles		
			Indirect: second-language use strategies	Rehearsal	
				Retrieval	
				Communication	
				Cover	
			Direct: second-language learning strategies	Literacy, oracy strategies	
				Cognitive, meta-cognitive, and social-affective strategies	
	Academic survival strategies (indirect and direct)	Cultural skills	NL cultural skills		
			TL cultural skills		
			Academic (TL) cultural skills		
		Study skills	Time management		
			Text processing		

FIGURE 5.1 ◆ A model of strategies to achieve academic competence (Table 4.1 in figure form).

Source: Adapted from Yeh, 2001.

TABLE 5.1 • Academic Competence (Figure 5.1 in Outline Form)

Academic Competence
I. Learner Strategies (indirect and direct)
   A. General strategies applied to non-SLA context
   B. Learner strategies applied to SLA context
      1. Indirect: learning styles
      2. Indirect: second language use strategies
         i. Rehearsal
         ii. Retrieval
         iii. Communication
         iv. Cover
      3. Direct: second language
         i. Literacy, oracy strategies
         ii. Cognitive, metacognitive, and social-affective strategies
II. Academic survival strategies (indirect and direct)
   A. Cultural skills
      1. NL cultural skills
      2. TL cultural skills
      3. Academic (TL) cultural skills
   B. Study skills
      1. Time management
      2. Text processing

Source: Yeh, 2001.

have in their interlanguage; in contrast, language-learning strategies assist learners to learn new target language.

A third kind of learner strategy, learning styles, like other indirect strategies tends to originate at a level of unconscious or automated performance. Like other indirect strategies, these can be made explicit and used or altered in a conscious manner.

Academic/survival skills, the other aspect of academic competence, comprise cultural skills (native language, target language, and the culture of academia in the target language) and study skills (time management and text processing, among others). Although there may be other important strategies for the learner to acquire and use, this set will serve for now.

Most teachers have already applied various kinds of strategy-training activities in their classes. Almost every learning activity lends itself to a certain strategy use, and all learners are likely to accomplish any given task if they make use of one or more strategies successfully.

Learner Autonomy: Self-Motivation and Self-Management

Autonomy enables students to feel pride in their own achievements. If learning is too externally controlled, a student can feel other emotions (gratitude for the teacher's help, or relief not to have failed) but may not feel a personal sense of success. In SLA, the need for autonomy is especially important, yet especially difficult to attain. Intense pressure to acquire English, whether as a newcomer to American schools or as a student at a school in which English learning is mandated by examination competition, causes external obligations to succeed. Moreover, a second language is usually "owned" by native speakers, making a sense of autonomy elusive for nonnative speakers. In the final analysis, however, second-language proficiency is an individual achievement. One can *teach* the learner a second language—but only the learner can *learn* it.

Self-Management

What energizes and directs behavior? The explanation could be drives, needs, fear, goals, social pressure, interests, expectations, curiosity, and so forth. *Intrinsic motivation* is a term used to explain internal, personal traits. Raffini (1996) defined intrinsic motivation as "what motivates us to do something when we don't *have* to do it" (p. 3). The opposite is *extrinsic motivation,* when the activity is done for a reward or to avoid a punishment. Usually, students do not perform activities solely for either intrinsic or extrinsic reasons, but rather because of a combination of the two (Stipek & Seal, 2001). Teachers try to make activities interesting but also realize that self-motivated students are often those who are the most self-disciplined.

Self-Managed Instruction

Learner autonomy as a concept goes beyond internalized self-motivation to include the additional factor of self-managed instruction. Many teachers have had the experience of facing a classroom of highly disciplined yet passive learners, who will do everything necessary to achieve high grades but have little desire to learn anything that is not required. Given the choice, most teachers would prefer learners who are both self-motivated and self-managed. However, many teachers who are themselves highly motivated and highly managerial may find it difficult to cede control over learning.

Three areas of learner autonomy are particularly important for students: control over topics (goals), freedom of choice in activity (means), and belief in themselves as agents of their own success (self-efficacy). Students' control over topic was covered briefly in Chapter 3 (constructivist teaching), and because it involves curricular issues, it is a large issue that will be covered again in later chapters. Students' freedom of choice in activity (means) will be covered below in sections dealing with indirect and direct strategies.

Self-Efficacy

Students' belief in themselves as agents of their own success (self-efficacy) can be fostered systematically in language used by the teacher. At the beginning of the course, teachers who introduce the idea of autonomy set a tone of "working together" toward mutual goals. Consistent rhetoric that speaks of goals, together with strategies to achieve these goals, maintains the tone of self control. These who are successful as well as those who underachieve can learn to take responsibility for themselves. Doing so means also being able to undertake self-assessment to evaluate goal attainment (McNamara, 1998a).

The element of student choice promotes active learning and increases student motivation. Deci and Ryan (1985) claimed that activities in which choice was allowed are more compelling than similar activities in which no choice was given. Intrinsic motivation is enhanced, and stress is reduced, when individuals have a sense of control over their fate (Miller, 1980). One way to offer students more control is to let them have a say in instructional planning, especially in planning for assignments.

Autonomy can be fostered by encouraging students to access learning for themselves by going out on their own, drawing upon resources outside the classroom. Santás (1996) offered a checklist with which students can check their own self-access language-learning behavior. It includes suggestions such as, "Watch films in English with subtitles in your own language"; "read books, either in the original version or in simplified readers"; "remember that some readers come with an audiotape"; and "whenever you can afford it, go to a book shop and look at the English language section. Some of the many interesting materials are famous stories with audiotapes, videotapes with sing-along songs, simplified readers, comics, magazines, and computer games. Share what you find with your classmates" (p. 19).

Student Responsibility for Learning

Marshall (1999a, 1999b) offered classroom management strategies that foster a sense of responsibility for learning. These include assigning regular duties to all learners within the classroom; expecting all students to answer when a question is asked and using question-and-answer techniques to make this possible; and teaching critical thinking skills explicitly so that these can be used on a daily basis during instruction. These themes are addressed specifically in the competencies published by the Secretary's Commission on Achieving Necessary Skills (SCANS) for adult and vocational workers (for more on integrating SCANS skills into ESL instruction, see the Spring Institute for International Studies, ELT Technical Assistance Project [www.springinstitute.com]). Thus, the themes of responsibility, community, classroom discourse, and critical thinking are interwoven.

What Are Learner Strategies?

One must distinguish such terms as *strategy, megastrategy, tactic, technique, principle, practice,* and *method.* The term *strategy* denotes both general approaches and specific actions taken to learn a second language (see Cohen, 1996). Stern (1993) used both *strategy* and *technique,* and Seliger (1984) used the term *tactic.* Larsen-Freeman and Long (1991) used the terms *macrostrategies, microstrategies,* and *tactics;* Brown (2000) talked about *principles.* I use the term *megastrategy* to denote "a large idea that guides practice, and that hosts a set of matching strategies consonant with its theme."

In this book I use the term *strategy* to mean "an idea that a learner can employ to increase learning." Each strategy in this book is a direct strategy that the prospective teacher may acquire and use *as a learner of teacher education.* Some learner strategies in turn are appropriate for the second-language learner. Tudor (1996) supplied a definition for a second-language learner strategy: "any purposeful activity that learners engage in to promote their learning and knowledge of the target language (p. 38). So the term *strategy* is used in this book at two levels; it refers both to a strategy used by teachers and to learner strategies employed by English learners.

Indirect and Direct Strategies

Learner strategies are defined as "systematic plans, designs, procedures or maneuvers used during learning." These can be divided into *indirect* and *direct*. Indirect strategies tend to originate at a level of unconscious or automated performance and may or may not enter consciousness during operation. If the behavior is one that potentially can come under conscious control, however, it should be called a strategy.

As an example of an indirect strategy, suppose a given person has a preference for learning by listening rather than reading. The person probably did not consciously acquire this preference. Once the person becomes aware that listening is a preferred means of input, though, that person has a choice whether to maintain that preference or try to modify it by, for example, consciously trying to read more. While listening, however, the person is probably not consciously thinking, "There I go, listening again as a preference." Most people do not maintain self-consciousness while using cognitive functions, although they are conscious at the time.

Direct strategies, in contrast, are used by the learner in a directed way, that is, they tend to originate at a level of conscious performance and may or may not become unconscious, or automated, during operation. A person may be taught a strategy, try it, reflect upon its success, and eventually either decide to add it to the ongoing repertoire of behaviors or not, depending on its perceived utility. Like other acquired cognitive functions, once in the repertoire, the strategy may be used often or seldom.

In the domain of learning strategies there has been a lack of consensus on such issues as the role of consciousness in strategy acquisition and use; the distinction between teaching and learning strategies; and the difficulty of classifying strategies into those that are behavioral, mental, observable, explicit, and so forth. These difficulties are compounded, on the one hand, because research has depended on verbal self-reports from subjects and, on the other hand, by the fact that language itself can be considered "cognitive" only to a point. Language itself is, after all, a kind of mental "shortcut" used by the brain to automatize meaning for the purposes of communication. Only part of language was meant to be thought about consciously at all; in fact, most of the first language is acquired without self-consciousness, a key difference between first- and second-language acquisition as a whole. This reality has complicated the discussion of language strategies.

Strategy-Based Instruction

What can an educator hope to accomplish by the use of strategy-based instruction? Weaver and Cohen (1997) offered this explanation. The instructor can receive an introduction for the following purposes:

(1) raising students' awareness of strategies and learning style preferences; (2) introducing and reinforcing systematic strategy use among learners in the classroom; (3) in-

tegrating strategies-based activities into daily lesson plans; and (4) facilitating discussions of strategy effectiveness among the learners. (p. 9)

How does the instructor train learners to use these strategies? *Awareness training* (also called *consciousness raising* or *familiarization training*) helps the learner to become aware of strategies already in use, by such means as structured self-observation (taking open-ended notes or using checklists); interviews and think-aloud procedures; keeping notes, diaries, or journals; or taking self-report surveys (Oxford, 1990). "The Embedded Strategies" game (Oxford, 1990, pp. 24–30) uses a list of language-related activities (read and follow recipes in the target language; learn some "canned" routines by heart in the target language; listen to songs in the target language and try to learn lyrics). Learners match the activity to a chart of learning strategies. This helps the learner to become familiar with the overall schema of strategies. A second method of awareness training is to offer the learner brief scenarios or stories about second-language learners in a variety of task situations and ask the learner to match situation with strategy.

One-time strategy training is a second method to teach learning strategies. In this approach, the learner acquires and practices one or two strategies, matched to specific tasks. Although it does not provide long-term intervention, it is useful for the learner with a particular, focused need.

Long-term strategy training is the most valuable overall, being more prolonged and covering a broader terrain of strategies. This type of training may be tied to the objectives of the overall language program (Oxford, 1990). This book presents a pedagogical version of the language-learning strategy domain, at the risk of oversimplification. For a more nuanced treatment, see Cohen, 1996, and Oxford, 1990.

Indirect Strategies: Second-Language Acquisition and Use

* **STRATEGY 5.1:** Honor learners' second-language use strategies

What Are Second-Language Use Strategies?

A second-language use strategy is employed for transmitting an idea when the learner cannot produce precise linguistic forms. Cohen (1996) defined four second-language use strategies: *rehearsal, retrieval, communication,* and *cover.*

* Rehearsal is used to store a correct language form in long-term memory (LTM).
* Retrieval is used to call to mind the correct form from LTM.
* Communication indicates an attempt convey meaning even when no attempt is made to memorize a form.
* Cover strategies are used to create the impression that the learner is in control when in fact there are gaps in proficiency; for example, a speaker may fail to remember a word and must use gestures or a synonym to compensate.

Second-language use strategies are valuable not only as tools that facilitate the learner's language reception and production but also as a means to interpret the learner's interlanguage. Examining the learner's attempts to express or decode meaning in a given situation permits some analysis of the means by which the learner approximates the rules of the target language. This analysis provides interesting material not only for the teacher but also for the interlanguage researcher, because it emphasizes the learner's creativity in the face of difficulty, rather than focusing on the learner's errors.

Examples of Second-Language Use Strategies.   Learners used *reduction and achievement strategies* when faced with the challenge of conveying or interpreting messages for which existing linguistic resources are inadequate. They either adjust the message to the resources available (a reduction strategy) or increase the resources available in order to rise to the occasion (a resource expansion strategy) (see Corder, 1983). Reduction and achievement strategies result in differing solutions to problems of communication. One can see both of these types of solutions in the lists of communication strategies that follow.

Chesterfield and Chesterfield (1985) found that Mexican American children used a set of language use strategies when learning English that incorporated sociolinguistic, discourse, and strategic factors. Table 5.2 presents these strategies in sequential order of development.

Brown (2000) examined five broad categories of what he calls "communication strategies" based on Tarone's work (1981; see also Tarone, Cohen, & Dumas, 1983). These strategies (see Table 5.3) make conscious use of both verbal and nonverbal devices. The first category, prefabricated patterns, is the same as "formulaic expressions" (see above). The second, "appeals for help," is also covered above. The third

TABLE 5.2 • Language Use Strategies in Second-Language Acquisition

Language Use Strategy	Definition
Repetition	Imitating a word or structure used by another
Memorization	Recalling by rote songs, rhymes, or sequences
Formulaic expressions	Using words or phrases that function as units, such as greetings ("Hi! How are you?")
Verbal attention getters	Using language to initiate interaction ("Hey!" "I think . . .")
Answering in unison	Responding with others
Talking to self	Engaging in subvocal or internal monologue
Elaboration	Providing information beyond that which is necessary
Anticipatory answers	Responding to an expected question, or completing another's phrase or statement
Monitoring	Correcting one's own errors in vocabulary, style, grammar
Appeal for assistance	Asking another for help
Request for clarification	Asking the speaker to explain or repeat
Role play	Interacting with another by taking on roles

Source: Chesterfield & Chesterfield, 1985.

TABLE 5.3 ◆ Categories of Communication Strategies

Language Use Strategy	Definition
Prefabricated patterns	Memorizing stock phrases to rely on when all else fails
Appeals for help	Asking a conversant for help or pausing to consult a dictionary
Cognitive and personality styles	Employing one's personality to compensate for unknown language structures
Avoidance	Evading the use of sounds, structures, or topics that are beyond current proficiency.
Language switch	Falling back on the primary language for help in communication.

Source: Brown, 2000.

category, "cognitive and personality styles" will be covered at greater length in the next section.

Code Switching.   The last strategy, often called *code switching,* alternates between two languages on the word, phrase, clause, or sentence level (see Valdés-Fallis, 1978). In addition to its use as a second-language use strategy, code switching is also used to clarify or emphasize a point, to cross social or ethnic boundaries, to express group identity and status and/or to be accepted by a group, to quote someone, to interject in a conversation, to exclude someone, and to ease tension in a conversation (Baker, 1993). In classrooms, students should learn in whatever manner they feel most comfortable, including code switching, if it reduces anxiety or increases group solidarity.

❖ Tactics for teachers to facilitate second-language use:

- Familiarize language learners with second-language use strategies so that they can recognize them when they occur.
- Practice with students a set of formulaic expressions to cover most interactions so that they feel comfortable in routine language use.
- Recognize that in a bilingual context, code switching is common and relieves anxiety; too much code switching, however, may interfere with second-language use.

Indirect Strategies: Learning Style Preferences

- **STRATEGY 5.2:** Adapt instruction to learners' varying styles

Developing academically responsive classrooms promotes both equity and excellence. These may seem like competing values (adjusting to learner variance versus attaining learning standards), and they must be carefully balanced. This effort requires a serious reexamination of traditional schooling. Is it reasonable to expect a class of learners to do the same activities, with the same goals, in the same period of time?

The nature of teaching requires some kind of standardization and grouping, because class sizes are usually too large to treat each student in a unique manner. The reality in American classrooms, however, is that students are increasingly heterogeneous in an array of ways beyond language: religion; mainstreamed students with disabilities (see Kaye, 1997); race/ethnicity (one-third of the U.S. school population is nonwhite; see Marlowe & Page, 1999); and mobility (43 million people in the United States move every year; see Hodgkinson, 1998). The challenge is clear: how can curriculum, instruction, and assessment be responsive to this learner diversity?

A key element of diversity is learning style, defined by Brown (1987) as "a consistent and rather enduring tendency or preference within an individual" (p. 79). "Learning styles are the preferences students have for thinking, relating to others, and for particular types of classroom environments and experiences" (Grasha, 1990, p. 23). Knowing these preferences can assist instructors to anticipate the differing needs and perspectives of students, help students understand themselves as learners, and use the information to plan and modify certain aspects of courses and assignments. There are many typologies of learning styles.

Typologies of Learning Styles

Hruska-Reichmann and Grasha.   Hruska-Riechmann and Grasha (1982) offered three contrasting pairs of learning styles: competitive versus cooperative, dependent versus independent, and participant versus avoidant (see also Grasha, 1996). Students may show characteristics of more than one of these styles.

Keefe.   Keefe (1987) divided learning style variables into four categories: *physiological, affective, incentive,* and *cognitive.* Physiological variables influence personal nutrition, health, time-of-day preferences, sleeping and waking habits, need for mobility, and needs for and response to varying levels of light, sound, and temperature. Affective variables include the amount of structure or supervision students need, what anxiety and curiosity they display, and what degree of persistence they use to pursue a task in the face of frustration. Incentive variables cover students' personal interests; levels of achievement motivation; enjoyment of competition versus cooperation; risk taking versus caution; reaction to rewards and punishment; social motivation arising from family, school, and ethnic background; and locus of control (internal—seeing oneself as responsible for own behavior—or external—attributing circumstances to luck, chance, or other people).

Cognitive learning style variables for Keefe include *field independent* versus *field dependent; conceptual/analytical* versus *perceptual/concrete; broad* versus *focused* attention; *easily distracted* versus *capable of controlled concentration; leveling* (tendency to lump new experiences with previous ones) versus *sharpening* (the ability to distinguish small differences); and *high cognitive complexity* (accepting of diverse, perhaps conflicting input) versus *low cognitive complexity* (tendency to reduce conflicting information to a minimum).

Sonbuchner.   Sonbuchner (1991) referred to learning styles as a combination of *information-processing styles* (preferences for reading, writing, listening, speaking, visualizing, or manipulating) and *work environment preferences* (differences in motivation, concentration, length of study sessions, involvement with others, level of organization, prime times for study, amount of noise, amount of light, amount of heat, and need for food/drink).

Tharp.   Tharp (1989) suggested two sets of contrasting learning styles: *visual/verbal*, and *holistic/analytic*. Schools tend to reward students who are both verbal and analytic. In contrast, students who have a more visual orientation and learn by observing and doing rather than through verbal instructions may find schools mystifying until they adjust to a different cognitive style. Similarly, a student with more holistic thought processes dislikes reducing phenomena to disassembled parts. This person may understand pieces of a process only when the whole pattern is visible.

Cognitive style differences are evident in this excerpt from a dialog I had with Martha Chacon, the matriarch of the local Native Americans, when I wrote a book on their cultural beliefs. One can see here that the interviewer is struggling for precision, whereas the interviewee is comfortable with some degree of imprecision. Note the contrasting analytic and holistic cognitive styles:

> L D-R.   So, the *hukat* is the giant deer that appears when someone dies. When was the last time it came?
>
> M. C.   When my Aunt Luisa died. It was down on the road. When the ambulance came up the road, they said they saw it in their headlights.
>
> L D-R.   I'm not quite clear here. Are you saying that the deer came for Aunt Luisa?
>
> M. C.   It was because she died.
>
> L D-R.   Uh, did the deer come to, a . . . carry away her spirit? Or did Aunt Luisa . . . turn into the deer? Or do you mean that the deer . . . well, stood for her . . . like a symbol?
>
> M. C.   Yes.

Kolb.   The adult learner has been the focus of Kolb's theory of experiential learning. Kolb (1976) described this as a four-stage process: a learner's concrete experience forms the basis for observation and reflection, which in turn enables the learner to make decisions and solve problems, thus creating a basis for new experiences. Kolb's four learning types are cast into two dimensions; (1) active experimentation versus reflective observation and (2) abstract conceptualization versus concrete experience. Various types of learners fall along these two dimensions.

McCarthy.   Four learning styles similar to Kolb's are the result of McCarthy's 4MAT system (McCarthy, 1983): innovative, analytic, common sense, and dynamic. The innovative learner needs to be personally involved through social interaction. The analytic learner thinks through ideas and concepts. The common sense learner needs hands-on experience and enjoys solving practical problems. The dynamic learner uses intuition and trial and error, taking risks and jumping to conclusions. The underlying theme in this system is that "left-brained" and "right-brained" people approach tasks in distinct ways. This theory of learning style differences was a popular theme during the 1980s, when much of the learning style literature appeared; but subsequent research in neural anatomy has called into question distinctions in learning styles based on left-right brain differences.

Gregorc.   Gregorc (1982) explored the mismatch between teaching styles and student learning styles as a means of using style diagnostics to improve student learning. According to Gregorc, learners can be categorized into four types: (1) abstract random, (2) abstract sequential, (3) concrete random, and (4) concrete sequential. The abstract/concrete dimension resembles Kolb's abstract/concrete dimension, and the random/sequential distinction is reminiscent of Tharp's holistic/analytic dichotomy.

Myers/Briggs.   Carl Jung's theory of personality is the basis for the Myers/Briggs Type Indicator. Four opposing pairs of personality dimensions (introversion/ extroversion, sensing/perception, thinking/feeling, and judging/perceiving) make up the sixteen personality types. The Myers/Briggs Type Indicator has been extensively popularized in easy-to-understand versions such as Murphy's *The Eight Disciplines* (1998) and Keirsey's *Please Understand Me II* (1998).

Learning Styles Applied to the ESL/EFL Classroom

The use of learning styles is based on a few basic hypotheses: (1) that every learner—and teacher—has a learning style preference; (2) that all styles are equally valid, although the educational context may value some over others; (3) that learning about one's preferences, and acquiring styles other than one's preference, may assist students in learning; and (4) that learning strategies are linked to learning styles (Reid, 1995). Teachers can reduce the complexity of the learning style typologies by surveying various systems, analyzing themselves, and settling on one or two systems that both explain individual differences and offer a relatively easy way to accommodate instruction to learner differences.

Cultural Differences in Learning Styles

Some researchers claim that many aspects of cognitive style have demonstrated cultural differences (see Cohen, 1969). For example, Nelson (1995) characterized middle-class U.S. public school techniques as appealing to the field-independent, analytical, visual learner, whereas Native Hawaiian and Native American learning environments by contrast favored the field-sensitive, global, and kinesthetic learner. However, other researchers have considered the connection between cognitive styles and cultural styles overrated and divisive (O'Neil, 1990). Moreover, if a student is taking the inventory or self-report measure in the target language, there may be problems with understanding the terms (Eliason, 1995). Moreover, norms may not be available that help see the learner's response in the context of a native culture.

Measuring Learning Styles

Individuals' learning styles can be measured in four ways.

1. Self-report instruments or questionnaires, usually by means of a forced-choice task. (Kolb's self-test is a forced choice among four adjectives: are you receptive,

relevant, analytical, or impartial? Are you accepting, a risk taker, evaluative, or aware?)

2. An open-ended interview.
3. Observations of individuals as they work, tracked through anecdotal notes or by means of a checklist.
4. Review of what students produce, as seen in the results of their projects or in the types of errors they make.

Adapting Instruction to Learning Styles

In the typical classroom, some modification may be made that takes learning styles into account. If students as a group are both competitive and dependent, for example, assignments that enhance other characteristics (such as collaborative and independent learning) might be developed. Teachers can use a variety of learning activities to accommodate distinct learning styles. Students' awareness of their learning style preferences constitutes a metacognitive strategy (see below). Once aware of their own preferences, students can use this knowledge to support their learning.

Cognitive coaching is a peer-coaching process for teachers developed by Garmston and Costa (cf. Garmston, 1987) that helps teachers explore the thinking behind their classroom practices. As teachers talk aloud with a peer about their instruction, they become clearer about the underlying bases for their decisions and increase their awareness of how they might expand their teaching repertoire. This reflective process has been particularly effective in helping teachers become more aware of learner diversity and of the ways in which learners' styles differ from that of the teacher.

One teacher, Jan Whitaker, prided herself on detailed and organized lessons. Her questioning style while teaching tended to call for specific, quantitative answers. By means of cognitive coaching, she became aware that she was not including students' input in her lesson designs. By listening to her students more sensitively, she altered her

Teachers can coach one another to diversify their teaching.

style to draw forth creativity and higher-order thinking from students. She was able to relax and let students search for their own answers, building self-esteem and self-managed learning along the way (Garmston, Linder, & Whitaker, 1993).

A comprehensive source for the incorporation of learning styles into SLA instruction is Reid's *Learning Styles in the ESL/EFL Classroom* (1995), a compendium of articles on research and practice in this area. The book features various inventories of learning styles; suggestions for learners with visual, auditory, and kinesthetic preferences; and a look at crosscultural implications.

❖ Tactics for teachers to incorporate learning styles into SLA:

◆ Diagnose your own learning style preferences so that you understand yourself as a teacher.
◆ Settle on one system, or one set of preferences, that you find useful to know about your students.
◆ Find or create a questionnaire or observation survey that measures these preferences.
◆ Find a way to add variety to instructional plans that makes a difference on this set of preferences.

Direct Strategies: Cognitive

◆ **STRATEGY 5.3:** Teach cognitive strategies

The second category of learner strategies applied to SLA is second-language learning strategies. These include literacy and oracy strategies, which are treated in Chapter 6. The three kinds of direct strategies discussed here are *cognitive, metacognitive,* and *social-affective* (Chamot & O'Malley, 1987). Extensive work in identifying learning strategies has been done by O'Malley and Chamot (O'Malley, Chamot, Stewner-Manzanares, Kupper, & Russo, 1985a, 1985b), who have incorporated specific instruction in learning strategies in their Cognitive Academic Language Learning Approach (CALLA). Oxford (1990) is also a useful source for the application of learning strategies to second-language learning.

Cognitive strategies are the strategies a person thinks and acts on in order to complete a task. They can be divided into three areas: (1) brain-compatible teaching; (2) study skills; (3) and enhancement of cognitive functions by the use of specific psychological tools, including schema building, scaffolding, use of alternative information representations such as graphic organizers, and critical and creative thinking.

Schema Building

A *schema* (plural *schemata*) is a unit of understanding that can be used to store knowledge in LTM. Students use existing schemata when they recognize a connection between what they know and the learning experience. In addition to evoking prior knowledge, teachers build schemata, providing new experiences that arouse interest and attention to a topic. These may include field trips, guest speakers, films, experiments, classroom discovery centers, computer simulations, and so on. By recalling their own experiences and engaging in experiences with their classmates, students can associate what they already know with these new experiences. If there is little prior knowledge of the topic at hand, students will need more instructional support.

Scaffolding

In the world of construction, a scaffold is a temporary support for workers as they build a new edifice. In constructivist teaching, scaffolding is used to help the learner construct knowledge (see Berk & Winsler, 1995; Wood, Bruner, & Ross, 1976). During scaffolding, the teacher helps to focus the learner's attention on relevant parts of the task by asking key questions that help to determine the zone of proximal development for that student on that task. Using questions and verbalizations that give children the opportunity to think and talk about the task increases success, as does dividing the task into smaller, manageable subcomponents and sensitively withdrawing assistance when it is no longer required (Díaz, Neal, & Vachio, 1991). By using scaffolding techniques, teachers can help students build schemata.

CALLA (Chamot & O'Malley, 1987, 1994) was designed for English learners at the advanced-beginning and intermediate levels. The CALLA model includes the development of academic language skills and explicit instruction in learning strategies for both content and language acquisition. Content topics are introduced by using extensive contextual supports or by reducing language demands. Academic language skills include all four language modes in daily content lessons, as well as language functions important for specific curricular areas such as analyzing, evaluating, justifying, and persuading. Learning strategies are those used in scientific inquiry; gathering, analyzing, and interpreting data; explaining, inferring, and predicting; and communicating results.

Alternative Information Representation and Graphic Organizers

A graphic organizer is a visual frame used to represent and organize information, "a diagram showing how concepts are related" (McKenna & Robinson, 1997, p. 117). Graphic organizers present ideas visually. Many kinds of graphic organizers can also be used to help students focus their thoughts and reactions, for example, as they read a literature selection. Because graphic organizers balance visual with verbal representation, they can help to make visible the conceptual structures that underlie content. This technique helps students to make models for understanding ideas and outcomes.

Graphic organizers are particularly useful in classrooms in which English learners face challenging academic content. By using mind maps or other information organizers, students can interact with the concepts presented in various content areas in a way that supplements verbal text (Watson, Northcutt, & Rydell, 1989; Flynn, 1995). Thus, English learners can access core content even when their reading skills are weak. As a result, students becoming more engaged in their learning.

Graphic organizers have at least three major applications. First, *generative*: They are used to promote language related to content. Students can talk or write about the information presented on a chart. Second, *representative/explanatory*: They are used to increase content understanding, either to build background knowledge before reading a text, to read interactively with the help of an organizer, or to synthesize new information that is gained from a text. Third, *evaluative*: They are used to assess understanding of content (Early, 1990).

Sequential organizers show events in order. Sequential organizers include the use of the alphabet, parts of a book, parts of a letter, parts of a paragraph, parts of an essay, a chain of events in a story plot, and a set of steps in written directions (Kagan, 1998). Figure 5.2 shows a sample sequential organizer used to list the beginning, middle, and end of a story. Figure 5.3 shows the problem-solution chain in a Native American "coyote" story. A picture of a chain of boxes horizontally or vertically can represent a sequence, as can a picture of the steps of a ladder. If the events repeat, a cycle graph may be used. A sequence of pictures makes a cartoon or picture strip, and a set of dates can be sequenced on a time line. A step chart with lower to higher steps set up from left to right can represent a set of steps in written directions.

Compare-contrast organizers can be used in language arts to compare characters in the same story or in different stories, types of correspondence (business versus friendly letters), or genres of reading (fiction versus nonfiction). Visually, these comparison charts can be of three types: a Venn diagram (see Figure 5.4), a T-chart (see Figure 5.5), or a comparison chart (see Figure 5.6).

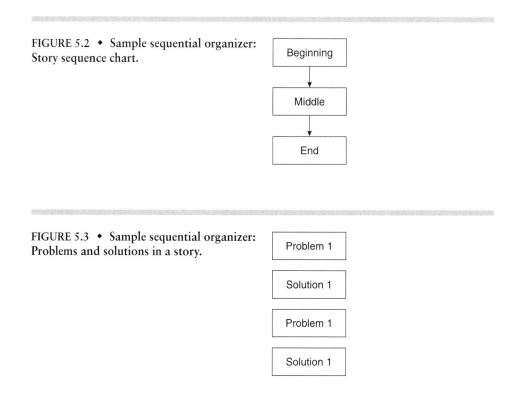

FIGURE 5.2 ◆ Sample sequential organizer: Story sequence chart.

FIGURE 5.3 ◆ Sample sequential organizer: Problems and solutions in a story.

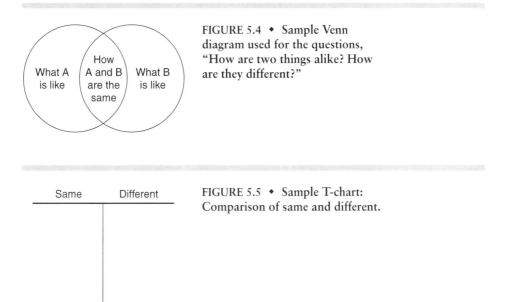

FIGURE 5.4 ◆ Sample Venn diagram used for the questions, "How are two things alike? How are they different?"

FIGURE 5.5 ◆ Sample T-chart: Comparison of same and different.

Comparison of Civilizations		
	Egypt	United States
Duration	over 4,000 years	about 400 years
Political structure	Towns united by centralized government	Hierarchy: towns, counties, states, federal government
Religion	Pharaotic, later Islam	Predominantly Protestant Christian, then Catholic Christian, then Jewish, Islam, other
(etc.)		

FIGURE 5.6 ◆ Sample comparison chart: Comparison by attributes.

Relational organizers other than compare-and-contrast models show concepts that are embedded (see Figure 5.7), whole-part (see Figure 5.8), or cause-effect (see Figure 5.9).

Classification organizers are used to create hierarchies, matrixes, or other concept relations that show specific structures. Figure 5.10 shows a hierarchy format,

FIGURE 5.7 ◆ Sample relational organizer: Embedded concepts (a teacher's phenomenal field of person relations in the role of teacher).

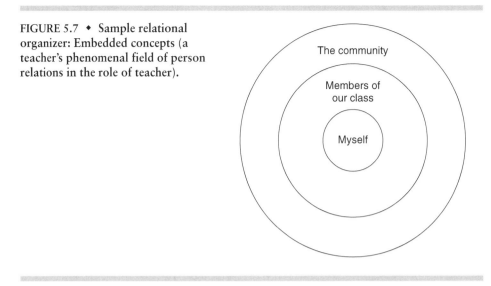

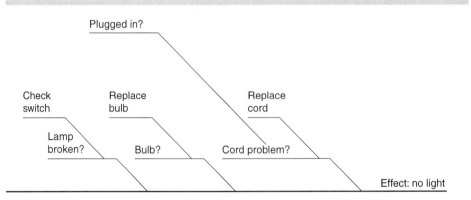

Atom	Nucleus	Protons
		Neutrons
	Electrons	

FIGURE 5.8 ◆ Sample relational organizer: Whole-part (parts of the atom).

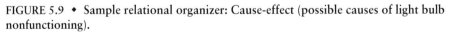

FIGURE 5.9 ◆ Sample relational organizer: Cause-effect (possible causes of light bulb nonfunctioning).

FIGURE 5.10 ◆ Sample classification chart: Main ideas.

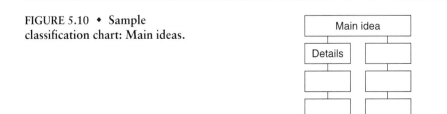

118

Figure 5.11 shows a matrix, Figure 5.12 shows a two-dimensional plot, and Figure 5.13 shows an alternative way to display a hierarchy.

Concept development organizers are used to brainstorm. The K-W-L chart is used to introduce a theme, a lesson, or a reading. It can help generate student interest

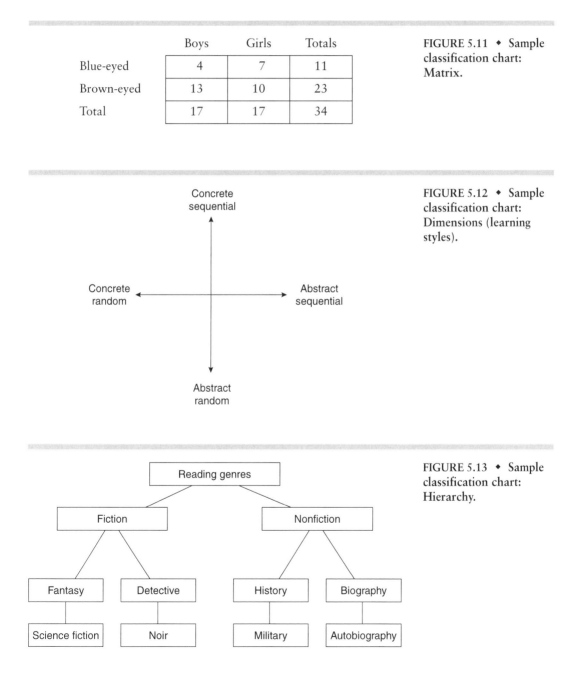

	Boys	Girls	Totals
Blue-eyed	4	7	11
Brown-eyed	13	10	23
Total	17	17	34

FIGURE 5.11 ◆ Sample classification chart: Matrix.

FIGURE 5.12 ◆ Sample classification chart: Dimensions (learning styles).

FIGURE 5.13 ◆ Sample classification chart: Hierarchy.

in a topic and assist students in using their prior knowledge as they read. Students can enter K (what we Know), W (what we Want to know), and L (what we Learned), completing the chart at the end of the unit or lesson (see Figure 5.14). The Mind Map is basically a circle with the concept or topic in the center, surrounded by lines, bubbles, arrows, or other connectors that group students' ideas to the concept or topic (see Figures 5.15 and 5.16). Concept charts are concept development organizers, primarily lists in no particular order encased in boxes (see Figures 5.17 and 5.18).

Evaluation organizers show degree of positivity (Kagan, 1998). These can be grade scales (A–F); Likert scales (1 = strongly disagree and, at the other extreme, 1 = strongly agree); rubric scales (needs work → satisfactory → good → excellent); two boxes ("I like/agree with" versus "I dislike/disagree with"); or three boxes, indicating plus/minus interest. One teacher uses three shapes as an evaluation tool: a square ("things I am square with," as students write one thing with which they agree on each of four sides); a triangle ("points that made me think," as students write three concepts they gained at each of the points), and a circle ("things I am still going around about," as students write in the center of the circle a concept they do not quite understand).

Semantic mapping proved to be a successful approach for the three English learners, two boys ages 5 and 9 and their sister, age 10, whom Judy was tutoring. She searched for an interesting topic that would increase their vocabulary in English. The children chose "Halloween." Starting with words they knew in English (skeleton, witch), Judy

What we know	What we want to know	What we have learned

FIGURE 5.14 ◆ Sample concept development chart: K-W-L.

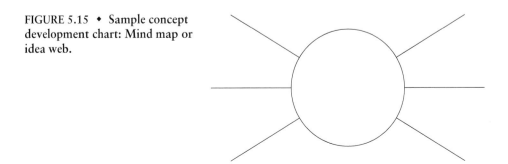

FIGURE 5.15 ◆ Sample concept development chart: Mind map or idea web.

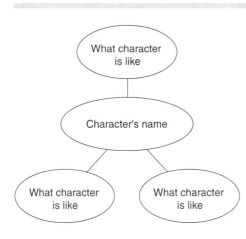

FIGURE 5.16 ◆ Sample concept development chart: Character trait web.

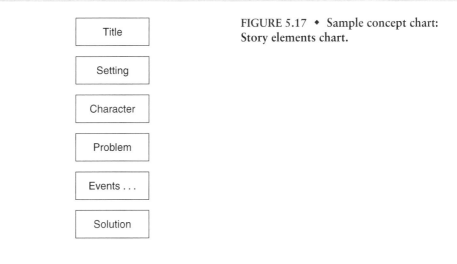

FIGURE 5.17 ◆ Sample concept chart: Story elements chart.

FIGURE 5.18 ◆ Sample concept chart: Word log.

wrote the words on chart paper and the children copied the words in their notebooks. The children gave other words in Spanish, and Judy found the English equivalents and wrote them, too. Using a fresh piece of chart paper, Judy asked the students how the list of words could be grouped into categories. The activity continued until the words had been grouped into categories, Animals, Monsters, and Trick-or-Treat. Judy followed this activity by reading a book on Halloween, *Rotten Ralph's Trick or Treat.* When they came to a word on the chart, Judy pointed this out for reinforcement. (Brisk & Harrington, 2000, pp. 71–72)

Once students and teachers become familiar with graphic organizers, they can help English learners grasp basic concepts without depending on language as the sole source of understanding. Two excellent sources are Bell's *Visualizing and Verbalizing* (1986) and Parks and Black's *Organizing Thinking: Graphic Organizers* (1990).

Critical Thinking

An important aspect of schooling in a democracy is the ability to think for oneself, analyze ideas, separate fact from opinion, support opinions from reading, draw inferences, and solve problems. Critical thinking can create self-understanding, as a person might approach significant issues in life differently following the acquisition of analytic skills. Paul, Binker, Jensen, and Kreklau (1990) offered a strategy list of the dimensions of critical thought as an organized introduction to this complex field.

Materials are available that incorporate the teaching of critical thinking into ESOL education directly. Other materials widely available for mainstream teaching can be adapted to ESOL. Little and Greenberg (1991), in their book *Problem Solving: Critical Thinking and Communication Skills*, provide activities for junior and senior high school English learners that combine reading, dialogue, and discussion. The characters involved in the vignettes are drawn from a wide variety of cultures. *Developing Critical Thinking and Problem Solving Abilities* (Stice, 1987) presents methods for successfully teaching problem solving and critical analysis across disciplines and offers exercises that students could use to improve critical thinking skills. The four-volume set *Critical Thinking Handbook* (grades K–3, 4–6, 7–9, and high school) presents lesson plans that have been remodeled to include critical thinking strategies (available from the Center for Critical Thinking at Sonoma State University).

The book *Teaching for Thinking: Theory, Strategies, and Activities for the Classroom* (Raths, Wasserman, Jonas, & Rothstein, 1986) features practical suggestions on how to implement critical thinking through classroom applications at both the elementary and secondary levels. Special attention is given to the teacher's role as well as to problems that may be preventing more widespread acceptance of thinking programs. In addition, educators will find ample entries in publishers' catalogs arranged by grade level. The series *Into English* (Tinajero & Schifini) has incorporated critical thinking as an integral part of ESOL lessons.

Creative Thinking and Risk Taking

Creativity is a part of cognition and should not be confined to music and art classes. During problem solving and project-based learning, for example, once the requirements of a problem or project have been surveyed and the goals determined, creative thinking can be used to generate possible solutions. Creative thinking can be used in every reading lesson to generate alternatives and expand the point of view of reading comprehension: What if the main character were female rather than male? What if the book were set in the seventeenth century rather than in the modern era? What if the setting were Thailand rather than the United States? Can we imagine a different outcome?

This focus opens the door to fertile terrain, the imaginary world where possibilities are unlimited and constraints of reality do not pinch. In addition, use of the imaginary can stimulate scholars to explore other cultures, other times in history, and nonhuman worlds such as those of science fiction, myths, or animal tales. The use of the imaginary in language teaching will be further explored in Chapter 7.

A whole range of activities, from creative movement and manipulatory activities to brainstorming and story creation, can promote creative thinking. Turner (1990) featured "101 Things to Be: And Then Some"—ideas for creative movement, including being a ball in a pinball machine, a letter of the alphabet, an angry animal, a kite, an umbrella opening and closing, and so on. In "Name Puzzle" students print their names in large block letters in brown paper and paint the names and the surrounding space. The students then cut the paper into a puzzle, each keeping a puzzle piece as a souvenir. In "Magic Auction" students make a list of things they would wish for (a formula for instant water, a flying carpet) and then hold an auction in groups for these items using play money.

The genre of brain puzzles is also mentally stimulating. *Brain Puzzles* (Tyler & Round, 1987), part of the Usborne *Brainbenders* series, offers visual and verbal puzzles and includes an answer key in the back of the book. The *MENSA Mind Maze Challenge* (Bremmer, 1999) is one huge puzzle from the front to the back of the book, with more than 150 interlinked brainteasers. *Brain Quest* (Feder, 1992) is a series of grade-appropriate card sets with questions and answers that draw upon a student's general cultural knowledge. Students can play these in pairs or teams of four. Here are some sample questions from Deck 2: "Order from east to west: India, Japan, Vietnam, Iran"; "What star is closest to earth?"; "Where is a person's diaphragm?"

Both critical and creative thinking are integral parts of the human mind that enrich any part of the curriculum. Thinking is the key to the creation of meaning, in which children learn to react not just in response to the real world immediately before them but also in accord with their internal world, the world of ideas. Channeling the power of thought is an important part of language education in the context of cognitive development.

❖ **Tactics for teachers to develop students' cognitive strategies:**

♦ Match cognitive strategies to specific contexts of content knowledge.
♦ Remodel lessons to teach critical thinking explicitly.
♦ Include creative thinking as a specific cognitive strategy rather than as a curricular add-on.

Direct Strategies: Metacognitive

Metacognitive development involves direct teaching of strategies that help students plan what and how they want to learn; monitor, manage, and motivate while they are learning; and evaluate what they have learned and how they did so. Self-management and self-motivation have been discussed together earlier in this chapter as "autonomy." Metacognition is "the ability to think about your thinking—to make your thinking visible. Metacognition results in critical but healthy reflection and evaluation of your thinking, both of which may result in specific changes in how you teach or learn" (Anderson, 2002).

♦ STRATEGY 5.4: Teach metacognitive strategies

The term *metacognition* means "beyond cognition." Wellman (1985, p. 1) defined metacognition as "a person's cognition about cognition." Jacobson (1998) uses the term "metacognition" to describe the self-monitoring, and conscious use, of learning strategies. Metacognition is an invaluable skill, an important part of long-term cognitive development. It can also been defined as "learning about learning."

Vygotsky (1934/1982) is credited with being the first person to investigate the idea of what is now known as metamemory, which serves as a theoretical basis of the concept of metacognition. Vygotsky found that the roots of self-directed development stem from social interaction. Awareness and control strategies are learned through interaction with teachers and more capable peers; once these processes have been practiced and internalized, the student is able to carry out individual metacognitive activity (Wertsch, 1978).

Flavell's research on metamemory (see Flavell, 1979, 1985) showed that children's awareness of memory develops gradually over the school years, until they are able to choose selectively which memory strategies are most effective with what kinds of memory tasks. Control over one's own cognition involves the ability to think about thought, to integrate several mental processes simultaneously, to be aware of the relative difficulty of mental tasks and to adjust mental performance in accord with these differences, and to assess and monitor the state of one's own mind (Pressley, Barkowski, & O'Sullivan, 1985).

Metacognitive strategies are executive in nature; that is, they direct and supervise other thinking processes (Vaidya, 1999). Seven distinct processes facilitate students' learning processes (see Table 5.4).

Chamot and O'Malley (1994) divided metacognitive strategies into three areas: planning, monitoring, and evaluating. *Planning strategies* help students learn how to organize themselves for a learning task. *Monitoring strategies* help students to check their comprehension in listening and reading and their production while speaking and writing. *Performance evaluation strategies* teach students how to assess their own performance on a task, using learning logs or other reflective tools to keep track of their progress.

Planning strategies play a role in instruction. For example, if students know that an essay is due in one week, they can plan to gather information for the first three days, draft their composition over the next two days, and finally proofread

TABLE 5.4 ♦ Metacognitive Strategies: Overview

Strategy	Function
Self-management	Rearranging learning activities to suit personal preferences
Functional planning	Identifying and organizing strategies to perform tasks
Advanced organization	Skimming concepts of task material beforehand
Organizational planning	Sequencing or ordering task features
Selective attention	Deciding in advance on which specific aspects of task to focus
Self-monitoring	Correcting cognitive processes during use
Self-evaluation	Judging how well a task has been accomplished

Source: Adapted from Chamot, 1987.

their writing. Students learn to plan the main concepts, key ideas, and specific information that must be included. Monitoring strategies can be student-used comprehension checks that help students pause and quiz themselves periodically to see if they comprehend the main ideas when reading, or to see if they are writing what they intend to say in a rough draft. Students can self-evaluate outcomes to judge how much they have learned, and this self-evaluation can be compared to the teacher's assessment.

Additional kinds of metacognition in the area of self-knowledge are knowledge of one's own learning styles and preferences, knowledge of one's own strategy repertoire, and knowledge of one's own schemata.

Metacognition literally means transcending knowledge by monitoring the state of learning (Forget & Morgan, 1997). To this end a double mental process must take place during such events as reading a text. The reader must plan before reading, adjust effort during reading, and evaluate the success of the ongoing effort of making meaning from the text—all in addition to the reading itself.

Although to some extent metacognition is innate, it is not self-evident to everyone. Instead, like other strategy training, it must be modeled and integrated into learning through regular guided practice. Metacognitive strategy use takes its place as one more piece within the overall framework of cognitively stimulating teaching.

❖ Tactics for teachers to develop students' metacognitive strategies:

- Model metacognitive processes such as self-checks and self-awareness.
- Make time during instruction to plan, monitor, and reflect as a group.
- Match self-reflection to replanning and setting new goals.

Direct Strategies: Social-Affective

Social-affective strategies teach how to elicit needed clarification, how to work co-operatively with peers in problem solving, and how to use mental techniques or self-talk to reduce anxiety and increase a sense of personal competency.

◆ STRATEGY 5.5: Teach social-affective strategies

Social strategies represent the actions that learners choose to take in order to interact or communicate with other learners, the teacher, or with native speakers. They might ask for clarification, explanation, or feedback about their language use. This supports or advances learning and helps the learner to "take control of the social environment in learning tasks and/or situations of use" (Tudor, 1996, p. 207).

Affective strategies are defined by Oxford (1990) as "emotions, attitudes, motivations, and values" (p. 140). They "help create and maintain suitable internal and external climates for learning" (Weinstein, 1988, p. 291). These strategies help language learners to lower their anxiety, encourage themselves through positive self-talk and positive attitudes, and find ways to reward themselves when they have accomplished their learning goals.

However, beyond the control and fostering of positive emotional states, teachers may promote positive character traits. Paul, Binker, Jensen, and Kreklau (1990) listed affective traits that assist in critical thinking, including thinking independently; exercising fair-mindedness; and developing intellectual humility, courage, integrity, and perseverance. These dispositions combine thinking with affective aspects of the disposition toward reflective thought.

Student Opportunities to Cooperate

In planning for the development of a positive emotional climate in the classroom, many teachers include opportunities for students to talk about key concepts, using their primary language to clarify the concepts. Teachers ensure that students have numerous conversational partners and opportunities to interact within the context of lessons. Interaction patterns include teacher to student, student to teacher, student to student, student to content, and student to self.

A *noncompetitive environment* can be established through cooperative learning activities, both formally and informally structured. Individual work as a follow-up to cooperative work expands the students' areas of interest, stimulating a positive affective response. Heterogeneous groups encourage language development, as students talk about learning experiences with one another. *Literature and Cooperative Learning* (Whisler & Williams, 1990) details a variety of cooperative learning activities for the literature classroom.

Material presented in a mainstream class may be difficult for English learners if the topics are cognitively complex and highly language dependent. Using cooperative learning, English learners have increased opportunities to verify their comprehension by receiving explanations from their peers and sharing prior knowledge. This technique helps them to clarify and familiarize themselves with the lesson content. Cooperative learning strategies are offered in Chapter 7 in the context of engagement with the community.

Support in the affective domain for English learners outside the classroom may include special home visits by released time teachers, counselors, or outreach workers and informal counseling by teachers. Monitoring of academic progress by counselors helps to encourage students with language needs (Romero, 1991).

Maintaining the First Language as an Affective Strategy

Students achieve more when they use and develop their native language (Ramírez, 1992). Teachers can use several strategies to support students' L1 in the classroom. Students can also keep reading logs or journals in their native language. Aides and tutors can assist in explaining difficult passages and help students summarize their understanding. Books, magazines, films and other materials in the native language relating to the topic or theme of the lesson can support and augment students' learning (Tikunoff, Ward, Romero, Lucas, Katz, Van Broekhuisen, & Castaneda, 1991).

❖ **Tactics for teachers to develop students' social-affective strategies:**

- Help students identify their own characteristic negative affective thoughts and formulate positive verbal affirmations.
- Watch for signs of discouragement and pause for encouragement at that point.
- Discuss positive character traits with students and praise students when they exercise them.
- Use L1 support strategies.

Direct Strategies: Academic Survival and Study Skills

Academic survival skills are an aspect of academic competence comprising cultural skills (native-language cultural skills, target-culture skills, and knowledge of target-culture academia) and study skills. For English learners, academic experiences in the first language provide a foundation for L2 educational success. These students then acquire target-language skills to supplement this prior experience. The American classroom is often like a third culture that English learners must master; in addition, each teacher creates a classroom microculture with its own rules and practices.

- **STRATEGY 5.6:** Teach academic survival and study skills

Academic Survival Skills

For many students college is a necessity, not an option. New technologies mandate education beyond high school. In order to bridge the gap between ESL and college content courses, students must grapple with academic material that is challenging and relatively complex (Gardner, 1997). EFL college preparation issues are similar in many ways to those of ESL. EFL students who aim to attend college in English must also learn what is expected of them and how to approach new learning and study demands. Many aspects of higher education follow unwritten cultural rules and practices that may take time to acquire. Discourse practices in the American K–12 classrooms are discussed in Chapter 10. Hemmert & O'Connell (1998) offered an excellent overview of college-level communication skills.

Native-Language Cultural Skills and Experiences

Students with prior success in schooling may know how to use reference materials; how to act like serious students; and how and when to ask for help from peers and authority figures. ESL and EFL students both have access to a cultural body of knowledge that can be used as topics for essays, term papers, or autobiographic writing. Leki (1995) described an international student in a writing class at a U.S. university who consistently used the native culture as a theme. Even when the instructor asked her to find other themes, she persisted, gradually wearing down the instructor's protests, and received an A in the course. One might call this native-culture guerrilla warfare!

Target-Language Cultural Skills

Students can use target-language cultural skills to achieve academically. In addition to acquiring academic language, knowing how to solicit cooperation from English-speaking peers is vital. Moreover, in many ways appearances are important in American culture. Presenting oneself as a cultural "player" with access to pop culture, slang expressions, and other accoutrements of "cool" helps gain the respect of peers. Learning one's way around a campus and its activities is a key to success. Those who participate in after-class activities are more likely to be successful in school than those who do not (McWhorter, 1995).

Knowledge about the Culture of Academia in the Target Language

Both for immigrants and international students, speaking and listening in class is a hurdle. Instructors in U.S. classrooms tend to expect students to be active participants in class discussion under highly structured conditions. However, this is difficult for many English learners. The students may have learned English by means of curricula based on grammar, reading, and vocabulary without the opportunity to speak English or interact with native English-speakers. Often, U.S. teachers spend too much time talking or lecturing, or they interact verbally in question-and-answer sessions with students; again, this behavior follows traditional cultural patterns (see Chapter 10).

Instructors in U.S. college classrooms often say they want students to express their own ideas freely, to get involved in discussion, and even to challenge the instructor's opinions. However, few international students risk open disagreement, because some instructors are insulted when their opinions are challenged. In some ways, the American classroom resembles that of many other countries. The instructor is still in control, and some use the attention as a personal show. In turn, many students have learned to be passive, preferring to listen and not to express their opinions.

Use of clarifying strategies is the preeminent speaking/listening skill (Leki, 1995). Students use these to make sure they understand the assignment and the tasks they are expected to do. In American classrooms, it is accepted that students may negotiate with the professor as a group. If, for example, more time is needed to complete an assignment, one of the students may request an extension for the whole class. Asking for an extension as an individual, however, is considered to be asking for special favors and is frowned on.

Behavioral expectations in an academic setting govern both students and instructors. Students are expected to be on time to class, and good attendance may be a critical factor in regard to the grades received. Students remain sitting during class unless instructed otherwise and are expected to listen while the instructor is speaking. Students are responsible for their own work, and it must be submitted when due. Students are also responsible for their own learning. If a student has a particular question or does not understand, it is incumbent on that student to ask for clarification.

Proper forms of address may vary from context to context, but K–12 teachers are generally addressed as "Mr.," "Miss," or "Mrs." Many teachers are annoyed when a student addresses them as "Teacher." Parts of the United States may be more formal than others; for example, instructors in the southeastern United States may require more formal address, with answers accompanied by "Sir" or "Ma'am," because this culture is often more formal and traditional.

The environment of a classroom is expected to be sociable, but nonacademic activities such as buying or selling items or promoting social clubs are frowned on. Making friends in class is optional. Students may not smoke or use drugs and alcohol in class. Food may sometimes be eaten, but usually only with the permission of the instructor. Informal racial resegregation is common in classrooms, with students from similar backgrounds clustering together. The instructor has discretion in assigning seats or mixing people within working groups. Most K–12 schools have a dress code for students as well as instructors, but customs vary across U.S. universities.

A printed syllabus is often used to set the objectives and requirements for a course. Explicit office hours are offered, although instructors need to emphasize the importance of individual advising, because in many cultures, people visit authority figures only when they are summoned. Professors are expected to respect students and treat them as equals without "talking down" to them. Students are responsible for completing the coursework in their major and monitoring their own progress toward completion of a degree. Students may apply for scholarships and student loans, although funds may be available only to U.S. citizens.

Public and private schools in the United States exhibit cultural, legal, and ethical differences. Private universities may restrict a student's freedom of speech if it is contrary to the university's beliefs and values. All students are expected to honor the intellectual property rights of others by not copying the ideas of others without adequate acknowledgment, but actual sanctions for plagiarism vary. Unethical practices such as selling exams, papers, and assignments should be avoided. Although it is not uncommon for a person to risk cheating on tests and papers, one who commits these acts risks expulsion.

The laws of the state in which the institution is incorporated govern American schools. Public universities, for example, cannot deny the public from using their buildings during the course of a business day. A private university, on the contrary, can refuse entry to its grounds and buildings. The university may regulate some other aspects of its life more strictly than the state (for example, may prohibit liquor) but may not be more liberal than the state (may not, for example, permit minors to imbibe liquor).

Professional boundaries between teachers and students are expected. Sexual harassment is not ethical on the part of either student or teacher and is against the law; instructors are expected to prohibit students from harassing each other in class for any reason. Instructors are expected to grade students fairly without racial, gender, age, or other bias. Personal relationships are not supposed to influence the evaluation of students, and students are not supposed to bribe teachers or solicit preferential treatment.

Athletes may be held to different standards in many secondary and postsecondary schools because some schools are dependent on the fame and revenue generated by sports. Admission to the university may be granted based on athletic ability rather than solely on academic performance. Misconduct such as underage drinking or drug abuse may be overlooked by the administration in the case of such athletes.

Handbooks or other school publications contain regulations that govern the lives of students, and once these are made publicly available, students and/or their families are responsible for abiding by them. Cultural practices are not so publicly stated, but this does not mean that they are not enforced. Minor or inadvertent transgressions may be met with social punishment. For the most part, mainstream Americans do not help induct foreigners into their culture. The newcomer is expected to bear the burden of assimilation or accommodation—to "sink or swim" culturally.

Study Skills

One might think that knowing how to study is a universal skill, but study skills vary across cultures. Some students are trained to memorize, and the instructor is expected to define and delimit exactly what must be learned by rote. These students may not function well when the expectation shifts from dutiful pupil to active scholar. Students may need explicit training from an instructor on specific required skills, such as taking notes, making an outline, writing an opinion essay, and using a library. For example, to help students prepare for writing a term paper, step-by-step preparation may be needed that includes partial credit for an early reference list or draft, as well as provision for in-class peer editing and review.

Keeping track of assignments and notes is an important academic skill. Some students need reminders to copy assignments and to marshal the necessary materials, such as taking the relevant textbook home from school (Gonzales & Watson, 1986). At the college level, many students can benefit from specific training in adjusting to the academic culture. Time management, textbook reading, academic scheduling, and stress management are integral to academic success. Gardner and Jewell's (1997) handbook includes many such strategies for academic success.

The ability to take tests is another aspect of study skills. However, some strategies that are commonly assumed to be helpful are actually not. The adage, "Work as quickly as you can" contradicts research showing that it is not the total time spent on a task that is important, but rather how one allocates and budgets one's time. Also, it may be useless to "read everything carefully." In some reading comprehension tasks, one must read for detail, while others require analysis or application, that is, reading for the main idea. The important skill is to know *what* and *what not* to read carefully, and to allocate reading time accordingly. One should prepare a range of strategies and be able to select strategies intelligently.

Assistance from organizations and volunteers outside the classroom is often available to English learners. This assistance can come from academic summer programs, additional instructional services such as after-school programs and peer tutoring, and Dial-a-Teacher for homework help in both English and the primary language.

Text Processing and Time Management

Academic reading presents the biggest challenge for English learners. During the period of an average academic semester, students may be faced with hundreds of pages of reading, with the expectation that the material must be thoroughly mastered. The term *text processing* is distinct from reading comprehension in that it connotes strategic planning: the ability to manage large reading assignments wisely and to prepare to respond to large amounts of information. Strategic reading is a natural part of this process (see Chapter 6).

Requirements vary depending on the type of assessment. A given reading assignment may require broad, comprehensive thinking (such as examining underlying causes); creative thinking (such as research needed to expand the topic); specific types of critical thinking (such as comparing or contrasting); or memorization of facts. The type of text processing needed depends on the type of thinking that will be required; a good student presses the instructor early in the course for indications about the assessment keyed to the reading.

Pacing the reading load is needed no matter what type of reading is required. Using the academic syllabus provided by the instructor, the scholar identifies the *sources* of reading required (text that must be purchased, text that is reserved in the library for limited access borrowing, or text that must be retrieved independently using research skills). Gauging the *number of pages* required for each assignment, the scholar notes when in the semester the heaviest load will fall in each course, such as scheduled midterm and final examination periods, and *plans ahead for those times*.

> Julie processes text in a variety of ways. She matches the Table of Contents with the print headings of the text in each chapter to confirm the structure of information. Then she uses a colored marker to highlight key ideas. To memorize or compare, she locates sections in the text in which lists of causes, reasons, or explanations are provided. She checks the glossary for definitions. Then she uses the margin of the textbook or a notepad to add memory-enhancement cues to the text.

Effective time management divides text processing into phases: early, middle, and late. In the early phase of any assignment, the scholar identifies requirements and assembles materials, setting aside additional time for research-related reading. In the middle phase of the assignment, the scholar processes the text, allowing extra time for difficult reading and distributing the reading evenly over the time allotted. In the late phase, cramming for examinations or pounding out a term paper for a deadline, the scholar takes advantage of prior preparation, and does not frantically stay up all night at the expense of other responsibilities.

❖ Tactics for teachers to develop students' academic/survival strategies:

◆ Native culture: Remind students that as scholars they already know how to do well in class.
◆ Target culture: Provide cooperative tasks during class time that pair native and non-native speakers of English, and encourage assignments in groups so students can make friends with their classmates.
◆ Academic culture: Provide specific orientation to classroom operations and school rules, including an introduction to library procedures, support personnel, and research skills.
◆ Study skills: Include in-class test review and term paper draft editing; give students course credit for assembling class notes; provide outlines of class lectures for the purpose of note taking.
◆ Time management: Employ frequent reminders for longer assignments; require partial products such as notes from reading; call in students who do not perform well at midterm for extra supervision.

ESL and the Content Areas

With the increase of English learners in K–12 schools, school personnel recognize that these students need to keep up academically with their native–English-speaking peers while learning English. Two approaches, *content-based ESL* and *sheltered instruction* (or SDAIE), are used to connect ESL teaching with academic work in K–12 content areas such as mathematics, social studies, and science. The term *content-based ESL* is used less frequently in EFL contexts; if English is taught to help students master specialized subjects such as business and engineering, it is considered ESP (English for Special Purposes, also called English for Specific Purposes, or English for Science and Technology), with instruction usually taking place in the native language.

◆ **STRATEGY 5.7**: Combine English and content teaching

Content-Based Instruction in ESL

Content literacy is one of four main types of literacy, according to McKenna and Robinson (1997); the others are emergent literacy, functional literacy, and workplace literacy. Content literacy is "the ability to use reading and writing for the acquisition of new content in a given discipline" (McKenna & Robinson, 1997, p. 8). In content-based instruction (CBI) ESL classrooms, ESL educators, collaborating with content teachers, organize learning objectives around academic subjects in order to prepare students to master grade-level curricula as a supplement to the students' English class.

Content literacy is more than "having knowledge" in a particular discipline; it represents skills needed to acquire knowledge of content and make it easier for the student to read and write in the discipline. This literacy is content-specific; an individual who can read and write about science may not be able to do so in mathematics. However, being able to think clearly, understand key concepts, and express oneself are cognitive skills that do generalize across disciplines, so that efforts to promote content literacy in one subject can positively affect learning in other subjects.

CBI-ESL is currently one of the methods for English learners that helps them achieve some of the national standards. In the standards document developed by TESOL (1997) mentioned earlier, three standards determine whether EL students are able to use English to achieve academically in all content areas: (1) use of English to interact in the classroom; (2) use of English to obtain, process, construct, and provide subject matter information in spoken and written form; and (3) use of appropriate learning strategies to construct and apply academic knowledge.

CBI-ESL classes develop not only language proficiency but also content knowledge, cognitive strategies, and study skills. Teachers familiarize students with the difference in the style and structure of texts and the type of vocabulary featured in the particular discipline. Reference may be made to background knowledge that is restricted to that discipline (Addison, 1988; Gunderson, 1991), along with abstract, specialized, and difficult vocabulary.

CBI can be of great benefit if learners, content instructors, and language teachers can work together to provide comprehensible input to the learner, as well as design tasks that are both comprehensible and important. Systematic, planned instruction must present vocabulary, concepts, and structures that are required for mastery of the content (Snow, 1993). Whether an adjunct model—having the language teacher assist in content teaching by providing additional contact and support—(see Snow & Brinton, 1988) or a collaborative model—having the ESL teacher coteaching the content course—is chosen, providing English instruction coupled with CBI increases the likelihood of academic success.

Collaboration and Reciprocity

Is the collaboration between ESL and content instructors reciprocal? If ESL teachers teach content, the content teachers should include language development objectives along with content objectives. This is an important feature of SDAIE instruction. If this reciprocity is not the case, then CBI-ESL unfortunately positions the ESL teachers as adjunct content instructors, which leads instructors of other disciplines to believe that ESL is not a content domain in its own right. This attitude tends to undermine the professional status of ESL instructors.

Some content instructors resist including language development objectives along with discipline-based objectives, for a number of reasons. Some instructors deny that students need help in reading and writing to master the content, or they underestimate the literacy demands of the discipline. Other instructors may think that time spent on enhancing the reading and writing skills of the students infringes on content instruction time. Whatever the reasons, the content instructor who does promote content literacy is a more responsible and active partner for collaborative CBI-ESL (Kinsella, 1992).

One successful collaboration between a content instructor and an EFL educator took place in a Japanese college, using CBI in a team-teaching partnership that teaches the course "Introduction to History" in English. Miyazaki International College, located in Kyushu, is designed to graduate students whose problem-solving skills are useful in a global context. Toward this end, students learn to use such critical thinking tools as graphic organizers, compare-contrast essays, charts and illustrations, teacher-created fact cards, and a student-created fact card game. The small class size (4 to 20 students) and the high level of written English skills achieved by students in their previous high school study made this experiment possible. (Sagliano & Greenfield, 1998)

CBI-ESL and ESP are connected. Those instructors who can collaborate successfully with science and mathematics teachers in ESL can also teach ESP abroad. Medical schools and engineering programs in many countries are open to visiting educators who are able to prepare international students for the reading, writing, and vocabulary tasks required in specialized undergraduate and graduate programs. More about ESP is offered in Master and Brinton's (1998) compendium of activities and lesson plans; moreover, Duff (2001) presents an overview of the research needed to further understanding of research issues in ESP.

CBI-ESL: Lesson Planning

In CBI-ESL, the content to be taught, general instructional goals, and time available for instruction are negotiated with the content teacher. One important factor in the success of CBI-ESL is the ESL teacher's past experiences in teaching similar content or ability to transfer knowledge gained from teaching similar concepts in other disciplines.

Five types of lesson plans are commonly used in CBI-ESL (McKenna & Robinson, 1997). Table 5.5 describes the five lesson types in detail.

TESOL, Inc. has published a four-volume series (*Integrating the ESL Standards into Classroom Practice*, Agor, 2000; Irujo, 2000; Samway, 2000; and Smallwood, 2000), which shows TESOL standards incorporated into classroom practice, especially in the content areas.

❖ Tactics for teachers to develop students' content-based strategies:

- Develop a collaboration with content instructors that is two-way: Include language objectives if ESL includes assistance in learning in the content domain.
- Include a wide range of learning strategies.
- Build performance indicators into the collaboration that clearly assign credit to the CBI-ESL class for student success where appropriate.

Specially Designed Academic Instruction in English (SDAIE)

Many schools and teachers today use SDAIE to address the academic learning needs of English learners whose English is in an early developmental stage. SDAIE provides additional support to these students, rather than leaving them to "sink or swim" in a content class designed for native English-speakers. SDAIE combines SLA principles with teaching modifications to make a lesson understandable to students (Echevarria, Vogt, & Short, 2000)

TABLE 5.5 ◆ Types of Lesson Plans in CBI-ESL Reading

Lesson Plan Type	Directions to Teacher
Directed reading activity 　Advantages: 　　Flexible, purposeful 　Disadvantages: 　　May be too teacher-directed	Establish readiness for reading, relating to students' prior knowledge and preteaching vocabulary or specialized skills (maps or charts, etc.). Set purposes for reading (analyze goals and communicate these goals to students). Arrange for students to read silently. Discuss the reading. Extend students' understanding by using supplementary materials or by assigning a writing task.
Directed reading-thinking activity 　Advantages: 　　Emphasizes the reading-thinking connection 　　Encourages students to set own purposes 　Disadvantages: 　　Not well suited to new or unfamiliar material	Assist students to set purposes for reading; check students' prior knowledge, preteaching concepts if necessary; encourage students to predict content using cues. Facilitate reasoning as students read. Help students to test their predictions, locating and discussing bases for conclusions.
K-W-L (what students *Know*, *Want* to learn, and *Learn*) 　Advantages: 　　Activates prior knowledge 　　Establishes group purposes 　Disadvantages: 　　Not well suited to unfamiliar material	Brainstorm with students to bring out prior knowledge of the topic; then discuss, grouping ideas into subtopics. Select subtopics of interest based on what they need to know; have students write out their interests. Assess what was learned by the reading.
Explicit teaching 　Advantages: 　　Permits clear-cut, sequential planning 　Disadvantages: 　　May encourage overreliance on teacher for direction 　　May avoid literacy activities when planning	Create readiness by positive set and by communicating objectives clearly. Teach concepts directly, checking for understanding, reteaching if needed. Provide opportunities for guided and independent practice.
Listen-read-discuss 　Advantages: 　　Effective with low-ability readers 　Disadvantages: 　　Does not appear to improve actual reading skills 　　May encourage overreliance on teacher for direction 　　Highly teacher-directed	Present complete text through lecture and demonstration. Give students a chance to read the material silently. Conduct a discussion of the selection.

Source: McKenna & Robinson, 1997.

The distinction between SDAIE and CBI-ESL is that SDAIE features content instruction taught by content-area teachers (science, history, mathematics) with English-language support. In contrast, CBI-ESL is taught by ESL teachers using content-area materials as texts. SDAIE helps English learners to learn grade-appropriate content featuring "academic" English. In addition, they are exposed to the academic culture of the school, including established routines of turn taking and participation.

SDAIE teachers not only address the content objectives of the discipline they teach but also support students' academic English by the use of visuals, hands-on props and manipulatives, and cooperative learning. However, the use of such materials may inadvertently be misused to water down content, a practice that decreases the information available to students rather than increasing their ability to comprehend complex content. SDAIE instructional techniques help students to master demanding content areas without overly simplifying the curriculum. SDAIE teachers also modify their oral teaching to make themselves more understandable to English learners.

SDAIE: Determining Content, Language, and Learning Strategy Objectives. An SDAIE teacher incorporates tasks in the content area and language that take into account the vocabulary of the discipline. In reviewing the language objectives, the teacher can keep the following questions in mind: (1) What are the key concepts to demonstrate and illustrate? (2) What structures and discourse of the discipline are included in the language objectives? (3) Are all four language modes—listening, speaking, reading, writing—included in planning? Of course, SDAIE lessons should also include learning strategy objectives, as shown in Table 5.6.

SDAIE: Modifying Instructional Materials and Activities. The teacher selects, modifies, and organizes text material to accommodate the needs of English learners. In modifying text, the goal is to improve comprehensibility through such means as providing study guides or defining new content vocabulary by showing vocabulary pictorially (Brinton, Snow, & Wesche, 1989). Focus questions or concept maps serve as advance organizers. Selected passages may be tape-recorded for students to listen to as they read along in the text. These adaptations increase readability. As students' language proficiency increases, so should the complexity of their reading material. The goal is for students to progress toward the ability to work with unmodified texts (Richard-Amato & Snow, 1992).

Student learning activities should develop interactive language but not disadvantage an English learner. Collaborative, problem-solving teams include member roles that provide a variety of input and output modalities to balance the English skills and nonverbal talents of students. English learners can benefit from the use of media, realia, science equipment, diagrams, models, experiments, manipulatives, and other modalities that make language more comprehensible.

SDAIE: Increasing Teacher Understandability. Teachers must ensure that students understand what is said in the classroom. Teachers in SDAIE classrooms devote particular attention to four communication strategies: (1) language contextualization, (2) teacher's speech modification, (3) use of paraphrase and repetition, and (4) use of clarification checks.

TABLE 5.6 • Rain Forest Unit: Content, Language, and Learning Strategy Objectives

Science

To name four layers of the rain forest and distinguish the different species that live in the different layers

To compare life cycles of these species for similarities and differences

To study the effect of the surrounding environment on various animals' life cycles

Language

To predict what will happen in the story "The Great Kapok Tree" by looking at the pictures

To explain why the Great Kapok tree was so special

To read aloud parts of the story using appropriate voices to represent characters

To read information from a nonfiction source and compare it with information gained from the story

To recognize vocabulary from the story and pronounce it correctly when reading to a peer

Learning Strategy

To work cooperatively with a learning group

To keep a personal vocabulary "new word" book

To create a comparison chart for information gained from the story and nonfiction sources

Language contextualization means focusing teaching on the context of the immediate task, augmenting vocabulary with gestures, pictures, realia, and so on to convey instructions or key words and concepts. This approach provides a rich visual and/or kinesthetic environment (e.g., through drama and skits). Verbal markers are used to organize the lesson, such as "note this" to denote importance, or "now," "first," "second," and "last" to mark a sequence. To help with directions, teachers can determine the ten most frequently used verbal markers and teach these through mini-TPR-type lessons. The teacher might also learn how to say simple directions in the students' language(s).

Teacher's speech modification means adjusting speech from the customary native speech patterns. This takes place at many linguistic levels: phonological (precise articulation); syntactic (shorter sentences, with subject-verb-object word order); semantic (more concrete, basic vocabulary, with fewer idioms); pragmatic (frequent and longer pauses; slower delivery; and exaggerated intonation, especially placing more stress on important new concepts); and discourse (self-repetition; main idea easily recognized and supporting information following immediately). Teachers in SDAIE classrooms also talk less in the classroom, encouraging students to talk.

Use of repetition and paraphrase involves verbal repetition (for example, using the same type of directions throughout various lessons); and organizational repetition (lessons that occur at specific times, lessons with clearly marked verbal and nonverbal boundaries, such as "Now it's time to . . . ,") or the use of location or materials change (Wong-Fillmore, 1985). Concepts are presented numerous times through various means. Elaboration, in which the teacher supplies redundant information through repetition and paraphrase, may prove effective (Nunan, 1991).

Clarification checks are strategies to monitor listening and reading comprehension at intervals to give the teacher a sense of the students' ability to understand. Teachers may need to rephrase questions and information. The teacher might pause to ask a question requiring a simple response, such as, "Show me how you are going to begin your work," or ask individual students to restate the instruction using their own words. The teacher may also teach students to express their need for clarification by accepting questions that are written on index cards (Díaz-Rico, 1991).

Skilled questioning using a linguistic hierarchy of question types helps teachers to ascertain students' understanding. For students in the "silent period," questions elicit a nonverbal response—a head movement, pointing, or manipulation of materials. Once students begin to speak, they can choose the correct word or phrase to demonstrate understanding of either/or questions: "Is the water evaporating or condensing?" "Did explorers come to the Americas from Europe or Asia?" Once students are more comfortable in producing language, *wh-* questions are used: "What is happening to the water?" "Which countries sent explorers to the Americas?" "What was the purpose of their exploration?" (Díaz-Rico & Weed, 2002).

Although SDAIE teaching involves presentation of subject matter in English, opportunities are available throughout the lesson for students to clarify their understanding using their primary language, supplemented whenever possible by primary-language resources (print, electronic, personnel) that can help students with key concepts.

The scope of this book does not permit an exhaustive discussion of SDAIE. For an excellent, in-depth treatment refer to *Making Content Comprehensible for English Language learners: The SIOP Model* (Echevarria, Vogt, & Short, 2000).

❖ Tactics for teachers using SDAIE strategies:

- Teach content and language with two modalities if possible; for example, supplement listening with pictures.
- Cover content with as much richness and depth as possible, without watering down the curriculum or slowing the pace.
- Strive to give students comprehensible input.

Computer-Assisted Language Learning/ Computer-Mediated Communication

Computer-assisted instruction (CAI) has been available for classroom use since the earliest days of word processing (late 1970s). Tutoring programs soon followed. The early 1980s saw the advent of commercially available instructional software, in which multiple-choice answer formats enabled the individual user to attempt repeated answers and receive error feedback without public embarrassment. Computer-assisted language learning (CALL) applied to English learning soon moved beyond skill drills into more innovative applications (Egbert & Hanson-Smith, 1999). Computer-mediated communication (CMC) is a term that describes the role of computers in allowing people to communicate virtually (see Herring, 1996).

- **STRATEGY 5.8**: Use computers to assist language learning

Language classrooms have been transformed through multimedia computing and the Internet. The digital revolution is changing the way people spend their free time—playing video and computer games, chatting on the Internet, conducting business transactions, and much more—and also changing the way people learn. From home, people can access educational experiences that formerly required attending classes (Peabody, 2001). CALL has the potential to extend learning far beyond the four walls of the classroom. Websites offer lesson plans, quizzes, chat rooms, and bulletin boards that allow the learner to sample English idioms, prepare for standardized tests, or connect with English learners in other parts of the world. Many language teachers benefit from an Internet hookup in the classroom or language laboratory.

Professional training in CALL for language educators maximizes the benefit to students. This training should provide an introduction to the issues in the field of CALL/CMC, including ways in which students can interact with others meaningfully, become involved with authentic tasks, and maximize the feeling of self-directed learning. It is important that educators learn fundamental principles of computer use within CALL/CMC so that language acquisition theory is fully integrated.

CALL and Second-Language Acquisition

SLA theory meshes with CALL in *CALL Environments* (Egbert & Hanson-Smith, 1999), a general introductory text in this field. Various authors review the contribution of Vygotsky to classroom interaction theory; address the physical design of the classroom to facilitate student interaction; provide an overview of language-learning tasks; and survey a variety of software and hardware configurations, noting their uses, strengths, and weaknesses. The book also features a chapter on computer-based language assessment, as well as one on the assessment of the computer-assisted environment itself. It is important that CALL include discussion of pedagogical issues, because the earliest uses of the computer did not foster constructivist pedagogy (cf. Perkins, 1992).

Laboratory Skills.   Hands-on laboratory skills are necessary in addition to a general introduction to CALL to demonstrate the instructional and communicative use of the Internet, CD-ROM–based software, and other CMC tools. Many such courses include an introduction to audio and video production using computers, although in the process it is probably true that older, noncomputer-based tools of multimedia production are falling by the wayside (see Herrell, 2000, pp. 134–138 for tips on the use of a variety of multimedia formats, including camcorder and overhead projector). Some such courses introduce computer-managed instruction (CMI) techniques such as the use of programs that manage students' grades and perform database management.

In contrast and perhaps supplementary to Egbert and Hanson-Smith's overview of CALL, Boswood's *New Ways of Using Computers in Language Teaching* (1997), tends to be somewhat miscellaneous, in that teachers who are working in all kinds of situations have contributed reports of activities that involve computers in language acquisition. The virtue of this approach is the emphasis on teaching methodologies and lesson planning, rather than on the technology per se, and the wealth of suggestions across a wide range of contexts, both ESL and EFL.

Strategic CALL.   CALL supports strategic language learning. For example, word processing supports the formal writing process by allowing students to organize, draft, revise, edit, and even publish their work electronically. They can write informal e-mails with "keypals" in different areas of the world or use writing-based "chat" rooms online in real time (Warschauer, 1995). Students can develop oral skills by using presentation or authoring software to create professional-looking oral presentations, and they can use both aural and oral skills in Web-enabled telephone conversations.

Both software programs and online resources are used in classrooms involved in CALL to help students achieve their language-learning goals. Software programs include traditional drill-and-practice programs that focus on vocabulary or discrete grammar points; tutorials; games; simulations that present students with real-life situations in the language and culture they are learning; productivity tools, such as word processing, databases, spreadsheets, graphics, and desktop publishing (DTP); and presentation or authoring programs. Material from encyclopedias and even the *National Geographic* are available on CD-ROMs.

Instant communication afforded through the Internet connects students with other parts of the world, with speakers of English, and with rich sources of information. The World Wide Web delivers authentic materials including texts, images, sound recording, video clips, virtual reality worlds, and dynamic interactive presentations. Streaming audio and video connect students with native speakers and authentic audiovisual materials by virtually transporting the target-language environment to the second-language classroom. Students can listen to live radio stations from around the world or hear prerecorded broadcasts of music, news, sports, and weather (see Media Info at http://emedia1.mediainfo.com/emedia/ and Leloup & Ponterio [2000]). Search

Computers can be used in a dual language immersion setting for second language acquisition.

engines (e.g., Yahoo, Altavista, Excite) help the student find authentic materials on classroom, group, or individual research topics.

CALL Supports Learner Autonomy.   The computer is a powerful learning tool that requires the teacher to organize, plan, teach, and monitor. Egbert and Hanson-Smith (1999) found that computer technology can provide students with the means to control their own learning, to construct meaning, and to evaluate and monitor their own performance.

> Abdel uses the Internet in the language-learning lab to research current events and cultural topics for a conversation class at the International Extension Program (IEP). He also converses with native speakers who are paired with class members via e-mail. To practice pronunciation, he uses software that enables him to click on a word or sentence to hear it repeatedly, look up a meaning, see a related picture or video clip and/or read a related text, listen to a sentence, compare his voice to a computer model of the correct response, and have the computer judge the accuracy of his attempts.

Computer-Mediated Communication.   Computer-mediated communication (CMC) is a new field in which publications are burgeoning (see Murray [2000] for an overview of research in the field). Lam (2000) recounted teenage English users' construction of virtual identities; Kamhi-Stein (2000) described the use of peer-mediated feedback on writing; and Nunan (1999) reported on the use of the computer for graduate study. Articles have appeared on hypertext poetics, visual rhetoric, cyberspace aesthetics, hyperrhetoric, electronic literacy, metamedia literacy, iconology, teletheory, hybrid literacies, and design discourse (see Handa [2001] for a selected bibliography of digital literacy and rhetoric). English is fast becoming fused to an iconic or visually enhanced version of itself, as the sociology of knowledge undergoes a concomitant rapid transformation. It is not clear at this time in what direction the volatile mix of English as an international language and CMC will lead.

CALL teachers help students carefully plan and organize learning experiences, rehearse useful language, and understand the physical operation of the Internet. For a well-organized, highly readable guide to using the computer in the language classroom, see *Internet for English Teaching* (Warschauer, Shetzer, & Meloni, 2000).

Technological Literacy.   Technological literacy involves both technology and CALL. Charp (1996) stated, "literacy goes beyond the basic skills of reading, writing, and arithmetic and includes computer and other technology-related skills in the context of the workplace" (p. 6). Hansen (2000) defined technological literacy as "a personal ability to adopt, adapt, or invent proper technological tools in an information society to positively affect his or her life, community, and environment" (p. 31). More than five million jobs added to the workforce since 1993 require professional, management, or technical skills (Charp, 1996). As people recognize its importance, technological literacy will become a growing field, standing as it does at the intersection of ESP, CALL/CMC, and Vocational ESL (VESL)/workplace ESL.

❖ Tactics for teachers using CALL to enhance students' SLA:

- Use CALL not as an end in itself but as a means to enhance other learning strategies.
- Expose students to a variety of CALL modes of interaction for reading, listening, speaking, writing, and critical thinking.
- Encourage students to work collaboratively with others to see CALL as a group activity that encourages face-to-face language use.

Equipped with strategies for language learning and use as well as academic and survival skills, students can take more responsibility for improving both their language abilities and their learning processes. Teachers who directly teach strategies will see students gain in language proficiency and self-confidence. Teachers can also encourage students to share their favorite strategies for accomplishing certain tasks during class. As students learn how to succeed with second-language learning, they gain the tools they need to become lifelong learners.

Learning Processes That Build on the First Language

According to Plato, the only knowledge humans acquire is that which they already learned in the pure world of Forms. If this were true, then teachers would be in the business of teaching people what they already know! In a sense, this is exactly what happens in classrooms. Students learn best when they already know something about the subject matter and can draw from this prior knowledge. The most profound prior knowledge that English learners possess is knowledge *of* their first language and knowledge *in* their first language. This is, as Bourdieu puts it, their "cultural capital." This is the capital that teachers build on in dual-language acquisition. This chapter discusses the learning processes—how people learn to read, write, listen, and speak in a second language—that make academic success possible.

❖ **MEGASTRATEGY 6:** Teach skills systematically, building on primary-language skills

Vygotsky believed that children learn to engage in higher-level thinking by learning first how to communicate (including speaking, listening, writing, and reading). The more that students can use language in the classroom environment, the more they will learn how to think. Writing and reading, like speech, are social acts. This means that the natural sociability of children in their first language is the foundation for their intellectual development. This chapter presents ways in which literacy and oracy develop within a social context and are enhanced by strategic teaching, based on a foundation of how the mind functions. Imaginative ways of using literacy and oracy are addressed in Chapter 7.

Literacy and Power

Whose purposes does literacy serve? One cannot "simply" teach English learners to read, write, speak, listen, or think. Learners must select and acquire those aspects of the target language and culture that offer the most reward for their investment of time and energy and provide them with the basis for transforming their lives, rather than simply finding a place in the existing social order (Giroux & McLaren, 1986).

Unfortunately, too often English learners' best interests are sacrificed in the call for mastery of a common national language, accompanied by the call for statistics to show that this task is being successfully accomplished. Gramsci (1971) identified this as a movement toward *hegemony* (defined as the attempt by the dominant class to persuade the subordinated classes to act in the interests of the dominant class). When

English learners are led to believe that only literacy in English is socially useful and acceptable—and are then given literacy education that emphasizes narrow decoding skills at the expense of their reading and writing about the world as they see it—the literacy that they acquire, often imperfectly, serves the interests of others.

Macedo cautioned that educators of English learners must pay greater attention to sociocultural context in order for literacy to be transformational:

> I want to propose that the attempt to institute proper and more effective methods of educating non-English-speaking students cannot be reduced to issues of language but rests on a full understanding of the ideological elements that generate and sustain linguistic, racial, and sex discrimination. (1994, p. 126)

During the entire process of teaching reading, educators who also function as sensitive ethnographers and "child watchers" take note of what reading "lights a fire" in the learners and take care to balance students' receptive and productive skills within a learning environment that respects culture, human interests, and imagination.

Reading Processes

Reading has become an essential skill. Adults who cannot read are hampered when shopping for groceries, filling out applications for work, or obtaining a driver's license. Children who do not learn to read in elementary school enter secondary education as severe underachievers and are at risk for dropping out. Research has shown that English learners often learn to read by becoming efficient "word callers" (Goldenberg, 1992) but may fail to attain comprehension or higher-order thinking skills. How can teachers encourage English learners to acquire skills that will result in academic achievement and an enjoyment of reading?

Reading has become an arena of conflict between advocates of literature-based, whole-language approaches and supporters of bottom-up phonics (see Taylor, 1988; and Wolfe & Poynor, 2001 for a discussion of the politics of reading instruction). Politics aside, this chapter examines various approaches to reading, along with the integration of reading with writing, listening, and speaking. More complete instruction in reading pedagogy can be found in Peregoy and Boyle's *Reading, Writing, and Learning in ESL* (2001); and Hadaway, Vardell, and Young's *Literature-Based Instruction with English Language Learners, K–12* (2002).

♦ **STRATEGY 6.1:** Teach reading in a way that builds interest, information acquisition, and lifelong literacy

Purposes for Reading

During the advent of the era of television, critics asked, "Is reading dead?" Again, in the advent of the Internet, people are asking the same question, as they see young people inundated with images and sounds that flout classic print conventions. At the same time, however, more individuals are expected to be literate than ever before, as employment in modern technology requires advanced reading and writing skills. English-language cultures, for a variety of reasons, are not the most literate *per capita*; Japan, for example, has almost 100 percent literacy (Japan Culture Institute, 1978).

However, in the midst of calls for enhanced workplace literacy (which are often reminiscent of the survival adult education curriculum), McLaren (1995) has called for a more comprehensive approach to literacy, one that teaches a critical stance, especially toward the media. He observed that too often, "media literacies" (p. 100) (e.g., print, radio, television, film) create simulations in which human dreams and desires are artificially adjusted to fit within the narrow parameters of a consuming citizenry. McLaren called for media studies to be a central focus of school curricula, lest learners divest themselves of their specific culture in the attempt to gain access to the social and economic resources they see displayed before them in mass media marketing, the "mall culture" (Shepard, 2001, p. 603). This puts into perspective the impulse to impose upon learners a functional literacy that serves the purpose of the school but perhaps not the purpose of the individual (see Barton, Hamilton, & Ivanič, 2000).

The search for reading strategies that fit the generic learner quickly runs afoul not only of current calls for situated literacy but also of the impossibility of finding a "best" method (see Prabhu, 1990). Certainly, contextual and instructional variation complicates matters. Older learners need different reading instruction than do children, learners' goals deviate from official policy mandates, and variety in the target language makes even the choice of reading materials problematic. In spite of these shortcomings, it is clear that *some* instruction in reading is better than *no* instruction in reading. This foundation in reading instruction can be applied situationally and experimentally until some wisdom is reached about best practices for the particular context and learners.

Standards-Based Reading Instruction

New reading basals in the market reflect the current insistence on standards-based instruction. For example, *Launch into Reading, Level I* (Heinle & Heinle), an ESL reading series, specifically refers to the particular California English Language Development standard to which each lesson is connected. Lesson 13 "'Flowers' (A Poem by E. Greenfield)" addresses Reading 6, 3.4, "Define how tone or meaning is conveyed in poetry." Follow-up exercises ask students to use a continuum scale to rank five "ways you can learn about people's feelings and ideas" (short story, poem, magazine or newspaper article, movie or television program, and conversation), which addresses Reading 2, 2.7 "Interpret information from diagrams and charts" (Heinle & Heinle, 2002a).

Later in the lesson, students are asked to find the rhyming words in the poem "Flowers" (Reading 1, 1.6, "Create and state a series of rhyming words") and then work with a partner to interpret a poem (Writing 6, 2.4, "Write responses to literature: Organize the interpretation around several clear ideas, premises or images"). All teaching materials, the teacher's resource book, the student workbook, and the student reading book contain explicit references to standards on each page. The assessment guide (Heinle & Heinle, 2002b) contains a Language Proficiency Assessment chart, with a summary of the standards across three levels of each of the six domains (Oral Reading, Reading Comprehension, Vocabulary, Spelling, Conventions, and Writing).

High Points from Hampton-Brown (Schifini, Short, & Tinajero, 2002) is an excellent ESL series, complete with teaching tips designed to facilitate comprehensible input, decodable small books, learning strategies for enhancing cognitive academic language, ways to increase reading fluency, writing support for students with non-Roman alphabets, and cultural tips. The introductory material in the teacher's edition (p. 12) states that curriculum standards provided the foundation for the design of the book. The texts themselves do not contain ESL standards, however, leaving the integration of standards and instruction to a separate supplemental document.

Emergent Literacy

When children—or adolescents or adults, for that matter—are first learning to read, they are in the stage of *emergent literacy*. This can be defined as "the reading and writing behaviors that precede and develop into conventional literacy" (Sulzby, 1986, p. 84). Educators now realize that most "nonreaders" actually have had much exposure to print in the culture at large and may have engaged in various informal kinds of reading. Therefore, it is the teacher's job to build on these nascent skills so that these students can "grow into reading."

Emergent literacy involves a combination of components. Emergent readers must learn to do the following tasks:

- Draw upon their prior knowledge of the world to connect the printed word with its semiotic meaning. For example, most preschool children understand that a red octagonal sign at a street corner means "stop."
- Enhance their phonemic awareness by coming to understand that sounds correspond to symbols.
- Recognize a set of sight words that are frequently used in English but may not be phonetically predictable (*the* is not "ta-ha-ay").
- Acquire reading behaviors, such as handling books, borrowing and returning books to the class library, and reading for enjoyment.
- Participate in a culture of reading, sharing their pleasure in reading with others and working in the company of others to acquire meaning from books.

Most people learn new skills in an integrated way, starting from the need to learn for some purpose. May and Rizzardi (2002) use the example of a child learning to ride a bicycle. She does not spend thirty days practicing how to pedal, jumping on and off the seat twenty times, and then trying to ride; at a certain point she just gets on the bike and goes, wobbling and falling at times, but riding. The joy of the first ride is exhilarating. In a similar way, we do not teach children to speak by having them repeat syllables until they can put together a whole word. Children speak in holophrastic utterances, because they mean to communicate. Reading is a cognitive activity that must be learned in a brain-compatible way, as an organized, meaningful event.

Why? Because humans like stories.

". . . we are story-making animals. . . . something deep within us impels us to cherish the product of the writer. . . . Given a modicum of reading skill, some free time, and accessibility to literary materials, people read . . . not every person, but most. People read in cramped bunks under the Arctic ice. They read 40,000 feet above the earth. They read as they have their hair cut and dried, and while they wait for the dentist. People read in bed, in the bath tub, and occasionally, sitting upright in a chair. We are literature-creating and literature consuming animals. (Carlsen, 1974, p. 24)

Most learners read and write because they see others doing it—reading directions, newspapers, or road signs for information, or notes they have written to themselves to jog their memory, or novels just to pass the time. However, it is important to remember that reading is optional to human life. Only within the last five hundred years have masses of people been reading, and people were living on earth for eons before reading was invented. Many English learners do not see their families reading or writing. Therefore, it takes a leap of imagination for them to see themselves as readers. It is important, then, for the classroom as a community to be a place in which reading is an everyday, enjoyable feature. This environment socializes students into a culture of literacy.

Until recently, ESL teaching for students at the stage of emergent literacy involved direct teaching of English vocabulary and sentence syntax, particularly focusing on oral English as a necessary prerequisite to introducing written forms (Hudelson, 1984). With the advent of a communicative model of SLA, however, instructional approaches that integrate language, reading, and writing skills have gained increasing favor as a means of promoting emergent biliteracy (Abramson, Seda, & Johnson, 1990). Oral and written language are now seen as interactional, and writing is seen as an important means of mediating meaning (Sulzby, 1986).

> By creating shared contexts, mediating students' learning through ongoing literacy activities, providing vocabulary, modeling language and literacy behaviors such as reading and writing, encouraging peer interactions, relating to students' cultural background and according high status to LEP students' first language, teachers can successfully develop language and literacy skills in multilingual classrooms. (Abramson et al., 1990, p. 72)

Teachers can draw upon students' everyday activities to help them to use the tools of literacy for their own purposes. Vygotsky commented that children can draw speech as well as objects. From their drawings, students' interests become evident, and teachers who converse with students can find natural ways to introduce written words into their stories. Finding books that correspond to children's natural interactions while playing also helps students to feel that literacy supports their interests. One teacher overheard two children playing with a caterpillar and as a result read Eric Carle's *The Hungry Caterpillar* to the class (Britsch, 1993). A context of shared enjoyment is the key to making literacy an everyday part of life.

Language Experience Approach

The language experience approach (LEA) encourages students to describe events in their own words, which the teacher writes down and reads back so that students can eventually read the text for themselves. This process develops language by connecting students to their own experiences and activities. LEA reinforces the notion that sounds can be transcribed into specific symbols and that those symbols can then be used to re-create ideas. Because students provide their own phrases and sentences, they find the text relevant and interesting, and generally have little trouble reading it. The texts they create can be used for specific lessons on vocabulary, grammar, writing conventions, structure, and more. Heald-Taylor (1986) calls these texts "individual dictated stories" and comments, "Once students recognize that you accept their initial oral attempts, their trust and self-esteem grows, which gives them confidence in composing extended oral stories" (p. 19).

The use of stories is probably the most important means by which teachers can develop oral and written language in young children. Stories come naturally to children, and in the telling and retelling they gain vocabulary enrichment, sensitivity to audience, and mastery over oral language. The same holds true for written stories as they learn to read.

> The sounds of children bathed in language—in and out of school—are not those of structured language lessons; no one is repeating sentences like "This my pencil." Instead, children create their own meanings for the drawings they design, the stories they invent, and the ideas that grow out of the many experiences they have . . . child-oriented classrooms lack drill-like, repetitive language, but they do have a rhythm and stability that enable children to repeat—or more accurately, replay—what they are learning in the context of activities that make human sense. A word may be repeated 20 times or more, not in the senseless context of an isolated sentence, but in a range of contexts: a poem, a child-created song of drama, a caption for a drawing, a chant, a story that children beg to hear again, a game that a child plays and replays with friends, or a conversation with children or the teacher. (Genishi, 1988, p. 22)

Young children will enjoy making and reading their own Big Books. The teacher prints the words of a book with predictable text that students will be reading that week onto large sheets of manila paper. These sheets are assembled in order but not attached. After reading the story in the original book aloud, the teacher reads the same story as individual sentences in the Big Book. Each page of the Big Book is given to a child to illustrate. The books can be bound with large metal rings or cord, with the binding edge reinforced with masking tape. A reading stand made of plywood can be kept in a corner so that students can rest the book on the stand as they read (Heald-Taylor, 1987). This gives students a sense of ownership.

Direct Teaching of Reading

Despite the success of approaches based on the social construction of knowledge, a generation of students is being taught how to read through a series of controlled, behaviorally based lessons. Such programs as Reading Mastery, Open Court, and Direct Instruction employ teacher-centered methods in step-by-step curricula that follow highly structured, interactive scripts (Groves, 2001). Reading Mastery requires students to be grouped in precisely measured skill levels, and Open Court expects teachers to follow a script verbatim day by day to reinforce skills (Vega, 2000). Only time will tell if the students taught in this manner learn to read for academics and for enjoyment. Groves (2001) made the point that gifted students are not taught in such a prescriptive manner. It may be that being taught to read in such a prescriptive manner is yet another marker of social class in America.

❖ **Tactics for fostering emergent literacy in children (from Gunning, 1996):**

- Provide an accessible, appealing literacy environment with attractive reading and writing materials.
- Include in classroom reading materials extra copies of books the teacher has read aloud, books by the same author, commercial books, student-written books, comic or cartoon books (with words), magazines, encyclopedias, and age-appropriate bilingual dictionaries.
- Encourage children to role-play or play-act reading and writing activities.
- Incorporate shared book experiences using big books or enlarged text.
- Follow up shared reading with independent reading, small-group review of the big book, or work with language skills such as phonics.
- Bolster reading with chanting or singing based on reading the lyrics together.

Emergent literacy for adolescents and adults is a challenge. Many people who have never learned to read have internalized a sense of shame, stemming from a background that precluded schooling or from a deep sense of failure at having attended school with a poor outcome. Many need to experience immediate success. Collecting words from environmental print and helping students to decode it sometimes reassures the nonreaders that they can read. Freire's approach was designed for programs of adult literacy in the native language (see Chapter 2).

The Basics of Learning to Read

Within the social context of shared enjoyment among a group of readers, there are four important facets of learning to read: skill with print, prior knowledge, comprehension, and seeking meaning (Barr & Johnson, 1997). When these four elements are present, it is more likely that reading will take place (see Figure 6.1).

Skill with print involves understanding that the printed text contains words carrying meaning and that printed words correspond to spoken language. Often prereaders connect meaning with text in signs and advertising, but they may be engaged in logographic reading without understanding the alphabetic principle of sound-letter correspondence. Reading begins when the emergent reader matches specific letters to

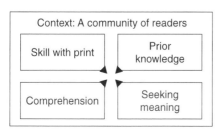

FIGURE 6.1 ◆ **Four facets of learning to read within a community of readers.**

Source: Barr & Johnson, 1997.

spoken sounds and begins to look for recognizable words or parts of words in text. Skill with print comprises ten concepts:

- ◆ Language is divided into words.
- ◆ Words can be written down.
- ◆ Space separates written words.
- ◆ Letters make words, and words make sentences.
- ◆ Sentences begin with capital letters.
- ◆ Sentences end with punctuation.
- ◆ A book is read from front to back.
- ◆ Reading goes left to right and top to bottom.
- ◆ Words, not pictures, are read.
- ◆ A book has a title, an author, and sometimes an illustrator. (Gunning, 1996)

In a print-rich environment, children see print wherever they turn (see Box 6.1).

Prior Knowledge that Is Useful for Reading.   Word knowledge (vocabulary) is the chief hurdle faced by English learners, because reading a word successfully depends on knowing the word in the first place (Tikunoff, 1988). Beyond vocabulary are the experience and understanding of situational context that help make sense of the world.

BOX 6.1
❖ Ideas for a Print-Rich Environment

A rich literacy environment presents ample opportunities for reading:

- ◆ Bulletin boards with words and pictures
- ◆ Aquariums and terrariums labeled with the names of their inhabitants
- ◆ Calendar with children's birthdays and other important events
- ◆ Displays of students' stories and booklets
- ◆ Student-run post office
- ◆ Library corner with book displays
- ◆ Labels on objects in several languages
- ◆ Magnetic letters, printing sets, typewriter, computers available
- ◆ Picture dictionaries, both commercial and student-made
- ◆ Listening centers with audiotaped books for read-along
- ◆ Order blanks, notepads, shopping lists at play centers

Source: Gunning, 1996, pp. 26–28.

- ◆ Menus available from restaurants
- ◆ Advertising flyers to cut and paste
- ◆ Weekly words collected on hanger "mobiles"
- ◆ "Living" bulletin board that accumulates evidence of the week's learning

Source: Lipton & Hubble, 1997.

- ◆ Displays around the classroom can include different scripts and languages, other alphabets and number systems. This can help to position bilingual pupils in the role of "expert" as they share their knowledge with the class.
- ◆ Labels around the room in the bilingual child's primary language can help students feel that the classroom is hospitable to diversity.
- ◆ A display of appropriate books other than English might be featured, accompanied with language tapes and pictures of a country in which that language is spoken.

Source: Morgan, 1992.

Once students start to read, vocabulary acquisition accelerates, because general comprehension of a text allows readers to predict and infer meaning of unknown words they encounter. The teacher's job is to help students develop background knowledge by the use of other books, oral discussion, exposure to media, or use of pictures or other visual prompts combined with text in order to build schemata, that is, construct a framework of concepts that show the relationships of old and new learning and how they are connected.

Reading Comprehension.   *Comprehension* is the key to meaning. Readers generally form some initial hypothesis about the content or main idea of a book or a reading passage based upon their expectations, title, first sentence, previous knowledge of genre, or other clues. Reading further, the reader modifies the initial prediction (Gunning, 1996). Getting the gist of a reading passage is the most important concept a reader can develop, because getting the main idea makes further reading more purposeful, facilitates recall, and helps to make sense of the supporting details.

Sight Words and Phonics.   Using *sight words*, the learner relies on visual memory to match sound with writing. Using *phonics*, the learner explicitly constructs the sound-symbol connection. Each of these techniques has its place in learning basic words. Lists of sight words can be obtained from reading texts. These include frequently used words with unpredictable spelling such as *the, might, could*, etc. Phonics can be taught using the synthetic method (bottom-up), with students first learning phonemes in isolation, then learning to blend them, and finally seeing them in the context of words. Or students can learn using the analytic method, beginning with contrasting words that contain the target phonemes and then hearing classmates generate similar words. The analytic method is illustrated in Box 6.2.

BOX 6.2
❖ Teaching Reading via the Analytic Method of Phonics

Tactics for teaching via the analytic method of phonics:

1. Planning: Make a list of easy words that include the target phonic element, for example the digraph *sh*: *cash*, *crash*, *mash*, *dish*, *fish*, and so forth. Write simple, meaningful sentences for each one, or a little story if possible that contains the words. Find pages in a common reading book that have these or other *sh-* words, including *-sh* as a final sound.

2. Teaching: Read the sentences aloud to the students, in a smooth and informal fashion. Have the students echo-read the sentences, repeating after the teacher, then repeating each underlined target word after the teacher, looking to see what sound the words have in common.

3. Guided practice: Students each make the target sound and look again at the letters that make the sound. Have students say other words with the same sound. Students choral-read the sentences and then take turns reading them aloud.

Source: May & Rizzardi, 2002, p. 177.

Phonemic Awareness.   Phonemic awareness has been found to be an important precursor to learning to read. Phonemic awareness, "the insight that every spoken word is made up of a sequence of phonemes" (California Department of Education, 1999b, p. 278), is considered by many to be a prerequisite for learning to read (Tunmer & Nesdale, 1985). Once children grasp the principles that words are made of phonemes represented by letters, they can benefit from phonics instruction (Tompkins, 1997).

Pre-Reading Activities.   In a typical bottom-up reading approach designed for English-speakers, prereading activities help to develop visual discrimination, including such tasks as matching pictures and patterns, sequencing story cards in a meaningful order, matching uppercase letters to lowercase letters. Teaching letters phonetically takes place in a sequence. First, alphabet cards introduce the name of each consonant letter and the sound it makes. Matching objects and pictures to letters helps learners to identify initial sounds. (Ending sounds can be treated in a similar way.) Then short vowels are introduced, usually in the order *a, i, o, u,* and *e*; next come the short vowels blended with consonants. Sight words (those that do not conform to phonetic rules—about 10 percent of English written words) are memorized. Simple stories featuring short vowels help to create early success. Long vowels and vowel blends are taught next, followed by digraphs (consonants which together make a single sound, like "th").

Drawbacks of Structural Approaches.   However, reading based on phonetic awareness may not be the best approach for English learners (Flood, Lapp, Tinajero, & Hurley, 1997). Hamayan (1994) cites four reasons why structural (phonics-based and grammar-based) approaches fail to meet the needs of preliterate English learners: (1) they do not meet the learner's need to acquire an understanding of the functional aspects of literacy; (2) literacy is forced to emerge in an unnatural way and in an artificial form; (3) a focus on form without a functional context makes learning abstract, meaningless, and difficult; and (4) literacy becomes a boring chore.

Emerging Sound/Symbol Awareness.   Written English is based on the alphabetic principle, and children do need to understand that sounds correspond to letters. Teachers of English learners are encouraged to provide students with rich language experiences, including word play, which lead them to understand sound-symbol correspondences. During and after read-alouds, for example, teachers point out specific sound and letter patterns that occurred in the texts. According to Peregoy and Boyle (2001), specific instruction in sound-symbol correspondence emerges best through students' own writing. Their invented or temporary spelling represents "an important step on the way to conventional spelling while providing individualized phonics practice that will assist both reading and writing development" (p. 153).

Strategies for Making Meaning.   When attempting a sentence with an unknown word, different readers use distinct strategies. One type of reader uses *semantic knowledge*. If the sentence reads, "Joey pushed open the door of the haunted . . ." that reader might guess that the next word is not *hose,* because the meaning would not make sense. Another type of reader might use *syntactic knowledge* to understand the sentence, "Joey drives a small . . ." to reject the word *care* as the wrong choice for that part of the sentence. Still a third type of reader might use *orthographic shape* in decoding the sentence, "Joey drove a load of trees to the paper mill," knowing that the words *pap* and *paperwork* look wrong. A single reader might use these three types of making meaning equally often or might develop a preference for one type of decoding. Interventions would be designed accordingly (Newman, 1985a).

Seeking meaning is natural to the mind. Some readers seek precision and are satisfied only when they can state the writer's intention with certainty. For others, a general feeling for the topic seems to satisfy. Nonetheless, the goal of the reading instructor is for students to come away from a reading passage with meaning. Because this meaning is constructed by the reader, there will always be some imperfect match between the meaning as taught and the meaning as attained by each reader. The richest of text evokes the most fundamentally meaningful, yet passionate and idiosyncratic, response. Anything less is reductionistic, to be doomed to accept the exact understandings of others rather than to glory in our own, however unique. This is the chief reason for the existence of literature.

The Three-Stage Reading Process

A common approach used in working with literature is captured by the phrase *into*, *through*, and *beyond*. Activities prior to reading prepare students to get "into" the reading. Other strategies help students read "through" the material. Finally, follow-up activities help students organize and retain their understanding "beyond" the act of reading. This three-part, sequential approach, although a popular organizing device, actually misrepresents the complexity of a classroom in which literacy is socially constructed. In reality, students are moving into, through, and beyond their own reading on an individual basis as they dip into some books, pick up and discard others, or use the table of contents and index wisely to be able to choose to read what they need. Other students "surf" the Internet, following links that fizzle out, downloading information to look at later, or stumbling onto topics much more exciting than their original area of interest. Therefore the into, through, and beyond approach represents reading for an entire topic, rather than for a single book.

Schemata for the Reading Process

A useful overall method of teaching reading to English learners is to think of three types of schemata: cultural or content schemata, text-processing schemata, and linguistic/grammatical schemata. These three types of schemata are applied at every stage of the reading process by using specific strategies (see Figure 6.2).

Cultural and content schemata include the categories that humans deploy to make sense of new knowledge. For example, in a recent class, prospective TESOL educators were comparing Chinese writing with alphabetic scripts. Because it was close to the Chinese New Year, a small red envelope was part of the display of Chinese writing. When non-Chinese students found that this envelope had something to do with intergenerational money transfer, their attention was immediately alerted. They asked the Chinese students, "How much money is customarily given?" "When does this occur?" "How old are you when your parents no longer give you this money?" On

Schemata Type → Reading Process	Cultural and Content	Text-Processing	Linguistic and Grammatical
Into			
Through			
Beyond			

FIGURE 6.2 ◆ **Strategies used "into, through, and beyond" to build cultural and content, text-processing, and linguistic and grammatical schemata.**
Source: Jo, 1999.

the other hand, interest in the writing on the envelope was low. The native English-speakers had a cultural category of their own as a schema (parents giving money to children) but, conversely, had little experience with an ideographic writing system and were relatively incurious about it.

Many topics in target-language reading shut out English learners because of their lack of knowledge about the culture or the content. One teacher found teaching Jack London's story "To Build a Fire" to a middle school class frustrating because the students did not care about dog sleds or Arctic travel. Establishing a historical context is a particular challenge. Table 6.1 shows a variety of "into, through, and beyond" strategies that can be used to build students' cultural/content schemata.

Text-processing schemata are used to assist students to read. These can take place in all phases of the reading process (see Table 6.2) as students prepare to read, perform silent or oral reading, or evaluate what has been read. Text-processing schemata permit readers to accelerate their reading and yet retain more information.

Linguistic and grammatical schemata are built when an instructor devotes explicit attention to analysis of the structure, usage, or even dialect of a text. Native speakers often find it necessary to do this in order to understand a writer's intent. When employing these schemata with nonnative speakers of English, an occasional focus on form is helpful, as they strive to understand and create longer, more intricate, and more elegant sentences. Table 6.3 specifically lists strategies that focus on form rather than content.

Into Reading. "Into" activities activate students' prior knowledge by drawing from their past experiences or helping them to develop background knowledge through new experiences. Films, texts, field trips, visual aids, and graphic organizers can clarify meaning and help students anticipate the work. Brainstorming ideas about a topic is one way to activate prior knowledge and stimulate students' ideas by generating those of others. Some teachers have students make predictions about the content of a story and then put these predictions into "time capsules" that can be opened and analyzed once the text has been read. Students can discuss what happened later in the book to confirm or disprove their original predictions.

Another classroom activity that activates or develops background knowledge using all of the language processes is K-W-L (What do I *Know*? What do I *Want to*

TABLE 6.1 ◆ **Strategies Used to Build Students' Cultural and Content Schemata during Phases of the Reading Process**

Phases of the Reading Process	Strategies	Suggestions for Implementation
Into	Setting goals for reading	Goals make sense in the cultural context of the classroom.
	Gaining background knowledge	Use background notes or a content or cultural briefing to understand relevant aspects of culture.
	Recognizing discipline-specific knowledge	Define particular technical terms.
	Brainstorming	Students pool their existing knowledge.
	Tactics for lexical acquisition: ◆ Previewing a glossary	If book has no glossary, students can keep a private dictionary.
Through	Understanding cultural terms and practices	Terms, beliefs, and behaviors are explained as they occur in the reading.
	Crosscultural comparison	Compare/contrast matrix or Venn diagram is used to make explicit cultural differences and similarities or to explicate content.
Beyond	Tactics for cultural understanding: ◆ Cultural perspectives	Characters are understood in their cultural contexts; rewrite ending to story from other perspectives.
	◆ Cultural immersions	Students put themselves in the shoes of characters of other cultures.
	◆ Intercultural communication	Students talk with a guest from another culture or content expert about issues raised in reading.
	Tactics for content application: ◆ Project-based learning	Read for problem solving.
	◆ Making posters, doing experiments	Gain additional content knowledge through hands-on experience, then read/write to report findings.

learn? What have I Learned?). Asking, "What do I know?" allows students to place new knowledge in the context of their own episodic memories and existing concepts, even if they have misconceptions that have to be "unlearned." Some prior knowledge may be based on experiences in the students' home cultures that are beyond the teacher's conceptualization.

It is especially important for English learners that during brainstorming and K-W-L, all ideas should be accepted. A comment made by a student may be highly relevant within that student's experience or cultural background even though it may appear inappropriate to the teacher. In the follow-up to brainstorming, the teacher can

TABLE 6.2 ◆ Strategies Used to Build Students' Text-Processing Schemata during Phases of the Reading Process

Phases of the Reading Process	Strategies	Suggestions for Implementation
Into	Literary lore: • Identifying genre (e.g., fiction, reflective essay) • Identifying literary terms	What structure characterizes this genre? What poetic/literary characteristics make the reading appealing?
	Previewing text: • Skimming • Scanning • Previewing • Formulating questions • Semantic mapping	What techniques can be used to process text to evaluate its usability or worth before much time is invested? What can a picture or graphic reveal about the conceptual structure?
Through	Metacognition	Self-monitor and adjust.
	Tactics for text comprehension: • Identifying the main idea and supporting details	Use group discussion—the instructional conversation format, for example—to identify possible main ideas; evaluate; vote.
	Tactics for critical thinking about text: • Making inferences • Problem solving	What is implied but not stated outright? What problems does the character create for others?
Beyond	Tactics for review: • Taking notes • Study buddies	Make flash cards, underline, make annotations, pose questions.
	Strategies for text comprehension: • Summarizing • Storytelling	Retell the text from an outline. Recall key ideas. Conduct "what if?" discussion to generate alternative possibilities.
	Tactics for application: • Telegraph plot	If you had only forty words to tell the plot, what would you say?

ask the student to give more detail about the comment. Once ideas are exhausted, the students and teacher together can organize the list, grouping and selecting appropriate category labels to create a beginning model from which they can work and learn.

K-W-L not only taps into what students already know but also draws from them what they would like to learn. The students list everything they know about a topic and then tell the teacher what they would like to learn. The chart is kept up throughout the duration of the unit for students to refer to from time to time. They have the opportunity to make additions and change incorrect information. When the unit is

TABLE 6.3 ◆ Strategies Used to Build Students' Linguistic and Grammatical Schemata during Phases of the Reading Process

Phases of the Reading Process	Strategies	Definition
Into	Tactics for sociolinguistic competence: • Observing dialect, idiosyncratic speech, social class distinctions	How does dialogue reflect differences between characters? How does dialogue reflect the social class of the speakers or characters?
	Tactics for discourse competence: • Observing point of view	Is there a narrator? Whose point of view is represented?
	Tactics for metacognition: • Time management • Planning	Will the text be difficult? How much time should be allocated for mastery?
Through	Tactics for vocabulary acquisition: • Guessing meaning using context	
Beyond	Tactics for paragraph analysis:	What role does every part of the reading play in creating and sustaining meaning?
	• Identifying the topic sentence	Do the paragraphs have clear, coherent content?
	• Identifying logical argument	Does the order of paragraphs create an accurate flow of ideas?
	Tactics for discourse competence: • Identifying story, grammar	Are the beginning, middle, and end apparent to the reader? Does the plot hold the reader's attention?

completed, they return to the chart and talk about what they have learned. By starting each topic or unit with an activity that actively engages students in reviewing their own experiences relevant to the topic, the teacher gains valuable insights.

While Reading.   "Through" activities help students as they work with the text. Many teachers find reading aloud a useful strategy that gives the students an opportunity to hear a proficient reader, get a sense of the format and story line, and listen to the teacher "think aloud" about the reading. In the "think aloud," teachers can model how they monitor a sequence of events, identify foreshadowing and flashbacks, visualize a setting, analyze character and motive, comprehend mood and theme, and recognize irony and symbols (Anstrom, 1998). To help students develop a sense of inflection, pronunciation, rhythm, and stress, a commercial tape recording of a work of literature can be obtained for listening and review; alternatively, native English-speakers may be willing to make a recording.

Teachers using literature in their classrooms may find that English-language literature does not elicit the same responses from English learners as from native English-speakers. By selecting materials judiciously, slowing the pace slightly, portioning work into manageable chunks, and increasing the depth of each lesson, the teacher can ensure that English learners have a fulfilling experience with literature. Myths and folktales from many cultures are now commonly available in high-quality editions with vibrant illustrations, and these can be used as a bridge to more complex works of literature. These tales often evoke a familiar response. Students can move from these folktales and myths to selected short stories by authors of many cultural backgrounds, go on to portions of a longer work, and finally progress to reading entire works (Sasser, 1992).

Various ways can be used for students to perform the actual reading. Table 6.4 offers a variety of reading methods for in-class use.

To sustain students' interests in a longer work of literature, class time may be used to review the narrative to date and discuss and compare students' understanding of the assigned reading. A preview of the next reading can feature interesting aspects of the new passage. *In Literature in the Language Classroom*, Collie and Slater (1987) suggested ways in which a teacher can structure literature homework. "Gap summary" is a technique in which the teacher provides an almost complete and simply phrased description of the main points of the section assigned for home reading. Gaps are usually key words or expressions that only a reading of the passage can reveal. "Charac-

TABLE 6.4 • In-Class Reading Methods for English Learners

Method	Description
Page and paragraph	Teacher or fluent reader reads a page; English learner reads a paragraph; group discusses what has been read.
Equal portions	Students work in pairs, and each reads aloud the same amount of text.
Silent with support	Students read silently in pairs and can ask each other for help with a difficult word or phrase.
Choral reading	Passage is divided into sections, and various parts of the audience read various sections.
Radio reading	One student reads while others close their books and listen. After reading, the reader can question each student about what was read.
Repeated reading	Students read silently a book that has been read aloud or independently reread books of their choice.
Interactive read-aloud	Students can join in on repetitious parts or take parts of a dialogue.
Echo reading	For rhythmic text, students echo or repeat lines.
Cloze reading	When reading big books, teacher covers certain words and students try to guess the word in context.
Nonprint media support	Students can follow along with a taped version of the book.

Source: Hadaway, Vardell, & Young, 2002.

ter diary" is an ongoing record of what each character is feeling that helps students step within the character. "What's missing" encourages students to make inferences about missing aspects of the story: What were the characters like at school? What were their favorite subjects? Did they have friends? Were they close to their parents?

"Story mapping" is a way for students to use a graphic organizer to summarize the plot. Younger students can work with four boxes (Who? Wants? But? So?) to fill in their knowledge of what happens in the story (Peregoy & Boyle, 2001). Older students can use the terms "characters," "intent," "opposition," and "resolution." Using this device, students can follow the story grammar, the progression of events in the plot.

After Reading.   "Beyond" activities are designed to extend the students' appreciation of literature, usually in another medium. Poems can be written and shared with other classes or parents at a Poetry Night. Reviews of literature works can be written for the school or classroom newspaper. Letters to authors or to pen pals encourage students to express their reactions to certain pieces of literature. Students can be movie critics and view the film representation of a text studied in class, comparing the pros and cons of the two media. Favorite parts of selections can be rewritten as a play and enacted for other classes. Using reminder sheets, students in pairs restate various parts of what they have read to one another (cued retelling) (Whisler & Williams, 1990). Students can plan a mock television show, for example, a game show, in which a host asks contestants to answer questions or to act as characters or objects in the story.

In the traditional grammar-translation classroom, "beyond" becomes an extensive review of the grammatical forms contained in the reading. This is consistent with the "fishbowl" approach to EFL (Yoshida, 2001/2002), in which students depend on the teacher to provide them with everything they need to know to pass an entrance examination, much as the caretaker of a fish keeps the captive pet supplied

Teachers can encourage English learners to enjoy reading using drama as an extension activity.

with food. "Beyond" activities in the communicative classroom, however, prepare students for the "open seas" of English use. Although grammatical and linguistic training may continue to be a part of the "into, through, and beyond" phases of instruction, cultural, content, and text-processing strategies are a priority in preparing students for the larger world of English in international settings.

Focus on Acquisition Vocabulary

New words can be introduced before a reading lesson, or meaning can be inferred from context during reading. Explicit work with new vocabulary words, though, is usually reserved for the after-reading phase. Students can study words in a number of ways. The *word element approach* isolates roots, prefixes, and suffixes and uses word families to expand a new word into its host of relations (e.g., biology, sociology, psychology are relatives of anthropology). Specific vocabulary acquisition strategies teach students to infer from context, find synonyms in apposition, make use of a subsequent list of examples of a new word, use a dictionary. *Technical word acquisition strategies* include a glossary, side-bar, chart, or graphs. Worksheets or other kinds of practice may also help students to recognize meaning. *Word formation practice* involves compounding (room + mate = roommate), blending (motor hotel = motel), and acronyms (self-contained underwater breathing apparatus = scuba) (see Justice, 2001). However, moving a new word from students' acquisition vocabulary (used in reading or listening) to their production vocabulary (used in writing or speaking) requires far more guided practice (Rosenthal & Rowland, 1986).

Collocation is growing in importance as a teaching tool because it enables students to learn vocabulary as it is used in real contexts. Using concordances, or sets of corpus, students can see "how words combine in predictable ways," in order to see recurring patterns (Hill, 2000). Although students must still devote study to individual words, seeing the word as it is actually used in a natural context permits words to be learned in appropriate phrases. Students can see verb + noun sequences ("dispute findings"); adjective + noun sequences ("unaccompanied minor"); verb + preposition sequences ("hear about") or adverb + adjective + noun sequences ("highly irregular situation") (Conzett, 2000).

Transition Reading

Educators emphasize that students should be taught to read first in their primary language, because the sound-symbol correspondence draws upon words they know. Primary-language usage continues as English is acquired, so that students can sustain higher-order thinking. With primary-language reading well under way, learners begin slowly to acquire English as an additional language. Sometimes reading instruction in English resembles reading instruction in the L1, and sometimes it does not. Because Spanish has an excellent sound-symbol correspondence, Spanish reading instruction has traditionally relied on phonics and syllabic decoding. In contrast, Chinese is traditionally taught using kinesthetic memorization, with emphasis on drawing ideographs.

Depending on the L1, some students must learn the Roman alphabet. As students who speak other Roman alphabetic languages make the transition into English, they must learn to distinguish phonemes in their L1 that differ in sound but are spelled the same (ll, b, v, and t, in Spanish and English, for example), as well as learn the many exceptions to the sound-syllable correspondence between oral and written English. Students must translate many words they already know in their L1 into English, as well as acquire many new words and concepts directly in English from their reading. These various similarities and differences (in script system, pedagogy, and prior knowledge) between English and the L1 result in some students learning English more quickly than others.

Stages of Reading Development for English Learners

Teaching reading on the basis of proficiency as the organizing principle (Higgs, 1984) implies that reading activities can be matched to the language proficiency level of the student. Omaggio (1986, pp. 153–155) provides tactics that she considers appropriate for each of the four reading levels corresponding to the American Council for Teaching Foreign Languages' (ACTFL) proficiency levels.

❖ Tactics for teaching reading to students at various levels of proficiency:

- Novice: anticipating/predicting, skimming, gisting, scanning, extracting specific information, contextual guessing, prereading activities, simple cloze, filling out forms
- Intermediate: Comprehension checks, guessing from context, clue searching, making inferences, scrambled stories, extracting specific information, skimming, scanning, paraphrasing, gisting/resume, note taking/outlining, passage completion, identifying sociolinguistic factors, understanding idioms, understanding discourse structures, understanding link words and referents
- Advanced: Comprehension checks, guessing from context, clue searching, making inferences, cloze techniques, reverse cloze, scrambled stories, extracting specific information, skimming, scanning, paraphrasing, gisting/resume, passage completion, identifying sociolinguistic factors, filling out forms, anticipating/predicting, understanding discourse structures, understanding link words and referents

---

Teaching Strategies for Comprehension

Too often students do not know what to do when they cannot comprehend a text. Table 6.5 presents several strategies that are useful when comprehension fails.

Each of these strategies can be developed using a variety of reading selections. When introducing a new comprehension strategy, the teacher explains when the strategy is useful, models the process, and then gives the students guided practice. Pearson & Gallagher (1983) call this the "Gradual Release of Responsibility" model.

Directed reading-thinking activity (DR-TA) is an activity that boosts reading comprehension by helping students understand how proficient readers make predictions as they read (Stauffer, 1970). Teachers guide students through the prediction process until they are able to do it on their own, by asking students to make predictions and then reading to confirm their ideas. The teacher's goal is to help students see that correctness—a prediction that is exactly right—is not as important as plausibility—

TABLE 6.5 • Strategies That Readers Can Use When Comprehension Fails

Strategy	Description
Rereading: text-based answers	One can skim the text and find the answer. (1)
"Right there" answers	Answer is easily found in the book. (2)
"Think and search" answers	Reader needs to put together different parts of the reading to obtain solution. (2)
Rereading: reader-based answers	The reader must infer the answer: Look for answers clues from text. (1)
"Author and you" answers	Solution lies in a combination of what is in story plus reader's experience. (2)
"On my own" answers	Answer comes from one's own experience. (2)
Visual imagery	Before rereading, students discuss what pictures come to mind. Younger children can draw these pictures, and older children can use verbal description. Ask students to form mental images while rereading. (3)
Thinking aloud	Students self-monitor comprehension by asking, "Does this make sense?" as they read. What question can they ask that will help to focus what they need in order for it to make sense? (1)
Suspending judgment	Students read ahead when a new concept is not well explained, seeking information to develop clarity. (1)
Reciprocal teaching	Students predict, summarize, ask questions, and suspend judgment, using these techniques with one another. (4)
Mine, yours, and ours	Students make individual summaries and compare with a partner; then they write a joint paragraph outlining their similarities and differences. (5)
Summary pairs	Students read aloud to one another and summarize what they have read. (5)
Shrinking stories	Students write their own versions of a passage in twenty-five words or less. (6)
Simply put	Students rewrite a selection so that students two or three years younger might understand it. (6)

Sources: Barr & Johnson, 1997 (1); Raphael, 1986 (2); Gambrell & Bales, 1986 (3); Palinscar & Brown, 1984 (4); Lipton & Hubble, 1997 (5); Suid & Lincoln, 1992 (6).

a prediction that is possible—and that they need to check the text continually as new information is revealed.

Teaching Literature

More and more teachers are using literature as the core of their reading program. For an overview of the use of literature in a children's reading program, see Tunnell and Jacobs (2000). A literature-based approach to reading uses *controlled readers, text sets, core books,* and *thematic units* to provide reading experiences that are rich in meaning and interest for students. Controlled readers can be literature-based basal readers, in which vocabulary and length are tailored to the target reading level, or book sets (Story Box and Sunshine Series from the Wright Group, Literacy 2000 from Rigby) that feature big books and matching reader sets. Text sets are books that are related thematically (such as books on sports and hobbies, or sets of multicultural readers on the Cinderella theme) or feature the same characters in a series of adventures. Using the *Sweet Valley High* series as a text set, for example, Cho and Krashen (1995) were able to induce a group of Korean mothers to read English for enjoyment.

Core books are those that are specifically featured in a statewide adoption list for all classrooms to use. These books are selected to appeal to a wide range of interests and abilities. Box 6.3 demonstrates how to introduce students to a core book so that they will want to read further.

Thematic Units. Thematic units integrate literature with science, social studies, and art/music/performing arts. The unit may be on the rain forest, the settling of the West, or other interdisciplinary topics. *Family Vacation,* a thematic unit designed by Ann García, combines five types of reading. In Lesson 1, "Visiting National Parks," the focus is on reading for facts. In Lesson 2, "Joshua Tree National Park," the students read for interest. Lesson 3, "Family Vacation at a National Park," includes reading fiction. Lesson 4, "Lake Perris, Your State Park," teaches how to read for technical information. In Lesson 5, "Local Park," students collate, compare, and evaluate

---

BOX 6.3
❖ Tactics to Introduce a Core Book

If a whole class is to read the same book, the following tactics may inspire them to want to read it.

- Read the title and ask students to speculate about its significance.
- Begin with questions that raise issues that are dealt with in the book, or create a scenario similar to one in the book and ask students how they would react.
- Bring in a poem that speaks to a central issue of one of the characters in the book.
- Read the first few pages or the first chapter aloud. Have students predict the kinds of situations that will develop or what will happen to the characters.
- Read the first few pages aloud and ask students to write about or sketch the images or pictures they see in their minds.

- Draw students into the book by asking them to share experiences that parallel those that the character will experience.
- Make up startling or interesting statements about a key character.
- Give students a partial list of values that are important to a main character and have them rank these in order of importance to them.
- Read a provocative paragraph or scene to raise students' interest.
- Pass out a survey or questionnaire or sentence starters that you composed based on issues that surfaced during the book.

Source: Tchudi & Mitchell, 1999, pp. 217–218.

information. Lastly, "Plan Your Own Park" (Lesson 6) leads students through an information search as they brainstorm what items an "ideal" park for their family would have and then draw a map (complete with map legend) that lays out the recreation area, picnicking facilities, restrooms, and parking lots.

Multicultural Literature.   Multicultural literature helps students to see life from a variety of points of view, to compare cultures on different aspects of life, and to see their own culture represented in the curriculum. Anthologies of multicultural literature present a wealth of materials, some grouped thematically (see Harris, 1997; Monroe, 1999). *The Literature Connection* (Smallwood, 1991) offers a selection of literature chosen for use as read-aloud material and includes criteria for selecting books (attractiveness, curricular tie-in, age-appropriate theme, easy-to-follow story line, clear illustrations, predictable pattern, skillful use of dialogue, and *i* + 1 structures). *Multicultural Voices in Contemporary Literature* (Day, 1994) presents thirty-nine authors and illustrators from twenty different cultures. A follow-up book, *Latina and Latino Voices in Literature for Children and Teenagers* (Day, 1997) has biographies of thirty-eight authors with synopses of their work, as well as an extensive list of resources for books in English on Latino themes. Day (2003) is a follow-up extending the Latina and Latino theme.

Reader Response.   Reader response theory holds that in order to make sense of a text, readers must first make connections with it (see Rosenblatt, 1978). The teacher must create an atmosphere of trust and acceptance, so that students are free to reveal their perceptions, personal feelings, thoughts, and feelings in relation to a text in a cooperative setting. Students must feel free to be both tentative and flexible, so that they can modify or clarify their first thoughts as they read further into a text. Despite the emphasis on personal intellectual and emotional reactions, reader response must be guided by faithfulness to the text. The texts themselves must be of high quality, yet close enough to the readers' interest to inspire investment in the ideas (Probst, 1988).

Literature Response.   Literature response groups can develop a community of readers and help students understand the richness of literature. After reading a piece of literature (with the teacher, other adult, cross-age tutors, buddies, or individually), a group of students and the teacher meet for discussion. After each student expresses ideas about the story, the teacher opens the discussion with a thought-provoking question. As points are made, the teacher guides the students to deeper understandings, for example, by asking them to support their point with words from the text and asking what words or devices the author used to invoke a mood, establish a setting, describe a character, move the plot along, and so on.

Independent Reading.   As students become better readers, they begin to read their own *self-selected books*. As they read independently, they are encouraged to use familiar techniques for comprehension—making mental images, surveying the book and making predictions, and monitoring their reading to make sure they understand. Students keep a simple reading log of the books they finish. Atwell (1987) suggested that students use a bookmark to track difficult words or a passage they do not understand. Many bookmarks may indicate that a book is too hard for them to understand. Students who have difficulty finding books to read might benefit from a peer "book hunt" in which students interview one another and then go off to the library to find books that fulfill the partner's interests.

Several sources are available that suggest *age-level appropriate reading material.* Public libraries have detailed reference books that list thousands of children's books, including winners of the Caldecott and Newbery Medals. Sometimes a school will send out a list of recommended books to every family. At one school fourth graders prepared their own list of books and duplicated it for every child in the school. *A Parent's Guide to Reading* (Larrick, 1982) is an excellent resource of annotated books for every age and grade level. Generally speaking, children respect their teacher's recommendations and enjoy what the teacher enjoys, but if a recommended book is not interesting or understandable, the teacher's opinion begins to account for less.

Book Conferences.   Book conferences with the teacher, if there is time, allow students to benefit from direct guidance. Students can use this time to share what they liked about the book, what they do not understand or what puzzled them about the book, and other personal responses (Reynolds, 1988). Dialogue with an interested party makes reading literature sociable and fun. Hornsby, Sukarna, and Parry (1986) suggest this format for a reading conference: The teacher first listens to students' responses as they summarize a story or retell a particular scene and then asks students questions that encourage speculation or divergent thinking. If students confer in a group, they can ask one another questions. Occasionally, students can read their favorite passages aloud. The conference ends as students make a plan for an extension activity or for the next book they will read.

Sociocultural Affects on Literacy.   When students do not like to read, schooling becomes a cycle of failure: Poor reading habits exacerbate poor academic work, leading in turn to the dislike to read. Minority students reported to Zanger (1994) that their literacy was adversely affected in high school by their feelings of low status, negative classroom experiences due to a curriculum that alienated them from the teacher and from other students, and failure to include their home language and cultures in a respectful and meaningful way. Nieto (2000) and others have called for inclusionary, multicultural learning environments in which English learners will feel accepted and productive and will therefore work to become literate and successful in school.

Writing Processes

Hand in hand with reading goes writing. Writing is no longer an activity that can be postponed until English learners can speak English fluently. "Child ESL learners, early in their development of English, can write English and can do so for various purposes" (Hudelson, 1984, p. 221). Writing in English is not only a key to academic success, it is also an outlet for self-expression. Hadaway and colleagues (2002) put it this way:

> The permanence of writing allows us to communicate with others across distance and across time. Yet, at the same time writing allows us to reach beyond ourselves, it also

furnishes a means of looking inward. Writing is an expression outlet for self-communication, a way to chronicle our personal reactions and journeys. Finally, writing is truly the most complex of the communicative arts, incorporating reading as well as oral language. (p. 137)

Although much has been written about "the writing process," it is more accurate to use the term "writing processes." Most writers do not simply draft, revise, edit, and publish. Rather, the process is recursive; there is much back-and-forth work—drafting to redrafting, editing to redrafting, revising to redrafting, and so forth. Many teachers teach a five-step writing process, but in a classroom with a rich learning environment, students actually work in various stages simultaneously. It is worthwhile to do as Emig (1981) did, namely, take a look at students' actual process and teach students writing in the most brain-compatible way. Most often, the brain carries out a fuzzy, holistic process of learning (see Chapter 3). If teachers honor the reality of the learning process rather than trying to impose a lockstep system, the mind stays engaged throughout the struggle to "write down" and clarify thinking.

• **STRATEGY 6.2:** Teach writing in a way that sustains interest, information acquisition, and lifelong self-expression

The Role of Writing in Academic Literacies

Students who are still in the process of acquiring English are entering colleges and universities at an unprecedented rate. The good news is that English learners are being encouraged to pursue higher education. The bad news is that few are ready to perform college-level work. In the California State University system of twenty-two campuses, for example, 46 percent of the 36,655 freshmen who enrolled in fall 2001 failed the English Placement Test and therefore could not enroll in English 101 (Tresaugue, 2002). Why are so many students unprepared for college writing? Students' prior academic work and social situation may hamper their ability to participate in discourse at the university level (Bizzell, 1982). In order to become insiders in the world of academic culture, students must learn to write essays that bring forth their own personal values, experiences, knowledge, and questions. In this way students can discover an "enlarging horizon that every discourse can open to [their] view," and "gradually enter the community of 'knowers' while retaining their own voice" (Spellmeyer, 1989, p. 274).

Academic writing seems to serve a variety of functions. Some instructors use writing so that students can draw upon their prior knowledge in preparation for new activities (for example, stimulating students' interests through freewriting). Some instructors expect writing to enable students to consolidate and review new information and experiences (using, for example, learning logs, journals, note taking, reaction papers, summaries, and study exercises). Others hope that by writing, students can reformulate and extend their knowledge using formal, structured reflection assignments such as lab reports, essay exams, or impromptu writing (Langer & Applebee, 1987).

Just what language is needed to accomplish academic work and how students can attain mastery of that language are topics of much debate. Attempts to address the preparation of students are varied (e.g. Reid, 1993; Strauch, 1997). College English departments have tried to involve university faculty across disciplines in improving undergraduate students' writing through "writing across the curriculum" (Applebee, 1977), and a growing number of experts are working as writing center coordinators to train tutors to work with instructors and students to improve writing. In fact, the tutoring of writing at the university level is a growing area of expertise; see Maxwell (2000) for an excellent introduction to interpersonal and professional issues in this field.

The field of teaching undergraduate writing and other academic skills to underprepared English learners at the college level has been called English for Academic Purposes (see Benesch, 2001), and is burgeoning in response to the "Generation 1.5" population of U.S.-educated ESL learners (Harklau, Losey, & Siegal, 1999). TESOL educators are collaborating with content-area instructors to improve the targeted writing of English learners in specific academic and technical fields (Flowerdew, 2001). This chapter attempts to treat writing issues as generic across age levels of ESOL learners. For further reading in the emerging literature on academic literacy, see Zamel & Spack (1998) as an entry point.

Writing as a Social Construction

Writing is no longer seen as a lone pursuit of the individual. As far back as 1981, Szwed argued that reader, writer, function, text, and context were a "nexus" for literacy (p. 15). Farr (1994) reiterated this theme when she studied the motivation of a group of Mexican immigrants in Chicago. The motivation for many students to improve their writing is not so much internal or intrinsic but rather lies embedded in the social context in which the writing takes place. As Rodby (1999) pointed out:

> . . . motivation is not located in the individual, per se. Motivation results from a combination of factors often beyond the individual's control. It is produced by a confluence of relationships, ideologies, institutions, and activities with and in which the individual is engaged. Second, as these factors change from one context to another, either synchronously or chronologically, so does motivation. (p. 48)

Rodby (1999) described case studies of ESL students who were more or less able to draw upon multiple and overlapping systems of support from work, home, church, clubs, peer interactions, faculty, and social and cultural systems to revise their writing in a prefreshman English class. These students are examples of the powerful role played by the systems in which they are immersed in influencing their literacy behavior, which in turn influenced their academic potential. This type of ethnographic study now facilitates the careful analysis of these intersecting forces as a means of designing interventions that are sensitive to context and culture.

What Do Writers Need?

Learners need *time and opportunity* to write as a regular means to develop their fluency. They need *a real reason for writing*, such as a letter exchange with a pen pal. They need a *genuine audience*; if students know they will be sharing their writing with their classmates, their investment increases. Students need *role models*, people who are using writing to fulfill life purposes. They need a *safe environment* for writing, with voluntary sharing, one-on-one conferences, and support for the writing at different phases of the work. They need useful *feedback* that blends a moderate level of error marking with a thoughtful response to the writer's composing efforts. The final need is for a *sense of community*, in this case others who can collaborate, validate, and support one another's efforts (Hadaway et al., 2002).

Authentic Purposes for Writing.   Sometimes writing, if it does not stem from or fulfill an authentic purpose, becomes a ghost of itself, an empty form that looks like writing but is hollow. Although some teachers assign students to write invitations, journals, and stories so as to avoid having children complete work sheets, the writing on these teacher-assigned topics is often wooden and perfunctory. In contrast, Edelsky (1989) gave several examples of authentic writing: Students scolded their pen pals, offered medical advice in get-well letters, and gave Santa Claus directions so that he could deliver a motorcycle. Students who are writing just to fulfill an assignment cannot really write with a spirit that is their own. Luckily, teachers who work with students on each phase of the writing process can help them to find topics that interest them and to which they can then do justice with a dedicated effort (Roen, 1989).

Dialogue Journals.   *Dialogue journals* enjoyed a surge of popularity as a part of whole-language methodology, and many teachers employ them as a means of increasing fluency and promoting interpersonal communication. Jones (1991) provided a definition:

> Dialogue journals are essentially written conversations between a student and teacher, kept in a bound notebook or on a computer disk or file. Both partners write back and forth, frequently, over a period of time about whatever interests them. Their goal is to communicate in writing, to exchange ideas and information free of the concern for form and correctness so often imposed on developing writers. (p. 3)

Topics in dialogue journals are typically not assigned, so that the partners are free to discuss whatever they wish. The writing is not corrected, graded, or evaluated. Most teachers keep the writing private, promising not to show the journal to a third party. The focus on communication provides a nonthreatening, high-interest interchange that features a sense of equality between partners and renders the relationship between teacher and learner less hierarchical. Students like dialogue journals because the interaction focuses on student-generated topics; the process emphasizes meaning, rather than form; the language input that the learner receives from the teacher is comprehensible; correct grammatical forms are modeled by the teacher, thus taught indirectly; and the dialogue occurs in a private, supportive context (Peyton, 1990).

A central issue, of course, concerns the role that dialogue journals play in an overall writing curriculum, because accuracy in form or usage is not a priority in this genre. Peyton (1990) found that the value of dialogue journals is that students can express themselves in written English long before they have mastered its forms and structures and are able to write narratives, describe events and problems, and even argue their points of view. This type of success is a recommendation for the acquisition of grammar in a meaningful, integrated context (see Chapter 8). A general introduction to the use of journals for adult basic literacy education can be found in Peyton and Staton (1991).

Stages of Writing Development for Young English Learners

Writing behavior on the part of children who are native speakers of English reflects a series of developmental stages. The first is *scribbling and drawing*, as the writer attempts to emulate adult writing. At the *prephonemic* stage, the writer uses real letters, but the meaning stands for whole ideas. Moving on to the *early phonemic* stage, the writer uses letters, usually consonants, to stand for words; as the *letter-naming* stage follows, vowels may accompany the consonants in an attempt to approximate phonemic sequences. The writer then moves through a *transitional* phase toward *conventional* spelling, using "invented" or "temporary" spelling to convey meaning. If children are held to correct spelling, they write much less (Hadaway et al., 2002).

The actual spelling that children write is a fascinating indicator of their thinking and their emotions, as well as their progress in learning conventional forms. Kress (2000) looked at one child's form, *dided* ("died"), and speculated that the child was struggling with overregularization of past tense; another child, Emily, printed the uppercase *E* with four horizontal strokes instead of three, perhaps indicating that this letter carried extra signification as the first letter of her name. Emergent spelling, whether it stems from first- or second-language acquisition, is a rich source of knowledge about intellectual and interlanguage development.

Beginning English learners usually enter English in the transitional phase, that is, they generally catch on to the sound-symbol principle of the alphabet, even if their own language is ideographic. The more similar their first-language alphabet is to the English alphabet, the more easily their writing skills will transfer to English (Odlin, 1989). Beginning English learners need to become familiar with beginning vocabulary. Word banks can be a rich source of vocabulary building; students can collect words on index cards and then alphabetize them, classify them, illustrate them, or nominate them for Word of the Week contests (Lipton & Hubble, 1997). Beginning students can engage in interactive journal writing with their teacher or complete simple frame sentences such as "I like _____ because _____." They can copy words and sentences, or they can make their own books by copying and illustrating simple books (Hadaway et al., 2002).

Intermediate English learners increase their vocabulary as they attempt more complex sentences while writing. They can try their hand at various genres of personal and expressive writing, such as letter writing, as well as various types of academic writing such as note taking, short essays, and lists (Raimes, 1983). Exercises in combining sentences help English learners to extend the length and variety of their writing. Students at this level of English acquisition are struggling with subject-verb agreement and the correct forms of plural nouns, pronouns, and verb tenses. Many errors occur at the sentence level, involving adverbial and adjectival phrases and clauses, sentence fragments and run-on constructions, and collocation errors (incorrect verb + preposition combinations) (Leki, 1992).

Advanced English learners write responses to many academic assignments, such as personal or literary essays and completed work sheets, laboratory manuals, and test questions. Their writing may feature many of the issues with which native speakers struggle, such as topic focus, parallel sentence structure, and paragraph cohesion.

The Writing Workshop

Williams and Snipper (1990) labeled the process approach "the classroom as workshop." In this "workshop" environment students are free to talk with one another as they write. English learners can draw on other students, not just the teacher, as a resource, and can in turn use their own experiences to enrich their writing and that of their peers. The teacher's role then becomes that of facilitator and listener.

Writing is often more fun if students write collaboratively. Students can first brainstorm and share ideas and then list them in a form that resembles poetry. One useful convention is the phrase, "I used to _____, but now_____." Once the story is completed, it can be copied onto a chart and used for reading practice (Cantoni-Harvey, 1987). This is a group version of the LEA that connects students to their own experiences and activities by having them express themselves orally. It reinforces the notion that sounds can be transcribed into specific symbols and that those symbols can then be used to re-create the ideas expressed; it also provides texts for specific lessons on vocabulary, grammar, writing conventions, structure, and more.

Students may enjoy writing buddy journals, a sort of diary in which a pair of students write back and forth to each other (Bromley, 1989). The teacher models this by suggesting sample topics and perhaps putting a daily journal entry on the board: "Today I feel excited about the field trip. I got up extra early to find something to pack in my lunch!" (The buddy journals are less private than a teacher-student dialogue journal, because every two weeks or so the students change buddies, and the new buddies have access to previous entries.)

The process approach involves several stages: planning or prewriting, writing, and feedback and editing.

The Writing Process: Prewriting

During *prewriting*, students are involved in using oral language to develop their need and desire to write. These activities may include talking about and listening to shared experiences, reading literature, brainstorming, or creating role-playing or other fantasy activities (Enright & McCloskey, 1988). Mind mapping (see Chapter 5) encourages students to generate and organize their ideas graphically on chart paper or on the blackboard. Some classes may use Inspiration, a computer program that facilitates mind mapping.

The prewriting phase helps to generate, incubate, explore, test, and integrate ideas. Most writers find it often helps to talk about a topic, bouncing ideas off others, benefiting from the questions others ask as they shape and explore ideas (Newman, 1985b). Not only does this help students to build a representation of the topic about which they are writing, but the challenges, prompts, and questions from collaborators help to fashion a working representation of the assignment or task (Flower, 1994).

Some writers experience prolonged silent periods, whereas others report heightened emotional states or sudden bursts of productivity (Smith, 1982). Just because writing in school is tidily penciled into thirty-minute lessons does not mean that each writer can wax eloquent in a timely way. The best writing springs from creative sources within the person that may manifest themselves as the individual becomes "distracted, preoccupied, or temperamental. If new ideas are bubbling, the individual may become restless, excitable, emphatic even, while lack of manifest progress may result in gloom and despondency" (Smith, 1982, p. 126). The most profound education reaches deep into the individual, and in reaching deeply, evokes emotional reaction. Teachers who respect this passion sympathize with its companion emotions. The alternative? Apathy.

The Writing Process: Drafting

The drafting stage involves quickly capturing ideas. There may be several false starts, changes of mind, and searches for more ideas. Writers do the best they can in spelling, vocabulary, and syntax, without a concern for accuracy. This stage is followed by revision, during which students share and discuss the content and clarity of their writing, drawing on the teacher as a resource for advice and support. This step helps students to expand their thinking and communicate more expressively before editing perfects the form and grammar.

A useful aid for English learners is a *word wall* or *word bank,* which provides a visual representation of words they may need to draw on while writing. For example, a pictorial word wall for a unit on fairy tales might include matched pictures and printed words of a queen, a king, a castle, a crown, and other words that a writer might need to use. This device helps English learners to be more fluent as they draft their ideas.

Self-Correction and Revision

Writers face similar problems as they draft. Moxley (1994) suggested using the following questions for self-evaluation as part of the revision process (questions have been shortened from the original):

1. Have I provided the details that my audience will need in order to understand the subject? What changes can I make to simplify the presentation?
2. Is my essay unified by a clear purpose or thesis? Have I provided sufficient forecasting statements so that readers will understand the organization of the essay? Have I followed the organization I promised in the introduction? Have I mixed together any stages that could be kept separate? Have I neglected any stages or steps?
3. How well developed is the content? Are all important concepts well defined?
4. Will readers find fault with my logic? Have I provided sufficient information for readers to understand my reasoning? What additional comparisons, illustrations, or analogies could I add?
5. Is the report visually appealing? Would readers better understand how I have organized my information if I used more subheadings, tables, flow charts, or other visual aids?
6. Is my writing economical? Can I combine and edit some of the sentences to make them more vigorous?
7. Is the report grammatically and mechanically correct? (p. 109)

Feedback through Peer Response and Writing Conferences

Students can give one another feedback through formal "sharing" meetings organized by the teacher, in which students explain where they are in the writing and what help they need, read their work, and ask peers for comments; or they can be informal, student-initiated interactions (Calkins, 1983). Peer response can be more valuable than teacher feedback in helping writers analyze their own drafts (Reid, 1993). Simply putting students together in groups to react to the strength and weaknesses of a paper read aloud is unlikely to be successful with ESL students (Kroll, 1991). To be useful, peer responding must be modeled and taught as part of the writing process from the beginning, so that students are aware of writing for their peers as well as for the teacher (Mittan, 1989).

One way to shape peer response is to provide students with a peer-review feedback sheet that is specifically designed for the writing prompt (Mittan, 1989) or the evaluation criteria for the final paper (Campbell, 1998). In a college-level writing class, these might include the following:

- specific title, related to the central idea
- introductory paragraph previewing the entire paper
- clearly stated thesis, tying the ideas together
- logically organized paragraphs, with claims supported by evidence
- clear differentiation between writer's ideas and those of other authors
- concluding paragraph, discussing the significance of the ideas
- appropriate grammar and usage

Group Review.   Peers are most successful as respondents when they are grouped with two other writers whose topic is similar. They can read two papers and respond to one of them. In this way they are better prepared to become more deeply involved in the discussion of ideas and topic development, use of sources, and other substantive issues (Campbell, 1998). Peer response to writing is not about editing (Leki, 1990). It should include feedback about the content, point of view, and tone of the work. The point is to focus on the communicative content of the writing and draw students together in a more respectful sharing of the messages they intend.

Writing Conferences.   *Individual writing conferences with the teacher* are interviews in which the teacher listens to each student talk about the work in progress, commenting and asking "following" questions (those that follow or reflect the student's comment), which lead the student toward control of the topic; "process" questions, which help the student organize and focus the writing; or "basic" questions, which ask the student to focus on the basic structure (Graves, 1983). This questioning helps the teacher understand the student's topic and focus and models appropriate questions that students can later ask themselves as they put their thoughts on paper.

Ideally, the tone of the conference is that the writer is in charge. The writer speaks first to set the agenda and communicate the intended meaning. The teacher may then respond to specific sections ("What is the main point of this part?"), offer suggestions as alternatives, or check for understanding. The student who can restate what the instructor suggests is more likely to make substantial revisions in subsequent drafts (Goldstein & Conrad, 1990).

The Writing Process: Editing

Editing takes place after the message is complete. In this stage, which is particularly important when writing is going to be shared in a formal way, errors or mistakes in usage and spelling are corrected. Students who learn to self-edit can examine their own writing critically and improve it. The teacher's proofreading is useful only if the students can use it to improve their own writing.

If a perfected, or final, version is not necessary, students may archive their rough drafts in a portfolio without rewriting. The process has generated writing that is satisfying in its ability to capture and share ideas, which is the essence of writing for the purpose of communication. If, however, the writing is to be published or publicly shared, and students are to achieve pride of authorship, accuracy in such areas as spelling is warranted.

Error Correction

In the early stages of writing English, fluency is a much more vital goal than accuracy. With ESL students, the teacher must consider the level of their general language proficiency before making decisions about error correction. Law and Eckes (2000) suggested that with younger children and newcomers, one should encourage expression of ideas without correcting grammar. Writers should be rewarded for their courage in trying new formats and more complicated sentence syntax, and risk taking should be actively encouraged. Error correction is the process of tactfully leading students to enjoy perfecting their vocabulary, grammar, and usage. As Gadda, Peitzman, and Walsh (1988) pointed out, correcting an essay is like fine-tuning an engine: An essay must "run" before a tune-up is needed.

Correcting "errors" means offering the student feedback not on *mistakes*, one-time random occurrences caused by carelessness or memory lapses, but rather on errors, imperfect language structures that are systematic and part of the learner's developing language system (Corder, 1981). Leki (1986) found that students are grateful for specific kinds of feedback that improve their sentence-level writing. An instructor's optimal response to any written composition errors should follow two cardinal principles: (1) Attention to the communication of meaning is paramount; and (2) the learner is better served who is guided toward self-correction.

Proofreading.   Raimes (1983) suggested using proofreading marks to indicate just twelve types of error (new paragraph needed, error in spelling, capitalization, punctuation, verb form, verb tense, word order, word form, vocabulary, grammar, sentence structure or boundary, and missing letter or word). Moreover, teachers may wish to use *restrictive correcting*, focusing on only a few types of errors at one time (Bartram & Walton, 1994, p. 80). Some instructors may set certain standards of submission before accepting a paper, such as requiring that a word-processed paper be electronically spell-checked.

Correcting Spelling.   Correcting spelling in English is easier for instructor and student alike if it is done systematically. Gable, Henrickson, and Meeks (1988) suggested a five-step method of diagnosing and correcting spelling errors:

1. Sample students' spelling to gain an understanding of what kinds of errors are frequent.
2. Interview students, asking if they can tell what words they find confusing or difficult to spell.
3. Analyze and classify the errors into three types:
   (a) *Regular* words that have a consistent sound-symbol connection (*nap, pig*; errors in these may indicate a phonics problem).
   (b) *Predictable* sound-symbol connection words (*may, day*) that while not exactly phonics-compatible, can be explained in an expected way.
   (c) *Irregular* words (*melon, might, through*) that must be taught through visual memory.
4. Devise interventions or corrective strategies. For regular words, practice letter-sound connections; for predictable words, practice rhyming words and word pairs, or review spelling rules; for irregular words, use pair work with flash cards, a look-cover-copy-compare drill, or some other means of enhancing visual memory. (pp. 112–117)
5. Implement and evaluate the strategy.

Table 6.6 lists frequently asked questions about correcting errors in composition and experts' responses.

Publishing

Ways of publishing may vary: A play is performed, a story is bound into a book for circulation in the class library, a poem is read aloud, an essay is posted on a bulletin board, a video is made of a student reading aloud, a class newspaper is circulated to the community (Enright & McCloskey, 1988). Desktop-publishing software, usually a simple page-layout program combined with a word processor, has made more readily accessible the look of professional typesetting and layout. Teachers of writing may find themselves incorporating principles of page layout, type font manipulation, and other aspects of journalism into their composition courses in order to help students prepare their work for a wider audience. It is easy to master the principles of laying out a newsletter page:

- Put the most important information near the top left of the page.
- Do not put two headlines side by side.
- Do not mix too many different type fonts on the same page.
- Do not place a continuation column higher on the page than the original headline.
- Make columns at least two inches wide.

Issues with ESL Writing

Selecting a topic can sometimes be a concern for English learners. Not all writers find a topic of a personal nature, such as a childhood experience, fruitful for generating ideas. Such topics may be paradoxically difficult for English learners—experiences that took place in one's native country or in one's native language may

TABLE 6.6 ◆ Questions and Answers about Error Correction in Composition

Questions about Error Correction	Expert Answers
What is the instructor's role when responding to ESL learners' papers?	• "Collaborator in response to content" • "Constructive critic in response to sentence errors" (p. 5)
Why is it important to respond to content in writing?	Evidence shows that in subsequent drafts, writers do at least attempt to address content issues that have been raised during the process of feedback from instructors. ESL students find this desirable because they can understand how their rhetoric structures differ from those in English, and they can understand if they are communicating well with the target audience.
How can the instructor effectively respond to content?	• Write comments that reflect a personal response. • Provide specific suggestions. • Refer to specific text segments in the feedback. • Balance positive and negative comments.
Where in a paper should content feedback be given?	• Write in right margin or left margin, not both, and/or write endnotes, referring to specific text sections.
When in the writing process should content feedback be given?	• On early drafts, mostly suggest ideas for content (make use of peer review here, too). • On later drafts, perhaps provide pregrading feedback. • On final drafts only, give content feedback; works well if there is a process of peer review.
How can the instructor respond systematically to sentence-level errors?	Use a system, with codes. Be selective; concentrate on global errors, especially those addressed in whole-class discussion.
Should grades be given on content and sentence errors?	Some systems allow for three grades: Organization (focus and coherence), Development (logic of paragraph structure), and Language (sentence structure, word choice, usage). A rubric used in grading tells students what value is placed on which element.
How can the instructor help students to improve their writing?	• Determine the most serious and frequent sentence-level errors. • Prioritize the errors and target some for improvement. • Develop strategies for working on these targets, examining cause and cure. • Encourage the student to monitor these with enough focus to improve and not too much anxiety.

Source: Bates, Lane, & Lange, 1993.

be more difficult for nonnative speakers of English to write about than topics drawn from an English-language context (Friedlander, 1990). Being familiar with a topic is no guarantee of writing ease. The fact that a topic is popular with native English-speakers is no guarantee that it will enable English learners. Crosscultural differences abound: Japanese writers are reluctant to discuss religion, for example (see McKay, 1989), while students of the Islamic faith usually like nothing better (Leki, 1992).

Academic Register.   Establishing a tone suitable for school writing may be difficult for English learners, especially at the young adult level. International students who are asked to write essays while sojourning at American universities may adopt several stances that are not conducive to authentic voice. First, they may prefer topics that are exotic to others who are not of their culture (e.g., Chinese New Year) in order for the topic itself to appear engaging; yet as they write about these topics it may be evident that it is not easy to discuss their culture without insight into the origins of its customs or values. This difficulty may result in a superficial tone. Topics about which the student knows little (divorce, drug use) may be treated with naïveté or an excessively judgmental tone (Leki, 1992). Other tones to avoid are flippancy (disrespectful levity), sarcasm (contemptuous remarks), sentimentality (shallow feeling), self-righteousness (making a special claim to virtue), belligerence (trying to bully the reader into agreement), and apology ("poor little me") (Packer & Timpane, 1997).

Plagiarism.   The unacceptability of plagiarism may be difficult to convey. Students from other cultures may not understand the Western emphasis on originality. They may have been taught that mimicry is the highest form of respect and thus literally feel negative sanction for altering words as they are written. Students may also feel pressure to help others by letting them copy; or they may simply work together, resulting in identical copies of student work (Leki, 1992). Other students may come from cultures in which an end-run around authority is considered clever, or in which individual achievement is meaningless because rules are routinely bent to accommodate the wealthy and powerful.

On a deeper level, however, plagiarism may occur because English learners feel coerced into writing in English, perhaps on account of social, academic, or economic demands on their lives; or they may feel lack of ownership over English (Pennycook, 1998). Lastly, students may feel that the pressure to succeed in the United States is so strong that any means justifies the end. Plagiarism has been taken to new levels by the advent of the Internet and electronic databases, which allow instant access to global sources of information as well as multiple sources of term papers for sale (Bloch, 2001). The best solution to the problem of plagiarism is to invest in the writing process, give students support and accurate feedback at various stages in their writing, and offer specific guidelines and training in "textual borrowing" strategies (Barks & Watts, 2001, p. 246).

Reference Materials.   The use of dictionaries and the use of the library are two areas in which English learners may need guidance and direction. Many students rely on bilingual dictionaries, which in their brevity do not always supply accurate translations. On the other hand, if dictionaries are not frequently used in the primary language, the student may not use one in English either (Leki, 1992). Explicitly teaching dictionary skills can be of great help to students, especially those whose first language shares the same alphabet as English (see Feuerstein & Schcolnik, 1995, for an example of such instruction). International students sometimes rely on pocket translating devices, which do not always supply accurate translations:

> Once in a TESOL methods class I was discussing the topic of self-esteem in SLA. A Japanese student sitting at the back of the class was punching keys on the pocket translator and frowning. I stopped the discussion to ask her what was wrong. She called me over to point out that the machine's translation for *self-esteem* was *egotism*. It bothered her to think that I was advocating selfishness as a boost to second-language learning. I was later to find that many Japanese translations involving the term "self" may not carry positive connotations.

English learners may not be familiar with the use of a library, especially if such resources are not available in their native culture. Students who know how to use a library may simply need special training in order to be able to make use of the library's features, such as the electronic card catalog (Leki, 1992). In other cases, students may have come to rely on the libraries within their own families, if they are among the elite; or they may never have had occasion to use a library. For example, during the eight years in which I lived in Puerto Rico, the public library in San Juan, established by Andrew Carnegie, was unfortunately closed, due to lack of air conditioning. As far as I knew, people did not use public libraries there, and there was no public outcry for the library's reopening.

In summary, current approaches to writing instruction vary in emphasis, but the best teaching supports the following principles: (1) integration of language and content teaching, (2) use of authentic language and materials, (3) recognition of student diversity and learning styles, (4) development of cognitive strategies, (5) use and support of students' first languages and cultures, (6) importance of interaction and collaborative learning, and (7) student engagement in purposeful learning tasks (Díaz-Rico & Weed, 2002).

Listening Processes

Part of the knowledge needed to comprehend oral discourse is the ability to separate meaningful units from the stream of speech. Although listening may be seen as a "receptive" skill, it is by no means a passive act. According to the sociocognitive approach to learning, listening is an act of constructing meaning. Listeners draw on their store of background knowledge and their expectation of the message to be conveyed as they actively work at understanding a conversation or oral presentation. The role of the teacher is to set up situations in which students can develop their own purposes and goals for listening, acquire the English that is most useful in their daily lives, feel a sense of purpose, and engage in real communication.

♦ **STRATEGY 6.3:** Teach listening in a way that builds interest, information acquisition, and lifelong literacy

Although the current emphasis is on communicating for authentic purposes, a number of guided listening techniques have come from more traditional language-teaching methodologies. Long (1987) separated the act of listening into two sets of factors: message factors and medium factors. Message factors entail understanding the propositions that the message contains—the semantic information, the intention of the speaker, and the background knowledge of the listener through which the message can be interpreted. Medium factors include provision for the constituents of speech (usually clauses) and the efficiency of speech (perhaps featuring reduced and elliptical forms); the possibility of ungrammatical forms; provision for pausing, errors, pace of speech, rhythm, and stress; inclusion of cohesive devices; and provision for co-construction of meaning among interlocutors.

Long (1987) divides listening into conversational listening and academic listening, each containing a host of subskills. For purposes of simplification, listening activities will be discussed here under the categories of listening to repeat, listening to understand, and listening for communication.

Listening to Repeat: The Audiolingual Legacy

In audiolingual teaching, students repeat exactly what they hear, with an emphasis on correct pronunciation. Minimal pair pattern practice is a common strategy; students are asked to repeat simple phrases that differ by only one phoneme, for example: "It is a ship/It is a sheep." "He is barking/He is parking." Another typical listen/repeat format is backward buildup: Students are given the end of a sentence or phrase to repeat; when they are successful, earlier parts of the sentence are added until the complete phrase is mastered ("store/the store/to the store/walked to the store/Peter walked to the store"). Both these procedures require little attention to meaning.

Current methods encourage students to listen to minimal pairs within meaningful contexts. Teachers use poems, nursery rhymes, and songs to introduce "rhyming words," asking students to fill in the blanks at the end of lines to demonstrate their knowledge of phonemic difference and context-appropriate words. In addition, teachers can read aloud books featuring word play, alliteration, and tongue twisters, encouraging students to talk about how the author manipulates words. Such activities help students to hear the language and to develop phonemic awareness.

Jazz chants provide rhythmic presentations of the sentence intonation patterns of English. "The rhythm, stress, and intonation pattern of the chant should be an *exact* replica of what the student would hear from a native speaker in natural conversation" (Graham, 1992, p. 3). *Jazz Chants* and subsequent books by Carol Graham (1978a, 1978b, 1986, 1988) offer entertaining verbal interchanges set to catchy rhythms, such as the toe-tapping singalong, "I'll have a chicken salad sandwich on toast" or the woeful, "I'm sorry, I'm so sorry, I'm really sorry, I'm terribly sorry." Graham (1988) has also created jazz chants from fairy tales, giving younger and less proficient students the opportunity to work with longer texts.

Listening to Understand: The Task Approach

As the audiolingual tradition fades, students are being asked to demonstrate comprehension as well, not through exact repetition but through performing tasks such as writing the correct response or selecting the correct answer (Morley, 1991). To be successful, they must listen carefully. Typical classroom tasks are listening to an audiotape and completing true/false exercises based on the content, listening to a prerecorded speech and circling vocabulary items on a list, and listening to a lecture and completing an outline of the notes. Students may be asked to listen for the main idea, for specific information, for synonyms, or for vocabulary in context (Leshinsky, 1995). Other listening activities may include listening for focal stress or listening for syllables (Kozyrev, 1998a).

Autonomy in language learning is encouraged by assigning students to create listening journal entries. Three times a week students summarize what they have listened to—for example, a television program, a video, a movie, or a lecture—with a minimum requirement of thirty minutes of listening at a time (Leshinsky, 1995).

Contemporary language-teaching methods emphasize the interactional aspects of language and recognize the importance of the listener's construction of meaning. The first stage of language acquisition is now seen as listening rather than repeating. During the initial "silent period," learners actively listen, segmenting the sound stream, absorbing intonation patterns, and becoming comfortable in the second-language environment. They demonstrate comprehension through nonverbal means. With this methodology, academic subjects can be included, even in the early stages of language acquisition (see TPR and Natural Approach, Chapter 3).

Even though students are just asked to listen, not pressured to speak, the listening is for the purposes of comprehension. For example, in *Bridge to Communication Primary Level A* (Santillana Press), Unit 9, Lesson 6 ("Animal Riddles"), students view a poster of animals in a barn. The teacher might ask a student in the preproduction stage, "Are people *safe* around these tame animals?", pointing to the sheep, cat, and calf. The response of a nod to the word "safe" indicates comprehension. In Unit 12, Lesson 5 ("Sniff and Tell"), the teacher asks a student who is in the preproduction stage, "Which odors do you like?", pointing to the Sense of Smell exhibit. The student can show comprehension by pointing.

Listening to understand features listening activities based primarily on three types of sources. The first type of source is prerecorded selections by various speakers, usually, though not always, native speakers. At this level excerpts are usually based on simulations of actual conversations or other input. For example, Randall's Listening Lab (www.esl-lab.com) uses a limited range of speakers, and topics vary.

A second source of listening material is audiotaped selections culled from a variety of sources. To create listening input materials for *The Heart of the Matter* (Vai, 1998), the author used a Sony Professional to interview a wide array of musicians, artists, entrepreneurs, and other professionals on a host of topics. Each lesson was organized around a brief, formal lecture that introduced a topic, a listening activity that presented material of a more informal and subjective nature, and a third listening exercise that asked several speakers "from the street" for their reaction to the second exercise. The usual workbook activities rounded out these listening opportunities with comprehension, vocabulary development, and critical thinking exercises.

A third type of source consists of listening to the "real world." *Talk It Over!* (Kozyrev, 1998b) assigns students the task of watching a television game show and answering workbook questions about the nature of the contestants, the content and format of the show, and the kinds of possible prizes. In another section of the same series, students watch television commercials and decide if they are effective tools of persuasion. Thus students are expected to seek out their own input and do a task based on the assigned listening.

Academic listening might be classified as listening for understanding. Lecture comprehension is of vital importance in the lives of many ESOL learners who enroll in English-language university programs. Flowerdew's *Academic Listening: Research Perspectives* (1994) provides a general introduction to the issues in academic listening, including the effect on ESL students' listening comprehension of the various genres featured by distinct academic disciplines, and ways in which lecturers might be trained to facilitate comprehension for international students.

For a more interactive adaptation of these listening procedures, the teacher and students can discuss the topic of an upcoming talk by a guest speaker and brainstorm questions and comments the students might like to make. During the talk, students listen for answers to their questions. The talk can be tape-recorded and the tape subsequently put into a listening center. Students can then listen again, making note of ideas they want to share in the class follow-up activities. The tape also serves as a mediator when students have varying recollections of a particular point. The students can listen carefully to the tape in order to reconcile their points of view.

Listening for Communication

The emphasis at this level is on developing students' abilities to communicate fluently and accurately by integrating listening, speaking, and pronunciation practice and developing skills in anticipating questions, understanding suggestions, and note taking. Once listeners are beyond the initial stage, interviews are often used to augment listening skills in the communicative approach. *The Complete ESL/EFL Cooperative and Communicative Activity Book* (Sloan, 1991) offers various interview formats and subjects that can be used cooperatively among students. Listening can also be used in problem-solving situations by means of riddles, logic puzzles, and brain teasers as well as more traditional mathematical problems. Listening, far from being a merely receptive skill, can be successfully combined with other language modes as part of an integrated approach to English-language acquisition.

Table 6.7 provides listening comprehension activities within each of the three levels discussed above.

Before Listening

Explicit instruction in listening can be organized in "into, through, and beyond" stages in a similar fashion to reading instruction. Prelistening tasks can include a preview of vocabulary, a cue to the type of rhetoric expected (such as chronological order), or attention to a map that cues a spatial setting for the listening task. Chapter 1, "The American Civil War," in Unit 5 of Dunkel and Lim's *Intermediate Listening Comprehension* (1994) offers a prelistening preparation task defining "civil

TABLE 6.7 ⬩ Activities for Listening Comprehension

Repetition	Understanding	Communication

To hear sound patterns:
  Rhyming poems
  Songs
  Couplets
  Tongue twisters
  Jingles
  Alliterative poems and books
	Listening to answer factual
	questions orally or in writing:
	  Dialogues
	  Talks
	  Lectures
	  Arguments
		Playing games:
		  Twenty questions
		  Pictionary
		  Password
		  Simon Says
		  Mother, May I?

To listen to sentences:
  Jazz chants
  Dialogues
  Skits
	Listening to make notes:
	  Support an argument
	  Persuade
		Open-ended sentences
		
		Conversation starters
		
		Cooperative problem-
		solving activities:
		  Riddles
		  Logic puzzles
		  Brain teasers

Source: Díaz-Rico & Weed, 2002.

war," introducing key vocabulary, and previewing the rhetorical structure of causal explanation. At a more advanced level, Dunkel, Pialorsi, and Kozyrev's *Advanced Listening Comprehension* (1996) presents a preview of the content of the listening tasks as well as a lengthy outline to help the listener understand the rhetorical organization of the excerpt. In contrast, in Chapter 8 of *Talk It Over!* (Kozyrev, 1998b) students first interview classmates or people outside class to find out why they watch television and then listen to an interview with David Bianculi, television critic for the *New York Daily News*. This prepares students to listen in a different way.

While Listening

Students can follow an outline as they listen, take notes cued by a set of questions, or take notes in a variety of ways, using idea maps, outlines, paragraphs, or lists. They can listen several times with a slightly different purpose each time: main idea, supporting details, or attitude of the speaker. They can listen to the lecture or conversation recorded several times, using speakers from contrasting dialects. The purposes of listening might be to detect emotional cues; I once attended a training session for hypnotists in which we were instructed to listen to a woman who related an anecdote twice in Russian, once telling the truth and once lying. Our task was to distinguish the truth from the lie.

If the teacher feels the need to lecture, a helpful strategy for English learners is to videotape a lesson while students simply listen to the lecture, concentrating on understanding and writing down only questions or parts of the lecture they do not fully understand. Later, the videotape is played, and the teacher and several students take notes on the board. The teacher can model the type of outline that indicates the main ideas and supporting details. After a few minutes, the videotape is stopped and the discussion then highlights various note-taking and other strategies. This activity can be used on a periodic basis to enhance students' ability to comprehend lectures and take effective notes (Adamson, 1993).

Teachers in content classes in which English learners are "mainstreamed" need to attend to the listening skills of these students. Frequent comprehension checks are helpful. When a difficult concept is presented, the teacher can ask the entire class to indicate with a (chest-high) thumbs up/thumbs-down sign if they understand a new concept well enough for the class to continue. This public, yet private, gesture can offer feedback to the instructor about the general level of comprehension without stigmatizing the English learners.

Unfortunately, people do not always pay attention when they should be doing so. Table 6.8 presents six common bad listening habits and their cures (from Dale & Wolf, 1988).

After Listening

Many kinds of activities can follow up a listening task. Students can write, discuss, read, draw, or act out their interpretation of the content. They can attend to the linguistic aspects of what they have heard by completing work sheets on word meaning, idiomatic usage, formal versus informal English, words that compare and contrast, or words that introduce causal statements. The focus can be on cultural aspects of the reading, content applications across the disciplines, or critical thinking including problem solving. In Leshinsky (1995), students listen to a recording about two people who have just signed a lease; following this activity they work on paraphrasing, discussing the relaxed pronunciation of the speakers (use of filler words like "y'know" and con-

TABLE 6.8 • Six Common Bad Listening Habits and Their Cures

Bad Habit	Cure
Being distracted by the speaker's appearance/delivery	Concentrate on the message, not the messenger.
Deciding the topic is boring	Make an effort to listen for information that might later be useful in a job or in conversation with friends and family.
Faking attention	Be sincere and take a real interest in the person speaking. If you are too busy to listen, be honest and ask if you can hear the story later when you have more time to listen.
Looking for distractions	Concentrate; refuse to take your mind from the speaker.
Overconcentrating on unimportant facts	Pay attention to the general purpose and main idea first; then take note of supporting facts.
Reacting emotionally to trigger words	Make a list of the trigger words that upset you. When they occur, recognize them as such and postpone reactions.

Source: Dale & Wolf, 1988.

tractions), writing a summary of what was learned about the rights and responsibilities of landlords and tenants, or role-playing renegotiating a lease.

Authentic Tasks in and out of the Real World

An effective listening curriculum exposes students to a variety of speakers for a variety of tasks on a variety of topics for a variety of purposes. Language should resemble speech used in real life, whether short and direct, rambling and indirect, formal or informal, or curt and incoherent. How is one to assess the response to such varied stimuli? Clearly, a prepackaged test, based on correct answers to work sheet exercises, exerts the most convergent control. At the other end of the curriculum, service learning exerts pressure to listen for the needs of the community. The most useful approach is one that increases in complexity as students become more capable and exposes them to the "real world" when they can handle authentic interactions. The teacher is the judge of the appropriate balance between what is real and what is contrived, and between convergent and divergent goals.

Of course, aside from classroom exercises, the real listening skill is going out into the real world, "swimming in the open seas of language" (Yoshida, 2001/2002, p. 5). Comprehending carefully selected three- to seven-minute chunks of language is much simpler than listening to actual spoken discourse. Comprehension must be balanced between the actual utterances of real speakers and their intended meanings. Listeners must bring a relatively sophisticated set of understandings to bear on a number of factors: what to expect from the speaker, the setting in time and place, the topic, the genre of the text and the co-text, or accompanying clues to meaning. In face-to-face conversation, the speaker is supposed to give the listener cues to help sustain coherence and clarity (Brown & Yule, 1983). A great deal of unconscious work goes into the task of real-world listening to create both cultural and linguistic understanding.

But despite the complexity of listening tasks and the emphasis on communicative approaches, listening is only half the work; one must also learn to speak.

Speaking Processes

Oral work in English has generally been considered to rest on the concept that oracy lacks a social or political dimension. Being able to speak, or to participate in a discourse community or exchange by listening, was a transparent way of communicating meaning and intent. However, not acknowledging that discourses are influenced by uneven distributions of power amounts to teaching skills that are not grounded in the realities of knowledge and power practices. Teachers of English must become aware that oracy is inextricably joined with cultural identity and social differences, and that opportunities to listen and speak are differentiated according to the individual's relationship to institutions and sociocultural contexts. As Peim (1993) put it, it is not the case that any oral activity in class simply and directly enhances language development. Direct connections to the community and to the circulation of power (Foucault, 1980, 1984) strengthen the chance that individuals' investments in learning to speak and listen will actually enhance their cultural capital.

Speaking involves a number of complex skills and strategies, but because spoken language leaves no visible trace, its complexity and organizational features are hard to track. In spoken discourse, words must not only be strung together in proper grammatical sequence, they must also make sense. This process produces an oral text that has inherent form, meaning, purpose, and function. Spoken discourse can be informal, as in conversations between friends, or formal, as in academic lectures. Informal conversations are interactive; speaker and listener share common knowledge and support one another with nonverbal cues. On the other hand, a lecturer assumes that the listener can supply a complex background or context; the listener is less able to interact with the speaker to negotiate meaning.

Part of the role of the teacher is to help students assimilate and produce discourse not only for the purpose of basic interpersonal communication (informal) but also for the comprehension and production of cognitive/academic language (formal). In addition, the teacher provides opportunities for students to express themselves in a wide range of language functions.

◆ **STRATEGY 6.4:** Teach speaking in a way that sustains self-esteem and lifelong self-expression

Difficulties with Spoken Discourse

Today's universities enroll many undergraduates whose first language is not English, including an increasing number of foreign students. Many international students who sojourn in the United States or elsewhere and have learned English as a second or foreign language experience some reticence in oral speech. It is not uncommon for these students to attend class for an entire semester without speaking once in class. Kehe and Kehe (1998) describe the challenge:

> A complaint often heard from both ESOL and subject-matter instructors is that their international students are passive in group and whole-class discussions. At the same time, international students tell us they're quiet because they feel that they don't know what to say, they don't feel they have anything interesting to say, or they have difficulty understanding what others say but are embarrassed to admit it. Furthermore, they may say they come from cultures where spontaneous give-and-take interaction in class isn't valued (or is even discouraged), and they don't know the "rules" for participating in this kind of interaction. (p. 211)

Despite the difficulties of getting these "silent types" to interact, the emphasis on communicative methodology mandates that teachers try (e.g., Savignon, 1983; Taylor, 1983; Nattinger, 1984; and thereafter a groundswell of publications). Similar situations exist in K–12 classrooms in American schools, in which large numbers of English learners are "mainstreamed" into contexts that render them silent as a result. Multiple avenues of communication are needed in order for students who are English learners to meet the double challenge of what to say and when to say it. Research shows that language learners develop best when they have opportunities to interact (see Wells, 1981). It is therefore vital that teachers help students overcome their oral language quietude and help them to develop their speaking abilities.

Basic Interpersonal Communication Skills

A newcomer to the English language needs to learn basic interpersonal communication skills (BICS) that permit adjustment to the routines of schooling and the comforts of peer interaction. This accomplishment enables the student to perform classroom chores, chat with peers, or consume instructional media. The importance of BICS is that students can begin to understand and communicate with their teacher, develop and fine-tune their interpersonal skills, and begin to overcome culture shock.

School-age children use BICS to communicate basic needs to others or to share informal social interactions with peers. The focus in BICS is on getting across a message, with little regard for sentence structure and word choice. BICS is clearly more than words. Some exchanges with people involve no words at all; for instance, a nod of the head while passing in the hallway at work may serve as a greeting. Cummins (1984) calls BICS *context embedded*, because factors apart from the linguistic code can furnish meaning. For example, one student asks another for an eraser: "Mine's gone. You got one?" The student points to the pencil eraser and beckons for a loan. The item itself provides the context rather than the language. Other cues that add meaning to BICS in this situation are the tone of voice (supplicating) and the gesture ("Give me.")

Successful results support early acquisition of BICS; children who seek admission to a playground game using English may receive quick support for their attempts. Studies have shown that conversational skills can approach native-like levels within two years of exposure to English (Collier, 1987; Cummins, 1981a). Fluency in BICS often leads parents or other adults to assume that the child has mastered English. Students themselves may feel that BICS is equivalent to English mastery: In a poll taken in 2000, 86 percent of children aged five to seventeen whose home language is Spanish reported that they speak English "well" or "very well," and 90 percent of youths who speak a language from Asian or Pacific Island countries reported that they spoke English "well" or "very well" (U.S. Census Bureau, 2001c). However, this apparent fluency can be misleading. Students who may appear to be fluent enough in English to survive in an all-English classroom may in fact have significant gaps in the development of academic aspects of English.

Teachers can encourage newcomers' acquisition of basic social language in several ways. First, pairing a new student with a bilingual buddy who speaks the same primary language as well as English eases the pain of culture shock. Although much of the first communication with this buddy takes place in the primary language, the buddy can teach the student BICS. When there are no other students who speak the language of the newcomer, the ideal buddy is one who is outgoing and can communicate with body language, gestures, or facial expressions. Seating newcomers so that they can be involved with other pupils and can participate with other students can help to keep the new students alert and interactive.

A "Newcomer Handbook" is helpful during the earliest stages of BICS acquisition. Students can help to create this orientation guide. Sections of this guide may feature simple school rules and procedures; English phrases to use for various social functions (asking for help, volunteering for class jobs, etc.); and guides for homework help. It may include a simple map of the school with bilingual labels. Teachers may wish to check Amery's (1979) *The First Thousand Words: A Picture Word Book* and its companions, such as Amery & Milá's (1979) *The First Thousand Words In Spanish* for vocabulary items that match in English and other languages.

Cooperative tasks of all kinds provide opportunities for students to speak with one another. Students in the earliest stages of acquiring BICS should not be isolated from high-achieving peers during their "silent period." Cooperative groups with mixed abilities permit students some measure of participation even though it may not be a role requiring a high level of verbal ability in English. Cohen's Complex Instruction model (see Cohen, Lotan, & Catanzarite, 1990), is built on providing equal opportunity for student participation in order to eliminate notions of high and low status within the group. Students are assigned well-defined roles that rotate among all members of the class, so that students can practice cooperative rules while working with content materials.

Developing Oral Language

Morgan (1992) offered a host of ways in which teachers can develop oral language in the classroom. An encouraging classroom climate helps students to feel confident, to speak freely and make mistakes, and to believe that their way of speaking is respected and their opinions are taken seriously. A noncompetitive atmosphere encourages the sharing of ideas through interaction, especially at a dedicated "sharing time" every day. A "productively talkative" work environment is not so noisy that a timid child feels overwhelmed. Even in a "normally noisy" class, a shy student may need a "home corner" where he or she can listen to tapes in the primary language or engage in nonverbal play in which English is not necessary. This space provides a respite from the stress of foreign-language immersion.

A listening area can be set up in which the English learners can listen to books on tape, with picture books or models nearby to support understanding of what is heard. Two such stations may be set up side by side so that students can share this listening experience with a friend. It may be comforting to a child if the voice on the tape speaks English that is accented the same way that people from her primary-language community sound. This is an important contribution that a bilingual English speaker who lives in the neighborhood of the child can make.

❖ Tactics for teachers to develop students' BICS:

◆ Provide academic opportunities for talking and working together, ranging from informal (work-related chit-chat) to highly structured (for example, each person in a cooperative group is responsible for one section of an oral report).
◆ Listen to students with enthusiasm and interest to communicate that their thoughts are valued.
◆ Fill a "pocket chart" with slots for every student with a paper flower after a student has spoken at sharing time, with no student receiving a second turn until everyone has had a chance to volunteer a personal anecdote.
◆ Make sure a quiet area is available where a child can "escape" English for a while.
◆ Have the voices of other speakers of English available on tape or in person to provide aural exposure to more than a single speaker.

Situations for Spoken Discourse

Students need opportunities to talk in natural interactional contexts and for a variety of purposes: to establish and maintain social relationships; to express reactions; to give and seek information; to solve problems, discuss ideas, or teach and learn a skill; to entertain or play with language; or to display achievement (Rivers & Temperley, 1978). In addition, students need to learn to interact with a variety of conversational partners: other students, the teacher, other adults at school, cross-age peers, guests, and so on.

English learners need environments that help them to meet the social, emotional, cognitive, and linguistic demands of their lives in and out of school. Students need an *emotional setting*, a climate of trust and respect, in which they need not fear ridicule from their peers or correction from the teacher. Teachers can encourage students to respect the language of their peers, can model respectful listening when students speak, and can work with students to establish classroom rules of respect and support. Students need a *physical setting for talk* that features flexibility for working and interacting: round or rectangular tables, clusters of desks, work stations, and centers. In addition, classrooms need to contain *things to talk about*: fish tanks and nature displays; flags, maps, and artifacts; and a variety of print material. Finally, students need *frequent opportunities to talk*; flexible grouping allows work with a variety of classmates, cross-age tutors, aides, parent volunteers, and volunteer "grandparents" (Dudley-Marling & Searle, 1991).

Speaking can be integrated with other literacy and oracy activities (Morgan, 1992). Students can retell the stories they hear in storytelling or sharing time and finish them in new ways. They can listen to the sharing time of others and use these as starting points for their own "adventures." As they become aware of the patterns within stories and the needs of the audience, they can embellish their storytelling. Inviting storytellers and community elders to tell stories in class provides rich stimuli; and when the visitors are gone, the students can finish these stories to continue the entertainment.

Speaking reinforces listening comprehension. To ensure comprehension, the content or SDAIE teacher needs to solicit feedback from students about the course content. To find out who is comprehending the material, one must ask. If no one asks questions, the teacher finds other ways to check for understanding. Cooperative speaking activities are a part of every SDAIE lesson (Gonzales & Watson, 1986). Some instructors stop for a "pair/share" break every five minutes, during which each student can ask a partner one question.

If structured public speaking is important in the content of the class, students are given a tight outline and timetable for each presentation. The teacher might invite students to meet outside class to rehearse before the presentation. Other students can help by participating in a peer-scoring rubric in which content is emphasized over understandability. It is wise not to surprise students with requests for extemporaneous speaking.

Resources for Spoken Discourse

Opportunities for oral discourse range from those that are carefully constructed to those that are completely student-generated. Several kinds of speaking activities can be included in daily lessons, including problem solving in small groups, practicing persuasive or entertaining speeches, role plays, interviews, chain stories, talks, problems, and discussions (see Zelman, 1996). *Discussion Starters* (Folse, 1996) offers speaking activities that build oral fluency using exercises specifically designed for group participation. The discussion prompts are based upon role plays, "finish-the-story" situations, problems that can be solved only if members of a group work together, and real court cases for groups to play "judge."

Table 6.9 organizes representative oral activities into the three categories suggested by Allen and Vallette (1977). These categories range from tightly structured on the left to freely constructed on the right.

Improving Pronunciation

English learners need a comprehensible control of the English sound system. Pronunciation involves the correct *articulation* of the individual sounds of English as well as the proper *stress* and *pitch* within syllables, words, and phrases. Longer stretches of speech require correct *intonation* patterns. However, the goal of teaching English pronunciation is not necessarily to make second-language speakers sound like native speakers of English. Some English learners do not wish to have a native-like pronunciation but prefer instead to retain an accent that indicates their first-language roots and allows them to be identified with their ethnic community. Still others may wish to integrate actively into the mainstream culture and thus are motivated to try to attain a native accent in English. Teachers need to recognize these individual goals and enable learners to achieve pronunciation that does not detract from their ability to communicate.

TABLE 6.9 ◆ Formats for Oral Practice in the ELD Classroom

Guided Practice	Communicative Practice	Free Conversation

Formulaic exchanges
    Greetings
    Congratulations
    Apologies
    Leave taking
	Simulations	Discussion groups

	Guessing games	Debates
	Group puzzles	Panel discussions
	Rank-order problems	Group picture story
Dialogues	Values continuum	Socializing
Mini-conversations	Categories of preference:	Storytelling/retelling

Role plays	Opinion polls
	    Survey taking
	    Interviews
		Discussions of
		    Films

Skits		Shared experiences
Oral descriptions	Brainstorming	Literature
Strip stories	News reports	
Oral games	Research reports	
	Storytelling	

Source: Díaz-Rico & Weed, 2002.

Students' attempts to reproduce correct word stress, sentence rhythm, and intonation may improve by exposure to native-speaker models. The teacher's role in this case is to create a nonthreatening environment that stimulates and interests students enough for them to participate actively in producing speech. Teachers may also take a more direct role in improving pronunciation. Clarification checks may be interjected politely when communication is impaired. Correction or completion by the teacher may be given after the teacher has allowed ample "wait time." Older students may be given the task of comparing speech sounds in their native language with sounds in English in order to understand the contrast better.

Communicative games are useful for practicing various aspects of intonation, syllabification, stress, and so on. "Syl/la/bles and Linking" is an activity proposed by Benson (1999): Students in pairs practice separating words into syllables by clapping along with the instructor as words are said in syllables. Then students mark the syllables in a written paragraph as the instructor reads. Decide which syllables students will learn to link (example: hear_us, told_us). Students in pairs play a game; the instructor reads a list of word phrases, some of which have linked words and some of which do not. Students link arms if the words are linked. Students are out of the game if they link arms incorrectly.

Cogan (1999) proposed a game for practicing stress and sentence intonation. Students working in pairs each receive a card containing a dialogue. Student A mimics the stress and intonation of one of the sentences on the card using a nonsense syllable. B tries to guess which is the target sentence. Another game to practice stress is "Stress Clapping." A student comes to the front of the room, pulls a sentence written on a folded overhead transparency strip out of a box, and displays the sentence on the overhead projector (sentences are taken from song lyrics, poems, or limericks). The student must read the sentence aloud and clap each time there is a stressed word. The student's team receives a point for each stressed word correctly identified (Mahoney, 1999b).

Using a computer program for practice is a self-tutoring way in which students can improve their pronunciation. Such programs as Pronunciation Plus™ are fun and easy to use.

Before Speaking

Prespeaking activities warm the students to the topic and activate or provide some prior knowledge. In Kehe and Kehe's (1998) Unit 11 ("Your Hometown and Childhood Home"), students write their answers to several questions about their hometown before beginning the discussion. In Hynes and Baichman's (1989) *Breaking the Ice* (Chapter 12, "Romance on the Horizon"), students think about how they offer advice before they discuss three common difficulties people have in starting a romantic relationship. In Huizenga and Thomas-Ruzic's (1992) *All Talk*, Unit 13 ("Pick Your Perfect Vacation"), students warm up to the task of interviewing a partner by circling new words in vacation ads. These activities help students to practice vocabulary and survey the content terrain before speaking.

Students can prepare for an impromptu speech on the subject of a news story by watching the evening news on television, listening to a news radio station, reading the editorial page of a local newspaper, reading a newsmagazine such as *Time* or

Newsweek, and/or talking to people outside the class about selected issues. Students who must prepare for a formal public presentation need a more structured approach, with an advance outline that includes an attention-getting opener, a preview of what will be said, enough substance to complete the main body of the speech, a summary of the main points, and a memorable conclusion (Dale & Wolf, 1988). What prior knowledge does the audience have about the topic at hand? An outline helps the presentation to stay on topic and enables the speaker to balance thought-provoking statements with quotes, anecdotes, and statistics where applicable. Rehearsal in advance of the delivery—whether out loud to oneself, via an audio- or videotape, or before a critical audience—helps the presenter pace the delivery, create a natural tone, and practice difficult pronunciation (Wong, 1998).

While Speaking

Teachers working in mixed-ability classrooms can plan group activities that help students in different ways. Students can work in homogeneous groups when the goal of the activity is accuracy and in heterogeneous groups when the goal is fluency. For example, to develop accuracy, first-grade students can listen to a reading of the story "The Three Little Pigs." A group of beginning students can retell the story using pictures and then talk about the pictures. Intermediate students can retell the story to the teacher or a cross-age tutor who can write their story for them; students can then reread, illustrate, and rearrange the story from sentence strips. A group of more proficient students can create a new group story.

Informal class discussions are a low-key way to practice speaking. While speaking, eye contact is made with listeners, and the volume is appropriate to the distance between the speakers. A speaker usually does not use notes when chatting with a classmate, but sometimes such notes are available from a previous brainstorming session. Turns are usually shared in small groups, and one person does not monopolize discussion.

A public speech or formal presentation requires a more formal approach, with a neat public appearance that shows respect for the situation and audience. Visual aids in the form of charts or overhead projections help listeners to see as well as hear the presentation. Memorizing the presentation is not advisable, for it may lead to a stiff and forced delivery. Stance should be facing the audience, with hands and feet appearing calm and under control (Wong, 1998). If the public speech is in the form of a debate, courtesy toward one's opponents shows grace under pressure.

Correction while a person is speaking is seldom appropriate. A teacher who does correct may seem overly dominant and cause the speaker to become tense and unable to be fluent or creative. If the speaker is genuinely unable to be understood, the teacher may pretend to misunderstand so that the student may rephrase—or may genuinely not understand and be honest about it. However, the teacher who expects an imperfect sentence to be repeated correctly impedes communication. Reformulation is the best alternative; if the teacher hears an incorrect utterance, a similar sentence can be repeated to the student naturally and in the context of the conversation without embarrassing the student (Bartram & Walton, 1994).

Oral presentations can be assessed using *holistic scoring* (see Table 6.10) or *analytic scoring* (see Figure 6.3).

After Speaking

Sometimes the class as a whole supplies feedback to the speaker in the form of structured peer review. Many kinds of activities can follow up a speaking task. As in the listening task, students can write, discuss, read, draw, or act out their interpretation of the content, attending to the linguistic or cultural aspects of what they have heard. For the most part, oral discussion is a vital part of any other task and should be developed as a top priority. When students have been outside the classroom on a service-learning project, debriefing is needed in order for students to reflect on and share with one another what they have learned.

Strategic speaking involves a combination of cognitive, social, and emotional factors. Table 6.11 offers a compendium of strategies from experts in the field.

Speaking Games and Tasks

Shameem and Tickoo (1999) have compiled a variety of listening and speaking games that can be used in a variety of contexts. Table 6.12 lists these and their contributors.

TABLE 6.10 • A Holistic Scoring Criteria for Seventh- or Eighth-Grade Oral Presentations

---

A good presentation:
1. Falls within the assigned time limit (or is reasonably close)
2. Has a clearly identifiable speech purpose and a thesis statement
3. Has an introduction, body, and conclusion
4. Shows a basic understanding of effective verbal and nonverbal delivery
5. Shows respect for the audience

An excellent presentation, in addition to meeting the above criteria:
1. Deals with an interesting and challenging topic (if student was allowed to choose topic)
2. Includes both a strong introduction and conclusion that achieve all their major functions
3. Is well organized
4. Develops points with appropriate supporting materials (relevant, credible)
5. Is skillfully delivered (verbal and nonverbal delivery)

A superior presentation meets all of the above criteria, and:
1. Uses clear, appropriate, and vivid oral language
2. Is delivered fluently and in a polished manner
3. Is interesting and well adapted to the audience
4. Supports points with provocative and compelling supporting material
5. Constitutes a general contribution to the knowledge and/or beliefs of the audience

A fair presentation meets some, but not all, of the grading criteria for a good presentation.

A poor presentation meets almost none of the requirements for a good presentation.

Source: Chaney & Burk, 1998, p. 119.

Speaker's Name: _____	Topic: _____				
CONTENT	Superior	Excellent	Good	Fair	Poor
Introduction Caught attention, stated topic and purpose of speech; previewed main points	5	4	3	2	1
Body Main points were clear, distinct, and supported the purpose of the speech	5	4	3	2	1
Organization was clear and consistent throughout	5	4	3	2	1
Logic and analysis (if a persuasive speech) were strong	5	4	3	2	1
Supporting materials were credible, useful, appropriately cited, and adequate for each main point	5	4	3	2	1
Language choice was interesting, appropriate for the occasion and audience, with appropriate grammar	5	4	3	2	1
Conclusion Concluded with psychological impact, summarized main points, brought closure to the speech	5	4	3	2	1
DELIVERY					
Audience Adaptation Adapted to the physical characteristics of the speaking situation	5	4	3	2	1
Adapted to the background and perspective of the audience	5	4	3	2	1
Chose words and language that were meaningful to, and demonstrated respect for, the audience	5	4	3	2	1
Vocal Delivery Appropriate volume, rate, pitch, and variety of expression	5	4	3	2	1
Avoided too many non-fluencies (e.g., "uh," "um," "like," "okay," "y'know")	5	4	3	2	1
Used pauses and silences effectively (if a speech that lends itself to drama)	5	4	3	2	1
Physical Delivery Good posture; absence of nervous shifting of body weight, twisting at the waist, leaning on podium, etc.	5	4	3	2	1
Gestures and facial expressions were well-timed, natural, expressive	5	4	3	2	1
Eye contact was direct, sustained, inclusive	5	4	3	2	1

Additional comments:

Total Score: _____ (out of a possible 80 points)

FIGURE 6.3 ◆ **An analytic scoring evaluation for an oral presentation.**

Source: Chaney & Burk, 1998, p. 122.

TABLE 6.11 ♦ Some Strategies Useful for Speaking a Foreign Language

Phase of the Speaking Process	Sample Strategies
Before speaking	Lower anxiety by taking a few deep breaths, visualizing success, repeating positive self-talk phrases.
	Review the purpose of the talk; ask for clarification if unsure of goal.
	Activate background knowledge; make associations with similar situations.
	Predict what will happen and what language is needed; practice difficult vocabulary in advance.
	Plan the talk, using an outline; rehearse with a partner if it is a joint presentation.
While speaking	Recognize tenseness and channel stress as energy from body to mind.
	Ask for clarification or help if necessary.
	Concentrate on the task; avoid distractions.
	Stay involved with others; negotiate meaning with listeners; take reasonable language risks; think in the target language.
	Monitor speech, paying attention to vocabulary, grammar, and pronunciation; try new words; back up and fix mistakes if necessary; try to imitate native speakers.
	Compensate for vocabulary shortcomings by using circumlocutions, cognates, synonyms, gestures, or guesses; simplify message if necessary; base talk on information about which you have some prior knowledge.
After speaking	Reward yourself with positive affirmations.
	Evaluate accomplishment, reviewing goals and strategies, asking for feedback and tuning in to the reactions of others.
	Identify problem areas, looking up grammar and vocabulary that were troublesome and finding new ways to relax.
	Make a plan for improvement, noting strategies of classmates or instructor's suggestions.
	Ask for help or correction from more proficient speakers.
	Keep a learning log, writing down reflections, strategies, reactions, and outcomes.

Source: Alcaya, Lybeck, Mougel, & Weaver, 1995.

Oral Discourse and Critical Communicative Competence

Since the time of Socrates, educators have advocated a type of teaching that does more than transmit knowledge and skills. Contemporary educators have sought discussion formats that engage students in critical thinking and intellectually productive social interaction. The Instructional Conversation (IC) is a small-group, semistructured discourse format in which the instructor functions as "thinker leader" while encouraging

TABLE 6.12 • Activities for Listening and Speaking

Name of Activity	Directions for the Teacher
Shadow tableaux	Pass around a bag, and have each student put in a small personal object. Spread the objects out on an overhead projector so that only their shadows can be seen. Have students work in pairs to name all the objects. (1)
Headline news	Cut out interesting headlines and their corresponding photographs from newspapers. Cut the headlines in half (do not split word phrases). Paste the beginnings and ending of the headlines onto index cards. Students in group A receive photographs, group B receives headline beginnings, and group C receives headline endings. Students move around the room, asking one another (not showing) the content of their card. The first group to identify its members wins the game. (2)
Animal psychology	Pair off students and have them jot on index cards three main characteristics or activities of their favorite animal. Then have partners swap index cards and read each other's phrases, guessing the animal by writing it on the front of the card. After this activity, use the phrases and cards on the overhead projector to generate and practice vocabulary. (3)
Give me a word that . . .	Prepare index cards (one for each student) with fifteen to twenty vocabulary questions starting with the phrase, "Give me a word that . . ." For example, A word that dances . . . (ballerina, Madonna) A word that runs . . . (runner, river) A blue word (sky) A cold word (ice, winter) Student A reads the word; first student in group B and C has thirty seconds to give an answer. Whoever is first wins that round. (4)
So did I	Students report something they did over the weekend ("I visited my grandmother"). Other learners respond, "So did I" or, "I didn't." The learner must come up with a new idea if someone answers, "So did I." (After three reports, move on to the next student.) (5)
Spontaneous oral developemnt of group stories	Seat students in groups of three to six and give them a number corresponding to the order of their sentence in the story. The first student gives the opening sentence of the story; the second gives the second. Before the third, the first two repeat their sentences in order. When the story is completed, one of the students transcribes it, and when all groups are ready, they tell their stories to the class, each repeating one sentence. (6)

Sources: Mahoney, 1999a (1); Hetherton, 1999 (2); Becker, 1999 (3); Mansour, 1999 (4); Sick, 1999 (5); Larking, 1999 (6).

voluntary oral participation (see Chapter 10). *CommuniConfidence* is an oral language development program specifically tailored for university students that took place for several years at California State University, San Bernardino (Díaz-Rico & Young, 1998). *CommuniConfidence* sessions were designed to bring together native and nonnative speakers of English in a weekly one-hour chat session.

Students can assess each others' oral presentations.

Discussions were based upon a discussion prompt consisting of a one-paragraph vignette that described some small, complex situation involving a protagonist aged twenty-one to thirty (for a sample prompt, see Box 6.4). The prompts were intentionally written to encourage some opinionated interchanges based upon participants' personal experiences. The prompts also called forth some deeper understandings of human motivation and values; however, in each situation there were no right or wrong answers. For each conversation (the ideal size for each small group is six to eight members) a thinker-leader guided the flow of the discourse.

Graduate students in the master's program Teaching Speakers of Other Languages option in the College of Education acted as thinker-leaders for the discussions. These included both English learners who had originally learned English without attaining oral fluency and native speakers of English. The opportunity to assume the

---

BOX 6.4
❖ Sample Prompt for CommuniConfidence

Prompt: "Marriage at Her Age?"

All of Brenda's aunts and uncles, as well as her parents, are upset because Frances, Brenda's grandmother, has a new boyfriend. Frances is 80 years old and has been visiting the Senior Citizens' Center to play mah-jongg twice a week. She met Harvey, who is 78 years old, at the center. Harvey is a widower, and Frances is a widow. Brenda's grandfather died at the age of 75, just three years ago. Frances and Harvey have been talking about getting married so that they can live together. Brenda's family is afraid that if Frances remarries, she will alter her will to leave her money to Harvey when she dies. Harvey has three daughters who are always asking him for money. Besides, Brenda's family thinks Frances is too old to remarry.

leader function in discussions permitted these students to practice thinking fast on their feet as well as to achieve oral and aural proficiency. The thinker-leaders were given two one-hour preliminary training sessions so that they understood how to begin, sustain, and close a discussion.

CommuniConfidence was held in the informal environment of a staff lounge. This provided a relaxing environment that helped to create a sense of community among participants. At the beginning of each hour, participants were welcomed to the session as they signed in and donned name tags, so that participants could address one another by first name in conversation if they so wished. This system also ensured that participants became acquainted with one another. Each participant was then given a copy of a prompt.

First-time participants were given a welcome sheet that explained the discourse procedure and offered suggestions about turn taking (see Box 6.5 and Box 6.6). A few students were silent for the first few sessions and then gradually spoke more. Other students were fairly fluent as soon as they acquired the specific turn-taking skills. No feedback was given to participants after each discussion, except for general praise offered by the thinker-leader. New participants who remained silent throughout the conversation were approached individually after each discussion to see if they needed help understanding how to obtain a turn.

Naturally, some prompts were better than others in triggering rich thematic material from participants. One successful prompt was the story of a young man whose mother always bragged about and overstated his academic achievements at family gatherings, ignoring his achievements in art, his desired vocation. Several students from Asian family backgrounds found much in common with this protagonist, and the conversation was long and lively. On the other hand, the following vignette was unsuccessful in provoking conversation. In this story a young man was dissatisfied with the suspended sentence meted out to a drunken driver who had killed his sister in a car crash and wanted to take revenge, much to his family's consternation. This desire for revenge was far from the personal experience of participants.

The IC Model.   The IC model developed by Goldenberg and Gallimore (1991) has both instructional and conversational elements. The most important instructional element is the establishment of a thematic focus. The text that participants all read before beginning the conversation provides the basis for the theme. Because the goal of

---

BOX 6.5
❖ Are You Here for the First Time? (handout for participants)

Are You Here for the First Time?
CommuniConfidence organizes participants into informal talk groups led by a volunteer leader. Everyone reads the same short paragraph. Then the group discusses the situation.

During the discussion, participants take turns without needing permission from the leader. There are no right or wrong answers; any idea is welcome. Each discussion takes approximately twenty minutes. Then the group discusses how the discussion went.

BOX 6.6
❖ Get Your Turn (handout for participants)

Get Your Turn
Even when you have something to say, it is sometimes hard to get a turn in the conversation.

Two ways to get a turn

Nonverbal
- Make eye contact with the current speaker.
- Lean forward as if you will be next.
- Interrupt in a small way and then stop.
- Be ready to start your turn at the slightest pause.

Verbal
- When your idea is *connected* to the current speaker:

- I'd like to add to that . . .
- Oh, yes, and besides . . .
- Yes, and . . .
- Well, I see it like this . . .

- When your idea has *no connection* to the current one:

  - Here's a different idea . . .
  - I see things a little differently . . .
  - Going back to what _____ said, . . .
  - Changing the topic somewhat, I'd like to mention . . .

---

the IC is to develop a more complex understanding of the prompt, a good theme is one that is flexible enough to grow out of the ideas of the participants, without being superimposed upon the group by the leader. This flexibility encourages the participants to share responsibility for the discussion. At the same time, however, the leader's responsibility is to see that the theme has a genuine connection to the prompt.

The conversation elements include those aspects that defuse anxiety and promote verbal interaction. Another conversational element is the establishment of a challenging, nonthreatening atmosphere for the participants. It is helpful, for example, to talk while seated in a circle of chairs versus sitting around a conference table. The circle gives individuals equal access to turns and facilitates eye contact. Disagreement and differences of opinion are protected, although part of the challenging atmosphere is for students to find a way to evaluate one another's viewpoints.

CommuniConfidence encouraged oral participation in a setting that is social as well as somewhat academic. The IC format gave students an opportunity to speak openly and frankly in a small-group setting, with the understanding that their turn was voluntary. The small-group setting made it easier for the thinker-leader to equalize the input from participants and also made it more difficult for a small number of students to dominate the conversation. Participants were encouraged to speak; grammar was not corrected, nor were opinions judged. The group members were stimulated to talk with one another in everyday English on topics that elicited opinions, without necessarily requiring expertise or prior knowledge.

The oral language skills developed by participating in *CommuniConfidence* benefit all undergraduate students. The prompts have been designed to appeal to a broad cross-section of students. *CommuniConfidence* afforded students a chance to exchange ideas, compare values, and become better acquainted with students from other countries. It further provided the opportunity for low intermediate students to use English interpersonally. In addition, advanced students were more fully able to voice in English the depth of their thinking. This, more than anything else, gave students a broader range of language proficiency to support their academic participation.

For future teachers of English as a foreign language, the opportunity to lead a discussion in English trains them to think swiftly and encourage others to become fluent. The *CommuniConfidence* prompts may not be ideal for the types of discussions they may lead with *their* students, particularly if they find themselves teaching in junior or senior high schools in Taiwan, Japan, Mexico, or other countries; but they at least will have had practice with the IC format. Several of the thinker-leaders volunteered themes and ideas of interest to them as possible prompts, and several of their ideas were incorporated into successful prompts. This gave them practice in generating ideas for prompts.

Using IC in the Classroom.   Many instructors are eager to find ways to promote oral participation in the classroom as an alternative to lectures. However, educators may perceive that IC is hard to use in a class with fixed seating and a tradition of lectures. Despite these drawbacks, IC as a discussion format has broad utility in education. In classes of between twenty and thirty-five students, students can break up into small groups using peers as thinker-leaders. Other instructors may offer after-hours sessions with interested students on a voluntary basis on selected course-related topics of interest to students. Students who are assigned group projects as a course requirement may be able to use class time for planning while the instructor pulls aside a discussion group on a rotating basis.

The conversational elements of IC are perhaps the most difficult to incorporate in a traditional classroom because students are not often given the opportunity to converse. However, the instructor may function as a thinker-leader by asking open-ended questions, responding positively to student ideas, and weaving ideas that are volunteered by class members into the instructional content. A tone of challenging, nonthreatening, intellectual give and take promotes critical thinking and speaking. Grouping students into pairs for in-class self-expression can allow students to verbalize their ideas to one another. Pausing during a lecture to allow students to comment on an idea with one another is a way to encourage students to construct their own knowledge.

Summary: The Conversant Student

CommuniConfidence helps its participants learn to speak English more fluently, to have faith that their opinions will be recognized and honored, and to believe that their ideas are important and valued. When asked how this program had helped him, one participant responded, "Now I feel more confident to speak out in classes. This has taught me to participate in discussions with others in class." Another student added, "This program helps me a lot. Now I can talk to Americans when I'm shopping or even making some phone calls such as the phone company, TV shopping or ordering pizza." A third student felt that the program had helped him to become more assertive with native English-speakers. "When I have an argument, I speak up more. Example,

I fixed my car, and I paid money. But I drove the car on my way. I noticed the car had still problem. I complained about the car. I got angry. But now I could speak more than usual. The important thing is when I want to tell to somebody, I can." A fourth student noticed that the program had helped him to speak up in public. "I feel more confident than I did before when I'm speaking in English." A Hispanic female thinker-leader, a graduate student in the M.A. in Education, TESOL Option, indicated that her ability to participate in class had been strengthened by the *CommuniConfidence* program. "I never knew how to get a turn," she stated. "I always had plenty of opinions and never knew how to make myself heard."

A second outcome is that the conversational prompts have helped students from other countries learn about the cultures of the United States, including the appropriate behaviors for American academia. They have learned how some Americans think about selected topics. Moreover, because *CommuniConfidence* drew students from many countries, the participants were able to compare their reactions and values with those of students from other countries. In one student's words, "Especially, I learned about lots of cultural aspects of people's thinking." In addition to crosscultural comparisons, students benefited from learning how the other gender reacted to the various issues. This type of male-female dialogue and interaction was completely new to many of the participants. The women learned to voice their opinions, some of which were a real surprise to the men, and vice versa.

A third outcome of *CommuniConfidence* has been the formation of a community, a discourse group of people who enjoy meeting on a regular basis and enjoy each other's company. The students feel that they have friends in other countries, the beginning of feeling a part of a global community. Another consequence of *CommuniConfidence* is that the American facilitators have found their own cultural perspectives immeasurably broadened by exchanging views with the international students in depth. The American students benefited from the opportunity to act as thinker-leaders and to interact with the international students. IC proved to be an excellent format for intellectual and cultural exchange. This is what U.S. academia does best.

Overall, the learning processes discussed in this chapter—retaining information, reading, writing, listening, and speaking in a second language—share the characteristic that if they are performed naturally in the context of a rich, interesting experience, the learner acquires the skill almost unnoticed. If the pressure is on, however—a test, a public performance—the skill must be learned with focus and determination, with full faculties devoted to the process involved. Both kinds of learning have their place. If no one had to work hard, to labor and sweat over reading and writing, books would not be completed—this one included!

Learning Processes and the Imaginary

No one has fully fathomed the power of the human mind. Human history has recorded amazing feats of mental prowess: bards, the oral historians of the ancient cultures, were capable of reciting entire epics from memory. For example, the *paha* (ceremonial singer) of the Native American tribal group *Serrano* was responsible for a week of oral storytelling, singing/chanting the entire history of the tribe from creation to the present during the yearly mourning ritual. Genius is manifest in many domains of human endeavor, including the literary productions of Shakespeare, Cervantes, and Solzhenitzyn; the works of mathematics savants and visionaries (Einstein, Gauss); the prodigious musical accomplishmnets of Mozart; and the artistic brilliance of Cassant or Nevelson.

What constitutes genius in second language acquisition (SLA)? How many languages can a human acquire in a lifetime, and to what degree? And more important for the study of SLA, what features of the human mind can be tapped to help the rest of us, the population of nongenius learners for whom SLA is "1 percent inspiration and 99 percent perspiration"?

Chapters 5 and 6 covered many strategies that behavioral, cognitive, and humanistic psychologists, linguists, educational researchers, and teachers have proposed to assist the process of SLA. Yet one senses that more powerful strategies await discovery if one could tap as yet undiscovered powers of the human mind. In what domain would these lie? One answer lies in the domain of the *imaginary.* Common definitions of the imaginary include such terms as "illusory, hallucinatory, fictitious, fantastic/fanciful, visionary, unreal, sham." Clearly these terms connote a distrust in things not real. Imagination is also the art and practice of producing ideal creations and forming clear mental images. Overall, the imaginary is an avenue toward things not yet seen. It defies definition.

❖ MEGASTRATEGY 7: Use English to explore the imaginary

Imagination is probably the oldest mental trait that is typically human; it roils through human history, surfacing in myth, dream, poetry, and the arts. The imaginary is a realm of language that can enrich us emotionally and expand our creative powers. Everyone spends time not only in the world of language, but in the imaginary; the human being "hovers between the imaginary and symbolic orders, divided into conscious and unconscious systems" (Peim, 1993, p. 62). But how can the imagination be used in SLA, which, like so many other aspects of the modern world, has long emphasized the supremacy of rationalism?

Vygotsky saw the imagination as the key to the creation of meaning. In creating imaginary situations, children learn to react not just in response to the real world immediately before them but also in accord with their internal world, the world of ideas. Imagination helps the child to separate thought from the surrounding world and rely on ideas to guide behavior. During the third year of life, the mind begins to imagine objects and events without any direct support from the real world (Berk & Winsler, 1995). Thus, for Vygotsky, the process of imaginary play is key to the creation of meaning. Channeling this imaginative power is an important part of education and cognitive development.

Exploring the Imagination

◆ **STRATEGY 7.1:** Explore the concept of the imaginary

Lozanov's Suggestopedia Revisited

One answer may be found in Lozanov's *Suggestology and Suggestopedia* (1982). Although Lozanov proposed learning methods that were unorthodox at the time, two strands of his work loom ever larger in importance. The first is his use of music to stimulate the brain. Recent discoveries in cognitive science have affirmed the connection between exposure to music—particularly music from the baroque era such as Bach, just as Lozanov predicted—and brain development in children. This idea will be further explored later in this chapter.

The second aspect of Lozanov's work that may prove momentous in future language learning is his use of alterations in human personality to further second-language learning. He proposed that the learner assume a second identity in the second language, even taking a new L2 name, and have that persona assume the role of L2 learner. This suggestion has implications far beyond Suggestopedic technique. The assumption of an altered personality opens the door to the imaginary.

The imaginary as an underexplored realm of the human mind has potentially vast implications for the education of English learners. In the past, educators have considered the exercise of the imagination a marginal pursuit, one relegated to the visual and performing arts. Traditionally, neither of these arts has had a strong theoretical or methodological connection to SLA, perhaps because of the strong modernist rational bias in the historical and philosophical traditions of Western civilization since the Enlightenment. Lozanov, a Bulgarian, carried out his research at the fringes of Europe, enough removed from the reaches of Western rationalism to be able to explore alternative approaches. His work using the personality in language learning offered a depth to learning theory that may be more important than previously realized.

As postmodern theorists, as well as psychanalyst Carl Jung, have pointed out, the rational bias of Western education has led to certain limitations. Despite the Western belief in progress through rational decision making, the Western world has been held hostage by world wars of unprecedented savagery. Yet in traditional cultures such as Bali, in which the average person spends time developing skills in, and participating in, art, music, and drama, these creative and imaginative activities help to balance "rational" pursuits, to the benefit of the whole community. How can the work of the imagination lead to increased language learning and, even more important, to increased wholeness and balance in society?

Lacan's Personality Theory and the Imaginary

Jacques Lacan, the French psychoanalyst, has had a profound influence on postmodernists through his reconceptions of personality development and his emphasis on the importance of language as a means of personal development. Lacan's work (1977) has wide-ranging potential impact for the field of linguistics (albeit Lacan never contributed directly to SLA theory). A brief exploration of his work is offered here to expand a vision of possibility for educators in the creative and generative realm of the imaginary.

Lacan was a post-Freudian in the sense that he relentlessly pursued research into the function and effects of the unconscious. Perhaps even more than Sigmund Freud, he insisted that the human mind in its nonconscious functioning was heterogeneous and opaque to conscious intention. Yet Lacan furthered Freud's research on the unconscious by insisting that it was a profoundly linguistic domain, with its own drives toward the production and articulation of knowledge (Grosz, 1990). At the risk of radically simplifying the work of an extremely complex thinker and writer, I will summarize Lacan's explanation of the early development of the child and draw forth what I believe this implies for learning theory, particularly language-learning capability.

Freud viewed the ego as the mental agent that is motivated by principles of rational compromise between the demands of physical and social reality ("beware of the dangers of the world, conform to group norms and rules") and the impulses of the unconscious ("please thyself, seek pleasure"). He equates successful ego functioning with successful negotiation of reality. In contrast, Lacan argued that reality is not to be equated with successful ego functioning. The real cannot be experienced by the ego; it is a terrain without borders, boundaries, or divisions, a continuum of "raw materials" capable of representation or conceptualization only through the inferential work of the imaginary.

According to Lacan, soon after birth the child receives the first dose of reality: Mother is a part of the world just beyond control. Frustrating! To deal with this frustration, the child creates images that, in a sense, seek in the imaginary the satisfaction sought for the needs the mother cannot fill. The imaginary is the key to the child's entry into social life (Grosz, 1990), for it is the vehicle by which the child first distinguishes his or her identity from the mother and is able to interact. Through the imaginary the child turns needs into demands, creating the earliest mechanism of self-satisfaction through the use of a symbolic system that is individual, unique, unregulated, and unrestricted. This, then, describes the freedom of the imaginary.

The stage following the use of the imagination is the use of language as a symbolic means of seeking satisfaction. Hence the use of the imagination precedes language. Although Lacan did not offer much in the way of first-language acquisition theory, it is clear that the "mother tongue" becomes a flexible and powerful tool for obtaining satisfaction not only from the first caretakers but from the larger world. In a major way it replaces the use of the imaginary for many people, as the dominant brain hemisphere seizes upon language as a tool and pushes the other, more idiosyncratic symbol system—the imaginary—into subdominance.

The Imaginary and English Learning

How, then, can this affect SLA? Probably the chief factor inhibiting SLA is its marginal utility. The first language fulfills so many basic needs—for family kinship, emotional security, and job satisfaction—that there is little room for the L2 to be deeply fulfilling in the same way. Therefore, in order to access some motivational drive within the learner, the second language must somehow reach beyond the powers of the first language and address social and emotional functions that the first language does not. To access motivational power, the second language must reconnect with a symbolic system that is subdominant in the first language but lies dormant, connected with powerful emotions, in a sense waiting for a portal of expression. Hence the door opens to the imaginary.

Picture a darkened theater. The curtain rises. The actors step into the spotlight wearing elaborate costumes, singing exquisite music heard nowhere else, portraying emotions exaggerated for theatrical effect. Opera, in Western culture, is often sung in a language unfamiliar to the audience. Yet tickets for major productions are sold out far in advance. Why do opera buffs submit themselves voluntarily to hours of exposure to a foreign language in an opera house when they would not do so at the office, at the beauty parlor, or in their neighborhoods?

The answer lies in the imaginary. Imagination is stimulated at the opera in a manner that is attractive, intriguing, and motivating. Hollywood films make money throughout the world for the same reason. People throughout the world routinely stand in line to see a new release in English—not waiting for the film to be dubbed into their native tongue—because the sheen of celebrity and the siren call of special effects open doors to the imaginary that are supremely enticing.

Although Lacan conceived of the imaginary primarily as a visual domain (Grosz, 1990), Julia Kristeva, a contemporary of Lacan, postulated that the imaginary was synaesthetic, involving all sensory registers (Kristeva, 1980). This premise sets the preconditions for language acquisition. As Grosz (1990) explained, "Kristeva's analyses of music, painting, and cinema as well as linguistics make it clear that the preconditions of these cultural practices also provide the preconditions of verbalization" (pp. 157–158). However, in SLA the energy required to convert the primordial semiotic nature of the imaginary into a new symbolic system is often dissipated in the need for obtaining and stabilizing meaning.

The Imaginary and the Development of Personality

Second-language learners must develop some capacity to imagine themselves speaking a different language. Some learners find this easier than others. Some small children may "cluck" like a chicken at the appropriate point in the story "The Little Red Hen," whereas others might prefer remaining silent. Kristeva might interpret the use of this story as a cultural practice that provides the preconditions of verbalization to some children more than others. Teachers use many techniques to promote verbalization and facilitate students' ability to link their image of themselves as speakers of their native language to a new image of themselves as speakers of another tongue.

Students at different ages have differing access to the imaginary and link this to language acquisition in age-predictable ways. Elementary school children who are in the personality stage characterized by Erik Erikson (1963, 1980) as "industry versus inferiority" (ages six to twelve) may see second-language learning in school as just another form of work; if they can imagine themselves as industrious workers, then they can deal with the demands of learning a new skill and thus avoid a sense of inferiority.

According to Erikson, however, adolescents are in the throes of questioning their identity. The sense of self they have been developing since birth is faced with new challenges, such as choices about work, values, ideology, and commitments to people and ideas that may be new (see Marcia, 1980). Peer pressure, which at times includes social mockery from one teen to another, may inhibit students' ability to alter their image of themselves as native-language speakers and take on images of themselves as speakers of another language.

On the other hand, older, adolescent or adult learners have other personality drives, according to Erikson: the need to become intimate with the other sex, or the need to contribute to society at large. These may involve the imagination in new and compelling ways as one uses a second language to attract romance in accordance with one's image of the ideal lover, or uses a second language vocationally or socially.

Research on the role of personality in SLA seems to have been limited to date to the study of the role of affective variables, such as inhibition, anxiety, extroversion, and so forth. No study to date has linked developmental changes in personality to the idea that SLA suffers after the learner has passed the "critical period" (see Lenneberg, 1967). In other words, researchers have not, to date, asked the question, "Is the difficulty in language acquisition that the learner experiences after adolescence due to personality changes?" In addition to the relative paucity of research connecting personality theory to SLA, research is also lacking on the link between the imagination and SLA. That is, no systematic effort has been made to connect developmental changes in the use of the imagination to SLA.

The Imaginative Function of Language

Halliday's (1978) seven categories of language function included the *imaginative* function as that which allows the individual to create a personal world, freed from everyday boundaries, in which language is used for sheer pleasure. Despite the fact that communicative language teaching has facilitated the switch from behavioral approaches to those eliciting communicative competence and has succeeded in building curricula based on social function theory, the personal and imaginative functions SLA remain underdeveloped.

Yet it is these functions, ironically, that have the most potential for intercultural communication. The result of SLA is often biculturality; the bicultural person actually has a personality structure and identity that is flexible and capable of operating in two or more very different social, intellectual, and emotional contexts. As Lozanov predicted, work on developing a separate second-language identity facilitates SLA. Therefore, working directly to use the personal and imaginative functions of language, that is, working with identity development and reaching into the imaginary as a semiotic system that precedes language, provides a fertile avenue of curricular development.

❖ **Tactics for honoring the imagination of language learners:**

◆ Help learners embrace the notion that learning a second language involves an enjoyable leap away from everyday reality.
◆ Create a classroom ambience that encourages risk taking and fun.
◆ Reward approximations, "fuzzy logic," and "half-baked ideas."
◆ Give public recognition to acts of imagination, fancy, and whimsy.

Stimulating the Imagination Directly

Throughout the recent history of education, various techniques have been proposed to stimulate the imagination directly. Several of these can be adapted to the education of English learners.

◆ **STRATEGY 7.2:** Respect the power of the imaginary as a language-learning tool

Guided Imagery

De Mille's classic *Put Your Mother on the Ceiling* (1976) offers directed mental play to children that encourages them to practice creating specific visual images. The book contains a series of themed exercises that the teacher reads aloud as the students follow along in their minds; for example, "Squeeze" is an exercise in changing the imaginary size of objects; "Being Things" is an exercise in changing into things ("Be a rock. Be a mountain. Be the moon"); "Camera" is an exercise in turning the eyes into a camera and seeing in new ways. The excerpt below, which can be used as a listening task for ESOL learners, provides the flavor of exercising the imagination:

> This game is called Animals. We are going to start with one little mouse, and see what we can do. Let us imagine that there is a little mouse somewhere in the room. Where would you like to put him? All right, have him sit up and wave to you./ Have him turn green./ Change his color again./ Change it again./ Have him stand on his hands./ Have him run up the wall./ Have him sit upside down on the ceiling./ Turn him right side up and put him in a corner up there./ Put another mouse in the corner up there./ Put a mouse in each of the other two corners up there./ . . . Turn them all yellow./ Have them all say "Hello" at the same time. . . . (De Mille, 1976, pp. 57–58)

Guided Fantasy Stories.   Guided fantasy stories can be used to stimulate mental creativity and personal imagery. Walker (1987) suggested a guided fantasy that begins with a teacher-directed journey that uses the framework of an imaginary trip to elicit vivid imagery. The journey begins by creating an atmosphere of relaxation and sensory awareness ("Close your eyes and just listen to the sounds around you . . ."). Note that each

section of suggested wording should contain five or six such sentences. Rather than spontaneously creating such sentences, the teacher should write them out in advance. Sensory
awareness is followed by wording that suggests a setting ("You hear the soft sounds of
a green mountain meadow"); following this, action statements are mixed with calming
statements ("A soft breeze is blowing across your face as you climb the mountain").

Further events in this sequence evoke images and actions that may include meeting a wise man, seeing far in the distance, or seeing images in cloud formations that
carry a meaning or a message. As students are guided back, the wording features closing and separation statements such as, "When you are ready, you can return to the
classroom." Although Walker (1987) followed such mental experiences with the exercise of writing a story, productive output is optional. For English learners, the listening experience is rich enough to provide practice in language skills.

Guided imagery as a writing prompt stimulates fluency. Magy (1991) suggested
that the teacher begin with a relaxing episode and, when students are relaxed and receptive, present an image. The writing prompt, "Someone I Remember" is generated
by the following imagery:

> Bring to mind a picture of a feeling of a person important to you when you were grow-
> ing up . . . Someone who is still living now, or someone who has died . . . someone for
> whom you have loving thoughts . . . your mother . . . father . . . grandmother . . . grand-
> father . . . aunt . . . uncle . . . or family . . . a friend. . . . Allow a picture of them to come
> into your mind. . . . Notice what they look like . . . their face . . . eyes . . . hair . . . the size
> of their body. . . . Notice their clothing . . . pants . . . skirt . . . sweater . . . blouse . . .
> shirt . . . dress . . . maybe traditional clothing from your country. . . . How do you feel
> when you are with them? What smells or sounds do you associate with them? . . . cook-
> ing . . . animals . . . machines . . . perfumes . . . musical sounds . . . work sounds . . .
>
> Share with them something about your life . . . what you are doing . . . what you
> are feeling. . . . Listen to them as they speak to you. . . . Listen to what they are say-
> ing. . . . Take a moment to talk with them. . . . Thank them for being with you . . . for
> sharing with you. . . . Look at them again. . . . Notice how you feel with them. . . . Now,
> slowly come back to the classroom. . . . Breathe in and breathe out slowly. . . . Open
> your eyes. . . . Share with a partner who you saw, what they looked like, and what you
> talked about. (p. 81)

Turning Imagery into Language.   Talking and then writing after this guided imagery
experience helps students to share what they saw or felt with a partner or with the
whole class. Students may "pass" if they do not wish to speak. Then each student
writes the first draft of a composition on this theme. The role of the teacher is to read
what students have written and encourage them all to stretch and expand their descriptions. They may then go through several cycles of reading the story to their peers,
soliciting feedback, having the teacher correct the draft, and then writing a final version. Other topics that may stimulate the imagination and result in interesting stories
are "About Me," "Early Memories," "An Important Experience," "Problems and
Choices," and "Plans for the Future" (Magy, 1991).

Other Uses of Fantasy.   *Directing an inner movie* is another way of using the imagination that connects to the increased use of mental imagery to affect goal setting, boost

self-esteem, and defuse anxiety. Movies of the mind (Bry, 1976) are inner pictures that bypass the limitations of the rational, analytic mind and provide an outlet for visual memory and visual imagery. Visualizing is appropriate, for example, as a means of setting in motion realistic events that may occur in the future. It is distinguished from fantasizing in that fantasies, although useful in the practice of generating images (see de Mille's 1976 work, above), are generally distinct from possible reality—unless one really believes an individual is likely to win $300 million by purchasing a $1 lottery ticket!

Programmed visualization (Bry, 1976, p. 51) has been used effectively in sports psychology to direct athletes to perform well under stress (cf. Murphy, 1973). Teachers can employ programmed visualization much as sports psychologists do to help learners defuse anxiety, for example, in preparing for oral class reports. The teacher may lead the class members through a preliminary "movie of the mind" in which each individual visualizes the prospective audience as friendly and supportive, the information to be presented as interesting and useful, and the vocabulary involved as easy to pronounce (although the previsualization does not preclude cognitive preparation such as incorporating extra practice for multisyllabic words). This functions not only as a listening exercise but also as one that both stimulates the imagination and provides relaxation and emotional support.

Creative Environments

Fashioning an environment that promotes creativity is vital to the stimulation of imaginative skills (Csikszentmihalyi, 1996). Creative thinkers have long sought out places of beauty and harmony in order to produce art. "Think tanks" are creative laboratories, for example, Xerox Park in Palo Alto and the Media Lab at The Massachusetts Institute of Technology, that attract original thinkers who wish to work in an environment that encourages creative group brainstorming.

A classroom bright with posters, unusual visual images, and colorful cultural materials sparks the emotions and invigorates the spirit. Although schools around the world vary in the degree to which they permit decoration, many exercises that stimulate the imagination depend on the introduction of a stimulating visual image. Current issues of magazines such as those in the Internet industry supply arresting visual images that may be used to promote creative language use in poetry, role play, or creative writing.

Comics

While on the topic of visual images, one cannot neglect the use of comics and cartoons as tools to teach English. *Comics and Conversation* (Aragones, 1985, 1991, and 2000) uses witty, uncaptioned cartoons that can be used to stimulate discussion. One example is a three-part comic strip in which a customer calls a waiter to his table to complain about a bug in the soup; the waiter pulls a can of insect spray from his jacket and douses the dish. This incident can be used for a quick writing exercise in which the students retell the cartoon in words or predict what happens next. Small (1993) is another source of cartoons for English-language teaching. Each cartoon is accompanied by a short vocabulary list. One cartoon, in which a child protests at the dinner table,

"This isn't about eating my peas, this is about the struggle of men everywhere to throw off the yoke of tyranny" (p. 70), could certainly function as a code (see Chapter 2) to provoke a discussion about comparative child-rearing practices in the United States and elsewhere! Using the same cartoon, students may want to use their imagination to construct their own "kid" speech, or the parent's response.

❖ **Tactics for explicitly evoking the imagination:**

- Set aside a time each day for direct attention to the imagination.
- Discuss the imagination with students so that they recognize its functioning.
- Provide students with a public space for posting works of the imagination.
- Give periodic awards for acts of imagination.

Curriculum That Stimulates the Imagination

Teachers can use the imagination explicitly to facilitate SLA. This chapter presents many ways to evoke imaginative responses from elementary school children and link these to English learning. Especially in the new elementary EFL programs being instituted in Japan, Korea, and Taiwan, new methods are needed to energize English instruction. One cannot rely upon grammar translation for children—it is surely boring, and it will ultimately prove counterproductive as children simply learned to be bored by English at an ever earlier age.

In an EFL context, one cannot rely upon the standard survival motivation used to assimilate immigrants to the United States. An ESL student needs to learn quickly the English terms for such common classroom objects as chalk and functional vocabulary such as "bathroom," but it is probably not such a high priority for young EFL students to know this type of vocabulary in English, as they will be using the native-language term throughout their schooling. It would be more stimulating for them instead to learn words that fulfill imaginative social functions that are less frequent in the native language.

Avoiding nonsense and providing meaning are both necessary steps to stimulate the imagination. It is probably better to avoid the traditional rhymes found in Mother Goose ("Wee Willie Winkie runs through the town, upstairs and downstairs in his nightgown"—a strange message, to be sure, and not crossculturally communicative!). Rather than relying on techniques that have been used in traditional contexts for native speakers of English, new curricular demands call for creativity and imagination.

Adolescent identity is flexible, but adolescents may find it particularly difficult to risk communicative efforts in a foreign language. It may be wise for teachers to address the identity issue openly and creatively. In an EFL class incorporating Suggestopedia, for example, the teacher might encourage shy Hans to take on the role of Gene the waiter, a friendly, outgoing personality. This kind of identity shift encourages students to associate the second-language use with alternative personality features that they can freely try on and discard.

Immigrants' identities may be at risk in ESL education. Pierce (1995) reported that for immigrants, identity issues are intimately bound up with motivation to acquire a new language; each human relationship in which the immigrant is invested becomes both the source and target of differential language use and investment. Immigrants may feel threatened by being asked to become "Joe" rather than "José" and may sense assimilation pressure from a teacher if asked to use an English-sounding name. Assuming a temporary identity only for the purpose of role play, and using a name that is not phonetically similar to the original, may help to sidestep this issue.

Imagination is part of a cycle in the 4MAT learning styles system (see Chapter 5). McCarthy (1983) recommended that all instructional units begin with a personal experience that helps to connect the learner to the concepts of the unit. Throughout the unit, a return to concrete experience builds a foundation for conceptual development at a more abstract level. The cyclic use of the imagination as a vehicle for exploration, coupled with concrete experience and reflective observation, becomes a manner of teaching that appeals to multiple learning styles. This is an excellent use of the imagination for purposes of learning.

The sections that follow feature a variety of ways in which teachers can use the imaginary to develop English language skills, including creative dramatics, poetry, and music. This is by no means an exhaustive presentation. The creative educator can invent a myriad of activities that stimulate the imagination and promote language skills.

Drama in the Classroom

Theatrical drama may be as old as human culture. The earliest dramas were connected with religious rituals, as the human stepped into a special arena of performance to call forth the divine. The theater holds a mirror to human life to show us ourselves—the "complicated, contradictory, joyful and sorrowing things that were are, the pattern of tensions between hopes and fears that constitutes human life, the inward and outward conflicts that accompany and comprise human existence" (Roberts, 1971, p. 3).

◆ STRATEGY 7.3: Empower the emotional imagination with drama

The opportunity to perform in a play or dramatic reading allows an ESOL student to step into the spotlight, however briefly, and experience the sense of heightened reality that is peculiar to dramatic performance. Plays are a holistic experience involving not only language but also the physical body and emotions on a conscious and unconscious level (Schiffler, 1992). Theater has long been accepted as part of English-language instruction, both for native speakers (cf. Via, 1975) and in EFL courses of study (cf. Hall, 1982). McCaslin (2000) described the connection between the imagination and drama:

> Imagination is the beginning of our work. To work creatively, it is necessary, first, to push beyond the boundaries of the here and now, to project oneself into another situation or into the life of another person. Few activities have greater potential for developing the imagination than playmaking. Little children move easily into a world of make-believe, but as they grow older, this amazing human capacity is often ignored or even discouraged. The development of the imagination to the point where the student

responds spontaneously may take time in some cases, but it is the first step toward satisfying participation. (p. 14)

Drama helps explore the world of emotions and nonverbal communication in the ESL/EFL classroom. Drama not only helps students to internalize language patterns by memorizing dialogue or to enhance listening skills by attending to dramatized stories but also to express themselves despite the frustration of learning a new language. Drama helps students to use reading to find meaning and then to enact that meaning in an interpersonal context. In this sense, drama and reading join forces to promote learning. "They develop the same personal resources in students, building links between print and experience, dream and reality, and self and other" (Booth, 1985, in Ernst-Slavit & Wenger, 1998, p. 31).

Drama helps students to develop problem-solving skills. The *persona* that students assume as they take on roles in plays or dramatic readings is the one who does the talking in English and makes the errors. This freedom to take risks allows students to relax, reduce their self-criticism, and protect their self-esteem. Taken together, drama activities have the power to transform the social structure of the classroom (see O'Neill, 1989), bringing out dormant talent, having teachers and students cooperate on projects, and bringing forth new kinds of face-to-face interactions.

Drama in the classroom usually takes on a variety of forms: use of classroom dramatics, whether developed by class members or performed by visitors; use of playscripts as literary text; the use of role play; readers theater; puppetry; and storytelling. Each of these is examined in turn.

Classroom Dramatics

Classroom dramatics offer a range of performance opportunities, some as simple as role-playing from a prepared script, others as complex as staging the school version of a Broadway musical. Creative dramatics include pantomimes, improvised stories and skits, movement activities, and dramatic songs and games in which students do not need sophisticated theater skills. Dramatics provide students with a format for exploring self-perceptions and attitudes toward self and others, stimulating creative imagination, developing an understanding of human behavior, and participating in group work (Heinig & Stillwell, 1974; Fox, 1987).

Drama is a language laboratory for oral communication skills, enabling students to acquire speaker-listener experiences and increase their ability to decode and encode ideas. Drama makes it possible for both teachers and students to escape from familiar patterns of language interaction and invent a new range of possibilities (Cottrell, 1987). Moreover, the use of drama can stimulate other language skills, such as writing and vocabulary usage. As students practice dramatic improvisation and characterization, their deeper understanding of human motivation and character can give them topics for composition (Evans, 1984).

Drama builds vocabulary. Students meet new words and move these words from their passive to their active vocabulary, helping them to clarify meaning and permitting the repeated practice of unfamiliar pronunciation (Schuman, 1978). This section features a variety of ways in which ESOL students can use drama to access the imaginary.

Types of Enactment.   *Participation theater* is a technique that originated in England (Way, 1981). Plays are enacted in the classroom by a children's theater group. During the enactment, the action is stopped from time to time to invite children to suggest ideas to the actors. Children become actively engaged as they become vocally, verbally, and physically involved with the action. *Process drama* is a way of having a group work on a dramatic interaction by stepping back to create a "backstory" that motivates and explains the interaction (McCaslin, 2000).

Drama in education encourages students to become emotionally involved in the content they are studying by becoming the person they are studying or enacting the event: a tourist visiting the Statue of Liberty, an international student being interviewed at the U.S. consulate for a visa approval, or Paul Revere getting ready to undertake his historic ride to warn the patriots that the British soldiers are advancing on Concord. The teacher guides the study and furnishes direction and materials.

Theater in education uses professional actors to visit schools, enacting productions that provoke discussion. The touring company provides curricular materials that help teachers to introduce the play and integrate the theme of the play into curriculum units. *Forum theater* is a dramatic technique that presents to students a difficult social situation and invites the audience to step into the action as protagonists and change the outcome. Each of these types of drama has potential benefits for language development.

Two Complementary Aspects of Drama.   *Informal and formal drama* are two complementary aspects: On the one hand, students learn to act informally and use their imagination to develop their talents in characterization and movement. On the other hand, if a formal play is staged, students become involved in reading the script; auditioning for roles; staging the play with costuming, rehearsals, and memorization; and, finally, performing it. These two processes aid one another, and each incorporates strategies that have been covered in earlier chapters, such as the use of multiple intelligence theory to develop talent, TPR to develop movement and listening skills, team building to promote cooperation, and social function theory to develop an understanding of language routines (see Figure 7.1).

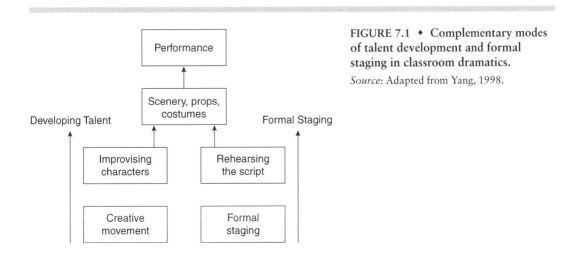

FIGURE 7.1 ◆ Complementary modes of talent development and formal staging in classroom dramatics.

Source: Adapted from Yang, 1998.

Practice in sense awareness and movement precedes creative dramatics. English learners love language games such as Simon Says (described in Chapter 3) and Fruit Basket (each student receives a card bearing the name of a fruit; they take a chair in a circle, and when their fruit is called they must exchange places with the other fruit that is called). They may also improvise physical movements to match vocabulary words in games such as Charades. (In a simple version of Charades, each student receives a card with an action verb to act out; they call upon a peer to guess, and if that peer guesses correctly, he or she keeps the card; the person with the most cards at the end wins). These and similar routines help students to relax as they enjoy listening and learning vocabulary.

McCaslin (2000) emphasized the importance of the teacher's support for nascent play acting on the part of students:

> The sensitive teacher will not demand too much in the beginning but will accept with enthusiasm the first attempts of a beginner to use imagination to solve a problem. After the players have had the fun of seeing, hearing, feeling, touching, tasting, or smelling something that is not there, they will find that their capacity grows quickly. Through drama, the imagination is stimulated and strengthened to the student's everlasting pleasure and profit. We learn through experience. Through participation in drama and vicariously through attendance at plays, children are provided with many experiences in acceptable and exciting ways. (p. 14)

Improvisation is an important part of talent development for creative dramatization. In "Object Imagination" students stare at an object provided by the teacher and make up a story about it to share with others. McCaslin (2000) suggested the following objects: a velvet jewelry box, an artificial rose, a foreign coin, an old hat, a cane, a quill pen, a headset radio, a pair of athletic shoes, a silver whistle, an old dog leash. As an additional stimulus, the teacher can provide a setting in place or time for the object: a settler's cabin one hundred years ago, or the town dump.

Character improvisation can take place by providing a setting, such as a bus stop, in which one by one characters come and join a group conversation. McCaslin (2000) suggested the use of an imaginary character named August, whom other characters visit with ideas for inventing an August holiday, which he lacks. Other types of improvisation include costume improvisation, in which a vest or hat assists in imaginative thinking about character development. Improvisations that lead to interactive skits or scenes might be considered role play (see below). At times, the response to an improvisation is rich enough to become a whole play, complete with script, characters, setting, and costumes.

Character development starts with characters that are as "neurotic and unusual" as possible (p. 34), as well as those who lend themselves to dramatic situations, such as policemen. Students work first from character introductions ("I am the thief who . . .") and then the characters interact. Each character belongs to the whole class, so the class as a whole can suggest that the character, say, falls in love, be kidnapped, or so forth (Wilhelm & Leverett, 1998).

Students can stage scenes from the plays they read, exercising creativity by being able to rewrite the scenes in their own words or reworking the scenes in creative ways (Schiffler, 1992). Some rehearsal is necessary to create a successful staging, with the teacher providing assistance in blocking out the actors' movements on stage and help-ing the actors to convey effective emotional communication accordance with the script.

The teacher's role in scripting is to move the script along by correcting gram-mar, making the lines more colorful based on the character's personality, and helping the actors to face the audience and speak loudly. Dialogue in a scene should be bal-anced so that all characters have approximately the same number of lines. Perfor-mances can be small, for the class only, or large, with audiences drawn from school staff, families, and other classes.

The teacher's role in rehearsal may vary. The teacher may act as a coach on the sidelines, offering suggestions to enhance staging, prompting with lines from a script, or taking actors aside for individual rehearsal. The teacher may actually take on a role in the play or assume a part briefly to get a scene back on track; such participa-tion helps students to view the teacher as willing to experiment with characterization (Ernst-Slavit & Wenger, 1998). The teacher may act as a group facilitator, running several scenes simultaneously and moving from one to the other to provide support and direction (McCaslin, 2000). Seldom can a group of novices reach emotional depth and focus without the direction provided by the teacher.

Student-Made Plays.   Plays can be developed and written by students using such lit-erary sources as myths, fairy tales, and scenes from novels, stories, or popular televi-sion shows. Students can act out fables such as "King Midas and the Golden Touch." The teacher evokes the mood by asking students, "If you had only one wish, what would it be?" The teacher then intensifies the mood by showing pictures of ancient Greece while reading the story. Students choose their favorite characters and close their eyes to picture that character in a pose from the play: a princess picking flowers in the

Plays involve authentic and creative use of oral and written language skills.

garden, or Mercury watching the king from Mount Olympus. Students then develop the play from their characters (McIntyre, 1974).

> One class reads an Aesop fable every week, and each student writes a story based on that fable. The story can adhere to the original moral (such as the Hare and the Tortoise's "Slow and steady wins the race"), or it can end with a twist, showing the moral is not always true. The stories are peer-critiqued, and then the stories are turned into scripts with dialogue. Students take turns in groups turning each script into a play, and every student has a part in each script. Over a period of time, students improve their playwriting and their performance skills—and boost the cognitive level of the class considerably. (Strohmeyer, 1991-1992)

No matter what the source, the process of writing the script, rehearsing, and performing stimulates both the creative imagination and the use of English. Myths, legends, and fairy tales provide fertile story lines for drama, because they are based on archetypes (the poor lad, the fairy godmother, rages to riches, the frog prince) that have evoked strong feelings and ideas through the ages. Two sources of multicultural stories that can be used for dramatization are Stern's *Tales from Many Lands: An Anthology of Multicultural Folk Literature* (1996) and Kasser and Silverman's *Stories We Brought with Us* (1994), which includes "Juan Bobo and the Pot," and "Don't Make a Bargain with a Fox." Fables open the door to creative use of scenery, music, and costume in ways that realistic stories do not.

Play Scripts as Literary Text

Play scripts as reading texts can be used to teach English in various ways. Most teachers who use drama tend to use plays for which a videotaped version is available. Students can read plays in sections, perhaps after viewing a videotape of the entire performance and discussing the production and its context, language, and plot. Scripts have particular elements that must be taught explicitly, such as directions to the actors. Some plays, such as the libretto to the musical drama *West Side Story,* may need an introductory passage (written by the teacher) that explains the social context for the plot and functions as a prereading warm-up (Beniston, 1996).

Reading the Play.   Dialogue is a means of focusing on conversation when reading a play. A deeper understanding of conversational discourse emerges as students use dialogue to probe characters' motivations. Having the entire plot of the play as the context helps make this exercise more meaningful than, for example, the arbitrary dialogue and without context associated with language instruction in the audiolingual era. One advantage of this technique is that the study of the second language is used to further understanding of discourse in general, thus avoiding the view of SLA as a compensatory or remedial activity.

Postreading exercises may be used to recap the plot and explore the characters. Each student can draw a picture of a plot event and then pair with other students to discover whose plot event comes first or last or features a given character. Students can write brief biographies of the characters that actors might use as "backstory" to prepare to act out their roles. As a class, they can brainstorm a list of questions they could ask each character for their opinions on the events of the plot. Students might also volunteer to be interviewed in character to answer these questions.

Viewing a Play.   Seeing plays performed is a memorable experience. A field trip to a theater is a first-time experience for many English learners. If a major theater company is beyond the classroom budget, local high school or amateur productions may be a reasonable alternative. Local amateur actors have skills that range from the gifted to the histrionic, and the stagecraft also varies widely in quality. These people provide models for students of community members' talent and enthusiasm and may spur the class to stage their own group performance. Students may enjoy studying a play before attending.

The analysis of a play to be read or viewed begins with a plot summary. What happens? Working in pairs, students tell the overall story briefly in their own words. Next, they try to recall what language they found memorable, working from their notes. What mental images does the playwright create with words? Were the words highly emotional? Was the language understandable?

Emotional impact is essential. What is the overall feeling of the scene? What emotions do the characters feel? Did the characters really interact with one another emotionally? Were the students affected by the actors? Which actors were most successful in creating a convincing character? Were the actor's lines understandable? Did any of the actors overact (make the character too much of a stereotype or make the emotions too obvious)?

Staging is an important feature to note. Did the design of the set convey a message? Was the setting realistic or tending toward the symbolic? Did the actors use the space well? Was the staging creative or boring? Were the props used well to convey the intent of each scene? Finally, encourage students to state the message of the scene in their own words. Was it hard to understand? Do they agree with it, or not?

Role Play

People are natural actors; after all, each person likely assumes a variety of roles every day. Role play is not only an excellent communicative activity in its own right, it can also be used as a warm-up for other kinds of dramatics. Role-play activities in the ESOL classroom range from rehearsal of relatively routine social interactions such as cashing a check at a bank to problem solving that involves complex conversations, whether authentic or staged. Students can practice talking by asking questions, making suggestions, demanding things, pretending to be other people, organizing themselves to solve problems, and reflecting on what happens.

Communicative Role Play.   Communicative language teaching uses role play extensively, but in a different way from the scripts used in audiolingual teaching. In communicative language teaching, the social functions of language are the organizational basis for turn taking. The role play is organized in linguistic terms as a *script* (Schank, 1981), with specific slots that fulfill specific social functions and variable filler that offers choices for each slot (in this context, "script" does not denote the Hollywood-type script, in which exact speeches for each role are specified. To avoid this connotation, the term "pattern" might be more appropriate to describe the format).

Slots and fillers are variable forms that fulfill social functions. For example, the common pattern for a restaurant involves a sequence of communicative slots. The first slot is "The Welcome," in which the hostess or maître d' greets the customer with such phrases as "Hello, and welcome to Friday's. How many will there be?" or "Good evening! Do you have reservations?" Any of these filler phrases is acceptable. The next slot might be labeled "Being Seated at the Table," and so forth. In communicative terms, showing the role players various filler phrases helps to acknowledge that the social function can be fulfilled creatively, within the framework of socially acceptable responses.

Suggestopedic Role Play.   The absence of tension and the inclusion of relaxation elements characterize role play in suggestopedia. Such conditions allow students "undisturbed intellectual and creative activity" (Lozanov, 1982, p. 155) through access to mental reserves untapped in other learning environments. Once material is introduced in the relaxed, supportive atmosphere, students engage in "elaborations"—reading dialogues, songs, games, and conversations. In role plays students can take on new identities when they wish but are never forced to perform.

Scenarios.   Scenarios for learning language bring the same dynamic tension to the classroom as occurs in real life. Di Pietro (1987) provides a complete training for educators in adapting foreign-language instruction from textbooks to active and interactive classroom exchanges among students, with wide applicability at multiple levels of proficiency.

Role plays can be imaginative or realistic. One simple scene takes place at a newsstand in a subway station, where a variety of customers interact with the newsstand owner. Young children can simulate a scene at a toy shop after customers have gone home, in which various toys discuss their desires. Customers in a laundromat can pretend they have lost money in a coin slot and try to obtain a refund from the laundromat manager. A floral delivery person can give flowers to a person at the wrong address and then try to get them back. Most problem-solving role plays are open-ended, encouraging the players to shape the conclusion (McCaslin, 2000).

Decision Dramas.   Decision dramas combine discussion and role play. An instructional unit poses a "weighty" problem. One student in a pair takes on the role of decision maker, and the other takes the role of advice giver. The topics can be designed to be suitable for adults, young adults, or younger students. Dramatizing family scenes, school situations, and other kinds of interactions helps ESOL students to compare their reactions to certain problems with those of other students. Thus can they clarify differing points of view, attitudes, and values. The teacher might further the discussion by asking leading questions, such as, "How do you think the father felt?" Repeating the role play with characters exchanging roles also furthers understanding of other people's feelings and gives all players the opportunity to experience both sides of an issue (Radin, 2000). *Personal journals* can be used to explore the issues that a role play has dramatized, allowing students to reflect on their learning.

Crosscultural Role Play.   Role plays of crosscultural misunderstanding in *Our Own Stories* (Dresser, 1993) are based on short narratives used as prompts. Each vignette tells the experience of an immigrant to the United States from a first-person point of view. After students read the narrative together, answer a set of comprehension questions, and discuss the crosscultural differences that are evident in the story, they role-play the misunderstood interaction. After the role play, students discuss the scene from the point of view of both actors. This can be useful both in the ESL context, in which students may actually experience these misunderstandings, and in the EFL context as a book about intercultural communication. A sample story compares the treatment of grandparents in the Mexican culture.

A small segment of one vignette represents the type of anecdotes featured in the book.

> My name is Cristina. I was born in Mexico and came to the United States when I was three months old. . . . My parents taught us we should respect grandparents more than anyone else in the world. . . . We were taught that hugging or kissing grandparents was disrespectful and that we should greet them by kissing their hand. . . . [She goes to a friend's birthday party and kisses the grandfather's hand.]. . . . I noticed that he looked at me in a strange way, as if he didn't like what I had done. Everyone else in the room looked at me, and my friend started laughing. (p. 56–57)

Readers Theater

Readers theater is a reading activity in which readers read stories or plays with expressive voices and use gestures to help the audience to visualize the action (Sloyer, 1982). Through voice and bodily tension, the audience is led to imagine the scenes and characters (Laughlin, Black, & Loberg, 1991). Because the players are reading aloud, there is no energy expended on memorization, props, costumes, scenery, music, or lighting, although the performance may be enhanced with elements of stage theater (Wold, 1993).

Readers theater engages students in group work that can enhance classroom language learning. This activity motivates students' enjoyment of literature by means of creative activity and promotes reading fluency, as students are provided with opportunities to read and reread the same texts (Martínez, Roser, & Strecker, 1998). It particularly benefits weak readers, as their need for additional mediation is met as the text is rehearsed (Busching, 1981).

Texts for readers theater are chosen based on the age of the students, the length of the text, and the suitability of the language and plot to oral adaptation. Interesting characters help students to project understanding and care for their characters as they read.

Adapting Text.   To adapt a text to readers theater, the teacher reproduces a selection that appeals to the students as a script, eliminating parts that are unnecessary and highlighting the characters' names on the left margin along with their lines (Young & Vardell, 1993). Dialogue sections are short, and characters use direct speech. Parts are distributed so that characters have a proportionate number of lines. The program has a clear beginning, middle, and end, giving it the unity of a finished production. A narrator introduces the play and provides background not told in dialogue (Hill, 1990). McCaslin (2000) offers a sample readers theater script, an adaptation of the folktale "The Musicians of Bremen."

Practicing and Performing.   Preperformance preparation may include language development activities. The teacher reads the selection to the class, clarifying the meaning of unfamiliar vocabulary. On the second reading students repeat each line in a choral response after the teacher. As an alternative, the teacher may read two lines and then wait for student repetition, or teachers and students may alternate lines. Students continue practicing in small groups, after which the teacher may ask for volunteers to read individual parts (Root & Dumicich, 1998). Parts may then be assigned for the reading.

During the performance, readers usually hold the script in their left hand so that the right hand is free to gesture. Pages are fastened securely to a binder, using loose rings or spiral binding so that pages turn easily and stay flat. All performers wear similar clothes to present a uniform appearance onstage (Shepard, 1994). Performers are arranged to create an interesting stage picture. Sometimes readers whose characters are not present in a particular scene turn their backs to the audience to indicate that they are absent. Music can be used to indicate transitions between scenes. As a performer is reading, he or she directs the speech to another character if it is intended that way. Otherwise, the reader uses an offstage focus, looking up from the script as often as possible to establish eye contact with the audience

Following the performance, students can talk about their experience, either as performers or as listeners, or write a review for a local newspaper. Teachers can use observational checklists or rating scales as a means of evaluating students' performances, using such criteria as smooth delivery of lines, clear and distinct speech and fluent reading, creation of believable characters, listening and reacting to other characters appropriately, and mature behavior onstage. With these qualities in mind, readers theater makes a substantial contribution to students' growth in reading skills, communicative competence, and social awareness and interpersonal cooperation in the English development classroom.

Classroom drama helps students to exercise the imagination.

> ❖ Tactics for promoting classroom dramatics:
>
> - Provide a set of large wooden boxes of various sizes made of ¾" plywood for flexible use in staging.
> - Set aside a stage in the classroom illuminated by a strong lamp with a gooseneck stem; rig a portable curtain; provide a microphone stand with a heavy base on which cardboard can be taped for stand-alone props.
> - Provide readers theater scripts with each character's parts prehighlighted.
> - Write versions of readers theater scripts with parts for a chorus that comments on the action; this involves class members who may not have a speaking part in that scene.

Puppetry

In many parts of the world, puppetry is enjoyed as a fine art, whereas in Western culture it is generally considered a child's entertainment. In recent years, with the popularity of innovative forms of theater, the use of puppets has entered the mainstream. The musical *Lion King*, adapted from the animated movie, features giant costumes with actors dressed as puppets. Although masks and puppets go hand in hand, for the purposes of SLA, hand puppets are better than facial masks, which make it harder to produce and listen to oral language. Puppets are particularly useful for English learners if shyness, anxiety, or fear of error are inhibiting factors.

Puppet plays with cultural content can portray legends, fairy tales, or historical events, whether from the native culture or the target culture. An excellent example is the instructional unit entitled *Chinese Animal Zodiac* (Yang, 1999) which features a puppet show starring the animals of the twelve-year Chinese zodiac cycle (rat, bull, tiger, rabbit, dragon, snake, horse, sheep, monkey, cock, dog, and boar). Instructions for making the animal hand puppets are available on the Internet (http://familyplay.com/activities/actpuppets.html); these can then be used to act out the *Story of the Chinese Zodiac* (Chang, 1994, available from Shen's Books and Supplies in Arcadia, California).

"The Magic Sieve" is another Chinese fable that is amenable to puppetry. A bamboo tea strainer can be used as the magic sieve. More Chinese fables are available in the book *Favorite Children's Stories from China and Tibet* (Hume, 1962/1993). A wealth of multicultural literature is now available so that puppet shows can teach cross-cultural values as well as English-language development, both in EFL and ESL classrooms.

Puppets are constructed from a variety of materials. "Puppets are 'actors' who come to life with the help of a puppeteer" (McCaslin, 2000). Some hand puppets hang from strings; others are fastened to sticks, fit over the hand or fingers like a glove, or are made of everyday materials like paper bags, bandannas, or socks. The puppeteer can manipulate the puppet in full sight of the audience or can hide behind a cloth or below the edge of a table.

Puppet theaters can be handmade or purchased. For example, the Castle Tabletop Theater is a commercial product made of colorful wooden pieces that measures 28 inches by 28 inches by 9 inches. Another avenue for puppetry is the use of Create-a-Scene Magnetic Playsets by Smethport. The FELTkids Play System uses felt costumes that stick to dolls and matching scenery and is available in themes such as Cool Clothes, Fun on Wheels, Country Garden, and Playhouse. English learners can use these to play with one another in pairs.

Puppet scenery can be simple, with the setting established by means of dialogue. Props should match the size of the puppet in scale. Using easily available materials, students can construct their own puppets, following written or oral directions from the teacher and writing their own puppet plays or adapting material from stories, poems, or fairy tales used in class. The wide range of material that can be used in puppet shows demonstrates the usefulness of puppets as language teachers.

Storytelling

In the world predating the printing press, storytelling was employed by many cultures not only as entertainment but also as a means of educating the young, preserving history, and transmitting cultural values and beliefs. The narrative approach to ESL and EFL education provides students with interesting and comprehensible language in a low-anxiety setting. When students hear and see stories, they are exposed to a wide variety of vocabulary and structures.

Storytelling foundations such as the New York City Storytelling Center and the Jewish Storytelling Center, together with celebrations such as the Jonesboro (Tennessee) annual storytelling festival, are promoting the return of storytelling as a human art form. Storytellers who are booked through organizations such as Art in the Schools visit schools to engage students in the firsthand immediacy of oral language events.

Delivery.   Storytelling delivery takes much practice with characterization, vocal exaggeration for effect, strong facial expressions, and dramatic use of emotion and suspense. Some storytellers add musical accompaniment or work in conjunction with a traveling minstrel. Stories may be told standing or sitting in front of the class with a dramatic flair, using props or costumes, or in a tight circle with the class drawn closely together. Visual effects, such as reduced lighting, a spotlight, or special staging can heighten the mood. The best training for storytelling is to watch experts and learn from them, and to collect stories that are interesting and entertaining for the listener.

Children absorb meaning by investing their attention and interest in the plot and characters of a story as the storyteller makes use of inflection, intonation, emphasis, change of pitch, and use of facial expressions, eye contact, gestures, and body language. Whether using heroic tales, science fiction, biography, or history, the storyteller has a unique opportunity to build positive social attitudes and values, while transporting the listener by means of the imagination to remote times, places, and cultures.

Picture-enhanced listening can more fully engage young English learners. As they listen to a story, each child holds a picture that corresponds to the characters in the story. As the children listen attentively, they each hold up the picture of the character who is featured in that part of the story. The storyteller pauses to check the children's pictures, saying the name of the character with the child. After the story is over, the children repeat the names of the pictures one by one and then work with a partner to retell the story using the character pictures. A sequential story like "The Little Red Hen" (in which the hen goes from animal to animal trying to get help with baking) works well with this exercise (Malkina, 1998).

Telling stories from their native cultures is one way in which ESOL students may benefit, but they may certainly enjoy a well-told story from any culture of origin. Older ESOL students may enjoy preparing stories to tell younger children and thus develop poise in speaking before a group. Students may enjoy working together to prepare stories using props or other types of prompts.

Creating Stories. Students can create stories using a flannel board with flannel characters, or act out fairy tales. Many different flannel board sets, including Castle Stories (featuring six fairy tales), Dinosaurs, People (twenty-seven figures of various ages and ethnicities), Cottage Classics (interior scene for Snow White, etc.), Aesop's Fables, and others are available from Storyteller online (www.thestoryteller.com). Alternatively, a magnet board with magnetic characters (see World Discoveries) may provide a shy storyteller with props that help move the story forward.

Strip stories are fun activities in which each student in order adds a line to a story based on an intriguing picture or photo (Hadaway, Vardell, & Young, 2002). One way to involve students in groups is the use of *story theater* (Gunning, 1996). A narrator, a student who may have stronger reading skills, reads a story aloud, while others in the group perform the actions of characters or objects. This format helps students to listen and work cooperatively.

Aesop's Fables may work well in this format. Students may also work cooperatively to find an alternative ending to a story, giving it a creative twist as it is retold (Barr & Johnson, 1997). Students enjoy retelling stories they have heard, using props such as stuffed animals or telling the story to a favorite stuffed animal in a classroom storytelling center. Storytelling differs from story retelling, however, in that storytelling requires students to memorize some of the language in the story so that the retelling is more dramatic and communicative with the audience (Tompkins & McGee, 1993).

> Marna Bunce-Crim sets the stage for writing in the classroom by using storytelling to arouse students' interest. She begins by raising a question: "How many of you have a pet?" She then instructs them to think of funny or sad stories about their pets—where they got the pets, their names, and so on. As hands rise, children are invited to share their pet stories with the class. Additional "How many of you . . ." questions include, "How many of you have broken a bone or had an injury? How many of you have a funny story to tell about a brother or sister? How many of you have taken a trip or a vacation?" She also shares stories about herself and her family. By having everyone in the room share a story, she creates a feeling of intimacy and an understanding of everyone's similarities and differences. (Bunce-Crim, 1991, p. 16)

Personal Stories. Family stories may provide anecdotes for retelling. Every family has stories—my family often retold the Christmas story of my grandmother's getting drunk on Brandy Alexanders (she thought they were chocolate milk) and passing out over a plate of green beans! Students may prompt stories from their relatives using openers like, "Tell me about the town where you lived as a child" or, "Tell me about your favorite toy when you were a child."

Personal experience stories are often best told in small groups or to a partner, because the storyteller is sharing something personal (Mallan, 1991). Students may enjoy sharing these unrehearsed anecdotes with classmates, thus practicing the use of story structure: plot, characterization, elaborative details, climax, resolution, and conclusion (what Peregoy and Boyle [2001] call story elements).

"Time-Travel Mirror" is an exercise that helps students to tell their own stories (Morgan & Rinvolucri, 1983). One student draws a large, ornate mirror on the blackboard, and others copy it onto a sheet of blank paper. Students each "time-travel" to the past to draw a scene from memory. They then stand up and move about the room to find a partner to whom to explain the scene. The worse the drawing, the more necessary and productive the oral explanation. Students can regroup several times to obtain a different partner. In a variation on this theme, students can draw a scene from yesterday or a wish for the future to share with a partner.

Stories to Tell Our Children (Weinstein-Shr, 1992) is a collection of short quotes from immigrants to the United States. Each "story" is accompanied by a picture of its author. Readers are asked first simply to react to the story and discuss its theme briefly with a peer. After a few workbook exercises to familiarize themselves with the vocabulary, students use given discussion questions to deepen their experience with the story. They then tell a similar story to a classmate, using sentence completion as a prompt. They can meld these sentences into their own story and save these stories in a portfolio. The teacher's personal stories are also a part of the class's shared experience. Both are a part of the telling, writing, and sharing process of the class.

Steps to Storytelling.   Four main steps in the process of storytelling begin with a very short story and culminate in students creating stories and books independently. These steps are listed in Table 7.1.

TPR storytelling uses mini-stories to introduce and practice vocabulary for beginning students (see Ray & Seely, 1997). A list of "guide words," core vocabulary that will move the story forward, begins each story. These are presented visually and

TABLE 7.1 ◆ Steps to Using the Narrative Approach

Steps	Instructions to the Teacher
1. Telling the core story	Begin with a simple story, assisted by drawings, with props or gestures. Retell several times, adding characters, setting, and vocabulary by writing directly on the drawings.
2. Revising the story	Retell the story, using different characters, altering the plot, or telling the story from a different character's point of view.
3. Creating a story as a class	At the preproduction stage, students are given yes/no options to alter the story as it is told. When they can produce short phrases, they can suggest more alternatives. Draw their versions and retell them to the class.
4. Creating stories and books independently	Preproduction students can draw figures, with the teacher adding their ideas as text. More advanced students can create their own storyboards and narratives to share with the class.

Source: Adapted from McQuillan & Tse, 1998.

taught through hand gestures and basic TPR techniques. The guide words act as the anchor of the storytelling. Next, a few students act out the given "mini-situation." The teacher then retells the mini-situation, using questions to boost comprehension (example: "Did she *jump* or did she *fall*?"). One or two students then retell the story, using all the guide words. The students tell one another the story in pairs and then repeat it without seeing the guide words. Finally, various students tell parts of the story to the whole group. This procedure is replicated at higher levels of language learning and extended to student-created stories.

Stories are introduced by means of a picture cue, a mysterious object, or a photograph. As an ice-breaker, intriguing sentences from a story may be cut in half and the halves distributed to all the students; each student must then find the match for his or her half. As the story is told, students may listen for their sentence. After the story, the students can sequence the sentences as a story review. In a different setting, the language laboratory, half of the students can listen to one story while the other half hear a different story. After listening, students form pairs to tell the missing story to their peer. Some stories can be used to teach grammar ("Goldilocks" for the present perfect progressive—"Who's been eating my porridge?" and "The Three Little Pigs" for contractions—"I won't let you in" and "I'll huff and puff and blow your house down") (Morgan & Rinvolucri, 1983, pp. 55–56). Students in pairs can practice telling the story to one another, emphasizing the target form with exaggerated intonation.

Students develop fictional stories of their own by bringing to class a recent newspaper article and turning it into a fairy tale. One way to expand students' descriptive powers as they begin writing stories is to give pairs of students a fairy tale cut up into sentences. After each sentence of the story, students must stop to describe at greater length the character, place, or physical action.

Alternatively, each pair of students may be given an index card bearing a small anecdote, with three words highlighted. Using the highlighted words only, the students must create a different story. Another option is to divide students into groups of four and make each person responsible for the time, people, action, or place. They can create story openings made up of a sentence that contains one of each element (Wong, 1996). The key that makes these exercises useful for storytelling is the final phase, in which students tell their stories in pairs to another pair (pair/share).

Resources for Stories.   One source for stories to use in class is Morgan and Rinvolucri's *Once Upon a Time: Using Stories in the Language Classroom* (1983). An excellent source of ideas and activities for developing the talents of children as storytellers is *Children as Storytellers* (Mallan, 1991), which includes specific exercises for developing imagination, visualization skills, innovative story structures, and enhanced narrative memory. Mallan also suggests a variety of story activities that can be used across the curriculum, such as rewriting a folktale or historical event as a radio news bulletin. Stories from around the world can be retold as a part of the social studies curriculum, and biographies of famous scientists or historical figures can be retold as stories.

Something about the narrative, with its structured beginning and ending, ritual performance, and patterned sequence of events, is deeply satisfying to the emotions, powerfully stimulating to language acquisition, memorable to the mind, and conducive to crosscultural comparison and cultural enrichment. This is exactly the kind of technique sought by TESOL educators around the world.

❖ Tactics for promoting storytelling:

◆ Coach students to practice storytelling often.
◆ Select stories with vivid emotional appeal, engaging characters, and a clearly defined theme.
◆ Encourage vivid and vital use of voice, face, hands, body, and props to make story-telling come alive.
◆ Give students training and practice in becoming attentive and responsible members of the audience.

Poetry and the Muse

The Greeks believed that poetry was a gift of the Muses, a group of goddesses who acted as the source of inspiration for poets (at that time also musicians). Although some people still believe that gifted musicians and poets have a special connection to mysterious wellsprings of talent, the love of poetry can be taught, as can the use of the imagination to produce creative writing in this genre.

◆ **STRATEGY 7.4: Stimulate the linguistic imagination with poetry**

Poetry was excluded from second-language teaching during the era of behaviorist teach-ing, because language for the classroom was deliberately simplified into structured pat-terns with limited, controlled vocabulary. Even in the era of communicative-based teaching, the emphasis has been on utilitarian, practical language. Any literature that is used is molded into texts, which are the basis for analysis or comprehension questions. Poetry is too often an optional extra. Yet poetry can be used as the central focus of a language-teaching lesson, integrated with other forms of reading, writing, speaking, lis-tening, and critical/creative thinking to teach English in a satisfying manner.

A Universal Language

Poetry is universal across languages. All cultures deal with its nontrivial themes such as love, nature, religion, joy, and despair. All languages employ devices of rhythm, rhyme, allusion, and figurative language to express deep emotions. From poetry we receive the language tools that make life more beautiful, meaningful, and personal. Just as important, students who write poetry can be encouraged to make the second language their own by coining words, using new words in old ways, and being freer to be more imaginative and more creative in the second language than they could be in their first (Maley & Duff, 1989).

In fact, poetry written by second-language speakers of English can provide the native speaker with fresh insights. I'll never forget a conversation with two students who were writing a poem about a young man's summer lover. Her name, they said, was "Julie." How limited was my imagination—I tried to talk them out of spelling the name "July"! Another student tried to tell me that a taste could be deep. In fact, to delve deeply in to the taste of a fruit, one could "plum" it! (Well, it *is* a better explanation than a "plumb" line). Another student, in a poem, broke through a portal of "pained" glass. (I'm sure he had heard that glass comes in panes.) In truth, I had never considered that not only the hand that breaks the glass, but the breaking glass itself might suffer hurt!

Poetry is a gateway to personal growth. This is especially true of poetry enacted in performance. In poetic imagination, if old, we are young again; if Chinese, we can become Persian; we can become our own brother, mother, uncle; we can transmogrify into a hawk, a chrysanthemum, a syringe, or a raisin in the sun. In the poetic imagination, identity, culture, past, and future are open to change. In poetry we can share with others the journey that has brought us to the present or the bridge that connects us to the future. Poetry uses contemporary language and does not trap students in fusty archaisms. Rather, it opens doors to compacted, intense meanings that lift the language classroom, even momentarily, from the humdrum to the sublime.

Poetry is used in many ways in the SLA classroom: to reinforce English pronunciation patterns by taking advantage of the sounds and natural rhythms of a poem; to introduce students to the insights into human nature revealed through literature; and as a vehicle for discussing culture. Both reading the poems of others and creating one's own poetry stimulate the imagination and can lead to an increase in appreciation for the beauty of English as a language.

The Sound of Poetry

Language games such as tongue twisters teach sound values without being truly poetic, but they can lead to other kinds of word fun based on short rhyming verse such as the work of poet Ogden Nash (see Harmon's *Oxford Book of American Light Verse*, 1979). Students working in pairs can generate lists of English words that rhyme (Humphries [1998] used *pen*, *red*, *feet*, *sing*, *cake*, and *hat* as starting words), just for the fun of using language or to teach irregular homonyms (*way* rhymes with *say*, but so does *weigh*). Making poems directly from rhymes, however, may undercut the connection between the imaginary and poetry; I believe poetry is based on communicating an insight, image, or emotion, and the rhyme serves to enhance this original impulse. As Koch reminded us, "The effort of finding rhyme stops the free flow of . . . feelings and associations, and poetry gives way to sing-song" (1970, p. 8).

Traditional poetic structures are organized by sound. If the sound value of a particular poem is salient, poetry is worth studying for this feature alone. Using Poe's "Annabel Lee" (Poe, in Sullivan, 1978) to teach such concepts as *end rhyme, internal rhyming, stanza*, and *verse*, and having students tap or clap along with the meter, helps to convey the rhythmic basis of poetry enjoyment. Students may be assigned to memorize the poem to encourage them to master the intonation and flow of the phrases (Meloni & Masters, 1988).

Using Poetry for Speech Improvement.   Poetry can teach pronunciation, if specific poems can be matched to a pronunciation pattern that the class is practicing. Solé (1998) gives practical suggestions on using poetry to teach pronunciation, joining the resources of a literature anthology (cf. McMichael, 1985) with a pronunciation text such as Orion (1988). Over a period of weeks, the teacher can take note of words that students are having trouble pronouncing, display these together, and ask students to make a sound poem. Reciting the poem together in pairs helps students to pronounce the words (Maley & Duff, 1989).

Poetry can teach intonation. Websites dedicated to rap musicians such as Tupak Shakur or the music of Bob Marley can teach students the rhythm of sentences. Choosing carefully poems that are appropriate for classroom use, the teacher can excerpt segments from rap music that feature rhymes made of longer, multisyllabic words. These examples assist students whose languages are monosyllabic to master the way longer words in English with multiple inflections (*inspirátion, rámificátion*) fit into sentence intonation.

Choral speaking has been used successfully with poetry to give students the opportunity for speech improvement by working on pitch, volume, rate, and tone quality of spoken English. Individual voices may alternate with the group as a whole for dramatic effect, or the group can be divided into *antiphonal* groups (two or more groups with differing timbre, or sound quality). The two groups may alternate lines or go back and forth in a call-and-response format. The choral reading may rise toward a climax, with individuals first blending into groups and then the groups into the whole.

Line-around reading gives each reader a line in turn. Sound effects (bells, drums, vocal sounds) may be added. McCaslin (2000) suggested many poems that can be used with choral speaking, including the majestic "The Creation" by James Weldon Johnson and Walt Whitman's "I Hear America Singing," which can be dramatized with pantomime. An excellent source of poems for choral reading is Fleischman's *A Joyful Noise: Poems for Two Voices* (1988) (about insects) and *I Am Phoenix: Poems for Two Voices* (1985) (about birds). Choral reading may be used effectively to build a sense of classroom community, such as in a morning routine that brings students into oral group unison (Lipton & Hubble, 1997).

Using Poetry Artistically.   Artistic recitation, writing or memorizing, is an objective when working with poetry. The teacher who models this type of recitation sets the pace (see the movie *Dead Poets Society* for an example of a teacher's dramatic poetic interpretation). An interpretive reading can be recorded at home with a small, handheld tape recorder and then played for the class. Dramatic lighting during the listening enhances the mood (Schiffler, 1992).

Poetry as Vocabulary Development

Poems are rich sources of vocabulary because words are part of the love of English that a poet demonstrates. To interest her second-grade students in acquiring difficult new words about dinosaurs from Jack Prelutsky's poetry book *Tyrannosaurus Was a Beast* (1988), Mrs. Washington duplicated rectangles of paper decorated to look like ten-dollar bills, but with a dinosaur in the center instead of the picture of a president. Students collected "ten-dollar words" from Prelutsky's poems, wrote them on the fake bills, and hung them on a clothesline. Students then volunteered to illustrate or define the words, attaching their work to the bill (sample words: *inedible, vacuous, cudgel,* and *ravenous*). With these words in hand, students clapped out the rhythm of the poems, dramatized the poems, wrote similar poems, and used "quickwrites" to tell what they liked about each poem (Tompkins & McGee, 1993).

Found poems are made from vocabulary words that students discover while reading. Collecting words and rearranging them in phrases to make a poem makes vocabulary acquisition also the work of the imaginary. Rather than having English learners simply translate a poem, Chatton (1993) suggested that they make a poem in their native language to match the English version. This could result in a dramatic dual-language choral reading.

Types of Poems

Poems can bring together vocabulary (meaning), form (meter, intonation) and sound (pronunciation). *Haiku* poems are written in three lines (5 syllables, 7 syllables, 5 syllables) for a total of 17 syllables, capturing a single image that transmits beautifully the sense of a single season of the year (see Box 7.1 and Box 7.2). The *tanka* follows the syllabic principle of the haiku, using the pattern 5, 7, 5, 7, 7 (see Box 7.3). The *cinquain* has five lines: the first line names the topic, the second uses two or three words to describe the topic; the third line expresses action in three or four words; the fourth line expresses personal attitude in four to five words; and the last line uses a word or two to rename or reframe the topic (see Box 7.4). The *concrete* or *figural* poem has a shape that reflects its content (see Box 7.5).

Cultural context in poetry is important. The haiku is of Japanese origin and has been used in Japan for three hundred years. A lightly sketched picture that the reader fills in from personal memories and experiences, it often juxtaposes two unrelated subjects, which the reader connects. The poem also implies a link to a specific season. The

---

BOX 7.1
❖ **Haiku: "Pretend Rain"**

Mist is not shower
Sympathy false, you're guilty
Crocodile tear-rain

BOX 7.2
❖ **Haiku: "Plum Blossoms"**

Snow-frozen white blooms
Unfurled too early, withered
Like fragile spring dreams

BOX 7.3
❖ Tanka: "Bicycle Lad"

Ped'ling, waves to me
Brown hair whipping in the wind
So far down the street . . .
I only know your hair whips
Because mine is rippling too

BOX 7.4
❖ Cinquain: "Puddle"

Puddle
After the rain
For sloshing, swashing, wading
New boots . . . I'm tempted . . .
I puddle . . .

BOX 7.5
❖ Figural Poem: Caracal Goes A-Hunting

Caracal goes   a-hunting
                            Nose
                            buried
                            deep
                            in
                            the
                            grass,
                            Ear-
                            tufts
                    sticking straight up above the meadow

root syllables of Japanese words, like Chinese characters, have sounds and meanings that evoke literary and historical meanings. Upon translation, the haiku is stripped of its cultural context and thrust unclothed into English. Yet even in translation, the subtlety lingers. Students can meet haiku from its masters. The local library may have access to a book of Japanese haiku in editions such as the Peter Pauper Press (1958). It is well worth the effort to preserve the flavor of the cultural origin as students write their own haiku.

Writing Poetry

Because each syllable of Chinese poetry represents a single image, poetry from China can be used to stimulate students to view English poetry in a different way. Rather than the word coming first, which often results in forced rhymes, letting the image come first tells a story or evokes a feeling by letting the poem emerge picture by picture. *The Heart of Chinese Poetry* (Whincup, 1987) offers the reader a bilingual translation of selected Chinese poems, including the original Chinese characters in an image-by-image translation. One does not have to be familiar with Chinese characters to absorb the logic of the poetry, and the visit to a dissimilar mental logic can be a refreshing stimulus to students' creativity. Students can translate the poem from the original characters, each putting the verse into English in a different way. Then they can view a short video segment such as a scene from the motion picture *Crouching Tiger Hidden Dragon* and put the scene into a poem image by image.

Poetic Listening.   Auditory input is sometimes even better than visual images, because listening alone, without seeing, evokes mental images. Listening to "The Highwayman" by Alfred Noyes can bring out a sequence of images. Perhaps the students might see a young man of the 1770s clothed in breeches and lace and review a list of words such as *inn, musket,* and *galleon*. After listening to the poem, they might try to write down images that came to mind. The teacher might help the class to put these images into words and write new verses to the poem, or write new poems that express emotions that the highwayman or the innkeeper's daughter may have felt (see Maley & Duff, 1989). The intensity of emotion conveyed by the poem might counter the stereotype of the English as emotionally reserved!

Writing Poetry with Students.   The private world of dreams and desires is an inspiring source for those who wish to write poetry with English learners. Koch's *Wishes, Lies, and Dreams* (1970) offers students the chance to finish the line, "I wish . . ." The world comes alive to the ear using the theme, "Noises." Changes in feelings over time are "poeticized" in the convention, "I used to . . . but now . . ." The theme "Lies" brings forth the "tall tale teller" in students. "I seem to be . . . but I really am . . ." allows students to compare their public face with their private, inner world. An interesting genre that Koch brought forth from students was "Poems using Spanish words." The words, usually nouns or adjectives, were inserted into English stanzas for cultural effect. This bilingual format may be highly generative for English learners.

Exposure to a rich poetic environment helps students to create poems in the classroom. Koch (1970, summarized in Cecil & Lauritzen, 1994) offered a few suggestions. First, poetry should be an in-class activity. Uses of the imagination in class may become drudgery if assigned as homework. However, if students are inspired to write at home and share their work, it is cause for celebration! Students who mingle with one another to share and borrow words and ideas can write collaboratively. Idea prompts that open up the world of "pretend" encourage students to exercise their imagination fully. If a line is unclear, asking for clarification rather than criticizing the work frees the poet from the burden of pleasing the teacher.

Scaffolding poetry, providing a temporary writing framework for a poetry pattern, is an important way to stimulate students. The scaffold can be a kind of formula for writing the poem (for example, "I dream . . ." in which each line contains a person, place, and color, as in "I dream I'm dancing with salamanders around a yellow desert campfire"). Other scaffolds can be the use of paintings that evoke mystery or a provoke a rich sensory response. When students have seen and heard the models of others, written and shared a group poem, and drafted their own versions, the teacher may wish to follow a group writing process in which students solicit feedback from a trusted peer editor, confer with the teacher, and then incorporate suggestions from both sources in a final work that they can read to an appreciative audience (see Cecil & Lauritzen, 1994).

Connecting Visual and Poetic

Visual Imaginary Dramatic Arts (VIDA) (Díaz-Rico, 2001a) is a process combining art with drama and poetry to help students explore their culture, dreams, and fantasies. Two types of visual prompts are used, depending on the age of the student. For adolescents and adults, a collection of art prints is employed that originates in the surreal. Each print features rich color and images that are figurative, but not constricted by an easy-to-label story line. For example, Dali's "Persistence of Memory" is visually arresting but too easy to label ("melting clocks") and thus not a suitable prompt. Conversely, Nash's "Landscape from a Dream" (1936–8) contains a beach, a hawk, transparent doors, and floating balls—all of which evoke ideas but do not constrain the imagination. The paintings are chosen with the goal of evoking archetypes and deep feelings, avoiding the display of nudity or overly disturbing images (see Appendix B for a list of paintings used in VIDA).

Students choose one from a laminated set of prints and work with a partner to create their own title for the artwork. They then find three decorator paint sample cards (obtained free from a hardware store) that match colors in the painting. The paint samples have names such as Malibu Blue or Thunder Gray. Students write the three color names on a display pad for the class to view, explaining or asking for explanations of the cultural allusions (Why "Malibu Blue"?) (Answer: Malibu is an upscale beach community in California). They then act out one of the names in a game of Charades. This is easy and rewarding for students. Using the color names and the paintings themselves as prompts, students write a brief poem using the scaffold, "Go through a portal in the painting. Meet the portal host. Bring back a message." They are encouraged to use words that evoke a rich sensory experience.

Inner Child Cards (Lerner & Lerner, 1992) function as the visual prompts for young children. These images feature fairies, dwarfs, and other fanciful creatures as well as the main characters of well-known fairy tales. Students can write poetry using the prompt, "You are invited to a party by the figures on the card. What do you see? What do you hear? What happens then?" For both groups, acting out the poem or performing a dramatic reading adds emotion and excitement.

For more information on using art in education, see Gardner (1990).

Poetry Interpretation

Interpreting poetry with students helps to bring out both literal and figurative meanings, as well as enabling students to appreciate the sound qualities of poetic language. The beginning element of analysis is the story line. In a few sentences, what is the poem about: who, what, when, and where (characters, setting)? The second element is the language of the poem—the word choice, sound value (including assonance and alliteration), rhythm, rhyme, and use of mental images. The third element of a poem is the emotional message. What words are used that convey feelings? How are the images used to evoke passion, sympathy, or horror? Finally, what is the meaning or theme that the reader or listener constructs from the poem? Is the message straightforward or ambiguous? What do we experience that is unique to this poem, and what do we learn about human condition?

To evaluate a student's presentation of a poem in class teachers may use criteria that assess such aspects as choice of poem; communication of meaning, emotion, and tone; quality of delivery in terms of stance, voice, gesture, and audience consideration; and overall impact (see Hadaway, Vardell, & Young, 2002). A teacher may use the presentation as a vehicle for informal feedback to the student, using an interactive journal to open the door to continued conversation about the theme, discussing favorite lines of the poem or the student's interpretation, composing a poem in return, or writing a short reminiscence about a related personal experience.

Poem in the pocket is a technique that invites spontaneous reading. On one special day, students copy favorite stanzas of poems, and throughout the day, whether in the classroom or elsewhere in the school, another student, the teacher, or anyone else may ask the student, "What poem is in *your* pocket?" The student then responds by reciting the poem (Cecil & Lauritzen, 1994).

Events in students' lives can provide occasions for poetry expression. Students who send birthday, graduation, or holiday cards to one another can write special poems for the occasion. This opportunity gives students authentic reasons for reading and writing poetry linked to communicative events (Christison, 1982).

> Mother's Day and Father's Day were poem opportunities for Mr. Stillwell's Level II ESL class. The class read poems from Myra Livingston's *Poems for Mother* (1988) and the companion volume, *Poems for Father* (1989). These poems describe many kinds of mothers and fathers, capturing the complexity of love and the warm memories of shared experience as well as the mixed feelings for parents who have moved away. The students each chose a poetic form to adapt, writing their own feelings and memories in a card to illustrate and bring home.

Poetry in the Curriculum.   Theme poems can tie poetry to the curriculum. Travel is a broad theme that brings out the poet in some students. Making an anthology of poems that focus on travel, students imagine a place that they would like to visit. After collecting pictures of that locale, students brainstorm words that describe their feelings about the site and write phrases that combine in a poem about the experience. A "wish book" is the result of combining the poem and pictures (Crenshaw, 1988). Making a transition from the imaginary to the real world, students research the climate and geographical features, compute the distance, decide the best mode of travel, and write a story about something that happens when they travel there.

Choosing poems for classroom use is based on poems having some innate, immediate appeal to the students. Poetry that goes too far beyond their developmental level may build resistance to the genre. An excellent source of poems for children is *The Random House Book of Poetry for Children* (Prelutsky, 2000); for adults, *The Norton Anthology of Modern Poetry* (Ellmann, 1988) is the classic. Shapiro (1990) recommended other ways in which poems can be discovered and used in addition to reliance upon poetry anthologies. Children's magazines such as *Cricket* and *Highlights* can show young students that poems are written by students their own age; they may wish to submit their own poems to these sources for publication.

Collections of poems adapted for classroom use are available in the Jamestown Literature Program's series *Reading and Understanding Poems* (1990). Each poem features a teaching follow-up that explores the meaning, form, or language of the poem in exercises and suggests questions for discussion. This systematic presentation educates the novice teacher about poetry, provides a poetry glossary, and includes suggestions about the use of poetry as a prompt for writing. However, the poems do not seem to be a prompt for writing other poems. Such anthologies are used more for analysis than for purposes of exercising the imagination. Overall, reading and analyzing poetry without a parallel process of creating poetry seems didactic, devoid of the vitality of students' own emotion and creativity.

"Hokey" poetry seems authentic but is not really literature. Lipson's *Audacious Poetry: Reflections of Adolescence* (1992) is a collection of numerous poems, most of them written by the author, that address adolescent themes such as the dirty bedroom, work at a fast-food restaurant, and teen slang. The book also features classroom activities that explore these topics. Overall, the book attempts to evoke issues that relate to the lives of teenagers, but the poems are rhyme-driven, with shallow poetic language. Adolescents, like other human beings, need to be exposed to language drawn from the heights and depths of the human experience, rather than pandered to with language that is trite.

Form poetry (alphabet poems, list poems, etc.) can help reluctant writers use and appreciate language in a new way. Kazemek and Rigg's *Enriching Our Lives: Poetry Lessons for Adult Literacy Teachers and Tutors* (cited in Peyton, 1997) includes advice on publishing student work, suggestions on how to work on language skills while reading and writing poetry, and also some background information on familiar, popular poems. For example, the poem "Apple" by Bruce Guernsey can prompt students to brainstorm ideas about apples and what they represent, leading them to write their own "apple" poems (Peyton, 1997).

❖ **Tactics for using poetry in the SLA classroom:**

- Stimulate the poetic imagination through prompts from other media.
- Involve students actively by producing as well as consuming poetry.
- Ask a poet to visit.
- Emphasize that emotion, image, and creative word use are more important than rhyme.
- Publish students' poetry whenever possible as a keepsake.

Good poetry has great benefit for English learners, with so many styles and topics that both student and teacher are bound to find some poems that are useful and memorable. A teacher who shares personal favorites communicates his or her love of English as a language, as well as a deep commitment to understanding what it means to be a human being. Inviting poems, or translations of poems, in students' native languages also communicates the value of bilinguality and models an openness to learning about other languages and cultures. A classroom in which poetry is featured invites learning about language and about life.

Music: Listening, Playing, Singing, Creating

✦ **STRATEGY 7.5:** Celebrate a sense of joy with music and other oral activities

Music has gained increasing prominence both as a way to develop the brain and as a way to help students acquire a second language. Cognitive psychologists have connected music to the development of the brain in general and the imagination in particular (see Jourdain, 1998; Storr, 1993), so much so that parents of newborns now routinely rush out to buy a Mozart CD along with disposable diapers.

Suggestopedia used music as a vital element, especially classical and early Romantic music of an emotional nature. The music accompanying Suggestopedic teaching is precise, with a clearly recognizable melody in the violin or string section and a steady bass accompaniment to the specific rhythm of sixty beats per minute (Rose, 1985). According to the tenets of accelerated learning, a set of educational methods based on Lozanov and neuro-linguistic programming (NLP), a musical piece that is specifically constructed to be harmonious has a harmonious effect on the mind and body. Music has become an accepted part of English-language development, and it is valued for its ability to engage students' interest, teach language forms and functions, and transmit target-language cultural content.

Popular Music

Songs drawn from traditional sources, films, and popular music are commonly used in EFL settings, as are songs created by ESL publishers exclusively for the classroom. The old Gold Rush song "Clementine" is known all around the world, although it is also rather depressing! ("Oh my darling . . . you are lost and gone forever/dreadful sorry, Clementine") and perhaps crossculturally obscure and grammatically incorrect ("herringboxes without topses/sandals were for Clementine").

Music in films adds a visual component as well as cultural elements. Switzerland is full of Japanese tourists chiefly because so many were taught the song "Edelweiss" in their English classes when they viewed the movie *The Sound of Music*, which the tourists associate with an Alpine setting. "My Favorite Things" and "Do Re Mi," from the same film, are still sung around the world, surely giving the film's star, Julie Andrews, honorary status as a TESOL educator. Technically speaking, however, American films marketed for home use cannot be shown in public contexts such as classrooms without paying royalties to the company and artist. Purchase of a karaoke version of popular songs may be legally acceptable, as these are marketed specifically for public use.

Popular music used educationally for language acquisition requires two main cautions: First the content should be appropriate for the age level and, second, the version used must not violate copyright restrictions. Lori Cleary presents an excellent choice of songs thoughtfully adapted to ESL/EFL teaching (cf. Cleary, 1997).

One example is her lesson plan on the song "My Heart Will Go On" from the film *Titanic*. The lesson begins with a vocabulary-matching game, to ensure that students can recognize words in the song that may be unfamiliar. Following this is a fill-in-the-blanks exercise, in which students supply missing words in the song's lyric from a word list. To check their work, students listen for the first time to the song itself. After listening again to the song, this time to focus on the meaning, students answer questions such as, "What does 'go on' mean in this song? What other meanings does it have? How does she know he 'goes on'?" Students are then asked to describe in their own words, "What kind of love did she have with him?" They then make a list of the adjectives in the song that describe the love it expresses. This lesson illustrates the use of song lyrics that are drawn from popular music and used to teach English. Other lesson plans might include the game of Bingo played with words from the song of the same name, a crossword puzzle created from words from song lyrics, and critical thinking exercises that include social issues addressed by other song lyrics.

Using popular music to teach vowel pronunciation is the goal of the program *Rock Talk* (Redding, 2001). Using pop and rock songs dating back to the 1960s, the program provides intensive practice on target vowels; for example, singing along with the Beatles' "Eight Days a Week" encourages students to practice the phoneme common to "eight" and "days" and contrast it with that of "week." The program comes with a tape of original recordings of the songs and a workbook that uses grammar, idiom, and essay exercises to reinforce language learning.

Music as a Cultural Tool.   Sharing cultural history with students through song is a way for many teachers to present their personal favorite songs. The Lennon-McCartney song, "In My Life" provides a lesson plan that encourages personal reflection. Before playing the song, the teacher may wish to introduce the context of the song, including a brief review of the Beatles era. Playing the song through once without a specific listening assignment communicates the idea that music is, after all, entertainment that is meant for personal enjoyment. During the second playing, students are asked to jot down phrases they hear and, after listening, to compare their phrases with those of a partner. Next, students read the lyric, and pick out key phrases that inspire them to think about their own lives. Using these key phrases, students write down two sentences about something in their life that has been unforgettable. This song can become part of a journal or songbook that they create throughout their course of study, in which lyrics are paired with introspective or personal writing.

Music and thematic units go together. Jane Nakagawa (2002) created an intermediate-level English course with a discussion emphasis in which the discussion prompts were all rock and pop songs (mainly from the 1990s) that discuss global issues. She arranged the lyrics by topic, sorting them into themes such as environment, war, youth culture, race, violence, beauty and fashion, growing old, modern romance, family, materialism, AIDs, anorexia, homophobia, domestic violence, gender issues, classism, and exploitation of peoples. These songs address social problems and social justice issues, obviously for use with high school or college students.

> Songs that promote justice are an integral part of Bob Peterson's teaching. Classroom discussions, "free writes," and a large spiral notebook entitled "Questions We Have" keep alive the idea that one's environment is not a given, but a process of creation, and that students themselves are active creators and shapers of that environment. Occasionally the "Questions We Have" are used as "triggers"—what Freire calls "codes" (see Chapter 2)—for classroom research projects.
>
> Peterson (1994) offered some of the students' questions: "Who tells television what to put on? How many presidents owned slaves? If we are free, why do we have to come to school?" Peterson provided a list of songs that he has used in his classroom, among them Holly Near's "I Cried," Stevie Wonder's "Happy Birthday, Martin Luther King," Woody Guthrie's "Deportee," Phil Ochs's "There but for Fortune," and The Neville Brothers' "Sister Rosa."

Culturally Authentic Music

Commercial ESL publishers often feature music that has been reinterpreted by studio musicians, and thus copyright issues have been covered. Typical songs include a range of selections from American musical heritage, including children's songs, spirituals, traditional folk songs, and pop music. The advantage of using commercially designed sources is that songs are often accompanied by practice exercises, tips on grammatical structures, and vocabulary explanations. Another source for commercially repackaged songs is the *Kids Songs* collection (see Cassidy, 1992), which contains audiocassette and CD versions of songs that are beautifully arranged and recorded, accompanied with a book containing sheet music. The downside of commercially repackaged music is that popular songs are not sung by the original artists (see Grenough, 1998).

Other commercial sources are *Walt Disney's Children's Favorites* recordings (e.g., volume 2, 1990) which include a singalong book. The Walt Disney Company has been known to aggressively protect materials that were designed for the home market from unauthorized educational use, however, and it is not clear if these materials are licensed for school use.

The loss of authenticity is cultural loss. Not using the original recording of a famous song means more than loss of a celebrity's voice. A case in point is the use of the Addison-Wesley version of "This Land Is Your Land." The Addison-Wesley version is upbeat, well arranged, and inviting. However, to hear the original voice of Woody Guthrie, and through that voice and that man's history to understand the Great Depression and the hope that the song conveyed in the darkest of eras, is to vote for the authentic over the ersatz. Moreover, the book *This Land Is Your Land* (Guthrie, 1998) contains several original verses to the song, which seldom appear in commercial versions, that raise some deeper questions about democracy and equity in America. The authentic version and voice undoubtedly convey a truer picture of American culture.

Teaching favorite songs is easier with a book of lyrics. A teacher with a guitar or piano will benefit from *Rise Up Singing*, a book containing 1,200 songs (with lyrics and source citations) drawn from the rich musical heritage of the United States. Many songs can be taught to classes even without musical accompaniment, if the teacher remembers the tune. The book has a title index as well as theme and culture indices. Broadway lyrics, old ballads, blues tunes, labor union songs—both famous and obscure—are featured, though not pop and rock songs of the last twenty years (Blood, 1992).

Jazz Chants

Teaching intonation is fun using *Jazz Chants,* and subsequent jazz chant books by Carol Graham (1978a, 1978b, 1986, 1988, 1992) offer entertaining verbal interchanges set to catchy rhythms. These can give students the opportunity to work with longer texts, songs, and plays.

Students can create their own chants to promote understanding of character and plot in a poem or story. Using a three-part chart (character, action, and sound), students list what characters do or say. The teacher then introduces the pattern of a chant, and students in groups write verses using the pattern (Hetherton, 1998). This works well with *Alice's Adventures in Wonderland* or other tales with a multitude of fanciful characters.

Singing Games

Ring games, or singing games, are social events; they stem from the Middle Ages, where they were originally used for courtship (Opie & Opie, 1985). These can be used in the language classroom in much the same way as jazz chants, but they incorporate movement and gesture. They also, as a part of the rhythmic events, encourage individuals to have speaking parts. Bell (1999) described the ring game as a kind of movement-enhanced choral speaking. A simple ring game is a five-beat chant, "When's your birthday?" with the accents on *when's, birth,* and *day.* Students form a ring, lining up in chronological order of their birthdays in the year. They then begin the chant, moving left three steps on each of *when's, birth,* and *day.* Then they snap their fingers twice: This is the time when first person in order says, "January 15" (fast, the month and day get only one beat each). Then the circle steps to the right, as all chant "When's your birthday?" This and other simple games, based on a chant with repetition and movement, break the ice and get students interacting physically as well as mentally with one another.

The best source for those interested in using music for TESOL education is Murphey's *Music & Song* (1992). Using song clips, video clips, song lyrics, discussions of the pop music industry, music with young children, even music alone, Murphey provides a complete "how to." Every activity includes a recommended language ability level and includes the approximate time to accomplish the activity. With this guide, even a tone-deaf educator has little excuse not to have the students "sing along."

> ❖ **Tactics for using music in the SLA classroom:**
>
> - Select music that illuminates some facet of the target culture.
> - Involve students actively by singing along, clapping, or playing rhythm instruments.
> - Ask a musician, such as a colleague who plays guitar, to entertain.
> - Ask students to bring in music from their native culture and see if they can provide a translation.

The Virtues of the Imaginary

Exercising the imagination directly through mental play or guided fantasy; using listening skills, visual arts, stories, or drama to stimulate language use; or practicing English through music or poetry emphasizes three facets:

- The imaginary serves the whole person; it develops new ways of thinking, new depths or understanding of emotion; and new avenues of expressing the complexity and wonder of the human experience.
- The imaginary develops language; although it is not primarily or even primordially a linguistic domain, it is a rich source of input to stimulate linguistic output, as well as providing powerful means and motivation, such as creative drama and poetry, to express language in new and creative ways.
- The imaginary is an "equal opportunity employer." It levels the playing field of language. Using imaginative functions of language, the teacher can encourage nonnative speakers to feel a sense of "pride of ownership" of English. Whatever refreshing form of language comes forth, the wise teacher rewards innovation and creativity in language use.

As a language, English is profoundly democratic. It is as a language that has accepted thousands of new words from cultures all over the world. The millions of speakers of English who are not native speakers nonetheless have equal rights to use English to their benefit and enjoyment. Although to the experienced linguist the spoken language conveys precise information about social origin, class, status, and education, the imaginary knows no such boundaries of class and culture. All users of English have an equal right to use English as their own personal door to a world in which love, joy, and freedom await, along with adventure and excitement, even loss and pain.

When a nonnative speaker writes, "The eagle overhead shrinks sorrowfully," does it matter that it might have been meant as, "shrieks sorrowfully?" In the imaginary, an eagle may well shrink in sorrow. The nonnative speaker, even in error, can juxtapose language in novel ways like the poet. Thus the teacher of English learners, if open to creative language use, finds delight in unusual turns of phrase. The process of language acquisition, when it takes creative turns and twists, opens language doors that the native speaker may not even know exist.

And in the imaginary, the children shall be teachers to us all. In fact, one linguist postulates that humans may owe the development of language to children:

> How, then did [language] begin? I suggest that it began with the children, and it probably began when the earliest settlements . . . reached a sufficient density of population so that there were plenty of young children in close contact with one another, a critical mass of children, playing together all day long. . . . When it first happened, it must have come as an overwhelming surprise to the adults. I can imagine the scene, the tribe gathered together in a communal compound of some sort. . . . The children have been noisier than ever on recent weeks, especially the three and four-year-olds. Now they begin a clamor never heard before, a tumult of sounds, words tumbling over words, the newest and wildest of all the human sounds ever made, rising in volume and intensity, exultant, and all of it totally incomprehensible to the adults. . . . In that moment, human culture was away and running. (Thomas, 1994, pp. 43–44)

In this vein, the person who acquires language with a sense of childlike wonder has an openness and curiosity that makes every day come alive with new learning. SLA, when done well, furthers the use and understanding of the first language as well. Time spent developing the imagination, in conjunction with time spent learning to communicate and learning how to learn, creates an agenda for English learning that uses powerful strategies to better the world.

Grammar through Integrated Language Skills and Wonderful English

Many learners of English have what Gardner and Lambert (1972) termed *instrumental motivation*: the desire to acquire a language for a specific purpose such as reading technical material or getting a job. Because in many countries a good command of English is a key to entrance into prestigious universities and attractive career prospects, students dutifully memorize vocabulary words and grammar structures. What may be missing, however, is a genuine appreciation for English as a language.

❖ **MEGASTRATEGY 8:** Teach language in a way that arouses a genuine interest in the history and beauty of English

The tongue spoken by Winston Churchill, Eliza Doolittle, Louis Armstrong, and Huckleberry Finn, to mention but a few of the characters—real and fictional—whose words have held the world's attention, is replete with history, spellbinding in its poetics, and rich in nuance and connotation. Many people, however, have learned English in the form of decontextualized sentences, puzzling over structure as one would solve equations. It could be that more English learners resent its complexity than love its gifts. How regrettable that one can devote so much time to mastering a language without acquiring a curiosity about word roots, a delight in witty puns, or appreciation of the turn of an elegant phrase!

English is the language of a fiercely independent people who struggled for millennia to attain personal freedoms. Freedom of speech is the first right that the American colonists demanded in exchange for approval of the Constitution. Freedom of speech is a far deeper right than a person's freedom to complain to a neighbor about high taxes. Freedom of speech includes the fundamental right of a learner to personal and social expression in reading, writing, speaking, and listening, and to study one's own personal and community culture as well as a larger target culture.

English as a language is not restricted by a national academy that decides what language is proper. In fact, language innovators—advertising copywriters and rap musicians, for example—continually exert pressure on English to change. The fundamental democracy of English is that all users have the right to torque the tongue to their needs and to their advantage. A learner should emerge from an English class with

239

more diverse and creative language than on entry. This best way to do this is to integrate the study of grammar—the structure of language—with other receptive, expressive, and processing skills.

Grammar should not be the prisonhouse of language, the subject of judgments about right versus wrong, correct versus incorrect, and acceptable versus nonacceptable. Instead of being taught as a mental puzzle to be solved or as a series of rules to be memorized, grammar should be subordinated to larger, nobler purposes: the empowerment of the learner as a full-fledged member of the English community, and the enhancing of the learner's freedom of expression and joy in learning English. Rules should serve not as shutters drawn against the storm of cacophony and chaos but as lenses to focus the rays of dawn at the birth of new words, postcolonial dialects, imaginative worlds of literary fancy, and calls to liberation and justice.

The sacred duty of a speaker of English is to treasure and respect the rights of others to honor English as only each individual can, by embedding in its words and phrases the depth and breadth of the struggle to be fully human. Teachers of English who remember and respect the role of English in the struggle for human rights will not use its current instrumental usefulness in the world as a tool to bind the learner to purposes that are ignoble, mean spirited, narrow, negative, or simply boring.

This chapter explores some ways in which proficiency in the structure of English can be combined creatively with other skills in the service of a deeper knowledge of the beauty, strengths, and challenges of English as a language. In this way each learner of English can gain equal access to the rights and privileges of English as a world language.

Why Integrated Skills?

Integrated skills is an approach in which teachers and students engage in long-range units of study so that language is used for many meaningful purposes. Speaking, listening, reading, and writing are not separate subjects, taught as though they were an end in themselves. Instead, they are tools to be used in the service of something greater: exploration of the world and its complexity.

◆ STRATEGY 8.1: Treat language as whole and integrate skills

Teachers who involve the learner in thematic units, problem solving, or service learning show by these engagements that language is a tool for analysis, examination, and investigation, as well as presentation and celebration. "As students use language to learn, teachers collaborate, respond, facilitate, and support their efforts" (Pappas, Kiefer, & Levstik, 1990, p. 1). As a part of integrated instruction, teachers provide a broad spectrum of activities that stimulate inquiry and advance language skills. Using language is a preeminent tool by which students construct their own wisdom.

In an integrated skills classroom, the skills comprised in language arts are not separated. In the reading class, students might also be writing, speaking, listening, or thinking. Thematic units combine disciplines. Home and school are integrated; there is no sharp break between knowledge that stays at school and knowledge that can be brought home to enrich the home and community. As Dewey (1956) wrote, "From the standpoint of the child, the great waste in school comes from his inability to utilize the experiences he gets outside of school in any complete and free way; while, on the other hand, he is unable to apply in daily life what he is learning in school" (p. 75). An integrated curriculum—for example, growing a garden to study science, math, social studies, and language arts—mirrors the unity of real life.

Integrated Instructional Activities

Before taking a closer look at how one might integrate classroom activities by combining language skills, it is important to reexamine some assumptions about how language is learned. Table 8.1 contrasts common assumptions about language learning held by those who teach through focusing on discrete skills with those held by teachers who emphasize integrated language skills.

Learner Output

Integrated skills furnish informative output. Output from language users gives the teacher three valuable kinds of information: a student's interests, preferred modality, and the nature of his or her interlanguage.

Students' interests are shown by their output. One student may be interested in pond fish, seek out books in English on the subject, and learn the Japanese names for *koi* coloration in the process. Other students may be fascinated by graphic illustration; intricately designed Web pages capture their full attention, and the words are noticed

TABLE 8.1 • Contrasting Common Assumptions about Language Learning

Discrete Skills	Integrated Language
Mastery of oral language is a prerequisite to acquiring written language.	Oral and written language develop simultaneously.
Seeing written language interferes with acquisition of oral language.	Oral and written language can facilitate and support one another.
Skills are best taught in isolation.	Skills are reinforced by other modalities, e.g., reading by writing.
Language must be explicitly taught.	Neither oral nor written language is learned exclusively through direct instruction or specific tutoring. People learn by interacting with adults or others (e.g., older or more knowledgeable peers); by exploring the world on their own and interacting with others; and by observing others.
The teacher's role is to be language expert, language source, or language "cop."	The teacher is co-learner, explorer, and language "delightee."

only if the visual design is appealing. Their own best work may take place using an integration of words with graphics. Some students are born busybodies whose favorite use of language is to manage the behavior of others. The language teacher capitalizes on these interests.

Students' preferred channels of production are signaled by output. One learner may prefer conversation and learn to speak fluently before acquiring other skills; another may need to be in continual motion, perhaps willing to practice pronunciation via headphones while lifting weights. With careful observation, the instructor can match activity to students' preferred information modality.

Interlanguage of the learner is revealed by output, the dynamic construction of what the learner understands about English. "Dynamic" means that the learner's system changes from day to day, even moment to moment. The learner's underlying knowledge, and hence interlanguage, is normally unstable. This instability is productive as long as the interlanguage is dynamic and growing toward improved English.

Productive Use of Errors.   Errors show students' rule making and are a window to the learner's interlanguage competence and learning strategies; they show the ways in which learners are thinking about English. Teachers need to see English from the learner's point of view, paying careful attention to learners' errors to see what hypotheses they are using. Language, like other mental processes, is learned through "best guessing." In most exploratory activities, the mind is satisfied with "almost right," and uses guesswork and approximation when practicing. An atmosphere of acceptance of error helps the learner to take risks. Persistent errors, rather than random mistakes, provide insight into the learner's rule set.

Complexification, not simplification is the key to language growth. As long as input is interesting, a learner can process a great deal of complexity and extract useful rules. Because this is not a conscious process, learners are often not aware of what they may know until they try to produce output. Output encourages a more complex, rather than a simply error-free, language environment. One job of the teacher at the intermediate level of English development is to engender in the learner sophisticated communication needs that require more advanced language. This keeps language acquisition moving forward.

Content: Flexible, Thematic Curriculum

Recognizing the wholeness of knowledge, instruction is organized around broad themes that engage students in meaningful activities and focus on areas of inquiry rather than on specific skills. This view is student-centered rather than teacher-centered and involves student-student interaction as well as teacher-student interaction. Students learn social studies by researching real-world questions that they have posed themselves. The "question-driven" format encourages focus on broader concepts that connect significant ideas and issues (Freeman & Freeman, 1998).

Thematic units provide a natural environment for the practice of language skills as students learn concepts in other areas of the curriculum. Through such means as filmstrips, films, videos, computer simulations, literature, nonfiction texts, and oral discussions, students are able to develop conceptual knowledge. Thematic units can incorporate history, geography, sociology, economics, values, information-seeking skills, group participation, and perhaps dramatic skills.

This move to a thematic approach to instruction has taken place primarily at the elementary level, although middle schools have also been reorganized so that content teachers can collaborate on instruction and can work together with the same groups of students. For examples of thematic integration at middle school, see Berman, Minicucci, McLaughlin, Nelson, and Woodworth, (1995).

One teacher used a mind map to generate ideas for a thematic unit on spiders. The organizer is displayed in Figure 8.1. This illustrates how subjects are interwoven in thematic planning.

❖ **Tactics to integrate language development curricula:**

♦ Observe students to discover what aspects of language fascinate them, and use this fascination as a key to academic content.
♦ Praise or reward students who bring information to class that connects with learning themes.
♦ Find links between input and output so that students talk about what they read, write about what they discuss, and think about what they hear.
♦ Teach students to use graphic organizers to explore content that encourages thinking skills.

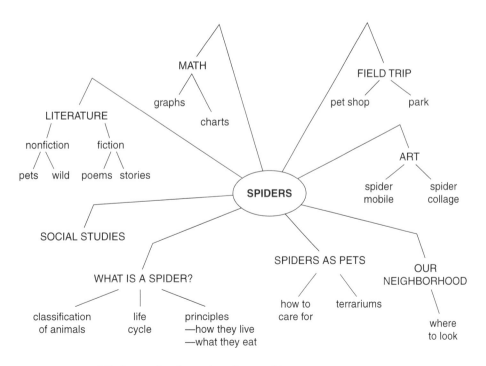

FIGURE 8.1 • Mind map for thematic unit on spiders.

Integrated curricula also open the door to language input from a wide range of sources. English as a language has a history of enrichment from multiple courses. Studying English as a language provides a rich, integrated look at history and linguistic change.

The History of English

♦ **STRATEGY 8.2:** Arouse interest in the history of English

The rise of English is a remarkable success story. When the Romans landed in Britain nearly two thousand years ago, English did not exist. Five hundred years later, English, which would be incomprehensible to modern ears, was still spoken by very few people. Nearly a thousand years later, at the end of the sixteenth century, the time of William Shakespeare, English was the native speech of between five and seven million English subjects.

Four hundred years later, the contrast is extraordinary. Today, English is used by at least 750 million people, barely half of whom speak it as a mother tongue. Of all the world's languages, it is arguably the richest in vocabulary. The Oxford English Dictionary lists about half a million words, with a further 250,000 technical terms that remain uncatalogued. Neighboring German has about 185,000, French fewer than 100,000.

English's teeming vocabulary is 80 percent foreign-born. Precisely because its roots are so varied—Celtic, Germanic, and Romance—it has words in common with virtually every other language in Europe. In addition, it contains extensive borrowings from Hebrew, Arabic, Hindi-Urdu, Malay, Chinese, and the languages of Java, Australia, Polynesia, and West Africa. The enormous range and varied source of this vocabulary, as much as the sheer numbers and geographical spread of its speakers, makes English a language of unique vitality.

Supple in grammar, maddeningly inconsistent in spelling and pronunciation, English has its strengths and weaknesses. English as a world language is sustained by another elusive quality, its own peculiar genius. This genius was, and still is, essentially democratic. It has given expression to the voice of freedom from Wat Tyler to Tom Paine, to Thomas Jefferson, to Edmund Burke, to the Chartists, to Abraham Lincoln, to the suffragettes, to Winston Churchill, to Martin Luther King, Jr. It is well equipped to be a world language, to give voice to the aspirations of the Third World as much as to the intercommunication of the First World.

From Old to Middle English

The story of English goes back to the earliest recorded days of Britain. Throughout its history, the island of Britain seemed to receive cultural innovation primarily through invasion and importation from overseas. Language was no exception. Little trace remains in Britain of the original inhabitants before the Saxon conquest save stone flints, earthworks, stone liths, and names for hills, mountains and streams. Even mighty Rome, which ruled Britain for centuries, left only stone walls, straight roadways, buried coins, and names of camps (place names ending in "chester" or "caster").

The warlike Saxons invaded England when Rome withdrew its protection, settling in the valleys where hay could be raised to feed livestock. They brought with them the language of Frisia, just across the English channel to the east. After the ordered civilization of Rome, with its well-planned cities, villas, markets, academies, arts, and literature, came the "dark ages," in which villages consisted of single-family huts and outbuildings, and social order depended on the swing of the ax.

With the conquest of England by the Saxons, new words came into English. For example, the Germanic prefix *wer-* meaning "turn" brought into English a host of words with the prefix *wer-* or *wr-* whose meaning involved turning. Some new words may have been necessary when people started to wear clothes made from finer rather than crude materials: Finer clothes, in contrast to leather, could be washed and dried by wringing (turning), but this caused wrinkles. To illustrate the response of English to this influence, Table 8.2 lists words that stem from the German prefix *wer-* (English *wr-*).

After the Saxons came the Vikings, who were at least partially sophisticated as a result of international trade with lands that knew of baths and silks. By the time the Danish Vikings were able to conquer Saxon England, the land was rich with Christian monasteries containing gold, silver, jewels, and stores of food and wine. In 871 at the Battle of Ashdown, Vikings met Saxons; each took the other's measure and found that neither could prevail, so they coexisted. English became part Norse. At the turn of the first millennium, Saxon and Dane bloodlines and dialects lived uneasily together in Britain.

The ancient Saxon names for days of the week (from Old Frisen *wike*) subsequently disappeared. Tiew's Day, the day for the god of war, became Tuesday; Woden's Day, the day for the god of wisdom, became Wednesday; and Thor's Day, the day of the thunder god, became Thursday. Daily life mixed Saxon emotion (*weep* from Old Frisen *wépa*, to cry aloud; *laugh* from Old Frisen *hlacka*) with Vikings' food lore (*cook* from Danish *kok*, *ale* from Norse *öl*), Vikings' love of plunder (*weapon*

TABLE 8.2 • English Words Beginning with *Wr-*, Connoting Turning

Word	Definition
wrap	to coil or twine about something
wreath	vines or branches twisted into a circle
wrench	to move with a violent twist
wrest	to twist something out of someone's hands
wrestle	to struggle, to twist the opponent to the ground
wriggle	to squirm, to make short writhing motions
wright	a worker who turns or forms wood on a lathe
wring	to extract water by turning cloth
wrinkle	a small furrow caused by twisting a fabric
wrist	bones that turn in the arm
writhe	to twist, as in distort
wroth	twisted up with anger
wry	to have a twisted shape or condition

has a cognate in Old Norse *vápna*), and Vikings' taste for personal comfort (rug from Norse *rugga*; silk from Danish *silke*).

Meanwhile, across the English channel, Vikings who settled in Normandy viewed England as rightfully theirs. The Norman duke William the Conqueror invaded England in 1066 and subdued the whole island little by little, bringing with him continental culture. William was a masterful administrator who ruled by organization without changing the daily life of the inhabitants. At first the Normans and the English did not mix, and the only Norman words used in English were words that a ruling class can force upon a lower: *prince, duke, noble, servant, messenger,* and so forth. But before long, the English learned French, and Saxon notables sent their sons to France for education (Churchill, 1956). Gradually the two peoples intermarried, and a language developed that blended the Latin-based French with English to form Middle English.

Middle English

The new language blending Anglo-Saxon and Norman French reflected a more sophisticated continental lifestyle and more abstract ways of thinking. Words from Latinate languages were used in conjunction with a noble lifestyle. Here are two descriptions of how English changed:

> The resident Saxon had already labeled their animals as oxen, sheep, calves, deer, and so on. But, with the arrival of the Normans, the words for the *meat* of these animals was [sic] borrowed from the more gastronomically conscious French. Thus, today, we don't eat *sheep,* we eat *mutton* (from the French word for "sheep"); similarly, we eat *beef* from *oxen,* and *veal* from *calves,* and *venison* from *deer.* (Axtell, 1995, p. 16)
> . . . a typical family lives in a Saxon *house* or *home,* or in a French *residence* or domicile. They eat a Saxon *breakfast* and a French *dinner* or *supper* at a Saxon *board* or a French *table,* seated on Saxon *benches* or *stools* or French *chairs.* Their Saxon *meal* or French *repast* consists of Anglo-Saxon foods like *milk, bread, broth, stew, baked meat, peas, beans, pie,* or of French foods like *cream, rolls, soup, roast, beef, pork, vegetables, fruit,* and *pastry.* They live in a Saxon *town* or *hamlet* or in a French *city* or *village.* Along the streets of the city or town you will see shops of Anglo-Saxon *bakers, builders, millers, shoemakers,* and *weavers,* alongside of French *carpenters, drapers, tailors, painters,* and *masons* . . . we see people wearing Saxon *shoes, hats, shirts, hose, gloves, coats,* and French *boots, robes, dresses, blouses, gowns, bonnets,* and *capes.* (Lambert, 1955, pp. 72–73)

The Dual Nature of English

As a result of the Norman invasion, English is a double language. For every Saxon-based word there is a conceptual double from the Latin side of the language. One may have a *heart trouble,* but also a *coronary occlusion.* One may *try hard,* or *persist;* one may *request,* or *ask.* At a *party, buffet,* or *banquet,* one may *mix* or *socialize.* One may take a *snapshot* or a *photograph.* One may buy an *icebox* or a *refrigerator.* One may be *thrilled* or *delighted, joyous* or *merry, saintly* or *holy, fearful* or *intimidated,* and *desire* or *wish.* Choosing carefully among these synonyms can help to achieve just the right shade of meaning or nuance. As Lambert put it, "*sincere amity* is a little different from *hearty friendship,* and to be *welcomed heartily* is a little different from being *received cordially,* although in each case the basic meaning is the same" (Lambert, 1955, p. 74).

The Latin side of the language is often used by bureaucrats who seek to use intellectual-sounding words to *hide* (*obfuscate*) simple truths: thus simple *slaughter* becomes *collateral damage,* and *war* becomes a *police action.* Being "let go" from a job can involve a series of euphemisms. Whether a worker hears *release of resources, involuntary separation from payroll, career-change opportunity, involuntary severance, career-transition program, reduction in force, elimination of employment security, repositioning, schedule adjustment,* or *focused reduction,* it means the same: "You're fired!"

The English-language poet is not seduced by words derived from Romance languages. Anglo-Saxon English has the emotional power that "governmentality" lacks. Witness this stanza from the poem "Winding Down":

Too hot! "Turn heater down." Too cold! We bicker . . .
Lukewarm our love; stale, now flown the flicker
That sparked that lust, so long awry.
Where once love flowed the stream's gone dry. (Wallace, 1999)

In this poem, could *bicker* be replaced by the more modern term *argue*? The Old English word *bicker* has the emotional power that the word *argue* lacks; it connotes a battle, especially a domestic quarrel, whereas *argue* can be used in a court of law, dealing with more abstract issues. Similarly, *sparked* is more powerful than its synonym, *initiated*; *awry* is more wrong, bitter, or twisted than its counterpart from French, *astray*. In these instances, the poet has chosen words that are older, more basic, primitive, with more concrete imagery. In the process the poet gains two more aspects of English that are poetic and pleasant: assonance and alliteration. These will be discussed in the next section.

Using the Dual Nature of English for Effect. This best writers in English have drawn conceptual elegance from the Latin side of English and emotional power and directness from Anglo-Saxon words. Shakespeare, for example, could tap from either the Anglo-Saxon, Anglo-Norman, or classical tradition. After Macbeth has murdered King Duncan, he laments what he has done:

Will all great Neptune's ocean wash this blood
Clean from my hand? No; this my hand will rather
The multitudinous seas incarnadine,
Making the green one red.

The allusion to Neptune flatters the listener who knows that Neptune is the Roman god of the sea; *multitudinous* is a long version of the word *many,* and in case the playgoers in the cheap seats miss the meaning of the graceful *incarnadine,* he translates the phrase into plainer terms: "Making the green one red."

The great writers of English have long taken advantage of the dual nature of English to draw upon both sides of the language when they needed emotional power in combination with the force of intellectual abstraction. In 1775, Patrick Henry delivered a famous speech in Virginia to arouse support for the revolution that was brewing in New England. His speech reached into the hearts of his listeners by using ancient words from Anglo-Saxon English. Of the eighty-six words in this speech, try to figure out how many come from Old (pre-A.D. 1066) English.

> Gentlemen may cry, "Peace, peace!"
> but there is no peace.
> The war is actually begun.
> The next gale that sweeps down from the north
> will bring to our ears
> the clash of resounding arms.
> Our brethren are already in the fields!
> Why stand we, here, idle?
> What is it that gentlemen wish?
> What would they have?
> Is life so dear, or peace so sweet, as to be
> purchased at the price of chains and slavery?
> Forbid it, Almighty God!
> I know not what course others may take,
> but as for me,
> give me liberty—or give me death!

Whether or not Henry was conscious of this effect, only six words have Latin origin. Four of these are strung together in the powerful phrase, "purchased at the price of chains and slavery"; ironically he uses words that harken back to a time when England was conquered by the Normans to remind the listener in Latinate terms of the threat of punishment if the British are successful. The last of the six, *liberty,* that most abstract of terms, is used as the pivot point of his last, immortal phrase, linked emotionally with the final term, *death.* This is a fine example of a great speaker drawing power from both sides of the language.

Abraham Lincoln was one of the greatest writers in the history of English, writing more total words than Shakespeare. His Gettysburg Address uses both facets of English for the sake of power: " . . . we cannot *dedicate,* we cannot *consecrate,* we cannot *hallow* this ground." Only a master would follow the Latinate "dedicate, consecrate" with the ancient synonym "hallow," with its connotation of both holiness and spookiness.

Winston Churchill's powerful language in his famous challenge to the Nazis during the Battle of Britain stems from the direct and concrete words of Anglo-Saxon English:

> We shall fight on the beaches; we shall fight on the landing grounds, we shall fight in the fields and in the streets, we shall fight in the hills; we shall never surrender.

In his expression of stubborn determination, Churchill used words that could have been used in A.D. 1066 to repel the previous invader. Only the last word, *surrender,* comes from continental French.

Dangers of Doublespeak.   The ability to express abstract ideas using the Norman French side of the English language has its drawbacks. It can result in Doublespeak, a term coined by George Orwell in his novel *1984* to indicate language that is vague or deliberately misleading. As Lutz remarks, "[we are in] an age of political correctness and hypersensitivity, not to mention rampant corporate and government linguistic fraud and deception" (1999, p. xiv). Witness the jargon in technical and governmental publications: *supplemental inflatable restraint system* (air bag), *transit coach operator* (bus driver), *instrumental anthropomorphic device* (crash dummy), and *public waste reception center* (garbage dump). Doublespeak seems to proliferate during wars, as the military dislike to speak of actually causing physical harm: *limited duration protective reaction strike* (bombing), *collateral damage* (civilian deaths), *ballistically induced aperture in the subcutaneous environment* (bullet wound), and *prematurely terminated flight* (crash). According to the military, wars do not harm people—only "personnel"! (Lutz, 1999)

Periodic complaints are made against the language of bureaucracy, especially in education. Teachers ("classroom managers") rarely test; they "implement an evaluation program"; this happens not in schools, but in "primary or secondary educational institutions." Few parents should complain, though: Teaching itself has been upgraded. Their children are been effectively processed in a "dual-communication mode of highly interactive student-oriented teacher methodology"! (Lutz, 1999, p. 109).

Fortunately, despite the Norman attempt to civilize the uncouth population, throughout the centuries English has lost little of its raw, earthy spirit. Although politically correct speech has replaced unbridled insult on the highways and byways of life, one can still draw upon Elizabethan English for a hearty insult if need be. In a fit of rage, one could call a transgressor one or more of the following: bawdy, beef-witted, beslubbering, boil-brained, dizzy-eyed, dog-hearted, elf-skinned, fen-sucked, flap-mouthed, fly-bitten, fool-born, logger-headed, hedge-born, knotty-pated, milk-livered, quailing, pox-marked, swag-bellied, toad-spotted, or whey-faced. What a pity these terms are obsolete!

English: Innovative and Unregulated

The English used in Shakepeare's day was as open to innovation as it is today. In Shakespeare's time people expected the playwrights to titillate them with new words, much as today's English users expect the same from advertisers. Shakespeare loved to experiment verbally. These words used by Shakespeare were all new to English in the sixteenth century: *allurements, armada, antipathy, critical, demonstrate, dire, emphasis, emulate, horrid, initiate, meditate, modest, prodigious,* and *vast.*

Disorderly Spelling.   In the centuries that followed, however, fiercely independent English writers considered it within their rights to spell words as they pleased. Only in the nineteenth century did people began to attend to spelling rules, but by then it was too late; English spelling had escaped logic almost entirely. The following two sentences show the various spellings of the long "e" sound (/i/ phoneme): *Did he believe that Caesar could see the people seize the seas?* and *The silly amoeba stole the key to the machine!* Other vowels are just as disorderly; there are ten ways of spelling the long "i" sound (*bite, sight, by, dye, aisle, choir, liar, island, sign, height*) and six ways of spelling the /u/ phoneme (*boot, lute, who, sewer, through , two, Louis*).

It is not just the vowels that are unruly in English; consonants have their own lunacy. Witness the thirteen spellings of the /sh/ phoneme in English: *shoe, sugar, issue, mansion, mission, nation, suspicion, ocean, conscious, chaperon, schist, fuchsia,* and *pshaw;* the four ways of spelling the /f/ phoneme (*fat, philosophy, cough,* and *coffee*), six ways of spelling the /z/ phoneme (*zip, jazz, pads, Xerox, design,* and *scissors*); and five ways of spelling the /zh/ phoneme (*measure, vision, azure, casual, rouge*). It seems that English spelling is already too far gone to return to a simple sound-symbol correspondence. English learners have to face the fact that *come* and *dome* do not rhyme, nor *how* and *low,* nor *war and far.* Then there is the phonetic absurdity of *heart, beard,* and *heard.* Kant we do beter?

Semantic Oddities.   Another confusing feature of English is the fact that the same word can be used to denote exactly opposite meanings. The word *constrain:* (to force, or compel to do something) can also mean to force someone *not* to do something (to check, limit, or stop from doing) (origin: Latin *con* (together) + *stringere* (to draw tight). The word *fast* can mean firmly fixed or immovable (stuck fast) or it can mean the opposite: rapid (to run fast) (origin: Old Gothic *faest,* strong, vigorous). The verb *trim* can mean to take off, to cut off irregularities (trim hedges); or it can mean to *add on,* as in decorate (trim a Christmas tree) (origin: Old English *trymman,* to make ready). The wealth of synonyms and ambiguity of meaning lend themselves to creative word play and riddles: Using synonyms, can you get from *good* to *bad* in five steps? (good = fine [very good]; fine = delicate [elegant]; delicate [precarious health] = ill [poor health]; ill [ill wind] = bad).

Lexical Innovation.   After 1066, England did not wait for waves of foreign language to wash ashore but went looking for it far and wide through international trade and, later, imperialism. For example, from what country are these English words taken? *Cummerbund, bandanna, bungalow, calico, jungle, chintz, verandah, juggernaut, pundit, coolie, curry,* and *guru.* These terms originated from the British Raj in India but have long since abandoned their tropical flavor.

Nowadays, few can keep up with the lexical demands of a language in which the cyberworld coins sixteen new words in a single edition of the magazine *Wired* (see Table 8.3). The pace of technology is, if anything, accelerating. Table 8.3 is dated 2000; an issue of *Wired* dated January 2003 contains at least twenty-four words and phrases not found in even the most recent dictionaries: *franken-chemicals, telezapper, killer app, baddies, granola lefties, newater, portal shield, post-traumatic job switcher, transponder, assistive bots, ibreakthrough, open source celeb, manga figure, loungecore, synthascapes, musicking, dot-commers, fraudsters, hack-prone, gigaplane, Bioes, blog backlash, cyberwar, infowar.*

Lest one think that the United States, because of its daily embrace of the new, is the sole source of language innovation, the British are capable of coining new words with flair. Try the quiz in Table 8.4, which lists new words and slang usages from a single edition of the *Financial Times.*

TABLE 8.3 • Words from the Magazine *Wired* (October, 2000)

Notice the way the bubbles catch the light? We did. **Photonic switching** from Agilent® can deliver the wide-open speed of an all-optical network by bending light with bubbles.

e-Recruiter allows Motive Communications® to proactively build a national and global talent community of qualified individuals.

Textosterone[3]: Office suite power for the Linus® desktop.

Dean Kamen, a multimillionaire **inventrepreneur,** is going global with a **robochair** that climbs stairs.

When you reach out for a hand to hold, that hand may well belong to a **thermoplastic animatron.**

Edelivery. DNet®is working with traditional retailers to offer same-day delivery service.

The **.kosher** controversy. Israel has a white-hot, **net-savvy** tech sector. But leaders of the country's ultra-Orthodox Jewish community view computers as a mixed blessing.

Brattitude adjustment. Razorfish® made a name and a mint dealing digital edge to corporate America.

One big problem with today's high-powered pharmaceuticals is that disease-fighting drugs often damage healthy tissue. The solution: a prototype subdermal "**micro-U-boat**" that will deliver drugs with pinpoint accuracy.

Public **listservant.** She's a leading contender in September's democratic race for the U.S. Senate.

Automata have lived among us since **toga days.**

Congratulations, it's a **bot!** Your new cyborg baby may be arriving shortly.

International **jock police** should forget about controlling technology's impact on sports.

"**Coopetition**" is to compete and cooperate with the same companies.

Pioneering **transhumanist** FM-2030, "launched" in Belgium October 1930, placed in liquid nitrogen at the Alcor Life Extension Foundation in Arizona July 2000.

PRC is working to cut tariffs and eliminate installation fees for Internet users—a Net-savvy form of "**telecom-munism.**"

TABLE 8.4 • New Words Appearing in the *Financial Times (U.S. Edition),* August 2, 1999

1. Minerva plans two "*groundscrapers*"	a. intensive focus with large force
2. Beijing aims to tighten grip on Hong Kong's "*redchips*"	b. pun on Bruce Willis' movies: failure to regulate Korean corporations
3. *Dae hard*	c. Chinese mainland–backed large companies
4. *3D blitz* brings new angle on radiation	d. building taking up excessive space on ground
5. Those who want to put the last conference behind them can travel in the *silence carriage*	e. no electronic communication permitted

(Answers: 1. d; 2. c; 3. b; 4. a; 5. e)

The ceaseless innovation of English speakers is partially driven by technology. In 1927, for example, two new words entered English, *airfield* and *co-pilot,* both due to airplanes. Other words entered English in 1930 that can be attributed not to technology but to cultural change in general: the verbs *debut* and *hang around,* as well as the nouns *grandparent, myth, melanoma, gold digger,* and *fair shake* (Merriam-Webster, 2001b). Even further back, in the year 1789, *aristocrat* first appeared in print, as did new words from the world of politics such as *federalism, federal court, district attorney,* and *public land.* But there were plenty of miscellaneous new words that year also: *lapel, ego, immigrant, roommate, washstand,* and *tomcat;* the verbs *remodel* and *arrange;* and the adjectives *philanthropic, sickening, weathered,* and *working class* (Merriam-Webster, 2001a).

Not all the changes to English are welcomed by English speakers. Each time a new edition of the Merriam-Webster dictionary appears in print, critics complain about the slang words that are sanctioned. In 1961, for example, many American cultural innovations and imports from the 1950s appeared in the new edition of Webster's: *breezeway, split-level, fringe benefit, astronaut, beatnik, den mother,* and *zen.* However, critics ignored these newcomers and raised a ruckus about *ain't* (Pei, 1962).

Five Languages in One.   Slang has been a big influence on new words in English, but it is not the only influence. In fact, one might accustom oneself to the fact that English is really five languages in one: the Anglo-Saxon tongue (Old English), words from Norman-influenced English, (after 1066), English that is borrowed from other languages, slang, and scientific-technical English. Table 8.5 gives examples of these.

How much time is wasted in the early stages of English language acquisition holding students to norms of accuracy in spelling and syntax, when the same time could be spent teaching them to love the sound of words, to create elegant phrases, and to forge fresh and original sentences!

❖ Tactics to teach students about the history of English:

♦ Post favorite quotes from famous poets, politicians, or leaders—and share with students why the language is extraordinary.
♦ Challenge students to learn words in families that share the same Latin root (engender, generous, gentile, heterogeneous).
♦ Display English words from foreign languages and what they mean.

The Curiosity and Beauty of English

ESL and EFL instruction alike have invested heavily in promoting the academic success of English learners. Yet the push for grade-level competency may underuse the beauty and expressive qualities of the English language. As a result, students may not be exposed to the love of English. Teachers may fail to stimulate interest in learning more about English, and exploring it to the limits of its immense and unique nature.

♦ **STRATEGY 8.3:** Arouse interest in English as a language

TABLE 8.5 ◆ Examples from the Five Languages of English

Anglo-Saxon (Old English)	Norman-Influenced English	English Borrowed from Other Languages	Slang	Scientific-Technical Vocabulary
hut	castle	hogan	pad space	cyberspace
like	relish		dig	:-)
seek	solicit		go for it	gopher
meet	encounter	powwow	hook up with	interfacewith
meeting	rendezvous	caucus	face time	synchronous interface
trade	interchange	swap		file transfer protocol
tool	machine	robot	tool	computer
get	obtain	swap	score	download
get mad	become furious	go on the warpath	go ballistic	flame
start	initiate		hit it	boot up
shoe	(podiatrist)	galoshes moccasins mukluks	Docs	boot-up (not a cognate)
mead, grog	vintner	tequila vodka alcohol	hootch	[rave drinks]
baby	infant	papoose	"babe"	generations of software
boss	executive	head honcho sahib	"chief"	Central Processing Unit
heaven	Celestial Kingdom	Valhalla happy hunting ground	bliss out	Nirvana Tao satori
gold	money	wampum	"bread"	credits/debits

Assets of English

The English language itself has three key assets. First, unlike other European languages, the gender of every noun is determined by its meaning; gender-matching articles (like French *le* and *la*) are not required. Second, English grammar is simple. Nouns and adjectives have simple endings, without a lot of morphemic declensions and inflections. Nouns can become verbs in a way that is impossible in many other languages (We can *park* our cars near the *park, bus* the children to school and *school* them in English). Third, the vocabulary can be as simple or complex as the learner can tolerate. A subset of English called Special English, often used by the Voice of America, has just 1,500 words, although the *American Heritage Dictionary* contains about 200,000 words of the 750,000 amassed by the *Oxford English Dictionary* (Wallraff, 2000).

Complexities of English

Each of these assets has an associated drawback. Although words are not declined with gendered endings, certain words are definitely associated with gender. One can be a *handsome* woman (although this seems to also indicate that the woman is not young); but to say a man is *beautiful, petite,* or *winsome* somehow undermines his masculinity. Conversely, one cannot call a woman a *hunk* or a *heavyweight* without impugning her femininity. These rules may not be obvious, but to violate them causes trouble.

The syntactic simplicity of English makes it easy to create idioms that conjoin verbs and prepositions. Who can quickly explain the differences between *sign up, sign on, sign over,* and *sign in*? Or distinguish *tune in, tune out,* and *tune up*? Or clarify the difference between *put up with, put down, put one over on,* or *put out*? And the fact that nouns can become verbs (to *milk,* to *shoulder* (to *cold-shoulder*), to *partner,* to *fellowship,* to *carpool*) means that perfectly good verbs may be pushed aside by their noun counterparts, as in the replacement of the humble verb *confer* with *to conference,* the simple verb *eat* with the pseudospecific *to breakfast,* and the unadorned *write* with the fancier *to journal*. Moreover, nouns used as adjectives are pushing out good old adjective forms, especially in headlines ("Peru Rebels Take Province"—the term "Peruvian" has all but disappeared).

And the ease with which new English terms are coined! Who can stay abreast of a language that can quickly combine nouns and verbs to form neologisms such as "hat hair" (mashed hairdo from wearing a hat), "helmet hair" (squashed hairdo from wearing a bicycle or motorcycle helmet), and "headphone hair" (squished hairdo from wearing a Walkman™).

English is curious, too, for the absurdity of some of its compound words. It is hard to explain how one can *drive* on a *parkway* but must *park* in a *driveway;* why there is no *egg* in an *eggplant* and no *ham* in a *hamburger;* or why *overlook* and *oversee* are opposites.

English has become even more complex with the accelerating jargon of the information age. English has even spawned subdialects consisting entirely of punctuation marks used in computer-mediated communication (emoticons, such as :-) [happy], ;-) [wink], :-o [surprised]; :-# [my-lips-are-sealed]). In addition, we now have Instant Messaging lingo such as BRB (be right back), TTYL (talk to you later) (Yost, 2000); INoUR (I know you are), YBS (you'll be sorry), *g* (giggle or grin) (Mander, 2001); pager codes (FONME [36663] for "Phone me"); and number codes used conversationally (24/7, pronounced "twenty-four-seven," meaning "all day and all night"). By June, 2002, 43 percent of cellular phone users between the ages of twelve and seventeen in the United States used text messaging, a written register that features abbreviations and common phrases turned into acronyms. WL C WHT HPNS 2 NGLISH as a result!

Not only are the spelling and rich synonym features and register freedoms of English confusing, but English is rife with other odd peculiarities. English is not the only language to use classifiers, words that must precede particular nouns in the singular or plural. For example, in Chinese one would say, "i-ben shu" (a book) but "i-ge" for many other kinds of things. But English certainly must score high among languages that feature weird classifiers (see Table 8.6).

In some ways English has already spread confusion enough in the world by proliferating systems of measurement that people in the rest of the world are forced to reckon with, however much they might prefer the scientific simplicity of the metric: *dots per inch, picas, points, letter size/legal size, micron, angstrom, inches, feet, tabloid size, yard, furlong, light-years, acres, miles, pint, quart, barrel, shot, fifth, carafe, peck, bushel, sack, carat, dram, ounce, pound per square inch, BTU, horse-power, cycle, Fahrenheit,* and *kilowatt-hour.* These terms are deeply implicated in both common life and technology, like it or not.

Despite its deceptive simplicity of morphemes and its neverending vocabulary innovation, English has retained its ability to host the best of the world's writers in its bosom. Naipaul, who writes in English as an Indian in exile who grew up in Trinidad, won the Nobel prize for literature in 2001. Nabokov, a renowned writer in English, was a native speaker of Russian. Joseph Conrad's native tongue was Polish. Joyce and Yeats were Irish, Dylan Thomas Welsh, and Faulkner American—all of the latter, I am sure, grew up not speaking "the king's English." Yet the world is the richer for the beauty of their language and the depth of their insights.

Beauty in Nuance and Sound

In poetry the beauty of language lies in the sound value of the words, as well as the ability of words to communicate subtle nuances of image, emotion, and meaning. Poetry permits a rarefied language that rises above the ordinary and says in a few compressed, well-chosen words what the orator cannot say in one hundred words, nor the tongue-tied lover say at all. Only in poetry could Shakespeare have a character look at the horizon and say, "But look, the morn in russet mantle clad/Walks o'er the dew of yon high eastward hill" (*Hamlet,* act 1, scene 1). He could have said, "Dawn is here," but this would have been the listener's loss.

Beauty, to the ear of the English speaker, lies in the combination of sound with meaning. Table 8.7 uses quotations from *Hamlet* to illustrate a variety of ways in which poetry can appeal to the English ear.

TABLE 8.6 • **Some Classifiers in English**

a pack of wolves	a piece, slice of cake
a herd of cows	a head of lettuce
a flock of birds	a scoop, dish of ice cream
a flurry of quail	a slice of apple
a gaggle of geese	a handful of cookies
a pride of lions	a piece, cut of meat
a school of fish	a stick, pat of butter
a pod of whales	a spoonful, gob of peanut butter
a cup of coffee	a bevy, group of young girls
a glass of water	a coven of witches
a bunch of grapes	a pack of needles
a slice, loaf of bread	a myriad, constellation of stars

TABLE 8.7 ◆ Some Sound Characteristics of Poetry*

Characteristic	Definition	Example from *Hamlet*
Assonance	Vowel sounds are repeated.	What is a man If his <u>chief</u> good and market of his time Be but to <u>sleep</u> and <u>feed</u>? A <u>beast</u>, no more . . . (act 4, scene 4)
Alliteration	Consonant sounds are repeated.	When <u>sorrows</u> come, they come not <u>single spies</u> But in battalions . . . (act 4, scene 5)
Anastrophe	Usual word order is reversed.	Madness in great ones must not <u>unwatched go</u>. (act 3, scene 1)
Internal rhyme	Rhyming words follow one another quickly.	<u>How now</u>, Ophelia! (act 3, scene 2)
End rhyme	Words rhyme at end of line.	The time is out of joint. O cursèd <u>spite</u>, That ever I was born to set it <u>right</u>. (act 1, scene 5)
Lexicon	Word choice is unusual.	Oh, Hamlet, thou has <u>cleft</u> my heart in <u>twain</u>. (act 3, scene 3)
Meter	Rhythm and flow of the line pleases the ear.	Good níght, sweet Prínce, And flíghts of ángels síng thee tó thy rést. (act 5, scene 2)
Epizeuxis (see Quinn, 1982)	Words repeat immediately.	<u>Tush, tush</u>, 'twill not appear. (act 1, scene 1)

*Underlining added for purposes of illustration

Of course these devices above can be combined to great effect, as in the following examples: internal rhyme combined with alliteration, as in "Till then sit still, my soul" (*Hamlet,* act 1, scene 2); assonance combined with alliteration, as in "Here's yet some liquor left" (*Hamlet,* act 5, scene 2); or meter and lexicon combined with assonance, as in "I could a tale unfold whose lightest word/Would harrow up thy soul" (*Hamlet,* act 1, scene 5). Good poetry is distinguished from the mediocre in that the sound serves the meaning, and serves to make the poem pleasing to the ear as well as the mind. Paradoxically, the better the poetry, the more creative a relationship it breeds to the rules of sounds and syntax, which leads directly to a look at the teaching of grammar.

❖ Tactics to help students learn to love English:

◆ Put up a "Wacky Word Wall" or bulletin board where students can post weird anomalies in English spelling or sounds.
◆ Give a prize for the week's strangest-sounding word.
◆ Collect and display word games or puzzles from the daily newspaper.

Teaching Grammar

According to Krashen and Terrell's (1983) Natural Approach, the need to pay explicit attention to language structure in a classroom is subordinated to the more important emphasis on a rich and stimulating learning environment. Second-language learners absorb and produce correctly formed sentences by listening and speaking, with the focus not on form, but rather on social or academic language functions.

This is not to discourage teachers from working with students to refine sentence structures at later stages of language acquisition. At the middle school level, even native speakers of English need explicit attention to grammar, especially before they start to learn a foreign language in middle or high school; many excellent grammar series are published to meet that need. Most Western European languages are taught to their native speakers using correct sentence structure and parts of speech as one feature of instruction. The explicit teaching of grammar, that is, use of a structured text and workbook, should be part of balanced language arts curriculum. Moreover, almost all EFL instruction is predicated on grammar, which carries through to the curriculum of the intensive English programs for international students on American college campuses.

However, at the elementary level many teachers begin daily instruction with a misnomer called "daily oral language" (DOL). Rather than promoting fluent oral language, as would happen in an alternative activity that Cazden (1988) calls "sharing time" (students take turns telling personal anecdotes), DOL features students taking turns correcting a sentence written incorrectly on the board. Like other forms of "display knowledge" (see Chapter 10), those who already know the usage or punctuation rule that is violated are quick to volunteer, while those who do not simply do not pay attention. Thus DOL does not promote oral language; neither does it teach usage nor grammar. A systematic program of grammar is recommended as a part of a comprehensive upper-elementary ESL program.

The topic of grammar seems to divide English teachers into three camps (Wilson, 2001). One camp, the *overt*, believes that students learn a language by mastering its grammar rules, usually by means of explicit teaching using memorization. The second camp prefers a *covert* approach, using directed inductive learning in a contextualized format. There is attention to grammar, but areas such as syntax might be taught using color-coded patterns, hands-on manipulation of sentence strips, and other ways to get students to internalize rules. The third approach to grammar, which might be called the *no-grammar* approach, expects that the mind will internalize rules by being exposed to language-rich situations. Each of these approaches might be useful in distinct situations. Which approach to use depends on the context.

◆ STRATEGY 8.4: Teach the structure of English explicitly but contextually

Without rules, language would be unpredictable, and speakers would have no common ground of agreement. The rules of a language govern what sounds right, for example, what is an acceptable phoneme in English. Phonemic errors cause speakers to have a foreign accent. Sometimes native speakers find this hilarious—think of Peter Sellers's character in the Pink Panther movies, Inspector Clouseau, who pronounced *bomb* as "bimb." More seriously, though, a foreign accent can serve as grounds for social and economic discrimination. Rules also govern semantics—remember how outraged Alice was in *Alice's Adventures in Wonderland* when Humpty Dumpty insisted that he could make words mean whatever he pleased! Syntax rules connect verb tense, morpheme use, and word order in a sentence.

Generally, people use the term *grammar* in two ways. One common use of the word considers what is proper and what is not; this definition uses grammar to create social class distinctions. The use of the subjunctive in English is often a social class marker. It takes years of schooling and exposure to those who use the subjunctive form correctly to say something like, "If he were related to me, I'd help him." Most commonly one would hear, "If he was related to me . . ." Thus the correct use of the subjunctive becomes a way in which native speakers communicate their level of education and exposure to the niceties of tense.

Grammar as System

At a more basic level, however, grammar is usually associated with whether sentences "work" correctly or not. One student wrote this sentence in a draft of his master's thesis:

> ESL teachers meet more challenges from many directions than before, ESL teaching is no longer just teaching English vocabulary, grammar, or logistic knowledge only, social and psychological effects of American culture is getting more complicated, especially tragic events of terrorism on New York the impacts on ESL teaching, immigrant education are changing at rapidly speed.

Certain facets of this piece of writing defy the rules of English. First, so many disparate ideas are crammed together that they strain the bounds of sentence logic. Certainly, this excerpt demands to be more than one sentence. Second, the central clause lacks subject-verb agreement (effects . . . is getting). Third, the final phrase offends in cardinal ways; the phrase "at rapidly speed" is one that no native speaker would utter, and the morphemic error (using an adverb in a prepositional phrase) clearly betrays the writer as a nonnative speaker. The other errors, such as using a noun in place of a verb ("the impacts on" for "impacts"), article errors ("especially tragic events" instead of "especially the tragic events"), and redundancy (just . . . only) might be of less concern in the overall scheme of things; it is the basic syntax flaws that undermine the understandability of this writing.

Teachers of writing at many levels of schooling can use peer editing to help writers identify grammar errors and receive feedback. Thus grammar is integrated into the oral conversation between editor and writer. Most teachers do not give students feedback on grammar errors in speech, preferring to recast sentences correctly as they respond to the content of students' talk. Thus grammar is integrated into conversation.

Grammar and Emotion

Learning the grammar of a foreign language is not just a cognitive act; it involves feeling. Rinvolucri (1984) relates many examples of the ways in which learners react to grammar emotionally. In one story, a young French speaker really liked the *-ando* (progressive ending in Spanish) because it feels ongoing and, well, progressive. Another speaker found out that many constructions in German begin with *wie* (how) instead of *was* (what) because young German-speaking children are taught that *was* is rude. A Brazilian speaker thought the English use of "I'm sorry" was insincere, routine, and falsely polite. No wonder incorrect use of grammar is so negatively sanctioned; people react to grammar with emotion. Rinvolucri uses this emotion in the service of teaching. He offers students sample sentences and asks them to enter them on the blackboard under two categories: NICE and UGH! Students use their emotions to accept and reject syntactic structures.

Grammar Games

Games for use in the service of grammar are presented in Table 8.8. Using games for this purpose serves several functions. Students have to take responsibility for learning the grammatical structures in order to play the game, and the teacher can use the game to take an informal inventory of students' mastery. The serious work of grammar mastery takes place in the context of fun, and games that last ten to fifteen minutes fully engage the learner during that time (Rinvolucri, 1984). The games in Table 8.8 are for beginning-level students, and none requires much advanced preparation.

Although some might argue that games teach grammar out of context, the social context of having fun might overrule that caveat. For the most part, grammar corrections are subordinated to the meaning that is conveyed. For example, when master's degree students are at the point of incorporating a theoretical framework into their theses, the conversation that ensues is about ideas. The last thing that comes to my mind as their adviser is to correct their grammar. The ideas that are conveyed are far more interesting and important. This same principle governs the integration of grammar into learning.

Correct Usage and Discourse Competence

◆ **STRATEGY 8.5:** Teach respect for correct usage in English

Prescriptive Language and Usage Wars

Should road signs read DRIVE SLOW or DRIVE SLOWLY? Which is grammatically correct? And what about the Apple Computer Company's slogan "Think Different": Is that poor grammar? If *hooks* is the plural of *hook*, what's wrong with *yous* as the plural of *you*? Are "between you and I" and "between you and me" both right, and who decides what's right and wrong in language, anyway? And who put *ain't* in the dictionary? (Finegan, 2001).

Linguistic variation is inevitable and natural. Languages often have alternative expressions for the same thing ("steal" and "appropriate"), and a given word can carry a different meaning as a different part of speech. Languages naturally adapt to their situations of use and also reflect the social identities of their speakers. In some countries, language academies have been established to settle such matters, but English has

TABLE 8.8 ◆ Cognitive, Affective, and Drama Activities That Teach Grammar

Activity	Description
An Article's Article (Definite and indefinite articles)	Students form two teams. A reader reads an article aloud but says "Bleep" instead of the articles. Students mark a score sheet with the missing article: *a, an, the,* or nothing (#). (Source: 1)
Jumping to conclusions (Comparisons with gerunds)	Students receive a survey sheet with the names of all class members. At the top of the page they write a comparison using two gerunds (Example: Swimming is more fun than riding a bicycle). They survey the class, entering answers *Agree* or *Disagree.* (Source: 1)
Conditional chain reaction (Conditional sentences)	Students are seated in a circle. Student A makes a conditional sentence ("If Fred took a trip, he would go to Paris.") The next student uses the final clause to make a new conditional sentence ("If Fred went to Paris, he would climb the Eiffel Tower."). (Source: 1)
Shopping list (Count and noncount nouns)	Half of the student are players seated in a circle and half are reserves standing outside the circle. The first player uses a count noun ("I went to the supermarket and bought a few lemons"). The second player repeats the previous entry and must add a noncount noun (. . . some sugar). Alternate using count and non-count nouns in the sentence. A player who fails to take a turn correctly is replaced by a reserve. (Source: 1)
Give a meaning (Varied structures)	Put on the board the sentence, "I am a hotel." Each student must change the sentence, adding one word only. Put sample answers on the board. (Examples: "I am a hotel manager." " I am running a hotel.") (Source: 2)
Brainstorming structures (Present perfect)	Give students sample prompts: Good Experiences I Have Never Had, and Bad Experiences I Have Never Had. Students brainstorm answers, and a recorder writes them on the board. (Source: 2)
Your words— My grammar (Present perfect continuous)	Write a sentence in the target structure on the board. Students must replace every word but the target with the same part of speech. (Example: Who's *been* eating my porridge?) Students write answers on board, and class votes yes or no for correctness. (Source: 2)
Surprise sack (Descriptive adjectives)	Each student brings a mystery object to class, along with a description of the item. Other students listen to the description and try to guess the object. (Source: 3)
I spy (Review vocabulary)	A student who is "it" says, "I spy something in the classroom. What is it?" Go around the room in order as the other students have to ask, "Is it the wastebasket?" etc. When someone guesses correctly, the next person is "it." (Source: 3)

(continued)

TABLE 8.8 • Continued

Activity	Description
Alphabet dash (Vocabulary recall)	Students are divided into teams. Each student receives a different numbered card. When the teacher calls out a number and a letter, the student has twenty seconds to give as many words as possible that begin with that letter. Team ending with most points wins. (Source: 3)
Buffet (Prefixes and suffixes)	Students receive a list of 40 prefixes (Appetizers), 18 roots (Main Courses), and 35 suffixes (Desserts). Students try to form correct words using two or three of each. (For example, "in-duct-ion") Students check answers with a dictionary; to receive credit, word must be accompanied by its meaning. (Source: 3) Hint: Use a book that features words of Greek and Latin origin such as Horowitz (1977).

Sources: (1) Kealey & Inness, 1997; (2) Rinvolucri, 1984; (3) Steinberg, 1983.

no such regulating body. Instead, those who write dictionaries and grammars and columns in daily newspapers are seen as authorities. It seems that many pundits moonlight as prescriptive grammarians, telling others how to use English correctly.

Descriptive grammarians ask the question, "What is English (or another language) like? What are its forms, and how do they function in various situations?" By contrast, prescriptive grammarians ask, "What should English be like? What forms

In English-as-a-foreign-language classrooms, grammar is often taught through direct instruction.

should people use, and what functions should they serve?" Descriptivists have no problem entering some forms—*ain't*, for example—in the dictionary and describing the context of their use. Descriptivists savor the range of regionalisms and "underground" use of language varieties, even if these language forms may be considered "ungrammatical." Prescriptivists who judge *ain't* to be wrong or inelegant might exclude it altogether or give it an entry with a prohibition.

Who decides whose language is right? Some observers claim that the real issue about prescribing right and wrong language usage is one of deciding who wields power and who does not. Stigmatized forms of language are typically used by social groups other than educated middle-class professional people such as lawyers, doctors, publishers, and so on. Linguists generally argue that the language of nonmiddle-class social groups is no better or worse than that of educated middle-class speakers. The expressions that appear in dictionaries and grammar books are not the only grammatical forms, merely the ones designated for use in circumstances of wider communication. Teachers who are careful to enjoy and honor the English that students produce balance that respect with concern that students know what is acceptable usage and are able to produce it when warranted.

A Schema for Literature, ESL, Grammar, and Usage

A beginning teacher called me one day and asked for help; she had so many language arts books that she needed advice on how to plan the best use of students' reading and language arts time.

> I arrived at her classroom to find her sitting behind a tall stack of fourth-grade curriculum materials. She had a basal literature anthology with supplementary workbook, teacher's manual, and testing booklet; an ESL series comprising a teacher's manual, student reading books, student homework book, and testing materials; a grammar series comprising a teacher's manual and workbook; and a spelling series comprising a teacher's manual and student workbook. In addition, she had a student library with books for independent reading and many reference materials that accompanied the social studies curriculum. If she were to teach from each of these elements, her language arts period would be ten hours long! How could I help her bring order out of teacher-planning chaos? And what was the role of explicit grammar teaching in a curriculum that depended heavily on promoting reading skills?
>
> Her class was composed of students who were nonnative English speakers. Although many of these students had never been taught in their primary language and had been immersed in English since beginning their schooling, the school district had mandated the use of an ESL curriculum, Into English,™ (Hampton Brown) with all students. She did not therefore face the additional challenge of a situation in which some students receive ESL and others do not. Into English™ was designed to accompany and complement the existing grade-level curriculum, facilitating the integration of ESL with various content areas and objectives that she was required to teach.

In response to the need expressed by the fourth-grade teacher above, I designed the following four-part schema to guide the teaching of reading and language arts (see Figure 8.2). Each quadrant is based on a different set of curricular materials. Assignments that combine objectives in more than one domain help to integrate these approaches. In this plan, acquisition vocabulary (learning new words) is separated from production vocabulary, which is associated with correct usage (spelling). Students are not expected to be able to spell the new words they acquire in literature, but simply to understand their meaning in context. The same might be said for concept vocabulary acquired through social studies or science. Moreover, the study of literature is an end in itself, and students should not be required to use it to learn spelling or social studies. Thus the selection of stories that students read is supplemented, not dictated, by thematic integration with other content domains. Lastly, correct usage such as punctuation, capitalization, and paragraph structure is emphasized in the context of composition, but that is by no means the sole goal of writing.

Integrating Grammar into the Curriculum

Awareness of sentence structure can be enhanced with various learning activities. Table 8.9 offers some ways to have students work creatively with sentences.

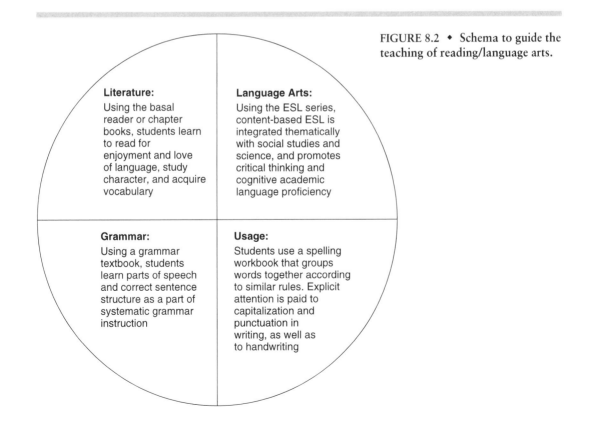

FIGURE 8.2 • Schema to guide the teaching of reading/language arts.

Literature:
Using the basal reader or chapter books, students learn to read for enjoyment and love of language, study character, and acquire vocabulary

Language Arts:
Using the ESL series, content-based ESL is integrated thematically with social studies and science, and promotes critical thinking and cognitive academic language proficiency

Grammar:
Using a grammar textbook, students learn parts of speech and correct sentence structure as a part of systematic grammar instruction

Usage:
Students use a spelling workbook that groups words together according to similar rules. Explicit attention is paid to capitalization and punctuation in writing, as well as to handwriting

TABLE 8.9 • Activities to Develop Awareness of Sentence Structure

Activity	Description
Sentence expanding	Students start with a simple sentence ("The jetliner flies.") and make it into a richer sentence by adding details ("The giant, four-engine Northwest jetliner flies above the skyscrapers.").
Sentence linking	Students chain sentences together by reading a detail-rich sentence and then using a phrase from that sentence to start a new sentence. ("This evening, a storm might drop six inches of snow." New sentence: "Six inches of snow is enough to cause a big traffic jam.")
Sentence shopping	From a passage that has varied sentences, students have a "shopping list" of sentence types to find (shortest; longest; compound subject, etc.).
Sentence slicing	Students cut up a given sentence and "stack" the phrases in a list.
Sentence swapping	One student starts a story about a common subject, such as getting dressed in the morning. After writing one sentence, the student passes the paper to the next person, who writes one sentence to continue the idea.

Source: Suid & Lincoln, 1992.

Explicit teaching of particular features of grammar and usage should, if possible, be drawn from actual (anonymous) student work. If an entire class has difficulty with a similar set of structures, it may be beneficial to use a workbook to make the instruction systematic. For example, almost all English learners have difficulty with the use of articles. This is certain to be the case, for example, with students from Japan or China who attend an intensive English program at a university. Cole's (1997) *The Article Book,* which has exercises that go through the use of articles and offers principles, examples, and quizzes, seems tailored for this population. It is exemplary professional practice to use the right workbook for the right application, rather than "reinventing the wheel."

Grammar Texts.   A grammar book that presents a systematic reference for ESL writers is an indispensable feature of the curriculum. Without such an aid, a teacher cannot be expected to explain grammar points with a suitable degree of accuracy. Byrd and Benson's *Problem-Solution: A Reference for ESL Writers* (1994) is an excellent resource, covering pedagogical grammar points with clear explanations and examples. Moreover, pedagogical grammar for students at every level is a must. An excellent grammar for TESOL educators and a classic in its field is Master's *Systems of English Grammar: An Introduction for Language Teachers* (1996).

A reason to work closely with students to improve their usage skills (handwriting, correct spelling, paragraph coherence, and correct use of punctuation) is that mainstream teachers often base their expectations for students on such salient features of their written production. Therefore, ESL teachers do students a great service by emphasizing—but not overemphasizing—correct usage. As students write—whether for purposes of critical thinking, reaction to literature, or in project-based learning—some part of that writing should become a final product in which correct usage is required.

Usage Games.   Games can be used to practice correct usage. "Ear for Punctuation" is an activity in which students are given a copy of a passage in a book retyped with the punctuation removed. Students in working groups restore the missing periods, commas, and so forth (Suid & Lincoln, 1992). This activity can be made into a game if students are given cards with punctuation marks and various teams compete to see which punctuation mark goes in the missing place. Correct usage can also be a part of various writing tasks. As students write about a trip they are planning to take around the United States, they pay particular attention to the correct use of capital letters. As they bring in a recipe from home for a class meal, they learn how to use the imperative form of the verb (Shoemaker & Polycarpou, 1993). Thus correct usage and grammar can be incorporated into a host of learning activities.

A Balanced Approach to Grammar.   Teaching ESL is one part of the overall reading and language arts and content curriculum and at best is integrated with these subjects. Teachers who achieve a balance between descriptive linguistics (enjoying students' language creativity and variety) and prescriptive linguistics (requiring adherence to rules of language) will promote English learning to high levels of academic achievement while fostering enjoyment of English. The effect that English learners have on English itself is to expand the language, as it has expanded before, to accommodate new speakers with new needs and desires. All living languages change, adapt, and grow. Those same language forms that are considered slang today may be tomorrow's canon. Contemporary English is undergoing exactly the same kinds of changes that have contributed to making it the rich, flexible, and adaptable language so popular throughout the world today. The only languages no longer in flux are those no longer in use. The job of grammarians is to describe language as it exists in real use. The job of TESOL educators is to teach that language to the world.

Culturally Based Language Teaching

Teachers of English learners are first and foremost language teachers. But unlike those who teach English to native speakers, they are also intercultural educators. Those educators who learned English in an English-speaking culture have the advantage of an unconscious understanding of this culture, whereas those who learned English but whose primary socialization took place in a non–English-speaking environment have a different perspective. Just because one is raised in a certain culture, however, does not mean necessarily that one can explain that culture to others. Teachers of English learners benefit from education about the mutual impact of language and culture. *Intercultural educators* are experts who understand culture to the extent that they can teach about culture to others.

Studying one's own culture is a domain of learning like any other, perhaps made more difficult because people, like fish trying to understand water, cannot see the invisible matrix in which they operate on a daily basis. Culture has many components that influence behavior at an unconscious level. Schools and teachers are cultural transmitters. Habits of teaching and learning are cultural products. Language teaching as an educational process is intimately involved with culture and its transmission.

❖ MEGASTRATEGY 9: Use culture to teach language

Before beginning to explore the language-culture connection, it is important to define what is meant by culture. The following definition serves as a reminder that culture is not only about art museums and folkloric dances, but also about people's everyday lives and worldviews:

> Culture is the explicit and implicit patterns for living, the dynamic system of commonly agreed-on symbols and meanings, knowledge, belief, art, morals, law, customs, behaviors, traditions, and/or habits that are shared and make up the total way of life of a people, as negotiated by individuals in the process of constructing a personal identity.

Culture involves not only observable behaviors, but also intangibles such as beliefs and values, rhythms, rules, and roles. Rather than seeing culture as an invisible, patterning force, it is more useful to see it as an active balance between the "social shortcuts" that make consensual society possible and the contributions and construction that each individual creates while fashioning a life that is satisfying.

Commenting on the language-culture connection, Strevens (1987) had this to say:

> . . . in the past decade, language teaching has paid increasingly greater attention to meaning—especially situational meaning, social and varietal meaning—and more recently still to discourse patterns as examples of a more holistic approach to the learning and teaching of languages. . . .
>
> In making these observations, certain fundamental assumptions or presuppositions are made, including, at least, the following:
>
> First, language is but one element of the complex, seamless fabric of the total culture of a society. Of course language is an immensely important element which informs and shapes other elements, yet is in turn shaped by them. It is not possible to say how far language influences the rest of the culture, and how far culture influences language. What is clear is that there are deep and indispensable links between the two.
>
> Second, 'language' . . . embraces much more than vocabulary, grammar, and phonology. It includes also the subtle and only partly comprehended mechanisms for interpersonal communication which are grouped under the general rubric of discourse. These mechanisms are partly linguistic, partly paralinguistic, and partly non-linguistic; they include the individual's rules for social comportment; they are subject to individual variability.
>
> Third, difficulties of understanding in cross-cultural circumstances are other cultural as much as—or more than—linguistic in nature. (pp. 170–171)

Teachers who function as intercultural educators acquire a sense of the difficulties faced by English learners. However, many prospective teachers initially are unaware of their own cultural values and behaviors and how these might be at odds with the home cultures of students. Those who are willing to engage in self-assessment activities are often richly rewarded with a deeper understanding of their professional and personal lives. The goal of such assessment is to enable prospective teachers to sustain intercultural contact, foster culturally responsive pedagogy, and develop the skills of advocacy for, and appreciation of, English learners.

Intercultural educators use a variety of terms in cultural education (see Table 9.1).

The Skills and Responsibilities of the Intercultural Educator

Culture influences the teaching of English to speakers of other languages in six basic ways. Each can become a component of instruction. First, the learner has learned how to learn by means of native culture patterns, values, and behaviors. Teachers who are acquainted with the norms and patterns of the native culture will better understand how students learn, especially how they learn L2. This component relates to *culturally derived learning styles and strategies*.

Second, the intercultural educator accommodates to students' culturally derived learning styles and strategies in order to deliver effective instruction. Because cultural patterns are difficult for the individual to analyze or alter, it seems unlikely that a group of learners can or will change their culturally based habits as they learn English.

TABLE 9.1 • Terminology Involving Culture

Term	Meaning
Intercultural communication	Exchange taking place between two or more speakers who have been socialized into different cultures
Intercultural education	Interchange between teacher and student who have been socialized into different primary cultures
Crosscultural education	The study of how people from different cultures view and practice education (Lustig & Koester, 1999)
Multicultural education	Educational practices that ensure students equal opportunity to learn in school regardless of their gender, socioeconomic status, ethnicity, religion, physical or mental abilities, or other cultural characteristics (Boutte, 1999)
Native culture (NC)	The culture in which the primary language was acquired along with the primary socialization
Target culture (TC)	The culture in which the target language is used (The target culture for English must be specified, because English as a target language varies depending on which culture is the model, for example, Australia, India, New Zealand, Canada, or South Africa, in addition to Britain or the United States; the pronunciation and lexicon vary distinctly depending on this choice.)
Bicultural	Having intimate knowledge of more than one culture
Long-term intercultural empathy	The ability to shift easily between cultural frames of reference (Bennett, 1996a, p. 15)

Teachers of English learners make whatever accommodations may be necessary. This component is called *culturally compatible instruction.*

Third, learning a language becomes easier when the whole personality of the learner is engaged. A certain amount of culture acquisition may accompany second-language acquisition (SLA). The learner who acquires English takes on a set of patterns, habits, and behaviors suitable to a multilingual lifestyle. Learning to add facets to one's identity rather than suffering identity conflict or loss might be called assuming a bicultural identity. The intercultural educator helps students to adapt to shifts in identity and values that may occur.

Fourth, the native culture and the target culture each provide rich content for instruction. Like all languages, English is a vehicle for ideas rather than a set of ideas in itself. However one defines culture—as literature, art, music, or as the daily life of a people—the *ideas* that language conveys give learning English meaning and purpose. Whether these ideas come from the native culture or from the traditions embodied within English, culture is serving as content.

Fifth, building on the idea of culture as content, English teaching can incorporate the comparison of cultures, both in terms of culturally based learning styles and strategies and in terms of ideas or behaviors. This component might be called the issue of crosscultural studies.

The sixth component is using intercultural communication to teach English. As an international language, English is learned by individuals who share no other common language. The use of English in intercultural education is most useful in a situation like the intensive English programs on American college campuses, in which speakers of many languages come together to improve their English skills before matriculating in a regular college course of study. This situation also pertains in adult basic English classes in the United States, in which adults of many nationalities come together to learn. In addition, many bilingual programs are set up so that English-only students can mix with non–English-speaking students during "mainstreaming" classes; all students then benefit from the opportunity to interact and to discuss this interaction as content. Students in various contexts can also communicate interculturally via Internet chat rooms.

This chapter outlines those general areas of culture that teachers will find most useful and then presents techniques for learning about students' cultures. Teachers can use their knowledge of students' cultures to design appropriate classroom organizational procedures and teach in a culturally responsive manner.

Culturally Derived Learning Styles and Strategies

Any learning that takes place is built on previous learning that took place in the context of families. Children learn verbal and nonverbal behaviors appropriate for their gender and age and observe their family members in various occupations and activities. The family teaches them about love and relationships with friends, kin, and community members. They watch as community members cooperate to learn in a variety of methods and modes. Their families give them a feeling for music and art. They learn to use language in the context of their homes and communities, to share feelings and knowledge and beliefs. Indeed, they are native speakers of the home language by the age of five, and as such can express their needs and delights.

◆ STRATEGY 9.1: Learn about how culture affects learning

The culture that students bring from the home is the foundation for their learning. All cultures provide an adequate pattern of living for their members. Therefore, no children are "culturally deprived." Certain communities may exist in relative poverty, that is, without middle-class resources. Poverty, however, should not be equated with cultural deprivation. Every community's culture incorporates vast knowledge about successful living. Teachers can use this cultural knowledge to enhance students' learning in schools.

Culture is not just a collection of artifacts used by a people; neither is it about types of food or celebrations, although people often equate these superficial elements with culture. Culture is not just symbols, souvenirs, or lifestyles. Culture does not mean "race." And although many people use "culture" to represent "high culture" or the high-status events of elite groups, culture is not about the activities of privileged social classes. Some aspect of culture belongs to every person within a society and is embodied by everyday objects and events.

In-depth background on the culture and history of all minority groups in the United States is clearly beyond the scope of this book (see Díaz-Rico & Weed, 2002).

However, all cultures share general features. These features will be discussed here along with ways in which insightful teachers can use this general knowledge in their classrooms. For further reading, Buckley (2000) features a set of common parameters shared by cultures that help to organize the complex terrain of intercultural communication.

Values, Beliefs, and Practices

Values are "what people regard as good or bad, beautiful or ugly, clean or dirty . . . right or wrong, kind or cruel, just or unjust, and appropriate or inappropriate" (Lustig, 1988). Each culture uses a set of values to manage social life. Values cannot be seen, heard, or tasted, but they deeply influence social customs. Teachers concerned about the success of all their students make every effort to understand the different ways in which cultures organize individual and community behavior, ways that on the surface may not seem compatible with school practices and beliefs. To understand these differences is to help students bridge home and school differences.

Social Customs

Social customs dictate norms of daily life. These customs are paced and structured by habitual use of time and space. Conflicts may arise when teachers use *time* in different ways than families do. For example, teachers who demand abrupt endings to activities in which children are deeply engaged or pace instruction very strictly by the clock may confuse and depress students whose family life is not regulated in this manner. Many teachers find themselves in the role of "time mediator," helping students meet their learning needs within the school's schedules.

Use of space is another aspect of cultural experience. Personal space varies; in some cultures individuals touch each other frequently, whereas in others, touch and proximity may cause feelings of tension and embarrassment. In the United States, touching often shows dominance—a higher-status individual may throw an arm around the shoulder of a lower-ranking individual, but the reverse is not acceptable. Middle-class, European American teachers sometimes hug boys and girls from minority cultures more than they touch European American boys, thinking they are conveying warmth. In reality, dominance is another explanation for this behavior.

A cultural sense of space influences the rooms and buildings in which people feel comfortable. Large classrooms may overwhelm students whose family activities are carried out in intimate spaces, but others who are used to open spaces may feel confined when expected to remain indoors all day. The organization of the space in the classroom sends messages to students: how free they are to move about the classroom, and how much of the classroom they "own." Space can be negotiated to provide a classroom setting in which ownership is shared.

Other symbolic systems, such as dress, personal appearance, and facial makeup also convey meaning. In fact, these are prominent class markers in American schools. The "right" clothing and accessories are considered status symbols; conversely, the "wrong" ones mark some students for ridicule. Other symbolic systems are intrinsic, such as beliefs about natural phenomena, luck, and fate. Because European American culture views nature as something to be conquered, natural forces greater than human control cause great anxiety. People's behavior during harsh weather often demonstrates this.

Rites, Rituals, and Ceremonies

Each culture celebrates formal events such as holidays, births, marriages, and deaths with specific rites. Schools have ceremonies; in the United States, assemblies often begin with the Pledge of Allegiance. Rituals in some elementary classrooms in the United States are also relatively formal; students must line up and wait for the teacher. Hmong students from Laos are accustomed to even more formality; when it is time for lunch, students rise and stand by their seats, waiting for permission to leave the room, and when passing the teacher, they clasp their hands in front of their faces in respect (Bliatout, Downing, Lewis, & Yang, 1988). Greeting and welcome behaviors vary across cultures. The sensitive teacher understands how parents expect to be greeted and incorporates some of these behaviors in the exchange.

Work and Leisure Systems

Crosscultural variation is evident in work and leisure activities (Schultz & Theophano, 1987). In mainstream U.S. cultures, work is valued over play, that is, one's status is directly related to one's productivity, salary, or job description. Play often reinforces this status; for example, executives conduct business informally on the golf course. Young people are trained to use specific tools of play, and their time is structured to attain these skills. In contrast, other cultures expect children to engage in adult-type labor. In still other cultures, such as that of the Hopi Nation in Arizona, children's playtime is relatively unstructured, and parents do not interfere with play. The typical work and play activities expected of girls and boys also vary by culture.

In work and play groups, the orientation may be to the *individual* or to the *group*. U.S. society is widely regarded as one in which the individual is paramount. In Japan, by contrast, individuals compete fiercely, but accompanying this value is a sense that one must establish oneself within a group; being singled out for attention or praise by teachers may therefore result in embarrassment (Furey, 1986). In another example, American Indian children who come from group-directed cultures may enjoy competing against one another in teams but not as individuals (Philips, 1972).

Health and Medicine

Health and medical practices involve deep-seated beliefs because the stakes are high: life and death. Each culture has certain beliefs about sickness and health that may affect schooling, and when students come to school with health issues, teachers need to react in culturally compatible ways. Students may have health problems stemming from war trauma, culture shock, poverty, family violence, or crime; but teachers and the family may view these problems in very different ways (Witte, 1991), resulting in miscommunication. Students from some cultures may respond negatively to attention from mental health professionals or counselors.

Institutional Influences: Economic, Legal, Political, and Religious

The institutions that support and govern family and community life are embedded within cultural behavior and beliefs. In the United States, for example, religious practices are heavily embedded but formally bounded: Some citizens complain about Christmas trees in schools, but retail businesses depend on increased consumer spending at the close of the calendar year. When immigrants with strong religious beliefs encounter the largely secular institutions of the United States, cultural patterns may be challenged or cause conflict within the family (Chung, 1989).

Language-Related Behaviors and Beliefs

The role of language and nonverbal expression in communication varies widely by culture. Most language educators are oriented toward verbal expression and are less likely to accord importance to "silent language." However, most cultures use *kinesic* behavior, including facial expressions, body movements, postures, and gestures, to enhance a message. People from such cultures and are highly tuned to nonverbal messages that a teacher may be sending. *Paralanguage,* the nonverbal elements of the voice, can affirm or belie a verbal message. *Proxemics,* the communication of interpersonal distance, varies widely across cultures. Last, but not least, *olfactics,* the role of smell in interpersonal communication, may constitute a factor that is powerful yet often overlooked. Even the use of silence differs dramatically across cultures. In the United States, silence is interpreted as expressing embarrassment, regret, obligation, criticism, disagreement or sorrow; in many Asian cultures, however, silence is a token of respect. Similarly, in many Native American cultures, silence is used to create and communicate rapport in ways that language cannot.

Attitudes toward language are also a part of the messages teachers send. In the example below, Hang Nguyen and her family were immersed in a new language and culture when they fled Vietnam to seek sanctuary in the United States in 1983. Hang felt that the messages that her daughter received caused much conflict and unhappiness within the family:

> My daughter is bilingual, but only half bilingual because she doesn't know how to read and write. She only speaks Vietnamese. She was four years old when she came over, and she started kindergarten early. So since she was five years old she has been bombarded with the ideas "You live here. You have to speak the language. You have to learn the way to live here. Your language is not important. Your language is an embarrassment. If you learn your language you will not be able to learn English. English is the main language here." That's the message she got. It was not always obvious, but she would be told, "You need to go home and practice your English. You need this . . . you need that . . ." and I think that was enough to poison her mind against what she stands for. (Stiel, 2002, p. 187)

Educational Systems

Educational systems in the past were designed to pass on cultural knowledge and traditions; however, in the increasingly complex and technological society of the United

States, schools have shifted their emphasis. Students come to school already steeped in the learning practices of their own family and community. Many of these practices may not support the type of learning to which students are exposed in school.

For immigrant children with previous schooling, experience in U.S. classrooms may engender severe conflicts. For example, Indochinese students expect to listen, watch, and imitate. They may be reluctant to ask questions or volunteer answers and embarrassed or reluctant to participate in individual demonstrations of a skill or project (Armour, Knudson, & Meeks, 1981). The teacher may wish to support their initial dependence while gradually introducing student-centered practices.

Teachers who seek to understand the value of education within the community can examine the following questions: What methods for teaching and learning are used in the home (e.g., modeling and imitation, stories and proverbs, direct verbal instruction)? What role does language play in learning and teaching? How are children expected to interact (observe only, ask questions, volunteer)? Understanding differing perceptions of schooling is an important step toward accommodating these differences.

Culturally Compatible Instruction

+ **STRATEGY 9.2:** Align the culture of schooling and the learner's culture

Teachers can play an important role by learning about their students' communities and cultures and thus reducing the cultural shock between home and school. The best way for a teacher to understand culture is to understand his or her own teaching and learning styles and then investigate to what extent each student is similar or dissimilar. Direct personal observation of social behavior or ethnographic study may be used to understand students' cultures from the perspective of the members of those cultures. This understanding can then be used to organize classroom activities in ways that promote educational achievement for all students.

The study of culture is important because groups of students may be similar in their reaction to schooling. With this cultural knowledge, classroom routines can be organized to encourage more effective learning, and information about the students' cultures can be incorporated into the content of instruction. In a multicultural classroom, there may be no single best way for students to learn. Using a variety of activities that appeal to different students in turn may be an effective strategy. The observation cycle continues as teachers watch students to see *which* approaches meet *whose* needs. The intercultural educator is sensitive and flexible.

Ethnographic Study

Ethnography seeks to provide cultural explanations for behavior and attitudes. This field of inquiry is useful in exploring the ways in which students' cultural experiences at home and in their community compare with the culture of their schools. Culture is described from the insider's point of view, as the classroom teacher becomes not only an observer of the students' cultures but also an active participant (Erickson, 1977; Mehan, 1981). To understand the home and community cultures, teachers may participate in community life, interview community members, and visit homes. To understand the school culture, teachers may observe in a variety of classrooms; record and/or video-tape classroom interaction; and talk with other teachers and administrators.

Self-Study

Teachers who engage in self-exploration activities that help them understand and appreciate their own origins and values may find it easier to understand the cultural behaviors of others. One can start a cultural inquiry by investigating one's personal name, asking, "Where did I get my name? Who am I named for? In which culture did the name originate?" Self-examination includes identifying one's favorite cultural customs, such as holiday traditions, home decor, and favorite foods, as well as one's stance on such issues as individual freedom, competition, and the value of work. Introspective questions help to pinpoint one's own cultural attitudes (see Box 9.1). The process is challenging and ongoing.

Cultural Observations

Observations of students' cultures include looking at students' use of language within the community; etiquettes of speaking, listening, greeting, getting or giving information; values; and aspirations—in short, the categories of culture described in this chapter. When

---

BOX 9.1
❖ Cultural Self-Study: Self-Exploration Questions

Describe yourself as a preschool child. Were you compliant, curious, adventuresome, goody-goody, physically active, nature-loving? Have you observed your parents with other children? Do they encourage open-ended exploration, or would they prefer children to play quietly with approved toys? Do they encourage initiative?

What was the knowledge environment like in your home? What type of reading did your father and mother do? Was there a time when the members of the family had discussions about current events or ideas and issues? How much dissent was tolerated from parental viewpoints? Were children encouraged to question the status quo? What was it like to learn to talk and think in your family?

What kind of a grade-school pupil were you? What is your best memory from elementary school? What was your favorite teacher like? Were you an avid reader? How would you characterize your cognitive style and learning style preferences? Was the school you attended ethnically diverse? What about your secondary school experience? Did you have a diverse group of friends in high school?

What is your ethnic group? What symbols or traditions did you participate in that derived from this group? What do you like about your ethnic identity? Is there a time now when your group celebrates its traditions together? What was the neighborhood or community like in which you grew up?

What was your experience with ethnic diversity? What were your first images of race or color? Was there a time in your life when you sought out diverse contacts to expand your experience?

What contact do you have now with people of very dissimilar racial and ethnic backgrounds? How would you characterize your desire to learn more? Given your learning style preferences, how would you go about this?

Source: Díaz-Rico & Weed, 2002.

analyzing the culture of the classroom, one might look at classroom management and routines; affective factors (students' attitudes toward activities, teachers' attitudes toward students); classroom talk in general; and nonverbal behaviors and communication.

Interviews

Interviews are *structured* or *unstructured*. Structured interviews use a set of preselected questions to gather specific kinds of information. Unstructured interviews are more like conversations on a wide variety of topics. When learning about a new culture, the classroom teacher would be well served initially to begin with general questions and be guided in follow-up questions by the interviewee's responses. The result of the initial interview may lead to a second interview. Agar's *The Professional Stranger: An Informal Introduction to Ethnography* (1980) is a useful book about ethnographic interviewing.

Home Visits

The home visit can be a "social call" or a brief report on the student's progress that enhances rapport with students and parents and helps teachers learn what is familiar and important to their students. Families in some cultures may require an invitation, but in other cultures scheduling an appointment ahead of time is not necessary. A short visit (twenty to thirty minutes) is best, but some hosts may expect a longer stay. Viewing the child in the context of the home provides an opportunity to observe the parent-child interaction, the resources of the home, and the child's role in the family.

Sources for Learning about Cultures

Teachers can use books, magazines, and videos to learn about other cultures; or they can draw on students, parents, and community members for insights about values, attitudes, and habits. Students generally provide teachers with their initial contact with other cultures. Through observations, shared conversations during or after school, and group participation, teachers gain understanding about various individuals and their cultures. Asking students to map their own neighborhood is another source of knowledge from the students' perspective.

Educators who form relationships with parents can talk about culture and schooling. Teachers can ask students to interview their parents about common topics such as work, interests, and family history. In this way students and parents together can supply knowledge about community life. Although it may be more difficult to involve working parents, asking about the work that they perform can provide useful information about the knowledge and expertise in the community.

Community members are an equally rich source of cultural knowledge, especially about such areas as housing, popular meeting places for different age groups, and sources of food, furniture, and services. Much can be learned about a community by walking or driving through it, or stopping at local stores and markets. Through community representatives, respected elders, or religious leaders, teachers can become familiar with important living patterns of a community. They can also attend local ceremonies and activities to learn more about community dynamics.

Websites on the Internet can introduce the curious to other cultures. Students may be able to provide the names of such sites, which would be difficult to access without such insider knowledge. The Internet can also be a source of materials for the study of students' cultures. The California Department of Education *Handbooks for Teaching Students from Diverse Cultures* (*Cantonese-Speaking Students* [1989a]; *Japanese-Speaking Students* [1987]; *Korean-American Students* [1992]; *Pilipino-Speaking Students* [1986]; *Portuguese-Speaking Students* [1989b]; and *Vietnamese-Speaking Students* [1994]) are designed to help school personnel understand and work with these second language students. To order online, go to the website www.cde.ca.gov/cdepress and click on "catalog."

Culturally Responsive Pedagogy

The selection of a particular teaching method often reflects cultural values, whether conscious or unconscious (Andersen & Powell, 1988). There may be conflict between the patterns acquired at home and those demanded by the school. However, it is not enough simply to explain children's differential school success as a cultural mismatch between home and school. Teachers who understand students' cultures invite students to learn by welcoming them, making them feel that they belong, and presenting learning as a task at which they can succeed. Teaching styles, interaction patterns, classroom organization, curriculum, and involvement with parents and the community are all factors that are within the teacher's power to adapt to achieve the goal of culturally compatible teaching.

Teaching Styles (Cultural Orientation)

Teachers raised in a certain culture have elements of that culture embedded in their personal teaching approach. Fischer and Fischer (1979) have identified six teaching styles that might affect students from a variety of cultural backgrounds. The *task-oriented teacher* expects students to be independent of the social environment when working. The teacher who is a *cooperative planner* involves students in setting objectives and choosing activities, which may be a shock for a student accustomed to a high level of teacher direction. The *emotionally exciting teacher* may be stimulating for some students but distracting and overstimulating for others. The *child-centered teacher* wishes students to find and pursue their own best means of learning, but students raised in adult-centered cultures may find this approach disorienting. *Subject-centered teachers* strive to "cover" the curriculum, but the relevance of the curriculum may not always be clear to students. A *learning-centered teacher* focuses on each individual student's ability, but goal-focused students may just want to get good grades.

Even in monocultural classrooms, the teacher's style suits some students better than others. Flexibility becomes the key to reaching more students. With knowledge of various teaching styles, teachers can examine their own styles, observe students' reactions, ask questions about the community's expectations for the teacher, and modify their styles as necessary.

Teacher-Student Interactions

Teacher-student interaction may derive from parent-child relationships or from values transmitted by the parent toward teachers and schooling. Attitudes toward authority, teacher-student relationships, and teachers' expectations of student achievement vary widely. In the United States, respect is shown to teachers by looking at them, but in some cultures looking at the teacher is a sign of disrespect. In general, one must not conclude that a particular behavior is disrespectful; it may be that the child has learned different customs for communicating with those in authority. In some parts of the world it is acceptable to call a teacher by his or her first name, indicating that relations between teachers and students are warm, close, and informal. In other cultures teacher-student relations are formal, without an emphasis on rapport.

Classroom Organization and Curriculum

The typical classroom is that of a teacher-leader who gives assignments or demonstrates to the students, who act as audience. Teacher presentations are usually followed by some form of individual study. Learning is then assessed through recitation, quizzes, or some other performance. Any deviation from this—group work, individual projects, group problem solving, or class discussion—requires explicit cultural adaptation for students to these new ways of behaving and speaking. Teachers can help students adapt by providing clear instructions and models, by calling on more self-confident students first, and by assigning self-conscious students minor roles at first in order not to embarrass them.

Many aspects of the school curriculum are highly abstract and contain themes and activities for which some students have little point of reference. The biggest challenge for all educators is to engage students of all backgrounds equally in a stimulating, yet understandable, curriculum, with instruction organized in a way that meets their learning needs.

Assuming a Bicultural Identity

♦ **STRATEGY 9.3:** Motivate the learner to achieve cultural fluency

People communicate their identities (personality, intellectual ability, interests) to one another by means of culturally based interaction patterns. Emotional bonds (love, fear, respect) and ways of showing this bond through language (oral, written, body) are also culturally based. These aspects of identity are not only individual but are characteristic of subgroups in a society, and they circulate through society by means of discourse (Foucault, 1984). Cummins (1996) has argued that students' success or failure is determined largely through the process of identity negotiations between teachers and students. When students learn another language and then learn by means of the second language, maintaining and supporting a strong sense of identity and self-esteem are important (Cummins, 2000b).

When people use language in any discourse context, the meaning is shaped and constrained by that context, whether it is interpersonal, institutional, or sociocultural.

"As subjects of discourse, we are 'interpellated'; we make imaginary identifications with culturally constructed positions and identities" (Peim, 1993, p. 63). This identification in turn influences the discourse that the individual produces. Identity is shaped and determined by social configurations, distinctions, categories, and practices. Taking on new language practices inevitably requires a new set of intrapersonal configurations.

Shen (1998) found the act of academic writing in English to require cultural and ideological reformulation: "learning the rules of English composition is, to a certain extent, learning the values of Anglo-American society" (p. 124). Shen found that to obey the dictum to express her "voice" ("Just be yourself!") she had to construct an American self, different from her Chinese self, and become *that* self: a mask that was confident, assertive, even aggressive. In the end, the identity she forged was a balance between these two aspects. In retrospect, she would have liked the instructor to help her to confront the cultural differences more directly, rather than assuming that the "real" self was the Western construct.

Technologies of the Self Toward Identity Development.   Teachers who use humanistic techniques, including interactive journals and self-esteem exercises, draw upon what Foucault calls a "technology of the self," which he defines as a set of techniques that permit individuals to transform themselves (Foucault, 1988). But what exactly is the "self"? In fact, *self* is an elusive concept, because concepts of identity differ across cultures.

Many students from collectivist cultures see the United States as a culture that values individualism, in contrast to cultures in which self-identity is grounded at least in part by the thoughts and feelings of others in a specific referent group. In Japan, for example, self-identity is predicated on interactive reflection, with strong social pressure to subordinate one's individualism to the well-being of others. "Even the word 'individualism' (*kojinshugi*) is still an ambivalent word in Japan . . . suggesting as it does to the Japanese selfishness rather than personal responsibility" (Reischauer, 1977, p. 147). Doutrich (2000) commented on this sense of self in others:

> Without this projected image, many Japanese experience a loss of self. Without knowing one's position and without the caring of others, the sense of self may fade. . . . Significantly, the Japanese have language to label this phenomenon; they call it *jibun ga nai* (no self). (p. 147)

Many English learners are aware that their sense of "self" shifts as they move back and forth from their native language to English. Doutrich described the ability to move back and forth freely between cultures, smoothly, with grace and flexibility, as "cultural fluency" (p. 142), borrowing the term from Poyatos (1984). This means one must be able to change and undergo personal transformation, as well as maintain flexibility and openness to change.

This does not always mean becoming more responsive to context. For the Japanese in Doutrich's study, the transforming act that allowed them to fit more easily into American culture was becoming *less* responsive to social context, more task oriented and direct, and somewhat less willing to accommodate to others. The shifts (in this case from a high-context to a low-context culture) may be along any dimension that affects language and culture, including ways of thinking, acting, and believing.

Senses of the Self.   The idea of the "self" in postmodern thinking has taken on certain characteristics: as multiple rather than unified identity; as a decentered site of struggle rather than a centered, essentialist core; and as a flexible, changing response to the contexts of the external and internal world rather than a fixed structure of personality (Pierce, 1995; Weedon, 1987). Modern themes of self-expression, self-fulfillment, and self-actualization have been gradually replaced in the postmodern mythos with a realization that the external world is pushing against the self with its own forms of restraint, including threats of ecological disaster, the decay of community, and the loss of universal values.

For many students, a subjective sense of self is secure within an identity based on traditional sources (family, race, neighborhood, nationality). But in the complex, technologically based contexts in which English is now used, traditional identities may not be as important as negotiated identities—specific, utilitarian aspects of personality suitable for the workplace or for instrumental relationships. Verbal language thus becomes increasingly important. Whatever else English accomplishes, it is important for students to preserve and enhance their sense of *sovereignty,* the sense that they are who they want to be, without the undue influence of internal forces (intrapersonal inhibitors, like anxiety) or external forces (interpersonal, institutional, or sociocultural inhibitors).

Cultural Marginality.   One might ask whether the English language, as a vehicle for postmodernity, is a Trojan horse, bringing the unwanted cargo of negotiated identity into a citadel of traditional context for the self. Even if this were true, little alternative exists to global cultural change except the defiant rejection of such influences. Probably a wiser course would be to embrace biculturality as a positive outgrowth of cultural marginality (see Bennett, 1993, for exploration of the concept of "dynamic in-betweenness"), so that those who learn English can feel themselves enriched by an expanded set of personal and cultural alternatives enabling them to maintain roots in the native culture while sprouting wings in English.

In postmodern terms, the margin is the place to be. As Yúdice (1988) claimed,

> There was a time when to be "marginal" meant to be excluded, forgotten, overlooked. Gradually, throughout this century, first in the discourses of anthropology, sociology, and psychoanalysis, "marginality" became a focus of interest through which "we" (Western culture) discovered otherness and our own ethnocentric perspectives. Today, it is declared, the "marginal" is no longer peripheral but central to all thought. . . . By demonstrating that the "marginal" constitutes the condition of possibility of all social, scientific, and cultural entities, the new "ethics of marginality" had emerged that is necessarily decentered and plural. . . . (p. 214)

It is easy to don and doff marginality when one has the luxury of taking a dose of otherness and then going on to other issues. Many students, though, do not have this privilege, being instead caught in the pressure to assimilate or accommodate. A useful position for educators is to accept a role at the margin, and as Bennett (1996a) recommended, choose to associate themselves with cultural difference, remembering that power circulates and staying "in the power loop."

"Knowledge emanating from the margins can be used to redefine the complex, multiple, heterogeneous realities that constitute those relations of difference making up the experiences of students through the cultural and political codes of a single, unitary culture" (Aronowitz & Giroux, 1991, p. 120). In short, teachers of English learners can play an important role in helping institutions accommodate students' needs. TESOL educators are quintessential candidates for leadership in postmodern education (Díaz-Rico, 1999a).

Culture as Content

Part of the richness and delight found in teaching English learners is the opportunity to teach and learn about culture. I confess I am a cultural traditionalist in some ways. I put ornaments on the Christmas tree every year, and I love to color Easter eggs and carve Jack O'Lanterns. At the same time, I can accept the gifts of cultural exchange: Christmas tree ornaments made of origami, celebration of Sweden's Santa Lucia Day, and multiple New Year's celebrations through the year. Students who are from other cultures enjoy learning the traditional symbols of American holidays and participating in seasonal pastimes, just as English-language cultures are opening up to the celebrations, customs, and beliefs of English learners. This cultural exchange brings forth deep feelings and emotions to enrich our mutual relations.

◆ **STRATEGY 9.4:** Teach English using the learner's culture as well as the target culture

Why Teach Language Using Culture?

Teaching English using the *learner's culture* as well as the *target culture* makes English more accessible. Teaching elementary students in Taiwan, for example, using the children's book *Legends of Ten Chinese Traditional Festivals* (Li, 1992) permits the students to draw on their cultural knowledge as they make sense of English. Teaching Mexican immigrant children English using a tour of Mexico as content helps them to feel pride in their heritage, and fluency is advanced much more if they know what they are talking about. Later in this section several sample native-language cultural units for English teaching will be described.

Culture of the Target Language

Teaching target language means presenting information to English learners about the cultural context of the language. If one is learning English in Australia, the target culture is that of Australian English-speaking peoples, whereas if one is in inner-city Detroit, the target culture is probably African American. In the rhetoric of English as an international language, there is no good reason for target cultures always to be those of native English-speakers. Yet for purposes of illustration, I will speak of the target culture as being mainstream United States American.

Resources for teaching American culture are vast. One might read about the Founders, country or punk rock music, African American women's liberation (hooks, 1989), schooling in Hawaii (Jordan, Tharp, & Baird-Vogt, 1992), or Native American art. Table 9.2 offers an annotated list of eight kinds of reading anthologies about

Bringing the students' culture into the classroom can motivate students to learn English.

TABLE 9.2 • Resources for Readings about American Culture

Source	Description
America Now: Short Readings from Recent Periodicals (Atwan, 1997)	English as an official language, television talk shows, interracial relationships—the book samples the discourse in current newspapers for advanced readers and native speakers.
American Picture Show (Mejia, Xiao, & Pasternak, 1992)	Authors use seven movies involving ethnicities in America to teach American culture. Each chapter provides background readings and vocabulary work.
American Street: A Multicultural Anthology of Voices (Mazer, 1993)	Fourteen stories from writers represent a spectrum of ethnicities.
American Topics (Lugton, 1986)	A reading vocabulary text that uses comprehension questions and prompts for writing and discussion.
American Voices: Webs of Diversity (Quintero & Rummel, 1998)	Readings about aspects of American culture (multicultural education, family values, social issues) are informed by critical theory perspectives.
American Ways (Althen, 1988)	Readings offer ways to understand Americans (for foreigners who are visiting or sojourning in the United States).
The American Ways (Datesman, Crandall, & Kearny, 1997)	Readings about aspects of American culture (education, family, leisure time) are accompanied by workbook-type comprehension and vocabulary exercises.
Spotlight on the USA (Falk, 1993)	Readings depict regions of America (cities, history, landmarks, famous representative people).
How to Live in America: A Guide for the Japanese (Collins, 1990)	Advice is given on intercultural communication for Japanese who sojourn in the United States.
The Yin and Yang of American Culture (Kim, 2001)	American culture—its virtues and vices—is viewed from an Eastern perspective.

American culture, all at an intermediate or advanced reading level. These readings range from specific kinds of cultural content (e.g., films) to tours of the United States, all with the goal of explaining aspects of American culture. Table 9.3 presents a sampling of books about Native American cultures on topics ranging from art and history to rituals, stories, and prayers.

American holidays are fun to teach about, especially when they involve family activities and even more when they are about love. Valentine's Day scores high on this index. Yet as with any other cultural content, it is not enough to relate to it only at a superficial level, one of behaviors or artifacts. The most important cultural content is at a deeper level, the level of values and beliefs. Box 9.2 presents an instructional plan that teaches about some typical American holidays and shows how to have fun with Valentine's Day. Table 9.4 presents a game that helps students to use the celebration of Valentine's Day to compare cultures. This game is fun for students, because it compares not only behaviors like dating rituals but also personal predilections, histories, and cultural values. Another activity uses the instructional conversation discourse format (see Chapter 10) to compare cultural values (see Box 9.3).

One interesting way to learn about the European roots of American culture is to use the *Inner Child Cards,* a fancifully illustrated deck of cards based on European folk and fairy tales (Lerner & Lerner, 1992). (See the demonstration lesson: "Contacting the Inner Child," Box 9.7). This promotes communicative activity and pair learning.

TABLE 9.3 • Resources for Information about Native American Cultures

Resource	Description
Chants and Prayers (Padilla, 1995)	Spiritual messages in the form of chants and prayers rooted in Native American oral traditions
Spirit Walker (Wood, 1993)	Poems with Native American themes, beautifully illustrated
Myths and Legends of the Indians of the Southwest (Dutton & Olin, 1995)	Brief introduction to the Hopi, Acoma, Tewa, and Zuni cultures
Dancing Teepees (Sneve, 1989)	Poems for American Indian youth: chants, bedtime songs, inspiration sayings
Great Native Americans (Copeland, 1997)	Brief illustrated biographies of forty-two outstanding Native Americans from the seventeenth to the twentieth centuries
A Rainbow at Night: The World in Word and Pictures by Navajo Children (Hucko, 1996)	Paintings by Navajo children, featuring their photographs and biographies
Native American Traditions (Versluis, 1994)	History of Native Americans in their contact with European culture, with many illustrations of cultural artifacts and historical personalities
Navajo Medicine Man Sandpainting (Reichard, 1977)	In-depth explanation of Navajo healing rituals, with color illustrations and diagrams

BOX 9.2
❖ Instructional Plan: American Holidays and Valentine's Day

Level: ESOL speech emergence or intermediate fluency, all age levels

Objectives:

1. To survey American holidays
2. To explain American Valentine's Day customs and compare with L1 customs for Valentine's Day or other similar holiday
3. To connect culture with language: candy heart messages
4. To make Valentine cards

Task Chain 1: American holidays

- Connect vocabulary and conceptual knowledge about holidays (use Focus Sheet 1a).
- Participants practice quizzing each other on vocabulary.

Task Chain 2: American Valentine's Day/crosscultural comparison

- Participants read box and compare with L1 culture (pair/share, group share).

Task Chain 3: Candy heart messages (see Box 9.5)

- Participants receive boxes of candy hearts.

- Choosing one candy heart, each person seeks another person whose heart has same message to be that person's "Valentine."
- "Valentines" with same color heart are on same team.
- Play Candy Heartbreak:

   Two teams in relays; (fly swatter game)

   Half of candy heart is on wall

   Instructor shows half heart; first person in line reads message, seeks matching half of heart (by message) to swat

Task Chain 4: Making Valentine cards

- Participants make cards for their "Valentines."
- Use construction paper, doilies, paste, glue, adhesive tape, ribbon, scissors, stickers, candy hearts, cookie cutter shapes.
- Draw names randomly from a hat. Put a Valentine's message inside the card by selecting three adjectives that you think represent this person (see Box 9.6).
- Exchange cards.

Assessment: Vocabulary

- Holiday matching quiz

English Teaching Using the Native Culture

English can be taught using themes derived from native cultures. Lesson plans might feature such topics as Japanese fairy tales (see Nishimoto, 1997); Chinese fairy tales; a puppet play based on Chinese horoscope animals; a dramatization of the Chinese folktale "The Magic Sieve"; Japanese cultural artifacts such as kites, dolls, and pottery; and other topics pertaining to the native culture. These are particularly useful at the elementary school level, a time when children should learn more about their own cultures. One instructional unit compared English and Chinese proverbs and folk sayings using as a resource Chinnery and Chu's *Corresponding English and Chinese Proverbs and Phrases* (1984), a source that is useful at several levels of instruction. A similar unit can be developed using Mexican folk sayings, or "dichos" (Sellers, 1994), or Hawaiian proverbs (Provenzano, 2001).

TABLE 9.4 ◆ U.S. Holiday Vocabulary

American Holiday	Vocabulary
New Year's Eve (December 31) New Year's Day (January 1)	Tournament of Roses parade (New Year's Day), noisemakers, "Happy New Year!"
Saint Valentine's Day (February 14)	Box of chocolate candy; Cupid; I love you, love notes; a dozen red roses; red and white; Will you be my _____?, paper lace doily, significant other
St. Patrick's Day (March 17)	Irish, shamrocks, green
Easter (First Sunday after first full moon after spring equinox)	Bunnies, crosses, Easter egg hunts
Fourth of July (July 4), Signing of Declaration of Independence	Firecrackers; red, white, and blue; parades; band concerts in the park; picnics; neighborhood parties
Halloween (October 31)	Candy corn, bobbing for apples, orange and black, skeletons, Boo!, costumes
Thanksgiving (fourth Thursday in November)	Parades (Macy's in New York), Indian corn, turkey dinner, gobble gobble, cranberries
Christmas (December 25)	"Jingle Bells," Season's Greetings, Kris Kringle, ornaments, red and green, office parties
Hanukkah (25th of the Hebrew month of Kislev—sometime between the end of November and the end of December)	Dreidel, menorah

---

BOX 9.3
❖ Sample Instructional Conversation Prompt

Leave the Party?

Jenny came to college from a small town in the surrounding area. She met Jake, a senior, the captain of the football team, who is a business major. They dated for two months, and she felt they had a committed relationship. On her birthday, Jake gave Jenny his fraternity ring. He invited her to a fraternity party for Valentine's Day.

At the party, Jake began to flirt with another girl. While he was dancing with the girl, Jenny began to talk with Akbar, another fraternity brother. Suddenly, Jenny realized that Akbar was someone she wanted to get to know, to see again. Akbar suggested they go for a walk where they could talk quietly. Should Jenny leave the party with Akbar?

BOX 9.4
❖ Valentine's Day Customs

Children exchange Valentine cards in elementary school. Each child brings one for each classmate. Adults buy Valentine cards for their significant other; sometimes they buy a box of chocolate for one another. A desperate lover may buy twelve red roses for his object of passion. Parents buy cards and candy for their children. The holiday used to be called "Saint Valentine's Day"; with the increasing secularization of United States culture, "Saint" has been dropped.

BOX 9.5
❖ **Focus Sheet for Valentine's Day Activity**

The Idiom of Candy Hearts

One of the traditions of Valentine's Day is the tiny candy heart. Below are the messages you may find on the hearts. Look before you eat—you may have messages from the new millennium!

Traditional Messages

SWEET TALK	CUTIE PIE
CALL ME	ONLY YOU
I HOPE	LOVER BOY
I'M SURE	LET'S KISS
YES DEAR	HUG ME
DEAR ONE	ANGEL
REAL LOVE	MY BABY
HOW NICE	SMILE
I DO	FOR YOU

"Twenty-First-Century" Messages

E-MAIL	PAGE ME
AS IF	U GO GIRL
GOT LOVE	EZ 2 LOVE
MUCH ADO	GET REAL
COOL DUDE	UR MINE
BE MY ICON	2000 HUGS
WHAT EVER	

BOX 9.6
❖ **Adjectives Used on Valentine Cards**

glamorous	focused	sincere	tender	easy-going
sensitive	secretive	competent	dependable	perky
adventurous	artistic	imaginative	magnetic	upbeat
even-tempered	friendly	sociable	thoughtful	elegant
proud	self-critical	coordinated	determined	personable
agile	attentive	inhibited	mystical	well-dressed
expressive	generous	stable	devoted	emotional
prudent	self-disciplined	courteous	outgoing	pleasant
agreeable	cautious	intense	tranquil	well-grounded
faithful	gentle	strong	domestic	energetic
resourceful	sensible	creative	passionate	poetic
ambitious	charming	introverted	trusting	well-informed
firm	traditional	sweet	domineering	entertaining
righteous	cheerful	decisive	patient	polite
amusing	graceful	intuitive	unpredictable	wise
flexible	serious	tactful	dynamic	enthusiastic
romantic	compassionate	deep	peace-loving	practical
articulate	hardworking	kind	unselfish	witty

Choose three adjectives that you think best describe you:

_____ _____ _____

Choose three adjectives that you would like to become:

_____ _____ _____

Interview your partner. Ask what traits he or she would like to acquire.
List three adjectives that your partner would like to become:

_____ _____ _____

BOX 9.7
❖ Demonstration Lesson: "Contacting the Inner Child"

Level: Adult (intermediate fluency)

Objectives:

1. To identify key European fairy tales
2. To experience personally target-culture mythical figures and compare these with native-culture figures
3. To explore means of thinking about personal decisions and choices

TESOL Standards:

Standard 2.2 Students will use English to obtain, process, construct, and provide subject matter information in spoken and written form.

Standard 2.3 Students will use appropriate learning strategies to construct and apply academic knowledge.

Warm-Up:

Brainstorm with students to see how many English-language fairy tales they can name.

Task Chain 1: European American Fairy Tales
- View *The Wizard of Oz* and identify key figures
- Identify key figures in *Sleeping Beauty*

Task Chain 2: Target-Culture Mythical Figures—Crosscultural Comparisons
- Cultural background: What are Tarot cards? Major Arcana versus Minor Arcana.

- Each person chooses three cards from the Inner Child pack (Lerner & Lerner, 1992).
- Each pair identifies and discusses the cards, offering crosscultural comparisons if available.
- Each member of a pair orally describes two cards.

Task Chain 3: Thinking about Personal Decisions and Choices

- Using the Inner Child cards, each pair plays "Turn the Corner." One partner thinks about a personal decision.
- "Turn the Corner" directions: Choose one card from the pack and lay it face up (card of the past). Choose another card from the pack. Lay it face up below the first card (card of the present, which "turns the corner" of your fate). Choose another card from the pack. Lay it face up beside the second card (card of the future)
- Given time, discuss personal anecdotes relating to game

Final Assessment: Thinking about Personal Decisions and Choices

1. Write a brief description of the cards that appeared in this activity. How did the images relate to your situation?
2. Self-assessment: Write in one or two sentences what you gained from this activity.

Using the learner's culture to teach English comes with a price—teachers need to take the time to use accurate information that represents the culture in an authentic way. It is important to have a native-culture consultant available with whom to verify cultural content. In addition to presenting information about the learners' culture(s), the teacher who can act as an advocate for that culture and its customs and values shows an adaptive, integrative view about culture. This serves as a model for students to acquire this view as well.

Bias in Teaching about Culture

Teachers with good intentions but lacking a solid foundation of cultural knowledge are often guilty of cultural bias. One type of bias is trivializing the cultural content of the curriculum. The sole cultural reference may be to holidays or food, or they may have "ethnic" bulletin boards only during certain times of the year (Black History Month). Books about children of color are read only on special occasions, and units about different cultures are taught once and never mentioned again. People from cultures outside the United States are seen only in "traditional" dress and rural settings or, if they are people of color, are always shown as poor. Native Americans may be represented as from the past. Moreover, students' cultures are often misrepresented; pictures and books about Mexico, for example, are used to teach about Mexican Americans, or books about Africa are used to teach about African Americans (Derman-Sparks and Anti-Bias Curriculum Task Force, 1988).

In her article "Educating Teachers for Cultural and Linguistic Diversity: A Model for All Teachers," Parla (1994) discussed issues related to the multicultural classroom and included information on cultural sensitivity, linguistic diversity, and teaching strategies to help teachers improve their understanding of cultural issues and translate that understanding into classroom practice. The article is available online at www.ncbe.gwu.edu/miscpubs/nysabe/vol9/model.htm.

The following checklist can help teachers assess the extent to which ethnic, linguistic, and gender biases exist in the curriculum:

* What groups are represented in texts, discussion, and bulletin board displays? Are certain groups invisible?
* Are the roles of minorities and women presented in a separate manner from other content, that is, isolated or treated as a distinct topic?
* Are minorities and women treated in a positive, diversified manner or stereotyped into traditional or rigid roles?
* Are the problems faced by minorities presented in a realistic fashion, with a problem-solving orientation?
* Are the materials written using inclusive language, or do they contain biased terms such as masculine forms (*mankind, mailman*)?
* Does the curriculum foster appreciation of cultural diversity?
* Are experiences and activities included besides those common to middle-class European American culture?

Crosscultural Studies

Comparing various aspects of cultures can result in rich thematic units used for teaching English. One such unit compares communication styles in Korea and the United States; yet another compares marketing, advertising, and product placement across several cultures. Simultaneous comparison of multiple cultures is fascinating. An instructional unit comparing Korean Chusook and American Thanksgiving, for example, should include a third celebration, El Dia de los Muertos, because many customs of Chusook are really close to the Aztec elements of picnicking at family graves. In fact, they may have originated in the same peoples, if one believes that the Aztecs migrated to the New World from the northern Asiatic peninsula.

♦ **STRATEGY 9.5:** Teach English by comparing cultures

Achieving Ethnorelativism

Bennett (1996a) called *ethnorelativism* the state of being able to accept cultural differences, adapt to them, and integrate them into our own personality. This means that one must understand culture not as artifacts, but rather as values, behaviors, and other patterns. In addition, ethnorelativism allows a discussion of cultural generalizations without stereotyping people and accepts that all cultures and races consist of varied groups of individuals, who may or may not exemplify a particular cultural predilection. Thus one can talk about the "primary tendency" of a cultural group in relation to some trait without insisting that all people fit a particular generalization.

Many students are particularly interested in crosscultural analyses of behaviors and values. Table 9.5 presents an annotated guide to several representative books from this genre. Intercultural Press (www.interculturalpress.com) is an excellent source for books in this genre. In contrast, Table 9.6 presents books relevant to minority cultures within the United States.

Deeper Crosscultural Comparison

The only concern when comparing cultures is to ensure that the content of such comparison goes beyond the superficial aspects of culture (holidays, food, and Cinderella

TABLE 9.5 ♦ Sample of Books on Crosscultural Behaviors and Values

Resource	Description
Understanding Spanish-speaking South Americans (Stephenson, 2002)	A study of cultural themes that underlie behaviors and beliefs in Latin America, with a focus on nine specific countries
Business Taiwan: A Practical Guide to Understanding Taiwan's Business Culture (Kenna & Lacy, 1994)	A concise guide to business practices and customs in Taiwan (including communication styles, body language and non-verbal cues, negotiating, and contracting)
Encountering the Chinese: A Guide for Americans (Hu & Grove, 1991)	A crosscultural analysis of behaviors and values geared toward Americans having closer relationships with mainland Chinese
Wtih Respect to the Japanese: A Guide for Americans (Condon, 1984)	A presentation of salient features of Japanese culture written to assist Americans in face-to-face encounters
Old World/New World, Bridging Cultural Differences: Britain, France, and the U.S. (Storti, 2001)	An assortment of dialogues illustrating fundamental differences in cultural behaviors and beliefs
Understanding Arabs: A Guide for Westerners (Nydell, 1997)	Insights into the complexities of nineteen distinct Arab cultures

TABLE 9.6 • **Books on Minority Cultures within the United States**

Resource	Description
Multicultural Education: A Teacher's Guide to Linking Context, Process, and Content (Hernández, 2001)	Strategies for studying students' backgrounds, and for adapting instruction accordingly
Educating for Diversity: An Anthology of Multicultural Voices (Grant, 1995)	Specific readings on fifteen American cultural groups, as well as other types of diversity
Multicultural Education: Issues and Perspectives (Banks & McGee Banks, 1997)	General approach to diversity, plus four-level schema on multicultural curricula (contributions, additive, transformational, and transformational + social change)
Sisters of the Yam: Black Women and Self-Discovery (hooks, 1993)	One in a series of provocative books by a black feminist writer
Crossing Cultural Borders: Education for Immigrant Families in America (Delgado-Gaitan & Trueba, 1991)	Ethnographic study of Mexican immigrants in California
¡Adelante mujeres! Video on the History of Mexican-American Chicana Women (National Women's History Project, 1992)	Videotape on the contributions of Chicana women (accompanied by curriculum/video guide)
Chicano School Failure and Success: Research and Policy Agendas for the 1990s (Valéncia, 1991)	Comprehensive look at education for Mexican Americans

tales) and delves into the values that people of differing cultures bring to their celebrations. This process may, however, bring some degree of discomfort.

For example, Americans who compare Halloween with the Mexican celebration El Dia de Los Muertos (Day of the Dead) may find superficial similarities in costumes and sugar candy. This superficial similarity masks deeper differences, however. The sugar candy in Mexico is in the shape of skulls, and most Americans probably find it distasteful to eat a skull because of the cultural avoidance of the subject of death. The underlying dissimilarity that might prove even more distasteful to some Americans, however, is the cultural belief of the Aztecs (who may have originated the celebration) that the dead are alive alongside the living. Conversely, Mexicans might look with disapproval on Americans who visit cemeteries only on a military holiday rather than for a family holiday or picnic. In this case crosscultural comparisons that are used to deepen understanding should not be avoided when the issues become tinged with deeper emotion.

One way of comparing cultures in depth using crosscultural psychology is through a unit on mandala design across cultures. Beginning with José and Miriam Argüelles' book *Mandala* (1972) as a source, lessons examine Crete's myth of the labyrinth and the Minotaur; Central American pre-Columbian circle motifs, Tibetan Buddhist yantra and meditation designs, the interwoven tracery of Celtic dragons and sacred trees, and the Japanese circle designs displayed on family crests. Moving back and forth from design to explanation uses visual import to support the language learning that takes place through this rich input.

Teaching Crosscultural Content

Crosscultural differences in greeting, complimenting, and showing appreciation are the bases for Nam's (2001) instructional unit on comparing customs in Korea and the United States. She uses a list of "dos" and "don'ts" as an acculturation strategy to get students talking about cultural differences. She also presents the concept of high-context culture and low-context culture (see Buckley, 2000) as a means of focusing the discussion on fundamental principles of crosscultural contrast. Key vocabulary words in this unit are such terms as "higher status," "modest and humble," "disrespectful," and "make eye contact." Nam then presents two dialogues, one in which a teacher who is a native speaker of English tries unsuccessfully to compliment a Korean student, and one in which the interaction appears to be more successful. Students complete a work sheet using a comparison circle diagram (see Chapter 5) to articulate the differences between the two dialogues; the instructor then presents a dialogue analysis that points out the cultural differences, which students discuss. This plan demonstrates the use of crosscultural comparison not only to teach English but also to compare the target and native cultures.

Using Intercultural Communication to Teach English

Classes of English learners that involve students from a variety of countries offer the opportunity to have the students communicate with one another in structured class activities. Almost any game or activity is valuable if it helps students to share their beliefs, values, and conceptions about the world.

⬥ **STRATEGY 9.6:** Use intercultural communication to teach English

Beyond Superficial Communication

A favorite activity on Valentine's Day in the American Culture and Language Program at California State University, San Bernardino, is the Language of Love game (MacKay, 2000). Using the game board provided, players take turns rolling dice, moving their token around the playing board, and drawing cards with questions that they must answer in the group (or they can pass). Sample questions are featured in Box 9.8. These questions create a deeper level of intercultural communication, involving sharing of values and personal anecdotes.

Intercultural Conflict

Occasionally, interaction occurs that is not so much fun: interethnic conflict. Should this occur, techniques exist for problem solving through carefully planned intervention. First, teachers can intervene in the early stages of conflicts to defuse the problem by talking to students privately, encouraging the sharing of perceptions on volatile issues, and communicating expectations that students will he able to resolve their differences. In this way, teachers allow students to vent their feelings as a group and provide a brief period of controlled verbal expression that can serve as an outlet for frustration. A teacher must resolve to be calm and should not tolerate violence or personal attacks. The most proactive stance is to modify the classroom learning envi-

BOX 9.8
❖ Sample Questions from "The Love Game"

Category	Sample Questions
About You	Do you think it's OK for a girl to ask a boy for a date?
Cultural Question	What kinds of things do people do on a first date in your country?
	How do people meet other people in your country?
New Expressions and Idioms	What does "to go steady" or "to go with someone" mean?
	What does "to be stood up" mean?

Source: MacKay, 2000.

ronment to include a variety of cultural content and to make provisions for varied learning approaches (Díaz-Rico, 2000).

In summary, cultural studies are a rich and rewarding part of educating English learners, whether students are learning about American culture from a distance or learning about their host culture as immigrants to an English-speaking country. Teachers of English learners play an integral role in the success of their students. In effect, the teacher is the gatekeeper for academic success, serving as an everyday implementer of social policies and values.

In order for prospective teachers to accept the work of achieving equity in education, they must at some point examine their own complicity in the privilege of being a native speaker of a colonial language. To sustain professional lives committed to ideals of multicultural equity and private lives enriched by intercultural participation, individuals must be able to interact with speakers of the native language using dimensions of intercultural understanding. It is useful for prospective teachers of English learners to use tools like the ethnographic case study to obtain rich, descriptive data about the contexts, activities, and beliefs of diverse community members.

Overall, instructors who can "teach with a difference" are the best cultural ambassadors. Infusing the domains of intercultural communication and cultural study into the education of English learners has the potential of strengthening the capacity of educators to prepare diverse students to be strong, caring, contributing community members in the cultures of the future.

Discourse in the Classrooms of English Learners

You must know who is the object and who is the subject of a sentence in order to know if you are the object or the subject of history. If you can't control a sentence you don't know how to put yourself in history, to trace your own origin in the country, to vocalize, to use your voice.

Nelida Piñon (in Aronowitz & Giroux, 1991, p. 114)

What Is Classroom Discourse?

Discourse analysis can be defined as the analysis of language "beyond the sentence" (Tannen, 2001). A discourse might be characterized as "a language form associated with a particular activity, a particular kind of knowledge, a particular group of people or a particular institution" (Peim, 1993, p. 37). The study of discourse looks at language in its larger units, such as oral text (classroom talk, speeches, casual conversation) and written text (magazine articles, school assignments, signs and posters). Discourse specialists have looked at such behavior as how people take turns, how speakers use contextual cues as they interact, and how people show others they are listening. These features are heavily influenced by culture. Educators who understand how culture affects schooling can help English learners to adapt to new patterns of language use.

❖ **MEGASTRATEGY 10:** Understand cultural patterns of instruction

Linguists who analyze classroom discourse, the language that is used in teaching and learning, note that schooling in some ways sounds like everyday life yet in other ways has its own peculiar patterns of interaction. This chapter has two goals. The first is to understand the ways in which schools use language separately from the experience of everyday life, exploring in the process how this separation (which is powerful, inevitable, and potentially positive) can work to the benefit of English learners. The second is to ask how educators can affirm the voices that students bring to school. Teachers of English learners are gifted with the marginality of the profession. The next step is to take full advantage of English teaching as a border pedagogy.

Language Teachers at the Edge

In a surprising sense, at the beginning of the twenty-first century we have all become second-language learners. The various discourses that are circulating keep us all on edge. This "edge," or boundary, appeared in the discourse of Los Angeles early in the 1990s, when people began to use "edgy" as a complimentary term meaning that a person was somehow interesting, complicated, and unpredictable but still socially acceptable. The "edge" surfaced in New York City as the boundary around Ground Zero beyond which only rescue workers could pass. The "edge" in nature is the growing tip of the root where growth is possible. If possible, this is where the expert educator works, at the edge where learning takes place, a social and cultural border that functions as a horizon of opportunity.

> Central to the notion of border pedagogy are a number of important pedagogical issues regarding the role that teachers might play at the interface of modern and postmodern concerns . . . the concept of border pedagogy suggests that teachers exist within social, political, and cultural boundaries, which are both multiple and historical in nature. . . . As part of the process of developing a pedagogy of difference, teachers need to deal with the plethora of voices . . . that constitute any course, class, or curriculum, so as to make problematic not only the stories that give meanings to the lives of their students but also the ethical and political lineaments that inform their students' subjectivities and identities. (Aronowitz & Giroux, 1991, p. 130)

The Language and Culture of Schooling

Culture is constantly changing and accumulates based on individuals' past experiences. When someone learns a foreign language, the culture acts as a guide to the way people think, feel, and act. Culture aids in understanding not only daily life but also the ways in which people bring meaning and joy, creativity and enrichment to this daily life. Ideally, the language used in school promotes this sense of meaning.

⬥ **STRATEGY 10.1**: Understand the role of language and culture in instruction

Schooling is an enterprise in which people use language to express their culture. Schooling involves cultural indoctrination, the reinforcement and refinement of cultural expression. The language of schooling is one element in a whole set of discursive practices that shape behavior and remind the student that society is serious about participation. Nonverbal signals reinforce this message: most school buildings are huge compared to homes; surfaces are hard, official flags wave, and shrill bells ring. Given these practices, how can the language of schooling function as a tool of improvement?

Classroom discourse is a special type of conversation. Conversation is an enterprise in which one person speaks and another listens. Intonation, pausing, and phrasing determine when one person's turn is over and the next person's turn begins. Markers signal the circulation of power. As Foucault (1979) noted, discursive practices in the modern world prepare the individual for power. Schooling can shape an average person into a "good" student using discourse. The postmodern shift has allowed teachers for the first time to use the power of language knowingly and equitably.

Good language learners are able to gain access to a variety of conversations in their communities rather than simply to acquire or control a variety of linguistic forms and meanings (Norton & Toohey, 2001). The communities of practice (Lave & Wenger, 1991) in which they participate, even peripherally, provide access to the utterances of others and the cultural practices they need to become engaged in community life. This means that the community of practice in a classroom does more to create a good learner than the individual's cognition and striving.

Linguistic Features of Classroom Discourse

Linguistic features are useful ways to examine classroom discourse. Speaking is signaled by turn markers that govern who takes the floor, but listenership too may be signaled in different ways. Some speakers expect frequent nodding, and some kind of listener feedback such as "hmm," "uhuh," and "yeah." In a room full of people, one might expect listening to be signaled by eye contact. The type of listener response a speaker gets can change the presentation: If someone seems uninterested or uncomprehending (whether or not they truly are), the speaker tends to slow down, repeat, or overexplain, giving the impression of "talking down."

Discourse is classified using four dimensions. One dimension is *written versus spoken*; another is *register* (formal ↔ informal); a third is *genre* (a combination of communicative purpose, audience, and format); the fourth is *monologic*, *dialogic*, or *multiparty* (how many are involved) (Celce-Murcia & Olshtain, 2000). Many kinds of analysis have been applied to the study of discourse: studies of information structure, coherence, cohesion, turn taking, and critical language analysis. This chapter focuses on the educational anthropologists' look at patterns of discourse, as well as on cognitive academic language proficiency and its incorporation into instruction.

What Discourse Genres Are Common in U.S. Classrooms?

Chapter 3 provided an introduction to communicative competence theory and looked at the social functions of language. The seven categories of language function outlined

Classroom discourse patterns involve students as active language users.

by Halliday (1978) are *instrumental* (manipulating the environment to cause certain events to happen), *regulatory* (controlling events or the behavior of others), *representational* (communicating information), *interactional* (maintaining social communication), *personal* (expressing feelings and emotions), *heuristic* (acquiring knowledge), and *imaginative* (creating a world freed from the boundaries of everyday).

A curriculum might encourage students to perform a wide variety of verbal functions such as reporting, evaluating, questioning, and critiquing. Many other functions are not necessarily encouraged by schools but take place in schools nonetheless: interrupting, shifting the blame, threatening, accusing, arguing, demanding, and making excuses. Learners must acquire written as well as spoken competence in the effort to match forms with functions.

Academic language functions, which supplement these social functions, include explaining, informing, justifying, comparing, describing, proving, debating, and so on. Since accomplishing these functions successfully with academic content requires the use of thinking skills, there is some overlap in the terminology of academic functions and thinking skills. Chamot & O'Malley (1994) listed and described these functions.

Academic English, also called cognitive academic language proficiency (CALP), is designed for abstract, decontextualized performance across a variety of content domains. Students acquire this level of proficiency in English only after a long period of successful schooling; exposure to academic language; feedback and support in its use; and explicit instruction in vocabulary, morphology, syntax, and cognitive strategies. TESOL's Statement on the Acquisition of Academic Proficiency in English reaffirms the importance of CALP: "In the past decade, research has shown that content-based instruction that focuses on the development of academic language proficiency is critical in school. LEP students are expected to learn academic content in English in order to compete academically with their native-English speaking peers." (TESOL, 2002).

Academic genres of discourse are academic functions within content areas. This chapter looks at discourse patterns to see how these are used to foster academic English.

◆ **STRATEGY 10.2:** Understand typical American classroom instructional patterns

The Recitation Pattern: A Typical Learning Encounter

Classrooms in the United States often follow a model of instruction based upon what Mehan (1979) labeled "recitation." Typically, the pattern falls into three parts, called the IRE sequence. First, the teacher invites (I) an interaction by asking a question; a student responds (R), and the teacher follows with evaluation (E). Alternatively, this may be called the IRF pattern if the term "evaluation" is replaced by the term "feedback." "Feedback" is a more accurate term, because this step involves not only praise or disguised evaluation but also reformulation, repetition of the student's answer, and a summary or delivery of information.

The IRF pattern shares characteristics of other kinds of teacher talk. The teacher not only produces the most language but also takes the most turns. Questions asked in this way usually call for simple information recall, and the responses are limited to this type of thinking. The teacher tends to ask "known answer" questions in which students' responses can be easily evaluated (Pridham, 2001). The IRF pattern is easy to identify, partially because of its prevalence.

Invitation to respond:

> TEACHER: "Who knows why names are capitalized?" (Some students are wildly waving their hands, begging to be chosen to respond; others are averting their eyes, hoping *not* to be called on) José?

Response:

> JOSÉ: It's somebody's name.

Evaluation, or Feedback:

> TEACHER: That's true. Good, José.

Invitation to respond: (pattern repeats)

> TEACHER: But who can tell me what the term for that is?

Sociohistorical Features of the Recitation Pattern

The IRF pattern may have become dominant in American classrooms because it matches deep-seated discourse habits of the mainstream culture. Some evidence of this exists in Heath's *Ways with Words* (1983b), an ethnographic study of two communities in the rural South conducted approximately in the 1970s. One community, which Heath called Roadville, is white and working class, while the other, Trackton, is African American. Heath described ways in which Roadville home-language practices patterned the discourse of white teachers in schools. Despite the fact that few mainstream teachers are raised in communities exactly like Roadville, the IRF is highly consonant with language patterns that Heath identified in Roadville homes.

For example, Heath detailed a typical question put to a Roadville child: "What color is that?" (p. 251). This pattern, which Heath calls *display knowledge*, follows an underlying Roadville discourse value: People respond when called upon by others to talk. Corollary principles are that children respond when called upon by adults to talk and that, in the company of adults, children speak only when called upon. One can see immediately the carry-over to the recitation pattern: In class, a student waits to be called upon, and when called upon, the good student is ready with the answer.

The IRF is not the only discourse pattern in which the teacher dominates. In *teacher-fronted* classrooms in general (Harel, 1992), the teacher takes the central role in controlling the flow of information, and students compete for the teacher's attention and for permission to speak. In such classrooms English learners are dependent on their ability to understand the teacher's explanations and directions. The IRF is the dominant pattern in American classrooms, but traditional educational contexts around the world feature their own versions of teacher-dominated talk. Although this chapter focuses on the IRF pattern, the suggestions that follow for altering this reliance on teacher talk may hold good for other types of teacher-fronted discourse.

Instructional Features of the Recitation Pattern

The recitation pattern has shown great persistence in American schools. Clearly, the IRF pattern has positive instructional features. It is often used to activate students' prior knowledge about a topic, to review material already covered, and to present new information. Teachers often use the IRF as a calming and control device, as a way of checking on the general state of group knowledge on a topic, and of evaluating the discipline and cooperation of individual students. This evaluation of the student seems to shape a teacher's academic expectations for that student. Table 10.1 shows features of the recitation pattern that work for the benefit of instruction.

Recitation Pattern: Critique

Despite its persistence, the recitation pattern is not successful for all students. Tables 10.2, 10.3, and 10.4 detail the ways in which the IRF pattern may inhibit learning for English learners. Table 10.2 looks at the Invitation to bid, Table 10.3 examines the Response turn, and Table 10.4 shows the Feedback part of the pattern.

Recitation Pattern: Questioning Strategies

Questions are a staple in American classrooms, and it is generally through skilled questioning that teachers lead discussions and ascertain students' understanding. Questions should be framed relative to the students' proficiency levels, the sociocultural aspects of displaying knowledge, and the level of critical thinking sought in the response.

A linguistic hierarchy of question types can be matched to proficiency levels. For students in the "silent period," a question requiring a nonverbal response—a head movement, pointing, manipulating materials—will elicit an appropriate and satisfactory answer. Once students are beginning to speak, "either/or" questions provide the necessary terms, and the student needs merely to choose the correct word or phrase to demonstrate understanding: "Does the water expand or contract to form ice?" "Did Russians come to California from the west or the north?" Once students are more comfortable in producing language, *wh-* questions are appropriate: "What is happening to the water?" "Which countries sent explorers to California?" "What was the purpose of their exploration?"

Teachers who are sensitive to varying cultural styles are aware that in some cultures students are reluctant to display knowledge before a large group. They will take care to organize other means for students to demonstrate language and content knowledge, such as small-group discussions.

If a teacher is seeking evaluative responses requiring critical thinking by means of questioning strategies, more wait time is necessary for students to understand the question and frame a thoughtful response. Bias is avoided if all respondents are given equal feedback and support in increasing the cognitive complexity of the answer.

Whether or not they use the IRF as a "default" discourse pattern, teachers of English learners cannot help using teacher-fronted discourse patterns to some extent, because of the legacy of traditional teaching discourse. However, awareness of its strengths (ease of use, usefulness in controlling attention and behavior, and diagnosis of learner's responsiveness) and weaknesses (limited learner oral production, limited peer interaction, and inequity of reinforcement) may encourage teachers to limit the use of teacher-fronted discourse in teaching English.

TABLE 10.1 • Instructional Benefits of the Recitation Pattern

Discourse Feature	Benefit to Instruction
Invitation to bid	Teacher waits for silence and imposes order on student behavior.
	Teacher controls the scope of the lesson by asking selected questions.
	Teacher determines order and importance of information by posing questions.
	Teacher controls the level of language displayed in class by choice of lexicon and complexity of sentence structure.
	Teacher controls pace and rhythm of discourse.
Response	Teacher evaluates behavior of individuals by looking to see who is willing and ready to participate.
	Teacher controls potential for reward by choosing respondent.
	By acting eager to answer, students can demonstrate responsiveness to instruction, attention, and cooperation—even if they do not really know the answer that the teacher expects to hear.
	Teacher controls behavior by calling upon students who may not be attentive.
	Students can practice risk taking by volunteering to answer.
	Students can show knowledge from prior instruction or experience.
Evaluation	Teacher is able to evaluate students' level of oral participation.
	Teacher is able to use teacher approval as a reinforcer.
	Teacher is able to establish public recognition for those who answer correctly.
	Teacher may use this stage to correct sentence grammar.
	Teacher can withhold negative evaluation by partially accepting an incomplete answer.
	Teacher can avoid direct negative evaluation by asking one student to "help" another to improve the answer.
	Teacher may evaluate students' success in the recitation pattern as an indicator of facility with "display knowledge" cultural pattern.
	Teacher can elaborate on answer and expand a concept by delivering direct instruction at this point.
	Teacher can improve a poor answer by substituting more accurate terminology or restating a sentence using correct grammar.
	As teacher evaluates students' responses, he or she determines what question comes next.
	Teacher rewards some students, for example, white boys (Sadker, Sadker, & Klein, 1991) by extending the response through corrective and thoughtful dialogue.
	Teacher rewards some students, for example compliant girls (Sadker & Sadker, 1986), for brief, exact responses that receive little extended feedback and correction.

TABLE 10.2 ◆ Instructional Shortcomings of the Recitation Pattern for English Learners (Discourse Feature: Invitation to Bid)

Beneficial Features in Mainstream Setting	Potential Shortcomings to Instruction for English Learners
Teacher waits for silence and imposes order on student behavior.	English learners may not appear as attentive as native-English speakers because they may have difficulty comprehending instructions.
Teacher determines order and importance of information by posing questions.	English learners may need more time than native-English speakers to understand questions and frame responses.
Teacher controls the scope of the lesson by asking selected questions.	Students with creative and individualistic thinking may wish to contribute related ideas outside the scope of the immediate topic.
Teacher controls the level of language displayed in class by choice of lexicon and complexity of sentence structure.	Instructional language, including vocabulary, may be too complex for English learners.
Teacher controls pace and rhythm of discourse.	Pace and rhythm of discourse may be different in students' native language, causing discomfort.

TABLE 10.3 ◆ Instructional Shortcomings of the Recitation Pattern for English Learners (Discourse Feature: Response)

Beneficial Features in Mainstream Setting	Potential Shortcomings to Instruction for English Learners
Teacher evaluates behavior of individuals by looking to see who is willing and ready to participate. Teacher controls potential for reward by choosing respondent.	English learners may be reluctant to bring attention to themselves, because they either feel insecure about their oral language, see such an action as incompatible with group cohesiveness and cultural norms, or are reluctant to display knowledge in front of others.
By acting eager to answer, students can demonstrate responsiveness to instruction, attention, and cooperation—even if they do not really know the answer that the teacher expects to hear.	
Students can show knowledge from prior instruction or experience.	Students may lack experience in particular topics under discussion, although their background may be rich in topics that are not curriculum-related.
Teacher controls behavior by calling upon students who may not be attentive.	Students from cultures in which children do not make direct eye contact with adults may not appear attentive during instruction.
Students can practice risk taking by volunteering to answer.	English learners may be reluctant to volunteer to answer if they are not 100 percent sure their idea is correct if their culture does not reward ambiguity.

TABLE 10.4 ✦ Instructional Shortcomings of the Recitation Pattern
for English Learners (Discourse Feature: Evaluation)

Features that May Be Beneficial for Mainstream Students	Potential Shortcomings to Instruction for English Learners
Teacher is able to evaluate students' level of oral participation.	Students may need prior language development in oral participation, including turn taking, listening, and speaking.
Teacher is able to use teacher approval as a reinforcer.	Students from certain cultures may not depend on teacher for approval.
Teacher is able to establish public recognition for those who answer correctly.	Individual public recognition may be a taboo in some cultures.
Teacher may use this stage to correct sentence grammar.	Research shows that second-language grammar is improved not by public correction of poor grammar, but rather by gradual acquisition of forms during language input and output.
Teacher can withhold negative evaluation by partially accepting an incomplete answer.	Indirect negative evaluation may be confusing for some students, leaving them with unclear concept formation.
Teacher can avoid direct negative evaluation by asking one student to "help" another to improve the answer.	
Teacher may evaluate students' success in the recitation pattern as an indicator of facility with "display knowledge" cultural pattern.	Students who are unfamiliar with the "display knowledge" cultural pattern may appear uncooperative.
Teacher can elaborate on an answer and expand a concept by delivering direct instruction at this point.	
Teacher can improve a poor answer by substituting more accurate terminology or restating a sentence using correct grammar.	
As teacher evaluates students' responses, he or she determines what question comes next.	

> ❖ Tactics for teachers to use to avoid overreliance on the teacher-fronted discourse:
>
> ◆ Use performance-based instruction to stipulate desirable language-learning goals.
> ◆ Use task chains to plan a variety of learner activities to accomplish language-learning goals.
> ◆ Use guided practice activities that strengthen the frequency of students' oral language production.

Cooperative Learning as an Alternative Pattern

The way discourse is organized is important for language acquisition in content classes. In contrast, classrooms that feature flexible grouping patterns and cooperative learning permit students greater access to the flow of information as they talk and listen to their peers, interact with the teacher or other adult in small groups, and use their home language for clarification purposes (see Wells, 1981).

In such classrooms, the style of teacher talk often changes: Teachers assist students with the learning task rather than providing error correction; they give fewer commands; and they impose less disciplinary control (Harel, 1992). The teacher orchestrates tasks so that students use language in academic ways. Students are placed in different groups for different activities. Teachers work with small groups to achieve specific instructional objectives (e.g., literature response groups, as discussed in Chapter 6, or instructional conversations, discussed below).

The Instructional Conversation (IC) as a Discourse Alternative

A collaborative team of teachers and researchers used Vygotsky's construct of the zone of proximal development to create the IC instructional discourse format. With a group of six to eight students in a circle of chairs, the teacher acts as a discussion leader, following up a literature reading (or a science, social studies, or math lesson) with a directed conversation that explores the focus of the lesson or invites a deeper understanding of the issues raised (Tharp & Gallimore, 1991). The smaller group size, as well as provision for assisted understanding of complex ideas, concepts, and texts, permits a more satisfying, interdependent intellectual relationship between teacher and students (see Chapter 6).

IC is not a "rap session" but a semistructured group discussion. The teacher selects a theme based on the ideas presented in the literature or content in question and permits open-ended but focused exploration. Students' prior knowledge is activated by the teacher during discussion or, if lacking, is quickly supplied by the teacher as direct instruction as the conversation progresses. Throughout the discussion the teacher draws out the participants, supporting the development of complex thinking and ensuring that statements made are supported by facts or texts (Goldenberg & Gallimore, 1991).

IC remains at its core a conversation. Participants take turns in a connected discourse in which, ideally, the leader has no more than 20 percent of the total talk (Díaz-Rico, 1994). The leader avoids "known answer" questions, using the students' own ideas as opportunities for follow-up turns. Overall, the atmosphere is challenging but not threatening. All turns are self-selected. If a participant does not volunteer a turn, the leader may take the student aside after the discussion for specific reminders and encouragement on how to obtain a turn. This is particularly important for nonnative speakers of English in a heterogeneous group with native English-speakers, who usually need to be reminded to talk less and listen more.

How can a teacher talk with eight students and leave the rest of the class unattended? An instructional aide or parent volunteer can supervise other language development centers and activities while the instructional conversation proceeds. Many teachers find that the increased attention paid to the assisted thinking of students reaps great benefit, not only in teachers' increased understanding of students' thought processes, ideas, and depth but also, unexpectedly, in improved classroom discipline and students' sense of instructional co-ownership.

Creating a Community of Scholarship with Instructional Conversations in a Transitional Bilingual Classroom (Patthey-Chavez, Clark, & Gallimore, 1995) and

Class discussion formats which mix native and non-native speakers of English must ensure that non-native speakers receive equal opportunities to speak.

Enacting Instructional Conversation with Spanish-Speaking Students in Middle School Mathematics (Dalton & Sison, 1995) are two articles about ICs, both available on the Internet (www.crede.uscs.edu), that provide both information about, and actual transcripts of, ICs.

Learning to manage and appreciate the IC takes time. A cognitively demanding activity, it challenges the teacher to become a conversational partner. The most difficult components for most teachers are learning to keep silent and let students think and volunteer their thoughts in good time, moving the conversation forward by building on students' ideas rather than the teacher's, selecting topics that students find genuinely interesting and comprehensible, and having the patience to listen as English learners' struggle to find the words for their thoughts. However, the rewards are great; a satisfying IC is an event for which, deep down, every good teacher yearns.

❖ **Tactics for teachers to use the instructional conversation (from Center for Research on Education, Diversity, and Excellence [CREDE], 1999):**

- ◆ Arrange the classroom to accommodate conversation between the teacher and a small group of students according to a regular and frequent schedule.
- ◆ Have a clear academic goal that guides conversation with students.
- ◆ Ensure that student talk occurs at higher rates than teacher talk and that all students are included in the conversation according to their preferences.
- ◆ Guide conversation to include students' views, judgments, and rationales, using text evidence and other substantive support.
- ◆ Listen carefully to assess levels of students' understanding.
- ◆ Assist students' learning throughout the conversation by questioning, restating, praising, encouraging, and so forth.

Cognitive Academic Language Proficiency

During the elementary school years, and even more so throughout middle and high school, students need to acquire a completely new kind of scholastic language. In contrast to Basic Interpersonal Communication Skills (BICS), the language used for social interaction and early school adjustment, CALP comprises academic language, is a highly complex set of language functions required for access to, and success in, the core curriculum. BICS and CALP overlap, with more complicated social language useful for cooperative learning and teamwork. Conversational skills have been found to approach nativelike levels within two years of exposure to English, but five or more years may be required for minority students to match native speakers in CALP (Collier, 1987; Cummins, 1981a; Hakuta, Butler & Witt, 2000). Students need skills in both kinds of language.

* **STRATEGY 10.3:** Promote the learner's use of cognitive academic language

CALP is the language needed to perform school tasks, which are often abstract and decontextualized. Students must rely primarily on language to attain meaning, especially reading and writing. Cummins (1984) calls CALP *context-reduced* communication, because there are few concrete cues to assist comprehension.

The Language of Thought

Beyond words, CALP also involves systematic thought processes. It provides the human brain with necessary tools to systematically categorize, compare, analyze, and accommodate new experiences. One cannot separate words from knowledge or learning; it is not possible to say that one understands a topic but does not understand the terminology. CALP represents the cognitive toolbox needed to encode and decode this thought. CALP is key to acquiring the in-depth knowledge that characterizes the well-educated individual in a complex modern society.

Academic language features specific linguistic functions such as persuading, arguing, and hypothesizing. Accurate use of grammar and precise differentiation of word meaning are increasingly important. CALP requires a transition from the simple *use* of language to the more complex ability to *think and talk about* language, that is, metalinguistic awareness (Scarcella & Rumberger, 2000). This takes place against a background of prior knowledge, a gradual accumulation of cultural capital that helps language users to understand the cultural and social uses of the language to which they are exposed. CALP is not gained entirely from either school or the home; one reinforces the other. Teachers who find ways for students' families to support CALP are able to expand those students' chances of academic success.

CALP requires complex growth in many linguistic areas simultaneously. This growth is highly dependent on the assistance of teachers, because for the most part CALP is learned in school. The complexity of CALP can be captured by examination of the five Cs: *c*onceptualization, *c*omplexity, *c*ontext, *c*ulture, and *c*ommunication (see Table 10.5). Many CALP skills are refinements of BICS, while others are more exclusively school centered.

TABLE 10.5 ◆ Components of Cognitive Academic Language Proficiency (from Díaz-Rico & Weed, 2002)

Component	Explanation
Communication	Reading: increases speed; uses context cues to guess vocabulary meaning; masters a variety of genres in fiction (poetry, short story) and nonfiction (encyclopedias, magazines, Internet sources); able to "read the world" (interpret comics, print advertising, road signs)
	Listening: follows verbal instructions; interprets nuances of intonation (e.g., in cases of teacher disciplinary warnings); solicits, and profits from, help of peers
	Speaking: gives oral presentations, answers correctly in class, and reads aloud smoothly
	Writing: uses conventions such as spelling, punctuation, report formats
Conceptualization	Concepts become abstract and are expressed in longer words with more general meaning (*rain* becomes *precipitation*).
	Concepts fit into larger theories (*precipitation* cycle).
	Concepts fit into hierarchies (rain → precipitation cycle → weather systems → climate).
	Concepts are finely differentiated from similar concepts (*sleet* from *hail*, *typhoons* from *hurricanes*).
	Conceptual relations become important (opposites, subsets, causality, correlation).
Critical thinking	Uses graphic organizers to represent the structure of thought (comparison charts, Venn diagrams, time lines, "spider" charts)
	Uses textual structures (outlines, paragraphing, titles, main idea)
	Uses symbolic representation: (math operators [<, >, +, =]; proofreading marks, grade indications [10/20 points, etc.])
	Reads between the lines (inference)
	Employs many other kinds of critical thinking
	Plans activities; monitors progress; evaluates results; employs self-knowledge (metacognition)
	Increases variety and efficiency in use of learning strategies
Context	Nonverbal: uses appropriate gestures (and is able to refrain from inappropriate ones); interprets nonverbal signs accurately
	Formality: behaves formally when required to do so
	Participation structures: fits in smoothly to classroom and schoolwide groups and procedures
Culture	Draws on experience in mainstream culture (background knowledge)
	Uses social class markers, such as "manners"
	Moves smoothly between home and school
	Marshals and controls parental support for school achievement
	Deploys primary-language resources when required
	Maintains uninterrupted primary-culture profile ("fits in" with neighborhood social structures)
	Develops and sustains supportive peer interactions

Source: Díaz-Rico & Weed, 2002.

The Teacher's Role in Promoting CALP

Teachers can promote the use of CALP by ensuring that students understand and use the vocabulary of specific subjects. When comparing two numbers, a teacher might ask, "Which number is greater?" The term "greater than" is specific to mathematics, because it eventually corresponds to the symbol ">"; "bigger" as a synonym is therefore not as useful. Teachers may encourage English learners to repeat a term to themselves for practice. Keeping a personal glossary of terms used academically is also useful for all students. In order not to single out English learners, the teacher should not require them to repeat phrases aloud in front of other students.

Some teachers confuse the terms BICS and CALP with correct versus incorrect usage of English. CALP is *not* just BICS that uses complete, grammatical sentences. Teachers further the acquisition of CALP by analyzing the conceptual and critical thinking requirements of the grade-level curriculum *and* taking the time to ensure that all students are explicitly taught such requirements. Good teachers use CALP with their students; excellent teachers ensure that students can use CALP themselves.

Without explicit attention to teaching CALP, one of three outcomes is all too common. First, educational "haves" prosper academically, whereas "have nots" do not. Those students who come to school already having acquired CALP as a benefit of a privileged home environment can draw on this prior knowledge, but English learners may lack this ability. Second, the curriculum for English learners may be watered down, on the assumption that those who lack CALP cannot perform academically at a high cognitive level. Third, the acquisition of CALP is heavily implicated in the type of participatory structure established in the classroom. Students lacking CALP in English are not able to participate knowledgeably in the IRF and are often instead given a skills-based, direct-instruction approach that does not encourage a constructivist learning environment.

Discourse That Affirms Students' Voices

Throughout this book we have emphasized the participation of the learner in learning. Classroom discourse will always be somewhat constrained, if not stilted, if the goal of discourse is to accomplish an agenda that is solely the teacher's. It is therefore imperative that teachers situate their practice in the language needed and desired by the student. If that desire does not exist, teachers must evoke those emotions and motivations as an integral part of instruction. Instruction, that is not meaningful and motivating to the learner, particularly in a second language, becomes empty.

♦ **STRATEGY 10.4:** Help the learner to construct meaning

What kind of participation enhances motivation and promotes acquisition? *Co-construction of meaning* permits the learner to plan, choose, and evaluate knowledge in relation to personal needs and goals. *Communities of practice* are local. Knowledge in the community sustains and reinforces classroom learning. The school and families must work together to extend academic discourse into the home.

Every community has a distinct kind of discourse into which children are socialized. *Participatory genres* help the student to bridge the home-school divide. The "talk-story" of Hawaiian culture, when brought into the classroom, opened up the discourse around reading (Jordan, Tharp, & Baird-Vogt, 1992). Philips (1972) found patterns and behaviors among Native American students in Warm Springs that differed in key ways from mainstream culture and was able to help teachers adapt instruction to meet students' needs. For example, the Native American students in Warm Springs were reluctant to volunteer or be singled out of a large group for individual praise, but in peer groups were they became willing to take major responsibility for group projects. By working in acknowledgment of, rather than at cross-purposes with, these community patterns of discourse, teachers can successfully modify teacher-fronted discourse for a particular group of learners.

In summary, teachers can use the tools of ethnography and community participation to learn what it means to have meaning, and how to help the learner gain that meaning through English-language instruction. A study of how the community uses discourse can help teachers to pattern their classroom activities in ways that increase the likelihood that students' English proficiency will grow.

Dual-Language Proficiency

Gadda ge. Dankie. Hioy'oy. Ghu long khu me-ah. Ju falem nderit. Amesegënallô. Shukran. Barak llahu fik. Merci. Mesi. Sag olun. Matur suksme. Nitsíniiyi'taki.

When I hear anyone state, "I can speak twelve languages" it always makes me wonder, "How much do people have to know in a language before they can say they can "speak" it? For example, if I say "thank you" in twelve languages—see above, and see Runner (2000) for more words in many languages—that does not mean I can "speak" twelve languages. How many people can say they are truly fluent in more than one language? On what level of proficiency is this based?

In many parts of the world, people undergo schooling in a language that is not their mother tongue because of government mandates, colonial legacies, or social pressure. For example, in the United States educators expect immigrants to function well in English before they graduate from high school. In Canada and elsewhere, the ability to read and write in two languages is encouraged. This chapter concerns the education of English learners in the context of bilingual programs, with an emphasis on programs that foster dual-language academic proficiency, what Cook (1999, p. 190) calls *multicompetent language use*.

❖ **MEGASTRATEGY 11:** Develop cognitive academic language proficiency in two languages

Why Dual-Language Acquisition?

Most of the world's population is bilingual or multilingual; only a minority of the world's peoples speak a single language. Each of the world's nations has groups of individuals living within its borders who use other languages in addition to the national language to function in their everyday lives (Valdés, 2001). The term *bilingual* means able to function in two languages, not necessarily as well in reading and writing as in speaking and listening. Although it is the case that some bilingual speakers possess very high levels of proficiency in both written and oral modes, others display varying degrees of proficiency in comprehension and/or speaking skills along a continuum, depending on how they use their two languages.

Bilingual individuals experience cognitive and linguistic advantages when compared to monolingual, performing better on tests of divergent thinking, pattern recognition, problem solving, and metalinguistic awareness (Cenoz & Genesee, 1998). Peal and Lambert (1962) found that highly bilingual ten-year-olds performed significantly better than their monolingual English-speaking peers in fifteen of eighteen activities associated with intelligence. Knowing a second language often opens doors into other cultures, leading to understanding of cultural differences and providing opportunities for intercultural communication. Proficiency in multiple languages is also a career enhancement in the modern world of international commerce.

◆ **STRATEGY 11.1:** Support enriched education in dual-language programs

Bilingual Education and the Teaching of English

TESOL, Inc. has taken the position that bilingual education is the best approach to the education of minority-language students (TESOL, 1976, 1992). The 1992 statement recommends that bilingual programs incorporate the following facets:

- ◆ Comprehensive English as a second language instruction for linguistically diverse students that prepares them to handle content area material in English.
- ◆ Instruction in the content areas that is not only academically challenging, but also tailored to the linguistic proficiency, educational background, and academic needs of students.
- ◆ Opportunities for students to further develop and/or use their first language to promote academic and social development.
- ◆ Professional development for both ESOL and other classroom teachers that prepares them to facilitate the language and academic growth of linguistically and culturally different children. (p. 12)

Bilingual education, in its most basic form, incorporates three characteristics: (1) continued development of the primary language; (2) acquisition of a second language, usually English; and (3) instruction in the content areas (Ovando & Collier, 1998). A fourth characteristic is the promotion of self-esteem and pride in the primary culture. However, it is not always feasible to implement a bilingual program. When there are too few English learners to justify primary-language support, TESOL recommends monolingual instruction with an ESL component (TESOL, 1976, 1992).

Because provision of educational services to immigrants in general, and Spanish-speaking immigrants in particular, is a highly contested political issue in the United States, bilingual education is controversial (see Crawford, 1992). This controversy will continue into the future as Spanish-speakers surpass African Americans as the largest minority population in the United States. Teachers of English learners, who cannot avoid being a part of this conversation, have a proactive role to play in advocating for services (Cazden, 1986).

This chapter specifically promotes dual immersion as the preferred model for educating English learners. In many local contexts this approach may not be feasible. However, teachers who teach in other types of programs can use the dual-immersion model to compare this with their own program, noting the strengths and shortcomings of each model.

Submersion (Sink or Swim)

The default mode for educating English learners in American classrooms is submersion in mainstream classrooms in which no provisions are made for the language and academic needs of EL students. Students receive instruction in English, with English monolingualism as the goal. The associated social difficulties experienced by English learners in a majority-language classroom are not addressed. As a result, the strongest may survive or even succeed academically (they "swim"), but the majority do not have the cognitive and academic foundation in the primary language at the time of their education in English and thus do not attain the level of success educators might wish (they "sink"). In addition to being academically disabling, submersion denies students their rights under law:

> Submersion is not a legal option for schools with non-native-English speakers; however, oversight and enforcement are lax, and many smaller schools with low populations of NNS [non–native-speaking] students are simply unaware that they are required to provide some sort of services to these students. Parents of these children, for cultural and other reasons, tend not to demand the services their children are entitled to; thus it is not uncommon to find submersion in U.S. public schools. (Roberts, 1995, pp. 80–81)

Transitional Bilingual and Structured Immersion Programs

Before examining dual-language programs, a look at two other programs will provide a contrast. Transitional bilingual education (TBE) programs support the use of the students' home languages in academic settings only during the period in which they acquire enough English proficiency to make the transition into English-only education. This subtractive view of bilingualism in effect requires English learners to discontinue the use of their native language as they increase their fluency in English (Nieto, 1997). In these programs, students receive initial instruction in most, if not all, content areas in their home language while they are being taught English.

There are numerous problems with a TBE program. It may be perceived as a remedial program and/or another form of segregated, compensatory education. It rests on the common misconception that two or three years is sufficient time to learn a second language for schooling purposes, whereas in fact this is not long enough for students to build cognitive academic language proficiency (CALP) either in their native tongue or in English. As a consequence, they may not be able to carry out cognitively demanding tasks either in English or in their home language.

The following vignette illustrates the challenge in teaching reading in a transitional bilingual education classroom.

> In Ann García's fourth grade classroom at Chaparral Hills Elementary School in Moreno Valley, California, the ethnic makeup of the 27 children consists of 22 students of Hispanic heritage, 2 European Americans, 1 African American, and 2 children of European/African American mix. Of the 22 Hispanic students, 17 are proficient in Spanish speaking and listening, and 5 are not. Of the 17 who are fluent in Spanish listening and speaking, 8 read fluently in Spanish, 6 read with a more limited capacity, and 4 do not read in Spanish. These students have attained mixed proficiency in Spanish for a number of reasons, including lack of parental support for schooling in Spanish, mixed prior exposure to Spanish reading programs, and insufficient number of qualified bilingual teachers.

In this school district, as in others in California, students may attend Spanish instruction only by parental request. Students who do not speak English are expected to undergo one year of structured English immersion (SEI) and then enter a mainstream classroom. Most students make the transition from education in Spanish to education in English no later than the fourth grade.

Mrs. García has established six different reading groups to meet the needs of the students. The first group are Spanish readers whose skills are at the fourth-grade level in Spanish; the second group reads at the second-grade level in Spanish. The third, fourth, and fifth groups comprise those who are reading at the second, third, and fourth grades in English. The sixth "group" consists of one Spanish speaker without previous schooling whose Spanish reading is "emergent." This student requires the services of a tutor. Mrs. García continually changes the composition of the reading groups throughout the year, as some students begin to read in English and others move up to higher levels. By the end of the year, transition into English is complete, and there are no more Spanish reading groups.

Reflection reveals problems with this scenario. First, those students who are in the top reading group in Spanish are not receiving grade-level instruction in English. They must devote extra time to English to catch up to the English-only readers, who are at the same time moving forward to the next grade level in their reading. Second, after transition, the top students in Spanish are not the top students in reading and language arts overall, as the school's exclusive use of English favors the English-only students. Third, the fact that they cannot continue to learn in Spanish, a subject to which they have devoted three years, is a blow to students' motivation. Imagine an athlete who trained daily for three years, only to find out in the end that the sport had been canceled!

Another shortcoming of TBE is its effect on home-language use. After transition to English, conversational fluency in the home language tends to erode. Frequently, students switch English as their primary language of communication. Research evidence suggests that this retards rather than expedites academic progress in English (Dolson, 1985), primarily because children and parents lose the benefit of a shared language for such purposes as homework help. For these and other reasons, TBE programs have not led to school success for many students (see Medina & Escamilla, 1992).

The same drawbacks that can be identified in the TBE model also hold true for students in structured English immersion (SEI) programs, in which students are taught solely in English supplemented with SDAIE strategies (see Chapter 5). Although supporters of SEI programs equate increased time spent immersed in English with increased classroom learning, a key missing factor in this research is that the opportunity for dual-language proficiency is lost. Whereas foreign-language teaching is increasing in elementary classrooms in developed countries around the world, neither SEI nor TBE classrooms of English learners in the United States take advantage of the chance to support dual-language proficiency.

Program models for English learners vary widely across the United States. One could find children who speak English only and Spanish only mixed in a shared kindergarten class or a two-way-immersion first grade; a second- and third-grade combination class mixed with English-only students plus native Spanish-speakers who have had previous schooling either in a Spanish-language class or in TBE; a third-grade TBE class; and other combinations of learner, language, and curriculum, including an ESL resource room. Genesee (1987) profiled a two-way immersion program in Cincinnati, Ohio, that involved African American speakers of English. These models offer a variety of alternatives, with varying degrees of success.

Dual-Literacy Programs: An Introduction

Four kinds of educational programs promote the acquisition of English side by side with acquisition or maintenance of other languages. These are *developmental bilingual, second- or foreign-language immersion, two-way immersion,* and *EFL foreign-language partial immersion.* The last model, EFL partial immersion, is described in Sagliano and Greenfield's (1998) content-based liberal studies program in Japan (see Chapter 4).

Dual-literacy programs are also dual-oracy programs; the four language modes of speaking, listening, reading, and writing are promoted in two languages. These programs are distinguished from foreign-language programs, in which the target language is not used for content instruction.

Developmental Bilingual Programs in the United States

Also called *late-exit bilingual* and *maintenance bilingual education* (MBE), developmental bilingual programs are designed for students who enter school speaking a primary language other than English. The goal of these programs is for students to preserve and advance academic proficiency in their heritage language as they become proficient in English, leading to additive bilingualism. The major assumption in such a program is that bilingualism is a valuable asset, not only for bilingual individuals but also for society as a whole.

The goal of advancing dual-language skills has not always been the focus of bilingual education. When the federal government passed the Bilingual Education Act of 1968 (Title VII, an amendment to the 1965 Elementary and Secondary Education Act), the purpose was compensatory. Children who were unable to speak English were considered to be educationally disadvantaged, and federal aid to bilingual education was seen as a "remedial" program (Wiese & García, 1998). The focus shifted again in 1989, when MBE programs were expanded. Since that time, maintaining and developing the native language of students has become an important goal for advocates of bilingual education.

Developmental programs have been implemented mainly at the elementary level. They are rarely continued into the intermediate grades. The goals of developmental bilingual programs are maintenance and full development of the student's primary language; full proficiency in all aspects of English; grade-appropriate achievement in all domains of academic study; integration into wholly English-language classrooms; and positive identity regarding the culture of both the primary- and majority-language group (Cloud, Genesee, & Hamayan, 2000).

Two studies (Ramírez, 1992; Collier, 1992) have provided considerable support for the idea that students in MBE programs have greater academic success than students who are educated in SEI or TBE programs. According to the studies, students in MBE programs, who continue to receive academic instruction in a language they can understand, are able to keep up with English-speaking students. In contrast, students in the SEI or TBE programs over time fall further behind in academic subjects. These studies lend empirical support to additive bilingual models.

One challenge for developmental bilingual programs is to achieve an adequate balance between support for the native language and ESL instruction. Children in a developmental bilingual program may be served by "pull-out" ESL instruction (Soto, 1991). If this is the case, the ESL instructor should be qualified. A far better approach is English instruction within the classroom in an integrated biliteracy model.

A particularly compelling illustration of MBE programs is the education of Native Americans. There are seventy-four schools operated by Native American organizations under grants or contracts with the Bureau for Indian Affairs that place a high priority on cultural and linguistic preservation (Reyhner, 1992). The attempt to increase the number of speakers of Native American languages is sometimes called "restorative" bilingual education.

Second- and Foreign-Language Immersion Programs for Majority-Language Students

Second-language immersion, also called enrichment education, provides academic and language instruction in two languages. The goal of immersion programs is additive bilingualism. Many such programs are found in Canada, where English and French both have high status for instructional purposes. In this model middle-class, English-speaking children are instructed in French, and English is incorporated into the programs both as a subject and as a medium of instruction (Lambert, 1984). In the United States a comparable schooling context is some private schools exclusive to the upper class, in which foreign languages are highly valued, even to the extent of having instruction delivered directly in those languages. In early immersion programs, the second language is introduced in kindergarten or first grade. Early partial immersion uses English about 50 percent of the time rather than solely delivering academic instruction through the second language (Cloud, Genesee, & Hamayan, 2000).

The enrichment immersion model is inadequate for English learners in the United States because the low status of the students' primary language puts it at risk for suppression (Hernández-Chávez, 1984). When the minority language is not a high-status language, few middle-class, English-speaking parents will favor having their children immersed in it for instructional purposes.

Two-Way Immersion Programs for Majority-Language and Minority-Language Students

Two-way immersion (TWI) (also called *two-way maintenance bilingual*) groups English learners from a single language background in the same classroom with approximately equal numbers of English-speaking students. The curriculum is provided approximately at grade level in both languages. Speakers of each language develop proficiency in both their native and second language, achieve academically through and in two languages, and come to appreciate one another's languages and cultures (Lindholm, 1994). This method enhances the status of both primary languages, promoting self-esteem and increased cultural pride (Lindholm, 1992) and leading to increased motivation.

TWI programs had been implemented in 182 schools in the United States by 1995 (Christian, Montone, Lindholm, & Carranza, 1997), and the number of schools is growing yearly. Sites are located in eighteen states ranging from Alaska to Florida, with the largest number in California and New York. Nearly all the schools (167) are Spanish-English in design, although other schools immerse students in Arabic, Cantonese, French, Japanese, Navajo, Portuguese, and Russian (with the other language in all cases being English). The grade levels served are predominantly K–6. Examples that follow focus on Spanish-English program designs.

Careful attention to a high-quality bilingual program in the context of primary-language maintenance is key to the success of TWI programs (Veeder & Tramutt, 2000). A highly successful dual-language program is operated by the Valley Center-Pauma Joint Unified School District in California (further information about this program is available at www.cal.org/db/2way/). In addition, the National Clearinghouse for English Language Acquisition has a wealth of information about two-way programs (available at www.ncela.gwu.edu).

Transfer of Literacy.   TWI is predicated on beginning literacy instruction for students in both languages. But how are skills transferred from beginning literacy instruction in Spanish to that of English? Goldenberg (1990) found that beginning literacy instruction in Spanish made extensive use of phonics-based, sound/syllable approaches that were weaker in providing opportunities to read connected text. Edelsky (1986) described attempts to introduce a reading-and-writing approach in a bilingual program in Arizona that took a phonics approach to Spanish reading. Both Goldenberg and Edelsky have advocated a balanced approach to Spanish reading instruction in which children have many occasions to interact with meaningful text.

Reading in a foreign language above the level of emergent literacy takes place through the use of both literature and subject area content, following many of the same principles as reading in the native language. Time is given in class for reading, so that students working in groups can facilitate one another's comprehension. To appeal to students' varied interests, all types of content are used (magazines, newspapers, plays, novels, stories, and poems), depending also on the proficiency level of students and the level of language studied. In this way, students are assured of receiving a challenging academic program in both languages.

One advocate of TWI finds that this model promises "mutual learning, enrichment, and respect"; is "the best possible vehicle for integration of language minority students, since these students are grouped with English-speakers for natural and equal exchange of skills"; and is "particularly appealing because it not only enhances the prestige of the minority language but also offers a rich opportunity for expanding genuine bilingualism to the majority population" (Porter, 1990, p, 154). Cummins

(2000a) argued that "a major advantage of two-way bilingual programs . . . is that they overcome segregation in a planned program that aims to enrich the learning opportunities of both minority- and majority-language students" (p. 142).

Criticisms of TWI.   Critics have argued that TWI delays English learning and fails to teach English to English learners. Because TWI programs teach content in the primary language, they do not emphasize communication in English, as do TBE programs. Amselle (1999) argued that "dual immersion programs are really nothing more than Spanish immersion, with Hispanic children used as teaching tools for English-speaking children." Experts concede that the greatest challenge in two-way bilingual programs is to "reduce the gap" between the language abilities of the two groups (English learners and SLLs). This gap appears as content classes in English are modified (slowed down) for English learners to "catch up," or as content delivery in the primary language is slowed for Spanish-as-a-second-language students. As Molina (2000) advised, "Without a watchful approach to the quality of two-way programs, schools will find themselves tragically exploiting the English learners they had hoped to help for the benefit of the language majority students."

Advocacy for Dual-Language Programs

Despite these criticisms, TWI is gaining in popularity in the United States. Parents of native English-speakers who support the establishment of such programs for their children later become advocates for language maintenance on the part of English learners. These parents see advantages in having their children learn academic and social skills in two languages, while parents of English learners see that the home language is valued. This is a win-win situation. Strong partnerships between schools and parents are needed, however, for these programs to be maintained.

One disadvantage of TWI programs is the difficulty they present for children whose home language is not one of the two used in the program. Such children must not only learn two more languages in order to participate but also forgo academic support for the home language. Another disadvantage is that middle-class parents who want a TWI program at their school often do not support such a program if it means that their child is bused to a low-income neighborhood. Therefore, unless the neighborhood is racially mixed, it is generally home-language speakers who are bused to schools in higher-income neighborhoods to create the language mix.

Parents who are looking into a TWI program generally have three major concerns. First, will the students attain as high a level of achievement in English and in the content areas as those in non-TWI programs, and will the students be able to transfer successfully to non-TWI programs after having been in the TWI program? Second, what will be the academic challenges in such a program? Will parents be able to help their children in the language they do not know? Lastly, will children be able to attain a high level of proficiency in the home language? Will the identity and self-esteem of the children be fostered and the primary culture maintained and transmitted, and will students feel able to converse with native speakers in both languages (Cloud, Genesee, & Hamayan, 2000)?

The Role of Monolingual English Instructors in a Dual-Language Program

Educators who teach English to speakers of other languages but are not themselves speakers of another language sometimes feel threatened by bilingual programs, fearing that individuals with dual-language skills will take their jobs. However, many TWI models are successful in pairing a bilingual teacher with one who is not. There are many ways in which monolingual teachers can demonstrate that they value students' languages and cultural experiences. These include making literature and learning resources available in two languages; encouraging students to write in more than one language, sharing that writing with others, and helping one another by speaking in both languages; using adults and community members who speak the primary language to assist in instruction; and advocating for literacy in two languages.

Biliteracy in a TWI Context

♦ **STRATEGY 11.2:** Teach literacy and oracy in two languages

Complexities of Biliteracy

A TWI context is complex because the contexts of the classroom and the school together influence how children learn to use language. Students in a TWI program do not merely absorb and produce two languages, they do so while immersed in a sea of covert messages about language derived from program structure and goals, tensions regarding social uses of two languages, effects upon instruction stemming from the similarities and differences between the languages, and complications resulting from the differing practices of literacy acquisition in the distinct languages (Pérez & Torres-Guzmán, 2002). This complexity is aggravated by social and educational discrimination that has historically existed in the attitudes toward, and treatment of, minority groups in the United States (Cummins, 1989), as well as by local social and political conditions in the community of a given school. In an integrated second-language program, the primary basis of instruction is the focus on academic goals. Language is taught not as an end in itself, but as a means toward academic achievement (Genesee, 1987). This is not to say that language instruction is incidental. As Ellis (1994) pointed out, the conscious, intentional teaching and learning of language is probably essential for the achievement of high-level literacy and oracy skills. This section addresses biliteracy, the acquisition and use of two languages in achieving academic goals.

Three interrelated questions help to tease apart the complex nature of biliteracy (Hornberger, 1994). First, what are the contexts in which biliteracy occurs? Examination of this context requires a look at the social context of texts and speech events, the use of literacy in the classroom and school context, the macro-context of the community and society, the relative relationships between oracy and literacy in the two languages, and the role that bilingualism and monolingualism play in the various contexts.

A second set of dimensions that Hornberger (1994) proposed relates reading/writing (first dimension) and speaking/listening skills (second dimension) in two languages (third dimension), which form a three-dimensional interlanguage space. Individuals may be high on one dimension in one language, and low on the others, making the issue of transfer between languages difficult to measure.

A last set of dimensions for analysis consists of the media used in biliteracy (Hornberger, 1994). One consideration is the issue of simultaneous or sequential exposure to literacy in the two languages. Two additional complicating factors are the relative similarity or dissimilarity of the languages, and the type of script they use. Hornberger's analysis offers the tools to understand why the process of language instruction within a framework of biliteracy is so intricate.

Questions about Biliteracy

The dimensions set forth by Hornberger raise a series of key questions about how to teach with respect to the complex nature and demands of biliteracy. In fact, if one were to set forth logically a grid of questions, one would have the following: how do micro/macro, monolingual/bilingual, and oral/literate contexts influence the receptive and productive skills of oracy/literacy in two languages with respect to simultaneous/successive exposure to languages that may differ to greater or smaller degrees of structure and script? This grid forms an interlocking set of three $2 \times 2 \times 2$ analyses, resulting in 512 separate questions about how these factors influence one another. With this in mind, it seems naive to offer Table 11.1, with a mere seven questions about dual-literacy development.

Despite the complexity of the context, language acquisition factors, and media situation in and across languages, several principles emerge. First, an analysis of these three sets of multiple dimensions begs for some simplification so that language educators can find a level of complexity that they tolerate. Few TESOL educators I know, for example, sojourn in multiple countries all over the world, teach for extended periods of time at multiple levels of schooling, and concern themselves with issues ranging from text selection to government policy. Most establish a comfort level concerning the number of different cultures with which they seek to interact, the level of literacy they instruct on a given day, and the number and level of sociopolitical battles they wish to fight. The same holds true for the other two sets of dimensions. Too much complexity in context, learner variation, or media heterogeneity can cause professional stress.

A Teaching Unit in Two Languages

Let's Go to Mexico/Vamos a México is an integrated teaching unit on the culture and traditions of Mexico that Christina Panzeri-Álvarez (1998), a second-grade teacher, developed with her students. The unit comprises twenty lessons combining social studies, language arts, mathematics, art, and music. Each lesson uses Spanish and English together.

> Students first create a passport for travel to various cities in Mexico. They identify regions and states using a geographical atlas of Mexico and briefly describe the historical background of Mexico. Using travel brochures, they first choose favorite vacation destinations and then write a persuasive letter to their parents, telling why they think such a trip would be enjoyable.

TABLE 11.1 ◆ Questions and Answers about Dual-Literacy Development

Question	Answer
What level of oral proficiency is necessary to teach literacy?	Younger children need to develop some oral and pre-requisite cognitive skills (e.g., retaining information in short-term memory). For older students, an integrated oral/literacy approach is recommended.
In what order should literacy be introduced when two languages are taught?	For speakers of a minority language, three to five years of primary-language reading instruction should take place before reading instruction in English begins. Some exposure to oral English is beneficial.
	For majority-language students in a dual-language program, some programs begin with non–English-language literacy and academics. Other programs begin with the respective primary languages in order to build upon existing oral language skills.
Why should literacy be taught in one language before beginning the second?	Students' reading rates, fluency, and comprehension may be compromised if both languages are begun simultaneously. Moreover, too much time may be spent on reading at the expense of other content.
How can reading be matched to a student's language proficiency level?	Students should be familiar with the core vocabulary used in the reading; the story line should be easy to grasp.
What cultural features of texts facilitate dual literacy?	Students possess the background knowledge and life experience required to understand the text; the materials represent and honor the cultural groups present in the school and their values.
How are materials used in dual literacy judged as authentic?	The language used is natural and predictable, and the level of colloquiality versus formality is appropriate; texts are based on the literary traditions of students.
What can be done with a student who reads well in the first language and performs poorly in the second language?	Strategies may be borrowed from those designed for special needs learners: use of high-interest/low-readability materials; cued text (underlining, highlighting, margin notes); modeling and demonstration; and peer tutoring and collaborative learning.

Source: Cloud, Genesee, & Hamayan, 2000.

Starting in La Ciudad de México, students explore the capital. They read "La Calle del Indio Triste" from Macías's (1996) *Leyendas Mexicanas*, draw and color a Mexican flag, and learn the "Himno Nacional Mexicano," translating it into English, noting similarities and differences in words and word order in English and Spanish, and comparing the anthem to "The Star Spangled Banner." The next lesson is a favorite: making corn tortillas, and listing and discussing the recipes that use tortillas as a basis.

Students next "travel" to the Guadalajara, "The Pearl of the West." They read about *mariachi* orchestras using the Website www.ifccsa.org/menumari.html. They tour the giant market (*mercado*) San Juan de Dios, also known as La Libertad (see www.mexweb.com/guadjara.htm). They role-play how to bargain at a Mexican market, use math to convert dollars to pesos, practice converting to the metric system of measurement, cook *nopales* (prickly pear cactus), and make a *piñata*. Moving on to Michoacán, Veracruz, and Oaxaca, they make *mole*, "attend" a Mexican wedding, and learn a traditional song of Veracruz, "La Bamba." At the end of the unit, students reflect upon their travels and write about their favorite places.

Although this unit did not originate in a TWI setting, its emphasis on biliteracy and its theme can easily be adapted to a TWI program. Families who are familiar with various cities in Mexico are invited to "show and tell." Students from Mexico sustain pride in their culture, and students who are not familiar with Mexico gain valuable skills in Spanish.

Another dual-language teaching unit is "El Jardín Curandero" ("The Healing Garden") developed by Ana Díez and Leandra Marchis (2001). Students in a matched set of Advanced Placement classes at a high school—one class for native speakers of Spanish and one class for non-native speakers—study plants that are used for treating various ailments, in Mexico, Southern California, and in the Philippines. They bring plant samples from home gardens, and discuss their medicinal properties. Students learn how to create specimens by drying the plants and write their own dual-language pharmaceutical manual.

As a service-learning project, the Spanish club grew an actual garden at a local park, and on the César Chávez Day of Service and Learning, students distributed dual-language information kits describing the medicinal uses of plants. In this way they used their bilingual skills to inform the larger community about knowledge drawn from their homes and families.

Principles of Language Transfer

According to Hornberger's analysis (see above), issues of language transfer are complicated not only by the complex nature of receptive and productive skills of oracy/literacy in two languages but also by the intersection of micro/macro, monolingual/bilingual, and oral/literate contexts. The type of media that literacy employs with respect to simultaneous/successive exposure to languages may also differ by greater or smaller degrees of structure and script. Across these three sets of three dimensions, expert use of strategies maximizes the probability that language acquisition will occur in sufficient depth and at a rapid pace.

◆ **STRATEGY 11.3:** Teach for transfer between the primary language and English

Metalinguistic Awareness and Common Underlying Proficiency

Educators once believed that not speaking the dominant language of the school (in the case of ESL students, not speaking English) was a handicap that interfered with and delayed cognitive growth. This belief assumes that content and skills learned through the primary language do not transfer to English. This notion of "no interrelationship between languages" has been termed *separate underlying proficiency (SUP)* (Cummins, 1981b). The contrasting notion, *common underlying proficiency (CUP)*, is the belief that the primary and second languages have a shared foundation, an idea that Cummins (1979, 1981b) has cited much evidence to support.

One common element is *metalinguistic awareness,* which refers to knowledge about the structural properties of language, including sounds, words, and grammar. It also means knowledge of language and its functions (Gombert, 1992) and awareness that there is more than one way to represent meaning, that to "realize the arbitrary nature of language in that form of language, either written or spoken language, is something different from meaning" (Yaden & Templeton, 1986, p. 9).

Metalinguistic awareness may develop either alongside primary-language acquisition or during middle childhood as the child learns to think about the linguistic system (Tunmer, Herriman, & Nesdale, 1988). A third view is that metalinguistic awareness is a result of schooling, particularly of learning to read. Up to a point, metalinguistic ability is a function of age, and students vary in this ability. Bilingual individuals outperform monolinguals on tasks requiring metalinguistic abilities (Hamers & Blanc, 1989). To summarize best practice in promoting metalinguistic awareness, knowledge, and skills, Table 11.2 divides these into four components and prescribes practices that enhance their various components.

Teaching for Transfer: Language Acquisition Processes

Language acquisition processes involve mental activities that people employ to be able to communicate ideas. Two of these processes involve general cognitive mechanisms that individuals use to learn: *transfer* and *generalization.* Transfer is applying old learning to new situations, whereas generalization involves inferring or drawing conclusions in order to respond to a situation.

Principles of Transfer.   Educators point out that transfer can be anticipated by closely aligning contexts or by engaging in immediate and varied practice through simulations, modeling, and problem-solving situations (Perkins, 1986). Abstract transfer depends on attaining a general principle before attempting to transfer, as well as using analogies, parallel problem solving, and metacognitive reflection to build bridges from one context to the next (Fogarty, Perkins, & Barell, 1992).

Language transfer occurs when the comprehension or production of a second language is influenced by the way the first language has been acquired (Odlin, 1989). Sometimes learners use rules from their first language that are not applicable to the second (*negative transfer*). As an illustration, Natheson-Mejia (1989) describes substitutions that Spanish speakers make when writing in English. These include *es* for *s* as in "estop," *d* for *t* or *th* as in "broder," *ch* for *sh* as in "chort," *j* for *h* as in "jelper," and *g* for *w* as in "sogen" (sewing).

Positive transfer allows people to respond appropriately and meaningfully in new language situations. The use of Spanish-English cognates, that is, words in two languages that look alike and have the same or similar meaning, is a helpful resource (Garrison,

TABLE 11.2 ◆ Practices That Promote Metalinguistic Awareness

Component of Metalinguistic Awareness	Definition	Suggestions to the Teacher to Enhance Awareness
Metaphonological	Identifying the phonological components in linguistic units and intentionally manipulating them (Gombert, 1992, pp. 15, 39, 63)	• Teach sound-symbol connection (phonics). • Teach word segmentation into syllables and onset-rime awareness (the idea that rhymes occur when the ending phonemes are the same sounds, even when beginning phonemes vary).
Metasyntactic	The ability to reason consciously about the syntactic aspects of language and to exercise intentional control over the application of grammatical rules (Gombert, 1992, p. 39)	• Teach students to separate the correctness of a sentence from its truth value; teach critical literacy (everything written is not necessarily true). • Have students make good/bad judgments on the correct form of sentences (could use peer editing).
Metapragmatic	Concerned with the awareness or knowledge one has about the relationships obtained between the linguistic system and the context in which the language is embedded (Pratt & Nesdale, 1984, p. 105)	• Help students to judge the adequacy of messages and their context. • Point out ironic, sarcastic, humorous, and polite forms of language.
Metasemantic	Refers both to the ability to recognize the language system as a conventional and arbitrary code and the ability to manipulate words or more extensive signifying elements, without the signified correspondents being automatically affected by this (Gombert, 1992, p. 63)	• Teach students about word denotation and connotation, and nuance of meaning. • Expand vocabulary of synonyms and antonyms. • Explore word oddities. • Help students to find cognates between languages.

1990; Nagy, García, Durgunoglu, & Hancin-Bhatt, 1993). The many predictable relations between Spanish and English words may assist students to expand their vocabularies with ease. For example, almost all nouns in English that end in *-ion* have a Spanish cognate stemming from the *-ar* series of verbs in Spanish: *preparation* (*preparación*, from *preparar*); *communication* (*communicación*, from *communicar*); *attention* (*atención*, from *atentar*); and *action* (*acción*, from *actuar*) are just a few examples.

Contrastive Analysis.   Numerous studies have been carried out comparing various features (phonological, syntactic, and semantic) of languages. Contrastive analysis, which compares features from L1 and L2 in order to predict learnability, rests heavily on behaviorist and structuralist tenets. Contemporary theory recognizes the importance of the first language in a global sense and does not encourage learners to compare minute surface forms of the first and second languages as they learn.

The second general cognitive strategy used by all learners is generalization. In first-language acquisition, this process is seen when young children begin to put labels on concepts. "Dada," a child may say to any male, or "ball," for any round object. In SLA, the term *overgeneralization* is more frequently used, referring to situations in which the learner incorrectly generalizes a rule to cases in which it does not apply. English learners may say, for example, "I don't can do that," overgeneralizing the rule "insert *do* in negative clauses."

What kind of transfer can be expected from the first language to the second? Students can transfer sensory motor skills (eye-hand coordination, fine-muscle control, spatial and directional skills, visual perception and memory); auditory skills (auditory perception, memory, discrimination, and sequencing); common features of writing systems (alphabets, punctuation rules); comprehension strategies (finding the main idea, inferring, predicting, use of cuing systems); study skills (taking notes, using reference sources); and habits and attitudes (self-esteem, task persistence, focus) (Cloud, Genesee, & Hamayan, 2000); the structure of language (speech-print relationships, concepts such as syllable, word, sentence, paragraph); and knowledge about the reading process (Thonis, 1981).

Teachers can transform positive transfer into a learning strategy by helping students to become aware of ways in which they can draw from prior knowledge of "how language works" to make English easier. They can explicitly foster this approach by welcoming dual-language use, understanding code switching, providing support for literacy in multiple languages, and honoring primary languages; and they can use specific strategies to help students build SLA on a firm foundation of primary-language proficiency.

Biliteracy and Biculturality

A bilingual/bicultural approach to teaching helps students to establish, maintain, and value the language and culture of their homes and communities as much as their skills in English (see Chapter 9).

◆ STRATEGY 11.4: Provide cultural support for dual language learning

Students who are supported in both languages and are able to attain a high level of scholarship can use both languages for literacy purposes. They can develop reading and writing in the second language simultaneously with speaking and listening skills, so that their skills are balanced (this is particularly challenging in Spanish, because of its long history of writing as a pursuit of the elite only). When students are provided functional use of two or more languages, they are able to read more widely, expanding their worldview. If the teachers can draw from students' cultural background to complement learning that goes on in the classroom, there is more potential for involving the community in a meaningful way. Students and teachers alike become cultural brokers, able to pass

TABLE 11.3 ♦ A Bilingual/Bicultural Approach to Teaching

Considerations That Guide Effective Practice	Description
Use both languages for literacy instruction.	Primary-language use permits students access to core concepts, shows respect for its value, and enhances SLA.
Develop reading and writing simultaneously with speaking and listening skills in L2.	A holistic approach does not delay literacy for the sake of oral skills. This permits students with a preference for writing to begin SLA immediately.
Provide functional use of the languages.	Students can choose to use either language to communicate, depending on what the situation seems to warrant. The teacher helps by creating situations in which the distinct languages are useful and appropriate.
Use students' cultural background as a tool for learning.	Students read books in their second language about which they have had experience. For example, Chinese students may be familiar with the topic of the book *Everybody Cooks Rice*.
Become cultural brokers.	Teachers help students to acquire knowledge and understanding of the use of the literacy skills they are acquiring, the cultural knowledge needed to comprehend text, and the structures and organization of text depending on the genre.
Engage homes and communities as partners of literacy development.	Teachers work with parents to achieve a balance between languages that is useful in the home, community, and the larger culture.
Have high expectations regardless of language proficiency.	Each student works to his or her potential in an environment that communicates the faith that all will succeed.
Provide appropriate support.	Teachers experiment with a combination of strategies to reach each student.

Source: Brisk & Harrington, 2000.

freely among many different communities—real, virtual, and imagined—engaging homes and families as partners of literacy development and sources of support (see Table 11.3).

The biliterate, bicultural community is a vision yet to be realized in the United States, yet models exist in other parts of the world. If English is one of the languages, it must take its place as a full, supportive partner of its sister and brother languages.

Teaching English in Context

Mr. Park was a student who had a successful business in Korea training students in grammar to pass the Test of English as a Foreign Language (TOEFL) so that they could apply to university programs in the United States. His teaching consisted of presenting sentence after sentence in English while speaking in Korean to explain the grammar structures. For him, English might have been algebra: a puzzle, a code, a complex system needing extensive explanation. However, when he applied to and was accepted into graduate school in the United States, his lack of ability to speak and understand spoken English became a challenge both for him and the instructors. In his graduate classes in the M.A. TESOL program, Mr. Park was silent, and after ten minutes of listening to English he would mentally drift away. Finally, I discussed with him the issue of his lack of oral/aural English. "Korean men don't have to talk," he said. I felt sorry for him, because he was somehow unable to learn to listen to or speak English.

But one of my colleagues gave me a different picture of the situation. "Quit pitying him," he said. "Mr. Park can speak English if he wants to—he just doesn't want to."

English learners have language rights, and one of those rights is not to speak English. In fact, many students of English will never need to speak English and will never learn to speak English. For them, English learning has other purposes: to attain high entrance examination scores, to read business documents, or to decode radio transmissions. In their contexts, oral/aural English may not be necessary. One kind of contextualized English is English for Special Purposes (ESP), English that is adapted specifically for science, technology, or business. Another kind of contextualized English is a dialect, a way of speaking that individuals have developed within the context of a special group of speakers. This chapter concerns dialects.

❖ MEGASTRATEGY 12: Teach respect for contextual usage of English

The reading and writing that are performed in various contexts—situated literacy—are influenced by the social and institutional practices and power relations of each specific context (Barton, Hamilton, & Ivanič, 2000). This chapter addresses two issues that are normally not grouped together: *situated oracy* (listening/speaking) and *situated literacy* (reading/writing). Situated oracy, including considerations of *oral dialect*, is evinced when people talk a certain way in order to feel appropriate within a given context. Situated literacy influences the way people read and write in a given context. This chapter explores situated oracy and situated literacy in turn, as the research traditions of the two differ greatly, and then discusses what teachers can do in the classroom to communicate respect and understanding of contextual influences on the use of the English language.

Dialects in English

♦ STRATEGY 12.1: Honor the dialect of the learner

Many people have had the experience of picking up the telephone and listening to the voice of a stranger. Within the first few seconds, I can usually tell if the speaker's voice is familiar. If I do not recognize the voice, I am left to rely on other cues, such as the accent and dialect of the speaker. As Wolfram (1991) noted, "It is surprising how little conversation it takes to draw conclusions about a speaker's 'background'; a sentence, a phrase, or even a word is adequate to trigger a regional, social, or ethnic classification" (p. 1). Using linguistics, I can usually figure out quickly who is a solicitor—even before hearing the content—and terminate the call!

English is spoken with regional dialects all over the world. *Dialect* refers to "any variety of language which is shared by a group of speakers" (Wolfram, 1991, p. 2). Dialects are important in many languages as markers of social class, ethnicity, regional background, and other social characteristics. In the United Kingdom, language is a fairly accurate marker of socioeconomic and class status. Although Americans like to believe they live in a casteless society, the United States seems to have inherited the tradition of using language as a marker of social class. As Wolfram (1991) noted, "In fact, there are some who feel that language differences serve as the single most reliable indicator of social position in our society. When we live a certain way, we are expected to match that lifestyle with our talk" (p. 2).

Language varies by region, social class, and ethnic origin. In some respects, the study of dialect overlaps with other aspects of cultural study, folklore, and literature. Some people enjoy the study of dialects as a way of understanding human differences, or as a way of learning more about their own culture. This leads people to listen to others when they speak, and to draw conclusions about what they hear.

As a native of Pittsburgh, Pennsylvania, I am able to identify others whose accent originates in that region. For example, they say, "still mill" ("steel mill") and "dantan" ("downtown"). Certain features of the dialect were then, and still are, negatively evaluated by others. At that time, a middle-class person, hearing the sentence, "I shoulda went" instead of "I should [have] gone," automatically disapproved. In southern California, however, the use of the simple past to replace the past participle is common in the middle class and is not as negatively stigmatized. I can now listen to "You shoulda went with us" and not wince—most of the time.

Dialects and the Education of English Learners

Language educators cannot help being influenced by dialect considerations. Wolfram (1995) emphasized the importance of dialect issues for educators of English learners:

> The standard version of English provided in most ESL curricula aims unrealistically at a dialect-neutral variety of English. At the same time, the majority of ESL learners are surrounded by an array of dialects, including some well-established vernacular dialects for those who live in economically impoverished conditions. The socialization of many ESL learners into U.S. culture may lead them to adopt the same uncharitable, biased opinion of vernaculars that is often found among native speakers of English. Further-

more, because many ESL learners may, in fact, speak vernacular varieties of their own languages that are comparable in status to the vernacular dialects of English, they may have already experienced language variation and bias. It thus seems appropriate to incorporate dimensions of langage variation into the ESL curriculum. (p. 1)

Issues of Dialect in EFL.   EFL and ESL contexts differ somewhat in the issues involving dialect. For those who teach English abroad, their own English dialect may be an issue. Many English-teaching programs abroad prefer to hire native speakers of English, on the assumption that native speakers are more expert on the target language and culture. At the point of hiring, they may be willing to pay a native speaker of English much more than they would pay a nonnative speaker, thus creating an unequal pay scale that favors native speakers. Native speakers of English who might be offered the modest pay of a local hire might have little financial incentive to remain in the job long enough to invest themselves in learning how to teach in that particular context.

A second issue is that of honoring the dialect of the learner. The English of native speakers may not be the English needed or used in the local context (Kirkpatrick, 2000). A more complex issue is that of teacher expectations. The EFL teacher may be tempted to reduce the standards of language use, believing that English used inside the artificial confines of the EFL classroom is "good enough." Finding the appropriate balance of language knowledge, pedagogical skill, dialect accommodation, and standard language modeling is a challenge for English education in the EFL context.

A third issue in the EFL context is prejudice on the part of international speakers of English. English educators who work abroad may find that nonnative speakers of English have a low regard for vernacular English in much the same way as native speakers do, but do not feel constrained when it comes to voicing these prejudices. They may discriminate against native speakers who speak a dialect, who are not white, or who do not represent mainstream culture.

Issues of Dialect in ESL.   In the ESL context, the issue of whether ESL teachers should model standard English is still relevant. In many urban school districts, where bilingual (Spanish-English) teachers are in demand, personnel administrators do not seem to see Spanish-accented English as a negative factor in elementary schools. However, the same personnel administrators still seem to prefer to hire high school English teachers who are native speakers, or who speak English without a "foreign" accent.

The second issue, that of honoring the dialect of the learner, means finding the appropriate balance between accepting and honoring the home dialect of the student, and modeling and teaching standard English. In many urban schools in the United States, English learners attend classes in schools with African American students, some of whom speak African American vernacular English (AAVE). Teachers of English learners in urban schools—or even in rural schools in which speakers of dialects interact with English learners—need to understand how to teach English in these contexts.

Prejudice is a third issue in ESL contexts. Often a speaker of a regional dialect (for example, a Puerto Rican dialect in Massachusetts) is not accorded the same respect as a speaker of standard English. Yet within a specific community, a dialect may be the norm. English teachers often enforce standard English as a norm even when it is not the norm in the students' community, believing that the community's norm is wrong or, conversely, that there is no point in teaching standard English. It is naïve to believe that any individual is totally free from these prejudices. Thus dialect issues are also issues of social power and status in society.

Teachers who understand dialects understand better how to teach. In a court case in Ann Arbor Michigan in 1979, teachers were ordered to attend workshops on dialects because of the potential impact on the school's achievement of vernacular dialect students (Wolfram, 1991). In my own case, if I had known more about the use of English on the part of men in Korea, namely, the English dialect used by Mr. Park (see the beginning of this chapter), I might have had a better idea how to motivate him to speak. In short, the knowledge of dialect might have made me a better teacher for him.

Students who speak nonstandard dialects are very aware that their speech creates potential difficulties in such areas as successfully acquiring standard forms for academic writing and avoiding stereotyping and discrimination if their dialect is negatively evaluated by others (see Nero, 1997). They are also aware that their very identity and deepest values are linked to their language, leading to potential conflicts in self-evaluation and acculturation. They can lead, however, to possible positive biculturality (Bosher, 1997). These factors make the role of dialect a complex variable in the language of English learners.

Before addressing the question of how a teacher deals with dialect, a look at dialect from a linguist's point of view is in order. The following section examines some common features that constitute dialects, ways in which dialects exhibit social and ethnic differences, typical attitudes toward dialects, ways in which gender influences dialect, and ways in which dialects affect speaking style. The section concludes with advice for educators.

Common Features That Constitute Dialects

Why do languages have dialects? Language differences go hand in hand with social differentiation. People may speak differently either because they are physically separated (regional dialects) or because they are socially separated (by means of economic ecology and/or social stratification). A third explanation is based on linguistic differences between the dialects themselves.

Regional Dialects.   *Regional dialects* emerge because groups of people settle in specific places, and the physical terrain keeps dialects isolated and intact. In the United States, the geographic isolation of some communities in Kentucky, Tennessee, North Carolina, Virginia, and West Virginia has given rise to so-called Appalachian English (see Wolfram, 1991). Not all geographic isolation results in regional dialects, however; the important factor is the communication links that the region maintains with other speakers. In Alaska, for example, English-speakers maintain links to the larger U.S. media and have not developed significant regional variations in speech.

The overall dialect terrain of the United States is an example of regional dialects. Various emigrants from the British Isles migrated to specific regions of the United States, bringing with them the dialects of their homeland; as they then migrated farther west, they took these regional dialects with them. As a result, most Americans recognize four distinct dialects in the United States today; these can be roughly characterized as (1) New York City, (2) New England, (3) the South, and (4) everyone else.

Dialects of English around the world are equally location-dependent. English-speakers from India or Pakistan have a characteristic lilt plus a British accent, while speakers from Scandinavia, Brazil, or Japan have another kind of word/sentence intonation/accent combination. As individuals from these parts of the world conduct business or pleasure in their local English, it serves them well enough. It is when English is used internationally—when it is the only common language for each speaker—that differences in dialect become an issue and speakers must learn to decode one another's speech. When complex international negotiations take place, such differences are not an issue, because experts are hired to translate. Dialects become important as international English is used on a daily basis, and in these cases the issues relating to dialect have cultural implications.

As an example of these cultural implications, in the colonizing of Puerto Rico, as well as in the diaspora of Puerto Ricans living in the United States, Puerto Ricans have most often interacted with people from New York and New England. Many people in the United States find New Englanders terse and think New Yorkers' speech is brusque. The way people from the southern United States speak English, in contrast, is more languid, more tropical in pace and rhythm; but southerners seldom travel to Puerto Rico. Therefore, Puerto Ricans often feel themselves remote in culture from "Americans," with little recognition of how much their values and lifestyles—even their speech habits—resemble those of other southerners. Thus, regional differences in English dialects can enhance intercultural communication or, conversely, hinder the process.

As English becomes more widely used as the language of international technology, attitudes toward English may change (Fishman, 1977). One prospect is that dialect speakers of English who represent the cutting edge of technology may lead the way in intercultural communication, leading others around the world to assume that their dialect of English, with its attendant cultural values, represents the mainstream. With the location of major centers of technology shifting from northern, urban populations, to southern and western cities of the United States, people speaking regional dialects of English will be finding their way around the world, and regional dialects will represent the United States to a greater degree.

Social Stratification.   Dialects reflect *social stratification* due to differences in the social groups with which people affiliate. People evaluate others by means of their language in order to establish and maintain social distinctions. If people want to be identified as part of a particular social group, they adopt the vocabulary, pronunciation, and grammatical patterns of this group (Wolfram, Adger, & Christian, 1999). This phenomenon is easy to see in the case of teenage slang. More complex is the fact that even when people's language receives negative social evaluation from mainstream English speakers, they continue to use the language of that group even if they have the choice of speaking a different way. Why is this the case?

One reason for the persistence of language dialects stigmatized by the larger society may be their association with ethnic solidarity; speaking like a mainstream person may cause the loss of one's friends or weakening of family ties. It is not uncommon for speakers to try to live in both worlds, to speak like a "hip" urbanite in the city and then to use the vernacular at home with the family.

Language can be used as a signal for social stratification consciously or unconsciously. A vernacular dialect associated with the underclass sometimes also connotes strength, toughness, and resolve. President Bush used this shift after the World Trade Center bombing when he declared he wanted terrorist leader Osama Bin Laden "dead or alive," using a phrase associated with the Wild West to convey the image of determination. Conversely, speakers may use the pronunciation associated with an elite social class to convey erudition or knowledgability. Thus dialect differences are socially sustained.

The Deep Syntax of Dialects.   Dialects may persist because of deeper syntactic causes. The third explanation for the origin and persistence of dialects is based on linguistic analysis. Double negation within a sentence ("He don't hardly know"), which resembles the AAVE construction "The dog didn't like nobody," is found in European languages. Deletion of the copula ("You ugly") is a feature of AAVE but also of Chinese and other languages. Lack of the 's in the possessive structure (that man hat) is correct for specific possessive structures in English (her hat); lack of plural endings (four girl) is common in many languages; and final stop deletion ("nin' war' " for "ninth ward") is common in other constructions in English that use midword stop deletion or change the unvoiced to voiced consonant (water). Thus dialects persist based on the ways in which languages are constructed.

Whether dialects have a regional, social, or linguistic explanation, speakers acquire a dialect of English based upon that which is used by others of their region, social class, and native language. The most obvious form of dialect usage is in the sound of the language, or *accent*. Just because someone speaks with an accent, it does not mean that they are less competent in the language (Wolfram, 2002). In fact, as Lippi-Green asserts, "degree of accentedness, whether from LI interference, or a socially or geographically marked language variety, cannot predict the level of an individual's competency in the target language. In fact . . . high degrees of competence are often attained by persons with especially strong L2 accents" (1997, p. 70).

How Dialects Exhibit Social and Ethnic Differences

The stakes are high when it comes to differences in social status, both in the United States and the United Kingdom. In the United States regional accents may be seen as quaint or charming, but listeners also use accent to judge on a range of personal qualities and capabilities, such as innate intelligence, morality, and employability (Wolfram, 1991).

Millions of U.S. residents, as well as millions of English-speaking people around the world, do not use the standard accent of the broadcast media, known in the United States as "general American" or "middle western," and in England as "received pronunciation" (Lippi-Green, 1997). Standard pronunciation has become associated with those in high-status occupations—doctors, lawyers, professionals, and executives of large companies—what Christensen (2002) calls the "cash language" (p. 176). Deviations from this standard are associated with unskilled laborers, or worse, as in the case of some Disney cartoons, vagabonds or criminals (Lippi-Green, 1997). Thus, language variation is associated with a person's economic activity. Economic discrimination based on language is enforced by means of informal, often invisible, social networks that intersect with social stratification.

Much of the social stratification that underlies linguistic discrimination is based on ethnic subcultures that manifest themselves in linguistic distinctions. Because of both racial class and prejudice, the extent of exclusion from the mainstream varies according to the number of people involved and the perceived threat these numbers create for the majority. In places like Texas, Spanish is seen as a major threat to the hegemony of English in the United States, whereas French, another language spoken just over the border, is not. This difference may also be due to the relative prestige of French compared to Spanish.

Linguistic influences from subcultures leak into English, and in the process the subcultures acquire some degree of acceptance. Sometimes the language sneaks in through specific customs. Japanese food has brought the language of *sushi* into major cities, while Spanish fast-food chains have created pseudo-Spanish food items like the "chalupa." Popular cinema can also bring subculture language into the mainstream, as in Arnold Schwarzenegger's "Hasta la vista, baby."

In a major example of subculture influence on English, when European Jewish immigrants brought Yiddish to New York City, its grammar, everyday phrases, and intonational patterns became so frequently heard on the city's streets that Yiddish expressions are associated to this day with New York dialect. Table 12.1 presents a sample of expressions or lexical items of Yiddish origin (Rosten, 1982).

Many people are multidialectic, living in communities in which multiple varieties of English coexist in relative harmony and switching back and forth easily between multiple languages, each with its own repertoire of styles. To disparage the use of code switching in the Spanish community as "Spanglish," or other such perjoratives, is, as Lippi-Green puts it, "just another subordination method with a long history" (1997, p. 233).

To overcome the negative effects of social stratification, many nonnative speakers of English seek to acquire an accent that will help them to assimilate into the mainstream. On the other hand, in many cultures the dialect they speak *is* the mainstream and to acquire any other accent risks social stigma. For example, in Taiwan, Taiwanese English is the norm and to deviate much from the phonological and linguistic features of that dialect might be to risk being accused of being too American. In some cultures, being bilingual is acceptable only to a limited degree.

Attitudes Toward Dialects

People who are forbidden by law or social custom from discriminating against others on the basis of race or ethnicity may use accent as a means of social stigmatization or exclusion (Lippi-Green, 1997). Children from outside mainstream cultures or languages may not find validation in school. For these students, as for others, school is not a power-neutral environment. As Foucault (1984) commented, "Any system of education is a political way of maintaining or modifying the appropriation of discourses, along with the knowledges and powers which they carry" (p. 123).

Teachers may unwittingly communicate a negative social evaluation to a student who is not a native English speaker by speaking louder, using shorter sentences,

TABLE 12.1 ♦ English Expressions Derived from Yiddish

Linguistic Term or Phrase	Example or Meaning
"again" fronted in irritation:	Again he forgot my birthday!
"again with" in question:	Again with the jealousy?
Alright already!	Enough!
cockamamy	ludicrous, unbelievable, cheap
chutzpa	brazen, shamelessness
sh- (contempt via reiteration)	clean, shmean; fancy-shmancy
dreck	utter trash; cheap, worthless
Eat your heart out!	you should feel envy
glitch	slip-up
How come . . .	why
icky	unpleasant, nauseating
Look who's talking!	pot calling the kettle black
-nik	devotee (peacenik)
curse + cancellation	May he drop dead, God forbid.
Now he tells us!	Finally we find out!
Phooey!	disgust
So sue me!	Just try to do something about it.
That's for sure.	agreement
That's what you say.	I don't believe you.
What gives?	What's going on?
Who knows?	I don't know.
Who needs it?	not necessary
yak, yakkety-yak	chatter

Source: Rosten, 1982.

slowing speech, restricting vocabulary and range of topics, or signaling a patronizing attitude (curiously enough, this attitude is also adopted toward the elderly). The nonnative speaker's status is thus demeaned, though teachers may be unaware of the attitudes they communicate.

Americans, consciously or unconsciously, view certain "foreign" languages as more prestigious than others. French, for example, is seen as a high-status language, although the French spoken by Haitians may not be evaluated positively due to racism. On the other hand, a Slavic accent may be seen as less acceptable because of the stigma attached to this accent during the Cold War. Status issues are prevalent in dialect differences among native speakers of English. Many Americans assign a positive value to British dialects (Wolfram, 1991). Pat Morrison (1994), a columnist for the *Los Angeles Times,* observed this in a radio broadcast: "Everyone knows an English accent gets you invited to lunch, but a Spanish accent gets you dirty looks."

In England some dialects are negatively evaluated by other speakers. An example of this is the conversation I had with a cashier named Francesca who was fixing the cash register before my transaction could be completed.

LDR: So what happened? The drawer got stuck?

F: It was jemmed. The coin rolls got jemmed.

LDR: Oh, jammed? Where are you from? England?

F: Surrey.

LDR: I'm writing a book chapter about dialects. What accent in English is the hardest for you to understand?

F: That would be Newcastle. Up there in the north, near the border. You can't tell what they are trying to say. It's awful.

LDR: So, Surrey, is that in the south of England?

F: South, yeeeah, way down. Our speech is, you know, the right one. Oh, I shouldn't say that, should I? It's the normal one, you know.

In many parts of the world, the prestigious form of British English is considered preferable to any form of American English, an attitude perpetuated through the requirement of the Cambridge certificate in order to teach English.

Language is central to the identification of self and group. Teachers who communicate dialect bias in the classroom do not merely damage the teacher-student relationship through prejudice or impair students' academic success through their lower academic expectations for them. Longer-term damage results from *symbolic-structural violence* (Skutnabb-Kangas, 1981, 1993) in which the student who is made to feel inferior for reasons of accent internalizes the shame associated with discrimination. Moreover, a student who is made to feel inferior internalizes a negative attitude toward learning English. As Lippi-Green (1997) stated,

> When persons who speak languages or dialects that are devalued or stigmatized consent to the standard language ideology, they become complicit in its propagation against themselves, their own interests and identities. Many are caught in a vacuum: When an individual cannot find any social acceptance for her language outside her own speech communities, she may come to denigrate her own language, even when she continues to use it. (p. 66)

The video *American Tongues* (information available at www.cnam.com/more_info/ameri3.html) provides an informative overview of various American dialects, American linguistic prejudice (regional, social, racial), the role of the mass media in fostering stereotypes, the way in which accents in one locale can differ by social class, and assessments and examples of AAVE. Also useful is the companion video, *Yeah You Rite*, which uses the city of New Orleans as a microcosm of dialectic variation. These tools help students hear examples of regional speech and attitudes and relate them to their own lives.

Dialects and Speaking Style

When the Australian actor Russell Crowe played a tobacco executive in the movie *The Insider*, he sounded just like a North Carolinian! How is it that actors can mimic particular regional and ethnic forms so well? Even more remarkably, how can the soccer mom sound so different when she is yelling at the kids in the back seat from how she sounds when speaking to the policeman who stops her for speeding violation? Speakers may shift back and forth from vernacular dialects to more standard forms for a variety of reasons, either to reaffirm ethnic solidarity, to appear well educated, or to sound "folksy." But why would a well-educated person deliberately use poor grammar?

When he was the chairman of the Joint Chiefs of Staff of the Armed Forces, Colin Powell appeared before a congressional committee. Powell testified as an advocate of a pay raise for military personnel, yet he confessed to the committee that his own salary was more than adequate. "I ain't done bad," he admitted.

Why would the top military official at the Pentagon appear before the United States Congress sounding like a street punk? One would think that Powell, as the child of an immigrant family from the West Indies, would feel some linguistic insecurity and be careful to use proper language before such an august body as the U.S. Senate. Quite the contrary. Powell's speech is an example of downshifting into "buddy talk" to appear manly. He was also playing a status-equalization game: He can go to the U.S. Senate and deliberately use colloquial grammar, defying negative evaluation. Thus this style shift worked to his advantage: He could be seen as powerful, confident, and manly. With this mastery of the language game, is it any wonder that Powell's next public position was secretary of state, a job for the quintessential diplomat?

Dialect Switchings.   One might think that people shift dialects solely to express or reject regional and ethnic affiliation, but the issue is complex. *Vertical dialect switching* from a more to a less stigmatized mode of speech in order to reduce negative social evaluation is frequent among all types of speakers; it is usually a function of the social

Students speaking a nonstandard dialect of English are a rich source of language input to English learners in urban schools.

setting, the person being addressed, the topic, and the purpose of the communication (Wolfram, 1991).

Style shifting has teaching implications for second-language educators. Although formal instruction in grammatical competence is common, especially in EFL, style shifting, like other types of sociolinguistic competence, is seldom formally taught. Yet for speakers of English as an international language, the ability to shift styles to accommodate speakers of other dialects of English is important. The auxiliary features of language, such as social distance and touching behaviors, that accompany style shifts can enhance rapport in intercultural communication.

Instructing about Dialects.   Explicit instruction in English dialects might include the use of videotapes showing people speaking various dialects; so that students could, by repeated exposure, learn to understand what is being said. *The Harder They Come* features Jamaican dialect; *My Left Foot*, Irish; and *Billy Elliot*, northern British English.

Students can use contrastive pattern drills to practice dialectic variation, just to increase awareness of the shift and to have some fun with dialects in English. Wolfram (1991) offers five kinds of drills: discrimination, identification, translation, substitution, and response (see Table 12.2). Wolfram's examples show how teachers can create awareness on the part of AAVE speakers of the differences between their dialect and standard English. I offer these drills for a different purpose, namely, allowing students to have fun with language as they practice southern speech by, for example, shifting the vowel in the word *hill* so that it sounds like the word *hail*.

Pronunciation software is excellent for the specific, repetitive drills needed to work on an accent. Many such programs allow the user to record speech and then compare the recording with a norm; some even show a graphic representation of the speech tone for purposes of comparison. Students can work in the privacy of a computer laboratory.

Gender and Language Variation

Traditional studies of dialect seldom included gender differences. Several studies of social dialect in American English have shown patterns in which the women in the study tend to have a higher incidence of prestige markers than their male counterparts from the same social class and region. What accounts for this? The most substantial male-female differences have been in samples taken from the lower middle class, a class typified by its desire to move up to the middle class. In this context, because women tend to be more sensitive to prestige norms they are more frequently seen to use language that is more characteristic of the class into which they wish to move (Labov, 1981).

Women's Speech.   Women tend to use more hypercorrect forms, such as "It is I" or "He's not as fast as I." They also use more hedges, or qualifiers, when speaking, such as "I guess I'll have soup" (Lakoff, 1975). Women change pitch more to show emotion ("Oh, that's awful!"), use more expressive adjectives and intensifiers (Brend, 1975), and speak more softly and with more breathiness and higher overall pitch than men do (Smith, 1985). They may speak more indirectly overall, using more polite

TABLE 12.2 ◆ Five Pattern Drills for Practicing Horizontal Dialect Shift (Southern Vowel Shift)

Type of Drill	Example	
Discrimination Drill *Explanation:* Teacher raises awareness of the difference between sounds.	Stimulus Pair She walked up the hail. She walked up the hill.	Student Response different
Identification Drill *Explanation:* Students identify which sentence shows southern accent features.	Stimulus Pair She walked up the hail. She walked up the hill.	Student Response southern not southern
Translation Drill *Explanation:* A sentence is given in standard English form. The student translates it into southern English, and vice versa.	Stimulus Pair She walked up the hill. She walked up the hail.	Student Response She walked up the hail. She walked up the hill.
Substitution Drill *Explanation:* The word that shifts in pronunciation is substituted for another in a variety of contexts.	Stimulus Flowers grow on the hill.	Student Response Flowers grow on the hail.
Response Drill *Explanation:* A response drill requires a student to change the format of the sentence in the response, while maintaining focus on the target form.	Stimulus Pair Where do flowers grow? (southern) Where do flowers grow? (standard)	Student Response On the hail. On the hill.

Source: Adapted from Wolfram, 1991.

speech conventions (see Brown & Levinson, 1987). O'Barr and Atkins (1980) found that characteristics of female speech are more related to powerlessness than to gender, suggesting that women have learned to use these linguistic forms because they have traditionally been relegated to relatively powerless social positions.

English educators, both in EFL and ESL contexts, may find that male and female learners acquire different dialects of English, transferring to English the different roles and speech patterns in the native language. For example, women students may be more reticent to speak than men, or vice versa. In such cases, a teacher may openly discuss the differences and find ways to equalize speaking opportunities; alternatively, the class might agree to divide into distinct gender groups and establish different norms. In some countries, the shifting values and social structures are permitting women to have a greater voice (Magnier, 2002), and in the long run gender differences in EFL students' learning may be less pronounced.

Both the gender differences in the local community and the families' values about gender roles may influence students' learning in the ESL classroom. This phenomenon affects such aspects as teacher expectations, communication patterns (Sadker &

Sadker, 1986; Sadker, Sadker, & Klein, 1991), and achievement aspirations. I once had a conversation with a teacher that revealed different achievement aspirations in a non–English-speaking family and indicated how the teacher had unconsciously mirrored the expectations of the family:

> I was observing a student teacher in a third-grade classroom that featured diverse ethnicities, predominantly European Americans, Mexican Americans, and a few others. One boy was from India. He appeared to be energetic and studious. I asked the teacher about his family. She beamed with pride. "Joseph," she whispered, "is very ambitious. He wants to be a surgeon. His family really pushes him."
>
> "What's his family like?" I asked.
>
> The teacher thought a moment, then replied. "I also had his sister last year. So different—she was so shy."
>
> "What did his sister want to be when she grew up?" I asked.
>
> The teacher frowned. "Why, that's funny," she answered. "They never told me."

Gender as Powerful/Powerless Speech.   Attempts to address power differences in speaking opportunities may or may not meet with success.

> In one college-level writing course in which were enrolled, among others, a group of Saudi men and Japanese women, the Saudi men refused to work in collaborative peer-editing groups with the Japanese women, insisting that the men be allowed to form their own groups. One of the men, when questioned privately, gave as the reason that "these women have nothing to teach us." Obviously the women's perceived lack of social prestige was an issue. When groups were mixed in gender, the men did all the talking. As an attempt to address this situation, the instructor made all peer editing anonymous.

Gender roles, and gender-influenced dialects of English in other cultures, may affect the TESOL educator returning from abroad. In an interview in my office at the university, a native speaker of English was applying for the master's program in TESOL. I could see clearly that she had picked up some Japanese cultural habits, even though she was speaking English. She was explaining that she had forgotten to bring her transcript for the admission interview.

> "Oh, I'm so sorry," she said. "I didn't bring it."
>
> "That's OK, you can send it in later," I said. "So you have been teaching in Japan?"
>
> "Oh, sorry," she replied. "Did I tell you I taught there for four years?"
>
> "Yes, you did," I said. "Whereabouts in Japan did you teach?"
>
> "Oh, sorry," she said. "I put Osaka on the admission form, but I should have put Hiroshima *and* Osaka—they had a branch school there where I also taught."

"That's OK, it's no big deal," I said. "You know, you really don't have to apologize so much."

"Oh, sorry," she said.

Vernacular Dialects and Language Teaching

Because people shift dialects to indicate identification with a social class even more than a regional or ethnic affiliation, one might wonder if teachers should pay more attention to accent and other dialect features in educating English learners. There is no easy answer to this question. One would hope that teachers could spend enough time teaching in the context of a dialect group to acquire a sense of local norms of English use. Using these norms, the educator could then use common sense in bringing students to the level of these norms. Education is, after all, an enterprise that enforces normative behavior (Gore, 1998).

Because accent and intonation patterns are important in making oneself understood when speaking a foreign language, it is important for students to understand four basic ideas about dialect usage in English: (1) one's dialect, if widely used by the surrounding racial, ethnic, or cultural community, is as valid a subset of English as any other dialect; (2) it is a fact that dialects are used as a basis for discrimination, but such discrimination is based more on underlying issues of power and race relations than on the dialect alone; (3) it is common for individuals all over the world to learn more than one dialect of English and to switch, depending on the demands of the context, from one dialect to another; and (4) such features of dialect as accent can be altered, if so desired, by specific, albeit time-intensive, drill.

❖ Tactics for teaching dialects:

- Teach students pride in their community's dialect.
- Emphasize that the ability to communicate is more important than the sound of one's accent.
- Tell students that learning to switch from formal English to informal, and from standard English to colloquial usages, is part of learning English.
- Explain that pronunciation software is useful for accent reduction.

Teaching Standard English: Whose Standard?

In a language as varied as English, there are naturally some who feel that it is important to establish a standard, or norm, against which usage is measured. Experts who publish grammar and usage books usually prescribe correct or standard language forms. As Finegan (1980) put it, standard English is the language of the educated, especially those who make their living by means of writing.

Although standard English is often referred to, in fact it does not exist. Because no particular dialect is inherently and universally standard, "the determination of what is and is not standard is usually made by people or groups of people in positions of power and status to make such a judgment" (Gollnick & Chinn, 2002). Generally speaking, standard American English is a composite of several subdialects spoken by the educated professional middle class. People seeking success in school and in the job market tend to adopt the language used by people in positions of power.

One example is the grammar books' distinction between the comparative modifies *less* for nonquantifiable nouns ("less sugar in the bag") and *fewer* for quantifiable nouns ("fewer fans at today's game"). The fact that one often hears "less people," "less papers to grade," and so on, demonstrates that this distinction is now relatively uncommon in informal speech. The *who/whom* distinction is also dying out as English becomes less formal.

Informal standard English is a continuum, with some speakers speaking much as they would write formal standard English. Many speakers practice sociocultural shifts in their usage, speaking an informal vernacular with friends, coworkers, and car mechanics and then shifting to a more formal speech with superiors at work. To be bidialectic may mean shifting back and forth vertically, using language as a means to navigate the particular social environment.

Despite this facility, many educators feel it is their right and privilege to enforce standard English on their students. Teachers may subordinate the language of their students using a variety of messages, both overt and covert. Covert messages may range from, "English is too complex for a nonnative speaker to master" to, "Your language is quaint, cute, funny, or incorrect and unacceptable" to, "No one will employ you if you talk that way." Some teachers act as though it is their right to correct students in public, to reprimand them for incorrect usage, or to refuse to acknowledge them until a standard is reached ("You must answer in a complete sentence," "I can't understand you—say it again") (Lippi-Green, 1997).

Varieties of language are a result of normal social processes, rather than inadequacies on the part of individual speakers. In the case of English as an international language, the youth of the world associate American English with the latest in trends and styles; and individual speakers differentiate their language with regard to these trends (Kahane & Kahane, 1977). Rap music and hip-hop culture have spread as exemplars of language and style. Japanese pop music culture adds another layer to the linguistic mix, resulting in a pastiche and jargon that only loosely resembles its host language. Today's international English is moving at rapid speed, making it difficult to enforce standards of correctness.

The unique voice of the student is lost if educators insist on standard English exclusively in the classroom, along with the irreplaceable and priceless gift of knowledge about that individual's inner universe. Just as the worldview of the Native American is lost if the indigenous language dies away, so is the interlanguage of the student lost if no one listens. An approach that balances the need to teach standard English with the desire to find zest and delight in each individual's vernacular, can make education a reservoir of English-language diversity.

Language Variety as a Goal of Instruction

The heterogeneity of the modern world presents vast register and stylistic diversity in English. These enrich language learning.

◆ **STRATEGY 12.2:** Teach a variety of registers and styles

What is a *register*? A register is a type of language used in accordance with overt or covert rules of formality and informality in a specific situation. These rules may involve conventions of intonation, vocabulary, or topic that meet the needs of the people and the tasks to be performed in that situation. A *register shift* enables a language user to adapt to these rules. Registers are usually features of situated oracy, but the term can also be applied to the use of various conventions in reading and writing that relate to the adoption of a tone of formality. For example, the tone of voice in which one reads sacred texts in church constitutes a register shift.

Some Sample Registers in Oracy

A church is a common site of what might be termed *ceremonial register*. The words of a cleric at a wedding or funeral may have the tone of solemnity, including the choice of words, "Dearly beloved, we are gathered here. . . ." Charismatic preachers may have a characteristic lift and stridency—one could call this an "evangelical register." Kindergarten teachers who read fairy tales aloud use *storytelling register*, featuring a tone of wonder and suppressed excitement. Airline pilots who use the public address system of the airplane adopt a folksy, reassuring, and paternal tone—"captain register"? Automobile commercials filmed locally often use "car advertising register," a kind of frenzied tone performed by a man speaking loudly and quickly.

Some Sample Registers in Literacy

Reading and writing are as contextualized as oral activities. Reading a pornography magazine at a PTA meeting, or a gun magazine at a women's club meeting, would certainly raise eyebrows. These activities would set an inappropriate tone, which is a register issue. Literacy register in the United States seems to be affected by gender, class, and occupation; teachers in the average elementary school, for example, might read *Instructor*, but probably not *Business Week*. Automobile repair waiting rooms might have racing car magazines available for customers, and hospitals or clinics might offer patients a general-interest publication such as *National Geographic* in the waiting room. I once got angry when I saw *Investor's Weekly* in a medical specialist's office, thinking that it indicated that the doctor charged such high fees that he could invest large sums in the stock market (although the doctor may have provided this reading for the benefit of patients who are stockbrokers). Literacy registers sometimes reveal more about a context than we care to know.

Register shifts seem to be age-related. By the age of nine, preferences seem to be established for reading independently. Middle-class parents may struggle to get their child to put away a favorite magazine to finish homework. One difficult register for a child to master while growing up is the thank-you letter for gifts received by mail. Letter writing in general is a difficult register for most people to master, for it generally requires the writer to set an appropriate tone that mirrors the relationship between reader and writer, which ranges from business ("please make good on the product warranty") to long-distance relations ("sorry I haven't written/how are Joe and the kids?").

Gender-Typical Registers

Because certain registers are traditional, they tend to sound more acceptable if performed by the appropriate gender. For example, some people have trouble accepting a woman's voice in ceremonial register as authoritative, because church ceremonies in English were traditionally performed by men. Men, on the other hand, do not seem to enjoy spending time on the telephone and thus seldom use "gossip register," that intimate tone of chit-chat some women often use with their best friends. Radio programs feature characteristic registers that attract specific audiences. Tuning into the radio, one can distinguish stations immediately by the announcer's topic and tone of voice.

Teaching Oral Register Shifts

Students can be encouraged to practice a variety of oral registers in the classroom. One is *student response register*, a firm tone, spoken confidently, that reaches all other students in the room. Students can be trained to use *leadership register*, the voice of roll call, the call to line up for lunch, or the call to be quiet and listen. *Classroom presentation register* involves eye contact with an audience, confident bearing, pleasing and varied tone of voice, and an inviting sense of two-way communication with listeners. *Dramatic register* is used in a play, in the role of narrator or announcer, or in the role of storyteller. It is "larger than life," with exaggerated emotion and voice. The *storytelling* register features simplification and a sense of warmth and intimacy, no matter what the size of the crowd. Each of these registers requires situated practice with the appropriate setting, topic, and audience.

❖ Tactics for training students in oracy register shifts:

- Set up opportunities for situated practice, require oral presentations, and stage dramatic events and storytelling-to-children episodes for students.
- Provide repeated trials with feedback to help students improve their ability to shift registers to achieve situated oracy.
- Students who take the initiative in creating settings and events for a variety of register usages acquire leadership and talent in language use.

Situated Literacy and Academic Registers

What does it mean to use language for academic purposes? Chapter 10 covered in depth the academic functions of language within the cultural context of ESL, detailing those practices that promote the learner's use of academic language. Because this chapter focuses on contextualized language use, we return to the topic of cognitive academic language from the standpoint of register. Academic competence makes demands on the learner that in some ways require activities and attitudes not found in other, less literacy-dependent situations.

- **STRATEGY 12.3:** Teach academic registers and standard usage

The Individual World of Literacy

If an educated person kept a daily reading and writing log, it might become obvious to that person that both skills are used for a wide range of purposes. In the morning the individual might read the morning paper and perhaps make a shopping or "to do" list for the day. On the way to work, he or she might pass advertisements by the roadside. At work, literacy is situated in the workplace setting and varies greatly depending on the work tasks. For many, literacy at work has become highly computer-related, depending on word processing, databases, telephone number files, e-mail, and Web-based activities; work literacy also remains highly paper-related, with piles of various folders containing information, not to mention books, journals, and newsletters. At home, personal literacy may involve cookbooks, hobby materials, newsmagazines, correspondence, and bill paying. All these reading materials have their own place, time, and task orientation—situated literacy.

Situated Literacy: Synthesis of Practices

One of the best ways for students to understand literacy and its relationship to settings, people, and tasks is for them to reflect on their own literacy practices and the everyday practices around them. Barton (2000) posed a series of questions to students: How might literacy depend on the particular roles that people take? How does gender influence participation in literacy events? How do people learn new literacies? Some students observed events in the everyday life of the community—such as rugby games, sports betting shops, or wallpaper sales—concentrating on everyday literacies rather than on those demanded by their academic tasks. In researching these practices, students developed new insights into the role of literacy in people's lives, their own in particular.

Everyday life provided an amazing range of types of situated literacy. Students investigated literacy in mundane events, for example, having a baby, being arrested, getting a tattoo, drinking wine, playing the lottery; in working life, for example, conducting a job search at an employment bureau, consulting a staff notice board at a supermarket, selling to customers at a home decor store; in running errands in town, at the post office, in a fish-and-chip shop, at the dentist; in travel, for example, signs on roads, buses, and trains, as well as travel brochures; during sports activities, for example, playing darts, reading sports magazines, and attending a soccer match; and in student life, for example, reading message boards, writing graffiti, or using the laundromat.

International students at U.S. colleges may use literacy to try to figure out how the host culture works. They may find themselves studying bulletin boards around campus, inundated by notices they have no way of sorting through to separate the significant from the insignificant. They have to learn new computer literacy habits, such as using the Internet and e-mail to keep in contact with their home culture. For these students, being in an unfamiliar culture makes them reliant on the written word as a means of cultural survival and accommodation.

Gee (2000) pointed out that the New Literacy Studies described by Barton (1994), Gee (1996), and Street (1995), among others, are part of a larger movement away from the focus on the behavior of individuals that constituted behaviorist research in the early twentieth century and cognitivist research in the latter part of the same century. Gee related this change of focus toward investigating the social and cultural effects on literacy to fifteen collateral movements, in addition to the New Literacy Studies, as shown in Table 12.3. The table lists only a few key references for each movement (Gee, 2000, p. 180); please see the text for more citations.

The individual does not exist in a vacuum, but rather within a social milieu with historical, cultural, and political aspects. Literacy practices are activities within larger sets of structures that form discourses of the culture or society at large (see Mills, 1997). The literacy practices of the group shape the individual, and the individual in turn plays a part in the larger whole. The New Literacy Studies, which situate literacy in a cultural matrix, are relevant to educational literacy practices. Attention to the larger social and cultural contexts is a vital part of the work of literacy educators.

Teaching Academic Registers

Table 12.4 lists and describes the types of academic tasks faced by undergraduate and graduate students of psychology, biology, and history in a large, urban university in the United States, which is fairly representative of other, similar American institutions of higher learning (from Carson, 2001). This list permits a discussion of the distinctive nature of academic discourse, in order to distinguish it from other types of cognitive and linguistic activity.

Differences between academic work at the undergraduate and graduate level are summarized anecdotally by Campbell (1998):

> I finally learned ways to write academic papers in graduate school. Maybe I finally learned how to read and make connections among ideas from one course to another at that time since I was focusing on a unified course of study. A broad liberal arts education may have its merits, but I never read much of anything in depth as an undergraduate except German literature, given my major in that language. It was in graduate school that I began to see links between what I was studying in various courses, and I began to draw on my growing understsanding of a field of knowledge to understand new readings and discussions. I also found that in reading and listening to discussions, I was able to learn new ideas as well as analyze how an argument was developed. I may well have developed the ability to analyze the structure of arguments during my undergraduate study of German literature. But what was new for me in graduate school was that I took my understanding of a framework of an argument and deposited that framework somewhere in my mind for later use as a rhetorical strategy for my own writing. . . .
>
> I've seen from examining my own history as a writing student that my early schooling, even in college, involved what we now refer to as product-oriented writing pedagogy. The focus of the teacher's and the student's attention was the final written product, the essay. There was little discussion or experimentation with various strategies for producing these final written products. . . . (pp. 2–3)

Campbell points out here that graduate work calls for depth and range of thinking skills in order to transform static knowledge by means of one's own perspective. Students need to have a mature response to the demands of academic literacy in these

TABLE 12.3 ◆ Movements toward a Social and Cultural View of Literacy

Movement	Description	Key Sources
Ethnomethodology and conversational analysis	Study of moment-by-moment social and verbal interaction.	Goodwin & Heritage, 1990; Schiffrin, 1994
Discursive psychology	Analysis of the individual's memories and emotions as a part of social interaction.	Edwards & Potter, 1992; Harre & Stearns, 1995
Ethnography of speaking	Study of how people use cues available in a context to infer and construct meaning.	Gumperz, 1982; Hymes, 1974
Sociohistorical psychology	Thinking is mediated by cultural tools and by appropriating meaning from social interaction.	Vygotsky, Bakhtin; see Wertsch, 1985, 1991, 1998
Situated cognition	Knowledge and intelligence are distributed across the semiotic systems of a community of practice.	Lave, 1996; Lave & Wenger, 1991
Activity theory	The social activity of a community affects the availability of tools, techniques, and learning.	Engeström, 1990; Leont'ev, 1978
Cultural models theory	People make sense of their experiences by applying tacit explanatory theories originating in their cultural socialization.	D'Andrade & Strauss, 1992; Holland & Quinn, 1987
Cognitive linguistics	Human languages are organized by means of metaphors that help us to interpret the material and social world.	Lakoff & Johnson, 1980; Ungerer & Schmid, 1996
New science and technology studies	Scientists live and work in a collegial matrix that conditions their thinking and practice.	Latour, 1987, 1991
Modern composition theory	Knowledge and meaning are situated within genres that discipline their possibilities.	Bazerman, 1989; Swales, 1990
Connectionism	Thinking is a matter of using stored patterns derived from previous experiences.	Clark, 1993; Gee, 1992
Narrative studies	People make sense out of reality by interpreting it through culturally specific stories.	Bruner, 1986; Ricoeur, 1984
Evolutionary approaches to mind and behavior	Human intelligence is the result of a long process of adaptation to the social and physical environment.	Clark, 1997; Kauffman, 1993
Modern sociology	Human thinking and interaction shapes, and is shaped by, human institutions, both being radically transformed by global social changes.	Beck, Giddens, & Lash, 1994; Giddens, 1987
Poststructuralism, postmodernism	Certain discursive practices are positioned as normal or deviant, depending on social and cultural norms.	Bourdieu, 1979/1984; Fairclough 1992; Foucault 1973, 1979

Source: Gee, 2000.

TABLE 12.4 ✦ **Types of Literacy Required of University Students**

Unit of Analysis	Type of Analysis	Description
Course objectives	Course syllabi, or from professor/student	Undergraduate objective involved a broad introduction to a discipline, expecting students to absorb existing knowledge.
		Graduate objectives expected students to be critical of methods used and knowledge attained to date.
Texts (primary)	Textbooks, lectures, laboratory manuals	One main book and the course lecture were the primary texts at both levels. Reading difficulty varied among disciplines, as did dependence on graphics to convey information.
Texts (secondary)	Syllabi, study guides, handouts, references, course reading packets	Disciplinary differences were evident in expectations for use of the study guide.
Text topics	Subject matter included in evaluated products	Topics offered a view of content, but also a history of discovery of knowledge. Students were responsible for both process (how one arrived at the content) and content for each topic.
Text amount	Total pages per assignment, per chapter, per class, per exam	Amount of reading varied greatly across disciplines.
Text characteristics: prose	Organization, amount, content parameters (number of references, pedagogical aids provided, use of examples, themes, etc.), language demands	There was little use of references and little pedagogical support (how to study) in the primary texts.
Text characteristics: graphics	Organization, amount, content parameters (types, functions)	Biology and psychology depended heavily on graphics; history much less so.
Tasks (in class)	General parameters of tests, task of response/demand	On tests, students were expected to reproduce the basic concepts and principles in the course. Undergraduate tests had similar construction across disciplines (recognize/retrieve/identify). The history class featured an essay test. Students needed both literacy and oracy to do well: reading texts for detail, synthesis and integration of information; writing notes and study guide answers; listening to lectures, and asking clarifying questions.
		Graduate students had few in-class evaluated products such as tests.

(continued)

TABLE 12.4 ◆ Continued

Unit of Analysis	Type of Analysis	Description
Tasks (out of class)	Assignment description, task demands in preparation and production	Undergraduates had little out-of-class evaluated product. Graduate students needed reading skills for extensive archival work and critical thinking/writing skills to construct original responses and give oral presentations.

Source: Carson, 2001.

contexts. This means that academic competence comprises both psychological and sociocultural factors.

Academic Competence: Psychological Factors

Part of what a person needs to accomplish academic success depends on the psychological response of the individual, which is derived from patterns and habits learned in the sociocultural milieu. Important attributes are persistence, ability to achieve rapport with one's advisers and instructors, grasp of the demands of the tasks, and the ability to recognize if help is needed and to seek, obtain, and benefit from such help. These personality features help the individual to accommodate to the demands of the situation.

Academic Competence: Sociocultural Factors

Success in previous schooling makes present and future accommodations easier, assuming that previous schooling was demanding enough to act as a training context. Peers must set patterns of similar activity in order for the individual to feel supported by the peer culture; the parental/cultural standards of achievement must also be appropriately demanding and supportive. In this way, the individual is situated within a social and cultural context that sustains the academic activity.

Academic Competence Demanded to Perform Undergraduate-Level Academic Writing

It would be satisfying to believe that ESL and EFL courses invariably equip students to undertake successful undergraduate work at a college or university in the United States. In fact, in the United States the lines between ESL and non-ESL undergraduate students are blurring. Many children of non–English-speaking immigrants are now entering colleges and universities with weak skills in English, even after having been schooled in English in elementary and secondary schools. Given the level of demands identified in Carson's research, above, the list shown in Table 12.5 may be just a start.

TABLE 12.5 ◆ Academic Competence in Academic Writing at the Threshold Level

Component of Communicative Competence	Example
Grammatical competence	Sentence syntax intact (coherent phrases and clauses)
	Morphemic usage intact (no subject-verb number errors, verb tense markers are accurate)
	Register awareness (e.g., word choice not excessively colloquial)
	Uses idioms expressing intended meaning that make sense in context
	Verb tense usage consistent across sentences and paragraphs
	Denotative lexicon (word choices express correct meaning)
	Computer spell-check used to produce accurate spelling (except for the occasional homonym that computer spell-check passes)
	Average usage proficiency (capitalization and punctuation of sentences)
Discourse competence	Paragraph cohesion of ideas
	Main idea expressed in paragraph
	Logical heading structure (idea relations, e.g., subsumption)
	Lexical use of transition devices
Sociolinguistic competence	Aware of task demands (What is a summary paragraph?)
	Able to articulate relation of task demands to academic goal
	Use of a reference citation format in text
Strategic competence	Able to paraphrase ideas
	Able to verbalize information-seeking strategy
	Able to obtain adequate number and type of sources for research
	Able to take notes in class
	Able to word-process documents

Source: Díaz-Rico, 2001b.

Academic Competence Demanded to Perform Graduate-Level Academic Writing

To perform well on situated writing tasks at the graduate level, students need to enter the program with a threshold competence of academic writing (Díaz-Rico, 2001b) and then move beyond this level to achieve exit competence, for example to write the master's thesis. Table 12.6 uses Canale's (1983) four components of communicative competence as categories in order to contrast writing skills *below the threshold* (entry-level graduate skills) with those *above the threshold* (graduate-program exit level).

TABLE 12.6 ◆ Academic Competence in Academic Writing above the Threshold Level

Grammatical competence	Sentence syntax serving truth (logical phrases and clauses, including parallel structure)
	Sentence syntax serving beauty (elegant, balanced phrases and clauses; pleasing to ear)
	Morphemic usage correct (e.g., agreement, parts of speech)
	Register control (e.g., word choice academic)
	Idioms correct and logical (e.g., prepositions, determiners)
	Verb tense usage academic
	Connotative lexicon (expresses nuance, esp. use of "govern-mentality" lexicon)
	Human spell-check (detection of homonyms, etc.)
	Usage mastery (colons, semicolons, dashes, parenthetical expressions)
Discourse competence	Key-word cohesion
	Introductions and conclusions to sections
	Improved logical heading structure (correct idea relations)
	Logical use of transition devices
Sociolinguistic competence	Responsive to task demands (What is a *good* literature review?)
	Able to realize academic goal in key word review
	Mastery of APA* or MLA** citation format
	Mastery of APA or MLA rules
Strategic competence	Able to evaluate paraphrased ideas
	Able to exercise authority over information
	Strategic use of sources
	Able to manage large word-processed documents
	Mastery of APA or MLA rules for tables
	Able to use figures to serve cognition (e.g., model building)

*American Psychological Association
**Modern Language Association
Source: Díaz-Rico, 2001b.

Task Demands of Academic Writing in an MATESOL Program

As an example of graduate text and task demands, a master's degree program in TESOL requires students, among other tasks, to read texts, articles, and book chapters; write reaction papers in which they summarize and take a position on reading assignments; access computer-based instructional formats to read material, take both self-tutorial and evaluative quizzes, and communicate with one another; write grade-appropriate instructional plans; organize instruction and create instructional materials; write reflective self-analyses in which they examine their professional goals and teaching/learning styles; write a review of research literature with bibliography; and write an M.A. project that features individual research, including self-designed theoretical models. These tasks, which require a high level of critical, analytical, and integrative thinking, are situated within a social context that encourages students to collaborate and to draw upon the instruction, tutoring, and advising resources of the university faculty and staff.

A comprehensive look at writing situated within academia is presented in Flower's (1994) work, *The Construction of Negotiated Meaning: A Social Cognitive Theory of Writing*. Beginning with an examination of literacy and the meaning of literate acts, Flower explores what the metaphor of "construction" offers as a way of teaching students to write by means of collaborative cognitive acts, bolstered by strategic use of knowledge, metacognition, and reflection. Her definition of literate action deftly sums up the shift to a contextualized view of literacy:

> Literate action is a socially situated problem-solving process shaped not only by available language, practices, partners, and texts, but by the ways people interpret the rhetorical situation they find themselves in, the goals they set, and the strategies they control. When the discussion turns from the conventions of discourse to the practice of readers and writers within it, it becomes clear that literate acts are also moments of making meaning. Literate actions emerge out of a constructive process of negotiation in which individual readers and writers must juggle conflicting demands and chart a path among alternative goals, contraints, and possibilities. (p. 2)

This chapter has taken two positions, both of which may be controversial. First, it has argued that the concept of dialect may be seen as a facet of situated oracy. Knowing when to shift to standard English is a sociolinguistic issue, involving choice of register. Second, it posited that academic writing is an issue of situated literacy, again, knowing when to shift register. Rather than being solely a sociolinguistic shift, though, this register shift also involves grammatical, discourse, and strategic shifts and skills.

Language educators, as mentors of situated oracy and literacy, have the responsibility to create contexts in which English learners are fully supported by the activity system co-constructed by teacher and learners. This activity is purposeful, is satisfying to all members, and moves students forward in their understanding and use not only of English as their second language but also of language itself and the cultures that it conveys. This type of context brims with meaning and enjoyment. Learners deserve this high-quality environment.

Building a Community of Learners

Every neighborhood has a school. That simple building houses the American dream. In that school are classrooms, each a microcosm of society. In the best cases, that class is like a close-knit family, in which the members come together every day eager to share stories of their adventures, their triumphs, or their disasters. They learn together willingly, working on projects that enrich their quality of life, pushing the boundaries of their knowledge, confident that the world of learning is exciting and fulfilling.

In cities, suburbs, and rural areas across the United States, families speak languages other than English, and children depend on schooling to learn English. In some areas of the United States, it is the English-speaking immigrants who have settled in Native American lands, forcing indigenous people to function reluctantly in English. In EFL contexts, students grapple with the complexities of English as an academic language. Across these contexts, teachers face the challenge of building communities in the classroom in which students find positive affirmation.

McCaleb (1994) posed the issue succinctly:

> How can educators create a partnership with parents and young students that will nurture literacy and facilitate participation in the schools while celebrating and valuing the home culture and family and community concerns and aspirations? (p. x)

This chapter situates the education of English learners within the life of the community and offers strategies for opening the doors of the classroom to the world. These strategies include ways in which students can use their nascent English to improve community life and ways in which themes and projects important to the community become tools for classroom teaching.

❖ **MEGASTRATEGY 13:** Make the classroom a community, and bring the community into the classroom—parents, families, neighborhoods, and culture

What Is a Community of Learners?

In the traditional teacher-centered classroom, the language teacher sets educational goals, maintains an effective learning environment, dispenses linguistic and cultural content, initiates and organizes learning activities, motivates students, monitors progress, and evaluates achievement. Much of the success of the learner depends on the teacher. In a learner-centered classroom, in contrast, students develop self-discipline and accountability as they accomplish learning goals, work together collaboratively, make choices about language content, and follow their own interests and talents to develop ideas and turn them into projects. This change from teacher-centered to learner-centered pedagogy is accomplished largely through group collaboration (Bassano & Christison, 1995).

From a wider perspective, a community of learners is not only a group of learners working together in a classroom, but a classroom connected closely to a larger community, namely, the families of the learners. For English learners at the K–12 level, this environment ensures the support and active involvement of their parents or other family members and preserves the connection to their native culture that lives through their neighbors or friends. For adult English learners, the community may mean their children, their own elders, or the values and habitudes of their native culture. A "learning community" denotes a group of people who set about to gain knowledge by working together. The challenge in creating and sustaining such a community is to foster the sense of interdependency as well as productive learning.

◆ **STRATEGY 13.1:** Make the classroom a learning community

The Classroom as a Community

In a classroom community, students feel that they are free to work with others and that they have something to contribute to the whole (Tchudi & Mitchell, 1999). Involving the students actively in decision making and collaborative interaction requires a major shift from the traditional roles of teacher and student. Both are now learners as well as teachers.

Classrooms go beyond the use of cooperative learning to encourage students to be agents of change; they become sites of social transformation. What do classrooms look like when teachers listen to, and learn from, students?

In four contrasting scenarios that took place in Hong Kong, Lin (2001) compared classroom instruction in which students' *habitus* (Bourdieu's term for the dispositions/attitudes with which children are endowed, by virtue of their family or community socialization) was either compatible with that of the practices of schooling, incompatible with schooling, or transformed by schooling. Table 13.1 displays the four classrooms and describes briefly the contrasts in students' attitudes and teachers' behavior.

Using qualitative description, Lin showed how important it is for TESOL educators to match classroom teaching with students' social and cultural backgrounds. The teacher in classroom A benefited from the fact that students were habituated to the use of English in their lives, had learned to act cooperatively, and no doubt saw themselves as eventually being as successful as their parents were. English instruction was successful in this classroom because the students were already socialized at home to perform in consonance with the teacher's habits and expectations.

In contrast, classrooms B and C students disliked English because of their lack of interest, confidence, and competence. They did not expect to master English, even though they recognized its potential advantage, and this low expectation made the students feel angry and disenfranchised. These emotions were exacerbated by the

TABLE 13.1 ◆ Habitus and Discourse Patterns in Four Hong Kong Classrooms

Class	Socioeconomic Status/Habitus	Classroom Discourse Patterns	Outcome
A	Upper middle class/compatible with schooling	English is used as the language of instruction to engage students in higher-order critical thinking. Students are attentive and cooperative.	Students like English.
B	Working class/ incompatible with schooling	English is used as the language of instruction, but students are cynical, bored, and resistant. Teacher often chides boys for being off task.	Students dislike English.
C	Working class/ incompatible with schooling	English is used consistently by the teacher, but students are cynical, bored, and resistant. Teacher often has to rephrase questions into L1, and students respond in L1.	Students dislike English.
D	Working class/ transformed by schooling	L1 is used as the language of instruction and explanation. Teacher expects students to rephrase their answers in English. Teacher gives all students individual attention in and out of class to develop their interests, skills, and confidence in learning English.	Students like English.

Source: Adapted from Lin, 2001.

teacher's insistence that they use only English, although they were uncomfortable with it as the language of instruction.

In classroom D, students brought the same habitus in English as those in classrooms B and C, but they felt more comfortable. The instruction in L1 was relaxing, yet students were expected to take turns speaking English. Acceptance combined with challenge motivated students to learn English, even though they did not have the cultural capital or habitus enjoyed by the students in classroom A. The teacher was a full partner in classroom discourse. She spent extracurricular time getting to know each student individually. By using L1 as the language of instruction, she was able to bond with the learner, sustaining motivation when she pressured students toward high achievement. Lin (2001) called this teaching "transformative," because students made genuine progress toward investing their time and energy in activities for which there was a clear and attainable outcome.

To create a sense of community, then, it is helpful but not entirely necessary to be fluent in the L1 of the students. What *is* necessary is the investment in getting to know students as individuals, openness to students' creative impulses, and willingness to find ways for students to manage their own learning. However, even these ingredients are not sufficient to ensure that English teaching serves the ideals of democracy and social justice. Only the most fragile sense of community can grow within the classroom if the larger society is corrupt and uncaring.

Forming a Learning Community

At San Diego State University (SDSU), a Freshman Success Program (FSP) was formed in 1991 to increase the odds that entering students would be successful in their studies. Most of the students who enrolled in the FSP were ESL or bilingual students. Other students who were not considered ESL had failed the English Placement and thus needed one or more remedial English classes; some of these were Generation 1.5 students (see Harklau et al., 1999). Like many other FSP programs across the United States, SDSU's included a one-unit freshman seminar designed to orient students to the university and provide mentoring. What makes the FSP of interest to teachers of English learners is the composition/literacy class that was offered. This class helped students to acquire strategies for approaching different kinds of reading and writing tasks and genres, alternative discourse styles, and preparation for the exit exam that would demonstrate writing competence. This disciplinary-adjunct model not only helped the students with ESL needs but positioned the skills of the English-for-academic-purposes faculty as valuable to the university (Johns, 2001), creating positive feelings for both student and faculty participants in the community.

Critical Perspectives on Community Involvement

Critical language educators recognize that an effective curriculum is not simply a matter of "methods that work." Morgan (1998) brings the concerns of the community into course design through five key questions:

- ◆ Whose social values does this instruction serve?
- ◆ Whose expectations, desires, identities, and realities are reflected and promoted by the instructional activities?
- ◆ How does the classroom language complement the social concerns and priorities of the community?
- ◆ How can students learn to speak with authority in the face of a new culture in which networks of privilege may exclude them from higher education, employment, and the pursuit of happiness?
- ◆ How can dialogue with students and other members of the community help teachers to become aware of the values and habits that they may be taking for granted and that may or may not meet the needs of the community?

In community centers, classrooms, or wherever ESL and EFL are taught, students do not leave their lives as newcomers, parents, employees, and family members behind. The English they learn is not "an isolated topic disconnected from social concerns" (Morgan, 1998, p. 19). A focus on community is a way of achieving a more locally and socially responsive way of teaching. This means building language learning on experiences and activities that are real and immediate to students.

Introducing concepts such as politics and civil rights into the ESL/EFL classroom is a necessary way to position English teaching in the real world. In the past, language educators believed that theories and techniques could be used independent of the local context, as though one could learn a language "culture free," in a social vacuum. However, the economic and social circumstances of students' lives underlie the mental and emotional efforts they are able to make as language learners.

Listening to the Learner

The teacher in classroom D in Lin's examples above was able to engage her students because she was a genuine part of the communicative network of the class. She spent time with them to learn about them as individuals, and in turn she communicated to them that she was a real person who worked hard on their behalf and cared about them. Brian Morgan speaks of the importance of listening to the learner as he describes his early efforts to teach EFL:

> My initial training as an ESL teacher served several important purposes. It satisfied my early assumptions about the nature of language and provided me with a body of abstract methods and techniques that might safely guide me past the various land mines of the classroom. Soon after, however, I found myself fumbling with questions from students that went beyond my limited canon and experiences. Moreover, I tended to view such moments as disrespectful challenges to my newly sanctioned authority. Usually, in these times of threatened confidence, I would call upon some greater authority: the "latest" research, famous "expert," or in more desperate occasions, the "ultimate truth" on language. These responses were not specifically intended to deceive or mislead my students. Rather, they seemed to suit my idea of what a teacher should do, say, and know in a classroom.
>
> Later, during a stint as an instructor in the People's Republic of China, chinks in my protective armor began to appear. Unfortunately, my first private impulse was to berate the "willful ignorance" of students who resisted when presented with my "state-of-the-art" techniques to develop fluency. These methods, I assumed, were certain to work if only given a chance and a commitment. Of course, it didn't work that way, and I then embarked upon an unsettling adventure of listening to my students as much as telling them what to do. This proved more fruitful, and while I didn't always agree with them or comply with all of their requests, I started to gain a sense of their expectations and their histories, which informed their goals in learning. (1998, pp. 3–4)

The concept of listening to the learner is not new. Greene (1988) posed the question of what it might mean to listen to multiple voices in the classroom—one voice many times, one voice saying several things, or many voices, with overlapping or contradictory needs. Vella (2002) emphasized that the first need of adult learners is to feel that their needs are being met with understanding and immediacy. This need to listen to the learner has generated a host of teaching techniques based on the dialogue journal. Van Deusen-Scholl (1993) described ethnographic study as a way in which prospective teachers listen intensively to English learners in a semester-long series of interviews about the progress of their English learning.

When three male students in an English-for-academic-purposes class resisted the topic of anorexia, Benesch (2001) used dialogue journals to explore their attitudes toward women's bodies as well as their negative feelings about the topic. Encouraging students to express their discomfort with a teacher-imposed topic, helping these individuals to come to their own terms with the issues under discussion, and balancing this sort of topic with student-selected topics meant that the community created within the class could sustain a critical inquiry without causing the men to feel overrun.

Cultural Models within Communities.   Listening to the learner is a key to translating what is said into codes for critical work (see Chapter 2). Listening is also important because each community has what Gee (1990) called *cultural models*. Only by spending time within a community can one fully understand the meanings and nuance in the terms used by members of that community. Despite the overt meanings of words, one can only plumb the cultural connotations put on these words by spending time with people for whom they carry particular significance.

> When I moved to Puerto Rico and began learning Spanish as a second language, I naïvely assumed that when learning a second language, terms translated directly from one language to another. In the textbooks, the English "we" translated in Spanish as "nosotros." In English, "we" is used to mean, "you and I together." But over and over again, in Puerto Rican Spanish, "nosotros" was used to mean "We who are Puerto Rican." When used in my presence, it never meant "you and I together." Gradually I came to understand that because of my poor Spanish and the color of my skin, I was perceived as an "American." Therefore "nosotros" was never about me.

Listening to the way people use language helps to understand their cultural models. One can learn any number of languages and still interpret reality using one's original cultural models. Gee (1996) made the point that all meaning is local, *customized* within specific cultures and *activated* by cultural models. Only as teachers listen carefully to students can they design instruction that meets their needs and resist superimposing a pedagogical English that is "culture free" and thus relatively meaningless to them. Cultural models are not necessarily self-consistent and logical.

> Gee described an interview with a young Latina on the topic, "Why do you think there are relatively few African-American and Hispanic doctors?" In her response to this question, Marcella comes close to a cultural capital theory of society—that some people advance because their social class benefits from inherited privilege. Mixed with this tacit theory, however, is Marcella's insinuation that white people are inherently smarter than other races and thus succeed in medical school. She may have internalized a sense of racial inferiority as a result of the circulation of hegemonic ideas (in which lower classes participate in their own subjugation)—whatever the source of her belief, her cultural model is mixed, and the meaning of "success" to her is complicated by conflicting explanations for reality. (Gee, 1996)

Cultural Voices and Authentic Materials.   The concept of "listening" to language learners extends from the prompts used in discussions to the writing students do in journals, essays, and stories. Morgan (1998) presents lesson plans that bring many topics into his adult ESL classroom: the Gulf War, community policing, the impact of immigrants on society, and the morality of bringing children into a "dangerous world." The last topic sprang from a remark that a student made about the AIDS epidemic: that reading about this global health challenge had made her wish she didn't have children. In small groups, the class discussed the prompt, "Would you advise people against having children in a dangerous future?" This caused an outpouring of personal stories and opinions.

Morgan used writings as prompts that challenged "scientific" views. He asked questions like, "Whose interests does this article serve?" This stance enabled students to examine how a seemingly neutral grammatical structure such as passive voice helps to soothe antisocial or subversive tendencies against the social order. Morgan used critical language analysis in its three levels (text, institution, and sociocultural context) to help a class co-construct awareness of the interconnecting role that language plays with power and privilege to maintain controlling social structures. This work helped the class members to confront the challenge and oppression in the life of an immigrant.

Authentic materials can bring the concerns and voices of the community into the classroom. Pfingstag (1999) passed out copies of letters to the editor from the local paper. The class discussed not only the content of the letters but also how the writers used sentence structure and vocabulary to make their points, sometimes using sarcasm ("I feel really safe in the parks now, with the policy that replaces park rangers with work release prisoners"), loaded vocabulary, ("ludicrous thinking," "hoodwink voters"), rhetorical questions ("Why is it that people such as council members make decisions on matters they have no clue about?"), and dialect grammar ("This ain't your kind of town") (p. 62). Then the class wrote letters to the editor of the school newspaper to voice their opinions on controversial issues.

Not-So-Critical Perspectives on Community Involvement

Not all community involvement takes a critical stance. *A to Zany: Community Activities for Students of English* (Stafford-Yilmaz, 1998) takes a neutral approach. In contrast to Morgan's work (1998), in which students who had experienced inequities in community policing discussed their experience of discrimination, Stafford-Yilmaz's chapter on police compares police in the United States with that of the language learner's home country, discusses images of the police in the mass media, and suggests that the students invite a police officer to class. Students then write essays on whether they would want to be a police officer.

This and other activities in *A to Zany* position the class members as outsiders who interview "Americans" to ask their opinions ("Talk to an American about the speed of life in America. Ask if he or she would prefer a faster or slower life. Ask why" [p. 121]). When reading this assignment, a critical reader might ask when and where an English learner could ask such a question. Would such a conversation take place on the street, or in a neighborhood? The realities of the lives of newcomers seem to be missing from this perspective on community involvement, despite the range of suggested activities.

Authentic community concerns might serve as codes for critical educators but serve as neutral language input in the hands of other educators. "Protest!" is the topic of a lesson in which students discuss controversial issues (Connell, 1999). Class members skim the content of newspaper or newsmagazine articles for answers to a teacher-prepared work sheet, write one-paragraph summaries, and share their work in pairs or small groups. The whole class then discusses the issue, comparing attitudes that people in the United States might have with attitudes of people in other countries.

This approach uses authentic materials, but not those that originate in the concerns of the local community. Although this approach may engender critical thinking and discussion, it is strictly an academic exercise.

A Model for Community Involvement

Given the previous examples, one might imagine that the issue of community involvement is complex. Some people follow Bassano and Christison's approach, outlined at the beginning of the chapter, that "community" means the classroom as a community, without a systematic focus on concerns in the larger community outside. This kind of instruction positions the SLA educator as neutral to the concerns of the community. In return, critical educators have been accused of introducing content that is irrelevant to the survival skills needed by English learners.

One might think of the community-curriculum-instruction connection in four parts. Quadrant I is individually based English instruction disconnected from community concerns or social change. In quadrant II, students work in groups, but the learning does not reflect engagement with the local community. In quadrant III, the individual is engaged with the local community but not as a member of a proactive group. In quadrant IV, students are involved both in group learning and engagement with community concerns. Quadrants III and IV have the most potential for the learner's long-term growth and empowerment to influence society positively. This chapter uses this model to describe teaching from each quadrant.

Individual Learning.   The traditional approach to learning assumes that each learner's success is either independent of another's or negatively correlated, that is, individuals compete for learning in a "I win, you lose" situation. Quadrant I of Figure 13.1 posits individuals learning English without substantive connection to a learning community.

Individual Social Action.   The individual can learn in a community-neutral or a community-engaged learning context. The use of authentic sources represents the movement from community-neutral instructional materials toward the input of real language as used by the community. Using a sample map of San Francisco as well as

Learner Unit	Community Involvement	
Individual	I Individual Learning Community Neutral	III Individual Learning Community Engaged
Group	II Collaborative Learning Community Neutral	IV Collaborative Learning Community Engaged

FIGURE 13.1   ✦   A model of educational strategies for English learners and community involvement.

travel brochures, students in an English-language private school in Seoul wrote an account of an imaginary trip to the city (quadrant I).

Although this activity is a creative alternative to work sheets and other language drills, this specific use of authentic materials does not in itself engage the community. Two deeper aspects of engagement might shift this approach toward an authentic interaction with the community rather than an individualized, academic exercise. First, has anyone in the students' community actually visited San Francisco? The voice of authentic experience would be an invaluable resource. Second, is there a consulate that could recommend Korean speakers with whom to tour the city? What questions might one ask a denizen of San Francisco that would help to understand daily life there?

Collaborative Learning.   Probably more was written on cooperative and collaborative learning in the last twenty years of the twentieth century than in all the previous history of education. David and Robert Johnson (Johnson & Johnson, 1975, 1985; Johnson, Johnson, & Smith, 1991; Johnson, Johnson, & Holubec, 1993), Robert Slavin (1983, 1991) and Spencer Kagan (1998, 1999) advocated the use of cooperative learning for elementary students. Others documented the success of cooperative learning with elementary school English learners (Calderón, Tinajero, & Hertz-Lazarowitz, 1990; Cohen, 1986; Cohen, Lotan, & Catanzarite, 1990; Johns, 1992; Johnson & Johnson, 1994; and Kagan, 1986) as well as with secondary school ESL students (Holt, Chips, & Wallace, 1992).

Cooperative learning is well established as a methodology for language as well as content instruction. "How to" books abound in the use of cooperative learning in the education of English learners, an approach that came into its own simultaneously with the field's emphasis on communicative competence.

Cooperative learning helps to build a sense of community in the classroom.

Small-group learning provides English learners with a rich discourse environment and multiple opportunities for face-to-face interaction. This is particularly necessary when students must exchange information about academic content and procedures. When students are collaborating in small groups, they have substantially more chances to practice language without worrying if their production is exactly right. This lowers their anxiety and lets them concentrate on the content of learning. They can hear and say key words and phrases and repeat them in a variety of ways until they feel comfortable with their language mastery (Faltis, 2001).

Cooperative grouping also increases the possibility that English learners will feel a part of the culture of the classroom as a whole. "Cooperative grouping allows children to get to know each other in ways that do not happen in a whole-class setting. When left to their own devices, children tend to pick their friends from their own social or linguistic group. However, cooperative grouping gives students the opportunity to work with those they have never considered interacting with before. In such a setting, the likelihood of their becoming friends increases" (Johns & Espinoza, 1992).

Table 13.2 summarizes the instructional use of cooperative learning with English learners. This information represents a synthesis of tips and guidelines from Bassano and Christison (1995), Cantlon (1991), and Kagan (1998, 1999).

Even in the best of circumstances, cooperative learning has its challenges. Table 13.3 sets these forth, offering tactics for teachers to address these issues.

Many types of tasks have been designed that feature cooperative structures. These range from simply pairing students for discussion to more elaborate setups requiring extensive time for preparation and monitoring. Table 13.4 presents a few cooperative structures and tasks.

The jigsaw model of cooperative learning is particularly useful, in that students are individually accountable for learning their own material and for sharing their information effectively with other group members. In the jigsaw method, each member of the base team (see Table 13.4; teams are I, II, III, and IV) attends an expert group session (all the As huddle together) to study one aspect or section of the topic, and thus has one piece of the knowledge puzzle (hence the name *jigsaw*). The ultimate learning goal is for each member of the base team to have the whole set of information, so each member must communicate what has been learned in the expert group.

In one use of the jigsaw, fifth-grade students researched "Who Discovered America?" As a warm-up, students used a world map to identify the continents, and discussed the various land and sea routes to North America. Then students went to their expert groups and each read a statement of one point of view, such as that the Vikings were the first Europeans to come to the New World, or that the first people came by way of the Bering Strait. When students returned to their base groups, they compared the information and opinions in the four readings. (Coehlo, Winer, & Olsen, 1989)

In another example of jigsaw, intermediate ESL students studied the use of persuasion in advertising by looking at three different types of ads in three expert groups and completing work sheets with questions like, "How is the ad trying to persuade you? Is it using reason, an appeal to the emotions, or an appeal to a feeling of right or wrong? Is the advertisement effective? Why or why not?" Returning to their base group, they discussed the ad they studied and completed a second work sheet summarizing the types

TABLE 13.2 • Instructional Use of Cooperative Learning

Component of Cooperative Learning	Explanation or Example
Definition	"An approach to education and a repertoire of teaching strategies based on the philosophy that students can learn effectively in small groups. Cooperative learning restructures the traditional classroom into small, carefully planned learning groups to provide opportunities for all students to work together and to learn from one another." (Coehlo, Winer, & Olsen, 1989, p. 3)
Rationales for using cooperative learning	Practice speaking and listening.
	Share information.
	Create things together.
	Learn democratic processes.
	Practice negotiating and compromising (Bassano & Christison, 1995, p. 29).
	Develop leadership, communication, decision-making, and conflict management skills (Cantlon, 1991).
	Promote real-world team skills.
	Together Everyone Achieves More (TEAM)!
	Builds positive interpersonal relations.
	Transcend differences (cliques) (Kagan, 1999).
Roles in teams	Language monitor, task monitor, time-keeper, secretary, clarifier, encourager, reporter (Bassano & Christison, 1995, p. 29).
	Materials monitor, quiet captain (Kagan, 1993).
Optimal team size	For initial start-up, dyads (teams of two) are most successful (Cantlon, 1991).
	If teams of three are necessary, have them sit side by side (Cantlon, 1991).
	Teams of four are ideal, small enough for active participation and splits evenly for pair work (Kagan, 1993).
Frequency of use of cooperative structures	Minimum is three times a week, but simple structures (pair/share) can be used more often (Cantlon, 1991).
Room and seating arrangements	Partners should sit side by side. If students are in fours, provide two sets of materials. No student's back should be to the teacher (Cantlon, 1991).
Role of the teacher	Teacher is the source of task, arranger of materials, accountable authority, partner in learning (Bassano & Christison, 1995).
Team composition	Heterogeneous (mixed gender, ethnicity, ability), teacher-assigned, long-term teams are preferable (Kagan, 1998).
	To form groups of heterogeneous ability, list students in ability from high to low (1-28); divide into quartiles; then form one group from 1, 8, 15, 22; next group 2, 9, 16, 23, etc. (this avoids grouping highest with lowest).

(continued)

TABLE 13.2 ◆ Continued

Component of Cooperative Learning	Explanation or Example
Team composition (continued)	Random (randomly mixed ability, etc.) short-term teams break up the monotony (Kagan, 1998).
	Random teams may be a problem if all high-achieving students are in one group, or two students create mutual discipline problems (Cantlon, 1991).
	Random grouping: Use colored marbles or slips with group numbers in a jar; group students by month of birth; count off around class) (Bassano & Christison, 1995).
Team management	Inform students how much time is allotted to task; agree on a signal to stop working (clap pattern, ringing a bell, countdown) (Cantlon, 1991).
Rationale statement	Teacher explains why work is done in a team, what the benefits are, and what behavior is expected (Cantlon, 1991).
Necessary group skills	Form into groups quickly. Participate with muted voices. Establish turn-taking routines. Involve more hesitant members in group processes (Bassano & Christison, 1995).
Trustbuilding/bonding	Build rapport by discussing favorite foods, hobbies, likes, dislikes. Do nonacademic fun activities: games, puzzles. Do academic tasks: partner reading, checking homework together (staple papers together, teachers corrects top paper) (Cantlon, 1991).
Teaching social skills	Teacher models behavior: speaking in quiet voices, taking turns, everyone participating, encouraging partner, signaling to stop (Cantlon, 1991).
Appreciation statements by peers at debriefing	"(*Name*), you helped the team by _____" "(_____), you did a great job of _____" "(_____), I appreciated it when you _____" "(_____), you are very good at _____" (Cantlon, 1991)
Clarification statements by peers	"I don't understand" "Excuse me?" "Speak more slowly, please." "Okay?" (Bassano & Christison, 1995, p. 29)
Procedural statements by peers	"It's my/your/his/her turn." "Quickly! We have four minutes." "You first, then me." (Bassano & Christison, 1995, p. 29)
Peers asking for/ offering help	"Are you finished?" "I need help." "Do you need help?" (Bassano & Christison, 1995, p. 29)
Individual accountability	Students have progress conferences with instructor; groups are rated by teacher using monitoring chart; groups monitor themselves periodically using rating charts (Bassano & Christison, 1995).

(continued)

TABLE 13.2 ⬩ Continued

Component of Cooperative Learning	Explanation or Example
Rewards (nonmaterial), avoiding message that reward involves escape from work (extra recess)	Elementary: Provide "happy grams," suggest applause, display group work, give AV treat, play a special game. Middle/high school: Use library passes, computer time, daily announcements/ newsletter recognition, work displays, special privileges, team picture displays (Cantlon, 1991).
Feedback	At the close of activity, teammates write on index card: "Which question/ problem gave you difficulty?" "Give examples of what you might do differently next time." "List ways in which your partners helped the team to reach its goal." (Cantlon, 1991)
Anticipated difficulties	Aggression: Some students dominate and control others. Withdrawal: Some students are shy, embarrassed, and avoid participating. Apathy: Learners do not seem to care about the work of the group. Evasion: Students are off task. Egocentrism: Group members go off on their own or do not talk about their idea together. Complaints: Students reject one another's ideas and make negative comments. Disorderly conduct: Students damage materials, leave the group, or distress one another (Bassano & Christison, 1995).
Teacher-created difficulties	Instructions are unclear. Teacher fails to provide a rationale. Topic is boring, unfamiliar, or irrelevant. Product or process expectations are unrealistic. Strangers are expected to trust one another too quickly (Bassano & Christison, 1995).

and effectiveness of persuasion used in various ads. Students then worked cooperatively to write their own ads (Weatherly, 1999, p. 79). (These are examples of quadrant II activity.)

Community counseling (Curran, 1982) is a method of language learning designed for adult education in which members of a learning group sit in a circle, with (usually) two facilitators standing just outside the group. Members of the learning circle volunteer to speak to any other member, using one of the facilitators as a coach to frame the language of the message. This emphasis on communication was a forerunner of the communicative methodologies of the 1980s and 1990s.

Collaborative Social Action. Involving students in social action is a natural way to extend students' work (see quadrants III and IV). Project-based learning helps students to make school-community connections. *The Kid's Guide to Social Action* (Lewis, 1991) is a resource for teachers who wish to help students feel socially en-

TABLE 13.3 ◆ Challenges to Cooperative Learning and Tactics to Meet Them

Challenge	Tactics for Teachers
Students cannot get along.	Keep activities short and simple while students are learning how to work together.
	Group students wisely; place a socially immature student with two who are more mature.
	Teach social skills and review regularly.
Student prefers to work alone.	Provide encouragement by emphasizing importance of working in a group, giving examples from teacher's work.
	Give bonus points to class for working well together.
	Provide individual work occasionally as "safety valve."
Student is unmotivated.	Use an interest inventory to discover students' likes and dislikes.
	Ask previous teachers what works for the student.
	Give student a role in the group in which he or she will succeed.
Student cannot keep up with others.	Let student prepare some part of task prior to group work.
	Provide a modified work sheet for slow student.
	Provide an alternative way for student to perform.
Group finishes before others.	Provide an extension or enrichment task that extends the activity.
	Two groups who finish first can compare their products.
Group finishes last.	See if task can be modified so that all groups will finish together.
	Teacher or member of early-finishing group can spend some time to help slow group.
	Let individuals take home tasks.
There is too much noise.	Monitor groups and commend those who are quiet and on-task.
	Use a standard signal for noise, such as blinking room lights.
	Assign a member of each group as "noise control."

Source: Ellis & Whalen, 1992.

gaged. This guide explains how students can find worthwhile endeavors: acquire "power" skills such as writing letters to newspaper editors and public officials; gather information by interviewing and surveying people; influence public opinion by making speeches; circulate petitions and proposals; raise funds; have officials make proclamations; and obtain media coverage and advertising. In this way, students can feel that their energies make a difference in the world, and teachers can feel that they have a positive influence on students and their families.

Before leaving the topic of classroom community, one might look again to the theme of classroom culture (see Chapter 10). Toohey (1998) noted three instructional practices that communicate the value of individualism over collectivism. The first practice was exemplified by the maxim, "Sit at your own desk"; the second, "Use

TABLE 13.4 • Sample Cooperative Learning Activities

Name of Activity	Description
Relay	Four students learn a skill; they teach it to four others; eight teach it to eight more, until everyone knows it (Bassano & Christison, 1995).
Group memory	In groups of six, give each group a line to memorize. Group members receive extra credit if everyone can say it when time is up (Bassano & Christison, 1995).
Listen, please (also called "information gap")	In this paired activity, student A has words on various cards and student B has a matching set of picture cards. Listening to the description on a card, student B must pick out the matching card (Bassano & Christison, 1995).
Sequencing task	Students put a cut-up sequence in correct order, for example, scrambled dialogue from a phone call to a friend (Bassano & Christison, 1995).
Scavenger hunt	With a stack of newspapers, group finds one of each: some good news, some bad news, weather map, letter to editor, overseas news, etc. (Bassano & Christison, 1995).
Round robin	Each person solves a problem (using one color ink) and passes the paper to the next team member, who does the next problem. Teacher corrects one sheet (Cantlon, 1991).
Jigsaw	Students receive number and letter (Ex.: I–IV, A–D). Base teams: I, II, III, IVs. Students exit base team; all As group to study one aspect, etc., then return to base team to share expertise (Cantlon, 1991).
Numbered heads together	Each student in the group has a number (1 to 4); students huddle to make sure all can respond, then a number is called and that student responds (Kagan, 1998).
Rotating review	Students visit wall charts, each with different review question; they write answers, then rotate to next chart. If they agree with what is already written, they mark it with asterisk (Kagan, 1998).
Send-a-problem	Groups create problems and send them around the class for other teams to solve (Kagan, 1998).

your own things"; and the third, "Use your own words and ideas." Certain ways of seating children enabled the teacher to restrict them from conversing with others. Forbidding students to lend or borrow goods restricted social relations based on sharing. Prohibiting intellectual sharing reinforced the idea that cognition is individual and not co-constructed. These practices unfortunately restrained English learners from making maximal use of peer resources in learning English, reduced their legitimate peripheral practice (Lave & Wenger, 1991), and reinforced social stratification of language "insiders" and "outsiders."

In this excellent analysis of the circulation of power within the classroom community, Toohey includes a quote from Freire (1970):

> The truth is that the oppressed are not "marginals," are not people living "outside" society. They have always been "inside"—inside the structure that made them "beings for others." The solution is not to integrate them into the structure of oppression, but to transform that structure so that they can become "beings for themselves." (p. 55)

TABLE 13.4 • Continued

Name of Activity	Description of Activity
Pairs compare	Pairs come up with ideas to solve a problem. When pairs are through, two pairs make team of four and compare ideas, generating more ideas (Kagan, S., 1999).
4S Brainstorming	While brainstorming solutions to an open-ended prompt, team members take one of four roles: Speed Sergeant enourages many responses quickly. Sultan of Silly tries to come up with silly ideas. Synergy Guru helps members build on each other's ideas. Sergeant Support encourages all ideas, suspends judgment (Kagan, S., 1999).
Group memory	Students write everything they know about a topic they plan to study, including unanswered questions that come to them. In groups of three they read the paper to the group, and everybody adds ideas to the list. The group compiles unanswered questions and turns in a group memory sheet (Whisler & Williams, 1990).
Partner prediction	Teacher preidentifies places in a literature story where the students can stop and predict what happens next. They share predictions with a partner. They must then share aloud what the partner predicts.
2/4 Question some more	Teacher identifies key points in a read-aloud story. Partners talk about the story so far and then discuss what questions occur to them. They share these in a team of four, then with the class (Whisler & Williams, 1990).
Panel of experts	Students read selected passages, taking notes of possible comprehension questions. In a group, students agree on four questions. One group in the room forms a panel, and others question them. Play continues until panel gets two right or one wrong; then questioning group becomes panel (Whisler & Williams, 1990).
Picture dialogue	Before reading, teacher displays a picture from the book or sets a mental image using words. Working in pairs, students take character A or B and write a dialogue that characters say to each other. They read them aloud (Whisler & Williams, 1990).

Here we see the introduction of the concept of the margin. When the postmodernists see the margin as the terrain of possibility (Yúdice, 1988), they do not mean that the role of teachers of English learners is to induct these into the mainstream. Rather, cultural margins are a "zone of possibility"; the classroom as a community is interlaced with these possibilities in and among the individuals who are learning English.

Why Involve Families?

"Strong parent involvement is one factor that research has shown time and time again to have positive effects on academic achievement and school attitudes" (Ovando & Collier, 1998). The growing number of English learners in the school system clearly requires continued efforts to involve parents, families, and communities in public education. Successful program models are available to help school personnel, parents, and communities work successfully together.

◆ **STRATEGY 13.2:** Involve families as partners in learning

Changing Definitions of Family Involvement

Every society has its view of what kind of family involvement in schools is effective and appropriate. In addition, each school has its own version. Some schools want families to be involved only in specific ways and at times determined by the staff. Other schools are run completely by parents, who control expenditures, curriculum selection, and hiring and firing of staff. This perspective on the role of the family has shifted as society has seen the rise of nontraditional and alternative family structures (Jesse, 2001).

As modern society becomes more complex and demanding, many social institutions are disappearing that, in the past, helped children to grow and mature. Outside of school, members of the community spent time with children, taught them values, nourished their hobbies and interests, and helped them to feel that they were important. Schools must take on the role that small towns, neighbors, extended families, churches, and other community organizations used to play (Ada, 1995).

New beliefs are emerging about family involvement. The focus has shifted from parents to families, from a deficit view of urban families to an emphasis on the inherent strengths of families, from agendas that originate with teachers and administrators to a renewed respect for family priorities, and from the assumption that families do not want to be involved to an acknowledgment that some families are hard to reach (Davies, 1991). Because TESOL educators almost always teach in situations in which family members are non–English speaking, it is vital that teachers and administrators make a special effort to understand, and communicate with, these families.

Six types of family involvement are parenting, communicating, volunteering, learning at home, decision making, and liaison with the community (Epstein, 1995). Volunteering benefits specific classrooms as well as the school at large. Family members can help with small groups of individuals in classes, tutorial or remedial work, or planning projects and field trips. Another helpful role is that of community liaison, whereby one person who knows many others in the community explains school programs and needs, publicizes meetings and open-house activities, and musters support for extracurricular activities or parent training.

Recognizing Rights of Families

Parents in the United States have numerous rights that educators must honor. These include the right of their children to a free, appropriate public education; the right to receive information concerning education decisions and actions in the home language; the right to authorize consent before changes in educational placement occur; the right to be included in discussions concerning disciplinary action toward their children; the right to appeal actions when they do not agree; and the right to participate in meetings organized for public and parent information (Young & Helvie, 1996). In other parts of the world, parents may exert power in more informal ways, using family connections that influence the behavior of school administrators, personal relationships with the teacher, or external religious or political authorities. From the teacher's point of view, family involvement should promote achievement but not disrupt instruction.

A fundamental right of all parents is school support for the home language. To deny access to native-language literacy exploits minorities (Cummins, 1989). It is important that teachers help families to understand the advantages of bilingualism in connecting students to their heritage culture, adding a cognitive dimension in broadening and deepening students' thinking, and expanding career opportunities later in life. Family support for bilingualism helps to establish expectations for high academic performance in two languages (Molina et al., 1997).

Issues in Family Involvement

Schools that have grappled with how to increase parental involvement have encountered many of the same issues (Bermúdez & Márquez, 1996; Young & Helvie, 1996). Ovando and Collier (1998, pp. 301–309) organize these issues within five areas: language; survival and family structure; educational background and values; knowledge of and beliefs about education; and power and status. From each area questions arise that serve as guides for school personnel as they build collaborations with parents.

Questions about Language.   Questions about language include the following: How does language affect communication between the home and the school? Do teachers and parents value the use of the home language in school? How can educators bridge the gap between "schoolspeak" and everyday language?

Questions about Survival and Family Structure.   Questions about survival and family structure include these: How does the family's struggle for day-to-day survival affect the home-school partnership? How does a nontraditional family structure affect this relationship?

Questions about Knowledge and Beliefs about Education.   Questions about knowledge of and beliefs about education are these: How do parents' educational background and attitudes toward the value of schooling affect the home-school partnership? What assumptions do educators have about the attitudes of parents toward schooling? How much knowledge do parents have about school culture and the role of parents in schools in the United States? How much do parents know about the specific methods being used in their child's classroom, and how comfortable would they be reinforcing these methods at home? Do parents and teachers perceive the home-school relationship differently?

Questions about Power and Status.   Questions about power and status include the following: How does the inherent inequality of the educator-layperson relationship affect the quality of the partnership? Do programs for parents convey a message of cultural deficiency? To what degree are the parents of English learners part of the school instructional and administrative decision-making process? Some tactics that address these issues are presented in Table 13.5.

TABLE 13.5 ◆ Tactics for Teachers Based on Questions Regarding Parent-School Relationships

Area of Concern	Questions	Tactics for Teachers
Language	How does educators' language (jargon?) affect home-school communication?	Translate jargon into plain English and then into the home language.
	Do community members support using the home language in school?	Advocate maintenance of the home language in all parent communication.
Family structure	How do the struggles of day-to-day survival affect the home-school partnership?	Arrange conferences at convenient times for working families.
	How will differences in family structure affect the relationship?	Speak about "families" rather than "parents." Accept the relationships that exist.
Educational background, attitudes toward schooling	Do school expectations match the parents' educational backgrounds?	Discover the parents' aspirations for their children. Do everything possible to have the school and family agree on high standards.
	What do educators assume about the attitudes of parents toward schooling?	Ensure that communication with school is always honest and positive.
Knowledge of and beliefs about education	How do parents learn about school culture, their role in U.S. schools, and the specific methods being used in their child's classroom? Would they be comfortable reinforcing these methods at home?	Family education events, family literacy classes, primary-language written and oral information, formal and informal teacher-family talks, and family tutoring training are a part of the picture.
	How do parents and teachers differ in the perception of the home-school relationship?	Not only do teachers inform parents, but interest and communication is fully two-way.
Power and status	How does the inherent inequality of the educator-layperson relationship affect the partnership?	Try to have a "family space" at the school. Parents should be informed and involved in decisions.
	Do programs for parents convey a message of cultural deficiency?	"Funds of knowledge" approach affirms and respects the knowledge of the home.
	To what degree are minority-language community members a part of the school in instructional and administrative positions?	Bilingual speakers are paid well and are considered respected assets to the school as well as to the classroom.

Source: Adapted from Ovando and Collier, 1998, pp. 301–309.

Myths about Families and Other Communication Barriers

Often teachers think that families of English learners are not interested in what happens in school because they are not visible at parent meetings or traditional parent-school activities. However, surveys of parents show that an overwhelming number of parents express interest in being involved in school events, activities, and decisions. They report, however, that they are often not consulted about the type of involvement, scheduling of activities, or location of events. These reports show that the myth of so-called lack of interest that circulates in low-achieving schools may be due to poor communication between home and school.

Moreover, other studies have shown that parents feel intimidated by school staff and awkward about approaching school personnel (Chavkin, 1989). Parents are not comfortable dealing with school staff who appear to be too businesslike, or who talk down to them. Some parents may feel that it is disrespectful to talk to teachers about instruction, as doing so might appear to challenge the teachers' role. Other parents may feel inadequate to deal with school authorities or may be suspicious or angry about specific incidents. These and other communication problems can be lessened if teachers of English learners are trained in effective communication strategies.

Enhancing Home-School Communication

If the teacher does not speak the same language as the family, nonverbal messages assume an increased importance. Teachers who meet family members informally as they arrive to drop off their child, at a classroom open house, or during other school events should strive to make their body language "warm" rather than cold. Teachers can show respect toward family members by, for example, rising as guests enter the room, greeting guests at the door, and accompanying them to the door when they leave.

Any notes, letters, or newsletters sent home need to be translated into the home language. If communication sent home is positive, there is more chance that it will be read. Many teachers establish a positive communication pattern by sending a consistent stream of "happy grams" describing what a student has done well. However, if a student has a problem in class, communication between home and school must be consistent and sustained. Any useful program of home-school communication is predicated on having established a rapport with parents in person.

Teachers have modified a wide range of classroom behaviors through the use of home-school notes. The most effective notes are those that focus on the improvement of academic productivity, such as the amount or quality of completed classwork or homework. Work completion and accuracy are goals for all students, and when students are rewarded for increased outcomes, research shows that improvements in classroom conduct occur simultaneously. After all, few children can complete their work accurately and have time to misbehave. In contrast, a focus on disruptiveness does not cause an improvement in academic performance (Kelley, 1990).

Teacher-Family Conferences

Preparation for meetings with families enhances their chances of success. The concerned teacher makes sure that scheduled times are convenient for family members and prepares a portfolio of the student's successes. The conference might begin with a limited amount of small talk, especially if there has been a recent notable family event. Then the teacher reviews the student's performance, using the portfolio or other evidence of student work. Showing an anonymous example of a grade-level performance may make it easier for family members to put their child's performance in perspective. Listening to family members helps the teacher to get a more complete view of the child. If there needs to be a plan for improvement, the teacher sets in motion definite steps, including setting a time in the near future to compare notes on the child's progress.

Using an Interpreter.   The use of an interpreter for parent conferences shows respect for the home language of families. During the conference, the interpreter usually translates the client's own words as closely as possible to give a sense of the client's concepts, emotional state, and other important information. Despite the language difference, the teacher can watch nonverbal, affective responses and observe facial expressions, voice intonations, and body movements (Randall-David, 1989) to extend communication.

Partnership with the Family.   Partnership with the family is strengthened in several ways. A positive tone communicates that the teacher likes the student and has found strengths to appreciate in that student. Keeping careful records and samples of student work shows that the grading practices are fair and that the student is making adequate progress; if not, the family can be informed early if the child falls below expectations in some area. All family contact should be documented in an activity log that includes the date, subject, and parents' reactions. In this way, school administrators can see what communication efforts have been made.

Three-Way Conferences.   Three-way conferences that include the student invite family members into a dialogue about their children's schooling. Students can use this opportunity to demonstrate what they know, share their accomplishments, and set new learning goals. Family members find out about their child's learning, have the opportunity to ask questions and express their ideas, and help to plan for the child's learning at home. Teachers act as guides by clarifying ideas and issues and responding to specific questions (Davies, Cameron, Politano, & Gregory, 1992). In this way, students are encouraged to follow through on their self-regulated learning.

The three-way conference is based on four ideas:

1. A portfolio documents student learning; the student sees it in a positive light, has reflected on its contents, and has a sense of ownership about it.
2. The teacher has established ongoing informal means by which the family can see and comment on the student's work.
3. Students have practiced their part of the conference, perhaps with the aid of an older student, and are prepared to participate.
4. Teachers have communication training, such as the skills to guide a parent who sets a negative tone or a student who drifts off topic.

Reflection is an important part of this process and is the foundation for self-evaluation. Students can record reflections on journal pages to accompany their portfolios. The teacher can provide specific prompts, such as, "It was hard for me to learn . . . "; "Three things I want you to notice about my work are . . . "; "I wish I had been told more about . . . "; I had some trouble but I solved it by . . . "; "I was surprised to learn . . . "; and "I was on the right track with my idea about . . . " (Davies et al., 1992, p. 91; Appendix C). These and other aspects of the three-way conference, including forms by which teachers can inform parents and keep records, can be found in Davies and colleagues (1992).

Table 13.6 offers a brief overview of the process of three-way conferencing.

How Families Can Assist in a Child's Learning

Schools that have a take-home library of print- and media-based materials encourage learning activities outside school. In a dual-language setting, families can work with their children in either language.

Families' Attitudes toward Dual-Language Learning.   Families may not support learning in two languages. For example, Watahomigie (1995) describes the negative reaction of parents on the Hualapai Indian reservation in Peach Springs, Arizona, when educators proposed that schools establish a Hualapai/English bilingual program. The parents had been told for over one hundred years that the native language was unimportant, and they did not believe that such instruction would benefit their children. A "high-tech" approach based on CALL, built on efforts to convince parents of its value, was eventually successful.

TABLE 13.6 • Snapshot of the Three-Way Conference

Component of the Conference	Description
Preparatory work	The teacher builds rapport with parents, making sure that parents have a positive sense of the student's learning process.
Parent preparation	The teacher sends home a letter that helps parents to think ahead about how the conference will proceed.
Visiting and viewing	Before the conference, the student and parent take time to review the portfolio and view the displays in the classroom.
Student-led discussion	During the conference, the student presents the portfolio in the context of what has been learned, discusses what areas of improvement are needed, and outlines what the learning goals are for the next term.
Consensus on learning goals	The student, supported by the teacher, states the goals and means to achieve them, and parents and teacher together commit to providing specific support.
Role of the teacher	The teacher keeps a record of the conference, ensures that the conference runs smoothly, prompts the student if necessary, and helps to answer parent questions.

Source: Davies, Cameron, Politano, & Gregory, 1992, p. 26.

Family Literacy.   Family literacy projects help children achieve in school. Ada (1988) held parent literacy nights, in which children read stories that they had written to their parents. Eventually, parents wrote their own stories and read these aloud. The oral reading was videotaped, and the tapes were circulated to great enjoyment throughout the parent community. In Fresno, California, the Hmong Literacy Project was initiated by parents to help students appreciate their cultural roots, preserve oral history, and maintain the culture through written records. Parents asked for literacy lessons in Hmong (a language that has been written for only about thirty years) and in English. The program helped families to develop not only literacy skills but also skills in math and computers, thereby allowing them to help their children academically. The Hmong parents newsletter increased communication between the school and the community, leading to greater parent participation in school activities (Kang, Kuehn, & Herrell, 1996).

The following websites feature various models of family involvement: http://eric-web.tc.columbia.edu/families/strong/sfp.html, http://eric-web.tc.columbia.edu/families/strong/references.html, www.cyfc.umn.edu/Learn/family.html, and www.mmu.ac.uk/h-ss/sis/parents/danj~1.htm.

A Model of Home-School Relationships

Faltis (2001) provides a four-level sequence for home-school relationships based on an earlier model proposed by Rasinski and Fredericks (1989). Although teachers may not be able to reach the highest level of parental involvement at a particular school site, the model presents an overall view of the possibilities. This reciprocal process is summarized in Table 13.7.

Box 13.1 offers a host of tactics for involving parents in learning, ranging from providing information to learning from them about their views of education. These suggestions are drawn from Jones (1991), Díaz-Rico & Weed (2002), Fredericks & Rasinski (1990). Rather than including a separate list of suggestions from each source, I have amalgamated them in categories.

❖ Tactics for teachers to involve parents in policy decisions:

- Ask representative parent committees to advise and consent on practices that involve culturally and linguistically diverse students.
- Talk with parents before and after school to encourage them to get involved in school issues.
- Make school facilities available for meetings of community groups.

Community Funds of Knowledge

Sometimes teachers believe that English learners come from homes that have limited social and intellectual resources. This inaccurate perception, based on a "disadvantage/deficiency" model, has too often led to lowered academic expectations for these stu-

TABLE 13.7 ◆ A Two-Way Parent-School Involvement Model

Level of Involvement	Description of Activity
I. Teacher-parent contact	The teacher learns about parents' daily experiences and initiates positive home-school contact and dialogue by chatting, making home visits, talking with community workers, and arranging for after-school homework help or tutoring to promote students' success.
II. Sharing information in the home about schooling	The teacher keeps the parents informed (in the home language if possible) about important school and community events and meetings, changes in school schedules, help available from community-based organizations, and sources of academic support, using such means as student-produced newsletters, personal notes, telephone calls, and other notices.
III. Participation at home and school	Parents, caregivers, and other concerned adults are welcomed and encouraged to come to class and to attend school meetings and social events. Parents may linger in the morning to watch reading and writing take place or to see a little poetry reading, especially if it takes place in the home language. Students may be assigned to find out about their families' knowledge of planting, banking, etc. that teachers can find a way to use and elaborate on in class.
IV. Parental empowerment in curricular decisions	After the success of the previous three levels, teachers support parents who become involved as colleagues in professional activities and decisions. Some parents form advisory committees, start community tutoring centers, and find multiple means to influence school policy and support academic learning outside the classroom. The role of the teacher is to encourage and work with parents to make these possible.

Source: Faltis, 2001.

dents. To counteract this misconception, researchers have sent teachers as participant-observers into the homes of English learners to see what strategies and knowledge are used at home to sustain the families' well-being. Through these visits, it has become obvious that communities have "funds of knowledge" (Vélez-Ibáñez & Greenberg, 1992) that the community has developed and drawn on over generations to create success. This knowledge can be brought into the classroom to enrich, develop, and transform the curriculum.

◆ **STRATEGY 13.3:** Affirm and build on what the community values as knowledge

Teachers need to know what children do intellectually in the everyday context of their neighborhood and families. If teachers are not familiar with the activities and responsibilities that children perform in their homes and neighborhoods, their knowledge about children's cognitive abilities will be distorted, and they will not be able to connect the curriculum with students' daily thinking. Teacher research in the community accomplishes two purposes. First, teachers who interview community members and parents become familiar with the local expertise in many areas, and they use

BOX 13.1
❖ Tactics for Educators to Involve Families in Schooling

Providing information
- Informally chat with family members as they pick up their child after school.
- Use the telephone as an instrument of good news.
- Videotape programs for families.
- Operate a homework hotline.
- Encourage parent-to-parent communication.
- Hold workshops for family members to learn to help children with reading skills.
- Offer materials in the home language.
- Provide bilingual handouts that describe programs available through the school.
- Make available a list of parental rights under the Bilingual Education Act.
- Send home personal handwritten notes, using a translator if necessary.
- Send home notes when students are doing well.
- Create parent/student handbooks.
- Have students write classroom newsletters.
- Welcome new families with packets delivered to the home.

Ways to showcase English learners
- Enter students in poetry, essay, or art contests or exhibits sponsored by community or professional organizations.

- Offer to train students how to read aloud at libraries or children's centers.
- Encourage dual-language proficiency as a mark of prestige in school.

Ways to bring parents to school
- Encourage family members to come to class to make crafts with students or to discuss culture, calligraphy, or family history.
- Find out if teacher-family conferences or meetings conflict with work schedules.
- Ensure that siblings are welcome at teacher-family conferences or meetings.
- Provide baby-sitting services for teacher-family conferences.
- Maintain a friendly school office.
- Establish an explicit open-door policy so that families will know they are welcome; include welcoming signs in the primary language.
- Suggest specific ways family members can help to promote achievement.
- Help students to obtain remedial help if necessary in a timely way.
- Make meetings into social events, providing food and dramatic or musical performances if time permits.

---

this knowledge to teach in ways that make sense to students. Second, students feel a closer connection and increased respect for community members.

In the past, teachers may have made home visits to get to know parents or to discuss a particular student problem. In the "funds of knowledge" program (Moll, 1992), teachers visited homes to document families' knowledge in such areas as farming, animal care, construction, trade, business, and finance. By asking questions about these domains, the teacher-investigators opened up new channels of communication between home and school (Moll, Amanti, Neff, & González, 1992). Researchers found that practical activities (auto repair, music, etc.) provided rich possibilities for learning to occur (Moll & Greenberg, 1990). The ethnographic approach became a joint inquiry among the community, the teachers, and the university researchers working on the project; all met periodically to weave knowledge about family and school matters into academic content and lessons.

One teacher, aware that members of the community often built or remodeled their own homes, created a sixth-grade thematic unit on construction. Over twenty

BOX 13.1

❖ Continued

- Hold student-teacher-family breakfasts once a month.
- Schedule primary-language speakers at school events.
- Recognize family members for involvement at award ceremonies, send thank-you notes, and speak positively of parents to their child.

How families can teach teachers
- Suggest better ways to communicate.
- Provide a rich understanding of the students' role(s) in the family.
- Express the hopes they have for schooling.
- Describe students' hobbies, interests, and strengths.

Homework tips for families *(adapted from Jones, 1991)*
- Set aside a family quiet time when each person has homework or other activities to do that demand concentration.
- Establish a routine for finding out what assignments to expect.
- Make sure there is a place set aside for homework; provide paper, pencils, adequate lighting, etc.

- Check with the child to see if he or she understands the assignment. If needed, work through a sample problem. Have someone to call for help if necessary.
- Check the completed assignment with the child.
- Praise the work or offer constructive improvements.

Workshops and family support groups *(adapted from Jones, 1991)*
- Hold make-it-and-take-it workshops to construct home learning materials.
- Open a family learning center—school library or computer center—several nights a week, with learning activities for all ages.
- Hold learning fairs—in the evening, with single-topic sessions.
- Have community members host family support groups.
- Set aside a family room at school for families to drop in and participate in informal activities, play with toys, and talk with other parents.
- Hold child and adolescent development talks.
- Conduct special workshops on reading, math, study skills, self-esteem, etc.

---

parents and community members visited the class, sharing their knowledge and skills on various aspects of construction. As the unit culminated, students wrote and gave oral reports on their design of a model community. These authentic, relevant activities drew forth from students real communicative and problem-solving skills and added excitement, authenticity, and a community connection to the classroom (Moll, 1992).

Another teacher became aware that a student had experience in selling candy from Mexico in the United States. The teacher created a series of interdisciplinary lessons centered on the theme of candy production, enlisting the help of a parent who knew how to make the candy. In one week, the class studied math (average number of ingredients in U.S. versus Mexican candy), nutrition, food production, science, and social studies (crosscultural practices in making and selling candy). Language arts was an integral part of this project as students read about the subject and wrote about the knowledge they had gained (National Center for Research on Cultural Diversity and Second Language Learning, 1994).

Transformative School-Community Partnerships

The anthropological focus (based on culture) rather than the solely psychological approach (based on analysis of individual behavior) has widened the focus of SLA. Rather than looking at the classroom as a collection of individuals whose aptitudes, study behaviors, and motivation are responsible for achievement, educators now regard these learners as part of a larger community whose goals, aspirations, struggles, and resources form the basis on which school achievement rests. School-community partnerships are fundamental to TESOL education.

◆ **STRATEGY 13.4:** Form partnerships with the community to involve students in community activities and social action

Empowerment as a Goal

Some liberal educators look at their involvement with families and communities as "liberating" based on belief that education has the power to create social change. Although many educators describe community involvement programs as "empowering," Valdés (1996) questions the use of this term. Many such programs teach parents to help their children, but they may fail to address topics such as racism, social equality, and economic exploitation. Schools outside the United States also have economic issues: EFL programs may not receive textbooks comparable to those in other subjects, giving teacher the message that they must "make do" with an outdated curriculum. Thus TESOL education has a vested interest in the financial resources of schools and families.

According to Delgado-Gaitan (1994, p. 144) "empowerment" can be defined as a way in which a historically underrepresented group can recognize its potential and state its goals of access to resources, hence power. ESOL programs are often found in neighborhood schools that do not receive the same resources as schools in affluent neighborhoods do. The wealthiest school districts in the United States outspend the poorest by a factor of more than four to one (see Kozol, 1991). One might well channel the "empowerment" rhetoric into the election of officials who will enforce equal financial rights for neighborhood schools.

Family involvement programs may communicate the message that individual or family heroics are needed to overcome obstacles so that children can succeed. Many assumptions (individual heroics trump community building, poverty is an obstacle, students who succeed are valued the most, education should prepare students for a complex technological culture) underlie a particular set of middle-class values. If these school values do not match those of the community, some accommodation is needed.

Getting to Know the Community

Making friends in the community is the first step to forming and sustaining school-community partnerships. Some schools sponsor "Grandparents' Day" so that students can invite family members to class. Teachers may send home cards to mark the arrival of new babies or a change of residence. One teacher announces to the class at the beginning of the year that she is available to be asked to dinner on Friday nights.

Knowing in advance that their invitation is welcomed, parents and students book her for months ahead. Teachers who take the time to shop in the neighborhood, visit community centers, or attend religious services in the community often get to see another side of students' lives.

When investigating the daily life of the community, it is particularly valuable to look at the social practices that support learning. Delgado-Gaitan (1994) speaks of the "ecocultural niche" in which families exist, involving such factors as socioeconomic level; social and political relations; religious beliefs; and relationship to the neighborhood, media, health institutions, and schools. These influence the way in which the community uses learning as a means toward power. In a modern society that uses discursive practices to circulate power (see Foucault, 1979, 1980, 1984), it is important for the existing oracy and literacy practices to be seen in their sociocultural context as a way to begin to understand the culture of the community.

School Partnerships with Community-Based Organizations

Community-based organizations (CBOs) are groups committed to helping people obtain health, education, and other basic human services that can boost students' academic achievement in a variety of ways. Their activities include tutoring students in their first language; developing leadership skills and promoting higher education goals; and providing information and support on issues such as health care, pregnancy, gang involvement, and so on. Some programs help parents to assist their children by training the parents as tutors and homework helpers (Adger, 2000).

Community Support for English Learners

A supportive community offers a home for linguistic and cultural diversity. This support takes many forms, such as fund-raising for college scholarships for English learners and providing user-friendly community services. Students can be invited to the local library to offer their stories, books, and poetry to other students, in both English and the primary language. Policies of community agencies such as the library can be influenced by teacher involvement.

❖ Tactics for teachers to influence policies of local libraries:

- File lesson plans in the library and make specific materials accessible to students.
- Consult with those who purchase materials for school district and community libraries.
- Encourage parents to use the public library to check out books with their children.
- Justify to librarians the need for primary-language and ESOL materials.
- Ask if English learners can be involved in delivering storytelling and other programs at the library.

Community service organizations are often run by community leaders who set the tone for the community and sometimes have strong ideas about education. Teacher-led presentations to other teachers, staff, or community members can explain

ESOL pedagogy. Service clubs such as Rotary and Kiwanis provide opportunities for speakers to reach the business leaders of the community with current information about multicultural and linguistic issues. These activities deliver the message that teachers are knowledgeable and interested in the community at large.

Communities can foster a climate of support for English learners by featuring articles in local newspapers and newsletters about their achievements in the schools and prizes they have won, by sponsoring literature and art exhibitions that feature students, and by publishing their stories written in both languages. In this way, support for EL programs is orchestrated in the community at large.

Letters to the editor of the local paper can serve as a vehicle to persuade the public to support bilingual and ESOL instruction. Unfortunately, editorial letters are sometimes sources of misinformation or prejudice. Literate people need to protest to the editors of newspapers that publish overtly racist and misinformed letters and should write rebuttals to such opinions. Teachers and other staff members can influence community public opinion in several ways.

❖ **Tactics for teachers to influence local public opinion:**

- Give presentations to community groups about ESOL programs.
- Join or begin local education-community partnership foundations.
- Be proactive in gaining newspaper coverage for school events.
- Be heard in the local newspaper editorial pages.

This chapter suggests that the most successful educators are those who are connected with the communities in which they teach. In this situation, families are treated as partners, and are present and able to affirm and support students' efforts. Parents and community alike value what is learned as useful and compatible with what the community values as knowledge. In fact, the community acts in close harmony and partnership with the school, as students take initiative and responsibility in community activities and social action (Auerbach, 2002).

The Idea of Community

Not all communities, however, are in the immediate vicinity of the classroom, today virtual communities connect English learners with others around the world. The *idea* of community, the mere imagining that such a thing exists, is sometimes enough to inspire the deepest feelings of identification (see Anderson, 1983; Norton & Toohey, 2001). Language is one of the strongest markers of group identity, and linguistic conflict is one of the bitterest sources of discord (Thornborrow, 1999). This makes the role of speech communities—and those who manage, instruct, and transform them—into some of the world's strongest potential forces for cohesion or division.

Globalism affects the sense of community. "The production of electronic information radically alters notions of time, community, and history, while simultaneously blurring the distinction between reality and image" (Aronowitz & Giroux, 1991, p. 115). Global issues make peace education a priority, as members of ethnic groups who may never have spoken with one another before come together using English as a common language. Peace education may be defined as preparing students for "efforts to achieve human dignity for all people and to realize a viable global society on an ecologically healthy planet" (Reardon, 1988, in Brooks & Fox, 1998, p. vii).

Teachers of English learners face multiple challenges in connecting with community. Such education, for the most part, takes place in classrooms in which learners are socially marginalized, either because they are recent immigrants or because they live in neighborhoods in which English is not the native speech. TESOL educators who work in EFL settings may be expatriates who have much to learn from the societies in which they serve, and they may feel themselves marginalized too, by virtue of their visitor status. This means that involving the community will always be challenging, but rewarding. Building a community of learners means that these challenges and rewards are shared with others, multiplying both.

Project-Based Learning

14

Why Projects?

In many ways, school is inadequate preparation for real life. In school, problems are simplified, and there are usually right and wrong answers. Activities are neatly structured to fit within class periods. Teachers guide or provide knowledge, which is neatly divided into content domains. Teachers evaluate students' products and effort. Students know exactly what actions are required to produce good grades. Because all problems are simulations, no one lives or dies, eats or goes hungry, or is sheltered or homeless as a direct result of what goes on in class.

❖ **MEGASTRATEGY 14:** Involve the learner in projects that offer long-term, meaningful learning

Facing the Real World

In contrast to the delimited world of the classroom, the real world is relatively complex and unstructured, and the stakes are enormous. The efforts of individuals and groups make a difference. Project-based learning (PBL) is an opportunity for students to take on tasks that are consequential. Investigations based on real-world problems provide instructional tasks that are contextualized, and appropriately challenging for targeted students. The English that is practiced in class is connected with the English used in real-life environments (see Fried-Booth, 1997).

As in real situations, students may encounter ill-structured problems with insufficient information to solve them at the outset; the problem definition may change halfway through; or various participants may define the goal or desired outcome in radically dissimilar ways. In its sometimes messy character, PBL is excellent preparation for real life, and for real language use.

PBL is "an instructional approach that contextualizes learning by presenting learners with problems to solve or products to develop" (Moss, 1998, p. 1). PBL connects students with challenges that are motivating, putting students in charge of seeking knowledge and selecting and generating the activities they will pursue as part of completing the project (Roth-Vinson, 2001). The project approach is part of a balanced curriculum that supplements the curriculum of specific, sequential skills. Because a project is emergent and negotiated, rather than fully preplanned by the teacher, it encourages students to go beyond the minimum standards of engagement (Katz & Chard, 1989).

Characteristics of PBL

Four characteristics exemplify the use of PBL in the classroom (Blumenfeld, Soloway, Marx, Krajcik, Guzdial, & Palinscar, 1991). First, students are engaged with a *driving question* that is related to a real-world situation and applies across content areas. Second, students *conduct active research* that engages them in the study of concepts, analysis of data, and presentation of their findings. Third, *collaboration* takes place among students, teachers, and others in such a way that the learning is shared among members of the learning community. Fourth, *cognitive tools* are used that support student presentations, such as computer-based graphics, hypermedia, and telecommunication technology. Students become involved in long-term collaborative learning situations in which they identify what they need to know, assess what they already know, gather information, evaluate potential outcomes, and design and carry out activities.

Benefits of PBL

Students learn to take initiative, seek learning on their own, and take responsibility for the results of their inquiry. They experience diverse opinions and viewpoints; figure out how to negotiate with others to design a plan; and learn to agree about what to accomplish, who will be in charge of each task, and how information will be investigated and presented (Roth-Vinson, 2001). Students develop cognitive skills by posing questions, developing proposals, gathering and examining information, drawing conclusions, generating further questions, and completing artifacts (Stepien & Gallagher, 1993). Students use technology as they learn to systematize information and develop informative presentations (Land & Greene, 2000). Even students with low proficiency in English benefit from interacting cooperatively with others while working on a high-interest topic.

In addition to promoting students' academic skills, PBL helps students to feel more integrated into the community at large. This type of learning helps both international students studying in an English-speaking country and immigrants in a new setting to feel connected in more positive ways to life outside the classroom.

Projects Are Collaborative

Although the instructional content of projects may vary depending on the setting, language proficiency level, and target language skills, it is important for them to be collaborative. Six features of this collaborative effort are crucial (Wilhelm, 1997):

- Cooperative learning increases student collaboration (see Chapter 13).
- Individualized instructional planning and feedback is provided, even when students work in groups.
- Student self-assessment involves students in deciding their grades, combined with teacher evaluation.
- The teacher facilitates learning and provides feedback (see next sections).
- Authentic settings offer real-world significance.
- Reflection during and after the project is essential, because it is largely through reflection that people learn and develop.

*Projects outside the classroom encourage
language acquisition in a content-rich setting.*

Collaboration of any kind is based on interpersonal trust. Students working on projects need to become friends with one another so that they can build positive, productive working relationships, especially in classes of mixed nationality, primary languages, and cultural backgrounds. When students work together, cultural barriers fade, and students build communication skills.

The Teacher as Guide

Teachers act as coaches or tutors, providing not only cognitive help in framing issues and assessing possible solutions but also metacognitive help as they assist students to set goals, plan, monitor ongoing efforts, and evaluate progress. The role of the teacher may be to coax students along, drawing them into assuming responsibility in a given situation and then assuming the role of colleague on a problem-solving team (see Stepien & Gallagher, 1993). One of the best features of PBL is that teachers gain new opportunities to see their work as challenging. Taking on projects with students fosters the disposition to evoke creativity and problem-solving skills from students.

The way in which the students' learning is supported in the classroom has much to do with the teacher's vision of the learner. In the project-based early learning centers of the Reggio Emilia schools in Italy, teachers were interviewed about how they imagined the learner. The educators in Reggio Emilia saw the young children as "powerful, active, competent protagonists of their own growth; actors in their shared history, participants in society and culture, with the right (and obligation) to speak from their own perspective, and to act with others on the basis of their own particular experience and level of consciousness" (Edwards, 1998, p. 180). This view of the learner evolves just as the teacher's own identity evolves. In return, the role of the teacher constantly undergoes revision as students grow and mature, or occasionally regress under stress, and as the dynamics of the concerns and capacities of the students, parents, and community change.

Table 14.1 is a synopsis of Edwards's (1998) advice to teachers. I have taken the liberty of inventing names for each role by giving a label to the behaviors that Edwards prescribes for teachers.

Skill Integration

In the process of tackling projects large and small, students often integrate various content areas. They use a combination of receptive skills (reading and listening),

TABLE 14.1 • The Role of the Teacher in Project-Based Learning

Teacher's Role	Associated Behaviors
Listener	Being fully attentive, and at the same time recording and documenting what is observed as a basis for decision making
Organizer and provoker of occasions: "spark"	Originating intellectual dialogue that creates excitement and curiosity; writing down what students say; reading back their comments; searching for insights to motivate further questions and group activity
Co-actor in discoveries	Playing ball with students; catching ideas and throwing them back in a way that makes the student want to continue the game
Shaper	Taking ideas that emerge from a discussion or dispute and forming hypotheses to be tested, a representation that should be attempted, or the basis for a day's activity
"Knot" finder	Helping students pinpoint sticking points, need for more information, acquisition of necessary tools or skills, or launching points for new aspects of a project
Group "rememberer"	Observing and selectively documenting work by means of assigning benchmark reflection events, reminding groups to preserve notes, jotting down ideas overheard in discussions, making a record of observations
Intervener	Knowing when to nudge and when to step back and let a group solve its own problems
Colleague	Involving other adults in the process of a project
Expector of growth	Extending the students' stamina and attention span, increasing their range of techniques and strategies, and enhancing their concentration and effort.
One who is amazed	Expecting students to do wonderfully and to experience pleasure and joy in learning
Spiraler	Engaging in cyclical teaching and learning as ideas are revisited and represented a second time

Source: Edwards, 1998.

processing skills (critical and creative thinking, and use of graphic organizers), and productive skills (speaking and writing) as they research and discuss issues, propose and justify solutions, and design outcomes. In the process of completing projects, students learn to view knowledge as connected, rather than narrowly divided by subject matter. The integration of content knowledge and language development makes PBL an ideal mode of study for TESOL education.

Design, Documentation, and Discourse

Asking students to *design* a project requires them to keep records of their plans and intentions. *Documentation* records the process of creation and design, displaying what action or thought took place and explaining the thinking that went on. *Discourse* is the analysis of communication, "a metalinguistic process in which meaning is questioned in the name of growth and understanding" (Forman & Fyfe, 1998, p. 241). Together, Forman and Fyfe call these the three components of negotiated learning. Table 14.2, loosely based on Forman and Fyfe's 1998 description of the processes that underlie PBL, traces the evolution of a project from earliest discussion to culmination. This process is cyclical rather than linear, with many steps being revisited and deepened throughout the course of the project. Design leads to documentation, which engenders discourse, leading to new design, and so forth.

> A group of teachers of five-, six- and seven-year-olds at Marks Meadow Elementary School, a public school in Amherst, Massachusetts, embarked on a project called "The City in the Snow" (Forman, Langley, Oh, & Wrisley, 1998). Students prepared for the first snow of the year by recollecting how snow feels, how kids can play with it, and how the city deals with huge quantities. They drew snow scenes of skiers, snow falling on houses, and so forth. They constructed a toy village, sifted flour over the tiny buildings, and painted a large mural of a city—without snow—in anticipation. When teachers gave the children white paint to paint the snow, it became evident that some children did not fully understand that snow falls on horizontal surfaces (one child drew white snow vertically covering the walls of a house). When the students finally experienced real snow, they drew snow again, this time with more appreciation for the look of snow on the roofs and cornices of buildings. They then became fascinated with snowflakes—looking at them under a microscope, watching a video about snowflakes, and experimenting with freezing water. Lastly, some students tried to invent snow-making machines, revealing in their drawings their ideas about how snow is formed. Thus the study of snow generated some emergent objectives that were not part of the original discussion.

Representation

In the project described above, teachers started the project design with the language modality used most easily by children, talking, and then moved immediately to drawing. This connection between verbal and figural representation is important for ESOL

TABLE 14.2 ◆ Tracing the Process of Project Development

Stage of Development	Leads to . . .
Early discussion	Questions raised
Early explorations, such as drawings about questions raised	Descriptions of the problem
Descriptions from various points of view	Designs addressing the problem: plans, mind maps
Designs, symbols	More talking about the designs, becoming discourse as teachers help to deepen the dialogues creating shared vocabulary and meanings, with symbols becoming project language
Research and exploration	Facts, displays, artifacts, notes
Collections of information	Documentation, as teacher helps to wrap rationales and explanations around exploration, becoming part of formative assessment
Partial solutions	More documentation, more design
Disequilibration: partial solutions may not work	Provocation, more searching
Collaboration: student/student, student/teacher, teacher/colleague, class/community	Co-construction of designs, plans, meaning, final products
Design of culminating activity	Performance preparation, including formative assessment
Performance	Celebration, debriefing reflection, summative assessment

Source: Edwards, 1998.

learners, whose emergent oral language is thus supported by kinesthetic and visual activities. Viewing the drawings, the teacher learned how the students were thinking about the topic at hand, what aspects of the topic they depicted, and what were their hypotheses about how the world works. Moving to another mode of representation, in this situation the simulation of the snowfall with flour, allowed the teacher to offer students another nonverbal way of looking at the situation, which was then represented again in words during collaborative discussions. In the project "City in the Snow," the cycle of design-documentation-discourse was repeated as the students broadened and deepened their experience with the topic. Sometimes ready-made symbols were used as a catalyst (videos, pictures from books), but more often than not the students' intuitive representations drove the inquiry and generated the burning questions. Carefully documenting the development of students' ideas ensured that the children's initial questions were addressed, as well as providing a paper trail for purposes of accountability.

The following examples illustrate the use of PBL at a variety of educational levels. They range from short thematic units of two or three weeks' duration to investigations lasting several months, with students' ages ranging from second grade to college.

Thematic Units

Elementary ESL students can benefit from working on thematic units. Gordon (1992) described a project that involved studying different breeds of dogs. This combined relatively complicated vocabulary with comparatively simple syntax to boost students' English skills. For example, when students discussed dog breeds, the teacher employed "personality words" such as *affectionate, enthusiastic, obedient,* and *pugnacious* (p. 30). Student-generated topics sustained interest over the period of the project: Students took notes, duplicated pictures from source books into personal notebooks to use with mini-essays, and created their own books. This type of PBL helps students who are fluent in English but lacking in academic skills to sustain interest as their literacy skills in English catch up with their basic interpersonal communication skills.

Projects at Urban High Schools

The NET team is a two-year PBL program at Denver North High School, a large urban school with 1,500 students and a predominantly Hispanic (82 percent) student body, 8 percent of whom speak only Spanish and 25 percent of whom are English learners. Those students who have difficulty learning also often have poor attendance habits, low self-esteem, minimal study skills, and low math and reading scores. Students apply to the program and, once accepted, are assigned to teacher-composed, heterogeneous groups mixed by ability, cultural background, gender, or learning style, usually with three or four members. Instruction takes place in blocks of time, with two or more teachers working together in nearby classrooms (Giromini, 2001).

National History Day provided the stimulus for extensive research on the theme "Frontiers in History." Students were tasked with finding a "turning point" in history. They kept project logs, fact sheets, and annotated bibliographies; made a time line of significant dates and events; wrote a process paper explaining their research efforts; and completed a "metacognition," a five-paragraph essay that traced the project's success, failures, and lessons learned. The final project was presented to teammates, teachers, parents, and invited guests at the school's History Night. This project addressed content standards in English, history, science, and visual arts as well as workplace standards in technology, organizational skills, and communication skills.

Southeast Asian students at a high school in Sacramento, California, used the computer program Hyperstudio to create multimedia, multicultural family histories, which were then transferred to video for each student to take home. Students connected special effects, drawings, visual text, photos, and voice-over to present their families' stories. Balderas (2001) created family history projects in which students used photos, drawings, and word-processed text to create albums that could be shared with other family members or read aloud to other classes and community groups. A list of guiding questions early in the project helped students to structure intergenerational interviews with family members. The class periodically convened "author circles" to assist each writer with editing and revisions.

Community-Based Projects

Anderson Valley High School, on the north coast of California near Mendocino, worked with the Anderson Valley Nursery and the North Coast Rural Challenge network to collect seeds and cuttings of native plants and restore the plants to wetlands near the high school. Students refurbished an abandoned greenhouse, creating 1,000 square feet of growing space to propagate native plants for distribution throughout the valley. Meanwhile, at the junior high school, students spread out throughout the valley to record oral interviews with Anderson Valley elders, which they then typed and edited. Audio CDs were created to present the stories. Students collected photographs and prepared them for publication in book form. Three volumes of the oral history project have been completed to date (North Coast Rural Challenge Network, 2000).

Project-Based Learning in EFL

Sometimes a "vicious cycle" takes place in EFL classes in which lack of exposure to real-world English causes the learner not to use English, which in turn leads that learner to lack self-esteem and confidence in his or her English ability, which further exacerbates the lack of proficiency (Sarwar, 2000). PBL provides EFL learners a context for meaningful use of the target language outside the classroom. In Sarwar's EFL classes in Pakistan, groups of students created newsletters and books based on models they found in the library. Their products featured news, sports, business, advertisements, or whatever content they chose, with pictures to accompany the text. The final product was shared as a presentation and display.

Projects in Intensive English Programs

PBL can be used effectively in short, theme-focused classes for international students. Wilhelm (1999) describes seven different project classes in Levels 1–4 of an Intensive English program (IEP). These include Know Your City, Travel USA, The Midwest Yesterday and Today, Coffeehouse, School Visits, Creative Speaking/Drama, and Newsletter. In the Coffeehouse project, students working in groups organize a public performance in a local coffeehouse, reserving space, issuing invitations, creating the agenda, and documenting the event. In the Newsletter project class, students conduct surveys and write up the results in informative articles. The Travel USA project features students acting as travel agents, "selling" the travel packages they have assembled at an open-house exhibit. Communication in these classes is enhanced through the e-mail messages, activity surveys, and journal entries by which students keep the instructor informed about the progress of the projects.

At a Canadian university, fifty-seven Japanese exchange students worked on a three-month research project, producing a fifteen-page report complete with bibliography, illustrations, and other graphics. When the report was finished, they prepared an oral presentation on it (Beckett, Carmichael, Mohan, & Slater, 2000), which helped them to develop language skills (e.g., new vocabulary, writing), project skills (learning how to use a project format, conducting research, making a presentation), and content knowledge (specific information about the topic).

Projects in Teacher Education

Candidates for a teaching credential or master's degree in TESOL can benefit greatly from working on projects themselves during their career preparation. This brings into TESOL teacher preparation programs the element of individual research design. When assigned a project, TESOL candidates learn to focus the topic, design and carry out research, and represent the results to their peers and mentors. They thus both experience the power of a creative response to authentic learning and practice the skills they will be demanding of their students who take on supervised projects of their own while learning English.

> Sam's class engaged in the collection and presentation of a teaching portfolio. He chose to write a case study about his teaching in an intensive English program (IEP) program in a midsize university town. Sam's class, an oral conversation class, included immigrant students (mostly Puerto Rican) who worked in nearby manufacturing companies, spouses of Japanese international students enrolled at the university, and a Russian couple who were brought to town in a church-based resettlement program. Sam's portfolio posed the problem of these students' unequal oral participation in class, and documented the attempts he has made to address the challenge. These included ways that students could contribute their personal experiences to each lesson, and ways that students could make a personal commitment to increasing their participation through interactive journal communication with him. For Sam, the teaching portfolio became a useful tool in taking on the project of improving his teaching. (Johnson, 1996)

Many TESOL master's degree programs culminate in master's theses in which students perform research investigations or develop curriculum designs. For the M.A. in education TESOL program at California State University, San Bernardino, two students collaborated on a project in which they job-shadowed the administrator of the campus IEP and then designed their own proprietary language school. A student from Taiwan developed a theoretical model for teaching reading using film scripts and then designed a unit on Irish culture to provide students with background knowledge before viewing the movie *My Left Foot*. A student from Japan who teaches at a school for international business combined theoretical insights from three domains (situated discourse, intercultural communication, and negotiation theory) to design a teaching model for intercultural negotiation.

There are many aspects of a complex project that form an overall project "system." Figures 14.1 and 14.2 present these in graphic form.

Choosing a Project Topic

❖ **STRATEGY 14.1:** Negotiate the project topic with the learners

Teachers may wonder how to begin involving students in projects. In the Reggio Emilia schools described above, teachers observe what interests the children. Often these interests, as expressed by children's questions and speculations, evolve into a group unit. Using cycles of representation, teachers find ways to deepen the learning experience for students by combining language input (reading or listening) and output (speaking, writing, or drawing). Each class of students is unique; what works for one class may fall flat in another. Helping students to design and carry out projects is a process of trial and error.

These are the parts of "the big picture" of any project, job, business, or industry.

Planning

- What activities or duties need to be planned?
- Who will plan the activities that will help your project team meet its goals and objectives?
- Who are all the people who will help make this project happen (teachers, advisors, and people in your community)?

Management

- How are people, money, and materials "managed" in this project?
- Is there a supervisor or is the project managed by a group?
- How can all participants be more involved in the decision-making process within the project?
- Technical and production skills: Who is doing what (including yourself)? What project-specific skills are needed to get all the work done?

Underlying Principles of Technology

- What technical training do workers need to do all the jobs within the project?
- What academic background does one need to perform these jobs well?

Community Issues

- What is the impact of your project on the community?
- What service or benefit is the community receiving?
- How are other members of the community involved in your project?

Finance

- What is the cost of the project? This includes cost of materials and wages to pay workers (teachers, advisors, students, etc.).
- Who makes the decisions on how project money is spent?
- If you are paid for your services, how do you budget the money you earn?

Labor Issues

- What are the workers' (and supervisors') rights and responsibilities?
- How will the team make sure everyone does their fair share of the work?

Health, Safety, and Environment

- What is the work environment like at the project site?
- Are you working outdoors or indoors?
- What are the health and safety concerns?
- How does the project interact with and impact the natural world?

FIGURE 14.1 ◆ All Aspects of Your Project: Questions to Ask. When you understand "the big picture" of your project you can more easily see what work needs to be done and how best to make it happen. This "systems" approach helps you understand all the different aspects that contribute to a successful project.

Source: Edwards, K. M. (2000). *Everyone's guide to successful project planning: Tools for youth. Student Guide.* Portland, OR: Northwest Regional Educational Laboratory.

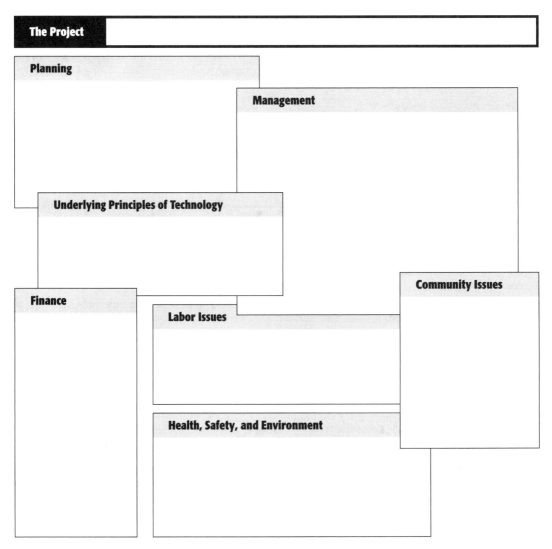

FIGURE 14.2 ◆ All Aspects of Your Project: Blank for Project Planning

Source: Edwards, K. M. (2000). *Everyone's guide to successful project planning: Tools for youth. Student Guide.* Portland, OR: Northwest Regional Educational Laboratory.

One teacher used the book *Esperanza Rising* (Ryan, 2000) two years in succession as a part of a fourth-grade unit on California history. In the first year, students showed interest in the young girl Esperanza's first home, a wealthy ranch in Mexico, by drawing, reporting on, and making up stories about *haciendas* in Mexico, and comparing them to *ranchero* life in early California. In the second year, students showed more interest in Esperanza's second life, which followed the migrant trail in California. Those students mapped Esperanza's journeys and planned family visits to various parts of California.

Of course, the teacher's passion is a factor. One fifth-grade teacher who is a great fan of detective fiction finds new ways to share this passion year after year by turning science, social studies, or even music into a detective game. Another teacher loves adventure stories, and students who come to share a love of this genre design projects that somehow involve adventure—imagining, planning, or carrying out group adventures. Yet another teacher is a cook and organizes student projects that always seem to have some eating component. No wonder!

What PBL teachers avoid is the repetition of units year after year. Like the hoary build-a-Spanish-mission projects carried out in the fourth grades of California elementary schools, eventually the project is "used up"; that is, a given group is not likely to discover ideas or facets of the topic that are new, and the teacher is not really involved in what Halliday (1978) called "heuristic" language use. In other words, the process of learning is no longer exciting.

Mapping the Project

In phase I of a project, the students and teacher devote several discussion periods to selecting and refining the topic. Good topics are those that are within the range of interest and comprehensibility for the students and closely related to their everyday experience so that they can raise relevant questions. Rich topics generate two or three weeks of exploration and cut across subject domains of the school curriculum. A "mind map" of the topic, delineating the questions raised and the prior knowledge of the students, helps to serve as an ongoing road map for the inquiry.

The journey of a PBL inquiry begins with questions for the class as a whole to consider. Guiding questions in this regard may be the following:

> Why are we doing this project? (What is the community issue, concern, or need this project is trying to address?) How does this project address this issue, concern or need? If we are dealing with a problem or concern, what has created it? What kind of knowledge needs to be acquired? What can be done to prevent the problem from recurring once our project is complete? (Roth-Vinson, 2001, n.p.)

Schools may not be the best source of interesting projects. In the search for a compelling project, one must take the community's needs into consideration. A teacher who takes the time to meet community members, listen to parents, and observe firsthand the life of the community can put into perspective the concerns brought forth by students. PBL, combined with critical pedagogy, makes sensitive use of stimulus codes to generate language that originates in the social context of the community.

> Deborah, a community college ESL teacher, had a Level I class in which half the students were Japanese exchange students and the other half were Mexican immigrants. The social interaction reminded her of oil and water in the same flask, that is, the students eyed one another warily, communicated in culturally homogeneous groups, and when paired across cultures had little to say to one another.
>
> Deborah turned to Gary Soto's *Pacific Crossing* (Soto, 1992), the story of a Mexican American youth who finds himself living with a Japanese

family during a study-abroad program. As they read the novel together, the Japanese students explained more fully the cultural customs of Japan, and in return the Mexican students clarified the protagonist's feelings of cultural shock. The novel opened doors to discussions of martial arts, communal bathing, and other areas of interest to both groups that kept the class lively and fun. The novel as code brought forth language, feeling, and cultural sharing that neither side alone would have been able to articulate, much less communicate.

There was spirited debate throughout the course as members discovered their mutual love: baseball. As a group project, the class members described the baseball leagues in their home countries and shared pictures of their favorite players. Although initially the topic seemed to be of greater interest to the male students than to the females, the class went together to a local baseball game, and the girls were grateful that they knew something about the game.

Topics across Disciplines

When PBL is interdisciplinary, collaboration takes place among teachers of different disciplines. Collaboration begins as teachers identify the central principles or concepts of each discipline and the target knowledge, skills, and dispositions that students will acquire. The next step is to create, discover, or define an engaging project that combines the required concepts or skills, achieving a balance between a problem that is both important and understandable for students. A division of labor among instructors distributes the work of supervision, coaching, and assessing results.

> "Zookeeper" is a collaborative project among the N.E.T. Team at Denver North High School, addressing content standards and involving teachers in English, history, visual arts, and science. Students design and build a habitat for a specific animal and plant, visiting a zoo and interviewing a zoo specialist in the process. At the beginning of the project, students amass a fact sheet for each plant and animal, with the goal of 50 facts for each. (Giromini, 2001)

Envisioning Success

When the students and teacher together develop a project, with input from the community if it is a service-learning project, the most compelling image that moves the project forward is the vision of what can be accomplished. The teacher next identifies the skills that will be needed to complete the project, such as writing, computer, or interview skills, and makes plans to teach or coach these skills. The teacher also matches the identified skills or content to district, state, or national curricular frameworks in order to justify the project as playing a substantive role in classroom learning. The next step is to select the performance indicators that will be used to determine the assessment of the project (presentation, product, etc.; "How will we know that it is good?") and to develop criteria for a successful project and/or product (Roth-Vinson, 2001).

> "Take Time in History" is a project that was developed with upper elementary students to emulate the *Time* magazine "Man or Woman of the Year" issue. Each student

chose a famous [historical] personality and wrote a feature story in the *Time* style, including an interview with the personality (what are five questions that you would ask if you could talk to him/her today?) and a narrative about an event that happened in that person's life. Supplements included a report from a fictional eyewitness about an event or person of the time or a narrative from a minor character. To augment the feature story, students made advertisements of products invented or used during the time of the famous personality. (Baker, 1987)

In this project, "success" was defined in three areas: attractive product, interesting and factually accurate information, and success of the collaborative effort.

Project Focus and Development

❖ **STRATEGY 14.2:** Delimit and focus project activities

Gathering and organizing information is an ongoing process as the project takes shape. The teacher as guide helps participants to locate sources relevant to the scope and focus of the project, whether books, magazines, Internet content, other print sources, or people with relevant expertise. Data that are gathered may be used to prepare a proposal or plan (for funding or other support); the plan may then include collecting further data to be analyzed as the project proceeds, data that will then be used to assess the success of the project.

Project Development

No matter what the goal or purpose of a project, the task of developing has a certain structure. The elements of this structure are represented in Table 14.3. Each of these will be discussed in turn in the sections that follow.

Students' projects engage them in long-term language use that can involve complex problem-solving.

TABLE 14.3 ◆ Common Structure for Development of a Project

Project Element	Description
Task representation	The information needed to perform the tasks provided, and the task is explained to the observer.
Example of the desired product	The project is based on a model or prototype.
Guided implementation	The project is supported by such means as assistance in information acquisition and advice on project design.
Self-check (quality control)	Project designers are able to obtain feedback, using specific criteria as a guide.
Recommendation for improvement	Project designers are able to modify and correct design flaws that have been identified during the quality-checking process.
Student presentation of product	Using a combination of designers' and audience's preferred mode of representation, the student/designer makes a formal presentation of project for purposes of assessment.
Feedback and reflection	Project designers are able to learn from feedback obtained through assessment.
Advice for mentors	Mentors are able to learn about learning by means of aggregated assessments across project results.

Source: Adapted from Loria, Shaltied, Pieterse, & Rosenfeld, 1999.

The Planning Cycle

The elements displayed in Table 14.3 seem to be in a linear, sequential order from the earliest to final stages of the project. This appearance of a linear order may, however, be illusory. Some projects contain loops in the planning cycle, in which the design changes multiple times during the project as participants' various points of view are incorporated to adjust and modify the ongoing design. The following project is an example of how plans can undergo modification during the design cycle due to such factors as the input of opinions, provision of expert data, and cost considerations:

> The fourth-grade teacher, Mrs. Shim, had the original idea: a four-part garden on the bare plot of ground beside the fourth-grade classrooms that would show various time periods of California history by means of four gardens: Native American, Mission, Chinese American, and Victory (World War II). Another fourth-grade teacher joined the project, suggesting a Ranchero period garden and a Japanese garden. A third teacher wanted a creek bed to demonstrate the Gold Rush. The space allotted to the project did not change, despite these added features, and the size of each of garden shrank as more components were added. Finally, each segment became one area 4 feet by 8-feet, connected by a "Walkway through Time." When research showed that the garden plants in the Mission and

Ranchero periods were similar, the two periods were combined. When the project went over budget, the Japanese garden became a Zen garden with sand, a rake, and beautiful rocks—but no plants. Thus the project changed in scope, focus, and design over an extended planning period.

Task Representation

The initial plan as imagined by the designers, the ongoing documentation, and the final product each are represented in a way that enables communication between project team members and the audience, stakeholders, or other participants in the project. The form of representation depends largely on four variables: the nature of the project; the preferred information style of the designers; the preferred information style of the audience or community participants; and the expertise and funds available. This may change during the course of the project. The following vignette illustrates how project designers struggled with the data available as a function of the nature of the project:

> As a final research project for a computer-assisted language-learning course, two students chose to document the successes and/or frustrations of a group of international students who were learning to use English pronunciation software in the campus foreign-language media laboratory. In the exploratory phase of the project, the researchers planned to make the software program available only in the presence of the researchers, who would observe and record student responses.
>
> Then one of the researchers suggested that the computer software itself could be used to store results from each usage attempt by an international student, thus allowing students to work unsupervised. The data would then be represented by computerized scores for each student. After consultation with the staff of the foreign-language media laboratory, the researchers decided that this was not feasible. Refusing to give up on the idea, the researcher called the software company to see if a research version of the software was available that could trace the process of the students as they used the software. However, no one in the company seemed to know if such a version existed.
>
> In frustration, the researchers decided to alter the research project to focus on six students (two each at three levels of pronunciation proficiency) and to monitor them three times each in supervised, half-hour sessions with the software, as well as record the computer's performance feedback. This would result in a total of eighteen sessions, a 4.5 hour commitment for each researcher. The data would then be represented by observational entries about each student supplemented by student feedback and pre- and post-session interviews with the six students.

The preferred information style of the designer usually influences the choice of project; people who do not prefer music and know little about it are rarely comfortable with a project based on music, for example. Because teachers of English learners work in a language domain, each project should serve as the stimulus for written or oral activity; that is, explanatory paragraphs should supplement a map, and a picture should not substitute for a verbal explanation. Charts, graphs, and other graphic organizers are not incompatible with words, but rather can support and express ideas along with verbal representation.

The preferred information style of the audience, stakeholders, or other participants governs how the final results will be conveyed. Pictures that show their children working in various stages of the project may be popular with parents. If the audience is comprised of school district authorities, an article with pictures in a district newsletter may simultaneously inform both insiders and the public at large. If dissemination of project results takes place at a culminating event, a slide show accompanied by music may be popular. Mariachi music and folkloric dance teams reinforced the cultural content of the César Chávez Day of Service and Learning:

> The César Chávez Day of Service and Learning was exciting for all participants. On the morning of March 31, teams of students from each of a dozen elementary, middle, and high schools set up their posters in the Expert Exposition area at the San Bernardino County Museum and took turns manning their booths. Each poster described a Sustainable Products project that had taken place during a service-learning partnership between their school and a community organization. The gardens that were showcased had a variety of themes. A first-grade class with a Bird and Butterfly school garden had learned to propagate plants, and donated several butterfly-attracting bushes to a nursing home. A class of sixth graders had traced the history of favorite recipes in the Mexican diet and had raised and donated six types of plants in an information kit to local families. As the students toured from booth to booth to look at other schools' projects, they experienced firsthand the social values of César Chávez: respect for life, service to others, determination, and celebration of community.

The expertise and funds available determine the long-range durability of project results and the extent of dissemination efforts. If a school can raise money for desktop publishing, each student can receive a colorful packet of pictures upon completion of a project. If a school has access to digital cameras and students can construct websites, project documentation can take the form of sites available on the Internet. Students can make up a song that commemorates the project and record it on audiotapes.

Example of the Desired Product

Not every project is brand-new. When a teacher implements a similar project for several years, the students in the second year have the benefit of seeing documentation or products from the first year. After students in a high school in Denver were invited to view the products from the Mexican Day of the Dead project prepared by a magnet program within the school, requests for admission to the program skyrocketed the next year. A student-run crafts market that took place in conjunction with International Day festivities was so popular that the following year parents began calling the school months in advance to be sure of the upcoming date.

Students can also benefit from viewing the efforts of others, even if those efforts are available only on a website or through other kinds of remote access.

> When high school students in Miami heard about the Memphis Blues project, in which students in Memphis, Tennessee, interviewed blues musicians to document the history and extent of the music tradition in their city, the Miami students wanted to do the same with Puerto Rican and Cuban music in Miami. Eventually they formed their own band—The Salsa Kids—and were invited to play at a national PBL conference, where they had the audience dancing in the aisles!

It is always a temptation to show students the best of past products, but it is more realistic to display a range of results as examples. Sometimes, products that turned out less successful than expected may nonetheless have a creative aspect that will inspire the next spark of creativity. In addition, it is wise to display as exemplars those that feature a range of representation styles and English skill levels.

Guided Implementation

The teacher in the role of guide plays a role long before the start of a project. The most difficult part of PBL is to involve the participants in worthy endeavors that are both comprehensible and manageable. Much background investigation must be done before a teacher can step into a complex situation and risk offering that complexity to students as a learning experience. Some research may be necessary to locate materials and make these accessible to students.

Community partners may have much to offer, such as a telephone list of contacts for reduced-price materials, a friend of a friend who knows an expert, or a shelf of books on a relevant topic. On the debit side, when the community is involved, it may be advisable to probe the goals and values of partners outside the school to ensure that students who participate are not exploited. Trust among community partners is established largely not by blind faith but by experience. Community partners often have their unique character flaws, such as procrastination over returning phone calls, change of heart about donating resources, tendency to spread their efforts too thinly, or preoccupation with other projects at a crucial moment. Part of what the teacher learns as guide is how to accommodate the labor, or lack thereof, of other partners.

Because a large part of students' initial motivation to become involved derives from the enthusiasm of the teacher, it is not unfair to say that the most successful projects seem to be those in which the teacher is invested, whether this be in prior knowledge, skills, or disposition. The challenge of the teacher is to build within students the desire and skills to become self-directed learners and then to fade into the background to take on such roles as supporter, colleague, clarifier, and reminder of deadlines.

At a certain point, it is necessary to formalize a master plan for the project. Students can use a chart called "Time Line with Responsibilities" (see Table 14.4) to organize their plans. When dividing up the work, students should start with the strengths and skills of each team member. When selecting project duties, however,

TABLE 14.4 ◆ Project-Based Learning Time Line with Responsibilities

Objectives of the Project	Person Responsible	Date of Proposed Completion

good project management leaves room for team members to branch out and learn new skills (Roth-Vinson, 2001). When completed, the master plan becomes a guide for the project and should be easily accessible so that team members can check off their work when completed.

Self-Checking (Quality Control)

Metacognition plays a large role in PBL, as it does in other parts of life. When criteria for successful performance are determined in advance, a valuable role of metacognition is to compare partial results or prototypical products against the desired criteria. At a certain point along the way, however, it may become obvious that some group members are too easily satisfied, whereas others are hard to please. Some point of satisfaction may have to be agreed on by the team as a whole, and the person(s) closest to an understanding of that point may become the agent of quality control.

> A new student, a recent immigrant from Guatemala, entered Mr. Olivo's second-grade class, which consisted predominantly of English learners. As a welcome gift, she gave the teacher a homemade "God's eye," a small wooden cross wrapped with brightly colored yarn in a diamond shape. Soon two Mexican girls came shyly to the front and informed Mr. Olivo that their mothers knew how to make the "God's eye" too; the next day one of the girls brought another to class. Within a week, a "God's eye" fad swept the second-grade class. Students came up with the idea to make "God's eyes" and sell them to other students at Christmas. Mr. Olivo bought yarn and several packets of craft sticks and presented the potential sales event as a project for students. As a group, they figured out the sale price, based on a fixed number of colors and a fixed length of yarn on each "God's eye."
>
> All went well until the actual creation of the "God's eyes." At that point it became obvious that some children's quality level was not as good as others. Students whose efforts were rejected by the perfectionists were hurt, and some began sneakily to sabotage the work of others. Mr. Olivo called a class meeting, at which it was decided that all finished products would be stored in flat cardboard boxes until just before the sale, when a panel of three would set a variable price for each. As it turned out, by the end of October the poor craftsmen has lost interest, while those motivated to continue worked at lunch or at recess. At the end of the sale, no one remembered whose work was whose; and the "God's eyes" that were not so

nice were sold anyway to those who had a nickel to spare for a present for their *abuelas.*

Recommendation for Improvement

Sometimes improvement is easy to attain by altering one's approach to a problem. However, when the project is still feasible based upon a few changes yet repeated attempts at problem solving fail and an impasse is reached, it may prove helpful to seek outside expertise and advice. Sometimes those with experience of a particular situation can suggest easier ways to deal with difficulties or offer the necessary advice that it is time to "cut one's losses." The frustrations along the way provide the greatest amount of learning, not only in problem solving but also in character building. Adequate prior analysis of the risks involved, finances needed, management and organization required, community's issues and values, and health and safety considerations makes projects no less challenging, but more assured of success.

Project Documentation and Evaluation

♦ **STRATEGY 14.3:** Document and assess the progress of the project

Process Counts

As the project proceeds, all parts of the process constitute learning. Participants should take pictures, preserve planning sketches, and keep a log of activities. Individuals who keep a chronological list of activities can share their lists with others periodically to make sure that everyone remembers events in a similar fashion. If one person is appointed archivist, someone may wish to check periodically to make sure that there are indeed archives. Notes from participant interviews, whether in person or by telephone, make worthy archive entries. When key decisions must be made, it is advisable for a member to record the minutes of the deliberations.

Student Presentation of Product

Culminating events trigger emotional investment as students experience anticipation, excitement, and suspense. They also supply clearly visible deadlines. Students need projects that include a public demonstration so that they can invite friends and family. Showcase events also create lifelong memories. Few people remember the day-to-day life of the classroom, the names of their peers in the third grade, or the pictures on the page of the ESL book they used. Few forget, however, the feeling of singing in a chorus or acting in a play. Life's events are the key to creating what psychologists call "episodic memory."

The culminating event can be a poster presentation or bulletin board display, play, songfest, or festival. If it is a poster presentation, peers from other sites who were involved in a similar event or competition are more likely to benefit from exposure to these products. As someone who attends county fairs each year, I can attest that displays of student work usually interest only those involved, unless they include high-quality, tangible products. The products of ESL are words, phrases, sentences, paragraphs, pamphlets, brochures—by themselves rarely as compelling as a steam engine exhibit. Perhaps language educators should focus on more dramatic linguistic products to showcase such as dramas.

> My first year as an English teacher was in a small Catholic school. I formed a drama club, and our first and only production was T. S. Eliot's *Murder in the Cathedral*. Thomas Becket was played by a girl, a wonderful actor only eleven years old. The knights were menacing killers, and the shrieks of the cleaning ladies after Becket's murder made the walls of the cafeteria resound. The bishop of the diocese shook my hand afterwards and said it was the best elementary production he had ever seen. But I suspected that this was an understatement: I'll wager it was the best *play* he had ever seen.

Feedback and Reflection

In any project, the learning that takes place does not come automatically, but rather results from introspection. Structured moments in which all pause and write down their feelings and thoughts capture a snapshot of ongoing activities. Here is a sample set of summative reflective questions:

> In your opinion, was the project a successful undertaking? In your evaluation, consider the following: What have you learned by participating in the project? How were project challenges met? How did the project make you feel? How may others have viewed the project? How do you think the community benefited? (Roth-Vinson, 2001, n.p.)

Planning for Assessment

Giving grades is part of the teacher's work. One of the goals of assessment is to organize learning so that it becomes visible and can be documented. Assessment should take place in multiple forms and be diverse enough to provide meaningful and relevant feedback to the participants. Multiple assessors (students, peers, teachers, and other mentors) in multiple formats ensure variety and completeness, avoiding a one-sided picture of student competence.

The teacher helps participants to keep their documentation organized, reminds participants to take pictures or record activities, pauses with the group for reflection and self-monitoring, and ensures that all team members share the workload. Moreover, the teacher—sometimes with the help of a teaching assistant or paraprofessional, if one is available—keeps records of project activities for the purpose of school records, for example, documenting growth of English skills, or making sure that the content standards are being met.

In addition, to lay the foundation for future community involvement, one must maintain good working relations with outside parties by keeping telephone numbers current, making sure that all parties who made a contribution receive credit, writing thank-you letters, arranging for publicity photos for donors when appropriate, and smoothing over misunderstandings that may occur as a part of the process.

Conducting Project Assessment

Part of the challenge of assessment is balancing high, focused expectations for achievement with the need for students to feel a sense of ownership of the project and freedom to explore its possibilities. Sometimes the process uses a form of "planning backwards," linking outcomes and standards (the end point) to student interests (the start point). A rich project environment demands resources, and teachers often steer students toward lines of inquiry in which the teacher has developed expertise and amassed supporting materials. A rich terrain of inquiry leaves room for students to make individual contributions and not feel that they are revisiting turf that is already well trod.

Quality Assessment.   Various kinds of assessments have been implemented in conjunction with PBL. Because the work that students produce is in some ways unique to the project, it might at first seem difficult to find assessments that measure the quality of such disparate types of work as a book report, a budget proposal, an informational brochure, the design for a museum exhibit, a survey report, or an interview-based personality profile (Morrison, 2001). Creating a documentation portfolio in the course of a project may achieve the goal of archiving the work, but evaluation is still necessary. The teacher, functioning as expert audience, forms the backbone of the assessment effort.

Within this terrain of expertise, the teacher's familiarity with the subject helps to set standards of quality. For example, in the Memphis Blues project, the teacher's interest in the blues as a musical form, combined with contacts already established in the community, gave students an entrée into blues players' homes to gather oral history and provided some background for the students about the kind of questions to ask. In turn, the teacher could assess the level of quality and degree of accuracy of the information obtained.

The teacher may draw on community expertise to help assess student work. What the community appreciates in a product may after all differ from the teacher's expectation, and this disparity may provide a healthy reality check on the relevance of the instruction. Students' goals and interests are a second pillar on which evaluation rests. As a group, students may find fascinating part of a project that the teacher has undervalued, due to generational differences or peculiarities of peer culture. To answer the question, "What constitutes a quality product?" one must draw on multiple points of view.

Assessing Language.   For purposes of second-language education, however, a vital criterion is the extent to which students' language skills have improved. Many final performances or products include reports, oral presentations, or multimedia exhibits that clearly demonstrate the use of language skills. Beyond such visible evidence as success in written essays and in standardized reading scores, however, lie deeper, more intangible measures of English communication ability. Does the student show more willingness to chat with peers? Does the student engage more often in self-selected reading? Is the student more comfortable with students of differing cultures and family backgrounds? Certainly, features of sociolinguistic and strategic competence, as well as measures of affect (comfort with English, self-esteem) are appropriate criteria for judging overall performance on a project.

Criteria for Project Assessment

As part of a master's degree course on research in SLA, graduate candidates were asked to study and monitor their attempts to increase proficiency in a second language for six weeks in a project titled "My SLA" (Díaz-Rico, 1999b). Native speakers of English were asked to study another language, and nonnative speakers of English could use English as their target language. Although candidates were free to try any methods or combination of activities they chose, the analysis was expected to employ Fairclough's technique of critical language analysis (CLA). Figure 14.3 presents the scoring criteria that accompanied this project as a reminder of critical features of CLA.

Projects offer a wealth of learning, and build real mastery of a subject because students can test themselves in real situations. Along the way they can incorporate new understandings and constructive feedback. In addition, they permit teachers to build more complex relationships with students by providing many opportunities for meaningful discussions in contexts where students may appreciate adult input. And the culminating events of PBL provide precious memories for all.

Designing a landmark for their city is one project that Steinberg and Stephen (1999) offer students in their book *City Works*. Through this and other such activities, students focus on community issues, learning to join adult conversations about the quality of life in their town and the role of young people within the fabric of city life. The work sheets and design activities suggested by Steinberg and Stephen may be used by teachers as templates for PBL, even though purists would hold out for students to design projects that originate wholly from the interests of the class rather than from such workbooks, inspirational as they might be.

That said, *City Works,* with its emphasis on community improvement, profusion of ideas for involving local experts, and wealth of sources for community-based learning, directly ties PBL to learning within the context of the community. *Community Activities A to Zany* (Stafford-Yilmaz, 1998), although activity-based rather than project-based, also has suggestions that could lead students to engage in longer projects, especially because the focus is on getting students out into the community.

The following student's reactions to the use of projects in the ESL classroom summarize well the language learning that is possible by means of PBL:

> I liked this course because there were a lot of chance to talk to classmates and American people. Especially, I liked the assignments to interview American people. I made some friends through this assignment.
>   It gave me a chance to broaden my conversational ability, not just simple sentence, not just simple idea, but ideas that make me think more. (Wilhelm, 1999, p. 15)

M.A. in Education, TESOL Option Program
Evaluation Criteria for Critical Language Analysis

Candidate _____   Course: EESL 615 *Research in TESOL*

Component	Point Value/ Critique
Description: Text Level	_____/30

- What language did you attempt to acquire? Describe.
  vocabulary; general reading level;
  formal or informal register;
  use of slang or jargon; expressive words;
  general complexity level of grammar;
  textual structures such as length of paragraphs;
  use of visuals, paralinguistic features (gestures, etc.);
  use of nonpaper media (computers)
- What insight accompanied the language that caused you to learn something?
- Where did the text originate? What interaction generated it?
- When did the learning take place?
- What psychological factors were involved in the learning?

Interpretation: Institutional Level	_____/30

- What is the institutional origin of the text
  (television, schooling, marriage, friendship, etc.)?
- How is the text influenced by an institution?
- How does the institution influence the psychological factors involved in learning?
- What interpretation do you make of your relationship to an institution as a result of the learning?
- What do you learn about the institution or about yourself?

Explanation: Social/Cultural Level	_____/30

- What sociocultural factors accompanied the text?
- How does society's attitudes/treatment of age, gender, culture influence the text?
- What insights about your own culture or the culture of others have you received as a result of the learning?

Format	_____/10

- Paper looks professional, word-processed
- Paper contains full citation of text source(s)

TOTAL	_____/100

FIGURE 14.3 • **Scoring criteria for SLA/critical language analysis project.**

Learning English through Service to the Community

15

Why Service Learning?

We learn as we serve. The maxim is simple, but the implications are profound. The world's greatest leaders—great in the sense of great in spirit—have urged a life of service. One example is the life of César Chávez. Chávez was a man who dedicated his life to bettering the conditions of farmworkers in California. He believed that service to others was a calling, a mission, and a way of life, not merely an obligation or an occasional act of charity. He once said, "we can choose to use our lives for others to bring about a better and more just world for our children. People who make that choice will know hardship and sacrifice—in giving of yourself you will discover a whole new life full of meaning and love." (GOSERV, p. 14).

Chávez was committed to the idea that service not only strengthens a community but also benefits those who serve. English learners have a strong need to feel part of the community, be that their classroom community, a community in which they are sojourners, or a community into which they have immigrated. Service learning helps students to improve their language skills, their social skills, and their understanding of the target culture. Service-learning pedagogy, with its focus on real-world experience, is a natural complement to potentially more abstract critical classroom learning. O'Grady & Chappell (2000) captured the essence of service learning as an activity in which "the academic and the experiential converge" (p. 209).

Some teachers of English learners may feel that service learning is not appropriate for their students, or that the community is not willing for English learners to be of service. These challenges may be addressed by strategies presented in this chapter.

❖ **MEGASTRATEGY 15:** We learn as we serve

Definitions

Service learning is a form of experiential education in which learning flows from service activities (Furco, 1996). The term has been used to describe a range of endeavors, including volunteer and community service projects, field studies, and internship programs. The National Society of Experiential Education defines service learning as any service experience that is monitored, involves intentional learning goals, and incorporates active reflection from the learner. Thus service learning requires a balance between learning goals and service outcomes.

Jacoby and Associates (1996) supply the following definition:

> Service learning is a form of experiential education in which students engage in activities that address human and community needs together with structured opportunities intentionally designed to promote student learning and development. Reflection and reciprocity are key concepts of service learning. (p. 5)

Across the United States, teachers are discovering that student service projects can be powerful learning tools:

> Whether children lend a hand to neighbors in need or assist their peers halfway around the world, service projects form a bridge between academic skills and real-life problem solving—and help students develop a sense of responsibility and self-worth along the way. (Bozzone, 1993, p. 65)

"Community" is a term that may refer to local neighborhoods or larger entities, national or global. It is important, however, that the needs identified and addressed are those defined *by the community,* which may be very different from those perceived by well-meaning outsiders. The involvement of community members in assessing needs and defining goals richly contributes to the learning outcomes of a given project.

To differentiate service learning from other types of experiential learning, Sigmon (1994) defined *community service* and *volunteerism* as types of involvement in which the focus is on service and the persons served are the chief beneficiaries. In contrast, in the case of *field education* and *internships,* the focus is largely on the learning that takes place, and the beneficiary is largely the service provider.

Service learning, as a combination of these, must be fully integrated into the curriculum of an ongoing course or program, so that the learning enhances the service and the service supports the learning. Learning objectives might involve *knowledge* (to recognize the recitation discourse pattern in a classroom and to note which students respond well to it); *skills* (to practice vocabulary development activities with students using audiovisual media); or *dispositions* (to feel empathy for parents' support role in schooling, or to foster civic responsibility and citizenship).

If the service learning addresses a short- or long-term problem needing a solution, then the service might involve project-based learning. On the other hand, the service can involve such efforts as tutoring, in which the person performing the service supplies labor in an already established program. The best service-learning projects provide students with an opportunity to develop skills and knowledge in real-life situations and meet a real community need. They reinforce the connections between school and community and teach students how to work collaboratively with others to create change.

Extent of Participation

Today's students are participating in community service in record numbers. A survey of students entering college in 1994 indicated that more then 70 percent of entering freshman reported involvement in community volunteer work in high school (Astin,

Korn, & Sax, 1994). In a simultaneous survey of 9,000 undergraduates, 64 percent were involved in volunteer activities (Levine, 1994). Such volunteerism is not a color-bound phenomenon: 65 percent of white students and 62 percent of nonwhite students were involved. As Coles (1993) observed, "today's students are likely to express their lofty political and social impulses and practical desires to change the world through community service" (p. 40).

Education in America has a long tradition of service. As Smith (1994) recalled, "From the beginning, the goals of American higher education have included the preparation of citizens for active involvement in community life" (p. 55). College student community service has long been involved in such agencies as the YMCA and Greek-letter organizations. In 1961, the Peace Corps was founded by President Kennedy, followed soon after by Volunteers in Service to America (VISTA) and the National Student Volunteer Program (1969), which became the Corporation for National and Community Service (www.learnandserve.org). In 1978, the National Society for Internships and Experiential Education was established (NSIEE; as of 1994, National Society for Experiential Education, NSEE).

The experience of the 1960s and 1970s demonstrated that volunteer work was not an integral part of the mission of either the community agencies or the educational institutions involved. Many well-intentioned programs succumbed to the pitfalls of performing charity work "for" others rather than supporting the community to meet its own needs. Simply placing young people in the vicinity of service needs ensured neither significant learning nor effective service (Kendell, 1990).

The White House Office of National Service was created by the National and Community Service Trust Act of 1990. During President Clinton's administration the Corporation for National and Community Service (generally referred to as the Corporation for National Service) was created, funding the AmeriCorps national service program as well as service-learning programs in both K–12 and higher education settings through Learn and Serve America. Service learning became an integral part of education.

Components of Service Learning

A beginning component of service learning is *preparation,* laying the groundwork for understanding the problem or topics to be addressed, identifying the host community agency or site and its perception of needs, and planning the learning objectives. The sponsor or partner at the host site is involved to a greater or lesser extent in these issues.

A second component is *performing the service.* This may be simple, requiring only fixed hours for all participants at a single site; or it may be complex, involving ill-defined problems, transportation difficulties, communication challenges in relation to the host site, and multiple coordination needs.

The third component is *reflection,* in which the learner analyzes the experience, absorbs lessons from the experience, identifies areas of maximum or minimum success, and refines insights. Were the service-learning goals fulfilled? What personal or professional growth took place? What positive change took place within the organization, neighborhood, or community as a result of the service? (Campus Compact, 2000).

Benefits of Service Learning

Traditional instruction that requires students to learn within a classroom setting may not develop intellectual habits, personal understanding of the content, or the desire and capacity for lifelong learning. By encountering and addressing problems in a real-world context, students can learn under conditions that are personally relevant to their own lives and interests (Bringle & Hatcher, 1999). Service in the community educates critical thinkers. Significant and authentic work in the community gives students the opportunity to examine social structures and their effects on people (Anderson & Guest, 1994).

Service learning has been shown to have positive effects on the learner, on faculty members who incorporate service-learning experiences into the curriculum, on the educational institutions that support such experiences, and on the communities that act as hosts. Eyler, Giles, and Gray (1999) presented a summary and list of research on the effects on the learner (see Table 15.1).

TABLE 15.1 • Effects of Service Learning on Students

Outcome by Category	Sample Positive Outcome
Personal development	Personal efficacy Personal identity Spiritual growth Moral development
Interpersonal development	Ability to work well with others Leadership Communication skills
Social cognition	Reduction of stereotypes Improved racial and cultural understanding
Sense of social responsibility	Citizenship skills Commitment to service Involvement with community service after graduation
Learning	General increase in learning and cognitive development Ability to apply learning to "real world" Improved grade point average (GPA)* Demonstrated complexity of understanding Problem analysis skills Critical thinking skills
Career development	General contribution
Relationship to institution of learning	Stronger faculty-student relationships Satisfaction with college Increased likelihood of graduating

*Other studies, however, show no difference in GPA between those students engaged in service learning and those who were not

Source: Eyler, Giles, and Gray, 1999.

In addition to listing the positive effects on students, Eyler, Giles, and Gray (1999) cited research that shows specific gains for educators: increased satisfaction with the quality of student learning, increased commitment to learning, and increased integration of service learning into courses. Communities that have been involved with service learning in return feel that service learning provides a useful service to the community and are satisfied with student participation (Eyler, Giles, & Gray, 1999).

What Constitutes Good Service-Learning Pedagogy?

Howard (1993) listed several principles that distinguish good practice in service learning. Among these are the following: The instructor supplies educationally sound ways in which students can benefit from service, is prepared for a redefinition of the instructor's role, and can accept some degree of uncertainty and variation in student learning outcomes.

Students Serving Others: Some Examples

Bozzone (1993) offered a glimpse of several service projects. A group of fourth-grade students in Ashton, Maryland, raised money to build a school in a small village in Somalia about five hundred miles from the capital, Mogadishu. Students held a bake sale, asked friends and merchants for donations, and wrote to foundations and major corporations for aid. Students in Holtwood, Pennsylvania, created books to help stock the classroom libraries of Chee Dodge, a school on the Navajo Reservation at Yah Tah Hey, New Mexico. Children in a third-grade class in Lynbrook, New York, wrote an informational booklet explaining the hazards associated with discarding used batteries and ran a collection agency so that dead batteries could be disposed of properly. These vignettes illustrate how curriculum topics can be extended to become service-learning projects.

In one such program, prospective TESOL educators could choose from a number of community sites, among them an ESL classroom at a nearby elementary or secondary school, an adult basic education ESL program, a public library, and a youth center that provided after-school recreation for youth. Participants attended their site for a total of twenty hours a semester, tutoring children or adults in small groups or individually. During the experience, students maintained a journal and wrote a number of papers on specific prompts. In addition, class discussion included references to, and descriptions of, students' individual experiences at their site and the relevance of assigned readings to the service-learning project. Using a combination of readings, reflections, classroom dialogue, and the service project, the goal was to pose problems, explore power relations, and encourage student commitment to activism (O'Grady & Chappell, 2000).

Building Relationships with Service Agencies

A phase of exploration begins service learning. In schools with a long-standing commitment to service learning, a wealth of partnerships may exist with community agencies. In newer situations, extended conversations with workers at potential community sites may be necessary in order to determine the goals and needs of the host.

◆ **STRATEGY 15.1:** Identify community agencies that need ESL/EFL

Reciprocity

Service learning fits well with the current overall emphasis on learning: "All parties in service-learning are learners and help determine what is to be learned. Both the server and those served teach, and both learn" (Kendall, 1990, p. 22). This approach precludes a model in which students perceive that a more competent person is coming to the aid of a less competent party. In many ways, an outsider to a community is by nature less competent in understanding the community's situation or causes for that situation. Everyone should expect to learn—and change—as service-learning projects engage people *with* others rather than *for* others.

Exposing prospective TESOL educators to diverse community settings is of great value. Merely subjecting students to readings on cultural diversity will not increase students' cultural awareness or sensitivity; they need exposure to a variety of racial and cultural groups in community-based experiences (Tellez, Hlebowitsh, Cohen, & Norwood, 1995). As Sleeter and McLaren (1995) pointed out, students and teachers are often situated, knowingly or not, in a "highly politicized field of power relations that partake of unjust race, class, and gender affiliations" (p. 6). Service-learning experiences help to create reciprocal exposure to these power relations.

White, middle-class students in particular often ignore the fact that *their* interests are being met through the curriculum and school structure, which tends to emphasize middle-class, European American values while not meeting the interests of more marginal groups. For instance, Aparicio and Jose-Kampfer (1995) described the educational downside for Latinos in public school: linguistic and cultural erasure, censure for speaking Spanish, low levels of motivation based on alienation, and inequitable placement policies. In service learning, students of diverse races, classes, and genders can mix in mutual, reciprocal projects, permitting a more open dialogue on these issues.

Types of Service-Learning Opportunities

A learning component must be present in order for students to feel that their efforts are part of a planned curriculum. The type of engagement varies depending on size of the group and the site (see Table 15.2).

Identification of Community Partners

In many instances, the manifold needs of a community partner, combined with chronic underfunding for community-based organizations, drive a community agency to seek out student help. The usefulness of each site for service learning is weighed taking into account peer support, proximity, ease of transportation, the abilities and interests of the students who will be placed at these sites, learning objectives of the curriculum, and personal and professional contacts of the instructor.

TABLE 15.2 ⬧ Types of Service Learning Opportunities

	Short Term		Long Term	
Type	*On Site*	*Off Site*	*On Site*	*Off Site*
Individual				
Team of 2 to 4				
Adult-led team				
Classroom size (3)				
Large group (200)				

Source: San Joaquin County Office of Education, 2001, p. 15. Used with Permission.

My most recent set of service-learning placements arose from the Native California Garden Partnership, a grant program I initiated at CSU, San Bernardino, in conjunction with a local school district. As a result, the M.A. in Education, TESOL Option students were invited to participate in a set of projects to design ten different local school and community gardens. Each had a curricular component linking the particular garden with the California English Language Development Standards. The students had the most fun designing a Japanese garden for one site, because the team had two native English-speakers from southern California, an international student from Japan, and an international student from Crete. Each brought a unique perspective to the design.

Community partners have their own interests to look after. The questions in Box 15.1 are posed from the point of view of a community agency as they look toward forming a partnership with a school.

Designing a Service-Learning Project

⬧ **STRATEGY 15.2:** Design a service-learning project

In a time of escalating costs of education and increased academic pressure on ESL/EFL students, it may be hard for instructors to design and supervise service-learning projects. For this reason, it is even more necessary for such projects to become an intrinsic part of the core educational effort (Jacoby & Associates, 1996). This also means that one must maintain a realistic perspective regarding what results are possible within the time allotted.

The most important steps are to determine the desired service and learning goals of the project. The community has the largest role in setting the service goals. Planning goals should be evenly distributed across community host and student participants. This distribution ensures that the outcomes are feasible given the amount of time and resources that can be realistically devoted to the project, and that both parties have a sense of ownership.

BOX 15.1

❖ Partnership with a School: Questions to Ask to Define Roles and Responsibilities

When beginning a partnership with a school, ask the following questions to build a clear set of goals and parameters for the project:

What are the goals of each partner?

What are the needs and expectations of each partner?

Are there concerns or issues about the distinct role of each partner?

What resource(s) will each partner provide?

What will each partner do: In preparation? During the activity? To evaluate success?

When and where will this occur?

What are the further responsibilities of each partner?

How will training/supervision/liability be handled?

How will we know when we have achieved our mission? What will have happened, been created, or changed?

What are the learning goals? The service goals?

What are the students responsibilities?

Are there other people who need to be included in the process?

Who will be the lead person? What is the best way to communicate (phone, fax, e-mail)?

Source: San Joaquin County Office of Education, 2001, p. 13. Used with permission.

Because the school year is limited and some time is consumed at the beginning in organizing student participation and establishing working relations, it is vital to set a time line. In this way, both parties can allocate their time accordingly. Key accomplishments should be planned along the way, from initial project stages to final report, with plans for documentation. Students often feel more secure if they can plan the structure of their reflection at the beginning so that they can anticipate the types of desirable outcomes of their participation.

Determining the Learning Goal(s)

Learning goals and objectives constitute the desired outcomes for student involvement (for example, goals and objectives for the M.A. in Education, TESOL Option at CSU, San Bernardino are outlined in the document *M.A. in Education, Teaching English to Speakers of Other Languages Option Framework for Outcomes Assessment* [Díaz-Rico, 1998a]). The learning objectives may balance cognitive, affective, and participation goals. Not all the goals and objectives of a course of study or program are involved in any given project. For example, the service-learning activity California Native Gardens Partnership of the M.A. in Education, TESOL Option Program, CSU, San Bernardino, involved three objectives drawn from the *Framework for Outcomes Assessment* (see Figure 15.1).

According to objective 3.3, in the reflective paper each student is expected to examine his or her own learning process and attitudes toward teaching, learning, and language; integrate past and present teaching and learning experiences in the light of

Objective 3.3   Examine one's own learning process and attitudes toward teaching, learning, and language, integrating past and present teaching and learning experiences in the light of various learning theories that correspond with teaching styles and philosophies; examine one's own assumptions, values, and attitudes stemming from personal and cultural sources

Objective 4.8   Educate students in ESL/EFL classes (grades K–12) at a designated level to increase proficiency in ESL/EFL by means of appropriate teaching methodology, learning theories, student-teacher interaction and mentoring, and accurate and valid assessment strategies across language domains; be able to develop effective lessons that include appropriate objectives, involvement of students, varied teaching strategies, and means of accommodating student diversity within a range of activities; use valid assessment of objectives; and employ activities that establish a classroom climate of teamwork, cooperation, acceptance, and security

Objective 8.2   Participate in team-building activities and service to the TESOL program and to the community at large, such as crosscultural discussions, recruitment, peer coaching, and community language learning

FIGURE 15.1 ◆ Learning goals of service-learning project, California Native Gardens Partnership (M.A. in Education, TESOL Option Program, CSU, San Bernardino).

various learning theories; and examine his or her assumptions, values, and attitudes. Moreover, to meet objective 4.8, each project must include an ELD (grades K–12 and adult) component containing effective lessons that feature appropriate objectives and performance goals, involvement of students, varied teaching strategies and activities, and means of accommodating student diversity within a range of activities. Such a project, if successful, accomplishes objective 8.2, to have candidates participate in team-building activities and service to the TESOL program and to the community at large.

Proposing Performance-Based Results

Because of the experimental nature of some service-learning projects (ill-defined problems needing creative solutions), there is often no clear-cut, concrete example of an exemplary result. Despite this drawback, a statement of specific, proposed outcomes is possible. The following is a statement of proposed outcomes for one of the twelve California native gardens that were proposed as a part of the California Native Gardens Partnership at CSU, San Bernardino:

> The Craftsman Garden (grade 5) at Mariposa Elementary School is a planning/planting project based on the Arts and Crafts movement of the 1920s and 1930s. The product of this project is twofold: (1) creation of a handbook for the Craftsman Garden theme, complete with connection to California curriculum standards in reading/language arts, ELD, science, and social studies; and (2) creation of an actual Craftsman Garden at Mariposa Elementary School.

Service learning involves students with the community in mutually beneficial activities.

It is evident from the statement above that the desired outcomes were first, a handbook, and second, an actual garden. More specific subgoals were determined during the partnership through extensive dialogue between host community members and student participants.

Monitoring and Evaluating Service Learning

+ **STRATEGY 15.3**: Perform and evaluate service

Frequent feedback sessions with supervising instructors and community members are essential to the successful completion of a complex project. Problems having no clear-cut, predetermined solution may provoke anxiety in students. It may be important to emphasize to participants that they are members of a team, that their team members may be feeling anxiety too, and that open communication is valuable. Partial goals, benchmark indicators, should be tied closely to fixed dates. All parties can check at these times to see if their expectations have been met.

The Reflective Component

According to John Dewey, reflection is an "active, persistent, and careful considera-tion of any belief or supported form of knowledge in light of the grounds that sup-port it" (1933, p. 146). The overall goals of reflection are to deepen students' understanding of their experience and to enable students to "recognize themselves, name their experiences, and learn how to change existing conditions for themselves as well as for others in the community" (Keith, 1997, p. 137).

Many kinds of reflective activities can be used to support the learning in service learning. Student journals help to distribute the reflection over the course of the engagement and tie summary thoughts to specific events. Bringle and Hatcher (1999) caution that more formal reflective activities may be more satisfying than unstructured journal entries, which tend to become a mere record of activities rather than a means of tying experiences to learning objectives. They recommend various reflective exercises (see Table 15.3).

The emphasis on reflection within service learning stresses dialogue between the student and the experience, between the student and the community members, and between the student and the course concepts. As O'Grady & Chappell (2000) reminded us, students are not mere receptacles to be filled; they must engage in an active way with their own experiences and with the social consequences of their service. Therefore, service-learning programs, must engage people in responsible action for the common good.

TABLE 15.3 • Types of Service-Learning Reflection Assignments

Assignment	Description
Experiential research paper	Students write a formal paper to identify a particular set of events at the service site; find an important social issue or issues underlying the circumstance; discuss multiple perspectives from which the situation could be analyzed; discover published research relevant to the issue or issues; and end with recommendations.
Ethical case study	Students raise issues that concern beliefs, values, and morals.
Class presentation	Students participate in bulletin board exhibits, panel discussions, speeches, or other creative displays. These can take electronic form such as home pages, chat room discussions, bulletin board discussions, or class listservs.
Key-phrase journal	Students incorporate select learning concepts into their entries.
Double-entry journal	Students use the left side of a spiral-bound notebook to record events and personal thoughts, keeping the right side for formal essays that connect these experiences to class readings, lectures, or presentations. Arrows may be used as links from left to right.
Critical incident journal	Students explore thoughts and reactions to a specific occurrence that took place, tying these explicitly to learning concepts and projecting possible alternative actions that might have been taken.
Three-part journal	Students list key incidents, decisions, and interactions that took place during service learning; then they make a connection to key learning concepts, personal goals, values, attitudes, or beliefs.
Directed writing	Students match specific learning concepts to relevant features of the service-learning experience.

Source: Adapted from Bringle and Hatcher, 1999.

Assessing Performance-Based Results

Bringle and Hatcher (1999) invoked Bradley's three-level set of criteria for assessing the level of reflection a participant has attained (see Table 15.4). Presenting these criteria to participants in advance of their reflective writing may elicit maturity and development in their perspective about the learning experience.

Measuring the impact on participants seems to be the chief focus of reflective evaluation, but Driscoll, Holland, Gelmon, and Kerrigan (1996) also looked at the effect of such experiences on the instructor, the community, and the institution. Their conclusions show an impact on participants' self-awareness, personal development, academic achievement, independence as learners, and overall academic achievement. Community benefits included enhanced capacity to meet the needs of individual clients, as well as economic and social benefits. These may be important results to keep in mind when designing a final evaluation of a service-learning project.

Linking the results of the service-learning experience directly to the desired goals and objectives seems the most straightforward approach to evaluating the experience (Jackson, 1993). Clearly, assessing service-learning experiences requires broadening the evaluation process and letting participants exercise a wide range of response. Promoting the active involvement of participants in evaluating their experience can be as valuable as their designing and execution of the experience itself.

Figure 15.2 suggests an evaluation plan for a service-learning project carried out in conjunction with an M.A. TESOL program. This combination offers participants some latitude in self-evaluation and connecting the learning goals to the experience.

TABLE 15.4 ◆ Criteria for Evaluating Service-Learning Reflection Assignment

Level (1 = lowest)	Description
Level 1	The reflection paper features a list or description of activities or events, with little or no apparent insight into deeper causes or reasons. The event may be described from a single perspective or aspect, without discriminating how varying perspectives did or could occur, and with some confusion of personal beliefs with facts.
Level 2	The paper evinces some broader context for events or incidents, gives cogent reasons for differing perspectives, and shows an effort to distinguish fact from opinion.
Level 3	The paper shows that the writer can view occurrences from multiple perspectives, acknowledge possible conflicting goals among participants and possible contextual factors influencing behavior; and draw conclusions based on facts versus opinions.

Source: Adapted from Bringle and Hatcher, 1999.

CALIFORNIA STATE UNIVERSITY, SAN BERNARDINO
M.A. in Education, TESOL Option Program
Outcome Assessment Criteria for *Service-Learning Project*

Candidate _____

Component of Paper	Point Value/ Critique
A Brief History of My Project	_____/5

- Specific details of my involvement
- Why did I choose this project?
- Accounting for the time I spent
- Who were the local contact people?

The Service Component	_____/15

- How were the community's needs determined?
- What was accomplished (attach documentation)?
- What provision was made for local cultural aspects?

The Learning Component	_____/15

- What were the learning goals (see course objectives)?
- What did I learn about the community?
- What did I learn about language and culture?
- What did I learn about myself and my partner?
- Is there growth in my critical perspective?

Relationship to TESOL and M.A. Project	_____/5

- What changes have taken place in my interest in TESOL?
  Does this paper suggest any topics for future research?

Format	_____/10

- Consistent throughout
- Professional appearance (use of word processor)

Relationship to Community

- Any interest in future involvement?

TOTAL	_____/50

Formative Assessment: Instructor of Record _____ Date _____

FIGURE 15.2 • Assessment criteria for service-learning project.

The Critical Component

Service learning is an integral part of inducting prospective teacher educators into a critical perspective on the relationship among schooling, democratic principles, and existing social and power structures. In fact, critical educators have probed the whole concept of service learning to ask if, indeed, such projects truly serve the interests of the community whose needs they purport to meet. In the project described above, the originators of the project explored this issue:

> The politics of the . . . service learning project can be analyzed in a systematic way by focusing on the relationship among interests, conflict, and power (Morgan, 1986). In this project, the interests of the predominantly white college students were being met. They were acquiring valuable personal and professional experience in working with students from diverse backgrounds. The interests of the ESL teachers also were being met, since they acquired additional aid in the classroom. The interests of the ESL students—at least some of the students—were being met as well, since they were getting valuable one-on-one tutoring, which had the potential to increase their agility with the language . . . it is the parents of the Latino students whose interests are missing. Rather, it is more correct to say that we do not know whether or not their interests were met, since they were an invisible component in this project. Within the schools their children attend, within the social structure of our community, and now within this project, they have little or no power to see if their interests are served. (O'Grady & Chappell, 2000, p. 218)

O'Grady & Chappell went on to question the relationship between service learning and multicultural education, cautioning that involving students without introducing a critical perspective or deeper analysis of social, political, and economic realities can at best perpetuate a superficial understanding of such issues as the cause of inequities in school achievement; at worst, it can exacerbate existing misconceptions about minority-language groups:

Other theorists have been more deeply pessimistic about the motives and activities of those who enter communities as outsiders, undergo brief experiences and service-learning encounters, and then move on:

> . . . in the context of conflicting interests and the historical dominance of one racial and gender group over another, it is possible that "service," in and of itself, can have racist or sexist outcomes despite good intentions. . . . I think that, in the context of a history of dominance of one group over others, there is an incipient racism in the practice of service that cannot be avoided even if the conceptualization of it includes values and ideals we can respect and the virtues of people who practice it are above question (Cruz, 1990, pp. 322–323).

In the light of these reservations, it is clear that reflection alone cannot provide students with a transformation impetus that characterizes long-term commitment to social justice. Hand in hand with real experience in the community, educators who are exposed to critical perspectives begin to see social conditions not as individual plights, but rather as communities that are in need of systematic access to economic and social reform. When students can learn through service learning to analyze, critically reflect, and transform oppressive situations through action, they are engaged in a social reconstructionist multicultural education approach (Sleeter & Grant, 1987).

Finding Out More about Service Learning

Useful books on service learning are Bringle, Games, and Malloy's *Colleges and Universities as Citizens* (1999), Eyler and Giles's *Where's the Learning in Service Learning?* (1999), Rhodes and Howard's *Academic Service Learning: A Pedagogy of Action and Reflection* (1998), Howard's *Praxis I: A Faculty Casebook on Community Service* (1993), and Galura and others' *Praxis III: Voices in Dialogue* (1995). Journal resources include the *Michigan Journal of Community Service Learning* (www.umich.edu/~ocs/MJCSL/) and the *Journal of Public Service & Outreach* (www.uga/~jpso/). Lewis's *The Kid's Guide to Service Projects* (1995) does not focus on service learning per se but offers a wealth of ideas for involving students in the community. Eyring (2001) writes about service learning as a part of second- or foreign-language education.

Campus Compact (http://compact.org) lists resources for service-learning practitioners, along with extensive links to websites, news, model programs, and sample syllabi. Other general organizations are those of the National Service-Learning Clearinghouse (www.servicelearning.org) and the Service-Learning Internet Community (www.slic.calstate.edu). Higher-education–oriented links are those of Learn and Serve American Training and Technical Assistance Exchange (www.lsaexchange.org), New England Resource Center for Higher Education (www.nerche.org), and the American Association of Higher Education Service-Learning Project (www.aahe.org/service/srv-lrn.htm). Community-college–oriented sites are those of the American Association of Community Colleges' service learning page (www.aace.nche.edu/initiatives/SERVICE/SERVICE.HTM) and the Campus Compact National Center for Community Colleges (www.mc.maricopa.edu/academic/compact).

The reflective practice component of service learning is particularly vital if teachers of English learners aspire to personal, social, and intellectual growth. Pedagogical knowledge alone is not enough, even if it incorporates a multitude of learning strategies and tactics. This knowledge must be combined with learning experiences within a full range of social, cultural, and linguistic contexts and reciprocal teaching and learning relationships. Service that teaches forms a balanced mission for English-language educators around the world.

Appendix A

Influencing Language Policies to Benefit English Learners

Both formal and informal policies have an impact on educators. Exerting an influence on policies that affect English learners is not only a right; it is a professional obligation. Such influence can be exerted at many levels.

Policy at the Classroom Level

In the classroom, language policy means creating an educational and social climate that makes school a place where all students can succeed. When students fail to learn, schools and teachers have failed. Teachers are best able to foster dual-language proficiency by carrying out equitable, empowering instruction.

Fair educational practices require discipline and vigilant self-observation on the part of the classroom teacher. Practicing gender, socioeconomic, racial, and cultural equity requires all students to have an equal opportunity to participate. Teachers must extend mentoring to all students. Referrals to special education or to programs for the gifted should be equitable.

Teachers can incorporate multicultural inclusion into instructional plans, obtaining unbiased materials that promote positive role models from a variety of ethnic groups (see Díaz-Rico, 1993). Multicultural educational materials are readily available (see Bennett, 1990; Harris, Nieto, 2000). Teachers can use multicultural examples to illustrate points of instruction, elicit the stories and voices of the students from various cultures, and knit together home and school for the benefit of the students. The following classroom policies promote equity and inclusion for English learners.

❖ **Tactics for teachers to promote policies of equity and multicultural inclusion:**

- Feature minority languages and cultures in school shows, written communications, and displays.
- Take students' interests, languages, and backgrounds into consideration when planning instruction.
- Use materials that depict successful individuals of both genders and of various races and cultures.
- Ask an outside observer to help you guarantee that you are giving boys and girls equal access to your attention.

The social environment of the classroom can support student achievement. Equitable cooperative grouping can address status differences among students in the classroom (Cohen, Lotan, & Catanzarite, 1990). School practices in noncurricular areas such as school clubs should be nondiscriminatory. If not, a resistance culture may develop among excluded students, leading those students to reject schooling and either drop out or carry out acts of school vandalism. The social climate of the school can be one of acceptance for all students in a variety of ways.

❖ Tactics for teachers to promote an equitable social environment:

- Group culturally and linguistically diverse students heterogeneously.
- Ensure that students can win prestige positions in extracurricular activities regardless of their ethnic or cultural backgrounds.

Policy at the School Level

Exemplary teachers provide leadership, goodwill, and academic models for students, advocating funding increases for ELD and bilingual instruction, working to configure classes and class sizes to the benefit of the English learners, acting as lead or mentor teachers to help new teachers to meet the needs of English learners, and developing a climate of acceptance for linguistic and cultural diversity. Teachers can collaborate and share resources to teach cooperatively, thus mutually increasing their expertise despite cultural, linguistic, or philosophical differences.

❖ Tactics for teachers to advocate a school climate of acceptance for linguistic and cultural diversity:

- Ask for teacher assistants to help students who are making a transition to English from primary-language instruction.
- Experts in ELD or primary-language instruction should be given time to assist other teachers.
- Negotiate so that ELD and primary-language teachers are given an equal share of mentoring and supervisory assistance.
- Vote that an equitable share of budgeted resources be available for bilingual and multicultural instructional materials.

Often intercultural educators must take the lead in opposing racism. If a colleague expresses opinions that are derogatory to individuals on the basis of race, language, or culture, a teacher might respond to such comments by saying, "Why, it surprises me to hear a person like you express that kind of opinion." In this way the person is affirmed while the derogatory sentiment is rejected.

❖ Tactics for teachers to oppose racism at school:

- Expect leaders in the school to set an example of respect and encouragement for diverse language abilities and cultures within the school.
- Make every effort to integrate primary-language, ESOL, and mainstream instructors socially.
- Ask school staff (e.g., office personnel) to be equally courteous to all students and visitors.
- Do not use dress codes to discriminate against some subcultures while allowing others to dress as they wish.
- Identify and abandon materials that contain images derogatory to certain races and cultures.

Schools attract community attention because of the academic excellence of their students. Certain schools garner academic laurels by means of academic competitions outside school. Activities such as academic decathlons are team efforts in which dedicated teachers can involve students from many ability levels and promote problem solving and inventive thinking. Schools can foster an academic ambience in a variety of ways.

❖ Tactics for teachers to promote English learner participation in academic extracurricular activities:

- Insist that teachers who sponsor academically oriented extracurricular activities receive extra pay.
- Arrange for the school to support students with funds to travel to intellectual competitions.
- Ensure that teams competing for academic awards actively solicit individuals from diverse cultural and linguistic backgrounds.
- Hold some intellectual activities, such as contests, in the primary language.

Involving Families in Policy Making

Encouraging family members to participate in school activities is vital. Chapter 13 features many ways in which families can support their children's English learning.

Policy Decisions in Local School Districts

The policies of the local school districts are shaped by the values of the community. School policies are determined by the beliefs of school board members as well as by legal precedents set by state and federal laws and court decisions. Cazden (1986) points out the need for teachers to advocate programs for English learners before local boards.

> ❖ Tactics for teachers to influence school board policies:
>
> ◆ Place policies before the school board in a timely manner, with clear, concise, well-researched presentations.
> ◆ Attend school board meetings to send the message that the meetings are monitored by experts on issues that affect English learners.

Professional Organizations and Service

Teachers of English learners may make presentations at districtwide conferences or school board meetings, or serve on curriculum committees. Commissions organized by state boards of education offer opportunities for teachers to be involved on advisory boards or in writing curricula or adopting textbooks. Reading articles in professional magazines can lead to submitting articles about successful classroom practices.

Participation in professional organizations such as attending district or regional conferences, serving on committees, drafting proposals, and attending committee meetings can lead to leadership positions. Professional conferences put educators in contact with language development specialists nationally and internationally. Such organizations enable new teachers to form relationships with peers outside their school site.

> ❖ Tactics for teachers to enhance professional expertise:
>
> ◆ Perform ESOL-related staff training and mentoring of others, and participate in leadership training for ESOL programs.
> ◆ Attend district and regional, state, and national professional events and submit proposals for professional participation and publication.

Influencing Community Public Opinion

A supportive community offers a home for linguistic and cultural diversity. Proactive publicity and public relations can present English learners as positive contributors in the community. Letters to the editor of a local paper can serve as a means to persuade the public to support the instruction of English learners or rebut overtly racist and misinformed letters. Teachers and other staff members can influence community public opinion in several ways.

> ❖ Tactics for teachers to influence local public opinion:
>
> ◆ Give presentations to community groups about ESOL programs.
> ◆ Join or begin local education-community partnership foundations.
> ◆ Be proactive in gaining newspaper coverage for school events.
> ◆ Be heard in the local newspaper editorial pages.

Influencing Legislation and Public Opinion

State and national legislators are responsive to popular opinion as expressed by letters of support and phone calls on controversial issues. It is important for legislators to hear from professionals in the field. Bilingual education and language issues often arouse strong emotions, perhaps because language policies affect the criteria set for success in the employment vital to economic survival and success in the United States (Heath, 1983a). Public policy can be shaped in a variety of ways.

> ❖ Tactics for teachers to influence legislatures and state policy makers:
>
> ◆ Ask your professional organizations to send subscriptions of the organization's publications to legislative libraries.
> ◆ Join an e-mail listserv to stay informed on policy issues.
> ◆ Organize letter-writing campaigns and visit legislators personally to convey interest in issues that affect English learners.

Influencing Federal Policies

In the history of the United States, decisions about subordinate languages have sometimes been supportive and sometimes repressive. Teachers, particularly through their professional organizations, play an important role in public debate. Federal funding for innovative programs can greatly benefit English learners. Federal funds are available to design innovative programs that provide success for all students. Public opinion and lobbying efforts play a large role in determining the continuation of programs that benefit English learners. Participating in lobbying that supports these programs is a chance for teachers to use the literacy they advocate.

> ❖ Tactics for teachers to influence federal educational policies:
>
> ◆ Become informed about federal legislation that has an impact on ESOL services, and support your professional organization's lobbying efforts to influence federal legislation.
> ◆ Organize letter-writing and e-mail campaigns to convey interest in issues that affect English learners.

The National Spirit

A national spirit is created in part by individuals who voice their opinions freely. Writing letters to national magazines on a regular basis helps editors sense the opinions of the readers, as national arguments are debated in the mass media. Controversial media figures also shape the national spirit. The population at large must take steps to defuse the voices of demagogues by writing letters to national networks voicing opposition to and distaste for racist viewpoints. Often, teachers of English learners who advocate on their behalf act as role models for English learners to speak for themselves and to be heard. Educators who share the culture and language of the minority communities have a natural function as community leaders.

❖ **Tactics for teachers to influence the national debate on topics such as immigration and support for English learners:**

- Write letters of support for television and radio shows that provide a fair, balanced discussion of controversial issues.
- Write or e-mail networks to express your approval or disapproval of the content of their programming.
- Write letters to national magazines to suggest or support content about issues that affect English learners.

Appendix B
Bibliography of Works Used for Visual Imaginary Dramatic Arts

1. "Ancient Greek I and II" by Gustav Klimt (Costantino, 1998, p. 28 only).
2. "Music I" by Gustav Klimt (Costantino, 1998, pp. 32–33).
3. "The Motley Life" by Wassily Kandinsky (Russell, 1969, p. 67).
4. "The Farm" by Joan Miró (Tomkins, 1966, pp. 144–145).
5. "Bikes Poster" by George Hardie (Hardie & Thorgerson, 1978, p. 77).
6. "Landscape from a Dream" by Paul Nash (Swinglehurst, 1995, pp. 40–41).
7. "The Mystery and Melancholy of a Street" by Giorgio de Chirico (Tomkins, 1966, p. 115).
8. "Mama, Papa Is Wounded!" by Yves Tanguy (Tomkins, 1966, p. 119).
9. "Dog Barking at the Moon" by Joan Miró (Tomkins, 1966, p. 145).
10. "Harlequin's Carnival" by Joan Miró (Swinglehurst, 1995, pp. 34–35).
11. "Blumenmythos" by Paul Klee (Swinglehurst, 1995, p. 8).
12. "Composition" by Edward Burra (Swinglehurst, 1995, p. 77).
13. "Bronze Ballet" by Edward Wadsworth (Swinglehurst, 1995, pp. 24–25).
14. "The Entire City" by Max Ernst (Swinglehurst, 1995, pp. 31–32).
15. Album cover, "Saucerful of Secrets" (Pink Floyd) by Hipgnosis (Hardie & Thorgerson, 1978, p. 34).
16. Album cover, "Elegy(Nice)" by Storm Thorgerson (Hardie & Thorgerson, 1978, p. 19 only).
17. "Apotheosis of El Tucuche" by LeRoy Clarke (Art Services International, 1995, p. 197).
18. "The Magic Wedding" by Phillipe Dodard (Art Services International, 1995, p. 138).
19. "El Mundo Mágico de JOP" by José Perdomo (Art Services International, 1995, p. 123).
20. "To Know a Veil" by Hipgnosis (Hardie & Thorgerson, 1978, p. 150).
21. "Carnival Dance" by Stafford Schliefer (Art Services International, 1995, p. 175).
22. "Gethsemane I" by Ras Akyem Ramsay (Art Services International, 1995, pp. 104).
23. "Blue Night" by Christopher Cozier (Art Services International, 1995, pp. 198–199).

24. "Las Meninas" by Pablo Picasso (Wertenbaker, 1967, pp. 160–161).
25. "Unterach on the Attersee" by Gustav Klimt (Costantino, 1998, p. 97).
26. "Baby" by Gustav Klimt (Costantino, 1998, p. 105).
27. "Water Snakes (Friends) I" by Gustav Klimt (Costantino, 1998, p. 51).
28. Album cover, "Uno" by Storm Thorgerson (Hardie & Thorgerson, 1978, p. 45).

Art Services International (1995). *Caribbean visions: Contemporary painting and sculpture* (pp. 104, 123, 138, 175, 197, 198–199). Alexandria, VA: Author.

Costantino, M. (1998). *Klimt* (pp. 28, 32–33, 51, 97, 105). New York: Knickerbocker Press.

Hardie, G., & Thorgerson, S. (1978). *The work of Hipgnosis ("Walk away René")* (pp. 19, 34, 45, 77, 150). New York: A. & W. Visual Library.

Russell, J. (1969). *The world of Matisse 1869–1954* (p. 67). New York: Time-Life Books

Swinglehurst, E. (1995). *The art of the surrealists* (pp. 8, 24–25, 31–32, 35, 41, 77). Bristol, UK: Parragon Book Service Ltd.

Tomkins, C. (1966). *The world of Marcel Duchamp 1887–* (pp. 115, 119, 144, 145). New York: Time-Life Books.

Wertenbaker, L. (1967). *The world of Picasso 1881–* (pp. 160–161). New York: Time-Life Books.

Bibliography

Abdoh, S. (2001). Interview on *Fresh Air*, National Public Radio, October 2.

Abramson, S., Seda, I., & Johnson, C. (1990). Literacy development in a multilingual kindergarten classroom. *Childhood Education, 67* (2), 68–72.

Ada, A. F. (1995). Fostering the home-school connection. In J. Frederickson (Ed.), *Reclaiming our voices: Bilingual education, critical pedagogy, and praxis* (pp. 163–178). Ontario, CA: California Association for Bilingual Education.

Ada, A. F. (1988). The Pájaro Valley experience: Working with Spanish-speaking parents to develop children's reading and writing skills in the home through the use of children's literature. In T. Skutnabb-Kangas & J. Cummins (Eds.), *Minority education: From shame to struggle* (pp. 223–238). Philadelphia: Multilingual Matters.

Adamson, H. D. (1993). *Academic competence.* New York: Longman.

Adamson, W. L. (1980). *Hegemony and revolution: A study of Antonio Gramsci's political and cultural theory.* Berkeley, CA: University of California Press.

Addison, A. (1988, November). Comprehensible textbooks in science for the nonnative English-speaker: Evidence from discourse analysis. *The CATESOL Journal, 1* (1), 49–66.

Adger, C. (2000). School/community partnerships to support language minority student success. *CREDE Research Brief #5.* Santa Cruz, CA: Center for Research on Education, Diversity and Excellence. Available online: www.crede.ucsc.edu.

Af Trampe, P. (1994). Monitor theory: Application and ethics. In R. Barasch & C. James (Eds.), *Beyond the monitor model.* Boston: Heinle & Heinle.

Agar, M. (1980). *The professional stranger: An informal introduction to ethnography.* Orlando, FL: Academic Press.

Agne, K. J. (1992). Caring: The expert teacher's edge. *Educational Horizons, 70* (3), 120–124.

Agor, B. (Ed.). (2000). *Integrating the ESL standards into classroom practice: Grades 9–12.* Alexandria, VA: Teachers of English to Speakers of Other Languages (TESOL).

Alcaya, C., Lybeck, K., Mougel, P., & Weaver, S. (1995). *Some strategies useful for speaking a foreign language.* Unpublished manuscript, University of Minnesota.

Alderson, J., Krahnke, K., & Stansfield, C. (Eds.) (1987). *Reviews of English language proficiency tests.* Washington, DC: Teachers of English to Speakers of Other Languages.

Allen, E., & Valette, R. (1977). *Classroom techniques. Foreign languages and English as a second language.* San Diego, CA: Harcourt Brace Jovanovich.

Allen, M. J., Noel, R. C., & Rienzi, B. M. (2001). *Program Assessment Consultation Team outcomes assessment handbook.* Bakersfield, CA: California State University, Bakersfield.

Althen, G. (1988). *American ways.* Yarmouth, ME: Intercultural Press.

Amery, H. (1979). *The first thousand words: A picture word book.* London: Usborne.

Amery, H., & Milá, R. (1979). *The first thousand words in Spanish.* London: Usborne.

Amselle, J. (1999). Dual immersion delays English. *American Language Review, 3* (5), 8.

Anderson, B. (1983). *Imagined communities.* London and New York: Verso.

Anderson, J. B., & Guest, K. (1994). Service learning in teacher education at Seattle University. In R. J. Kraft & M. Swadener (Eds.), *Building community: Service learning in the academic disciplines* (pp. 139–150). Denver: Colorado Campus Compact.

Andersen, J., & Powell, R. (1988). Cultural influences on educational processes. In L. Samovar & R. Porter (Eds.), *Intercultural communication: A reader* (5th ed.). Belmont, CA: Wadsworth.

Anderson, N. J. (2002). Using telescopes, microscopes, and kaleidoscopes to put metacognition into perspective. *TESOL Matters, 12* (4), 1, 4.

Anstrom, K. (1998). Preparing secondary education teachers to work with English language learners: English language arts. *NCBE Resource Collection Series, no. 10.* Washington, DC: National Clearinghouse for Bilingual Education. Available online: www.ncbe.gwu.edu/ncbepubs/resource/ells/language.htm.

Anyon, J. (1994). The retreat of Marxism and socialist feminism: Postmodern and poststructural theories in education. *Curriculum Inquiry, 24*, 115–133.

Aparicio, F. R., & Jose-Kampfer, C. (1995). Language, culture, and violence in the educational crisis of U.S. Latinos/as: Two courses for intervention. *Michigan Journal of Community Service Learning, 2* (fall), 95–105.

Applebee, A. N. (1977). Writing across the curriculum: The London projects. *English Journal, 66* (9), 81–85.

Aragones, S. (1985). *Comics and conversation.* Studio City, CA: JAG Publications.

Aragones, S. (1991). *More comics and conversation.* Studio City, CA: JAG Publications.

Aragones, S. (2000). *New comics and conversation.* Studio City, CA: JAG Publications.

Argüelles, J., & Argüelles, M. (1972). *Mandala.* Berkeley, CA: Shambala Press.

Armour, M., Knudson, P., & Meeks, J. (1981). *The Indochinese: New Americans.* Provo, UT: Brigham Young University Language Research Center.

Armstrong, T. (1993). *Seven kinds of smart: Identifying and developing your many intelligences.* New York: Dutton/Signet.

Armstrong, T. (1994). *Multiple intelligences in the classroom.* Alexandria, VA: Association for Supervision and Curriculum Development.

Aronowitz, S., & Giroux, H. A. (1991). *Postmodern education: Politics, culture, and social criticism.* Minneapolis and London: University of Minnesota Press.

Asher, J. (1982). *Learning another language through actions: The complete teachers' guidebook.* Los Gatos, CA: Sky Oaks.

Astin, A. W., Korn, W. S., & Sax, L. J. (1994). *The American freshman: National norms for fall 1994.* Los Angeles: Higher Education Research Institute, University of California.

Atwan, R. (1997). *America now: Short readings from recent periodicals* (2nd ed.). Boston: Bedford Books.

Atwell, N. (1987). *In the middle.* Portsmouth, NH: Boynton-Cook.

Auerbach, E. R. (1995). The politics of the ESL classroom: Issues of power in pedagogical choices. In J. W. Tollefson (Ed.), *Power and inequality in language education* (pp. 9–33). Cambridge: Cambridge University Press.

Auerbach, E. R. (2002). *Case studies in community partnership.* Alexandria, VA: Teachers of English to Speakers of Other Languages.

Auerbach, E. R., & Burgess, D. (1985). The hidden curriculum of survival ESL. *TESOL Quarterly, 10*, 475–495.

Auerbach, E. R., & Wallerstein, N. (1987). *ESL for action: Problem posing at work.* New York: Addison-Wesley.

August, D., & Pease-Alvarez, L. (1996). *Attributes of effective programs and classrooms serving English language learners.* Santa Cruz, CA: Center for Research on Cultural Diversity and Second Language Learning.

Axtell, R. (1995). *Do's and taboo's of using English around the world.* New York: John Wiley.

Baker, C. (1993). *Foundations of bilingual education and bilingualism.* Clevedon, UK: Multilingual Matters.

Baker, E. M. (1987). Take time in history. In D. J. Watson (Ed.), *Ideas and insights: Language arts in the elementary school* (pp. 153–154). Urbana, IL: National Council of Teachers of English.

Baker, E. L. (1994). Making performance assessment work: The road ahead. *Educational Leadership, 51* (6), 58–62.

Balderas, V. A. (2001). Words and images that provoke informed multicultural identities. In L. Ramírez & O. M. Gallardo (Eds.), *Portraits of teachers in multicultural settings: A critical literacy approach* (pp. 71–86). Boston: Allyn & Bacon.

Banks, J. (1991). A curriculum for empowerment, action, and change. In C. Sleeter (Ed.), *Empowerment through multicultural education.* Albany: State University of New York Press.

Banks, J. A., & McGee Banks, C. A. (Eds.). (1997). *Multicultural education: Issues and perspectives* (3rd ed.). Needham Heights, MA: Allyn & Bacon.

Barks, D., & Watts, P. (2001). Textual borrowing strategies for graduate-level ESL students. In D. Belcher & A. Hirvela (Eds.), *Linking literacies: Perspectives on L2 reading-writing connections* (pp. 246–267). Ann Arbor: University of Michigan Press.

Barr, R., & Johnson, B. (1997). *Teaching reading and writing in elementary classrooms* (2nd ed.). New York: Longman.

Barton, D. (1994). *Literacy : An introduction to the ecology of written language.* Oxford: Blackwell.

Barton, D. (2000). Researching literacy practices: Learning from activities with teachers and students. In D. Barton, M. Hamilton, & R. Ivanič (Eds.), *Situated literacies* (pp. 167–179). London and New York: Routledge.

Barton, D., Hamilton, M., & Ivanič, R. (2000). Introduction. In D. Barton, M. Hamilton, & R. Ivanič (Eds.), *Situated literacies* (pp. 1–15). London and New York: Routledge.

Bartram, M., & Walton, R. (1994). *Correction: A positive approach to language mistakes.* Hove, UK: Language Teaching Publications.

Bassano, S., & Christison, M. A. (1995). *Community spirit: A practical guide to collaborative language learning.* San Francisco: Alta Book Center.

Bates, L., Lane, J., & Lange, E. (1993). *Writing clearly: Responding to ESL compositions.* Boston, MA: Heinle & Heinle.

Battenberg, J. D. (1997). English versus French: Language rivalry in Tunisia. *World Englishes, 16* (2), 281–290.

Bazerman, C. (1989). *Shaping written knowledge.* Madison: University of Wisconsin Press.

Beane, J. A. (1991). Sorting out the self-esteem controversy. *Educational Leadership, 49* (1), 25–30.

Beck, U., Giddens, A., & Lash, S. (1994). *Reflexive modernization: Politics, traditions, and aesthetics in the modern social order.* Stanford, CA: Stanford University Press.

Becker, C. (1999). Animal psychology. In N. Shameem & M. Tickoo (Eds.), *New ways in using communicative games* (pp. 95–96). Alexandria, VA: Teachers of English to Speakers of Other Languages.

Beckett, G., Carmichael, M., Mohan, B., & Slater, T. (2000, March). *Framework for project-based language/content learning.* Presentation, annual conference, Teachers of English to Speakers of Other Languages, Vancouver, BC.

Bell, D. (1999, spring). Rise, Sally, rise: Communicating through dance. *TESOL Journal, 8* (1), 27–31.

Bell, J. (1991). *Teaching multilevel classes in ESL.* Carlsbad, CA: Dominie Press.

Bell, N. (1986). *Visualizing and verbalizing.* Paso Robles, CA: Academy of Reading Publications.

Bembridge, T. (1992). A MAP for reading assessment. *Educational Leadership, 49* (8), 46–48.

Benesch, S. (2001). *Critical English for academic purposes: Theory, politics, and practice.* Mahwah, NJ: Erlbaum.

Beniston, F. (1996). West Side Story: A lesson. In V. Whiteson (Ed.), *New ways of using drama and literature in language teaching* (pp. 100–103). Alexandria, VA: Teachers of English to Speakers of Other Languages.

Bennett, C. (1990). *Comprehensive multicultural education: Theory and practice* (2nd ed.). Boston: Allyn & Bacon.

Bennett, J. M. (1999). *Aspects of marginality in second language teaching.* Presentation, annual conference, Teachers of English to Speakers of Other Languages, New York.

Bennett, J. M. (1993). Cultural marginality: Identity issues in intercultural training. In R. M. Paige (Ed.), *Education for the intercultural experience* (pp. 109–135). Yarmouth, ME: Intercultural Press.

Bennett, M. (1996a). Beyond tolerance: Intercultural communication in a multicultural society (Part I). *TESOL Matters, 6* (2), 1, 15.

Bennett, M. (1996b). Beyond tolerance: Intercultural communication in a multicultural society (Part II). *TESOL Matters, 6* (3), 6.

Benson, V. A. (1999). Syl/la/bles and linking. In N. Shameem & M. Tickoo (Eds.), *New ways in using communicative games* (pp. 18–19). Alexandria, VA: Teachers of English to Speakers of Other Languages.

Berk, L. E. & Winsler, A. (1995). *Scaffolding children's learning: Vygotsky and early childhood education.* Washington, DC: National Association for the Education of Young Children.

Berman, P., Minicucci, C., McLaughlin, B., Nelson, B., & Woodworth, K. (1995). *School reform and student diversity: Case studies of exemplary practices for LEP students.* Emeryville, CA: Institute for Policy Analysis and Research. Available online: www.ncbe.gwu.edu/miscpubs/schoolreform/ipar.htm.

Bermúdez, A., & Márquez, J. (1996). An examination of a four-way collaborative to increase parental involvement in the schools. *The Journal of Educational Issues of Language Minority Students, 16.* Available online: www.ncbe.gwu.edu/miscpubs/jeilms/vol16/jeilms1601.htm.

Bider, M. (2001, February). Personal communication. San Bernardino, CA.

Bizzell, P. (1982). College composition: Initiation into the academic discourse community. *Curriculum Inquiry, 12,* 191–207.

Blair, R. W. (Ed.). (1982). *Innovative approaches to language teaching.* Boston: Heinle & Heinle.

Bliatout, B., Downing, B., Lewis, J., & Yang, D. (1988). *Handbook for teaching Hmong-speaking students.* Folsom, CA: Folsom Cordova Unified School District, Southeast Asia Community Resource Center.

Bloch, J. (2001). Plagiarism and the ESL student: From printed to electronic texts. In D. Belcher & A. Hirvela (Eds.), *Linking literacies: Perspectives on L2 reading-writing connections* (pp. 209–228). Ann Arbor: University of Michigan Press.

Blood, P. (1992). *Rise up singing: The group-singing song book.* Bethlehem, PA: Sing Out Corporation.

Blumenfeld, P. C., Soloway, E., Marx, R. W., Krajcik, J. S., Guzdial, M., & Palinscar, A. (1991). Motivating project-based learning: Sustaining the doing, supporting the learning. *Educational Psychologist, 26* (3&4), 369–398.

Booth, D. (1985). Imaginary gardens with real toads: Reading and drama in education. *Theory into Practice, 24,* 193–198.

Boseker, B. J. (1999/2000). The disappearance of American Indian languages. In I. A. Heath & C. J. Serrano (Eds.), *Teaching English as a second language* (pp. 40–47). Guilford, CT: Dushkin/McGraw-Hill. Originally published in *Journal of Multilingual and Multicultural Development*, 1994, *15* (2 & 3).

Bosher, S. (1997). Language and cultural identity: A study of Hmong students at the postsecondary level. *TESOL Quarterly, 31* (3), 593–603.

Boswood, T. (1997). *New ways of using computers in language teaching.* Alexandria, VA: Teachers of English to Speakers of Other Languages.

Bourdieu, P. (1977). *Reproduction in society, education, and culture* (with J. Passeron). Los Angeles: Sage.

Bourdieu, P. (1979/1984). *Distinction: A social critique of the judgement of taste.* Cambridge, MA: Harvard University Press.

Bourdieu, P. (1991). *Language and symbolic power* (trans. by G. Raymond and M. Anderson). Oxford: Polity Press in association with Blackwell.

Boutte, G. (1999). *Multicultural education: Raising consciousness.* London: International Thompson Publishing House.

Bozzone, M. A. (1993). Kids make a difference. *Instructor, 103* (4), 65–67.

Bremmer, J. (1999). *MENSA mind maze challenge.* London: Chartwell Books.

Brend, R. M. (1975). Male-female intonation patterns in American English. In B. Thorne & N. Henley (Eds.), *Language and sex: Differences and dominance.* Rowley, MA: Newbury House.

Bringle, R. G., Games, R., & Malloy, E. A. (1999). *Colleges and universities as citizens.* Boston: Allyn & Bacon.

Bringle, R. G., & Hatcher, J. A. (1999, summer). Reflection in service learning: Making meaning of experience. *Educational Horizons,* 179–185.

Brinton, D., Snow, M., & Wesche, M. (1989). *Content-based second language instruction.* New York: Newbury House.

Brisk, M. E., & Harrington, M. M. (2000). *Literacy and bilingualism.* Mahwah, NJ: Erlbaum.

Britsch, S. (1993). Experience and literacy. *Instructor, 103* (4), 48–49.

Brody, E., Goldspinner, J., Green, K., Leventhal, R., & Porcino, J. (Eds). (1992). *Spinning tales weaving hope. Stories of peace, justice, and the environment.* Philadelphia, PA: New Society.

Bromley, K. D. (1989). Buddy journals make the reading-writing connection. *The Reading Teacher, 43* (2), 122–129.

Brooks, E., & Fox, L. (1998). *Making peace: A reading/writing/thinking text on global community.* Cambridge: Cambridge University Press.

Brooks, J. & Brooks, M. (1993). *In search of understanding: The case for constructivist classrooms.* Alexandria, VA: Association for Supervision and Curriculum Development.

Brophy, J. (1983). Research on the self-fulfilling prophecy and teacher expectations. *Journal of Educational Psychology, 75,* 631–661.

Brophy, J. (1988). On motivating students. In D. Berliner & B. Rosenshine (Eds.), *Talks to teachers* (pp. 201–245). New York: Random House.

Brown, C. (1987). Literacy in thirty hours: Paulo Freire's process in northeast Brazil. In I. Shor (Ed.), *Freire for the classroom: A sourcebook for liberatory teaching.* Portsmouth, NH: Heinemann.

Brown, D. (1987). *Principles of language learning and teaching* (3rd ed.). Englewood Cliffs, NJ: Prentice-Hall.

Brown, D. (2000). *Principles of language learning and teaching* (4th ed.). Englewood Cliffs, NJ: Prentice-Hall.

Brown, G., & Yule, G. (1983). *Teaching the spoken language.* Cambridge: Cambridge University Press.

Brown, J. D. (Ed.). (1998). *New ways in classroom assessment.* Alexandria, VA: Teachers of English to Speakers of Other Languages.

Brown, K. (2001). World Englishes in TESOL progams: An infusion model of curricular innovation. In D. R. Hall & A. Hewings (Eds.), *Innovation in English language teaching* (pp. 108–117). London and New York: Routledge.

Brown, P. & Levinson, S. C. (1987). *Politeness: Some universals in language usage.* New York: Cambridge University Press.

Brown, S. C., & Kysilka, M. L. (2002). *Applying multicultural and global concepts in the classroom and beyond.* Boston: Allyn & Bacon.

Bruner, J. (1986). *Actual minds, possible worlds.* Cambridge: Harvard University Press.

Brutt-Griffler, J., & Samimy, K. K. (1999). Revisiting the colonial in the postcolonial: Critical praxis for the nonnative-English-speaking teachers in a TESOL program. *TESOL Quarterly, 33* (3), 413–431.

Bry, A. (1976). *Directing the movies of your mind.* New York: Harper & Row.

Buckley, L. C. (2000). A framework for understanding crosscultural issues in the English as a second language classroom. *CATESOL Journal, 12* (1), 53–72.

Bunce-Crim, M. (1991). Helping kids choose a topic. *Instructor, 101* (3), 16.

Busching, B. A. (1981). Readers theatre: An education for language and life. *Language Arts, 58* (3), 330–338.

Byrd, P., & Benson, B. (1994). *Problem-solution: A reference for ESL writers*. Boston: Heinle & Heinle.

Caine, R., & Caine, G. (1994). *Making connections:Teaching and the human brain*. Menlo Park, CA: Addison-Wesley.

Caine, R., & Caine, G. (1997). *Education at the edge of possibility*. Alexandria, VA: Association for Supervision and Curriculum Development.

Calderón, M., Tinajero, J., & Hertz-Lazarowitz, R. (1990, spring). Adapting cooperative integrated reading and composition to meet the needs of bilingual students. *Journal of Educational Issues of Language Minority Students, 10,* special issue, 79–106.

California Department of Education. (1986). *Handbook for teaching Pilipino-speaking students*. Sacramento: Author.

California Department of Education. (1987). *Handbook for teaching Japanese-speaking students*. Sacramento: Author.

California Department of Education. (1989a). *Handbook for teaching Cantonese-speaking students*. Sacramento: Author.

California Department of Education. (1989b). *Handbook for teaching Portuguese-speaking students*. Sacramento: Author.

California Department of Education. (1992). *Handbook for teaching Korean-American students*. Sacramento: Author.

California Department of Education. (1994). *Handbook for teaching Vietnamese-speaking students*. Sacramento: Author.

California Department of Education. (1999a). *English language development standards*. Sacramento: Author. Available online: www.cde.ca.gov/state tests/eld/eld_grd_span.pdf.

California Department of Education. (1999b). *Reading/ language arts framework for California public schools*. Sacramento: Author. Available online: www.cde.ca.gov/cdepress/lang_arts.pdf.

California Department of Education. (2001). *Resources for English learners*. Available online: www.cde.ca.gov/el.

Calkins, L. (1983). *Lessons from a child*. Portsmouth, NH: Heinemann.

Cameron, A. (1988). *The most beautiful place in the world*. New York: Random House.

Campbell, C. (1998). *Teaching second language writing: Interacting with text*. Pacific Grove, CA: Heinle & Heinle.

Campus Compact (2000). *Introduction to service learning toolkit: Reading and resources for faculty*. Providence, RI: Author.

Canale, M. (1983). From communicative competence to communicative language pedagogy. In J. Richards & R. Schmidt (Eds.), *Language and communication*. New York: Longman.

Canfield, J., & Wells, H. C. (1976). *100 ways to enhance self-concept in the classroom*. Englewood Cliffs, NJ: Prentice Hall.

Cantlon, T. L. (1991). *Structuring the classroom successfully for cooperative team learning*. Portland, OR: Prestige Publishers.

Cantoni-Harvey, G. (1987). *Content-area language instruction reading*. Reading, MA: Addison-Wesley.

Carlsen, G. R. (1974). Literature IS! *The English Journal, 24.*

Carson, J. G. (2001). A task analysis of reading and writing in academic contexts. In D. Belcher & A. Hirvela (Eds.), *Linking literacies: Perspectives on L2 reading-writing connections* (pp. 48–83). Ann Arbor: University of Michigan Press.

Cassidy, N. (1992). *Kids songs: Sleepyheads* (audio-cassette and book). Palo Alto, CA: Klutz Press.

Cazden, C. (1986). ESL teachers as language advocates for children. In P. Rigg & V. Allen (Eds.), *When they don't all speak English*. Urbana, IL: National Council of Teachers of English.

Cazden, C. (1988). *Classroom discourse*. Portsmouth, NH: Heinemann.

Cebollero, P. A. (1975). *The Puerto Rican experience*. New York: Arno.

Cecil, N. L., & Lauritzen, P. (1994). *Literacy and the arts for the integrated classroom*. White Plains, NY: Longman.

Celce-Murcia, M., & Olshtain, E. (2000). *Discourse and context in language teaching: A guide for language teachers*. Cambridge: Cambridge University Press.

Cenoz, J., & Genesee, F. (1998). Psycholinguistic perspectives on multilingualism and multilingual education. In J. Cenoz & F. Genesee (Eds.), *Beyond bilingualism: multilingualism and multilingual education* (pp. 16–34). Clevedon, UK: Multilingual Matters.

Center for Research on Education, Diversity, and Excellence (CREDE). (1999). *Five standards for effective pedagogy*. Santa Cruz, CA: Author. Available online: www.crede.ucsc.edu/Standards/standards.html.

Chamot, A. U. (1987). The learning strategies of ESL students. In A. Wenden & J. Rubin (Eds.), *Learner strategies in language learning*. Englewood Cliffs, NJ: Prentice-Hall.

Chamot, A. U., & O' Malley, J. (1987). The Cognitive Academic Language Learning Approach: A bridge to the mainstream. *TESOL Quarterly, 21* (2), June, 227–249.

Chamot, A. U., & O'Malley, J. M. (1994). *The CALLA handbook: Implementing the cognitive academic language learning approach*. Reading, MA: Addison-Wesley.

Chaney, A. L., & Burk, T. L. (1998). *Teaching oral communication in grades K–8*. Boston: Allyn & Bacon.

Chang, M. (1994) *Story of the Chinese zodiac*. Taipei: Yuan-Liou Publishers (available from Shen's Book and Supplies, Arcadia, CA).

Charp, S. (1996). Technological literacy for the workplace. *T. H. E. Journal, 23* (8), 6.

Chatton, B. (1993). *Using poetry across the curriculum: A whole language approach*. Phoenix, AZ: Oryx.

Chavkin, N. F. (1989, summer). Debunking the myth about minority parents. *Educational Horizons,* 119–123.

Cheng, L. (1987). English communicative competence of language minority children: Assessment and treatment of language "impaired" preschoolers. In H. Trueba (Ed.), *Success or failure? Learning and the language minority student*. Boston: Heinle & Heinle.

Chesterfield, R., & Chesterfield, K. (1985). Natural order in children's use of second language learning strategies. *Applied Linguistics, 6*, 45–59.

Cheung, O., & Solomon, L. (1991). *Summary of state practices concerning the assessment of and the data collection about limited English proficient (LEP) students*. Washington, DC: Council of Chief State School Officers.

Children's Defense Fund. (2000). *Booming economy leaves millions of children behind: 12.1 million children still living in poverty*. Washington, DC: Author.

Chinnery, J. D., & Chu, M. Q. (1984). *Corresponding English and Chinese proverbs and phrases*. Beijing: New World Press.

Cho, K. S., & Krashen, S. (1995). From *Sweet Valley Kids* to Harlequins in one year. *California English, 1*, 18–19.

Chomsky, N. (1959). Review of B. F. Skinner, "Verbal Behavior." *Language, 35*, 26–58.

Christensen, L. (2002). Whose standard? Teaching standard English. In B. M. Power & R. S. Hubbard (Eds.). *Language development: A reader for teachers* (2nd ed.) (pp. 173–177). Upper Saddle River, NJ and Columbus, OH: Merrill Prentice Hall.

Christian, D. & Genesee, F. (Eds.). (2001). *Bilingual Education*. Alexandria, VA: Teachers of English to Speakers of Other Languages.

Christian, D., Montone, C. L., Lindholm, K. L., & Carranza, I. (1997). *Profiles in two-way immersion education*. Washington, DC: Center for Applied Linguistics and Delta Systems.

Christison, M. (1982). *English through poetry*. Hayward, CA: Prentice Hall.

Chung, H. (1989). *Working with Vietnamese high school students*. Available from New Faces of Liberty/SFSC, P.O. Box 5646, San Francisco, CA 94101.

Churchill, W. S. (1956). *A history of the English-speaking peoples: The birth of Britain*. New York: Doud, Mead & Co.

Clark, A. (1993). *Associative engines: Connectionism, concepts, and representational change*. Cambridge: Cambridge University Press.

Clark, A. (1997). *Being there: Putting brain, body, and world together again*. Cambridge, MA: MIT Press.

Cleary, L. (1997). *ESL through music*. Presentation, annual conference, Teachers of English to Speakers of Other Languages.

Clifford, J. (2001). Facing down the enemy. *San Diego Tribune* (April 14), D1, D4.

Cloud, N., Genesee, F., & Hamayan, E. (2000). *Dual language instruction*. Boston: Heinle & Heinle.

Coehlo, E., Winer, L., & Olsen, J. W-B. (1989). *All sides of the issue: Activities for cooperative jigsaw groups*. Hayward, CA: Alemany Press.

Cogan, D. (1999). What am I saying? In N. Shameem & M. Tickoo (Eds.), *New ways in using communicative games* (pp. 22–23). Alexandria, VA: Teachers of English to Speakers of Other Languages.

Cohen, A. (1991). Second language testing. In M. Celce-Murcia (Ed.), *Teaching English as a second or foreign language* (2nd ed.). New York: Newbury House.

Cohen, A. (1996). *Second language learning and use strategies: Clarifying the issues. Working Paper Series #3*. Minneapolis, MN: University of Minnesota Center for Advanced Research on Language Acquisition.

Cohen, E. G. (1986). *Designing group work: Strategies for the heterogeneous classroom*. New York: Teachers College Press.

Cohen, E., Lotan, R., & Catanzarite, L. (1990). Treating status problems in the cooperative classroom. In S. Sharon (Ed.), *Cooperative learning: Theory and research*. New York: Praeger.

Cohen, R. (1969). Conceptual styles, cultural conflict, and nonverbal tests of intelligence. *American Anthropologist, 71*, 828–856.

Cole, M. (1998). *Cultural psychology: Can it help us think about diversity?* Presentation, annual meeting, American Educational Research Association, San Diego.

Cole, T. (1997) *The article book*. Upper Saddle River, NJ: Prentice Hall Regents.

Coles, R. (1993). *The call of service: A witness to idealism.* Boston: Houghton Mifflin.

Collie, J. & Slater, S. (1987). *Literature in the language classroom.* Cambridge: Cambridge University Press.

Collier, V. (1987). Age and rate of acquisition of second language for academic purposes. *TESOL Quarterly, 21* (4), 617–641.

Collier, V. (1992). A synthesis of studies examining long-term minority student data on academic achievement. *Bilingual Research Journal, 16,* 187–212.

Collins, A. M. (1990). *How to live in America: A guide for the Japanese.* Tokyo: Yohan Publications.

Condon, J. C. (1984). *With respect to the Japanese: A guide for Americans.* Yarmouth, ME: Intercultural Press.

Connell, E. L. (1999). Protest! In R. E. Larimer & L. Schleicher (Eds.), *New ways in using authentic materials in the classroom* (pp. 52–54). Alexandria, VA: Teachers of English to Speakers of Other Languages.

Conzett, J. (2000). Integrating collocation into a reading and writing course. In M. Lewis (Ed.), *Teaching collocation* (pp. 70–87). Hove, UK: Language Teaching Publications.

Cook, V. (1999). Going beyond the native speaker in language teaching. *TESOL Quarterly, 33* (2), 185–209.

Copeland, P. F. (1997). *Great Native Americans.* Mineola, NY: Dover Publications.

Corder, P. (1981). *Error analysis and interlanguage.* Oxford: Oxford University Press.

Corder, P. (1983). Strategies of communication. In C. Færch & G. Kasper (Eds.), *Strategies in interlanguage communication* (pp. 15–19). London and New York: Longman.

Corson, D. (1990). *Language policy across the curriculum.* Clevedon, UK: Multilingual Matters.

Corson, D. (1999). *Language policy in schools: A resource for teachers and administrators.* Mahwah, NJ: Erlbaum.

Cottrell, J. (1987). *Creative drama in the classroom.* Lincolnwood, IN: National Textbook Company.

Crain, S. (2001). *Language and brain.* In Linguistic Society of America, "Fields of Linguistics." Available online: www.lsadc.org/web2/fldcont.html.

Crawford, J. (1992). *Hold your tongue: Bilingualism and the politics of "English only."* Reading, MA: Addison-Wesley.

Crawford, L. (1993). *Language and literacy learning in multicultural classrooms.* Boston: Allyn & Bacon.

Crenshaw, S. R. (1988). Tripping on poetry. In C. Gilles, M. Bixby, P. Corwley, S. R. Crenshaw, M. Henrichs, F. E. Reynolds, & Donelle Pyle (Eds.), *Whole language strategies for secondary students* (p. 108). New York: Richard C. Owen Publishers.

Crookall, D., & Oxford, R. (1991). Dealing with anxiety: Some practical activities for language learners and teacher trainees. In E. Horwitz & D. Young (Eds.), *Language anxiety: From theory and research to classroom implications.* Englewood Cliffs, NJ: Prentice Hall.

Cruz, N. (1990). A challenge to the notion of service. In J. C. Kendell (Ed.), *Combining service and learning: A resource book for community and public service* (vol. 1, pp. 321–323). Raleigh, NC: National Society for Internships and Experiential Education.

Csikszentmihalyi, M. (1996). *Creativity: Flow and the discovery of invention.* New York: HarperCollins.

Cummins, J. (1979). Linguistic interdependence and the educational development of bilingual children. *Review of Education Research, 49,* 222–251.

Cummins, J. (1981a). Age on arrival and immigrant second language learning in Canada: A reassessment. *Applied Linguistics, 2* (2), 132–149.

Cummins, J. (1981b). The role of primary language development in promoting educational success for language minority students. In *Schooling and language minority students: A theoretical framework.* Sacramento: California State Department of Education.

Cummins, J. (1984). *Bilingualism and special education: Issues in assessment and pedagogy.* San Diego: College-Hill.

Cummins, J. (1989). *Empowering minority students.* Sacramento: California Association for Bilingual Education.

Cummins, J. (1996). *Negotiating identities: Education for empowerment in a diverse society.* Los Angeles: California Association for Bilingual Education.

Cummins, J. (2000a). Beyond adversarial discourse: Searching for common ground in the education of bilingual students. In P. McLaren & C. J. Ovando (Eds.), *The politics of multiculturalism and bilingual education* (pp. 126–147). Boston: McGraw-Hill Companies.

Cummins, J. (2000b). Negotiating intercultural identities in the multilingual classroom. *CATESOL Journal, 12* (1), 163–178.

Curran, C. (1982). Community language learning. In R. Blair (Ed.), *Innovative approaches to language teaching.* Rowley, MA: Newbury House.

Dale, P., & Wolf, J. C. (1988). *Speech communication for international students.* Englewood Cliffs, NJ: Prentice Hall Regents.

Dalton, S., & Sison, J. (1995). *Enacting instructional conversation with Spanish-speaking students in middle school mathematics.* (Research Report 12). Santa Cruz, CA: National Center for Research on Cultural Diversity and Second Language Learning. Available online: www.ncbe.gwu.edu/miscpubsncrcdsll/rr12/index.htm

D'Andrade, R., & Strauss, C. (Eds.). (1992). *Human motives and cultural models.* Cambridge: Cambridge University Press.

Danesi, M. (1985). *A guide to puzzles and games in second language pedagogy.* Toronto: Ontario Institute for Studies in Education.

D'Arcangelo, M. (1998). The brains behind brain. *Educational Leadership, 56* (3), 68–71.

Darder, A. (1991). *Culture and power in the classroom.* New York: Bergin and Garvey.

Darian, S. (2001). *Unpeeling the Soviet Union.* Available online: www.tesol.org/careers/counsel/articles/russia-01.html.

Darley, J. M., & Gross, P. H. (1983). A hypothesis-confirming bias in labeling effects. *Journal of Personality and Social Psychology, 44,* 20–33.

Datesman, M. K., Crandall, J., & Kearny, E. N. (1997). *The American ways.* Upper Saddle River, NJ: Prentice Hall Regents.

Davies, A., Cameron, C., Politano, C., & Gregory, K. (1992). *Together is better: Collaborative assessment, evaluation, and reporting.* Winnipeg, Canada: Peguis.

Davies, D. (1991). Schools reaching out: Family, school and community partnerships for student success. *Phi Delta Kappan, 72* (5), 376–382.

Day, F. A. (1994). *Multicultural voices in contemporary literature: A resource for teachers.* Portsmouth, NH: Heinemann.

Day, F. A. (1997). *Latina and Latino voices in literature for children and teenagers.* Portsmouth, NH: Heinemann.

Day, F. A. (2003). *Latina and Latino voices in literature: Lives and works.* Westport, CT: Greenwood Publishers.

Deci, W. L., & Ryan, R. M. (1985). *Intrinsic motivation and self-determination in human behavior.* New York: Plenum Press.

Deci, E. L., Nezlek, J., & Sheinman, L. (1981). Characteristics of the rewarder and intrinsic motivation of the rewardee. *Journal of Personality and Social Psychology, 40,* 1–10.

Deer, J. (2001). ESP in Colombia. *English for Specific Purposes News, 9* (2), 4, 8–9.

Delgado-Gaitan, C. (1994). Sociocultural change through literacy: Toward the empowerment of families. In B. M. Ferdman, R-M. Weber, & A. G. Ramírez (Eds.), *Literacy across languages and cultures* (pp. 143–169). Albany: SUNY Press.

Delgado-Gaitan, C., & Trueba, H. (1991). *Crossing cultural borders: Education for immigrant families in America.* London: Falmer Press.

Delton, J. (1974). *Two good friends.* New York: Crown.

De Mille, R. (1976). *Put your mother on the ceiling: Children's imagination games.* New York: Penguin Books.

Derman-Sparks, L., & Anti-Bias Curriculum Task Force. (1988). *Anti-bias curriculum: Tools for empowering young children.* Washington, DC: National Association for the Education of Young Children.

Dewey, J. (1933). *How we think: A restatement of the relation of reflective thinking to the educative process.* Boston: D. C. Heath.

Dewey, J. (1956). *The child and the curriculum and the school and society* (combined edition). Chicago: University of Chicago Press.

Dewey, J. (1916/1963). *Experience and education.* New York: Collier.

Díaz, L. T. (1988). *Motivating achievement in computer-assisted instruction of English as a second language.* Doctoral thesis, InterAmerican University of Puerto Rico.

Díaz, R. M., Neal, C. J., & Vachio, A. (1991). Maternal teaching in the zone of proximal development: A comparison of low- and high-risk dyads. *Merrill-Palmer Quarterly, 37,* 83–108.

Díaz-Rico, L. (1991). Increasing oral English in the university classroom: Strengthening the voice of the multinational student. *Fine Points.* San Bernardino: California State University, San Bernardino Office of Faculty Development.

Díaz-Rico, L. (1993). From monocultural to multicultural teaching in an inner-city middle school. In A. Woolfolk (Ed.), *Readings and cases in educational psychology.* Boston: Allyn & Bacon.

Díaz-Rico, L. T. (1994) *Teacher education of instructional conversants for multicultural contexts.* Presentation, American Educational Research Association annual meeting, New Orleans, LA.

Díaz-Rico, L. T. (1998a) *M.A. in Education, Teaching English to Speakers of Other Languages Option framework for outcomes assessment.* Document submitted to University Outcomes Assessment Committee, California State University, San Bernardino.

Díaz-Rico, L. T. (1998b). Towards a just society: Recalibrating multicultural teachers. In R. Chávez Chávez & J. O'Donnell, (Eds.), *Speaking the unpleasant: The politics of (non)engagement in the multicultural terrain.* Albany: SUNY Press.

Díaz-Rico, L. T. (1999a). The postmodern shift: A real revolution in ESOL teaching. *TESOL Matters, 9* (1), 20.

Díaz-Rico, L. T. (1999b). *Critical discourse analysis applied to second language acquisition.* Presentation, annual conference, Teachers of English to Speakers of Other Languages, New York, NY.

Díaz-Rico, L. T. (2000). Intercultural communication in teacher education: The knowledge base for CLAD teacher credential programs. *CATESOL Journal, 12* (1), 145–161.

Díaz-Rico, L. T. (2001a, February). *Visual Imaginary Dramatic Arts.* Presentation, annual conference, Teachers of English to Speakers of Other Languages, St. Louis, MO.

Díaz-Rico, L. T. (2001b, February). *Improving MATESOL students' academic writing.* Presentation, annual conference, Teachers of English to Speakers of Other Languages, St. Louis, MO.

Díaz-Rico, L. T., & Weed, K. (2002). *The crosscultural, language, and academic development handbook* (2nd ed.). Boston: Allyn & Bacon.

Díaz-Rico, L. T., & Young, L. H. (1998). Promoting oral language development and cultural socialization for international university students. *Phi Beta Delta International Review, 8,* 11–26.

Díez, A., & Marchis, L. (2001). "El jardín curandero" (thematic unit). Unpublished manuscript, California State University, San Bernardino.

Di Pietro, R. J. (1987). *Strategic interaction: Learning languages through scenarios.* Cambridge: Cambridge University Press.

Doggett, G. (1986). *Eight approaches to language teaching.* Washington, DC: Center for Applied Linguistics/ERIC Clearinghouse on Languages and Linguistics.

Dole, S. (2001). Dialogue: Does the current emphasis on student assessment help students learn? *NEA Higher Education Advocate, 18* (5), 11.

Dolson, D. (1985). The effects of Spanish home language use on the scholastic performance of Hispanic pupils. *Journal of Multilingual and Multicultural Development, 6,* 135–156.

Doutrich, D. (2000). Cultural fluency, marginality, and the sense of self. In H. Riggenbach (Ed.), *Perspectives on fluency* (pp. 141–159). Ann Arbor: University of Michigan Press.

Dresser, N. (1993). *Our own stories: Cross-cultural communication practice.* White Plains, NY: Longman.

Driscoll, A., Holland, B., Gelmon, S., & Kerrigan, S. (1996). An assessment model for service-learning: Comprehensive case studies of impact on faculty, students, community, and institution. *Michigan Journal of Community Service Learning, 3,* 66–71.

Dudley-Marling, C., & Searle, D. (1991). *When students have time to talk.* Portsmouth, NH: Heinemann.

Duff, P. A. (2001). Learning English for academic and occupational purposes. *TESOL Quarterly, 35* (4), 606–607.

Dunkel, P. & Lim, P., L. (1994). *Intermediate listening comprehension: Understanding and recalling spoken English.* Boston: Heinle & Heinle.

Dunkel, P. A., Pialorsi, F., & Kozyrev, J. (1996). *Advanced listening comprehension: Developing aural and notetaking skills.* Boston: Heinle & Heinle.

Dutton, B., & Olin, C. (1995). *Myths and legends of the Indians of the Southwest.* Santa Barbara, CA: Bellerophon Books.

Early, M. (1990). Enabling first and second language learners in the classroom. *Language Arts, 67* (6), 567–574.

Echevarria, J., Vogt, M. E., & Short, D. (2000). *Making content comprehensible for English language learners: The SIOP model.* Boston: Allyn & Bacon.

Edelman, G. (1992). *Bright air, brilliant fire: On the matter of the mind.* New York: Basic Books.

Edelsky, C. (1986). *Writing in a bilingual program: Habia una vez.* Norwood, NJ: Ablex.

Edelsky, C. (1989). Bilingual children's writing: Fact and fiction. In D. Johnson & D. H. Roen (Eds.), *Richness in writing* (pp. 165–176). New York: Longman.

Edwards, B., & Fitzpatrick, K. (2002). *Program evaluation: English as a Second Language.* Schaumburg, IL: National Study of School Evaluation.

Edwards, C. (1998). Partner, nurturer, and guide: The role of the teacher. In C. Edwards, L. Gandini, & G. Forman (Eds.), *The hundred languages of children: The Reggio Emilia approach— advanced reflections* (2nd ed.) (pp. 179–198). Norwood, NJ: Ablex.

Edwards, D., & Potter, J. (1992). *Discursive psychology.* London: Sage.

Edwards, K. M. (2000). *Everyone's guide to successful project planning: Tools for youth, student guide.* Portland, OR: Northwest Regional Educational Laboratory.

Egbert, J., & Hanson-Smith, E. (1999). *CALL environments: Research, practice, and critical issues.* Alexandria, VA: Teachers of English to Speakers of Other Languages.

Eliason, P. A. (1995). Difficulties in cross-cultural in learning styles assessment. In J. Reid (Ed.),

Learning styles in the ESL/EFL classroom (pp. 19–33). Boston: Heinle & Heinle.

Ellis, R. (1994). Variability and the natural order hypothesis. In R. Barasch & C. James (Eds.), *Beyond the monitor model*. Boston: Heinle & Heinle.

Ellis, S. S., & Whalen, S. F. (1992). Keys to cooperative learning: 35 ways to keep kids responsible, challenged, and most of all, cooperative. *Instructor, 101* (6), 34–37.

Ellmann, R. (Ed.). (1988) *The Norton anthology of modern poetry*. New York: W. W. Norton.

Emig, J. (1981). Non-magical thinking: Presenting writing developmentally in schools. In C. H. Frederickson & J. F. Dominic (Eds.), *Writing: Process, development, and communication* (pp. 21–30). Hillsdale, NJ: Erlbaum.

Engeström, Y. (1990). *Learning, working, and imagining: Twelve studies in activity theory*. Helsinki: Orienta-Konsultit.

Enright, D., & McCloskey, M. (1988). *Integrating English: Developing English language and literacy in the multilingual classroom*. Reading, MA: Addison-Wesley.

Epstein, J. L. (1995). School/family/community partnerships: Caring for the children we share. *Phi Delta Kappan, 76* (9), 701–712.

Erikson, E. (1963). *Childhood and society* (2nd ed.). New York: Norton.

Erikson, E. (1980). *Identity and the life cycle.* (2nd ed.). New York: Norton.

Erickson, F. (1977). Some approaches to inquiry in school-community ethnography. *Anthropology and Education Quarterly, 8* (2), 58–69.

Ernst-Slavit, G., & Wenger, K. J. (1998). Using creative drama in the elementary ESL classroom. *TESOL Journal, 7* (4), 30–33.

Evaluation Assistance Center-East. (1990, November). *State minimum competency testing practices*. Washington, DC: Georgetown University.

Evans, T. (1984). *Drama in English teaching*. Dover, UK: Croom Helm.

Ewald, F. (1992). Summary of discussions. In T. J. Armstrong (Ed. and trans.), *Michel Foucault philosopher* (p. 334). New York: Harvester Wheatsheaf.

Eyler, J., & Giles, D. E. (1999). *Where's the learning in service learning?* San Francisco: Jossey-Bass.

Eyler, J., Giles, D. E., & Gray, C. J. (1999). *Research at a glance: What we know about the effects of service-learning on students, faculty, institutions, and communities*. Knoxville, TN: Vanderbilt University.

Eyring, J. (2001). Experiential and negotiated language learning. In M. Celce-Murica (Ed.), *Teaching English as a second or foreign language* (3rd ed.). Boston: Heinle & Heinle.

Fairclough, N. (1989). *Language and power*. London and New York: Longman.

Fairclough, N. (1992). *Discourse and social change*. Cambridge: Polity Press.

Falk, R. (1993). *Spotlight on the USA*. New York: Oxford University Press.

Faltis, C. (2001). *Joinfostering* (3rd ed.). Upper Saddle River, NJ: Prentice-Hall.

Farr, M. (1994). En los dos idiomas: Literacy practices among Chicago Mexicanos. In B. Moss (Ed.), *Literacy across communities* (pp. 1–9). Cresskill. NJ: Hampton Press.

Feder, C. W. (1992). *Brain quest*. New York: Workman Publishing Co.

Feuerstein, T., & Schcolnik, M. (1995). *Enhancing reading comprehension in the language learning classroom*. San Francisco: Alta.

Finegan, E. (1980). *Attitudes toward English usage*. New York and London: Teachers College Press.

Finegan, E. (2001). *Prescriptive language and usage wars*. In Linguistic Society of America, "Fields of Linguistics." Available online: www.lsadc.org/web2/fldcont.html.

Finn, J. (1972). Expectations and the educational environment. *Review of Educational Research, 42,* 387–410.

Fischer, B., & Fischer, L. (1979, January). Styles in teaching and learning. *Educational Leadership, 36* (4), 245–251.

Fishman, J. A. (1977). Knowing, using, and liking English as an additional language. *TESOL Quarterly, 11* (2), 157–171.

Flavell, J. H. (1979). Metacognition and cognitive monitoring: A new area of cognitive developmental inquiry. *American Psychologist, 34* (10), 906–911.

Flavell, J. H. (1985). *Cognitive development* (2nd ed.). Englewood Cliffs, NJ: Prentice-Hall.

Fleischman, P. (1985). *I am phoenix: Poems for two voices*. New York: HarperCollins.

Fleischman, P. (1988). *A joyful noise: Poems for two voices*. New York: HarperCollins.

Flood, J., Lapp, D., Tinajero, J., & Hurley, S. (1997). Literacy instruction for students acquiring English: Moving beyond the immersion debate. *The Reading Teacher, 356–358.*

Flower, L. (1994). *The construction of negotiated meaning: A social cognitive theory of writing*. Carbondale and Edwardsville: Southern Illinois University Press.

Flowerdew, J. (1994). *Academic listening: Research perspectives*. Cambridge: Cambridge University Press.

Flowerdew, J. (2001). Toward authentic, specific-purpose writing at the lower levels of proficiency. In I. Leki (Ed.), *Academic writing programs* (pp. 21–35). Alexandria, VA: Teachers of English to Speakers of Other Languages.

Flynn, K. (1995). *Graphic organizers . . . helping kids think visually.* Cypress, CA: Creative Thinking Press.

Fogarty, R., Perkins, D., & Barell, J. (1992). *How to teach for transfer.* Arlington Heights, IL: Skylight.

Folse, K. S. (1996). *Discussion starters.* Ann Arbor: University of Michigan Press.

Forget, M. A., & Morgan, R. F. (1997). A brain-compatible learning environment for improving student metacognition. *Reading Improvement, 34,* 161–175.

Forman, G., & Fyfe, B. (1998). Negotiated learning through design, documentation, and discourse. In C. Edwards, L. Gandini, & G. Forman (Eds.), *The hundred languages of children: The Reggio Emilia approach—advanced reflections* (2nd ed.) (pp. 239–260). Norwood, NJ: Ablex.

Forman, G., Langley, J., Oh, M., & Wrisley, L. (1998). *The city in the snow: Applying the multisymbolic approach in Massachusetts.* In C. Edwards, L. Gandini, & G. Forman (Eds.), *The hundred languages of children: The Reggio Emilia approach—advanced reflections* (2nd ed.) (pp. 359–374). Norwood, NJ: Ablex.

Fosnot, C. T. (1989). *Enquiring teachers, enquiring learners: A constructivist approach for teaching.* New York: Teachers College Press.

Foucault, M. (1973). *The birth of the clinic: An archeology of medical perception.* New York: Vintage Books.

Foucault, M. (1979). *Discipline and punish: The birth of the prison.* New York: Vintage Books.

Foucault, M. (1980). *Power/knowledge: Selected interviews and other writings 1971–1977.* York: Pantheon Books.

Foucault, M. (1984). The order of discourse. In M. Shapiro (Ed.), *Language and politics* (pp. 108–138). New York: New York University Press.

Foucault, M. (1988). Technologies of the self. In L. H. Martin, H. Gutman, & P. H. Hutton, (Eds.), *Technologies of the self.* Amherst: University of Massachusetts Press.

Fox, M. (1987). *Teaching drama to young children.* Portsmouth, NH: Heinemann.

Freeman, Y., & Freeman, D. (1998). *ESL/EFL teaching: Principles for practice.* Portsmouth, NH: Heinemann.

Freire, P. (1970). *Pedagogy of the oppressed* (Trans. M. B. Ramos). New York: Continuum.

Freire, P. (1973). By learning they can teach. *Convergence, 6* (1), 78–84.

Freire, P. (1987). Letter to North American teachers. In I. Shor (Ed.), *Freire for the classroom* (pp. 211–214). Portsmouth, NH: Boynton/Cook.

Freire, P. (1994). *Pedagogy of hope* (Trans., R. R. Barr). New York: Continuum.

Freire, P. (1998). *Teachers as cultural workers* (Trans. D. Macedo, D. Koike, & A. Oliveira). Boulder, CO: Westview Press.

Fried-Booth, D. L. (1997). *Project work* (8th ed.). Oxford: Oxford University Press.

Friedlander, A. (1990). Composing in English: Effects of a first langue on writing in English as a second language. In B. Kroll (Ed.), *Second language writing: Research insights for the classroom* (pp. 109–125). Cambridge: Cambridge University Press.

From the Classroom. (1991). *Teachers seek a fair and meaningful assessment process to measure LEP students' progress.* Fountain Valley, CA: Teacher Designed Learning, 2 (1), 1, 3.

Furco, A. (1996). Service-learning: A balanced approach to experiential education. In Corporation for National Service (Eds.), *Expanding boundaries: Serving and learning.* Washington, DC: Author.

Furey, P. (1986). A framework for cross-cultural analysis of teaching methods. In P. Byrd (Ed.), *Teaching across cultures in the university ESL program.* Washington, DC: National Association of Foreign Student Advisors.

Gable, R. A., Henrickson, J. M., & Meeks, J. W. (1988). Assessing spelling errors of special needs students. *The Reading Teacher, 42* (2), 112–117.

Gadda, G., Peitzman, F., & Walsh, W. (1988). *Teaching analytical writing.* Los Angeles: UCLA Publishing.

Galura, J., Howard, J., Waterhouse, D., & Ross, R. (1995). *Praxis III: Voices in dialogue.* Ann Arbor, MI: Office of Community Service Learning.

Gambrell, L. B., & Bales, R. J. (1986). Mental imagery and the comprehension-monitoring performance of fourth- and fifth-grade poor readers. *Reading Research Quarterly, 21,* 454–464.

Gardner, H. (1983). *Frames of mind: The theory of multiple intelligences.* New York: Basic Books.

Gardner, H. (1990). Multiple intelligences: Implications for art and creativity. In W. Moody (Ed.), *Artistic intelligence: Implications for education.* New York: Teachers College Press.

Gardner, H. (1993). *Multiple intelligences: The theory in practice.* New York: Basic Books, 1993.

Gardner, J. N. (1997). Keys to success. In J. N. Gardner & A. J. Jewler (Eds.), *Your college experience: Strategies for success* (pp. 1–22). Albany, NY: Wadsworth Publishing Co.

Gardner, J. N., & Jewell, A. J. (Eds.). (1997). *Your college experience: Strategies for success* (pp. 1–22). Albany, NY: Wadsworth Publishing Co.

Gardner, R., & Lambert, W. (1972). *Attitudes and motivation in second language learning*. Rowley, MA: Newbury House.

Garmston, R. (1987). How administrators support peer coaching. *Educational Leadership, 44* (5), 18–28.

Garmston, R., Linder, C., & Whitaker, J. (1993). Reflections on cognitive coaching. *Educational Leadership, 51* (2), 57–61.

Garrison, D. (1990). Inductive strategies for teaching Spanish-English cognates. *Hispania, 73* (2), 508–512.

Gass, S. M., & Selinker, L. (2001). *Second language acquisition* (2nd ed). Hillsdale, NJ: Erlbaum.

Gee, J. (1990). *Social linguistics and literacies: Ideology in discourses*. New York: Falmer Press.

Gee, J. (1992). *The social mind: Language, ideology, and social practice*. New York: Bergin & Garvey.

Gee, J. (1996). *Social linguistics and literacies: Ideology in discourses (2nd ed.)*. London: Taylor & Francis.

Gee, J. (2000). The New Literacy Studies: From 'socially situated' to the work of the social. In D. Barton, M. Hamilton, & R. Ivanič (Eds.), *Situated literacies* (pp. 180–196). London and New York: Routledge.

Genesee, F. (1987). *Learning through two languages: Studies of immersion and bilingual education*. Cambridge, MA: Newbury House.

Genishi, C. (1988). Children's language: Learning words from experience. *Young Children, 44* (1), 16–23.

Giddens, A. (1987). *Social theory and modern sociology*. Stanford, CA: Stanford University Press.

Gillett, P. (1989). *Cambodian refugees: An introduction to their history and culture*. Available from New Faces of Liberty/SFSC, P.O. Box 5646, San Francisco, CA 94101.

Giromini, E. (2001, March). *PBL and the urban experience*. Presentation, the Ninth Annual Conference on Project-Based Learning, San Francisco.

Giroux, H. (1991). Modernism, postmodernism, and feminism: Rethinking the boundaries of educational discourse. In H. Giroux (Ed.), *Postmodernism, feminism, and cultural politics: Redrawing educational boundaries* (pp. 1–59). New York: SUNY Press.

Giroux, H., & McLaren, P. (1986). Teacher education and the politics of engagement: The case for democratic schooling. *Harvard Educational Review, 56* (3), 213–238.

Glaser, S., & Brown, C. (1993). *Portfolios and beyond: Collaborative assessment in reading and writing*. Norwood, MA: Christopher-Gordon.

Glass, R. D. (2001). On Paulo Freire's philosophy of praxis and the foundations of liberation education. *Educational Researcher, 30* (2), 15–25.

Goldenberg, C. (1990). Research directions: Beginning literacy instruction for Spanish-speaking children. *Language Arts, 67* (6), 590–597.

Goldenberg, C. (1992). *Let's talk*. Videotape, University of California, Los Angeles.

Goldenberg, C. & Gallimore, R. (1991). Changing teaching takes more than a one-shot workshop. *Educational Leadership, 49* (3), 69–72.

Goldstein, L. M., & Conrad, S. M. (1990). Student input and negotiation of meaning in ESL writing conferences. *TESOL Quarterly, 24*, 441–460.

Goleman, D. (1998). *Working with emotional intelligence*. New York: Bantam Books.

Gollnick, D. M., & Chinn, P. C. (2002). *Multicultural education in a pluralistic society* (6th ed.). Upper Saddle River, NJ: Merrill Prentice Hall.

Gombert, J. E. (1992). *Metalinguistic development*. Chicago: University of Chicago Press.

Gonzales, L. N., & Watson, D. (1986). *S. E. T.: Sheltered English teaching handbook*. San Marcos, CA: AM Graphics & Printing.

Goodale, M. (1987). *The language of meetings*. Hove, UK: Language Teaching Publications.

Goodwin, C., & Heritage, J. (1990). Conversational analysis. *Annual Review of Anthropology, 19*, 283–307.

Gordon, T. (1992). "We don't want to come to ESL": Teaching ESL to fluent, low-achieving students. *TESOL Journal, 2* (1), 30–32.

Gore, J. M. (1998). Disciplining bodies: On the continuity of power relations in pedagogy. In T. Popkewitz & M. Brennan (Eds.), *Foucault's challenge: Discourse, knowledge and power in education* (pp. 231–254). New York: Teachers College Press.

Gottlieb, M. (1995). Nurturing student learning through portfolios. *TESOL Journal, 5* (1), 12–14.

GOSERV (California Governor's Office on Service and Volunteerism). (2003). Available online: www.goserv.ca.gov

Graham, C. (1978a). *Jazz chants*. New York: Oxford University Press.

Graham, C. (1978b). *Jazz chants for children*. New York: Oxford University Press.

Graham, C. (1986). *Small talk*. New York: Oxford University Press.

Graham, C. (1988). *Jazz chant fairy tales*. New York: Oxford University Press.

Graham, C. (1992). *Singing, chanting, telling tales*. Englewood Cliffs, NJ: Regents/Prentice Hall.

Graham, S. (1991). A review of attribution theory in achievement contexts. *Educational Psychology Review, 3*, 5–39.

Graman, T. (1988). Education for humanization: Applying Paulo Freire's pedagogy to learning a second language. *Harvard Educational Review, 58* (4), 433–447.

Gramsci, A. (1971). *Selections from prison notebooks.* (Ed. and trans., Q. Hoare & G. Smith.) New York: International Publishers.

Grant, C. (1995). *Educating for diversity: An anthology of multicultural voices.* Boston: Allyn & Bacon.

Grasha, A. F. (1990). Using traditional versus naturalistic approaches to assess learning styles in college teaching. *Journal on Excellence in College Teaching, 1*, 23–38.

Grasha, A. F. (1996). *Your teaching style.* Pittsburgh, PA: International Alliance of Teacher Scholars.

Graves, D. (1983). *Writing: Teachers and children at work.* Portsmouth, NH: Heinemann.

Greene, M. (1988). *The dialectic of freedom.* New York: Teachers College Press.

Gregorc, A. (1982). *An adult's guide to style.* Maynard, MA: Gabriel Systems.

Grenough, M. (1998). *Sing it! Learn English through song,* Levels 1–6, New York: McGraw-Hill.

Grosz, E. (1990). *Jacques Lacan: A feminist introduction.* London and New York: Routledge.

Groves, M. (2000, January 26). Vast majority of state's schools lag in new index. *Los Angeles Times,* A1, A14.

Groves, M. (2001, August 20). "Direct instruction" paying off. *Los Angeles Times,* B1, B8.

Gumperz, J. J. (1982). *Discursive strategies.* Cambridge: Cambridge University Press.

Gunderson, L. (1991). *ESL literacy instruction: A guidebook to theory and practice.* Englewood Cliffs, NJ: Regents/Prentice-Hall.

Gunning, T. G. (1996). *Creating reading instruction for all children* (2nd ed.). Boston: Allyn & Bacon.

Guskey, T. R. (1994). What you assess may not be what you get. *Educational Leadership, 51* (6), 51–54.

Guthrie, W. (1998) *This land is your land.* Boston & New York: Little, Brown.

Hadaway, N. L., Vardell, S. M., & Young, T. A. (2002). *Literature-based instruction with English language learners, K–12.* Boston: Allyn & Bacon.

Hakuta, K., Butler, Y. G., & Witt, D. (2000). *How long does it take English learners to attain proficiency?* Santa Barbara: University of California Linguistic Minority Research Institute Policy Report 2000–1.

Hall, A. (1982). Drama in English language teaching: Two approaches at the university level in West Germany. *Applied Linguistics,* 144–160.

Halliday, M. A. K. (1978). *Language as a social semiotic.* Baltimore, MD: University Park Press.

Hamayan, E. (1994). Language development of low-literacy students. In F. Genesee (Ed.), *Educating second language children.* Cambridge: Cambridge University Press.

Hamers, J. F., & Blanc, M. A. H. (1989). *Bilinguality and bilingualism.* Cambridge: Cambridge University Press.

Hancock, C. (1994). Alternative assessment and second language study: What and why? *ERIC Digest.* Available online: www.cal.org/ericcll/digest/hancoc01.html.

Handa, C. (2001). Digital literacy and rhetoric: A selected bibliography. *Computers and Composition, 18*, 195–202.

Hansen, J. W. (2000). Parables of technological literacy. *Journal of Engineering Technology, 17* (2), 29–31.

Harel, Y. (1992). Teacher talk in the cooperative learning classroom. In C. Kessler (Ed.), *Cooperative language learning.* Englewood Cliffs, NJ: Prentice-Hall.

Harklau, L., Losey, K. M., & Siegal, M. (Eds.).(1999). *Generation 1.5 meets college composition: Issues in the teaching of writing to U.S.-educated learners of ESL.* Mahwah, NJ: Erlbaum.

Harmon, W. (Ed.). (1979). *The Oxford Book of American light verse.* New York: Oxford University Press.

Harre, R., & Stearns, P. (Eds.). (1995). *Discursive psychology in practice.* London: Sage.

Harris, V. (1997). *Teaching multicultural literature in grades K–8.* Norwood, MA: Christopher-Gordon.

Hart, L. (1975). *How the brain works: A new understanding of human learning, emotion, and thinking.* New York: Basic Books.

Hart, L. (1983). *Human brain, human learning.* New York: Longman.

Harvey, J. (1982). Communications approach: Games II. In R. W. Blair, (Ed.). (1982). *Innovative approaches to language teaching.* Boston: Heinle & Heinle.

Heald-Taylor, G. (1986). *Whole language strategies for ESL students.* San Diego, CA: Dormac.

Heald-Taylor, B. G. (1987). Big books. In D. J. Watson (Ed.), *Ideas and insights: Language arts in the elementary school* (p. 85). Urbana, IL: National Council of Teachers of English.

Heath, S. (1983a). Language policies. *Society, 20* (4), 56–63.

Heath, S. (1983b). *Ways with words*. Cambridge: Cambridge University Press.

Heine, H. (1982) *Friends*. Old Tappan, NJ: Simon & Schuster.

Heinig, R. B., & Stillwell, L. (1974). *Creative dramatics for the classroom teacher*. Englewood Cliffs, NJ: Prentice-Hall.

Heinle & Heinle (2002a). *Launch into reading, Level I: Teacher's resource book*. Boston: Author.

Heinle & Heinle (2002b). *Launch into reading, Level I: Assessment guide*. Boston: Author.

Hemmert, A., & O'Connell, G. (1998). *Communicating on campus*. Burlingame, CA: Alta.

Hernandez, H. (2001). *Multicultural education: A teacher's guide to linking context, process, and content*. Upper Saddle River, NJ: Merrill/Prentice-Hall.

Hernández, J. S. (1993). Bilingual metacognitive development. *The Educational Forum, 57*, 350–358.

Hernández-Chávez, E. (1984). The inadequacy of English immersion as an educational approach for language minority students. *Studies on immersion education: A collection for U.S. educators*. Sacramento: California State Department of Education.

Herrell, A. L. (2000). *Fifty strategies for teaching English language learners*. Upper Saddle River, NJ and Columbus, OH: Merrill/Prentice-Hall.

Herring, S. (1996). *Computer-mediated communication: Linguistic, social, and cross-cultural perspectives*. Amsterdam/Philadelphia: John Benjamins Publishing.

Hetherton, G. (1998). Choral chant. In V. Whiteson (Ed.), *New ways of using drama and literature in language teaching* (pp. 144–145). Alexandria, VA: Teachers of English to Speakers of Other Languages.

Hetherton, G. (1999). Headline news. In N. Shameem & M. Tickoo (Eds.), *New ways in using communicative games* (pp. 67–68). Alexandria, VA: Teachers of English to Speakers of Other Languages.

Higgs, T. V. (1984). *Teaching for proficiency: The organizing principle*. Lincolnwood, IL: National Textbook.

Hilgard, E. R., Atkinson, R. L., & Atkinson, R. C. (1979). *Introduction to psychology* (7th ed.). New York: Harcourt Brace Jovanovich.

Hill, J. (2000). Revising priorities: From grammatical failure to collocational success. In M. Lewis (Ed.), *Teaching collocation* (pp. 47–69). Hove, UK: Language Teaching Publications.

Hill, S. (1990). *Readers theatre: Performing the text*. Armadale, VI: Eleanor Curtain Publishing.

Hinton, L., & Montijo, Y. (1994). Living California Indian languages. In L. Hinton (Ed.), *Flutes of fire: Essays on California Indian languages* (pp. 21–33). Berkeley, CA: Heyday Books.

Hodgkinson, H. L. (1998). Demographics of diversity for the 21st century. *Education Digest, 64* (1), 4–7.

Holland, D., & Quinn, N. (Eds.). (1987). *Cultural models in language and thought*. Cambridge: Cambridge University Press.

Holt, D., Chips, B., & Wallace, D. (1992, summer). *Cooperative learning in the secondary school: Maximizing language acquisition, academic development, and social development*. Washington, DC: National Clearinghouse for Bilingual Education.

Hones, D. F. (1999). U. S. justice? Critical pedagogy and the case of Mumia Abu-Jamal. *TESOL Journal, 8* (4), 27–33.

hooks, b. (1989). *Talking back: Thinking feminist, thinking black*. Boston: South End Press.

hooks, b. (1993). *Sisters of the yam: Black women and self-discovery*. Boston: South End Press.

Hopkins, S., & Winters, J. (1990). *Discover the world: Empowering children to value themselves and the world*. Santa Cruz, CA: New Society.

Hornberger, N. H. (1994). Continua of biliteracy. In B. M. Ferdman, R-M. Weber, & A. G. Ramírez (Eds.), *Literacy across languages and cultures* (pp. 103–139). Albany: SUNY Press.

Hornsby, D., Sukarna, D., & Parry, J. (1986). *Read on: A conference approach to reading*. Portsmouth, NH: Heinemann.

Horowitz, E. (1977). *Words come in families*. New York: Hart Publishing.

Horwitz, E., Horwitz, M., & Cope, J. (1991). Foreign language classroom anxiety. In E. Horwitz & D. Young (Eds.), *Language anxiety: From theory and research to classroom implications*. Englewood Cliffs, NJ: Prentice Hall.

Hotz, R. L. (2001, July 2). Byte by byte, a map of the brain. *Los Angeles Times*, A12.

Howard, J. (1993). *Praxis I: A faculty casebook on community service*. Ann Arbor, MI: Office of Community Service Learning.

Hruska-Riechmann, S., & Grasha, A. F. (1982). The Grasha-Riechmann Student Learning Scales: Research findings and applications. In J. Keefe (Ed.), *Student learning styles and brain behavior*. Reston, VA: NASSP.

Hu, W., & Grove, C. L. (1991). *Encountering the Chinese: A guide for Americans*. Yarmouth, ME: Intercultural Press.

Hucko, B. (1996). *A rainbow at night: The world in word and pictures by Navajo children*. San Francisco: Chronicle Books.

Hudelson, S. (1984). Kan yu ret an rayt in Ingles: Children become literate in English as a second language. *TESOL Quarterly, 18,* 221–238.

Huizenga, J., & Thomas-Ruzic, M. (1992). *All talk: Problem solving for new students of English.* Boston: Heinle & Heinle.

Hume, L. C. (1962, reprinted in 1993). *Favorite children's stories from China and Tibet.* Rutland, VT, and Tokyo: Charles E. Tuttle (available from Shen's Book and Supplies, Arcadia, CA).

Humphries, R. (1998). Rhyme time. In V. Whiteson (Ed.), *New ways of using drama and literature in language teaching* (pp. 73–74). Alexandria, VA: Teachers of English to Speakers of Other Languages.

Hymes, D. (1972). On communicative competence. In J. Pride & J. Holmes (Eds.), *Sociolinguistics.* Harmondsworth, UK: Penguin.

Hymes, D. (1974). *Foundations of sociolinguistics.* Philadelphia: University of Pennsylvania Press.

Hynes, M., & Baichman, M. (1989). *Breaking the ice: Basic communication strategies.* White Plains, NY: Longman.

Ikenaga, K. (1979). Problems in English education in college level. In T. Sasaki (Ed.), *Today's English education.* Tokyo: Kenkyusha.

Irizar, T. (2001). English language education in Cuba. *ESL Magazine, 4* (1), 26–28.

Irujo, S. (Ed.). (2000). *Integrating the ESL standards into classroom practice: Grades 6–8.* Alexandria, VA: Teachers of English to Speakers of Other Languages (TESOL).

Irvine, M. (1998). What was Modernism? Available online: www.georgetown.edu/irvinemj/technoculture/pomo.html.

Jackson, F. M. (1993). Evaluating service learning. In Campus Compact (Ed.), *Rethinking tradition: Integrating service with academic study on college campuses* (pp. 129–135). Providence, RI: Author.

Jacobson, R. (1998). Teachers improving learning using metacognition with self-monitoring learning strategies. *Education, 118* (4), 579–589.

Jacoby, B., & Associates (1996). *Service learning in higher education: Concepts and practices.* San Francisco: Jossey-Bass.

James, S. (2000). Making bread together. In B. A. Smallwood (Ed.)., *Integrating the ESL standards into classroom practice: Grades pre-K–2* (pp. 25–42). Alexandria, VA: Teachers of English to Speakers of Other Languages (TESOL).

Jamestown Literature Program (1990). *Reading and understanding poems.* New York: McGraw-Hill/Glencoe Press.

Jametz, K. (1994). Making sure that assessment improves performance. *Educational Leadership, 51* (6), 55–57.

Japan Culture Institute (1978). *A hundred things Japanese.* Tokyo: Author.

Jasmine, J. (1993). *Portfolios and other assessments.* Huntington Beach, CA: Teacher Created Materials.

Jensen, E. (1998). *Teaching with the brain in mind.* Alexandria, VA: Association for Supervision and Curriculum Development.

Jesse, D. (2001). Increasing parental involvement: A key to school achievement. Available online: www.mmu.ac.uk/h-ss/sis/parents/danj~1.htm.

Jo, P. (1999). Unpublished master's thesis, California State University, San Bernardino.

Johns, A. M. (2001). An interdisciplinary, inter-institutional, learning communities program: Student involvement and student success. In I. Leki (Ed.), *Academic writing programs* (pp. 61–72). Alexandria, VA: Teachers of English to Speakers of Other Languages.

Johns, K. (1992). Mainstreaming language minority students through cooperative grouping. *The Journal of Educational Issues of Language Minority Students, 11,* Boise, ID: Boise State University Press.

Johns, K., & Espinoza, C. (1992). *Mainstreaming language minority children in reading and writing* (Fastback #340). Bloomington, IN: Phi Delta Kappa Educational Foundation.

Johnson, B. (1996). *The performance assessment handbook: Volume 1, portfolios and Socratic seminars.* Larchmont, NY: Eye on Education.

Johnson, D. W., & Johnson, R. (1975). *Learning together and alone: Cooperation, competition, and individualization.* Englewood Cliffs, NJ: Prentice-Hall.

Johnson, D. W., & Johnson, R. (1994). Cooperative learning in second language classes. *The Language Teacher, 18,* 4–7.

Johnson, D., & Johnson, R. (1985). Motivational processes in cooperative, competitive, and individualistic learning situations. In C. Ames & R. Ames (Eds.), *Research on motivation in education, vol 2: The classroom milieu* (pp. 249–286). New York: Academic Press.

Johnson, D., Johnson, R., & Smith, K. A. (1991). *Cooperative learning: Increasing instructional productivity.* Washington, DC: George Washington University.

Johnson, D. W., Johnson, R., & Holubec, E. (1993). *Circles of learning: Cooperation in the classroom.* (3rd ed.). Edina, MN: Interaction Book Company.

Johnson, D. W., & Johnson, R. (1994). Cooperative learning in second language classes. *The Language Teacher, 18,* 4–7.

Johnson, K. E. (1996). Portfolio assessment in second language teacher education. *TESOL Journal, 6* (2), 11–14.

Johnston, B. (1997). The expatriate teacher as postmodern paladin. *Research in the Teaching of English, 34,* 255–280.

Jones, L., & von Baeyer, C. (1983). *Functions of American English.* Cambridge: Cambridge University Press.

Jones, P. (1991). What are dialogue journals? In J. K. Peyton & J. Staton (Eds.), *Writing our lives: Reflections on dialogue journal writing with adults learning English* (pp. 3–10). Englewood Cliffs, NJ: Prentice Hall Regents.

Jordan, C., Tharp, R., & Baird-Vogt, L. (1992). "Just open the door": Cultural compatibility and classroom rapport. In M. Saravia-Shore & Arvizu, S. (Eds.), *Cross-cultural literacy.* New York & London: Garland.

Jourdain, R. (1998). *Music, the brain, and ecstasy: How music captures our imagination.* New York: Avon Books.

Jussim, L. (1986). Self-fulfilling prophecies: A theoretical and integrative review. *Psychological Review, 93,* 429–445.

Justice, P. W. (2001). *Relevant linguistics.* Stanford, CA: CSLI Publications.

Kagan, S. (1986). Cooperative learning and sociocultural factors in schooling. *Beyond language: Social and cultural factors in schooling language minority students.* Los Angeles, CA: Evaluation, Dissemination and Assessment Center, California State University, Los Angeles.

Kagan, S. (1998). *Cooperative learning smart card.* Kagan Cooperative Learning Available online: kaganonline.com.

Kagan, S. (1999). *Teambuilding smart card.* Kagan Cooperative Learning Available online: kagan online.com.

Kahane, H., & Kahane, R. (1977). Virtues and vices in the American language: A history of attitude. *TESOL Quarterly, 11* (2), 185–202.

Kamhi-Stein, L. D. (2000). Looking to the future of TESOL teacher education: Web-based bulletin board discussions in a methods course. *TESOL Quarterly, 34* (3), 423–455.

Kang, H-W., Kuehn, P., & Herrell, A. (1996). The Hmong literacy project: Parents working to preserve the past and ensure the future. *Journal of Educational Issues of Language Minority Students, 16.* Available online www.ncbe.gwu.edu/miscpubs/jeilms/vol16/jeilms1602.htm.

Kaplan, R. B. (2001). The language of policy and the policy of language. *Applied Linguistics Forum, 21* (1), 1, 9–11.

Kasser, C., & Silverman, A. (1994). *Stories we brought with us.* Englewood Cliffs, NJ: Prentice-Hall.

Katz, L. G., & Chard, S. C. (1989). *Engaging children's minds: The project approach.* Norwood, NJ: Ablex.

Kauffman, S. (1993). *The origins of order: Self-organization and selection in evolution.* New York: Oxford University Press.

Kaye, H. S. (1997). Education of children with disabilities. *Disability Statistics Abstracts, 19.* San Francisco: Disability Statistics Center.

Kealey, J., & Inness, D. (1997). *Shenanigames: Grammar focused interactive ESL/EFL activities and games.* Brattleboro, VT: Pro Lingua.

Keefe, M. W. (1987). *Learning style theory and practice.* Reston, VA: National Association of Secondary School Principals.

Kehe, D., & Kehe, P. D. (1998). *Discussion strategies.* Brattleboro, VT: Prolingua Associates.

Keirsey, D. (1998). *Please understand me II.* Del Mar, CA: Prometheus Nemesis Book Co.

Keith, N. Z. (1997). Doing service projects in urban settings. In A. S. Waterman (Ed.), *Service learning: Applications from the research* (pp. 127–149). Mahwah, NJ: Lawrence Erlbaum.

Keller, E., & Warner, S. T. (1988). *Conversation gambits.* Hove, UK: Language Teaching Publications.

Kelley, M. L. (1990). *School-home notes: Promoting children's classroom success.* New York: Guilford Press.

Kendell, J. C. (1990). Combining service and learning: An introduction. In J. C. Kendell (Ed.), *Combining service and learning: A resource book for community and public service* (vol. 1). Raleigh, NC: National Society for Internships and Experiential Education.

Kenna, P., & Lacy, S. (1994). *Business Taiwan: A practical guide to understanding Taiwan's business culture.* Lincolnwood, IL: Passport Books.

Kim, E. Y. (2001). *The yin and yang of American culture.* Yarmouth. ME: Intercultural Press.

Kinsella, K. (1992). How can we move from comprehensible input to active learning strategies in content-based instruction? *The CATESOL Journal, 5* (1), 127–132.

Kirkpatrick, A. (2000). English as an Asian language. *Manchester Guardian Weekly Learning English Supplement,* November 16, 3.

Kirschner, M. (1993). ESP for physiotherapy. *CATESOL News, 25* (4), 5, 12.

Klage, M. (1997). Structuralism and poststructuralism. Available online: www.colorado.edu/English/ENGL2012Klages/1derrida.html (Last accessed 5/4/01).

Koch, A., & Terrell, T. (1991). Affective reactions of foreign language students to natural approach activities and teaching techniques. In E. Horwitz & D. Young (Eds.), *Language anxiety: From theory and research to classroom implications.* Englewood Cliffs, NJ: Prentice-Hall.

Koch, K. (1970). *Wishes, lies, and dreams.* New York: Vintage Books.

Kolb, D. A. (1976). *The Learning Style Inventory technical manual.* Boston: McBer & Co.

Kottler, J. A., & Kottler, E. (1993). *Teacher as counselor: Developing the helping skills you need.* Newbury Park, CA: Corwin Press.

Kozol, J. (1991). *Savage inequalities: Children in America's schools.* New York: Crown Publishers.

Kozulin, A., & Presseisen, B. Z. (1995). Mediated learning, experience, and psychological tools: Vygotsky and Feuerstein's perspectives in a study of student learning. *Educational Psychologist, 30,* 67–75.

Kozyrev, J. R. (1998a). *Talk it up! Oral communication for the real world.* Boston: Houghton Mifflin.

Kozyrev, J. R. (1998b). *Talk it over! Oral communication for the real world.* Boston: Houghton Mifflin.

Krashen, S. (1981). Bilingual education and second language acquisition theory. In *Schooling and language minority students: A theoretical framework.* Los Angeles, CA: Evaluation, Dissemination and Assessment Center, California State University, Los Angeles.

Krashen, S. (1982). *Principles and practice in second language acquisition.* Oxford: Pergamon.

Krashen, S. (1985). *The input hypothesis: Issues and implications.* New York: Longman.

Krashen, S., & Terrell, T. (1983). *The Natural Approach: Language acquisition in the classroom.* Oxford: Pergamon.

Kress, G. (2000). *Early spelling: Between convention and creativity.* London and New York: Routledge.

Kristeva, J. (1980). *Desire in language.* Oxford: Basil Blackwell.

Kroll, B. (1991). Teaching writing in the ESL context. In M. Celce-Murcia (Ed.), *Teaching English as a second or foreign language* (2nd ed.). New York: Newbury House.

Kubota, R. (1998). Ideologies of English in Japan. *World Englishes, 17* (3), 295–306.

Labov, W. (1981). *The study of non-standard English.* Urbana, IL: National Council of Teachers of English.

Lacan, J. (1977). *The four fundamental concepts of psycho-analysis.* London: Hogarth Press.

Ladson-Billings, G. (1994). *The dreamkeepers: Successful teachers of African American children.* San Francisco: Jossey-Bass.

Lakoff, G., & Johnson, M. (1980). *Metaphors we live by.* Chicago: University of Chicago Press.

Lakoff, R. (1975). *Language and women's place.* New York: Harper & Row.

Lam, E. W. S. (2000). L2 literacy and the design of the self: A case study of a teenager writing on the Internet. *TESOL Quarterly, 34* (3), 457–482.

Lambert, E. (1955). *The story of the words we use.* New York: Lothrop, Lee & Shepard.

Lambert, W. (1984). An overview of issues in immersion education. In California Department of Education, *Studies on immersion education.* Sacramento: California Department of Education.

Land, S., & Greene, B. A. (2000). Project-based learning with the World Wide Web: A qualitative study of resource integration. *Educational Technology Research and Development, 48,* 45–67.

Langer, J. A., & Applebee, A. N. (1987). *How writing shapes thinking.* Urbana, IL: National Council of Teachers of English.

Larking, L. (1999). Spontaneous oral development of group stories. In N. Shameem & M. Tickoo (Eds.), *New ways in using communicative games* (pp. 144–145). Alexandria, VA: Teachers of English to Speakers of Other Languages.

Larrick, N. (1982). *A parent's guide to reading* (5th ed.). New York: Bantam Books.

Larsen-Freeman, D., & Long, M. (1991). *Introduction to second language acquisition research.* London: Longman.

Latour, B. (1987). *Science in action.* Cambridge, MA: Harvard University Press.

Latour, B. (1991). *We have never been modern.* Cambridge, MA: Harvard University Press.

Laughlin, M. K., Black, P. T., & Loberg, M. K. (1991). *Social studies readers theatre for children: Scripts and script development.* Englewood, CO: Teachers Ideas Press.

Lave, J. (1996). Teaching, as learning, in practice. *Mind, Culture, and Activity, 3,* 149–164.

Lave, J., & Wenger, E. (1991). *Situated learning: Legitimate peripheral participation.* New York: Cambridge University Press.

Law, B., & Eckes, M. (2000). *The more-than-just-surviving handbook* (2nd ed.). Winnipeg, Canada: Peguis.

Lazear, D. (1993). *Seven ways of learning.* Tucson, AZ: Zephyr.

Leki, I. (1986). The preferences of ESL students for error correction in college-level writing courses. *Foreign Language Annals, 24,* 203–218.

Leki, I. (1990). Potential problems with peer responding in ESL writing classes. *The CATESOL Journal, 3,* November, 5–19.

Leki, I. (1992). *Understanding ESL writers.* Portsmouth, NH: Boynton/ Cook.

Leki, I. (1995). Coping strategies of ESL students in writing tasks across the curriculum. *TESOL Quarterly, 29* (2), 235–260.

LeLoup, J., & Ponterio, R. (2000). *Enhancing authentic language learning experiences through internet technology.* ERIC Digest. Available online: www.cal.org/ericcll/digest/0002enhancing.html.

Lenneberg, E. (1967). *Biological foundations of language.* New York: John Wiley.

Leont'ev, A. N. (1978). *Activity, consciousness, and personality.* Englewood Cliffs, NJ: Prentice-Hall.

Lerner, I., & Lerner, M. (1992). *Inner child cards: A journey into fairy tales, myth, & nature.* Sante Fe, NM: Bear & Co.

Leshinsky, J. G. (1995). *Authentic listening and discussion for advanced students.* Englewood Cliffs, NJ: Prentice Hall Regents.

Levine, A. (1994, July/August). Service on campus. *Change,* pp. 4–5.

Levine, L. N. (2000). The most beautiful place in the world. In K. D. Samway (Ed.), *Integrating the ESL standards into classroom practice: Grades 3–5* (pp. 109–131). Alexandria, VA: Teachers of English to Speakers of Other Languages (TESOL).

Lewis, B. (1991). *The kid's guide to social action.* Minneapolis, MN: Free Spirit Publishing.

Lewis, B. (1995). *The kid's guide to service projects.* Minneapolis, MN: Free Spirit Publishing.

Lewis, G., & Bedson, G. (1999). *Games for children.* Oxford: Oxford University Press.

Lewis, M. (1997). *New ways in teaching adults.* Alexandria, VA: Teachers of English to Speakers of Other Languages.

Li, S. (1992). *Legends of ten Chinese traditional festivals.* Beijing: Dolphin Books.

Lin, A. M. Y. (2001). Doing-English-lessons in the reproduction or transformation of social worlds? In C. N. Candlin & N. Mercer (Eds.), *English language teaching in its social context* (pp. 271–286). New York and London: Routledge.

Lindholm, K. (1992). Two-way bilingual/immersion education: Theory, conceptual issues, and pedagogical implications. In R. Padilla & A. Benavides (Eds.), *Critical perspectives in bilingual education research.* Tucson. AZ: Bilingual Review/Press.

Lindholm, K. (1994). Promoting positive cross-cultural attitudes and perceived competence in culturally and linguistically diverse classrooms. In R. A. DeVillar, C. Faltis, & J. Cummins (Eds.), *Cultural diversity in schools: From rhetoric to practice* (pp. 189–206). Albany: SUNY Press.

Linn, R. L. (2000). Assessments and accountability. *Educational Researcher, 29* (2), (4–26).

Linn, R. L., Baker, E. L., & Dunbar, S. B. (1991). Complex, performance-based assessment: Expectations and validation criteria. *Educational Researcher, 20* (8), 15–21.

Lippi-Green, R. (1997). *English with an accent.* London and New York: Routledge.

Lipson, G. B. (1992). *Audacious poetry: Reflections of adolescence.* Torrance, CA: Good Apple.

Lipton, L., & Hubble, D. (1997). *More than 50 ways to learner-centered literacy.* Arlington Heights, IL: Skylight Professional Development.

Little, L. W., & Greenberg, I. W. (1991). *Problem solving: Critical thinking and communication skills.* White Plains, NY: Longman.

Livingston, M. (1988). *Poems for mother.* New York: Holiday House.

Livingston, M. (1989). *Poems for father.* New York: Holiday House.

Long, M. H. (1987). Listening comprehension: Approach, design, procedure. In M. H. Long & J. C. Richards (Eds.), *Methodology in TESOL: A book of readings* (pp. 161–176). New York: Newbury House.

Loria, Y., Shaltied, L., Pieterse, E., & Rosenfeld, S. (1999). The development of software to support teachers and their students in PBL: "The Golden Way." In B. Hasselgreen (Ed.), *Conference Proceedings for the 7th European Conference on Learning and Instruction* (EARLI). Gotenborg, Sweden: Gotenborg University.

Lozanov, G. (1982). Suggestology and suggestopedia. In R. Blair (Ed.), *Innovative approaches to language teaching.* Rowley, MA: Newbury House.

Lucas, T., & Wagner, S. (1999). Facilitating secondary English language learners' transition into the mainstream. *TESOL Journal, 8* (4), 6–13.

Lucero, S. S. (1999). *Increasing reading comprehension through joint mediated activity.* Unpublished master's project, California State University, San Bernardino.

Lugton, R. C. (1986). *American topics* (2nd ed.). Englewood Cliffs, NJ: Prentice Hall Regents.

Lustig, M. W. (1988). Value differences in intercultural communication. In L. Samovar & R. Porter (Eds.), *Intercultural communication: A reader* (5th ed.). Belmont, CA: Wadsworth.

Lustig, M. W., & Koester, J. (1999). *Intercultural competence.* New York: Longman.

Lutz, W. (1999). *Doublespeak defined*. New York: HarperResource.

McCabe, M., & Rhoades, J. (1988). *The nurturing classroom*. Willits, CA: ITA Publications.

McCaleb, S. P. (1994). *Building communities of learners*. New York: St. Martin's Press.

McCarthy, B. (1983). *The 4-MAT system: Teaching to learning styles with right-left mode techniques*. Oak Brook, IL: Excel, Inc.

McCaslin, N. (2000). *Creative drama in the classroom and beyond*. New York: Longman.

McCrum, R., Cran, W., & MacNeil, R. (1986). *The story of English*. New York: Viking.

Macedo, D. (1994). *Literacies of power*. Boulder, CO: Westview Press.

Macedo, D. & Freire, A. M. A. (1998). Foreword. In P. Freire, *Teachers as cultural workers* (pp. ix–xix). Boulder, CO: Westview Press.

Macías, R. F. (1979). The choice of language as a human right: Public policy implications in the United States. In R. V. Padilla (Ed.), *Bilingual education and public policy* (pp. 39–57). Ypsilanti, MI: Department of Foreign Languages and Bilingual Studies, Eastern Michigan University.

Macías, N. G. (1996). *Leyendas Mexicanas*. Selector.

McIntyre, B. M. (1974). *Creative drama in the elementary school*. Itasca, IL: F. E. Peacock Publishers.

MacKay, S. (2000). *The language of love*. Riverside, CA: Educational Alternatives for Students of English. Available online: www.learning-with-ease.com.

McKay, S. L. (1989). Topic development and written discourse accent. In D. Johnson & D. H. Roen (Eds.), *Richness in writing* (pp. 253–262). New York: Longman.

McKenna, M. C., & Robinson, R. D. (1997). *Teaching through text: A content literacy approach to content area reading* (2nd ed.). New York: Longman.

McLaren, P. (1989). *Life in schools: An introduction to critical pedagogy in the foundations of education*. New York: Longman.

McLaren, P. (1995). Critical multiculturalism, media literacy, and the politics of representation. In J. Frederickson (Ed.), *Reclaiming our voices: Bilingual education, critical pedagogy, and praxis* (pp. 99–138). Ontario, CA: California Association for Bilingual Education. New York: Longman.

McMichael, G. L. (Ed.). (1985). *Concise anthology of American literature* (2nd. ed.). New York: Macmillan.

McNamara, M. J. (1998a). Self-assessment: Preparing an English portfolio. In J. D. Brown (Ed.), *New ways in classroom assessment* (pp. 15–17).

Alexandria, VA: Teachers of English to Speakers of Other Languages.

McNamara, M. J. (1998b). Self-assessment: Keeping a language learning log. In J. D. Brown (Ed.), *New ways in classroom assessment* (pp. 38–41). Alexandria, VA: Teachers of English to Speakers of Other Languages.

McQuillan, J., & Tse, L. (1998). What's the story? Using the narrative approach in beginning language classrooms. *TESOL Journal, 7* (4), 18–23.

Maculaitis, J. (1988). *The complete ESL/EFL resource book: Strategies, acitivities, and units for the classroom*. Lincolnwood, IL: National Textbook Company.

McWhorter, K. T. (1995). *College reading and study skills* (6th ed.). New York: HarperCollins College Publishers.

Maeroff, G. (1991, December). Assessing alternative assessment. *Phi Delta Kappan, 73* (4), 272–281.

Magnier, M. (2002). Battery behind the *shoji* screen. *Los Angeles Times,* January 29, A1, A5.

Magy, R. (1991). *Stories from the heart*. Palatine, IL: Linmore Publishing.

Mahoney, D. (1999a). Shadow tableaux. In N. Shameem & M. Tickoo (Eds.), *New ways in using communicative games* (pp. 13–14). Alexandria, VA: Teachers of English to Speakers of Other Languages.

Mahoney, D. (1999b). Stress clapping. In N. Shameem & M. Tickoo (Eds.), *New ways in using communicative games* (pp. 20–21). Alexandria, VA: Teachers of English to Speakers of Other Languages.

Maley, A., & Duff, A. (1989). *The inward ear: Poetry in the language classroom*. Cambridge: Cambridge University Press.

Malkina, N. (1998). Fun with storytelling. In V. Whiteson (Ed.), *New ways of using drama and literature in language teaching* (pp. 41–42). Alexandria, VA: Teachers of English to Speakers of Other Languages.

Mallan, K. (1991). *Children as storytellers*. Portsmouth, NH: Heinemann.

Mander, G. (2001). *WAN2TLK? LTL BK of TXT MSGS*. New York: St. Martin's Griffin.

Mansour, W. (1999). Give me a word that . . . In N. Shameem & M. Tickoo (Eds.), *New ways in using communicative games* (pp. 103–104). Alexandria, VA: Teachers of English to Speakers of Other Languages.

Marcia, J. (1980). Ego identity development. In J. Adelson (Ed.)., *The handbook of adolescent psychology*. New York: John Wiley.

Marlowe, B. A. & Page, M. L. (1999). Making the most of the classroom mosaic: A constructivist perspective. *Multicultural Education, 6* (4), 19–21.

Marshall, B. (1999a). Making learning happen—whose responsibility is it? (Part 1). *CATESOL News, 30* (5), 11, 12, 14, 16.

Marshall, B. (1999b). Making learning happen—whose responsibility is it? (Part 2). *CATESOL News, 31* (1), 11, 12–14, 25.

Martínez, M., Roser, N. L., & Strecker, S. (1998). I never thought I could be a star: A readers theater ticket to fluency. *The Reading Teacher, 52* (4), 326–334.

Marzano, R. J. (1994). Lessons from the field about outcome-based performance assessments. *Educational Leadership, 51* (6), 44–50.

Master, P. (1996). *Systems of English grammar: An introduction for language teachers.* Upper Saddle River, NJ: Prentice Hall Regents.

Master, P., & Brinton, D. (Eds.).(1998). *New ways in English for specific purposes.* Alexandria, VA: Teachers of English to Speakers of Other Languages.

Maxwell, M. (Ed.). (2000). *When tutor meets student* (2nd. ed.). Ann Arbor, MI: University of Michigan.

May, F. B., & Rizzardi, L. (2002). *Reading as communication* (6th ed.). Upper Saddle River, NJ: Merrill Prentice Hall.

Mazer, A. (Ed.). (1993). *American street: A multicultural anthology of voices.* New York: Persea Books.

Medina, M. Jr., & Escamilla, K. (1992). Evaluation of transitional and maintenance bilingual programs. *Urban Education, 27* (3), 263–290.

Mehan, H. (1979). *Learning lessons.* Cambridge, MA: Harvard University Press.

Mehan, H. (1981). Ethnography of bilingual education. In H. Trueba, G. Guthrie, & K. Au (Eds.), *Culture and the bilingual classroom: Studies in classroom ethnography.* Rowley, MA: Newbury House.

Mejia, E. A., Xiao, M. K., & Pasternak, L. (1992). *American picture show.* Englewood Cliffs, NJ: Prentice-Hall.

Meloni, C., & Masters, C. (1998). Experiencing the music of poetry: Poe's "Annabel Lee." In V. Whiteson (Ed.), *New ways of using drama and literature in language teaching* (pp. 76–79). Alexandria, VA: Teachers of English to Speakers of Other Languages.

Menconi, M. (1996). Country profile: Russia. *TESOL Placement Bulletin, 6* (5), 1, 3–4.

Menn, L. (2001). *Neurolinguistics.* In Linguistic Society of America, "Fields of Linguistics." Available online: www.lsadc.org/web2/fldcont.html.

Merriam-Webster (2001a). *Word for the wise. Morning Edition,* National Public Radio, April 30.

Merriam-Webster (2001b). *Word for the wise. Morning Edition,* National Public Radio, September 18.

Mestel, R. (2001, April 25). Childhood bullying is common, study finds. *Los Angeles Times,* A10.

Mestel, R., & Groves, M. (2001, April 3). When push comes to shove. *Los Angeles Times,* E1, E3.

Miller, S. M. (1980). Why having control reduces stress: If I can stop the roller coaster, I don't want to get off. In J. G. Garger & D. P. Seligman (Eds.), *Human helplessness* (pp. 71–95). New York: Academic Press.

Miller, W. H. (1995). *Alternative assessment techniques for reading and writing.* West Nyack, NJ: Center for Applied Research in Education.

Mills, S. (1997). *Discourse.* London and New York: Routledge.

Mittan, R. (1989). The peer review process: Harnessing students' communicative power. In D. Johnson & D. H. Roen (Eds.), *Richness in writing* (pp. 207–219). New York: Longman.

Molina, H., Hanson, R. A., & Siegel, D. F. (1997). *Empowering the second-language classroom: Putting the parts together.* San Francisco: Caddo Gap Press.

Molina, R. (2000). Building equitable two-way programs. In N. Cloud, F. Genesee, & E. Hamayan (Eds.), *Dual language instruction* (pp. 11–12). Boston: Heinle & Heinle.

Moll, L. C. (1992). Bilingual classroom studies and community analysis: Some recent trends. *Educational Researcher, 21* (2), 20–24.

Moll, L. C., Amanti, C., Neff, D., & González, N. (1992). Funds of knowledge for teaching: Using a qualitative approach to connect homes and classrooms. *Theory into Practice, 31* (2), 132–141.

Moll, L. C., & Greenberg, J. (1990). Creating zones of possibilities: Combining social contexts for instructions. In L. C. Moll (Ed.), *Vygotsky and education* (pp. 319–348). Cambridge: Cambridge University Press.

Monroe, S. (1999). Multicultural children's literature: Canon of the future. Reprinted in *Annual editions 99/00: Teaching English as a second languagey.* Guilford, CT: Dushkin/McGraw-Hill.

Morgan, B. (1998). *The ESL classoom: Teaching, critical practice, and community development.* Toronto: University of Toronto Press.

Morgan, G. (1986). *Images of organizations.* Beverly Hills, CA: Sage.

Morgan, R. (1992). Distinctive voices—Developing oral language in multilingual classrooms. In P. Pinsent (Ed.), *Language, culture, and young children* (pp. 37–46). London: David Fulton.

Morgan, J., & Rinvolucri, M. (1983). *Once upon a time: Using stories in the language classroom.* Cambridge: Cambridge University Press.

Morley, J. (1991). Listening comprehension in second/foreign language instruction. In M. Celce-Murcia (Ed.), *Teaching English as a second or foreign language* (2nd ed.). New York: Newbury House.

Morrison, C. (2001). *Schoolwide portfolios for community acccountability: What standardized tests can't tell us.* Presentation, the 9th Annual Conference on Project-Based Learning, San Francisco.

Morrison, G. (1997). Working in Japan. *TESOL Placement Bulletin, 7* (5), 1, 3.

Morrison, P. (1994). *Commentary: Americans speak English—But we don't understand.* Morning Edition, National Public Radio, May 23. Transcript 940016680.

Moskowitz, G. (1978). *Caring and sharing in the foreign language classroom.* Cambridge, MA: Newbury House.

Moss, D. (1998). *Project-based learning and assessment: A resource manual for teachers.* Arlington, VA: The Arlington Education and Employment Program.

Mosteller, L., & Haight, M. (1994). *Survival English: English through conversations, Book II* (2nd ed.), Englewood Cliffs, NJ: Prentice-Hall.

Moxley, J. M. (1994). *Becoming an academic writer: A modern rhetoric.* Lexington, MA: D. C. Heath.

Moya, S., & O'Malley, M. (1994). A portfolio assessment model for ESL. *The Journal of Educational Issues of Language Minority Students, 13,* 13–36. Available online: www.ncbe.gwu.edu/miscpubs/jeilms/vol13/portfo13.htm.

Murphey, T. (1992). *Music & song.* Oxford: Oxford University Press.

Murphy, J. M. (1998). *The eight disciplines.* Grand Rapids, MI: Venture Management Co.

Murphy, M. (1973). *Golf in the kingdom.* New York: Dell Publishers.

Murray, D. E. (2000). Protean communication: The language of computer-mediated communication. *TESOL Quarterly, 34* (3), 397–421.

Nagy, W. E., García, G. E., Durgunoglu, A., & Hancin-Bhatt, B. (1993). Spanish-English bilingual students' use of cognates in English reading. *Bilingual Research Journal, 18,* 83–97.

Nakagawa, J. (2002). Personal communication.

Nam, J-Y. (2001). *Achieving English competence in Korea through computer-assisted language learning and crosscultural understanding.* Unpublished master's project. San Bernardino, CA: California State University, San Bernardino.

Natheson-Mejia, S. (1989). Writing in a second language. *Language Arts, 66* (5), 516–526.

Nation, P. (1994). *New ways in teaching vocabulary.* Alexandria, VA: Teachers of English to Speakers of Other Languages.

National Center for Research on Cultural Diversity and Second Language Learning (1994). Funds of knowledge: Learning from language minority households. *CATESOL News, 26* (3), 1, 7, 10, 15.

National Women's History Project. (1992). *¡Adelante mujeres! Video on the history of Mexican-American Chicana women.* Windsor, CA: Author.

Nattinger, J. R. (1984). Communicative language teaching: A new metaphor. *TESOL Quarterly, 18* (3), 391–407.

Navarrete, C., & Gustke, C. (1996). *A guide to performance assessment for linguistically diverse students.* Albuquerque, NM: EAC West, New Mexico Highlands University. Available online: www.ncbe.gwu.edu/miscpubs/eacwest/performance/index.htm#contents.

Nelson, G. (1995). Cultural differences in learning styles. In J. Reid (Ed.), *Learning styles in the ESL/EFL classroom* (pp. 3–18). Boston: Heinle & Heinle.

Nelson, S. S., & O'Reilly, R. (2000, August 30). Minorities became majority in state, census officials say. *Los Angeles Times,* A1, A16.

Nero, S. J. (1997). English is my native language . . . or so I believe. *TESOL Quarterly, 31* (3), 585–593.

Ness, V. (1998). China: A growth market for EFL teachers. *TESOL Placement Bulletin, 8* (8), 3–5.

Newman, J. M. (1985a). What about reading? In J. M. Newman (Ed.), *Whole language: Theory in use* (pp. 99–100). Portsmouth, NH: Heinemann.

Newman, J. M. (1985b). Conferencing: Writing as a collaborative activity. In J. M. Newman (Ed.), *Whole language: Theory in use* (pp. 123–129). Portsmouth, NH: Heinemann.

Nieto, S. (1997). We speak in many tongues: Language diversity and multicultural education. In J. V. Tinajero & A. F. Ada (Eds.), *The power of two languages* (pp. 37–48). New York: Macmillan/McGraw-Hill.

Nieto, S. (2000). *Affirming diversity* (3rd ed.). New York: Longman.

Nishimoto, K. (1997). *Japanese fairy tales* (vols. 1–4). Torrance, CA: Heian International.

North Coast Rural Challenge Network. (2000). *Voices of the valley (vols. I–III).* Boonville, CA: Author. (Contact: mmendosa@avusd.k12.ca.us).

Norton, B., & Toohey, K. (2001). Changing perspectives on good language learners. *TESOL Quarterly, 35* (2), 307–322.

Nummela, R., & Rosengren, T. (1986). What's happening in students' brains may redefine teaching. *Educational Leadership, 43* (8), 49–53.

Nunan, D. (1989). *Designing tasks for the communicative classroom.* Cambridge: Cambridge University Press.

Nunan, D. (1991). *Language teaching methodology: A textbook for teachers.* New York: Prentice-Hall.

Nunan, D. (1995). *Atlas: Teacher's extended edition, Level 2.* Boston, MA: Heinle & Heinle.

Nunan, D. (1999). A foot in the world of ideas: Graduate study through the Internet. *Language Learning & Technology, 3* (1), 52–74.

Nydell, M. K. (1997). *Understanding Arabs: A guide for Westerners.* Yarmouth. ME: Intercultural Press.

O'Barr, W. M., & Atkins, B. K. (1980). Women's language or powerless language. In S. McConnell-Ginet, R. Borker, & N. Furman (Eds.), *Women and language in literature and society* (pp. 93–110). New York: Praeger.

Odlin, T. (1989). *Language transfer: Cross-linguistic influence in language learning.* Cambridge: Cambridge University Press.

Ogbu, J., & Matute-Bianchi, M. (1986). Understanding sociocultural factors: Knowledge, identity, and school adjustment. In *Beyond language: Social and cultural factors in schooling language minority students.* Los Angeles: Evaluation, Dissemination and Assessment Center, California State University, Los Angeles.

O'Grady, C. R., & Chappell, B. (2000). With, not for: The politics of service learning in multicultural communities. In P. McLaren & C. J. Ovando (Eds.), *The politics of multiculturalism and bilingual education* (pp. 208–224). Boston: The McGraw-Hill Companies.

Omaggio, A. (1978). *Games and simulations in the foreign language classroom.* Washington, DC: Center for Applied Linguistics.

Omaggio, A. C. (1986). *Teaching language in context.* Boston: Heinle & Heinle.

O'Malley, J., Chamot, A., Stewner-Manzanares, G., Kupper, L., & Russo, R. (1985a). Learning strategies used by beginning and intermediate ESL students. *Language Learning, 35* (1), 21–40.

O'Malley, J., Chamot, A., Stewner-Manzanares, G., Kupper, L., & Russo, R. (1985b). Learning strategy applications with students of English as a second language. *TESOL Quarterly, 19* (3), 557–584.

O'Malley, J. M., & Pierce, L. V. (1996). *Authentic assessment for English language learners.* Menlo Park, CA: Addison-Wesley.

O'Neil, J. (1990). Link between style, culture proves divisive. *Educational Leadership, 48* (2), 8.

O'Neill, C. (1989). Dialogue and drama: The transformation of events, ideas, and teachers. *Language Arts, 66,* 528–540.

Opie, I., & Opie, P. (1985). *The singing game.* Oxford: Oxford University Press.

Orion, G. F. (1988). *Pronouncing American English.* New York: Newbury House.

Ovando, C., & Collier, V. (1998). *Bilingual and ESL classrooms: Teaching in multicultural contexts.* Boston: McGraw-Hill.

Owens, E. (1998). Ecuador. *TESOL Placement Bulletin, 6* (6), 1.

Oxford, R. (1990). *Language learning strategies: What every teacher should know.* Boston, MA: Allyn & Bacon.

Packer, N. H., & Timpane, J. (1997). *Writing worth reading: The critical process* (3rd ed.). Boston: Bedford Books.

Padilla, S. (1995). *Chants and prayers.* Summerton, TN: Book Publishing Co.

Palinscar, A. S., & Brown, A. L. (1984). Reciprocal teaching of comprehension-fostering and comprehension-monitoring activities. *Cognition and Instruction, 1,* 117–175.

Panzeri-Alvarez, C. (1998). *Metacognition and language transfer for an English language development transitional program.* Unpublished master's project. San Bernardino: California State University, San Bernardino.

Pappas, C. C., Kiefer, B. Z., & Levstik, L. S. (1990). *An integrated language perspective in the elementary school: Theory into action.* White Plains, NY: Longman.

Parker, R. (1995). *Mixed signals: Prospects for global television news.* New York: Twentieth Century Fund.

Parks, S., & Black, H. (1990). *Organizing thinking: Graphic organizers.* Pacific Grove, CA: Critical Thinking Press & Software.

Parla, J. (1994). Educating teachers for cultural and linguistic diversity: A model for all teachers. *New York State Association for Bilingual Education Journal, 9,* 1–6. Available online: www.ncbe.gwu.edu/miscpubs/nysabe/vol9/model.htm.

Patthey-Chavez, G., Clark, L., & Gallimore, R. (1995). *Creating a community of scholarship with instructional conversations in a transitional bilingual classroom.* Educational Practice Report 15. Santa Cruz, CA: National Center for Research on Cultural Diversity and Second Language Learning. Available online: www.ncbe.gwu.edu/miscpubs/ncrcdsll/epr15.htm.

Paul, R., Binker, A. J. A., Jensen, K., & Kreklau, H. (1990). *Critical thinking handbook: 4th–6th grades.* Rohnert Park, CA: Center for Critical Thinking and Moral Critique.

Paul, R., Binker, A. J. A., Jensen, K., & Kreklau, H. (1990). *Critical thinking handbook: 4th–6th grades.* Rohnert Park, CA: Center for Critical Thinking and Moral Critique.

Peabody, Z. (2001, September 27). College education online: Pass? Fail? *Los Angeles Times,* T1, T6.

Peal, E., & Lambert, W. (1962). The relationship of bilingualism to intelligence. *Psychological Monographs, 76* (27), 1–23.

Pearson, P. D., & Gallagher, M. C. (1983). The instruction of reading comprehension. *Contemporary Educational Psychology, 8,* 317–344.

Pei, M. (1962). 'Ain't' is in, 'raviolis' ain't. In J. Sledd & W. R. Ebbitt (Eds.), *Dictionaries and THAT dictionary* (pp. 82–83). Glenview, IL: Scott, Foresman and Co.

Peim, N. (1993). *Critical theory and the English teacher.* London and New York: Routledge.

Peñalosa, F. (1980). *Chicano sociolinguistics, a brief introduction.* Rowley, MA: Newbury House.

Pennycook, A. (1994). *The cultural politics of English as an international language.* New York and London: Longman.

Pennycook, A. (1998). Text, ownership, memory, and plagiarism. In V. Zamel & R. Spack (Eds.), *Negotiating academic literacies: Teaching and learning across languages and cultures* (pp. 265–292). Mahwah, NJ: Erlbaum.

Peregoy, S. F., & Boyle, O. F. (2001). *Reading, writing, and learning in ESL* (3rd ed.). New York: Addison Wesley Longman.

Pérez, B., & Torres-Guzmán, M. E. (2002). *Learning in two worlds* (3rd ed.). Boston: Allyn & Bacon.

Pérez, J. (1976). *Puerto Rico: U.S. colony in the Caribbean.* New York: Pathfinder Press.

Pérez de Lima, A. M. (1996). Country profile: Uruguay. *TESOL Placement Bulletin, 6* (3), 1, 3.

Perfection Learning (2000). *Who am I?* Logan, IA: Author.

Perkins, D. (1986). *Knowledge as design.* Hillsdale, NJ: Erlbaum.

Perkins, D. N. (1992). Technology meets constructivism: Do they make a marriage? In T. M. Duffy & D. H. Jonassen, (Eds.), *Constructivism and the technology of instruction: A conversation.* Hillsdale, NJ: Erlbaum.

Perrone, V. (1994). How to engage students in learning. *Educational Researcher, 51* (5), 11–13.

The Peter Pauper Press (1958). *The four seasons: Japanese haiku written by Basho, Buson, Issa, Shiki, and many others.* Mount Vernon, NY: Author.

Peterson, B. (1994). Teaching for social justice: One teacher's journey. In B. Bigelow, L. Christensen,

S. Karp, B. Miner, & B. Peterson (Eds.), *Rethinking our classrooms.* Milwaukee, WI: Rethinking Schools Limited.

Peyton, J. K. (1990). Dialogue journal writing and the acquisition of English grammatical morphology. In J. K. Peyton (Ed.), *Students and teachers writing together: Perspectives on journal writing* (pp. 67–97). Alexandria, VA: Teachers of English to Speakers of Other Languages.

Peyton, J. K. (1997). Book review of Kazemek and Rigg's "Enriching Our Lives: Poetry Lessons for Adult Literacy Teachers and Tutors." *TESOL Journal, 7* (2), 39.

Peyton, J. K., & Staton, J. (Eds.) (1991). *Writing our lives: Reflections on dialogue journal writing with adults learning English.* Englewood Cliffs, NJ: Prentice-Hall Regents.

Pfingstag, N. (1999). Hearing voices. In R. E. Larimer & L. Schleicher (Eds.), *New ways in using authentic materials in the classroom* (pp. 62–65). Alexandria, VA: Teachers of English to Speakers of Other Languages.

Philips, S. (1972). Participant structures and communicative competence: Warm Springs children in community and classroom. In C. Cazden, V. John, & D. Hymes (Eds.). *Functions of language in the classroom.* New York: Teachers College Press.

Phillipson, R. (2003). Union in need of language equality. *The Guardian Weekly, Learning English Supplement, 168* (6), 3.

Pierce, B. N. (1995). Social identity, investment, and language learning. *TESOL Quarterly, 29* (1), 9–31.

Pierce, L. V. (1998). Planning portfolios. In J. D. Brown (Ed.), *New ways in classroom assessment* (pp. 6–10). Alexandria, VA: Teachers of English to Speakers of Other Languages.

Porter, R. (1990). *Forked tongue: The politics of bilingual education.* New York: Basic Books.

Poyatos, F. (1984). Linguistic fluency and verbal-nonverbal cultural fluency. In A. Wolfgang (Ed.), *Nonverbal behavior: Perspectives, applications, intercultural insights* (pp. 139–167). Lewiston, NY: Hogrefe.

Prabhu, N. S. (1990). There is no best method—Why? *TESOL Quarterly, 24* (2), 161–176.

Pratt, C., & Nesdale, A. R. (1984). Pragmatic awareness in children. In W. E. Tunmer, C. Pratt, & M. L. Herriman (Eds.), *Metalinguistic awareness in children* (pp. 105–125). Berlin: Springer-Verlag.

Prelutsky, J. (1988). *Tyrannosaurus was a beast.* New York: Greenwillow.

Prelutsky, J. (2000). *The Random House book of poetry for children.* New York: Random House.

Pressley, M., Barkowski, J. G., & O'Sullivan, J. (1985). Children's metamemory and the teaching of memory strategies. In D. L. Forrest-Pressley, G. E. Mackinnon, & T. G. Waller (Eds.), *Metacognition, cognition, and human performance* (pp. 111–149). Orlando, FL: Academic Press.

Pridham, F. (2001). *The language of conversation.* New York and London: Routledge.

Probst, R. E. (1988). *Response and analysis: Teaching literature in junior and senior high school.* Portsmouth, NH: Heinemann.

Provenzano, R. (2001). *A little book of aloha.* Honolulu, HI: Mutual Publishing.

Pugliese, C. (2001, March 22). Languages go to the top of the class. *Manchester Daily Guardian,* Learning English Section, 1.

Quinn, A. (1982). *Figures of speech.* Davis, CA: Hermagoras Press.

Quintero, E. P., & Rummel, M. K. (1998). *American voices: Webs of diversity.* Upper Saddle River, NJ: Prentice-Hall.

Radin, B. (2000). *Decision dramas* (3rd. ed.). Studio City, CA: JAG Publications.

Raffini, J. P. (1996). *150 ways to increase intrinsic motivation in the classroom.* Boston: Allyn & Bacon.

Raimes, A. (Ed.). (1996). *Identities: Readings from contemporary culture.* Boston: Houghton Mifflin.

Raimes, A. (1983). *Techniques in teaching writing.* New York: Oxford University Press.

Ramírez, J. (1992, winter/spring). Executive summary, final report: Longitudinal study of structured English immersion strategy, early-exit, and late-exit transitional bilingual education programs for language-minority children. *Bilingual Research Journal, 16* (1&2), 1–62.

Randall-David, E. (1989). *Strategies for working with culturally diverse communities and clients.* Washington, DC: Office of Maternal and Child Health, United States Department of Health and Human Services. Available online: www.nmchc.org/html/cattoc.htm.

Raphael, T. E. (1986). Teaching question answer relationships, revisited. *The Reading Teacher, 39,* 516–523.

Rasinski, T., & Fredericks, A. (1989). Dimensions of parent involvement. *The Reading Teacher, 43* (2), 180–182.

Ratey, J. J. (2001). *User's guide to the brain: Perception, attention, and the four theaters of the brain.* New York: Pantheon Books.

Raths, L. E., Wasserman, S., Jonas, A., & Rothstein, A. J. (1986). *Teaching for thinking: Theory, strategies, and activities for the classroom* (2nd ed.). New York: Teachers College Press.

Ray, B., & Seely, C. (1997). *Fluency through TPR storytelling.* Berkeley, CA: Command Performance Institute.

Reardon, B. (1988). *Comprehensive peace education.* New York: Columbia University Teachers College Press.

Redding, J. (2001). *Music creating language experience: Rock Talk.* Presentation, CATESOL Annual State Conference, Ontario, CA.

Reichard, G. A. (1977). *Navajo medicine man sandpainting.* New York; Dover.

Reid, J. M. (1993). *Teaching ESL writing.* Englewood Cliffs, NJ: Prentice-Hall Regents.

Reid, J. M. (1995). Preface. In J. Reid (Ed.), *Learning styles in the ESL/EFL classroom* (pp. viii–xvii). Boston: Heinle & Heinle.

Reischauer, E. O. (1977). *The Japanese.* Tokyo: Tuttle.

Reyhner, J. (1992). American Indian bilingual education: The White House conference on Indian education and the tribal college movement. *NABE News, 15* (7), 7, 18.

Reynolds, F. (1988). Reading conferences. In C. Gilles, M. Bixby, P. Corwley, S. R. Crenshaw, M. Henrichs, F. E. Reynolds, & Donelle Pyle (Eds.), *Whole language strategies for secondary students* (pp. 138–140). New York: Richard C. Owen Publishers.

Rhodes, R. A., & Howard, J. P. F. (Eds.). (1998, spring). *Academic service learning: A pedagogy of action and reflection.* New Directions for Teaching and Learning. San Francisco: Jossey-Bass (73).

Richard-Amato, P., & Snow, M. A. (1992). Strategies for content-area teachers. In P. Richard-Amato & M. A. Snow (Eds). *The multicultural classroom.* White Plains, NY: Longman.

Richard-Amato, P. (1996). *Making it happen* (2nd ed.). White Plains, NY: Longman.

Rico, H. (2000). *Programs for English learners: Overview of federal and state requirements.* Sacramento, CA: California Department of Education. Available online: www.cde.ca.gov/ccpdiv/eng_learn/ccr2000-el/index.htm.

Ricoeur, P. (1984). *Time and narrative* (vol 1). (K. McLaughlin & D. Pellauer trans.). Chicago: University of Chicago Press.

Riles, G. B., & Lenarcic, C. (2000). Exploring world religions. In B. Agor (Ed.), *Integrating the ESL standards into classroom practice: Grades 9–12* (pp. 1–29). Alexandria, VA: Teachers of English to Speakers of Other Languages (TESOL).

Rinvolucri, M. (1984). *Grammar games: Cognitive, affective, and drama activities for EFL students.* Cambridge: Cambridge University Press.

Rivers, W., & Temperley, M. (1978). *A practical guide to the teaching of English as a second or foreign language*. New York: Oxford University Press.

Roberts, C. (1995, summer/fall). Bilingual education program models. *Bilingual Research Journal, 19* (3 & 4). Reprinted as Bilingual education program models: A framework for understanding. In L. Orozco (Ed.), (1998), *Perspectives: Educating diverse populations* (pp. 79–83). Boulder, CO: Coursewise Publishing.

Roberts, V. M. (1971). *The nature of theater*. New York: Harper & Row.

Rodby, J. (1999). Contingent literacy: The social construction of writing for nonnative English-speaking college freshman. In L. Harklau, K. M. Losey, & M. Siegal (Eds.). (1999). *Generation 1.5 meets college composition: Issues in the teaching of writing to U.S.-educated learners of ESL* (pp. 45–60). Mahwah, NJ: Erlbaum.

Roen, D. H. (1989). Developing effective assignments for second language writers. In D. Johnson & D. H. Roen (Eds.), *Richness in writing* (pp. 193–206). New York: Longman.

Romero, M. (1991). *Integrating English language development with content-area instruction*. Presentation, annual meeting, American Educational Research Association, Chicago.

Root, C., & Dumicich, J. (1998). Reader's theater: A primer on pronunciation. In V. Whiteson (Ed.), *New ways of using drama and literature in language teaching* (pp. 123–124). Alexandria, VA: Teachers of English to Speakers of Other Languages.

Rose, C. (1985). *Accelerated learning*. New York: Bantam Doubleday Dell.

Rose, D. (2001). Acronymonia. *CATESOL News, 33* (1), 8–9.

Rose, M. (1996). Tracking. In A. Raimes (Ed.), *Identities: Readings from contemporary culture* (pp. 370–377). Boston: Houghton Mifflin.

Rosenblatt, L. (1978). *The reader, the text, the poem: The transactional theory of the literary work*. Carbondale: Southern Illinois University.

Rosenthal, L., & Rowland, S. B. (1986). *Academic reading and study skills for international students*. Englewood Cliffs, NJ: Prentice-Hall Regents.

Rosenthal, R. (1987). Pygmalion effects: Existence, magnitude and social importance. A reply to Wineburg. *Educational Researcher, 16*, 37–41.

Rosenthal, R., & Jacobson, L. (1968). *Pygmalion in the classroom*. New York: Holt, Rinehart, Winston.

Rosten, L. C. (1982). *Hooray for Yiddish! A book about English*. New York: Simon & Schuster.

Roth-Vinson, C. (2001). *All aspects of project planning: Teaching tools for community-based learning*. Presentation, the 9th Annual Conference on Project-Based Learning, San Francisco, CA.

Ruíz, R. (1984). Orientations in language planning. *NABE Journal, 8* (2), 15–34.

Runner, J. (2000). *"Thank you" in over 465 languages*. Available online: www.elite.net/~runner/jennifers/thankyou.htm

Ryan, P. M. (2000). *Esperanza rising*. New York: Scholastic Signature.

Sadker, M., & Sadker, D. (1986). Sexism in the classroom: From grade school to graduate school. *Phi Delta Kappan, 68*, 512.

Sadker, M., Sadker, D., & Klein, S. (1991). The issue of gender in elementary and secondary education. *Review of Research in Education, 17*, 269–334.

Sagliano, M., & Greenfield, K. (1998). A collaborative model of content-based EFL instruction in the liberal arts. *TESOL Journal, 7* (3), 23–28.

Salovey, P., & Mayer, J. D. (1990). Emotional intelligence. *Imagination, Cognition, and Personality, 9* (3), 185–211.

Samway, K. D. (Ed.). (2000). *Integrating the ESL standards into classroom practice: Grades 3–5*. Alexandria, VA: Teachers of English to Speakers of Other Languages (TESOL).

San Joaquin County Office of Education (2001). *"Way to Grow!" Service learning—The seeds to your future*. Stockton, CA: Author.

Santás, C. (1996). In D. Gardner and L. Miller, (Eds.). *Tasks for independent language learning* (pp. 18–20). Alexandria, VA: Teachers of English to Speakers of Other Languages.

Santillana Publishing Company. (1989). *Bridge to communication primary level A*. Northvale, NJ: Author.

Sapon-Shevin, M. (1999). *Because we can change the world*. Boston: Allyn & Bacon.

Sarwar, Z. (2000). *Project-based learning*. Presentation, annual meeting, Teachers of English to Speakers of Other Languages, Vancouver, Canada.

Sasser, L. (1992). Teaching literature to language minority students. In P. Richard-Amato & M. Snow (Eds.), *The multicultural classroom*. White Plains, NY: Longman.

Sato, C. (1982). Ethnic styles in classroom discourse. In M. Hines & W. Rutherford (Eds.), *On TESOL '81*. Washington, DC: TESOL.

Savignon, S. J. (1983). *Communicative competence: Theory and classroom practice*. Reading, MA: Addison-Wesley.

Scarcella, R., & Rumberger, R. W. (2000). Academic English key to long-term success in school. *University of California Linguistic Minority Research Institute Newsletter, 9* (4), 1–2.

Schank, R. (1981). Language and memory. In D. A. Norman (Ed.), *Perspectives in cognitive science*. Norwood, NJ: Ablex.

Schiff, (1973). *Some things you just can't do by yourself*. Stanford, CA: New Seed Press.

Schiffler, L. (1992). *Suggestopedic methods and applications* (Trans., K. Herr). Yverdon, Switzerland: Gordon & Breach Science Publishers.

Schiffrin, D. (1994). *Approaches to discourse*. Chicago; University of Chicago Press.

Schifini, A., Short, D., & Tinajero, J. V. (2002). *High points: Teacher's edition*. Carmel, CA: Hampton Brown.

Schleppegrell, M. J. (1997). Problem-posing in teacher education. *TESOL Journal, 6* (3), 8–12.

Schultz, J., & Theophano, J. (1987). Saving place and marking time: Some aspects of the social lives of three-year-old children. In H. Trueba (Ed.), *Success or failure? Learning and the language minority student*. Cambridge, MA: Newbury House Publishers.

Schuman, R. B. (1978). *Educational drama for today's schools*. Metuchen, NJ: Scarecrow Press.

Seliger, H. (1984). Processing universals in second language acquisition. In F. Eckman, L. Ball, & D. Nelson (Eds.), *Universals of second language acquisition* (pp. 36–47). Rowley, MA: Newbury House.

Selinker, L. (1972). Interlanguage. *IRAL, 10* (3), 209–231.

Selinker, L. (1991). Along the way: Interlanguage systems in second language acquisition. In L. Malavé & G. Duquette (Eds.), *Language, culture and cognition*. Clevedon, UK: Multilingual Lingual Matters.

Sellers, J. (1994). *Folk wisdom of Mexico*. San Francisco, CA: Chronicle Books.

Shameem, N., & Tickoo, M. (Eds.). (1999). *New ways in using communicative games*. Alexandria, VA: Teachers of English to Speakers of Other Languages.

Shapiro, S. (1990). Beyond the anthology: Poetry readings in the classroom. In N. Cecil (Ed.), *Literacy in the 90's: Selected readings in the language arts* (pp. 122–127). Dubuque, IA: Kendall/ Hunt.

Shen, F. (1998). The classroom and the wider culture: Identity as a key to learning English composition. In V. Zamel & R. Speck (Eds.), *Negotiating academic literacies: Teaching and learning across language and cultures* (pp. 123–133). Mahwah, NJ: Erlbaum.

Shepard, A. (1994). From script to stage: Tips for readers theatre. *The English Teacher, 48* (2), 184–190.

Shepard, L. A. (2000). The role of assessment in a learning culture. *Educational Researcher, 29* (7), 4–14.

Shepard, S. L. (2001). Mall culture. In M. Petracca & M. Sorapure (Eds.), *Common culture: Reading and writing about American popular culture* (3rd. ed.), (pp. 603–607). Upper Saddle River, NJ: Prentice-Hall.

Shoemaker, C., & Polycarpou, S. (1993). *Write ideas: A beginning writing text*. Boston: Heinle & Heinle.

Shor, I. (1992). *Empowering education: Critical teaching for social change*. Chicago and London: University of Chicago Press.

Short, D. (1991). *Integrating language and content instruction: Strategies and techniques*. Washington, DC: National Clearinghouse for Bilingual Education.

Shuell, T. J. (1986). Cognitive conceptions of learning. *Review of Educational Research, 56*, 411–436.

Siccone, F. (1995). *Celebrating diversity*. Boston: Allyn & Bacon.

Sick, J. (1999). So did I. In N. Shameem & M. Tickoo (Eds.), *New ways in using communicative games* (p. 117). Alexandria, VA: Teachers of English to Speakers of Other Languages.

Sigmon, R. I. (1994). *Serving to learn, learning to serve: Linking service with learning*. Report, Council for Independent Colleges.

Sillivan, S. (2000). Mastering the art of persuasion: Marketing and the media. In S. Irujo (Ed.), *Integrating the ESL standards into classroom practice: Grades 6–8* (pp. 85–111). Alexandria, VA: Teachers of English to Speakers of Other Languages (TESOL).

Simon, R. (1982). *Gramsci's political thought*. London: Lawrence & Wishart.

Skutnabb-Kangas, T. (1981). *Bilingualism or not: The education of minorities*. (L. Malmberg & D. Crane, trans.). Clevedon, UK: Multilingual Matters.

Skutnabb-Kangas, T. (1993). *Linguistic genocide and bilingual education*. Presentation, annual conference, California Association for Bilingual Education, Anaheim, CA.

Skutnabb-Kangas, T. (2000). *Linguistic genocide in education—or worldwide diversity and human rights?* Mahwah, NJ: Erlbaum.

Skutnabb-Kangas, T. (2001, March 22). Murder that is a threat to survival. *Manchester Daily Guardian*, Learning English section, 3.

Slavin, R. E. (1983). *Cooperative learning*. New York: Longman.

Slavin, R. E. (1991). A synthesis of research on cooperative learning. *Educational Leadership, 48*, 71–82.

Sleeter, C. E., & Grant. C. A. (1987). An analysis of multicultural education in the United States. *Harvard Education Review, 57* (4), 421–444.

Sleeter, C. E., & McLaren, P. L. (1995). *Multicultural education, critical pedagogy, and the politics of difference.* Albany, NY: State University of New York Press.

Sloan, S. (1991). *The complete ESL/EFL cooperative and communicative activity book.* Lincolnwood, IL: National Textbook Company.

Sloyer, S. (1982). *Readers theatre: Story dramatization in the classroom.* Urbana, IL: National Council of Teachers of English.

Small, A. H. (1993). *English à la cartoon.* Lincolnwood, IL: NTC/Contemporary Publishing Company/Passport Books.

Smallwood, B. A. (Ed.). (2000). *Integrating the ESL standards into classroom practice: Grades pre-K–2.* Alexandria, VA: Teachers of English to Speakers of Other Languages (TESOL).

Smallwood, B. A. (1991). *The literature connection: A read-aloud guide for multicultural classrooms.* Reading, MA: Addison-Wesley.

Smith, F. (1982). *Writing and the writer.* New York: Holt, Rinehart, & Winston.

Smith, M. W. (1994). Issues in integrating service-learning into the higher education curriculum. In *Effective learning, effective teaching, effective service.* Washington, DC: Youth Service America.

Smith, P. M. (1985). *Language, the sexes and society.* New York: Basil Blackwell.

Sneve, V. D. H. (1989). *Dancing teepees.* New York: Holiday House.

Snow, M. A. (1993). Discipline-based foreign language teaching: Implications from ESL/EFL. In M. Krueger & F. Ryan (Eds.), *Language and content: Discipline- and content-based approaches to language study* (pp. 37–56). Lexington, MA: D. C. Heath.

Snow, M. A., & Brinton, D. M. (1988). Content-based language instruction: Investigating the effectiveness of the adjunct model. *TESOL Quarterly, 22* (3), 201–17.

Solé, D. (1998). Poetry for pronunciation, pronunciation for poetry. In V. Whiteson (Ed.), *New ways of using drama and literature in language teaching* (pp. 84–85). Alexandria, VA: Teachers of English to Speakers of Other Languages.

Sonbuchner, G. M. (1991). *How to take advantage of your learning styles.* Syracuse, NY: New Readers Press.

Soto, G. (1992). *Pacific crossing.* San Diego, New York, & London: Harcourt, Brace & Co.

Soto, L. D. (1991). Understanding bilingual/bicultural children. *Young Children, 46* (2), 30–36.

Spears, R. A. (1992). *Common American phrases.* Lincolnwood, IL: National Textbook Company.

Spellmeyer, K. (1989). A common ground: The essay in the academy. *College English, 51,* 262–276.

Spener, M. (1992). *The Freirean approach to adult literacy education.* National Center for ESL Literacy Education (NCLE). Available online: www.cal.org/ncle/digests/FreireQA.htm.

Stafford-Yilmaz, L. (1998). *A to zany: Community activities for students of English.* Ann Arbor: University of Michigan Press.

Stauffer, R. G. (1970). *The language-experience approach to the teaching of reading.* New York: Harper & Row.

Steig, W. (1972) *Amos and Boris.* New York: Farrar, Straus & Giroux.

Steinberg, J. (1983). *Games language people play.* Markham, Canada: Dominie Press.

Steinberg, A., & Stephen, D. (1999). *City works: Exploring your community.* New York: New Press.

Stephenson, S. (2002). *Understanding Spanish-speaking South Americans.* Yarmouth, ME: Intercultural Press.

Stepien, W., & Gallagher, S. (1993). Problem-based learning: As authentic as it gets. *Educational Leadership, 50* (7), 25–28.

Stern, H. (1993). *Fundamental concepts of language teaching.* Oxford: Oxford University Press.

Stern, A. (1996). *Tales from many lands : An anthology of multicultural folk literature.* Lincolnwood, IL: National Textbook Company.

Stice, J. E., (Ed.). (1987). *Developing critical thinking and problem solving abilities.* San Francisco: Jossey-Bass.

Stiel, S. (2002). An interview with Hang Nguyen. In B. M. Power & R. S. Hubbard (Eds.). *Language development: A reader for teachers* (2nd ed.) (pp. 185–188). Upper Saddle River, NJ and Columbus, OH: Merrill/Prentice-Hall.

Stipek, D. J., & Seal, K. (2001). *Motivated minds: Raising children to love learning.* New York: Owl.

Storr, A. (1993). *Music and the mind.* New York: Ballantine Books.

Storti, C. (2001). *Old world/new world, bridging cultural differences: Britain, France, and the U.S.* Yarmouth, ME: Intercultural Press.

Strauch, A. O. (1997). *Bridges to academic writing.* New York: St. Martin's Press.

Street, B. (1995). *Social literacies: Critical approaches to literacy in development, ethnography, and education.* London: Longman.

Strevens, P. (1987). Cultural barriers to language learning. In L. Smith (Ed.), *Discourse across cultures: Strategies in world Englishes*. New York: Prentice-Hall.

Strohmeyer, V. (1991–1992, winter). Fables in the ESOL classroom. *TESOL Journal, 1* (2), 33.

Suid, M., & Lincoln, W. (1992). *Ten-minute whole language warm-ups*. Palo Alto, CA: Monday Morning Books.

Sullivan, N. (Ed.). (1978). *The treasury of American poetry*. New York: Dorset Press.

Sulzby, E. (1986). Writing and reading: Signs of oral and written language organization in the young child. In W. H. Teale & E. Sulzby (Eds.), *Emergent literacy: Writing and reading* (pp. 50–89). Norwood, NJ: Ablex.

Swales, J. M. (1990). *Genre analysis: English in academic and research settings*. Cambridge: Cambridge University Press.

Swerdlow, J. L. (2001) Changing America. *National Geographic, 200* (3), 42–61.

Sylwester, R. (1995). *A celebration of neurons: An educator's guide to the brain*. Alexandria, VA: Association for Supervision and Curriculum Development.

Sylwester, R. & Cho, J-Y. (1992/1993). What brain research says about paying attention. *Educational Leadership, 50* (4), 71–75.

Szwed, J. (1981). The ethnography of literacy. In E. Kintgen, B. Kroll, & M. Rose (Eds.), *Perspectives on literacy* (pp. 303–311). Carbondale: Southern Illinois University Press.

Tannen, D. (2001). *Discourse analysis*. In Linguistic Society of America, "Fields of Linguistics." Available online: www.lsadc.org/web2/fldcont.html.

Tarone, E. (1981). Some thoughts on the notion of communication strategy. *TESOL Quarterly, 15* (3), 285–295.

Tarone, E., Cohen, A. D., & Dumas, G. (1983). A closer look at some interlanguage terminology: A framework for communication strategies. In C. Færch & G. Kasper (Eds.), *Strategies in interlanguage communication* (pp. 4–14). London and New York: Longman.

Taylor, B. P. (1983). Teaching ESL: Incorporating a communicative, student-centered component. *TESOL Quarterly, 17* (1), 69–88.

Taylor, B. P. (1987). In M. H. Long & J. C. Richards (Eds.), *Methodology in TESOL: A book of readings* (pp. 45–60). New York: Newbury House.

Taylor, D. (1988). *Beginning to read and the spin doctors of science: The political campaign to change America's mind about how children learn to read*. Urbana, IL: National Council of Teachers of English.

Tchudi, S., & Mitchell, D. (1999). *Exploring and teaching the English language arts*. New York: Longman.

Teachers of English to Speakers of Other Languages. (1976). *Position paper on the role of English as a second language in bilingual education*. Alexandria, VA: Author.

Teachers of English to Speakers of Other Languages. (1992). TESOL statement on the education of K–12 language minority students in the United States. In *TESOL resource packet: Is your school helping its language minority students meet the national education goals?* Alexandria, VA: Author.

Teachers of English to Speakers of Other Languages. (1997). *ESL standards for pre-K–12 students*. Alexandria, VA: Author. Available online: www.tesol.edu/assoc/k12standards/it/01.html.

Teachers of English to Speakers of Other Languages (TESOL). (2001). *Scenarios for ESL standards-based assessment*. Alexandria, VA: Author.

Teachers of English to Speakers of Other Languages. (2002). *Statement on the acquisition of academic proficiency in English*. Alexandria, VA: Author. Available online: www.tesol.edu.

Tellez, K., Hlebowitsh, P. S., Cohen, M., & Norwood, P. (1995). Social service field experiences and teacher education. In J. M. Larkin & C. E. Sleeter (Eds.), *Developing multicultural teacher education curricula* (pp. 65–78). Albany: State University of New York Press.

Tharp, R. (1989). Psychocultural variables and constants: Effects on teaching and learning in schools. *American Psychologist, 44* (2), 349–359.

Tharp, R., & Gallimore, R. (1988). *Rousing minds to life: Teaching, learning, and schooling in social context*. Cambridge: Cambridge University Press.

Tharp, R., & Gallimore, R. (1991). *The instructional conversation: Teaching and learning in social activity*. Washington, DC: National Center for Research on Cultural Diversity and Second Language Learning.

Thomas, L. (1994). Song of the canary. In V. P. Clark, P. A. Eschholz, & A. F. Rosa (Eds.), *Language: Introductory readings* (pp. 35–48). New York: St. Martin's Press.

Thonis, E. W. (1981). Reading instruction for language minority students, In California Department of Education (Ed.), *Schooling and language minority students: A theoretical framework*. Sacramento: Office of Bilingual Education.

Thornborrow, J. (1999). Language and identity. In L. Thomas & S. Wareing (Eds.), *Language, soci-*

ety, and power: An introduction (pp. 135–149). London and New York: Routledge.

Tikunoff, W. J. (1988). Mediation of instruction to obtain quality of effectives. In S. Fradd & W. J. Tikunoff (Eds.), Bilingual education and special education: A guide of instruction (pp. 99–132). Boston: Little, Brown.

Tikunoff, W., Ward, B., Romero, M., Lucas, T., Katz, A., Van Broekhuisen, L., & Castaneda, L. (1991). *Addressing the instructional needs of the limited English proficient student: Results of the exemplary SAIP descriptive study.* Symposium, annual meeting, American Educational Research Association, Chicago.

Tinajero, J. V., & Schifini, A. (1997). *Into English.* Carmel, CA: Hampton-Brown.

Tollefson, J. W. (1991). *Planning language, planning inequality.* London: Longman.

Tollefson, J. W. (Ed.). (1995). *Power and inequality in language education.* Cambridge: Cambridge University Press.

Tompkins, G. (1997). *Literacy for the 21st century: A balanced approach.* Upper Saddle River, NJ: Merrill.

Tompkins, G. E., & McGee, L. M. (1993). *Teaching reading with literature: Case studies to action plans.* New York: Merrill.

Toohey, K. (1998). "Breaking them up, taking them away": ESL students in grade 1. *TESOL Quarterly, 32* (1), 61–84.

Tresaugue, M. (2002). Back to the basics. *Riverside Press-Enterprise,* January 31, A1, A8.

Tudor, I. (1996). *Learner-centeredness as language education.* Cambridge: Cambridge University Press.

Tunmer, W. E., Herriman, M. L., & Nesdale, A. R. (1988). Metalinguistic abilities and beginning reading. *Reading Research Quarterly, 23* (2), 134–158.

Tunmer, W., & Nesdale, A. (1985). Phonemic segmentation skill and beginning reading. *Journal of Educational Psychology, 77,* 417–427.

Tunnell, M. O., & Jacobs, J. S. (2000). *Children's literature, briefly* (2nd ed.). Upper Saddle River, NJ, and Columbus, OH: Merrill/Prentice-Hall.

Turner, T. (1990). *Brainstorms: Creative problem solving.* Glenview, IL: Scott, Foresman.

Tyler, J., & Round, G. (1987). *Brain puzzles.* London: Usborne Publishing.

Ungerer, F., & Schmid, H-J. (1996). *An introduction to cognitive linguistics.* London: Longman.

United States Census Bureau (2001a). *The Asian and Pacific Islander population in the United States: March 1999* (update) (PPL-131). Washington, DC: Author. Available online: www.census.gov/population/www/socdemo/race/api99.html.

United States Census Bureau (2001b). *Hispanic population in the United States (2000 March CPS).* Washington, DC: Author. Available online: www.census.gov/population/www/socdemo/hispanic/ho00.html.

United States Census Bureau (2001c). *Census 2000 supplementary survey.* Washington, DC: Author.

Vai, M. (1998). *The heart of the matter.* Boston: Heinle & Heinle.

Vaidya, S. R. (1999). Metacognitive strategies for students with learning disabilities. *Education, 120* (1), 186–189.

Valdés, G. (1996). *Con respeto: Bridging the distance between culturally diverse families and schools: An ethnographic portrait.* New York: Teachers College Press.

Valdés, G. (2001). Multilingualism. In Linguistic Society of America, "Fields of Linguistics." Available online: www.lsadc.org/web2/fldcont.html.

Valdés-Fallis, G. (1978). *Code switching and the classroom teacher.* Washington, DC: Center for Applied Linguistics.

Valéncia, R. R. (Ed.). (1991) *Chicano school failure and success: Research and policy agendas for the 1990s.* London, New York: Falmer.

van der Woude, M. (1998). Korean students in the United States. *ESL Magazine, 1* (1), 28–30.

Van Deusen-Scholl, N. (1993). Ethnography and teacher training. In D. Freeman & S. Cornwall (Eds.), *New ways in teacher education* (pp. 187–190). Alexandria, VA: Teachers of English to Speakers of Other Languages. (1993)

Van Lier, L. (2000). From input to affordance. In J. P. Lantolf (Ed.), *Sociocultural theory and second language learning* (pp. 246–259). Oxford: Oxford University Press.

Vaughn, S. (2001, July 15). Common ground for differences. *Los Angeles Times,* W1, W3.

Veeder, K., & Tramutt, J. (2000). Strengthening literacy in both languages. In N. Cloud, F. Genesee, & E. Hamayan (Eds.), *Dual language instruction* (p. 91). Boston: Heinle & Heinle.

Vega, C. M. (2000). Reaching for literacy. *San Bernardino County Sun,* July 12, A1, A4.

Vélez-Ibáñez, C., & Greenberg, J. B. (1992). Formation and transformation of funds of knowledge among U.S. Mexican households. *Anthropology and Education Quarterly, 23* (4), 313–335.

Vella, J. (2002). *Learning to listen, learning to teach: The power of dialogue in educating adults* (2nd ed.). San Francisco: Jossey-Bass.

Versluis, A. (1994). *Native American traditions.* Shaftesbury, UK: Element.

Via, R. A. (1975). English through drama. *English Teaching Forum, 13,* 158–162.

Vygotsky, L. (1981). The genesis of higher mental functions. In J. V. Wertsch (Ed.), *The concept of activity in Soviet psychology.* Armonk, NY: Sharpe.

Vygotsky, L. (1982). *Thought and language.* (A. Kozulin, trans.). Cambridge, MA: MIT Press. (Original work published in 1934).

Walker, B. J. (1987). Guided fantasy series. In D. J. Watson (Ed.), *Ideas and insights: Language arts in the elementary school* (pp. 112–113). Urbana, IL: National Council of Teachers of English.

Wall, A. E. (2001). Teaching English in Mexico. Available online: www.tesol.org/careers/counsel/articles/mexico-01.html.

Wallace, L. (1999). "Winding down." Unpublished poem.

Wallerstein, N. (1983). *Language and culture in conflict: Problem-posing in the ESL classroom.* New York: Addison-Wesley.

Wallraff, B. (2000). What global language? *Atlantic Monthly, 286* (5), 52–66.

Walt Disney Company (1990). *Disney's children's favorites, volume 2* (audio cassette plus singalong book) Burbank, CA: Author.

Ward, A. W., & Murray-Ward, M. (1999). *Assessment in the classroom.* Belmont, CA: Wadsworth.

Wark, M. (2001). Cyberpunk—Subculture of mainstream? In M. Petracca & M. Sorapure (Eds.), *Common culture: Reading and writing about American popular culture* (3rd ed.), (pp. 352–358). Upper Saddle River, NJ: Prentice-Hall.

Warschauer, M. (1995). *E-mail for English teaching.* Alexandria, VA: Teachers of English to Speakers of Other Languages.

Warschauer, M., Shetzer, H., & Meloni, C. (2000). *Internet for English teaching.* Alexandria, VA: Teachers of English to Speakers of Other Languages.

Watahomigie, L. (1995). The power of American Indian parents and communiities. *Bilingual Research Journal, 19* (1), 99–115.

Watson, D. L., Northcutt, L., & Rydell, L. (1989). Teaching bilingual students successfully. *Educational Leadership, 46* (5), 59–61.

Way, B. (1981). *Audience participation.* Boston: Baker's Plays.

Weatherly, S. D. (1999). I'll buy it! In R. E. Larimer & L. Schleicher (Eds.), *New ways in using authentic materials in the classroom* (pp. 73–80). Alexandria, VA: Teachers of English to Speakers of Other Languages.

Weaver, S. J., & Cohen, A. D. (1997). *Strategies-based instruction: A teacher training manual. CARLA Working Paper Series #7.* Minneapolis, MN: University of Minnesota.

Weedon, C. (1987). *Feminist practice and poststructuralist theory.* London: Blackwell.

Weinstein, C. E. (1988). Assessment and training of student learning strategies. In R. R. Schmeck (Ed.), *Learning strategies and learning styles* (pp. 291–313). New York: Plenum Press.

Weinstein-Shr, G. (1992). *Stories to tell our children.* Boston: Heinle & Heinle.

Wellman, H. M. (1985). The origins of metacognition. In D. L. Forrest-Pressley, G. E. Mackinnon, & T. G. Waller (Eds.), *Metacognition, cognition, and human performance* (pp. 1–31). Orlando, FL: Academic Press.

Wells, C. G. (1981). *Learning through interaction: The study of language development.* Cambridge: Cambridge University Press.

Wells, G. (1998) Using the tool-kit of discourse in the activity of learning and teaching. In Wells, G. (Ed.), *Dialogic inquiry* (pp. 231–266). Cambridge: Cambridge University Press.

Wells, G., & Chang-Wells, G. L. (1992). *Constructing knowledge together: Classrooms as centers of inquiry and literacy.* Portsmouth, NH: Heinemann.

Wertsch, J. V. (1978). Adult-child interaction and the roots of metacognition. *Quarterly Newsletter of the Institute for Comparative Human Cognition, 2* (1), 15–18.

Wertsch, J. V. (1985). *Vygotsky and the social formation of mind.* Cambridge, MA: Harvard University Press.

Wertsch, J. V. (1991). *Voices of the mind: A sociocultural approach to mediated action.* Cambridge, MA: Harvard University Press.

Wertsch, J. V. (1998). *Mind as action.* Oxford: Oxford University Press.

Whincup. G. (1987). *The heart of Chinese poetry.* New York: Anchor/ Doubleday.

Whisler, N., & Williams, J. (1990). *Literature and cooperative learning: Pathway to literacy.* Sacramento: Literature Co-op.

Wiese, A. M., & García, E. E. (1998). The Bilingual Education Act: Language minority students and equal educational opportunity. *Bilingual Research Journal, 22* (1). Available online: http://brj.asu.edu/v221/indext.html.

Wiggins, G. (1989). A true test: Toward more authentic and equitable assessment. *Phi Delta Kappan, 70,* 703–713.

Wiggins, G. (1992). Creating tests worth taking. *Educational Leadership, 49,* 26–33.

Wilhelm, K. H. (1997). Sometimes kicking and screaming: Language teachers-in-training react to a collaborative learning model. *Modern Language Journal, 81* (4), 527–542.

Wilhelm, K. H. (1999). Collaborative "dos" and "don'ts." *TESOL Journal, 8* (2), 14–19.

Wilhelm, K. H., & Leverett, T. (1998). Lights, camera, interaction. *TESOL Journal, 7* (4), 34–35.

Williams, J. D., & Snipper, G. C. (1990). *Literacy and bilingualism.* White Plains, NY: Longman.

Wilson, H. (2001). *Three approaches to teaching grammar.* Presentation, annual conference, California Teachers of English to Speakers of Other Languages, Ontario, CA.

Wink, J. (2000). *Critical pedagogy: Notes from the real world.* New York: Addison-Wesley.

Witte, K. (1991). The role of culture in health and disease. In L. Samovar & R. Porter (Eds.), *Intercultural communication: A reader* (6th ed.). Belmont, CA: Wadsworth.

Wold, S. A. (1993). What's in a name? Labels and literacy in readers theatre. *Reading Teacher, 46* (7), 540–545.

Wolf, D. P., LeMathieu, P. G., & Eresh, J. (1991). Good measure: Assessment as a tool for educational reform. *Educational Leadership, 49* (8), 8–13.

Wolfe, P., & Poynor, L. (2001). Politics and the pendulum: An alternative understanding of the case of whole language as educational innovation. *Educational Researcher, 30* (1), 15–20.

Wolfe, P., & Sorgen, M. (1990). *Mind, memory, and learning.* Napa, CA: Author.

Wolfe-Quintero, K. (1998). ESL language portfolios: How do they work? In J. D. Brown (Ed.), *New ways in classroom assessment* (pp. 11–14). Alexandria, VA: Teachers of English to Speakers of Other Languages.

Wolfram, W. (1991). *Dialects and American English.* Englewood Cliffs, NJ: Prentice-Hall.

Wolfram, W. (1995). Reexamining dialect in TESOL. *TESOL Matters, 5* (2), 1, 22.

Wolfram, W. (2002). Everyone has an accent. In B. M. Power & R. S. Hubbard (Eds.). *Language development: A reader for teachers* (2nd ed.) (pp. 225–230). Upper Saddle River, NJ and Columbus, OH: Merrill/Prentice-Hall.

Wolfram, W., Adger, C., & Christian, D. (1999). *Dialects in schools and communities.* Mahwah, NJ: Erlbaum.

Wong, M. S. (1998). *You said it! Listening/speaking strategies and activities.* New York: St. Martin's Press.

Wong, M. M. W. (1996). Time-people-action-place. In L. Schinke-Llano & R. Rauff (Eds.), *New ways in teaching young children* (pp. 104–105). Alexandria, VA: Teachers of English to Speakers of Other Languages.

Wong-Fillmore, L. (1985). When does teacher talk work as input? In S. Gass & C. Madden (Eds.), *Input for second language acquisition.* Cambridge, MA: Newbury House.

Wood, D. J., Bruner, J., & Ross, G. (1976). The role of tutoring in problem solving. *Journal of Child Psychology and Psychiatry, 17,* 89–100.

Wood, N. (1993). *Spirit walker.* New York: Delacorte Press.

Woodbury, A. (2001). *Endangered languages.* In Linguistic Society of America, "Fields of Linguistics." Available online: www.lsadc.org/web2/fldcont.html.

Woolfolk, A. (1998). *Educational psychology* (7th ed.). Englewood Cliffs, NJ: Prentice-Hall.

Worthen, B., & Spandel, V. (1991). Putting the standardized test debate in perspective. *Educational Leadership, 48* (5), 65–69.

Yaden, D., & Templeton, S. (1986). Introduction: Metalinguistic awareness—an etymology. In D. Yaden & S. Templeton (Eds.), *Metalinguistic awareness and beginning literacy: Conceptualizing what it means to read and write* (pp. 3–10). Portsmouth, NH: Heinemann.

Yang, C. Y. (1999). *Promoting communicative competence through drama in elementary English as a foreign language.* Unpublished master's thesis, California State University, San Bernardino.

Yang, H-J. (1998). *The collaborative dramatic process in elementary English as a foreign language.* Unpublished master's thesis, California State University, San Bernardino.

Yeh, M. H. (2001). *Enhancing academic competence in English as a foreign language through multiple strategies.* Unpublished master's thesis, California State University, San Bernardino.

Yoshida, K. (2001/2002). From the fish bowl to the open seas: Taking a step toward the real world of communication. *TESOL Matters, 12* (1), 1, 5.

Yost, B. (2000, June 8). E-mail lingo is reshaping language. *San Bernardino Sun,* E1, E3.

Young, M., & Helvie, S. (1996). Parent power: A positive link to school success. *Journal of Educational Issues of Language Minority Students, 16.* Available online: www.ncbe.gwu.edu/miscpubs/jeilms/vol16/jeilms1611.htm.

Young, T. A., & Vardell, S. (1993). Weaving readers theatre and nonfiction into the curriculum. *Reading Teacher, 46* (5), 396–406.

Yúdice, G. (1988). Marginality and the ethics of survival. In A. Ross (Ed.), *Universal abandon? The politics of postmodernism*. Minneapolis, MN: University of Minnesota Press.

Zamel, V., & Spack, R. (1998). Preface. In V. Zamel and R. Spack (Eds.), *Negotiating academic literacies: Teaching and learning across languages and cultures* (pp. ix–xviii). Mahwah, NJ: Erlbaum.

Zanger, V. V. (1994). "Not joined in": The social context of English literacy development for His-

panic youth. In B. M. Ferdman, R-M. Weber, & A. G. Ramírez (Eds.), *Literacy across languages and cultures* (pp. 171–198). Albany: SUNY Press.

Zelman, N. (1996). *Conversational inspirations: Over 2000 conversation topics*. Brattleboro, VT: Pro Lingua Associates.

Zitkala-Sa (2000). The cutting of my long hair. In Perfection Learning (Ed.), *Who am I?* Logan, IA: Author.

Author Index

458

Subject Index

469

472

474